THEOLOGY IN HISTORY

HENRI DE LUBAC

THEOLOGY IN HISTORY

PART ONE

The Light of Christ

PART TWO

Disputed Questions and Resistance to Nazism

With a Foreword by Michel Sales, S.J.

Translated by Anne Englund Nash

SAN FRANCISCO IGNATIUS PRESS

Title of the French Original:
Théologie dans l'Histoire:
I. La Lumière du Christ
II. Questiones disputées
et résistance au nazisme

Cover by Roxanne Mei Lum

ISBN 978-0-89870-472-3
Library of Congress catalogue number 93-78537
Printed in the United States of America ♾

Contents

"*Omnem novitatem attulit semetipsum afferens, qui fuerat annuntiatus.*"

He has brought total newness
by bringing himself.

—Saint Irenaeus. *Adversus Haereses*, IV, 34, 1.

Foreword

This collection of articles and texts by Father de Lubac, some of which have not been published before, are being published here as a continuation of the volume entitled *Théologies d'occasion* (1984) [English translation: *Theological Fragments* (San Francisco: Ignatius Press, 1989)]. It has been compiled in the same spirit and with the same intention. If, overriding the excessive modesty of its author, we have given this collection another title and put the fine word *Théologie* in the singular, it is because, in our eyes, the fact that many of the texts it contains were written in order to respond to situations that were at times singularly serious for the Christian conscience, far from diminishing the greatness and the unity of true theological work, in fact manifests its true nature. It is true that many of these texts were occasional, either in the commonplace sense of acceding to a request for the purpose of some congress or some collection or some preface or, too, because a given situation whose stakes could be serious, as much for the Church as for the life of the world (as was the case with the Nazi peril), seemed to invite Father de Lubac to intervene in some debate. But other texts, such as the long article on "The Mystery of the Supernatural", without failing to have caused and still today to cause a great stir, go well beyond the occasion that gave rise to them to touch the substance of Christian revelation.

When useful, we have placed in an unnumbered note a few historical or bibliographical pieces of information capable of clarifying what was at stake in the published text. In addition, we offer here a few preliminary remarks on the rubrics by which we have regrouped the texts assembled into this collection. We hope the reader will find here both a guide and an invitation to enter into a better understanding of the selection that governed its composition.

Under the title "The Fathers and Christian Humanism", the reader will find, in addition to an article of great timeliness on the priesthood according to Saint John Chrysostom, an important study on the salvation of Origen. This text serves as a complement to the four volumes of *L'Exégèse médiévale* [Medieval exegesis], as do the prefaces that we have brought together on similar subjects. This section also contains an unpublished text on the famous thought of Pascal: "The eternal silence of these infinite spaces frightens me."

Under the title "Tripartite Anthropology" will be found the draft, entirely unpublished in French,[1] of a work to which Father de Lubac attributed great importance, even if he was unable to bring it to conclusion. These pages complete the text on "Mysticism and Mystery" published in *Theological Fragments* (35–69). Even unfinished, we believe it to be sufficiently perfected in its governing principles and especially capable of opening for future workers a sure and fruitful path of historical investigations as well as of systematic reflection.

At the end of the last work he published, Father de Lubac confided an invaluable secret.

> I cannot help thinking that it is a certain spiritual superficiality rather than the feeling of my intellectual deficiencies or even than the conviction that I am far too unequal to such a subject to dare ever to approach it head-on, that has always made me postpone undertaking that work on Jesus Christ that would have been dearer to me than all the others, and in view of which I did much reading and recorded many reflections but which I never really attacked. . . . Without claiming to refer to anything other than the Gospel such as the Church transmits it to me, I can nevertheless make my own the words of Moehler on Jesus, with little concern for the whiff of pietism that some of our adult minds would criticize in them: "I think I would no longer want to live if I were no longer to hear Him speak."[2]

We believed we could not satisfy the demands of such a confidence better than by concluding the first part of this collection with the beautiful study on "The Light of Christ",[3] published during the darkest hours of the twentieth century, when the Nazi barbarity seemed to be sweeping it away.

[1] This text in fact appears in volume 6 of the complete works of Cardinal de Lubac in Italian: *Mistica e Mistero cristiano* (Milan: Jaca Book, 1978), chaps. 2 and 4. Cf. *At the Service of the Church: Henri de Lubac Reflects on the Circumstances that Occasioned His Writings* (San Francisco: Ignatius Press, 1993), 157. See especially 113 and 141.

[2] *At the Service of the Church*, 147–48.

[3] About which he was told that, "Léon Brunschwicg, although he was an old man fleeing persecution from one hiding place to another and had had friendly conversations with his old comrade and adversary Blondel, had read it with attention and approval." *At the Service of the Church*, 58.

The contents of this first part justify its subtitle: "The Light of Christ", without any need for further explanation.

All that remains to be said is why and how we distributed the texts of the second part of *Theology in History*: Disputed Questions and Resistance to Nazism.

The long section entitled, "Disputed Theological Questions and Anticipations of Vatican II" is comprised of a series of texts written between the beginning of the forties and the beginning of the seventies. Opening with a twofold diagnosis of the religious and theological situation in 1942 and 1946, it contains several texts whose historical resonance and importance were considerable, given the circumstances. There is no need to dwell on the articles concerning "The Development of Dogma" and "The Mystery of the Supernatural". It would be worthwhile, on the other hand, to say a word about a text destined to find, paradoxically, an unexpected echo. Having remained unpublished because of unrelated reasons of the author, "The Doctrine of Father Lebreton on Revelation and Dogma according to His Anti-Modernist Writings" was written by Father de Lubac over the course of fifty years and several times proposed to the review of the theologians of the Society of Jesus consulted by the Superior General of the Order, who always refused to authorize its publication. Father de Lubac had to give up the idea of publishing these pages, whose principal ideas were to be found not only authorized but confirmed by the constitution *Dei Verbum* on Divine Revelation of the Second Vatican Council.

It will be noted that we have not included in this collection texts and articles written by Father de Lubac about the Second Vatican Council. The reason for this is that the major portion of the latter have already been published in other collections or in separate works that are still easily available today.[4] We would, however, point out that, for this entire period, the reader would find it of great interest to refer to the *Mémoire sur l'occasion de mes écrits*[5] and to the volume entitled *Entretiens autour de Vatican II* [Conversations about Vatican II] (Paris: Cerf,

[4] The principal titles of which are: *La Révélation divine*, 3d ed. (Paris: Cerf, 1983); *Paradoxe et mystère de l'Église* (Paris: Aubier, 1967); *Athéisme et sens de l'homme. Une double requête de Gaudium et spes* (Paris: Cerf, 1968); *Les Églises particulières dans l'Église universelle* (Paris: Aubier, 1971) [in English trans.: *The Motherhood of the Church* (San Francisco: Ignatius Press, 1982)]; *Petite Catéchèse sur Nature et Grâce*, Communio (Paris: Fayard, 1980) [English trans.: *A Brief Catechesis on Nature and Grace* (San Francisco: Ignatius Press, 1984)].

[5] *At the Service of the Church*, especially 145–51.

1985), which contains an invaluable diagnosis on the twenty years that followed the Council.

In a recent work, *Résistance chrétienne à l'antisémitisme: Souvenirs 1940–1944* (Paris: Fayard, 1988 [English translation: *Christian Resistance to Anti-Semitism: Memories from 1940–1944* (San Francisco: Ignatius Press, 1990)], Father de Lubac tried to strike an impartial balance in testifying, in a manner that is at once precise, nuanced and discreet, about events in which he participated in the front ranks. We have regrouped under the heading entitled "Resistance to Nazism and to Anti-Semitism" several of the principal texts published during the Occupation, except for the recently reprinted *Cahiers clandestins du Témoignage chrétien* (which is a collective work).[6]

The texts brought together under the title "The Thought of Father Teilhard de Chardin" call for some further explanation. Bound by a long and close friendship of over thirty years, Father de Lubac had known Teilhard in 1922 and had not ceased to correspond with him from that time on, as witnessed in all fundamental points by the document constituted by the *Lettres intimes de P. Teilhard de Chardin à ses amis Auguste Valensin, Bruno de Solages, Henri de Lubac et André Ravier* [Personal Correspondence of Father Teilhard de Chardin with his friends Auguste Valensin, Bruno de Solages, Henri de Lubac and André Ravier], in its second, revised and enlarged edition (Paris: Aubier, 1974).[7] During Teilhard's lifetime, he contributed significantly, along

[6] *Cahiers et Courriers clandestins du Témoignage chrétien 1941–1944*. Complete reprinting in facsimile, 2 vols. (Paris, 1980). Renée Bédarida, *Les Armes de l'Esprit, Témoignage chrétien (1941–1944)* (Paris: Ouvrières, 1977). By the same author: *Pierre Chaillet témoin de la résistance spirituelle* (Paris: Fayard, 1988). Pages 159–66 of this work, devoted to the crises of October-November 1945 at the *Témoignage chrétien*, contain some inaccuracies. It is useful to compare them to the version of the facts reported by Jean-Pierre Gault, *Histoire d'une fidélité, Témoignage chrétien 1944–1956* (Paris, n.d.), 295–306. All the facts reported here by J. P. Gault are confirmed by a copious file preserved in the archives of one of the principal actors in the matter, Father Gaston Fessard. Renée Bédarida did not have recourse to this file. Cf. also *Résistance chrétienne à l'antisémitisme* (Paris: Fayard, 1988), 264 [English trans.: *Christian Resistance to Anti-Semitism* (San Francisco: Ignatius Press, 1990)]. In his memoir, *At the Service of the Church*, Father de Lubac contests the interpretation given by Father Congar of the clandestine *Témoignage chrétien* (see 231).

[7] Among the principal publications, we will also point out: Maurice Blondel and Pierre Teilhard de Chardin: *Correspondance commentée*, Bibliothèque des Archives de Philosophie, new series, 1 (Paris: Beauchesne, 1965). *La Prière du P. Teilhard de Chardin: Note sur l'apologétique teilhardienne*, 2d ed. (Paris: Fayard, 1968) [English trans. of 1st ed.: *Teilhard de Chardin: The Man and His Meaning* (Burnes & Oates, 1965; New York: Hawthorn Books). On the Teilhardian publications of Father de Lubac, see *At the Service of the Church*, 103–12.

with Bishop Bruno de Solages, to the final editing of *Phénomène humain* (*The Phenomenon of Man* [New York: Harper, 1959]), the masterpiece of the great Jesuit.[8] After Teilhard's death, he published, in particular, texts as important for understanding the origin of his thought as his *Écrits du temps de la guerre* [Wartime writings].[9] But his contribution to the defense of his colleague was not confined to that. Through a conjunction of circumstances to which the documents we publish here give witness, he was led to take the lead, without having intended to, in presenting and defending Teilhard's work, doing so particularly on a twofold occasion that, with the perspective of time, one might call historical. It was he, first of all, who, at the explicit request of four French provincial superiors of the Society of Jesus, wrote the first important book on the theological thought of Father Teilhard de Chardin. Originally entitled, significantly: "La Doctrine spirituelle du P. Teilhard de Chardin" [The spiritual doctrine of Father Teilhard de Chardin], *La Pensée religieuse du P. Teilhard de Chardin* (Paris: Aubier, 1962) [English translation: *The Religion of Teilhard de Chardin* (London

---

[8] On the writing of *Phénomène humain*, see the first-hand information recorded in B. de Solages, *Teilhard de Chardin, Témoignage et étude sur le développement de sa pensée* (Toulouse, privately pub., 1967), 64, note 14. All the desired information on the writing and ecclesiastical mishaps of *Phénomène humain* will also be found in the notes for *Lettres intimes à ses amis Auguste Valensin . . .* , 2d ed. (Paris, 1974):

a. On the writing of the text, in mind since the month of September 1937 and begun in the beginning of June 1938, see letter 88 of May 25, 1938, to Father Valensin, note 10, pp. 334–35.

b. On the corrections introduced by Teilhard with the agreement of Bishop B. de Solages and Father de Lubac, after the first refusal to publish indicated by the Father General of the Society of Jesus, see letter 92 of July 31, 1946, to B. de Solages, notes 1, 2 and 4, pp. 346–47; letter 91 of June 26, 1946, to Father de Lubac, note 5; letter 93 of August 15, 1946, to Bishop B. de Solages, pp. 349–50; letter 96 of Christmas 1946, to Bishop B. de Solages, p. 352; letter 108 of November 9, 1948, to Father de Lubac, p. 376 (a very important letter on the relation of *Phénomène humain* to the Christian phenomenon and to the Roman Church).

c. On the meeting at Carmaux of January 6–8, 1947, during the course of which the published text of *Phénomène humain* was clarified by Teilhard, Father de Lubac and Bishop de Solages, see René d'Ouince, *Un Prophète en procès: Teilhard de Chardin*, 1:151, and letter 96 of Christmas 1946 to Bishop de Solages.

d. On the "Foreword" to *Phénomène humain* (21–23), see the letter of July 31, 1946, to Bishop de Solages, p. 347.

e. On the plan for the Summary or Conclusion of *Phénomène humain*, see letter 91, note 4.

[9] Paris: Grasset, 1965. This volume, reprinted without any changes except for the pagination, constitutes volume 12 in the works of Teilhard published by Éditions du Seuil. It is the only volume in that collection in which Teilhard's texts, carefully edited by chronological order, are accompanied in every instance by a detailed note giving the essential editorial information on the Teilhardian writings.

and Paris: William Collins and Desclée, 1967)] created quite a stir and was widely circulated everywhere in the world as well as in France. Another occasion, of an entirely different importance, although unknown to most of the public at large, was given to Father de Lubac to render justice to his colleague and friend. The text entitled "Tradition and Innovation in the Position of the Problem of God in Father Teilhard de Chardin" constituted by its date (autumn 1965), and especially the place where it was proposed, a small revolution whose initiative went back to the supreme Magisterium of the Church, breaking the ostracism that had been organized by a powerful coalition of influential theologians. It was in fact at the explicit request of Paul VI that Father Charles Boyer, Jesuit, Secretary of the Pontifical Academy of Saint Thomas Aquinas and organizer of the Thomist Congress, was directed to invite Father de Lubac to speak about the work and thought of Father Teilhard before an audience of theologians, many of whom were hostile to him. This report, presented to the Sixth International Thomist Congress, was given in Rome on September 10, 1965, in the great hall of the palace of the Cancelleria. This event and several others besides inspired Father de Lubac with some important reflections on the relations between the Magisterium and theologians in the work entitled *Teilhard posthume* [The posthumous Teilhard] (Paris: Fayard, 1977).[10]

[10] Let us note that Father de Lubac does not share, on this point, the opinion of his friend Father René d'Ouince (cf. *At the Service of the Church*, 111–12). On the most representative theses, influence and methods in the perspective of Neo-Thomism from the end of the nineteenth century up to immediate time of Vatican II, we should return to the *Lettres de M. Étienne Gilson au P. de Lubac* (Paris: Cerf, 1986) [English translation: *Letters of Étienne Gilson to Henri de Lubac* (San Francisco: Ignatius Press, 1988)]. The commentary and appendices in this volume constitute a significant document on the history of theology and its teaching in faculties, seminaries or scholasticates, beginning with those of the Society of Jesus, which were, by all means, far from always rejecting the best of Thomism. It will be seen there how, in a paradoxical way, all the disappointments that Father de Lubac experienced originated first with theologians in the Society of Jesus whose views were contradicted by his historical studies on natural desire and the supernatural in Saint Thomas Aquinas. Cf. again on this point, *Entretiens autour de Vatican II*, 11–12.

"When my book entitled *Surnaturel* appeared, the general outcry redoubled. It is true that in this book I criticized certain complications of a modern Scholasticism and proposed returning to a doctrine that was simpler, more traditional, more profound, better suited, as well, to guide us in the debates of our time, which had been that of Saint Thomas Aquinas. This was not done on the spur of the moment: I had undertaken my inquiry as early as 1924, at the suggestion of a revered mentor, Father Joseph Huby. Good authorities gave me their approval. . . . But like all constituted bodies, certain groups of theologians did not like

To bring these few details to a close, let us add in passing that, while understanding the importance of Teilhard's effort and while defending the orthodoxy of the essence of his views, Father de Lubac was never an unconditional partisan[11] or, with even greater reason, a blind zealot with respect to them, as witnessed, if necessary, by the recently published commentary on an anonymous 1962 article in *L'Osservatore romano.*[12]

> Is it not necessary [wrote Father de Lubac at the end of a diagnosis he gave in 1969 of the Church in the current crisis of civilization], when the gravity of the moment demands it, for the theologian to know how to suspend for a moment all his historical inquiries, his constructions and personal research—to which he would be wrong, moreover, to attach excessive importance at any time—in order to remember that his whole existence as a theologian and any authority that this profession can earn him are founded above all on the responsibility he has received in view of the defense and the elucidation of the Faith of the Church?[13]

Father de Lubac, who has always been a man of the Church, never failed to respond to this task each time he was presented with it. The celebrity, whether good or bad, that circumstances brought him throughout his life should not delude us about the roots from which he has drawn the fecundity of his work. If hidden from the eyes of the world and the worldly, the latter can be simply called to mind here: prayer, obscure but immense and persevering work and, finally, fidelity to the one Church of Christ.

having their habits upset. Moreover, as I was living then at Fourvière, a bugbear then developed about a mythical 'Fourvière School' (at the same time as a mythical 'new theology') of which I was supposedly the head. The fight increased in violence. I, however, took no part in this (I am passing over an earlier, short-lived debate of an entirely different kind): my Superior General had judged it wiser to take my defense upon himself with respect to the only legitimate Authority, using the memoranda he requested from me. Father Congar was right when he evoked the 'Tarasque of Tarascon' on this subject." See also: *At the Service of the Church*, passim.

[11] In his little work *The Theology of Henri de Lubac: An Overview* (San Francisco: Ignatius Press, 1991), Hans Urs von Balthasar has mischievously indexed all the passages from books where Father de Lubac expressed reservations regarding Teilhard's work, p. 83, note 82.

[12] See *At the Service of the Church*, 326–34.

[13] "L'Église dans la crise actuelle", *NRTh*, June 1969, 596. This was a conference given at the University of Saint Louis, Missouri, on May 29, 1969. Contrary to the very title of this text, hasty readers at that time attributed to Father de Lubac reflections about the crisis of the Church. . . .

On the eve of the extraordinary synod convoked by Pope John Paul II to celebrate the twentieth anniversary of Vatican II, both the reflection and the transmission of what the Lord gave him the grace to realize he was greeting in a few young Catholics, both priests and laymen, whom he had recently met, allowed him to see the canticle of the old Simeon rise from the depths of his heart.

> Those or others who have been pointed out to me [he would write in a postscript to his *Entretiens autour de Vatican II*] do not loudly proclaim their rights, however real, in the working of institutions: they quietly offer their services precisely where their self-sacrifice can be useful. If they group together here and there in small communities, it is not in order to move apart from the "institutional Church": they do not know and do not wish to know any other. Beyond disputes that seem not to hold their attention for long, their fidelity to the Church of Christ is not merely intact: it is a vital reflex. Faith is not a habit for them, nor is the liturgy an aesthetics or a refuge, nor charity a good feeling. Without seeking to, they reinvent in new forms the Christian life of all times. Realists, they turn their attention to their closest neighbor. They see very well that their Church is not triumphant. But they do not say every day, in some morbid fashion, with a morose delectation, that the only Christians left in France are "marginal". Without having made special inquiries, they have enough good sense not to confuse small numbers with marginality. They well know that numbers are not everything, that they resolve nothing, and their modest experience would allow them, if they had but the notion, to say that one single little hearth is capable of causing a vast conflagration. If they were familiar with them, they could take as their own these words of an unknown author of a letter to a certain Diognetes, who lived in the second century, lost with his little group in the immensity of the Roman Empire: "Christians are the soul of the world. They are so by vocation."[14]

The last section entitled "Figures" principally contains short texts. Their value derives less from the number of pages, which is often very limited, than from the gravity of the circumstances and the importance of the words that these testimonies contain in history and for all eternity about a man, a work, an act or a life.[15]

---

[14] *Entretiens autour de Vatican II*, 124–25.

[15] We have refrained from repeating here several texts reprinted in de Lubac's *At the Service of the Church*, in particular the articles published during the Liberation in *Témoignage chrétien* (232–37), the testimony given by Father de Lubac about Cardinal Daniélou after the latter's

To conclude the two parts of *Theology in History*, we thought it best simply to excerpt from the invaluable *At the Service of the Church* three pages where Father de Lubac tries to define what constitutes the unity of a work that is otherwise so diverse. These few lines, which are as precise as they are nuanced, every word of which is of consequence as much for historical information as for depth of thought, will reveal to anyone willing to read them with all the attention they deserve more than the texture of a work: they will reveal the soul of a life. As for the few verses from the Second Letter of Peter that we deemed a fitting epilogue, it is not enough to recall the importance that the author of *Exégèse médiévale* recognized in them: the admiration he does not cease to have for them, today more than ever, at the end of so vast and profound a work, is enough in itself to justify them.

MICHEL SALES

---

death (160–64) and the article on Paul VI published in *L'Osservatore romano* on June 20, 1978 (383–85).

PART ONE

The Light of Christ

I

THE FATHERS AND CHRISTIAN HUMANISM

1. The *Dialogue on the Priesthood* by Saint John Chrysostom

From his villa in Gentilly, Germain de Brie (Brixius), a native of Auxerre, canon of Notre Dame in Paris, wrote to Erasmus on August 11, 1526, on the subject of the ten books of our *Dialogue*, which the great patristics scholar had just published in its Greek text through Badius: "I devoted myself entirely, for several months, to their study, leaving completely aside other Greek and Latin authors, and I discovered that this dialogue, so gracious, so elegant and so profound, between Chrysostom (who is truly a golden author) and his friend Basil made an extraordinary impression on me."[1]

The voice of Germain de Brie is not an isolated voice. Many other readers have been seduced by this celebrated *Dialogue*. Everything has been said for centuries about its charm. As much here as in his discourses, John of Antioch deserves, as Erasmus' friend felt, the glorious surname "Golden Mouth". The charm has not been exhausted. Neither the digressions nor the commonplaces, which are not lacking,

This text, published in the *Nouvelle Revue Théologique*, November–December 1978, 822–31, had been requested of Father de Lubac as a theological introduction to the *Dialogue sur le sacerdoce* of Saint John Chrysostom for the *Sources chrétiennes* series. On this question, see also *Les Églises particulières dans l'Église universelle* (Paris: Aubier, 1972), appendix, 231–50 ("Le sacerdoce selon l'Écriture et la Tradition"); English trans.: *The Motherhood of the Church* (San Francisco: Ignatius Press, 1982), appendix, 337–63 ("The Priesthood according to Scripture and Tradition").

[1] Germain would spend many nights translating the *Dialogue* from Greek into Latin. Erasmus would insert this translation (judged better than an earlier one) into a later edition, published by Froben (1527). From the correspondence of Erasmus: Allen, 6 (1733).

nor even the occasional vague whiff of a Platonism that our age hunts down ruthlessly, prevents the reader from tasting, still today, a delicate pleasure. The work can also be considered as a historical document, invaluable but sometimes enigmatic, on the life and personality of its author as well as on the ecclesiastical customs of the region and period. We will consider only the doctrine here.[2]

Certainly, this is not a formal treatise. Nor is it a systematic study, a work of controversy or a theological manual. We will find here neither the biographical information about which we might be curious nor an explicit response to all the stirring questions of our time on the subject. It is a dialogue, rather nonchalant in appearance, which hangs together loosely in a meandering structure: quite the contrary of a didactic exposition. It is a work of art. It is also an argument, a personal defense, which even takes at times a rather lively tone. It is also, or rather, above all, a work of edification: the subject of faith is recalled only in view of tracing the behavior that should follow from it. This hymn to the greatness of the Christian priesthood is a call to the dignity of its exercise. It is in this that the major interest of the work lies, which causes it to be read and reread by many generations of bishops and priests. It is not difficult, however, to bring out its doctrinal core.

Had John, who had received the education of a monk,[3] already received Holy Orders the year he composed his dialogue? An insoluble question, it seems, although there may be several good reasons for an affirmative response: "probably four years after his ordination", judges Mademoiselle Anne-Marie Malingrey, who has studied the question very closely.[4] When, in his imaginary defense, he expounds on "the difficulties of the holy ministry", one has the vivid impression that he is speaking from experience, and one would even be tempted to believe that this experience had been long and varied. At the very end, he says again: "What is the use of enumerating all the other difficulties? To give or get some idea of it, one must truly have gone through it" (5, v. *finem*). This text, however, may not be decisive. One knows that it is characteristic of a genius to anticipate experience; and John, who was a

[2] Our analysis is confined strictly to the texts of the *Dialogue*.

[3] On the role of monasteries in education according to John Chrysostom, see A. J. Festugière, *Antioche païenne et chrétienne* (S. de Boccard, 1959), 181–210.

[4] In *Jean Chrysostome et Augustin*, Actes du Colloque de Chantilly (1974) (Beauchesne, 1975), 86.

good psychologist, had been able to observe or guess many things in a short time, before having had to practice or undergo them himself. In any case, this is of little importance for us. Nor is a certain vagueness in his vocabulary of much importance. For example, now he speaks of the priest, and now of the bishop, without the context always explaining the difference. Yet he could not have been ignorant about this, and in fact it is certain (as we will see) that he knew very well the essential hierarchical distinctions received from the most ancient tradition: deacon, priest and bishop;[5] he himself, as we know, exercised these three sacred functions successively. As another example, he happens to designate the priesthood by one word or another, according to the occasion, without there being any means of discovering any intention whatever behind his choice. Now it is legitimate to think, it is even, we believe, necessary to admit—and this is the first doctrinal finding we have to make—that what can appear mere imprecision to the less attentive reader stems, in reality, from the author's fundamental conviction that *the priesthood is one*.

As Mademoiselle Malingrey has remarked in her fine study on "the episcopal ministry in the work of John Chrysostom",[6] "this is very important". This one priesthood is defined above all by the episcopate. Which is the reason, whatever the incidental cause may have been, for the long hesitation about the very title of the work, whose variation in the manuscripts that have survived to our day does not allow us to know even now if it is "on the priesthood" or "on the episcopate". It seems that from now on the hesitation may be dispelled, since we will soon see it in the edition that *Sources chrétiennes* is about to give us; but it is remarkable that this variation is found again almost immediately in reading a passage from the first book (1, 8). Whether it is in fact that

[5] Together they form what the Latins called the *ordo clericorum*, what M. Charles Pietri, as a historian of society, names the "society of clerics" or "clerical society", which existed already much earlier in the Church, in the East as well as in the West: *Roma christiana* (Palais Farnèse, 1976), 1:144–56. On this triad, see, among others: Ignatius of Antioch, to the Magnesians and to the Trallians (ed. P. T. Camelot, *Sources chrétiennes* 10 [1951]: 95–99 and 113); Clement of Alexandria, *Stromates* 6, 13, 107; the *Apostolic Tradition* of Hippolytus (ed. B. Botte, *Sources chrétiennes* 11); Cyril of Jerusalem, *Catéchèses mystagogiques*, 2 (ed. Píedagnel, *Sources chrétiennes* 126 [1966]: 147–49); other texts quoted by Pierre Nautin, *Sources chrétiennes* 232 (1976): 109–10 (ed. of the *Homilies* of Origen on *Jeremiah*, vol. 1).

[6] Malingrey, *Jean Chrysostome*, 76. In his correspondence, Erasmus will make no distinction in saying that the *Dialogue* treats "the episcopal function" or "the priestly function". Allen, 6, 72 and 576.

of the bishop or that of the mere priest, John Chrysostom knows, and by his manner of expressing himself he suggests to us, that this one priesthood has its origin in Christ, that it derives its whole reality from Christ and that what it transmits to men, that with which it reclothes them, is Christ. He sees in it a function, a service, a "liturgy" essential to the Church. It is a ministry that is "great", "sublime, at the service of God first of all, and then of men", in order to lead them to God: in this "diaconia" (3, 8 and 16; 6, 13), the bishop or the priest "works for the people" (2, 4).

The author of this loose, meandering dialogue is not a confused mind. Without using dialectic rigor and without having recourse to precise definitions, he distinguishes very clearly between three things, or three kinds of functions, associated in the exercise of the sacerdotal ministry. The bishop is first of all the pastor of the flock (2, 1 and 4; 3, 7); he is the head of the faithful; if his responsibility is a service, it is as well, in Christ, an honor, a dignity (3, 6, 11, 12, 14)—which does not mean that it is honorary. He presides over his church, which is to say that he directs it (4, 7; 6, 7 and 8).[7] Besides the words ἐπισκοπή (3, 15 and 17), προστασία, προστῆναι (2, 2; 3, 9 and 10; 5, 4; 6, 7–8), ἐπιστασία (2, 1; 3, 9), the word that usually symbolizes this function of government is ἀρχή.[8] The bishop is, secondly, the one who, standing (3, 4), celebrates the sacred mysteries, the "heavenly mysteries" (3, 5), the "august", the "terrible mysteries" (3, 4); the one who enters into the sanctuary where he is surrounded by angels (6, 1), who invokes the Spirit with authority to make God himself descend, immolated, to the altar. Because of this, his responsibility is called ἱερωσύνη: he is the ἱερεύς. Finally, he is the guardian of doctrine, whose transmittal he must assure; he thus instructs the people, he forms them in Christian morals, he teaches with authority: this is his third responsibility: the διδασκαλία (4, 3 and 7; 5, 1).

Without ever indicating in what measure and under what conditions the simple priest participates in each of these three functions, which in their source and in their fullness are those of the bishop (the *Dialogue*

[7] The remark has often been made but is at times forgotten: the bishop (or priest) who presides over the Christian assembly is not a "president" in the modern civil or political sense; "it refers to something very different from a simple presidency; or rather, if one sticks to this word at any price, this presidency only expresses an infinitely more mysterious reality": Maurice Paissac, O.P., "Le Ministère du prêtre", in *Sources* (Fribourg) 3 (1977): 168.

[8] The faithful are ἀρχόμενοι (5, 1).

is no more a treatise on canon law than it is on theology), John reminds us in passing that the ministry of which he speaks is comprised of various degrees, that the bishop is assisted by different ministers (3, 15) placed below him, and it is clear that the work taken as a whole exalts, not the episcopate alone as such, but the priesthood in general (3, 7 and 8). On the other hand, the three functions that he recognizes in it are not, for him, separate but united and solidary: the one who directs and teaches the people is the very one who transmits God's gift to them; in this threefold and unique task, he is truly (although always ministerially) their father; he engenders them to the divine life as our parents engender us to this present life (3, 6).

John devotes long passages to the duty of preaching: "The priest must do everything to acquire the talent for it." Yet this incomparable orator stresses the first two aspects of the ministry perhaps more than this third, at least in the particularly doctrinal passages. He knows nothing of our present timidities concerning either the effective reality of a ministerial authority or the eminently sacred character of the priestly ministry. He does not seek to tone down formulas in their regard, quite the contrary. One sees that he is fully conscious that he is not giving out personal views or describing only a certain state of affairs, but rather is reproducing in its integrity the traditional Faith of the Church, coming from the apostles and, through them, from Christ. Far from watering down "authority" as a "sign", he uses the term ἐξουσία (3, 6) in all its force, as the New Testament itself does. He admires the greatness of the authority that the grace of the Spirit has conferred on the priest: authority that is not human but truly "celestial": to administer the mysteries, to engender to the divine life, to remit faults, to heal the wounds of the soul, to reunite in the body of the Church the members who have separated themselves from it (2, 4). . . . What the priest decides on earth, God confirms in heaven (3, 5). If the Father, he also says, has given judgment to his Son, the Son in turn has transmitted it to his priests (3, 5). John is not even afraid to use the military metaphor to affirm authority: if the Christian life is a battle in which one can never lay down arms, the bishop is the head of the army of Christ (6, 13).[9] Another, more intrinsic, analogy: Christ has confided his sheep, for whom he shed his blood, to Peter and his successors; now, when a bishop is placed at the head of his flock, he

[9] "In the war against the spirit of evil, it is not permitted to lay down one's arms. . . ."

finds himself installed in the same functions that a love greater than that of any other had reserved for Peter. Elsewhere, John Chrysostom will witness to the primacy of the bishop of Rome, successor of Peter, in the universal Church; in the dialogue on the priesthood, not departing from his subject, he is content to evoke Peter as the supreme example in order to show the greatness of the authority of the bishop in his own church (2, 1 and 2). And addressing the community of the faithful, he repeats the very terms of the exhortation that we read in the Letter to the Hebrews: "Obey your leaders and submit to them"—πείθεσθε τοῖς ἡγουμένοις ὑμῶν, καὶ ὑπείκετε (Heb 13:17) (3, 17).

To whatever degree one considers it, the priestly ministry never appears in this dialogue of John Chrysostom as if it were simply one kind of ministry or service among numerous others; it is not "in a series with" others, although clearly distinct from them by the fact that it is "ordained", as is sometimes said today, rather unfortunately in our opinion. It does not have the same origin. Within the Christian profession or Christian vocation, which is the same for all, which in all its forms tends to one, unique end: the glory of God and the building up of the Church (6, 5), the unicity of which John obviously never had the slightest thought of contesting (if by chance he had been tempted to think of it, it would rather have been with respect to the monk), the distinction between pastors and faithful, or priests and laity, is as clear as it is essential, and nothing permits classifying it under a larger genre. There is one clergy (κλῆρος), one order of clergy (κλήρου τάξις) (3, 15; 6, 8; cf. 5, 4) in the Church. To become a priest, one must be "called" and receive ordination, according to the rite in use from the first century, through the imposition of hands (4, 2; χειροτονεῖν, and so on). Let us note in passing that on two occasions John declares that there could be no question of women in the priestly ministry or in hierarchical government; their vocation is different. He considers the divine law (ὁ θεῖος νόμος) to be categorical on this subject (2, 2; 3, 9).

The second aspect of ministry is, if possible, emphasized even more. One is conscious of it in the frequency of the words ἱερεύς, ἱερωσύνη.[10] One sees it still better in the holy enthusiasm—this is the case to use that adjective—with which the author is seized when he comes to describe, in the third book, the celebration of the Eucharist (3, 4–5). He is no less aware than we that the properly "sacerdotal" vocabulary

[10] The two words, passim. Cf. ἱερωμένος (3, 4 and 10); ἱερατικὴ ἀξία (13, 15).

is absent from New Testament writings. But he knows better than some of us that from apostolic times the eucharistic mystery was at the heart of the life of the Church,[11] and that if there is any ministerial authority at all in the Church, it is above all for the act in which this mystery is realized that such an authority, such a "gift of God" is necessary.[12] Moreover, he, like every one of us, was able to ascertain the liturgical and sacramental atmosphere with which so many pages of the New Testament are permeated.[13] Any effort tending to "desacralize" the original Christian conception of the priest and bishop runs into the reality of a general situation that is well attested and that is soon manifest even in the words as soon as the danger of confusion either with the Jewish priesthood or even more with pagan priesthoods was dismissed. John Chrysostom is, in the fourth century, along with others, the witness of a language (assuredly analogical) that could at times develop in excessive proportions but no part of which had to overcome the least resistance in order to be accepted in the Church. Every time, on the contrary, that, under external influences, the organic links between the functions of authority and the liturgical functions were relaxed, this was to the detriment of both alike. In equal proportion, as the ecclesiastical authority was then distorted, conceived more or less in the way one would conceive of a secular authority (and consequently vulnerable to Christian sentiment), the Eucharist, losing its eminent place and involving the whole sacramental order in its disgrace, no longer opposed the force of its mystery to the invasion of secularism or to that of an aberrant "sacred". A twofold and inevitable disintegration. History offers many examples of it. On the contrary, it is because he is a ἱερεύς that the bishop according to Chrysostom can exercise in a Christian manner, without fear, his ἐξουσία.

One theory has been spreading for several years, in some writings with a popular bias, according to which we supposedly depend today, in the Catholic conception of the priestly ministry, on a late deviation, from which it would be appropriate to free ourselves. It is a question, some say, "of a synthesis worked out particularly in the Middle Ages, in a global situation that we can describe as sacral"; others, wishing

[11] Philippe H. Menoud, *Jésus-Christ et la Foi* (Neuchâtel, 1975), 74–76 and 354.

[12] Cf. Malingrey, *Jean Chrysostome*, 79, commenting on bk. 3, chaps. 4 and 5.

[13] Cf. Louis Bouyer, "L'Application au ministère apostolique des expressions sacerdotales", *Nova et vetera* 51 (1976), 179–87.

to be a bit less disrespectful of history, admit that "from the fifth century" a certain number of new factors supposedly stressed the ritualistic aspect of a ministry that was until then essentially, to its highest degree, a "ministry of the word". In short, more or less belatedly, "a kind of identification or freeze" was supposedly in operation "between the ecclesial presidency and the eucharistic presidency", or rather, as is sometimes said, "between the evangelizing function or the ministry of the word and the function of worship"; a freeze operated to the benefit of the latter and to the detriment of the former. The Council of Trent supposedly in some way canonized the result of this deviation. Nothing is less in conformity with historical reality. John Chrysostom, who does not belong "particularly in the Middle Ages"(!), or even to the fifth century, and who is not an innovator, is witness of this to us. In his conception of the unity of the (episcopal) priestly ministry in its threefold function, he reproduces that of earlier Christian generations. What some wish to call a "belated freeze" is quite the contrary a very early synthesis.[14] One should reread, for example, the letters of Ignatius of Antioch. This bishop did not invent the "monarchical episcopate": "it is clearly apparent that the situation" he describes, if it includes variations, is nevertheless "not new, and that it aroused no resistance, no surprise".[15] Now it is no less clearly apparent in these letters that, if this bishop "presides" over his church, with the assistance of his priests, in the strongest sense of this word, it is simultaneously over her teaching, over her worship and her government, in an indissoluble manner.[16]

It is obviously not out of the question that the liturgical flowering

[14] Here we have an example of that tendency toward dissociating and separating that, whether through a poorly understood concern for analysis or through a desire to promote reforms in view of a "new Church", appears in various publications between "word" and "worship", and also, on the subject of the Eucharist, between "meal" and "sacrifice", or again, between "reference to Christ" and "reference to the Church", etc.

[15] Camelot, *Sources chrètiennes* 10:46. Maurice Goguel, *L'Église primitive* (Payot, 1947), 147: "It is not accurate to say, as is sometimes done, that Ignatius is the father of the monarchical episcopate."

[16] In *Pour la vie du monde: Le sacrement de l'ordre*, Father Albert Chapelle remarks that the constitution *Lumen Gentium* of Vatican II "always speaks of the episcopal ministry in the singular; the *ministerium* is comprised of several *munera*, charges" (Brussels, Institute of Theological Studies, 1978), 63, note 70. If, breaking up the synthesis, one were to pull, so to speak, the *ministerium* into separate pieces, it would be very difficult to avoid, simultaneously or in turn, following the predominant tendencies, legalism in government, the magistery of professors in doctrine, superstition in worship.

in Antioch in the fourth century and the particular temperament of John Chrysostom had their part in certain accents in our *Dialogue*, in a certain emphasis as well as in the insistent comparisons of the officiating bishop with the Jewish high priest entering into the sanctuary or with Elias calling down fire over the sacrifice on Mount Carmel (3, 4).[17] One also senses in it the mystical sighing of homilies "on the Incomprehensible" that reveal to us an orator very different from the exegete, but no more than that[18]—the personality of this great man of the Church is as rich as it is likeable. The present work is also distinguished by several other traits that offer something of interest for the biography of its author or for the history of his milieu and his times, but without major consequences from a doctrinal point of view. It is thus that the very normal distinction between priests and monks or ascetics becomes here, in the heat of discussion, a kind of irreducible antithesis and takes on a quasi-obsessive relief; the reason for this is wholly personal:[19] sure of his monastic vocation, already experienced, Chrysostom is (or was) in awe of the ministry, its responsibilities and temptations; he would do everything to avoid the responsibility of the episcopate; in seeking to impose it on him, one was wishing, it seemed to him, to throw him into hell.[20] One thinks here too of Gregory the Great, who likewise groaned at having been torn away from his monastic condition and from his contemplation in order to exercise functions that involved him in the age and to be promoted finally to head of the Church.[21] Other points of a more general interest are also brought out: thus, the election of candidates to the priesthood or the episcopate, such as it was practiced at that time in Antioch (5, 10 and 15)—without this mode of designation being confused with any delegation whatever of priestly authority. That gives us a vivid scene traced

[17] See also, 6, 4, reminiscent of mystical vocabulary: εἰς οὕτως ἱερὰν τελετὴν . . . εἰσάγων. There was, moreover, nothing new about this.

[18] *Sources chrètiennes* 28. *Sur l'incompréhensibilité de Dieu*, by J. Daniélou, A. M. Malingrey, R. Flacelière (1970).

[19] An observation of Father Festugière would be applicable here, saying (191) that there is at times in John Chrysostom "a kind of inflexibility, a tendency to extreme solutions".

[20] The expression is F. Martin's; a free translation but summing up well the general impression given by chapters 8 to 15 of book 3 (*Classiques Garnier*, 54). Cf. l. 5, c. 8: "Waves assail the soul of the one who has received the priesthood, more numerous than the winds that stir the sea."

[21] Cf. Claude Dagens, *Saint Grégoire le Grand. Culture et expérience chrétienne*. Études augustiniennes (1977), 136–45.

by an observer "without illusions and without indulgence".[22] Those ambitious persons who intrigue in order to obtain votes and who grow impatient if the bishop is late in dying end in arguing among themselves in mixed truths. The meetings of the priest electors are no less tumultuous; plagued in addition by factions among the laity, they furnish our author with an occasion to observe that "the opinion of the crowd is subject to many errors" (2, 4; cf. 3, 15)—in which he repeats several disillusioned reflections of Origen.[23] "Tell me, what is the source", he ends by asking, "of the disorders that reign in the churches? As for me, I can see the principal one only in the ill-considered and reckless elections of those who are to govern them."

This brief analysis is in no way a summary of the *Dialogue*. Without pretending to do more than bring out the principal ideas of the doctrine of the priesthood presented there in scattered references, it would still be necessary to complete it with what John Chrysostom teaches, by mixing there all kinds of realistic matters, about the thousand obstacles of the priest (3, 8), about his formidable pastoral responsibilities, about the temptations of various orders of which he must beware, about spiritual discernment and all the high virtues, human and supernatural, that his responsibility demands of him (2, 4; 3, 10, and so on). He knows well that the qualities required of a Church leader are very different from those that make, for example, the accomplished monk. He does not forget the necessity of wise administration. He does not ignore the fact that the sanctifying role of the priest does not essentially derive from his personal holiness (he can recall on the occasion that it is the Holy Spirit who acts through him in the acts of his ministry); but he also knows that the unworthiness of the minister reflects inevitably on the esteem of his ministry and especially that only a holy priest will be able to guide the people of whom he is the pastor in the ways of holiness. Nothing is less like the priest fulfilling functions that remain totally external to him (half-time or full-time) than the portrait he traces (ἱερέως εἰκόνα), which is often inspired by "the admirable Saint Paul" (2, 3; 4, 7; 6, 5). Whence, above all, that fear in him, which he expresses retrospectively in the form of a dialogue with his friend Basil. "The Lord", he has him observe, "says clearly that the care exercised for his flock was a proof of love for him." "But then,"

[22] Malingrey, *Jean Chrysostome*, 86–87.

[23] Origen, *In Num*. hom. 22, n. 4; *In Gen*. hom. 3, n. 3.

Basil replies, "you, you do not, therefore, love Jesus Christ?" "I love him," responds John, "and I will never stop loving him; but I fear to offend the one I love" (2, 4).[24] Mademoiselle Malingrey, who quotes this passage and praises Basil's good sense, rightly concludes: "That is the key of the dialogue. The priesthood is a proof of love, but it is a thing so great that John feels unworthy to be ordained."[25]

We will leave the reader to discover for himself so many other pages, full of flavor. There is nothing, besides, that lacks timeliness. That will quickly be perceived. It is the characteristic of works that deserve the name of classics to cross centuries without ever ceasing to have something to say to us. It takes only a little historical imagination on our part and a slight effort to adapt. The *Dialogue on the Priesthood* is one of those works. Would it not be beneficial for us to reread it in a time when, as John Chrysostom once said, "the Church is more agitated than the waters of Euripus"?[26]

---

[24] "Nowhere else will those who aspire to the priestly or episcopal dignity learn better how dangerous is the responsibility they are taking on their shoulders." Erasmus to W. Pirckheimer, March 14, 1525. Allen, 6, 65.

[25] Malingrey, *Jean Chrysostome*, 78.

[26] Οὐδὲν Εὐρίπου τὴν ἐκκλησίαν διαφέρειν ποιοῦσιν (l. 3, c. 15). We are borrowing once again F. Martin's translation (57), which is literally a little forced.

2. Origenian Transposition

Celsus, in his *True Discourse*, quoted a passage from Plato's *Letter VII*, on the four elements that constitute knowledge: "The first is the name, the second the logos, the third the image, and the fourth the knowledge itself". Origen, who follows his adversary step by step in order to answer him, seizes this text and explains it in his own way. An explanation so strange at first glance, so enigmatic, that commentators who do not pass it by in silence admit their embarrassment, unless they decide boldly to declare that what we have here is simply a word puzzle.

Anyone who wishes should refer now, at the beginning of the second part of this work, to the paragraph in which Father Henri Crouzel proposes his interpretation. However little one may be familiar with Origen's thought, with his categories, with his customary behavior, one will not fail, we believe, to recognize him: *Father Crouzel has unraveled the enigma*. Day suddenly breaks; a curtain is rent open. Previously, one could see nothing; but once one has seen, doubt seems no longer possible: the meaning proposed is at once so well suited to the words, so coherent, so in conformity with the genius of the author, it also opens up so vast a perspective on the intention of his work that it compels conviction. Excellent analysts have been unable to discover its meaning, and the obscurity of the text is a sufficient excuse for them. It is nonetheless true that chance does not preside over such successes. The latter presuppose on the part of the historian an acquired familiarity with the subject of their study. It is one of those "good fortunes" that repay a long effort of penetration.

Plato frames knowledge in four stages, each summed up in one word. Origen likewise frames knowledge in four stages, copied from the four words of Plato. Only, the knowledge that he has in mind is of a different nature: it is the understanding of divine Scripture, or—for him, it is all one thing—the knowledge of Christ. Nothing more is needed to change everything, utterly. Thus it is very much a copy, to be sure; but

---

Preface to Henri Crouzel, *Origène et la connaissance mystique*, Museum Lessianum (DDB, 1961).

it is at the same time an opposition. It is an imitation of Platonism, and it is at the same stroke its antithesis. It has the same order of sequence, but with steps each one of which is profoundly different, to attain an end that is no longer at all the one of knowledge conceived by Plato—any more than any other human wisdom whatsoever. Here we have a fine example of that Origenian "transposition" of Platonism, the constant, though unsought, subject of Father Henri Crouzel's work. Or rather, we have here that totally complete transposition, in what makes the heart of it.

One can be particularly sensitive to Origen's "Platonism". One can also be sensitive to the "transposition" he brings about in Platonism. In the same way, among the historians of Plato himself, some apply themselves to diagnosing all the elements he borrows from poets, Orphism, the language of mysteries, mental schema received perhaps from ancient Iran—while others, more concerned with the essence, strive to show all these transposed elements in this original synthesis that we call Platonism. Both aims are just. The second is more so. The first is a historically indispensable preamble; but, alone, it would be misleading. The second includes the first; it takes it into consideration, it gives an account of it, and it measures its definite limits as it discerns its possible illusions. In Origen's case, it will be specified only that the new synthesis, made up in part of elements, or rather according to frameworks, of Platonian imprint, must be designated only secondarily "Origenian". For Origen professes to be above all a faithful interpreter of the Scriptures, such as the Christian tradition, to which he adheres with all his being, understands them. The success of his undertaking can obviously be only mixed. The synthesis obtained is not perfect; it is not difficult to note errors, incoherences, awkwardness, views that are still confused, as well as brief beginnings of long developments to come. But these faults themselves, as manifest as they may be, as serious as one judges them, can be well understood only if one perceives, in its clarity as in its vigor, the dominant thought of this extraordinary genius. It is Christianity that this "man of the Church" defends, against Celsus or against heresy; it is the doctrine of Christ that he sets forth before the bishops assembled in order to learn from him; it is the very person of Christ that he presents as the source of all renewal and the principle of final unity; it is the Christian life that he preaches tirelessly in his treatises and in his homilies; it is the Christian interpretation of all things, of which he is the first to try his hand at tracing the major principles. As personal as he may be, it is never his own thought that he wishes to construct.

After having shown how, in the spirit of Christianity such as Origen understands it, a law of transcendence is everywhere at work, Father Crouzel concludes: "Origenian exegesis is, like the Platonian dialectic, in this continual transcendence." This is perfectly illustrated by the Origenian commentary on the four words of Plato. Each step is there a stage calling for the next stage, and the last itself, which seems to reach the goal, does not place an end to the course: it in reality opens onto an endless beyond. That is again an analogy; but it must be understood in the proper sense of that word, which, in philosophical language, means both resemblance and difference—and difference even more. Imitation is transformed immediately into contrast. On both sides, here, a "continual transcendence": but, on one side, it is by means of a certain "exegesis", itself constituting a very different kind of dialectic, a new dialectic, as new as Christian revelation, all aspects of which it is trying to express successively. Now the "transcendence" itself is found to be necessarily other, according as the motive is such a dialectic or such an exegesis. . . .

The history of Christian thought offers other cases of these kinds of transpositions. One could almost say that it is the history of the succession of these cases. Always necessary—for supernatural revelation does not come to reign on a desert of thought, after having exterminated the fruits of natural research—these transpositions are at work thanks to the force of discernment and assimilation hidden at the heart of the Faith. If this force is always the same, it acts each time in very diverse conditions. Yet it never cuts down entirely the resistances of the given on which it operates. It is not, therefore, only with Origen that the result remains imperfect. A total success can only be dreamed of. . . . We could cite as an example of these great undertakings the work of Pseudo-Dionysius, in situating it with respect to the second Neoplatonism. But the must illustrious case of all, because of its fullness, its decisiveness and its success, is that of Saint Thomas Aquinas.

Through the diversity of the two historical situations, the work of Saint Thomas is comparable in this regard to the work of Origen. Aristotelianism is adopted in it, but not without being transposed—and if the adoption is frank and massive, the transposition that accompanies it is more radical than many of the interpreters of Thomism have perceived. The works of Étienne Gilson—who goes to the point of speaking of "metamorphosis"—have admirably shown this in our time. No more than Origen chose Plato, moreover—the passage from *Contra Celsum*, in this too, is symbolic, since the transposed text is found imposed by Celsus—did Saint Thomas, properly speaking, "choose" Aristotle. The doctrine of the "Philosopher" was for him, as for those whom he had to combat, Philosophy itself, in all its seductive brilliance. Origen and Saint Thomas both had, each in his time, the intuition of what constituted for their faith what would be called, according to the point of view, either the essential enemy or the fundamental need. No more in the domain of knowing than in that of acting did either of them wish to "overturn" everything: they believed it better to "purify". For neither of them was it a matter, except in a very partial way, of some "pious misconception" or, as has also been said, some "fortunate misunderstanding". Neither is what moves and guides them any sort of opportunistic tactic, for they are both ingenuous in their love for the truth. At the root of their effort there was much less conscious reflex than higher instinct—so completely did they identify themselves, so to speak, in the depth of their being, with the historical moment then lived by the Church.

Father Crouzel is not long in defining the kind of transposition that is proper to Origen, in measuring its depth, in describing its processes, in tracing its limits and in stressing its failures. He thought, with good reason, that it was better to provide simply whatever, with respect to the main subject he had chosen, might permit the reader to make his own judgment. Neither did he seek to follow a chronological order. A certain *consensus* of the best experts on Origen's work dissuaded him from having recourse to a method that can be imperative in certain subjects but which presented more inconveniences than advantages here. It is generally recognized, following Völker, Bardy, Lieske, Schérer and others, that there is not, in this work such as it presents itself to us, any distinguishable doctrinal evolution. At best, we note, with René Cadiou or with Mme. M. Harl, that "the doctrine's center of gravity gradually shifts", concern for the spiritual life taking precedence in the author over problems of a cosmological order, and that he "seems to have become increasingly simple". To the degree in which the different writings can be dated with precision, moreover, anyone can ascertain, on one point or another, the progress in the precision of the formulas or the variation in the nuances of the thought.

What is more important and demands a more synthetic exposition is a gathering of the parallel or complementary texts on each theme dealt with. For the differences that one notes from one text to another are most often explained by the occasion that dictates the literary genre and the point of view. Henri Charles Puech has remarked, with his customary perceptiveness: "It is appropriate to consider the passages taken as a whole. Origen is not complete in any one of them alone." More than one modern historian, beginning with Harnack, has made serious mistakes for having neglected this warning. At the risk of a certain slowness, Father Crouzel has made a strict rule of this, in a manner that could often be called exhaustive, and his interpretations are assured of a serious objectivity because of it.

Origen displays a thought that is often profound through a work that is rarely technical. This is what makes an examination of his vocabulary particularly indispensable, and this examination must be all the more minute as this vocabulary is the more elusive. Whence these three long chapters that open each of the three parts of the work. They introduce us successively to the subject of knowledge, its point of departure and its act, and already we avoid many missteps. Are we to say that all the conclusions to which we are directed are clearly imperative from the evidence? Assuredly not. No verbal precision, no precautions of method, no collation of texts will ever dictate the final interpretation, which one must still strive toward if one truly seeks to understand. Father Crouzel, in the end, invites us to see an ideal of a mystical nature in the Origenian ideal of knowing and a true mystic in Origen himself. At the end of his demonstration, it would be difficult to argue the first of these two theses, understanding, of course, that it is a question of Christian mysticism, founded on Scripture; a question of the ideal of the "vision" such as Origen found it enunciated in Saint Paul and Saint John, not of that universal mysticism of monist tendency, which is all that a number of our contemporaries have in mind. As for knowing if he himself was a mystic, it seems to us that the only ones who could have any serious doubts about this are those who would begin by setting up a certain dichotomy between doctrine and experience, such as has been in circulation for a few centuries. But is this dichotomy absolutely justified? Does it not constitute here, in any case, an anachronism? By the very fabric and thrust of his thought, which is not separable from the innermost part of his life, it seems to us that Origen is one of the greatest mystics of the Christian tradition. Without treating the subject in depth—that would be another volume

—Father Crouzel at least furnishes, through his fine and rich analyses, a solid point of departure and a sure orientation to anyone who would like to take up this new exploration.

3. Giovanni Pico della Mirandola and Pedro Garcia

Father Henri Crouzel has kindly proposed that I preface this work. Of course I would be unable to add or retract anything from his erudition, and how would it be possible to add any commentary to a commentator as diligent and penetrating, who leaves nothing in shadow? But then, how could I resist the pleasure of saying a word about our common friend, the Count of Concordia?

Once Father Crouzel had the text of Pedro Garcia in his hands, it surely did not take him long to perceive that only its rarity could make him deem it invaluable. None of the arguments that this established theologian accumulated against his young rival was capable of seducing Father Crouzel; no page of these *Determinationes* could prompt him to believe that he was going to bring back to light some misunderstood thinker. If, in his introductions and notes, he follows in the footsteps of our man, it is nearly always in order to catch him out in some error. Perhaps even one reader or another will be tempted to consider that Father Crouzel does him too much honor by applying himself to refuting him according to the rules, sometimes even, as in the course of the "disputes" of former times, by *distingo*, *concedo* and *nego*. But an exacting, professional conscience—to which it is permissible to think some mischievousness came to be joined—wanted it that way. Can we conclude from this that the exhumation of such a *factum* was not worth the trouble? Assuredly not! It not only furnishes us with a perfect specimen, perfectly explained, of the worst theology of the period: it constitutes a marvelous foil against which to place the prose of Giovanni Pico in relief. I was mistaken a while back: for this new reason, the text of Pedro Garcia does seem to us truly invaluable.

This is only one specimen. There are a dozen others, among which one would discover some more bizarre, more aberrant even (despite a few little intervals of good sense), more characteristic in showing what could be, at this end of the fifteenth century, a degenerate Scholasti-

Preface to Henri Crouzel, S.J., *Une Controverse sur Origène à la Renaissance* (Paris: Vrin, 1977).

cism. Garcia extols his own merit in having "spent a long time and very many sleepless nights" refuting the erroneous "Conclusions" of Pico. The latter would supposedly not have lost a minute, as we know, in trying to reply to him. He himself had spent only a few days, of intense work, it is true, in composing his *Apologia*, and what Father Crouzel admires in the chapter on Origen has its equivalent, and perhaps something even better, in more than one other chapter. The young author must have improvised the justification of theses for which he could not have known in advance he would be reproached. Under these conditions, this *Apologia* is an astonishing work, in the knowledge of which it gives proof as much as in the qualities of spirit that are manifest in it.

Father Crouzel indicates, with respect to the question of Origen, both the strength and the inevitable weaknesses of it. Let us also recognize an additional merit in it: let us admire it for what it does not say. Giovanni Pico's critical sense made him disdain completely a famous legend about the "fall" coming from a story by Saint Epiphanius, which for centuries everyone picked up to explain in his own way. For anyone interested in the classic question of the "salvation of Origen", that was the quasi-obligatory theme. Now Pico does not even feel the need to discuss it: from his pen, there is not the least allusion. He is content to brush aside with a word the apocryphal *Planctus* that was customarily linked to this legend, this *Planctus* that would be included by the scholar Merlin in the 1522 edition of Origen. He thereby freed himself from an old custom, which would continue to impose itself for centuries on the most serious historians: like Baronius and Denis Petau, Jean Daillé and Paganini, Daniel Huet and Antoine Pagi, and so forth, setting them in opposition to each other in a resolutionless battle and making them rant and rave for no purpose. Even people like Tillemont and Basnage would believe they still had to expend their critical forces to uproot a tenacious conviction, the echoes of which have not been completely subdued even in our own century. . . .

Giovanni Pico was not afraid to call things by their name. Of the theory that serves as the basis for the blame that is inflicted on him, he says, quite bluntly, that it is "foolishness". He proclaims that the criticism of the censors is "unjust", that their judgment "is not right": he makes fun of one of them, in passing, in a comic scene; he addresses them at the end of a severe preface by referring to the very words of the Lord in Deuteronomy. We should not see in that any bravado, any irreverence toward authority. The condemnation of which he complains is still only a "magisterial determination" and not "the determination of the Church"; those whom he criticizes, in turn, are not judges but only "masters", which is to say, experts—and Garcia himself, two years later, would have to recognize, all bishop that he was and all mandated by the pope as he says, that the long dissertation that he opposes to the defense of Pico is, itself, nothing more than a "magisterial determination". He will, moreover, weaken a bit, no longer daring to accuse the chivalrous champion of Origen of an opinion "smelling of heresy" but only of recklessness.

Poor Pico? Victim in his time of a handful of theologians, he was, after his death, to be the victim of a whole battalion of historians. It was recently written of him that he was "slandered". This is not the right word in all cases, for the historians of which we are thinking here, by exaggerating or by imagining the deviation of his positions with respect to the orthodoxy of the Church, were thinking much rather to glorify him. This affair of the 1487 "Dispute", of which Pedro Garcia's work was one of the consequences, has often been magnified by them. As painful as it may have been for the young count, attacked not only in his self-love but in his Catholic sentiment, it was never very serious and could not be counted among the signs that mark the great crises of thought that the Church has passed through in the course of her history. A closer examination of the texts, of the dates and facts has shown that there was never, on Pico's part, any intention or gesture of revolt or of disloyalty; and on the part of the Holy See (and of Garcia himself), no mark of any lack of esteem toward his person, quite the contrary. The inquisitorial tribunal that was for a moment constituted seems never really to have functioned at all. The *Apologia* that Pico presented of his theses prior to any sentence from the pope did not give rise to any examination followed by judgment, any more than the explanatory *Mémoires* accumulated two centuries later by Fénelon prior to the condemnation of the *Maximes des saints* were to incur censure. From the time the fugitive returned to Paris, a more or less tacit compromise was established, and the persistent bad humor of several members of the curia seems not to have had any appreciable effect. Finally, all was soon smoothed out by the Brief of Alexander VI.

As for the root of the matter, several of the historians about whom we are speaking had undoubtedly not explored the *Apologia* very closely, fearing to venture into the underground of thorny controversies, of which it is full. On the other hand, all had admired this "Discourse on the Dignity of Man", as it was called, in which they thought to see a "manifesto", the "manifesto of the Renaissance", considered in a spirit of opposition to traditional Catholicism. Such an interpretation has already, for some time, been shaken, thanks to a better knowledge of earlier tradition. Now here comes a recent discovery to shatter it even more, if possible. This celebrated discourse, which its author had neither given orally nor published, was widely known only after his death, when it appeared in a section devoted to minor writings. Far from raising a scandal, it was received very favorably in religious circles. Going through the libraries and archives of Rome, Father John W. O'Malley has found a whole series of sermons dating from the last years of the fifteenth century and from the first third of the sixteenth, in which several use—let us even say plagiarize—Pico's discourse. Some of them come from preachers at the Roman court and are not in any way worldly sermons. This discovery will contribute to restoring, for a wider circle, the true face of Pico della Mirandola.[1] The important publication that we owe today to Father Henri Crouzel will make us better understand some of its principal features.

[1] John W. O'Malley, University of Detroit, "Preaching for the Popes", in *The Pursuit of Holiness in Late Medieval and Renaissance Religion*, Papers from the University of Michigan conference, edited by Charles Trinkaus with Heiko A. Oberman (Leiden: E. J. Brill, 1974), 408–43.

4. Preface to Georges Chantraine's *"Mystère" et "Philosophie du Christ" selon Erasmus*

Erasmian studies are thriving. Never, without doubt, have they been more abundant. Never have their results been more substantial. At the same time as the work of the great humanist is taking on new dimensions, it appears in many respects to be of profound timeliness. If its Latin form protects it always and more and more inexorably from facile curiosity and hasty uses, a pleiad of good interpreters brings it close to us, making it live again. "It seems indeed that Colet's prophecy: 'The name of Erasmus will never perish' is being fulfilled. . . . At a time when national languages are flowering, it does not concede a word to them, and here it remains standing, monumental, in the wreck of latinity" (Manuel de Diéguez).

From the numerous works that were devoted to him in our century and that the five hundredth anniversary of his birth is multiplying at the present time, the most important knowledge acquired as well as the least debatable seems to me to be the following: if one wants to understand Erasmus, one must above all consider him as a theologian. The remark might seem banal. One might in fact be surprised that so many historians, and not the least of them, have for so long a time doubted this or, rather, even at times seemed not to suspect it. A whole tradition was thereby formed, at least in France, that presented Erasmus to what one calls the educated public under a false light. They ended in seeing nothing in his person any more but "scepticism" and "irony"; nothing in his activity as a scholar but love of the "old classical authors"; nothing in his most resounding writings but "manifestations of a lay spirit", and even in his fight against Luther, only the desire to save "the unrecognized interests of erudition". . . . Some much more serious works, in the first ranks of which must be placed the considerable work of Augustin Renaudet, have undoubtedly put an end to this absurd portrait; but too often they were once again invalidated at

---

Gembloux: Duculot, 1971, vii–x.

their base by a certain number of prejudices, the fruits of the liberal and modernizing context of the period. The monumental publication of the correspondence, however, which stretched out for more than half a century (1906–1958), has gradually necessitated a more just view of the man, of his behavior as well as of his thought. That Erasmus should be counted, in the proper sense of the word, among the theologians is the fact that results with increased evidence, notwithstanding a few hesitations, from a whole series of investigations. The long works by Pierre Imbart de La Tour and by Marcel Bataillon, the biography by Huizinga, opened the way. Others have advanced along it, such as Pierre Mesnard, Albert Hyma, Roland Bainton, J. B. Payne, C. Béné, Louis Bouyer, Léon E. Halkin. In 1966, Ernst Wilhelm Kohls defended at Erlangen a remarkable thesis with the significant title *Die Theologie des Erasmus*. A few methodological lacunae and a certain excess of systematization drew him some criticism. One can read in the *Revue d'histoire ecclésiastique* of 1969 the corrections carried out by Father Georges Chantraine, to whom the work of Erasmus had already been familiar for some time.

Kohls had taken as the basis for his study the celebrated *Enchiridion militis christiani*, which is still an early work and one whose doctrinal implications are not always apparent. Rather than start out by painting some vast fresco, Father Chantraine himself wanted to limit strictly his field of research and to proceed by analysis. But he chose a less narrow and more certain basis. He applied himself to two writings from the year 1518: the *Letter to Volz* and the *Ratio verae theologiae*. The reasons behind this choice are clear. These are two major works, although relatively brief, dating from what is rightly called the second period of Erasmus' literary activity. The *Ratio* is a methodical and serene treatise. As for the *Letter to Volz*, Erasmus himself made it an introduction to a new edition that he was giving the *Enchiridion*: it brings out the theological principles and confers a new fullness to the latter work. It thereby constitutes a privileged place for a genetic study of Erasmian thought. It will also be noted that the year 1518 is prior to the period of the great controversies that would soon surge, on the one hand, with Luther and, on the other, with a certain number of indomitable Scholastics and paganizing humanists. We can well imagine that there would be great interest in grasping at this crucial moment a theological thought already mature, fixed in a positive expression, before it is in danger of being warped in one way or another by the forces of polemics or at least before it is presented only under partial aspects.

For the first time, these two major works are thus submitted to a minute examination, according to all the rigor of a method that can be called at once semantic, structural and thematic. They are, besides, clarified in all their details by an abundant use of marvelously rich correspondence; finally, the comparison with earlier works allows the principal lines of force to be isolated: from the *Enchiridion* to the *Ratio*, through the *Eulogy in Praise of Folly*, the *Sermon on the Infant Jesus* and the *Commentary on the Psalm Beatus vir*, we watch the passage from an individual point of view and a mystical ascension to a Christian initiation in which the ecclesial point of view is resolutely affirmed. We see unfold an intellectual dialectic that seems indeed to have its source in a spiritual deepening.

The two principal themes that emerge, gaining greater clarity at the same time, are that of the *Mysterium* and that of the *Philosophia Christi*. Those two terms, particularly the second one, are well known by anyone who has even begun to approach the reading of Erasmus or consulted one of his historians; but the understanding of them is profoundly renewed by the analyses of them that are offered to us here. We will not undertake to set forth the main features of them: that would be to attempt a summary of the whole work. Let us say only that, contrary to numerous interpretations, the theology that is expressed in these two themes in no way appears to be reductive. Or rather, if it is so in some manner, it is not with respect to the substance of the Faith but with respect to the complications of the Scholasticism of that time. Erasmus undertakes a work of simplification but, at the same time, one of concentration. He refuses to recognize these *moderni* with whom he has clashed for some twenty years as the legitimate heirs of the Christian tradition. He reproaches them for distancing themselves from Scripture and for their infidelity to the mind of the Fathers. He also judges—he who, to tell the truth, was not much of a philosopher—that there is in the human spirit a depth of which their philosophy is not able to give an account, so that they are left powerless to understand the Mystery of Christ in all its depths—that Mystery that is not only the whole of his "Christian philosophy" but governs even the literary composition of his two writings. As he will again strive to do the following year in his *Apologia ad Latomum*, he wishes to renew the bond that has become too slack between exegesis and theology—

beyond preparatory disciplines and auxiliary techniques—thanks to a spiritual exegesis that reproduces in some way, under the action of the Spirit of Christ, the movement of Christian reflection and life. Such is the essence of his "Origenism".

Erasmus is not a "systematic" theologian. A humanist of very sure taste, he uses his elegance to veil the technical character of his thought in both his composition and his vocabulary. But he is indeed a theologian, and professes to be such. For him, the Christian reality is entirely contained in the "circle" within which "Christ moves"; it has its sources and also many of its developments in this *Christi Fabula*, real history in multiple dimensions, at once dramatic and symbolic, visible and invisible, human and divine, personal and collective, of which the Church has the understanding and whose continuous fecundity she assures. When he declares, in 1520 and 1521, that he is adopting as the rule of his faith that of the Catholic Church, recognized in the Roman Church, he is not thereby bringing about any change or truly new precision to his thinking. He does not become "Catholic" late in life through some accommodation to circumstances or through lassitude or for any other motive. He declares simply, because the situation demands it, the attitude dictated to him by reflection that had already long been ripe.

Prepared under the direction of the eminent master Roger Aubert, approved by the vote of the University of Louvain, the work of Father Georges Chantraine had no need of an extraneous introduction. It is a study that is masterful in all aspects, carried out according to demanding norms and with a concern for perfect objectivity. From beginning to end, Erasmus himself has provided the commentary. The author has not tried to paint a portrait but to examine a thought closely. If in doing so he has been able to "apply benevolence to the principle of understanding", he has just as well been able to guard against any tendency toward apology, as well as against any artificial search for novelty. The conclusions it draws are, we believe, of extreme interest for the history of Christian thought. They can also be of importance today even for enlivening and clarifying in the Church an effort for renewal that has been so laboriously begun. Toward that end, the reflection with which the work closes might be exemplary. After having shown us at length as a historian how Erasmus, this individual of the sixteenth century, has worked out according to his means and in the conditions of his times a certain type of theology, or of "Christian philosophy", Father

Chantraine invites us to work with him a reversal of perspective. It would then be a question, based on the same historically established facts, of seeing, in a light of faith, how this Christian philosophy, taken in its fruitful essence, has engendered the better part of Erasmian thinking, how it has vivified it by becoming alive in its author. Among a number of others before and after him, Erasmus could thus be for us a witness that ceaseless fecundity that must continue in us.

5. On a Thought by Pascal

The eternal silence of these infinite spaces frightens me.[1]

"In the churches where he followed the humble services, Pascal read his Psalm 128, and then he mused. . . ." He mused. . . . First of those who do not muse: the immense crowd (flock), knowing nothing of the one thing necessary, not even bothering about it. They live outside themselves, fascinated by a trifle. What tone of voice would be capable of drawing them from their "diversion". . . . He mused, too, about the little handful of those who, like him, "do not have the power to stop musing": often more unfortunate than the others, because their musing turns into distress. Unfortunate and dangerous Christians, some scold, wanting to apply to them the order of the Talmud: "Stop your children from musing!" A despicable order, unworthy of the Christian, unworthy of man; one has no right to renounce his nobility under the pretext of quenching its misery. Will the thinking reed stop thinking in order not to suffer at seeing the advantage the Universe has over it? A waste of time, besides! "There are some who do not have the power to stop such musing, and who would muse so much the more if it were forbidden. They challenge false religions, and even the true one, if they do not find sound discourses."

Pascal thus will understand their demand: he knows well that it is not pride. He will seek the sound discourse suited to strengthen them, he will give them those proofs of religion that they cannot give themselves and that they do not know where to find. But first it is necessary to be a brother to them. In order to help them effectively, he must pass through their distress. The works he dreams of accomplishing, the mission he has received from his Lord, demand nothing less. The disciple is not above his master. As Christ healed our infirmities only by clothing himself with them, so only by suffering more than all of them could he himself bring a remedy for the great evil of which the men of his time were in danger of dying. Not that, for this, he himself

Unpublished text.

[1] Ed. Brunschvicg, 206.

had to waver in his faith: Christ took our misery upon himself but not the sin. But he must not be ignorant of the distress of the one who doubts; but he must feel the darkness of the mystery to the point of the most vivid suffering. It is not enough for him to know this uneasiness and this ceaseless *cogitatio*, common to all great souls, and which, compatible not only with the firmness but with the serenity of faith, purify it, exalt it, give it all its radiance and all its splendor. His faith, just as firm, will not always enjoy an equal serenity. In order to lift the weight that bruises the shoulders of his brothers, *it will be necessary* for him to be overwhelmed by it first himself.

If we want to understand the anguish of Pascal, let us make an effort to recall the critical situation created at that time for the Christian Faith by the new orientation of the human mind. Many, within the Church, suspected nothing of it; many, for a long time afterward, still did not suspect it—never suspected it. So well protected that they were unaware they needed a protector! Ungrateful without knowing it, they sometimes went to the point of pursuing him like an enemy. Pascal himself realized this situation. He saw the tragedy of it in his soul. A half-century later, writing to a disciple of Father Malebranche, Bossuet, in a flash, will glimpse something of it. But he will still place in the future the "great battle that is being prepared against Christianity", he will singularly reduce the cause of it, and—this is the essential difference—he will see only an evil to be repelled, only an external struggle to sustain, only enemies to conquer, souls to save from peril. An intrepid bishop, he will worry only about others. How much more marvelous was Pascal's clearsightedness, and how much more poignant his anguish! It is not only at the name of Descartes that he sees this great combat break out. It is not only against a group of rationalists that he is preparing to sustain it. The struggle has long since begun, and nowhere does it rage more terribly than within himself. For he carries within himself, in reality, the solicitude for so many Christian souls, surprised, frightened, abandoned before the vision of the universe that has been ascending to the horizon for a century and which is, more and more, asserting itself.

It is not a matter of avoiding a temptation or dissipating a mirage. The battle has not only begun within, it has penetrated to the innermost part of the spirit. This new vision, so fraught with danger, can indeed be cursed, but it cannot be erased. Such an overthrow had not been seen for sixteen centuries. A dissolution of Christianity, the rebirth of ancient culture, the rapid development of scientific thought: under the combined action of these three prodigious forces, especially the third one, the world has changed in appearance. A new era has begun. All thought, all life takes another course. It is impossible to ignore it. Impossible, too, not to wonder if the old faith has not been carried away in the gust of wind.

. . . And, continuing to muse, the great Blaise calls to mind the time of his youth. It was at the beginning of his stay in Paris. His father took him to meetings of scholars organized by the illustrious Mersenne. What enthusiasm in this group! Oh! It was not the confused impulse that had roused the preceding generations. The volcanic period of the Renaissance was succeeded by an age of methodical lucidity. The heavy intoxication was transformed into a clear dream: after having sung, reeling, in the soul of a Giordano Bruno, it had just taken the forms of wisdom in the mind of René Descartes, impassioned with reason, with method and with clarity. But it was indeed still an intoxication. The "little edifice" of science, of which Renan was one day to write, was henceforth made of steel; under the fascinated eyes of these men, in their hands still surprised to find themselves so powerful, it rose, rose always and would rise to infinity. They did not wonder, then, if it might not be, by chance, that science did not suffice for everything: did they not believe themselves henceforth capable, along with that magician, science, "of overthrowing all resistance and of clearing away all obstacles, even, perhaps, death"? In religion, no concern. No opposition, as there would soon be around Clerselier; but, following the example of the master—*Scribo etiam Turcis*—forgetfulness. As if it were enough to relegate faith to the background of one's personal life in order to spare it any clash with the new mistress of minds.

In this atmosphere, the young Pascal "really held his own place", already master of himself. He was enchanted by the Cartesian hope. He had celebrated "the man who has produced only for infinity". He was carried away by the promises of science. . . . Today, matured by experience, touched by grace, he trembles, musing that he might have let himself be taken forever by this intoxication, like others he knows, for whom he no longer dares hope, the habit in which they are of submitting everything to their scientific proceedings so "distances them from their heart that they can no longer return to it". Poor creatures, condemned to wake from their illusions only to fall into "an eternal despair". Since, for anyone who wishes to reflect, the dream of dominating Nature, of making oneself its "master and possessor", is aground. Or rather, to the degree that it seems to be achieved, it is deceptive. "All sciences are infinite in the extent of their research"; their clearest result, in unveiling Nature "in its lofty and full majesty", is to show us better how it crushes us—and to make us fear that it might crush us completely.

Not that so many efforts have been in vain. Descartes sometimes enjoys feigning hypotheses, he is blamed for wanting to discover the last "principles of things"—which are hidden in nothingness; he has nevertheless determined a few sure principles. Experience and calculation, combined, have done marvels. The new astronomy compels recognition: the discoveries of Copernicus and Tycho Brahe are definitively established, Galileo is right against his adversaries. Science is thus the worker of truth. Now, truth, as troubling, as deadly as it may be, always has the right on its side. It forces one to recognize, admire, love it: and it is precisely here where the most painful conflicts are born. Up to his last moments, disdaining the too-easy solution that would proclaim its "failure", Pascal will believe in science, do science. He will not think, like Malebranche, that he must one day abandon it "in order to belong wholly to religion, to morality". Skilled at grasping the secret correspondences of things, the methods of science will even be a great assistance to him for his plan of defense. But, while waiting, his Christian soul is crushed by the results acquired. For he sees that science, while powerless to achieve the hopes that had been placed in it, does have the power to destroy. If it does not give what had been expected of it, it does, in return, tear away the most precious treasure.

Others around him are disturbed, already urge a warning cry. Wish to heaven they would be killed! Their intrigues are only going to bring down ruin. Offending the scholars, they provoke their sarcasm, they drive sincere minds crazy and prepare the way for an explosion of revolts. Good intentions, bad tactics, their attitude is not true. Such is that Father Cazrée, adjuring Gassendi to reject the new astronomy. By his relentless argumentation, he tries desperately to prove to him that if what Galileo says is right, it is all over with faith. Let's plug our ears to escape the siren! Otherwise, men soon "will be persuaded that the globe of the earth moves among the planets; then, since it has its inhabitants, it will be easy to believe there are also inhabitants on the other planets and even that they are not lacking on the stationary stars. . . . Then Genesis will be placed in doubt, when it says that the earth was made before the other heavenly bodies and that these latter were created on the fourth day to light the earth. . . . The whole economy of the incarnate Word and the truth of the Gospels will thereby be rendered suspect. Even more, the whole Christian Faith will be suspect, for it presupposes and teaches that all the heavenly bodies were produced . . . solely to light the earth . . . and to make it fruitful." So, in conclusion, hoping thereby to block most effectively the path to danger: "It is with good reason that, since the time of Copernicus, the Church has always opposed this error and that again recently, not a few Cardinals as you say, but the highest leader of the Church, by pontifical decree, has condemned it in the person of Galileo. . . ."

The folly of such logic! Renan will reason in exactly the same way: if the book of Judith is not historical, or if the book of Daniel dates from the time of the Maccabees, all Catholicism is aground. . . . Pascal, in his musing, sees the Cazrées engendering the Renans. Irritation seizes him. Why brace oneself against experience? It's too bad if one goes "against the universal teaching of the Fathers and the Scholastic Doctors" and, moreover, against Aristotle: authority is not acceptable here. It's too bad if one seems even in revolt against Moses. Constraint is unjust if used against duty and sincerity, and it will not prevail. . . .

But soon his irritation succumbs under the blow of a more penetrating pain. These men of the Church, they do not know that they are sinning against the spirit: "The world and Scripture are clear to them." Their reaction is inevitable, they believe themselves to be obliged to it in order to save the holy ark of doctrine. Unconscious actors in a drama that transcends them, they play a necessary role in it. And behind them, behind these unconscious others for whom, a few minutes ago, science was a potion, now come the principal actors, those in whom the drama is internalized. Here come the victims, in an ever-increasing flow! In an outburst of prophetic sympathy, condensing their anguish in himself, he passes through the horrors of their death—for, according to all appearances, it is indeed a question of a fight to the death. Cazrée himself, in his logic, had not gone all the way to the end: the truth of Scripture, the economy of the incarnate Word are not the only things at stake. Along with the Christian Faith, it is all human hope that is weakened. Man starts doubting his own dignity, or rather, he looks at it, a frail stem, broken by this newly looming giant, the enormous and brutal Universe.

Such is the crisis that, already, in thousands of consciences, is obscurely knotted. Pascal foresees the outcome of it. . . . Extending his gaze, he forms an evaluation of this new civilization, built upon science, having lost the sense of its eternal destinies, having repudiated its greatness. He sees it, unhappy and no longer even understanding its unhappiness. Even more, proud of its forfeiture, proclaiming: "Paradise does not tempt me." —The greatest of all miseries, which, more than anything else, "overwhelms him, grips him by the throat"! —He hears the remarks that this Humanity will one day make, this Humanity that considers itself adult at last, and is so in fact, but in a barbarity that its childhood had never known. Remarks whose cold serenity does not reveal even an echo of an agony of three centuries. . . . With an assurance given by something already judged, in impeccable formulas, as if to liquidate a definitively dead past, it says:

> The Universe is no longer the vast temple where everything reveals the presence of the God who created it, the building that is awe-inspiring but finished, whose clear plan, proportioned to human intelligence, arranged around a unique center, discloses the personal architect who has embraced the multiple elements of it in the unity of the same thought. The sky is no longer incorruptible, it no longer climbs degree by degree through the firmament up to the empyrean to the throne of God; the law of change and of becoming, the law of birth and death has invaded everything, and the glance that with an instinctive movement rises toward the Most High is lost in the infinite. The crystal spheres that turned under the impulse of the angels . . . are henceforth broken: the heavenly bodies sustain themselves in space, and they move there according to the laws of an inflexible mechanism. . . .
>
> The earth is no longer at the center of the world,
> it is a point in space,
> a minor star,
> Circling in its place between Venus and Mars!
>
> We can no longer imagine man on his planet, whom nothing distinguishes from so many others who can claim the same destinies, just like the principle and end of things. . . . Millions of suns, billions of planets raise equal claims to the divine solicitude: How many times has the miracle of the Incarnation been renewed? In how many worlds has this wandering God not had to be exiled? Undoubtedly he will never lack theologians to imagine some subtle "*distinguo*" that reconciles science with dogma. . . . But our whole life diverts us from it, it remains outside of all that is the subject of our thought. . . . One does not change the

universe without changing, whether one wishes to or not, the idea of God.

> If man [it adds] has fallen from the fictitious greatness that he naïvely attributed to himself, he is lifted up again by science. . . . We are no longer the slaves of things, we have unravelled their chaos in the knowledge of the laws found by means of an incomparable power. . . .

What irony, this end! Man remains the same in his suffering and in the necessity of dying. No progress will change that. If there is no longer a Father in heaven to hear his cry, if his will to survive and his desire for a better life are in vain, if the nobility that is in his heart gives birth to nothing eternal, the rest—material progress, the organization of the earth—is only deception. The earth rolls into an abyss, and the catastrophe into which it is rushing is already inscribed in these laws in which we think to find a support. Rather than lull ourselves with dreams, let us dare, then, to face the Power that has chased away our God. Let us raise our eyes in the night. Let us listen. . . . Pythagoras once perceived the harmony of the spheres, "biblical nights echoed the praises" of Yahweh. From then on, the concert of the heavenly bodies was silenced. These glances that shine in the firmament, immobile and taciturn, are glances without soul. But if our eyes grow tired of counting the stars, "let the imagination pass beyond", let it shoot out in all directions, let it ascend and descend across time as across space: "It will become more weary of conceiving than nature will of providing." And from these boundless courses, it will not report an atom of light, not a word of hope. "The ample bosom of Nature" is not a maternal breast. In this twofold infinity of space and time, we are engulfed. We are alone. Horror!

The eternal silence of these infinite spaces frightens me. . . .

One must be obsessed by the specter of Jansenism to find it in this famous thought, as if Pascal, insulting the Creator, wanted to indicate here that "outside the narrow provinces that the Redemption has ransomed, creation is evil." A fanciful interpretation, but less unjust than the one whose inventor, treating with condescension "this strange Christian" who "says he is frightened", cannot, he confides to us, keep "from thinking that there is some system and some work in this perfectly sad attitude and in this absolute of disgust". Commiseration for a genius who has gone astray, or a smile at some failed effect: that is what is proposed to us in the face of Pascal's anguish. A somber disciple of

Jansenius, or a comedian, an "author", putting up little resistance to his instinct for theatrics. . . . Worth just about as much as the romantic legend showing him "pursued by doubt up to the very arms of faith". A little more knowledge of the man and of history would have averted these mistakes.

Did the man wait for the Jansenist theology to moan, in the secret of his prayer, about the opacity of this world, which, before being a mirror, was too often a wall for him, "hiding God" from him? But this feeling, so natural for the Christian, was to acquire a different, formidable force at the time when scientific truth, taking hold of his mind, subjugated it like a new revelation. Believing only yesterday that he occupied the center of the World, with all harmony and light created entirely to serve him, he suddenly perceives, "as if led astray into a remote region", an indifferent Nature. How can we be surprised by the painful reaction provoked in him by the sight of a heaven abruptly stripped by Science of its divine reflection? A reaction that it is easy for us to find out of date today. It may in fact be becoming "a rarity and an object of curiosity for the psychologist", and when we read, in a modern poet:

Why, space, this silence?
Why, Universe, this speechlessness?

we are permitted to think it a little too literary. . . . But, let us not forget, if the eternal silence of infinite spaces no longer frightens us, as it once frightened Pascal, it is particularly to Pascal that we owe this. If the intoxication of science no longer goes to our head, the messenger of desperate alarms, it is thanks to him. He did not pass this anguish by in order that he might free us from it forever. For, while a necessary moment, it was nevertheless for him, to use the jargon of the Moderns, a dialectic moment. It was the first step toward deliverance. "The more man humbles himself, the more I raise him up." The greater the failure seemed, the more vivid the horror, the more magnificent the recovery will be. Pascal has not finished playing his strange organs. He is going to draw chords of triumph from them now.

Let us resume, then, the course of Pascal's musings. Let us readjust ourselves to the rhythm of his reflection.

The solitude of Pascal. Still in the image of his Master in agony. "The heaven and he are alone in this knowledge"; "Alone on the earth, not only he who feels and shares his pain, but he who knows it."

6. The Dispute in Modern Times about the Salvation of Origen

"A curious thing," wrote Lucien Febvre, "historians, who, by definition, make history of everything, never put any eagerness into reconstructing on the basis of the documents the consequence of the ideas, unless contradictory or at least fragmentary, that their predecessors have had about some man or problem that they, in their turn, are investigating again. Is the spirit of the modern sciences so foreign to them because they are perhaps dimly afraid of giving themselves, and even more of giving others, a severe and salutary lesson in relativism?"[1]

As if to illustrate his disillusioned reflection and to confirm it by the weight of a conspicuous example, Lucien Febvre, critical and personal historian that he was, manifests on occasion this lack of eagerness that he deplores. At the very moment when he was shaking a certain number of historical judgments wrongly transmitted as absolutes, he happened to be responsible for some others himself, proving that all of us, whoever we are, always need, in history, some of that "severe and salutary lesson in relativism". It is thus that, with respect to Origen, he unflinchingly repeats on faith a wholly legendary opinion of some predecessor. Even without having recourse to the simplest solution, which would have been to open an edition of Origen's works, if he had taken the trouble to "reconstruct on the basis of the documents" the series of ideas that some have had of this great man, he could not have missed seeing the wholly relative character of the opinion in which he, without even thinking, placed his confidence.[2]

If we bring up this fact, it is because Origen's case is precisely one of those privileged cases that verify to the utmost Lucien Febvre's reflection. Origen is one of the men who have most aroused opinions; none has received more praise, none has been the object of more anathemas;

This study appeared in the *Bulletin de Littérature ecclésiastique*, published by the Institut catholique of Toulouse, January–March 1982 and May–June 1982.

[1] *Au coeur religieux du XVIe siècle* (1957), 94.

[2] Cf. H. de Lubac, *Exégèse médiévale*, vol. 2 (Aubier, 1959), 463–64; see also vol. 4 (1964), 471–74.

some time after his death "this long process that is still being conducted began before the tribunal of posterity."[3] But, in this process, we have the same arguments, the same indictments over the centuries; there are the same contradictory clichés thrown in one's face, sometimes from the same invented facts, without ever returning methodically to the bases of the inquiry or without taking into consideration some of the rare serious studies that have now and then come to light.

We tried not long ago to reconstitute this "series" of ideas that people have had of Origen during the medieval period.[4] One would have thought that in modern times, beginning with the period when there was general agreement in celebrating the advent of criticism, the latter would have given place to better-founded judgments. Nothing of the kind. For a long time, the more or less false "series of ideas" has continued to unfold. It would take too long to observe them all. We will concentrate our gaze here on the fate of the legend that goes back to a page of Saint Epiphanius: the famous "fall" of Origen, when he was ordered to sacrifice to idols in order to prevent the violence of an "Ethiopian".

I. From Saint Antoninus of Florence to Erasmus of Rotterdam

Photius possessed at Constantinople, in his magnificent library, a whole parcel of "arguments for Origen". He neglected to describe these to us or even to indicate the names of their authors, judging that this was something "without interest".[5] The historians of patristics are disconsolate about it.[6] Yet the literary genre of these arguments did not remain dead and buried with Photius. A brilliant career was again opening up before it. It formed a part of a wider genre, in which the salvation of several celebrated men was discussed: principally Solomon for the history of Israel, Trajan for classical antiquity, Origen in the Christian centuries.[7] We know that the Englishman Robert de Cour-

---

[3] Msgr. Freppel, *Origène*, vol. 1 (1868), 16.

[4] *Exégèse médiévale*, 1:257–74.

[5] *Bibliotheca*, cod. 117 and 118 (PG 103, 393 and 396–97).

[6] Cf. Joseph de Ghellinck, *Patristique et Moyen Age*, 2:365.

[7] *Exégèse médiévale*, vol. 1 (1959), 287–88. Dante will make an allusion to the salvation of Cato, Trajan, Riphée of Troyes; he will recall the tradition according to which Trajan was

son[8] had written, in the thirteenth century, a work entitled *De Salvatione Origenis*, but the text of it has been lost.[9] In the same century, in his *Speculum historiale*[10] and in his *Speculum doctrinale*,[11] the Dominican Vincent de Beauvais (1264) had cited among the works of Origen the *Planctus Origenis*, which, he said, following common belief, was translated from Greek into Latin by Saint Jerome, and he had repeated in summary the account of Saint Epiphanius.[12] Others, however, while accepting this account as historical, rejected the *Planctus* among the apocryphal books, in conformity with the list contained in the "Decree of Pope Gelasius". Now this *Planctus*, or *Lamentum*, or *Paenitentia*, served as a substantial argument for all the partisans of Origen's salvation. From the moment that more or less all adversaries and admirers agreed to take as truthful the account of his unfortunate fall, which they read in Epiphanius, the adversaries were to triumph, since the touching testimony that Origen himself was presumed to have given of his repentance was held to be apocryphal.

In his *Book of Chronicles*, in the middle of the fifteenth century, the holy archbishop of Florence, Antoninus, referring to Vincent de Beauvais, also recalled the Decree of Gelasius, while giving, like others, a rather attenuated definition of the word apocryphal: "Liber ille (*De paenitentia Origenis*) ponitur inter Apocryphos . . . , id est, dubios de veritate eorum."[13] He, however, found a means of drawing from Origen himself an argument against the reality of his repentance: Had the Alexandrian not declared in his tenth homily on Leviticus that repen-

redeemed by the prayer of Saint Gregory. *Purgatory*, 10, 73–76; *Par.* 20, 47–48, 67–72, 106–17, 121.

[8] M. and C. Dickson, *Vie du cardinal Robert de Courson*. Archives d'histoire doctr. et litt. du Moyen Age, vol. 9 (1934), 53–142.

[9] The work is referred to by Balaeus, Centur. 3 *Scriptorum Britanniae*, and according to him, by Huet, *Origeniana* (PG 17, 1178 A), by Bayle, *Dictionnaire*, art. "Origène", by E. Tranner, *Bibliotheca Britannico-Hiberna* (London, 1748).

[10] L. 11, c. 13 (Douai ed., 1624, *Speculum majus*, vol. 4, 416).

[11] L. 17, c. 43; op. cit., vol. 2, col. 1579 A.

[12] *Speculum historiale*, l. 11, c. 8: "Fidem abjurasse dicitur cum exclamaverit se sacrificare malle, quam corpus ejus impudico Aethiope contaminare; atque inde a divina sententia, et gratia delapsus, alienas opiniones, Sathana instigante, induxit: per quas multis a saniore sententia seductis longo post tempore ab Ecclesia Christi per excommunicationem est prosecutus" (4:415). On Vincent and Origen: Jac. Echard, *Sancti Thomae Summa suo auctori vindicata, sive de V. F. Vincentii Bellovacensis scriptis Dissertatio* 1708), 55 and 70.

[13] *Chronicorum liber*, tit. 7, c. 6, n. 21 (vol. 1 [Lyons, 1586], 485).

tance is a very difficult thing?[14] Besides, as Epiphanius had not failed to show, the collection of his works was far from testifying in his favor. Undoubtedly he had said "many beautiful and useful things"; but one had nonetheless to consider him heretical, he who had invented so many perverse doctrines against the Faith and who had behaved like an enemy of the Church.[15]

To examine the matter closely, perhaps there is less distance between Antoninus of Florence and Vincent de Beauvais, and perhaps there is with both of them a little more critical sense, than first appears to be the case. While reporting Epiphanius' remarks, Vincent does not entirely adopt them as his own: "*Fidem abjurasse* dicitur. . . ." And while Antoninus contests the repentance of Origen, he does not insinuate that this repentance must have related to something else besides his doctrinal errors. As for the *Planctus*, if Antoninus casts a doubt on its authenticity, the way in which Vincent de Beauvais referred to this writing was circumspect enough to authorize this doubt. . . .[16] Yet this was too little, on both sides, to cut short the legend, to discourage the various attempts at explanation and to put an end to the disputes.[17]

But it was here, from the Renaissance Florentine milieu whose progress the old archbishop Antoninus had prudently encouraged, that Origen's avenger was to rise up. It was the young prince of Mirandola. Among the nine hundred theses, the list of which he prepared in the autumn of 1486, offering to go to Rome to support them, there was one that maintained that "Origen is not a master of lies."[18] There was

[14] *Hom.* 10, n. 2 (Baehrens, 442–45). To tell the truth, the passage is not at all convincing.

[15] *Chronicorum liber*, 486: ". . . Et, ut ait Epiphanius, si propter verbum unum aut duo, quae fidei sunt contraria, multae haereses abjectae sunt ab Ecclesia, quanto magis Origenes inter haereticos habebitur, qui tantas perversitates contra fidem Dei adinvenit, et Ecclesiae hostis extitit."

[16] *Speculum historiale*, l. 11, c. 13: "Extitit etiam libellus, qui *Planctus* dicitur Origenis, et a beato Hieronymo translatus inscribitur. In quo sic ex ejusdem Origenis persona legitur [a passage from the *Planctus* follows]." *Speculum majus*, 4:417.

[17] In his *Summa Theologiae*, l. 4, tit. 11, c. 3 (*Opera*, vol. 4 [Verona, 1740], col. 565–67), Antoninus unreservedly praises the spiritual exegesis of the Old Testament given by Origen, showing that the at first bitter and undrinkable water of the letter that kills "suaves factae sunt, misso in eis ligno crucis; ita ut omnis populus sapientum biberet. . . ." Gerson seems, on the contrary, to make his own the words that he quotes from Jerome, E. G. Ctésiphon, (PL 22, 1152, no. 3: "He drank too much from the cup of gold at Babylon." Quoted by Puech, *En quête de la Gnose*, vol. 1 (Paris: Gallimard, 1978), 229.

[18] We do not believe, despite André Chastel, *Art et humanisme à Florence au temps de Laurent le Magnifique*, 2d ed. (P.U.F., 1961), 85, that the interest then awakened for Origen's work

also another, more famous because it figured among the thirteen propositions that were condemned in 1487 by Innocent VIII and because, in his *Apologia*, Giovanni Pico explains it at length. Origen, the scholar Daniel Huet says on this subject, "could not have wished for a more learned defender".[19] It has been supposed that after his *Apologia*, Pico returned to the subject in a new writing entitled *Disputatio de salute Origenis*, dedicated to Lorenzo de Medici. After having been preserved for some time in the della Mirandola archives, the work was supposedly lost. What has given credence to this supposition is a passage from *Lezìoni di antichità toscana* (1766) by the scholar Giovanni Lami. The author recounts there that the Florentine Ricasoli, a lover of rare books, had had the original copied at the della Mirandola chateau. But it seems very likely that this in reality referred to the long dissertation on Origen that was a part of the *Apologia*.[20] Perhaps Ricasoli (born in 1581), who could hardly have been unaware that the *Apologia* had appeared in the edition of Giovanni Pico's *Complete Works*, in 1557, and had been reprinted, at Basel again, in 1572, judged the text to be incorrect (it is, in fact) and wanted to have an exact copy of the original. The *Apologia* is specifically dedicated to Lorenzo de Medici, and the "discussion on the salvation of Origen", which is the most fully developed part of it, constitutes a true treatise.[21]

> It is more reasonable to believe Origen saved than to believe him damned. These masters [the theologians of the pontifical commission charged with examining the theses of Giovanni Pico] have said that this conclusion is rash and blameworthy, that it smells of heresy, that it goes against the decision of the universal Church. . . . I want to show that their judgment is not right and that this conclusion is not contrary to the decision of the Church. . . .[22]

constituted "dangers for the Christian Faith", dangers that had supposedly been "minimized by the theologian friends of Careggi".

[19] *Origeniana*: "Maxima vero fuit. . . . Joannis Pici Mirandulani comitis in se litteraria laus et celebritas, ut neque doctiorem patronum sibi Origenes optare potuerit" (PG 17, 1178 D).

[20] Cf. I. V. Pouzyma, *Études sur la Renaissance italienne*, 216. G. Lami, *Lezioni . . .*, 1:145. A. Renaudet, *Préréforme et humanisme*, 254, note 161. E. Garin, *Pico della Mirandola* (Florence, 1937), 51 and 141; idem, ed. of Oeuvres, 52.

[21] Twenty-six large, compact, folio pages, from 1557.

[22] The *Disputatio de salute Origenis* was completely translated into French and studied closely by Father Henri Crouzel in three articles in the *Bulletin de litt. ecclésiastique* (Toulouse, 1965), 81–106, 174–94, 272–88; the translation corrected and accompanied with the Latin text and a fuller commentary in *Une controverse sur Origène à la Renaissance: Jean Pic de la Miran-*

Of the long argument in seven articles that this declaration introduces, we retain here only what treated directly Origen's "fall", "repentance" and "salvation". Giovanni Pico shows his critical mind in passing over in silence the absurd fable from Epiphanius and by rejecting as apocryphal the *Planctus Origenis* (also called *Lamentum*, or *Paenitentia*) that was claimed to have been translated from Greek by Saint Jerome. But, conceding that his hero did happen to give out some indiscreet opinions, he places the discussion on the true historical plane by admitting that Origen did in fact repent, in that letter to Pope Fabian recalled by Jerome himself. Consequently, by the very statement of his detractor, he did not persist in his error.[23] Giovanni Pico then recalls two conversations that he had had with two of the scholars who condemned his "conclusion". These are two scenes worthy of the *Provinciales*. To the first scholar, he wanted to prove on the evidence that Origen could not have been damned for his persistence, since his doctrines had been condemned only very long after his death; but "the good Father" does not understand Greek; he demands a Latin book:

> . . . Do we not have here, he says, the *Fasciculus temporum*,[24] which treats of all that elegantly? —Let them bring this *Fasciculus*, I say—it was brought, and we read what follows: "Origen, the eminent scholar, incomparable in the holiness of his life, very illustrious in the Church of God"; and . . . at the end: "Some weave a whole entangled plot on the subject of Samson, Solomon, Trajan and this Origen, in order to know if they were saved or not. There is no danger in ignoring all that, and the Church has said nothing certain on the subject; one must trust totally in the Lord." So speaks this good *Fasciculus*. When my contradictor heard that the damnation of Origen was not certified by the Church, he grew pale . . . and changed his opinion at once.[25]

dole et Pierre Garcia (Vrin, 1977). Pico had already spelled out his thought before his judges: "Sexta Conclusio declaranda. . . . Per haec verba formalia respondit: Haec fuit mens sua quod ex eo quo non invenitur Origenem errasse ex pertinacia voluntatis, verisimile est et pium credere quod Deus salvaverit eum" (Dorez and Thuasne, *Pic de la Mirandole en France*, 125).

[23] Fourth article, no. 41, of the Crouzel translation, *Bulletin*, 177–78; cf. nos. 44–45, pp. 181–83.

[24] A recent manual by the Carthusian Werner Rolewinck, published for the first time in Cologne in 1470.

[25] Fourth article, no. 42. Crouzel, *Bulletin*, 179–80.

The other scene, the next day, with the second scholar:[26]

> He pushed me rather bruskly, holding in his hands a fairly thick book: "How", he said, "can you dare to defend Origen against the punishments of hell? I am going to show you someone whose testimony you will not be able to reject. . . ."
>
> "Produce him," I said, "venerable sir."
>
> Then he began again: "Here is a great witness", and he told me his name. As for me, I will pass it by in silence: it is the author of sermons and preachings.
>
> Then I: "What do you bring me? Sermons! What nonsense!"
>
> "Nonsense", he replied, already in a complete furor.
>
> "Yes, nonsense", I said. "But here, on this subject, if it is a question of this (far be it from me never to read such things!), at least in order to find an explicit error in it, I want then to break with you the head of Origen on the wheel of Ixion."

"Burning with bile", the scholar began to read. And Giovanni Pico demonstrated to him, again on the testimony of Jerome, that his author was ignorant. "Then he began to turn red, and my cause was saved."[27]

In a fifth article, our apologist applies himself to proving that, "in admitting that nothing is known of Origen's repentance or persistence", it is "more reasonable", if one considers his admirable life, to believe him saved than damned. In a sixth article, he shows that it "does not belong to the Church to damn or save the souls of men: that is the affair solely of the One who is judge of the living and the dead." That is why it is ridiculous, when one reads in the Decrees: "We condemn Origen", to explain it like this: We doom his soul to infernal damnation. . . . Such expressions are still to be heard today because of the ways of speaking used by specialists for the condemnation of a doctrine, not of the soul. If, against all possibility, one were nevertheless to suppose that an ecclesiastical sentence had condemned Origen to hell, one would not be obliged to believe it any more than, according to Saint Thomas, one is obliged to believe as a necessary article of faith that the canonized saints are in glory: this is what the seventh and

[26] Ibid., no. 43; pp. 180–81. For the sake of brevity, we must leave out of these two scenes numerous comic details. Here Crouzel's translation comes not from the *Bulletin* but from *Une controverse*, see note 22.

[27] Pico was not unkind. With respect to his *Apologia*, in which he mistreats his adversary a bit, Paul Cortesi wrote: "Picus noster Mirandulanus . . . magis ambitu gloriae quam acerbiore odio quibusdam obtrectat." Cf. G. di Napoli, *Pico della Mirandola*, 189.

last article demonstrates. "Let my contradictors", concludes our Pico, "therefore beware of imposing on the faithful by their own authority new truths to believe. . . !"[28]

Such was not the opinion of Pico's fiercest adversary within the commission charged with examining his theses, the Spaniard Garcia, then bishop of Ales in Sardinia. "It is clear", he would say in the work he published against Pico, "that such an opinion is rash and that it goes against what the Church has determined. The proposition 'Whoever dies in mortal sin is damned in his soul' is an article of faith; now this proposition: 'Origen died in the mortal sin of heresy' is an article of the piety of the faith [*de pietate fidei*]; thus the conclusion: 'Origen is damned' is an article of the piety of the faith. . . . The Church is in fact certain, with a certitude of probability and of right, that one who is anathematized and declared heretical after his death in the judgment of the Church and in that of famous men, is damned, just like one who is canonized is saved."[29]

This absurd diatribe would, thank goodness, remain the private masterpiece of a theologian who seems to have been raised up to show historians the decadence into which one whole part of classical theology had fallen.[30] We would agree with Giovanni di Napoli that the validity of Pico's thesis needs no commentary.[31] Let us simply add that Garcia himself no longer interprets Origen's fall as anything but a definitive fall into heresy.

There are some weak points in Giovanni Pico's dissertation all the more easily explained by the fact that he could not have known Origen except in Latin: "The Greek Origen was probably nearly inaccessible to him, with the exception of the *Contra Celsum*." There are also a few lines of argument that are somewhat too hasty, notably the "little

---

[28] Crouzel, nos. 47–62; *Bulletin*, 184–94.

[29] Pedro Garcia, *Determinationes magistrales* (1489), 217–18, quoted by Giovanni di Napoli, *Giovanni Pico della Mirandola et la problematica dottrinale del suo tempo* (Rome and Paris, 1965), 182. Since Origen was condemned by a council after his death, it was because he persisted in his error up to the end: the *Lamentum* is thus apocryphal. It was in this way that Garcia linked up with, by a whole different path, the conclusions of the criticism.

[30] Other criticisms formulated by Garcia are even more aberrant. The long chapter devoted by G. di Napoli to the examination of the fifteen theses of Pico censured by the commission is entitled with good reason: "L'Ortodossia delle Tesi" (139–94). All were declared admissible in the explanations given in the *Apologia* by the brief of Alexander VI (1495). Cf. our *Pic de la Mirandole, études et discussions* (Aubier, 1974).

[31] *Giovanni Pico della Mirandola*, 182.

fairy tale built on two poorly interpreted texts of Eusebius" that shifts the responsibility for certain publications to Ambrose, Origen's wealthy and faithful secretary. It nevertheless contains "many elements that provide a solution to the Origenian problem and give evidence of critical and historical sense".[32] This *Apologia* is not at all characterized by a "spirit of concession and caution that smooths out by trying to tone down", as has been claimed.[33] As for the thesis itself on the salvation of Origen, it is impossible to see in it on Pico's part any kind of implicit self-defense: at the time when he enunciated it, before coming to Rome to support it, he was in no way suspect. The truth is more simple. If our young theologian—who was not immediately, from then on, an extemporaneous theologian—does not seem to have had a deep knowledge of the work he defended with passion, one senses that he loved the man, that he understood him,[34] and this is the reason for which, following many in the medieval period and against the opinion of several Scholastics of his time, he wanted to devote one of his nine hundred theses to the question of his salvation. In his *Apologia*, he also speaks, without specifics, about his "penitence": but he instinctively avoided the stupidities that had been going around for centuries concerning him, and, on the essence of the debate whose terms had been imposed on him by old habit, he brought to bear a voice of good sense, of Christian sense and of true theology.[35]

Paul Oskar Kristeller has remarked that, in the *Apologia* presented by Giovanni Pico, this part concerning Origen was much the longest and most eloquent. He wondered why this young man, in presenting his own defense, was so bent on saving Origen. The reasons he found for it are not lacking in truth. But two others, which we believe to be more determinative, seem to have escaped him. More than any particular doctrine, more than the depth or any particular characteristic of

---

[32] Crouzel, *Bulletin*, 195–288.

[33] *Dictionnaire des sciences philosophiques* by Adolphe Franck, article signed J. M. [Matter]; 2d ed. (Hachette, 1875), 1120.

[34] He complains of what "quis indoctior, cum intellexerit me de Origenis salute bene operari, non tam vitam, mores et poenitentiam Origenis, quam credita Origenis dogmata, a me amari, suspicetur", *Opera*, 236.

[35] Eugenio Garin, *Giovanni Pico della Mirandola, vita e dottrina* (Florence, 1937), 141, judges that, at least in the *Apologia*, Pico, in defending Origen, was defending himself. This hardly seems so, and in any case we would reject the conclusion he thereby manifests "le sua intima rebellione nei riguardi della dottrina chiesastica".

Origen's thought[36]—which, again, he could have known only rather poorly—what undoubtedly seduced the young thinker was the spiritual impulse he had received from it. In him was renewed that kind of miracle that is ascertained down through the centuries: between his soul and the soul of the great Alexandrian, a spark had flashed. And this mysterious sympathy had quite naturally found its expression in a literary genre long since established: Pico followed a venerable custom by writing, in his turn, a treatise *De salute Origenis*.[37]

Origen was nonetheless to remain "the most astounding 'sign of contradiction' of Christian thought".[38] This was soon to be shown by the "Merlin affair". We will note in this affair, on all sides, a new failure of the critical function.

The first edition of Origen's *Works*, procured by Josse Bade [or, Jodocus Badius] and Jean Petit, appeared in Paris in the autumn of 1512, in four folio volumes. That was again an entirely Latin Origen. A dedication to the bishop of Langres, Michel Boudel, was signed by Jacques Merlin, Victorine, doctor of the college of Navarre, who called himself *theologorum minimus*. At the end of the fourth volume was printed the *Threni, seu Planctus Origenis translatus ab Hieronymo*[39] (we know what this writing was), the two *Apologies* of Origen by Pamphilius and by Rufinus and, on the final page, an *Origenis per Badium* [Josse Bade] *Commendatio*. The third volume contained in addition an *Apologia pro Origene* owed to Jacques Merlin, written in a panegyrical tone:

> . . . Origenes Adamantius, inter sidera sol, inter volucres aquila, inter beluas bethmoth, inter gigantes atlas, inter israeliticos Saul, inter theosophos dignitatis gradum jure sibi vindicat. Eo sane nemo sanctior, eloquentiorve et omni disciplina promptior; cui tam sublimis ingenii acies, tam immortalis memoria, tam in dicendo vivax acrimonia, in religione pietas atque observantia, ut inter mortales nec primum similem visus, nec

[36] He was not the first among the Italian humanists to admire Origen so much. Cf. Coluccio Salutati, *De laboribus Herculis*, l. 2, c. 10: "Adamantius Origenes, quo non habuit insolens Graecia inter Christicolas doctiorem. . . ." Ed. B. L. Ullman (Turici, 1951), 1:119.

[37] *In L'Opere e Pensiero di Pico della Mirandola*, vol. I (1965), 79–80. Eugenio Anagnine, treatise on "De salute Origenis", in *Giovanni Pico della Mirandola, Sincretismo religiosio-filosofico* (Bari, 1937), 52–68.

[38] Crouzel, *Bulletin*, 81 and 288.

[39] In this same year, 1512, a volume of *Opera Sublimis Origenis* appeared in Venice, published by Constantius Hyerotheus. It included, also, the *Lamentum Origenis translatum a beato Hieronymo de graeco in latinum* (Crouzel, *Bibliographie critique d'Origène* [1971], 83).

habere sequentem[40] . . . Tam grandia Scripturarum educebat mysteria, ut nemo qui ad eum accessisset ineruditus abiret. . . .

Origen, Merlin also says, has completely opened the mysteries of the Scriptures to Christians:

. . . Jam procul dubio velum templi scissum est; jam non ultra loquitur Moyses in parabolis; jam in montis cacumine, apertis oculis transformationis mysteria cernimus: videtur Moyses remoto velamine; jam tota flagrat spiratque mysteriorum odore, vase litterae confracto, domus Ecclesiae, ut ne unus quidem sit qui ad nostrum Adamantium, discendi studio, accesserit, frustratus suorum unguentorum odore.

About which, in an impulse of wild admiration, the panegyrist sang a hymn to his hero:

Tuo, mi Adamanti, perfusa terra christianitatis semen restituit; tuo doctrinae splendore lumen indeficiens universus suscipit orbis. Tu contorta tabernaculi tapeta solvis; et bissum e purpura segregas. Tu Cherubim pedes et faciem revelas, et eorum alas explicas. Tu e rota rotam educis; oculus es caeco, pes claudo, et denique quod Abraham angelis officium, Joseph Aegyptiis, Moses Israeliticis, Job patientibus, Daniel captivis, tu Christicolis praestas. . . .

Coming back to earth, Merlin then endeavored to prove that Origen's doctrine had enjoyed great authority with all the ancients, who were "even envious", and that Origen himself had never mixed anything false with the true in his writings. Then he tried to explain how the works of so great and holy a Father had subsequently been profaned by so many errors and contaminated by so many blasphemies.[41] He finally concluded that it was impossible that a man who had lived and written uprightly, and thus whose life is a model of penitence, should not have ended his days innocently. Consequently, one must be assured of Origen's salvation.[42]

From the first quarter of the fifteenth century, in part under the influence of Cardinal Bessarion and of Pico della Mirandola,[43] Origen experienced a renewal of favor. The edition of his works was thus well

[40] Cf. Sedulius, *Carmel paschale* II, 68.

[41] This is what Isidore of Seville, in the registry of his library, had to say to Origen: "Nullus meos unquam tetigit blasphemia sensus."

[42] *Origenis Adamantii operum tertius* and *quartus tomi*.

[43] Merlin quoted Giovanni Pico twice among the authorities in favor of Origen.

received. But Merlin's excesses were to provoke a reaction. Intending to exalt Origen, he expressed himself, as Huet would say, "without sufficient prudence"[44] concerning Pope Gelasius as well as Saint Jerome, and his language was not the product of a considered theologian. A reprinting (already the fourth), in 1522, triggered the battle.

A theologian from Cambrai, Christian Masseeuw, a Brother of the Common Life, opened fire, through some "Dialogues", which circulated in manuscript. The matter would perhaps have been without consequence if the terrible Noël Bédier (Beda), trustee of the Sorbonne, had not become involved in it by accompanying the Dialogues of Masseeuw with a more virulent prose text.[45] Beda, who saw heresy everywhere, feared—who would have thought it?—that Origen's errors worked to reinforce the errors of Luther.[46] Despite their obvious differences, undoubtedly he ranked them all together, in company with Lefèvre and Erasmus, in the same vast condemned category of *humanistae theologizantes*. He published a whole book against Merlin's *Apologia*. The latter replied through an Apology for his Apology, in three volumes, which were deposited in manuscript form in the library of the Theology Faculty.[47] The quarrel was to last five years. It was to rage within the Theology Faculty in Paris. The "Register of Conclusions" of the Faculty contains nearly thirty articles that relate to it.[48]

One did not trifle with Beda! Witness the scene offered us by the account of the official proceedings of the Faculty, in barbarous Latin, dated Saturday, August 22, 1523. One of the professors, the Dominican de Novimagio (Noyon), had observed "in passing" that the biblical

[44] Huet, *Origeniana* (PG 17, 1179 C): "Jacobus Merlinus Victurniensis, theologus, canonicus et paenitentiarius Parisiensis. . . . Operi addidit *Pro Origene*, in qua de Gelasio et lata ab eo in concilio Romano sententia, tum et de Hieronymo, non satis prudenter locutus est, nec ut Catholicum ac pium verum, nedum theologum decuit."

[45] Beda to Erasmus, September 12, 1525 (Allen, 6:165; epist. 1609).

[46] Luther's aversion to Origen is well known. "Summopere interim Origenem aversabatur Martinus Luther, cujus eo vox fuit: 'Origenem jamdudum divis devovi' " (Huet [PG 17, 1180–81]). Melanchthon was to say much the same thing: *Depravat Paulum Origenes*; he observed in 1548 that in his time, "Jam caligo effusa erat doctrinae de fide et in Ecclesia late dominabantur philosophia platonica et superstitio" (Crouzel, 91).

[47] Huet (PG 17, 1179 CD).

[48] L. Delisle, *Notice sur le registre des procès-verbaux de la Faculté de théologie de Paris* (1899), 29–30: "This dispute created so much commotion that they [Beda and his party] carried their complaints to the King's Council, where they overlooked nothing in defaming Origen and his works"; but the Dominican Guillaume Parvi, confessor to the King, took Origen's defense. Richard Simon, *Lettres choisies* (Amsterdam, 1730), 1:129 (letter 12, 1683).

text used in the Church was incorrect. The meeting being in session, goaded on by the scandalized attitude of the conservative party, the Trustee requires the Dean to ask the guilty party if he persists in his assertion; in that case, let him proceed immediately to the deliberation on the measures to be taken. Seeing which, the poor Dominican backs down. He protests that he had not wished to affirm anything, that it was on his part only a statement submitted for discussion, and that he withdraws it. Upon which, the Faculty concludes through the medium of its Dean that corrected editions of the Bible are useless to the Church, that they must not be tolerated, that prelates must by all means eliminate them.[49] This was also the period (1525–1527) when the Faculty was beginning to support Beda in his fight against the writings of Jacques Lefèvre and Erasmus, to the point of entering into conflict with the royal authority.[50]

The dispute between Beda and Merlin had been almost immediately the subject of a parliamentary decree, dated June 6, 1522, which sent the matter back to the Theology Faculty. After various ups and downs, the latter finally registered its conclusions on January 4, 1525. But it did not succeed in calming their minds. So it ended in rendering a decree, on June 15 of the same year, declaring injuries on both sides: "With the mutual consent of MM. Beda and Merlin, the holy Faculty has ordained that the whole conflict calm down, in such a way that the books of both be expurgated by those whom they will designate of all that might appear injurious, or inappropriate, and that each of the two be free to maintain his opinion and to explain it in books." Merlin, undoubtedly, was asking for nothing more. But this was to reckon without Beda, who was infuriated by this act of semi-independence by the Faculty in his regard. On the spot, he wrote an opuscule that he entitled *Documentum quo docetur nullum Theologum debere arceri ab examine doctrinarum fidei, nisi fuerit suspectus in fide.* Now he, Beda, was himself not suspect! And the battle resumed was the finest. But a new sentence by the Faculty, rendered on August 19, 1526—*Sententia Deputatorum sacrae Facultatis in librum Merlini: Apologia pro Origene*—did not succeed

[49] Cf. *Exégèse médiévale*, vol. 3 (1961), 272. Delisle, 56. "Facultatem scandalizavit [Novimagio]; continuo per seniores reclamatum est et contradictum ferventer. . . ." "Dicens [Novimagio] quod nolebat illud asserere, sed quasi disputans dixerat, nec vellet in tali dicto persistere."

[50] Delisle, 29–30, etc.

in putting an end to it. Echoes of it are still found in the Register of the Faculty up to February 1527.[51]

This long storm did not hinder the success of Origen's works, which were then reprinted several times.[52] Despite his excesses and awkwardness, moreover, Merlin had well sensed the support that these works could offer for revitalizing Christian thought. But it was a setback with respect to Giovanni Pico. Agreeing to insert the *Planctus Origenis* into this edition, he contributed to the perpetuation of the legend that had its origin in the gossip once gathered by Saint Epiphanius, in defiance of any critical sense. A little later, in 1535, the *Planctus* was to appear in French translation: "*Les Regrets d'Origène et les larmes de sa pénitence* [Origen's regrets and the tears of his penitence], a work translated into Latin by Saint Jerome." This was still being called "Origen's last sermon".

After his meeting, in 1501, with Jean Vitrier, Superior of the Franciscan monastery of Saint-Omer,[53] Erasmus was no less an enthusiast of Origen than Merlin. But his head was sounder. In 1526, Noël Beda attacked him for it in a series of *Annotationes*, which reproached him for his Origenism, as the source of all his errors.[54] Without denying his sympathy, Erasmus responded to him: "Num ideo probo, si quid lapsus est Origenes?"[55] But this word "*lapsus*" evoked in this context, with regard to a fall, only the errors to which any writer is exposed. And in the new edition of Origen's *Works*, which was the last work of this great laborer and which appeared thanks to his friend Beatus Rhenanus, Erasmus wrote judiciously: "Lamentum hoc, nec ab Origine scriptum est, nec ab Hieronymo versum." This was the fabrication of some ignorant man, who doubtless had set his heart on defaming Origen.[56] Already in 1520, when he had published his revised *Anti-barbari*, Erasmus had introduced into it a protest against the pernicious obsession

[51] Du Plessis d'Argentré, *Collectio judiciorum* . . . , vol. 2 (1728), IX–X.

[52] There was a reprinting in Venice in 1530 and another one in Lyons in 1536.

[53] André Godin, *L'Homélie de Jean Vitrier* (Geneva: Droz, 1971), introduction.

[54] *Annotationes Natalis Bedae* . . . , l. 3 (Cologne, 1526), 236: censure of propositions 3 and 4. And *Apologia*, fol. 36 v., quoting the letter from Erasmus to Johan Eyck of May 15, 1518. Cf. D. P. Walker, *Origène en France au début du XVIe siècle* (P.U.F., 1959).

[55] *Responsio ad Notulas Bedae. Opera omnia* (Leyden), 9:708.

[56] "Sed figmentum est alicijus indocti qui studuerit colore Origenem infamare." Ed. of Origen (Basel and Lyons, 1586) pars prima. Gilbert Genebrard, who will produce a new edition of Origen in 1574 (still in Latin), and will reproduce there, with prudence, the *Lamentum*, "quod circumfertur nomine Origenis".

with usurping God's place in order to save some and damn others: "Quis istam judicandi petulantiam ferat, ut tanquam virga Mercuriali quos velint ad inferos demittant, quos velint ad superos evocent?" And although in this passage the reference is to discussions about the salvation of the Gentiles, the eulogy by Origen that follows immediately allows it to be understood that Erasmus also rejected as ridiculous the controversy endlessly resumed over the fate of his favorite scholar.[57]

Pico della Mirandola, Erasmus of Rotterdam: two very different spirits who were at one both in their reasoned admiration of Origen and in their rejection of the absurd legend. Antoninus of Florence and Jacques Merlin: one severe, the other enthusiastic, but both uncritical. For a long time yet, it would be the heirs of the latter who would carry the day.

II. From the Translation of Nicephorus to Father Étienne Binet

In the year 1555, *Histoire ecclésiastique de Nicéfore fils de Calliste Xanthoupolis, autheur grec, traduite nouvellement du latin en françois* [Ecclesiastical history by Nicephorus, son of Callistus Xanthoupolis, Greek author, newly translated from Latin to French] was published in Basel by J. Lange. This Nicephorus, who lived from around 1256 to 1335, was an historian and liturgist.[1] Already translated into Latin and well known by the scholarly world, this *Histoire ecclésiastique* was authoritative for many. The French translation was going to extend this into the literary world. Now here is what we can read there about Origen in the thirty-second chapter of the fifth book:

> Succumbing to the assaults of the enemy, he felt all of a sudden lacking in virtue, which had previously been perfect and accomplished in him: as one who forfeited submission and humility, the mother of all virtues. . . . It is therefore said that, in the time of the persecution under the Emperor Decius, he was apprehended, bound tightly and locked up: then at first

[57] *Opera omnia*, vol. 1 (Amsterdam, 1969), 79–80; p. 81: "Origenis libros in multis haereseos damnatos ad eruditionis fructum Christiana legit Ecclesia et eorum divina scripta fugimus de quorum moribus sine summa temeritate judicari non possit. Imo, ut melius dicam, de quibus in bonam partem cum laude, in malam non sine maximo vitio quisquam judicet."

[1] Cf. C. Zervos, *Michel Psellos* (Leroux, 1919), 231–32. One should avoid confusing our Nicephorus Callistus with Nicephorus Gregoras (1296–1360), who was a philosopher, theologian, astronomer, "essayist", hagiographer and also statesman.

> treated cruelly with serious torments . . . and after that lowered into a deep and harsh hole. . . . His body was very tightly bound and fitted with irons of great weight: and also, they threatened to kill him by fire. . . . They kept him for the space of several days, having four stocks of wood at his feet. Yet he was patient. . . . Now the criminal judge suddenly changed his judgment with a new cruelty. . . . He decided that gradually, by the diversity of tortures, life would be taken from him. In the end . . . he turned his mind to a wholly diabolical determination. For, recognizing his heart to be totally given to true philosophy, the conservator of chastity and guardian of modesty, this was the part through which he decided to make a breach in his perseverance. He thereby had him unchained and removed from his bonds; then ordained that he be led to the altar of their idols, to sacrifice and burn incense there. Now he had drawn close to him a nasty, lewd villain from the land of Ethiopia, with whom he threatened him if he was not willing to agree to offer sacrifices to their gods. For he told him that this detestable scoundrel would know him carnally and would defile his body through debauchery as abominable and execrable beyond all curses as it was against nature. Such was the threat that the judge brewed, mixed with threats. Origen therefore, choosing the thing that was worst, preferred to renounce the faith that he had previously had in Jesus Christ and by this means to defile his soul without any profit rather than to suffer seeing his body contaminated in any way. After this first fault, he forfeited the good opinion of the Divinity and lost the grace of God, in such a way that, through the instinct and pursuit of Satan, he put forward several strange, false and erroneous opinions; by means of which, several found themselves seduced and abused long afterward: and he was separated and banned from the unity of the Christian Church through excommunication.[2]

Nicephorus Callistus seems to have reproduced for the greater part of his work a history of the Church compiled in the tenth century and nearly contemporaneous with the *Souda* (it is difficult to specify the relations between the two works). Then comes, as an appendix to the fifth book of the French edition, the translation of a page of "Suidas", whose translator does not say if the text of it appeared in Nicephorus or if it is of his own accord: "Suidas speaks thus of Origen: The activity and curiosity about Origen was because he fell badly [into various errors]. He also says many other stupid, blasphemous things. . . ."

One recognizes in Nicephorus Callistus a disciple of that school of anti-Origenist historians that the ecclesiastical politics of Justinian had

[2] *L'Histoire ecclésiastique*. . . l. 5, c. 32; p. 114.

aroused and that accused Eusebius of having hidden the truth.[3] Even some of those in medieval times, like Vincent de Beauvais and others, referred to his work, whether or not they approved of it. Now the malicious legend found a wider distribution. An ironic echo of it would soon be found in Montaigne expatiating on the "man of conscience":

> When locked between two vices, he is set a severe choice, as was Origen, whether he practiced idolatry or whether he suffered carnal enjoyment at the hands of a great Ethiopian villain who was presented to him: he gave in to the first condition; and with fault, it is said.[4]

After having quoted "Suidas", the translator of Nicephorus proved to be more equitable than the Greek historians followed by his author. Without casting any doubt on the legend, he had specified in a note, with respect to some errors in which, according to Nicephorus, the Alexandrian supposedly gave way in the end: "Eusebius of Pamphilia and several other ancient Fathers have had greater esteem and a more sincere opinion of Origen. . . ." Then, in the appendix already quoted, he completed the account of Nicephorus with another anecdote, which also goes back to Saint Epiphanius:

> . . . Now Origen, having been banned by the Church and not being able to endure this injury, left the city of Alexandria in order to withdraw to the country of Judea. But when he had arrived in the city of Jerusalem, the order of priests begged him first (since he was a priest) to make a few statements to them in the church and to give a lecture: then forced him to do so. He therefore rose to his feet and recited only these words of the Psalmist: Now God said to the sinner, Why do you announce my justifications? and why do you take my testimony in your mouth? Then after having closed the book, he stopped and sat down, crying much and with abundant tears: so that everyone began to cry with him.[5]

This was once again an attempt to regain a certain balance by coupling the legend of the fall with the legend of repentance. Now the Protestant historians known by the name of the "Centuriators of Magdeburg" took up this twofold account again. In their third *Century*, they retraced the life of Origen with a very laudatory tone; referring to Vincent de Lérins, they also spoke highly of the writer; but Jerome and Theophilus

[3] Cf. *Exégèse médiévale*, 1:268–74.

[4] *Essais*, l. 3, c. 5. Ed. Thibaudet (Pleiade, 1946), 819. The editor returns us to "Callistus, in his *Histoire ecclésiastique*".

[5] *Histoire ecclésiastique de Nicéfore*, 115.

served them as witnesses to criticize his doctrine and particularly his use of allegory. They observed that Eusebius, "qui ubique laudibus ejus studiosissime favet", says nothing of the scandalous episode that supposedly took place under Decius and which Nicephorus, whom they had read, did not fail to report. They themselves, however, repeated it again,[6] and likewise repeated the pathetic scene of repentance in Jerusalem. . . . "What befell the unfortunate after this, neither he himself nor any historian has told us."[7]

Although severe, like Luther and like all the Reformed at that time, with respect to Origen's "allegorism", our Centuriators repeat again at the end of their account their admiration for Origen's life and even for his battle against heresy. What a difference from Luther, who declared: "I condemn Origen to the infernal gods!"[8] Their moderation is joined by a start at criticism, for if they express a possible suspicion about the silence of Eusebius, they nevertheless do not declare an opinion on the authenticity of the facts reported by the tradition inherited by Nicephorus. And as for the at least relative sympathy they demonstrate, they could up to a certain point be ranked, like Jacques Merlin, among the successors of the numerous medieval figures who reconciled their affection for Origen with their credulity and even, in the final account, turned the legendary accounts to the stirring glory of their hero.

The Jesuit Antoine Possevin took an interest himself in the life of Origen in order to draw a moral lesson from it. He was essentially an educator. What he wanted was to show thinkers the necessity of humility. So, although he had read Nicephorus and explicitly refers to it, he deliberately omits the scandalous episode—without feeling the need to express any doubt about it—in order to retain only the doctrinal "fall", a fall that was, at the evening of his life, he thinks, the punishment for a great scholar who was too sure of himself. Let us meditate on this sad example! Such is the theme that he unfolds, both in his *Biblioteca selecta* and in his *Apparatus sacer*:

> The more events are favorable to us, the more we must work out the salvation of our souls with fear, remembering what Nicephorus writes of the very learned Origen. The latter, he says, although he had sent before

---

[6] "Post varia Tormenta, quae forti et generoso animo Origenes pertulit, ductum eum esse ad arcam, ad quam impurissimus simul Aethiops. . . ."

[7] Cent. III, 175–89.

[8] "Origenem jamdudum divis devovi." Cf. Huet (PG 17, 1180–81).

> him to heaven numerous martyrs, among whom was his own father, and although he had provided immense labors in the conversion of souls . . . , fell in the end very miserably into numerous errors for not having been protected in humility. May he who is standing be careful therefore not to fall (1 Cor 10)![9]

Saint Francis de Sales, in his *Treatise on the Love of God*, would soon be less reserved:

> Origen, certainly, and Tertullian loved the purity of chastity so much that they violated its greatest rules of charity: the one having chosen to commit idolatry rather than suffer a horribly vile deed with which the tyrants wanted to defile his body; the other by separating himself from the most chaste Catholic Church, his Mother, in order better to establish, as he wished, the chastity of his wife.[10]

A superficial comparison, assuredly, due to the imaginative affectation with which Francis de Sales was endowed. Yet, as we will see in the following, this parallel established between Origen and Tertullian —which one chapter from the *Commonitorium* of Vincent de Lérins had been able to suggest[11]—was to make an impression on minds. It was to contribute to the perpetuation of the fallacious idea of a "fall" on Origen's part, in whatever way this fall was represented and at whatever period of his life it was placed.

Let us mention briefly the long poem by an Englishman, Stephen Jerom, in which are sung, after the threats of the Ethiopian and Origen's act of apostasy, his flight from Egypt into Palestine, his sermon of repentance and his tears: *Origen's Repentance After He Had Sacrificed to the Idols of the Heathen. . . .*[12]

---

[9] *Biblioteca selecta*, vol. 1 (Cologne, 1607), 160; l. 4. *De domesticis fidei juvandis*, c. 6: "Sed et ubi res e voto successerint, tum tanto magis salutem animarum cum timore operari debebimus, memores eorum, quae de Origene illo doctissimo scribit Nicephorus. Ille enim, ait, cum plures, atque ipsum suum genitorem, martyres praemisisset in coelum, summosque labores in convertendis animabus pertulisset. . . , tandem, quia humilitatem et seipsum non custodiunt [= custodivit], in multis errores miserrime cecidit. Itaque, qui stat, videat ne cadat. . . ." Cf. *Apparatus sacer*, l. 2, n. 179: "ut [lector Origenis] discat vero quilibet, vel doctissimus, timere, quando vir olim tanti ingenii, et [ut videri poterat] pietatis dotibus ornatissimus, corruit in errores, unde haereses aliae ex aliis pestilentes exortae. . . ."

[10] L. 15, c. 14. *Oeuvres*, ed. d'Annecy, vol. 5 (1894), 290. Note from the editors: "This accusation against Origen is based on an assertion by Saint Epiphanius (*Haer.* 64, 2) that Baronius (a. 253) believes to be an interpolation and of which Tillemont (*Histoire Eccl.*, vol. 3, n. 22 on Origen) has demonstrated the inaccuracy."

[11] Cf. *Exégèse médiévale*, 1:260–63.

[12] Cf. Crouzel, 101.

But now here are two serious historians: Cesare Baronius and Denis Petau. Faced with the account by Epiphanius, which continues to impress so many of their contemporaries, and faced with this *Planctus*, which has been reprinted again in order to offer edification to the faithful as well as a warning to scholars, they exercise their critical sense. What solutions are they going to propose to us?

Baronius interests himself with Origen several times, particularly during the years 229 and 253 of his *Annales ecclésiastiques.*[13] He devotes to our subject one whole dissertation entitled *Refellitur Origenis lapsus.* But we should not let this title mislead us: Baronius is not very favorably disposed toward Origen.

He begins by observing, like others already have but with a particular severity, that Eusebius expresses himself on this subject rather as a panegyrist than as a historian.[14] He nevertheless starts out with the account that Eusebius gives of the tortures suffered by Origen under the persecution of Decius: If Eusebius had lied in this regard, he would have aroused contradictions. But "how was Origen set free? Was it, like many other Christians, when religious peace was reestablished? Or rather, as some wished to think, did he offer incense? The thing is not clear." Certainly, Epiphanius affirms his act of apostasy, and he explains it by this "turpissima ac plane nefanda causa" with which we are familiar. But it must be admitted that all that is a little improbable: neither Eusebius nor Rufinus, who sought to cleanse Origen from the reproach of heresy, dreams of dismissing a grievance of impiety or apostasy; neither Dionysius nor adversaries such as Jerome and Theophilus, nor those who condemned Origen under Justinian, speak of the matter, nor does Porphyry, although he is happy to claim (wrongly) that Ammonius reverted to paganism; nor do Saint Augustine or Vincent de Lérins or many others seem to have had the least suspicion of it. It is therefore necessary to think, concludes Baronius, that this account that one reads in Epiphanius is only a fable, interpolated belatedly: an hypothesis made all the more convincing by the fact that in another place Epiphanius speaks of Origen without making the least allusion to it.[15]

---

[13] Rome, 1588.

[14] "Eusebius, dum agit de Origene, encomiasten potius quam historicum praebet"; he praises him "parum sincere"; the apology that he attributes to Pamphilius is in reality by him. *Annales ecclesiasticae*, ed. A. Theiner (1864), 2:555; 3:25–26.

[15] Ibid., 3:23–24 and 25–26.

Nor, however, does Baronius believe in the authenticity of the *Planctus*. But while it was generally viewed as the expression of repentance shown by Origen following his weakness before the impious judge, he observes rather judiciously that the text of it is very imprecise, that if he speaks of a fall he does not mention the nature of it, that one could not determine if its author is repenting for having been seduced by heretics or by pagans; the very tenor of the piece seems to him to be incompatible with the story one reads in Epiphanius.[16]

In his *Remarks* about the *Panarion* of Saint Epiphanius, Denis Petau will criticize these conclusions of Baronius. There is no reason, he declares, to consider the text of Epiphanius, which is completely in his style, to be apocryphal;[17] neither is there any reason to refuse to trust him. The various authors who, either before or after him, have said nothing about the event might have wanted to conceal it because of their love for Origen, or, indeed, they might have thought that it was not of interest in their perspective, or, too, they might have judged it fair to remain silent about a crime that had been followed by repentance, and they would not have wanted to seem to crush a man rather than combat his errors.[18] So as to be able to insert the fact in a less improbable way into the course of Origen's life, the ingenious Petau proposes therefore only to attribute to the persecution of Severus what Epiphanius placed under the persecution of Decius.

Thus, Baronius, who could not believe in the outrageous legend, got rid of it by rejecting the authenticity of the text read in Epiphanius, while Petau, who considered himself forced to recognize its authenticity, believed himself thereby obliged to give credence to the legend.[19] So great was the prestige of Saint Epiphanius for both of them! But

---

[16] Ibid., 3:24–25.

[17] *Ad Haeresim 64, Origenianorum:* "Falsissimum est intextam hanc Epiphanio laciniam esse, cum neque de stylo ipso dubitari possit. . . ."

[18] "Caeteri qui vel antiquiores Epiphanio vel illius temporis suppares erant, partim Origenis amore dissimularunt, partim, quod ad rem minime faceret, scribendo praetermiserunt. Atque Eusebius quidem, utpote Origenis admirator, consulto ut omitteret fecisse videtur. . . . Reliqui tam fautores quam adversarii Origenis, cum de impiis ejus dogmatibus atque erroribus in certamen disputationemque venissent, facile contempsere caetera. Ac profecto de eo crimine sileri a sanctissimis viris aequissimum fuit, cujus tantopere illum paenituisse scirent, ne hominis memoriae insultare obtrectarique velle potius quam errores damnare viderentur. . . ."

[19] "Epiphanium . . . , quo neque antiquiorem auctorem, neque graviorem requirere debemus, qui de Origene velut compertam rem minimeque dubiam illud ipsum retulit."

what seems incredible is that Petau imagined that he got the better of Baronius by critical clearsightedness. . . .[20]

In his *Histoire de la naissance, progrez et décadence de l'hérésie de ce siècle*, the Catholic polemicist Florimond de Raemond attributes the fall of Origen to pride and insists on comparing it to that of Tertullian; a comparison that, as we will see, was to know a long good fortune:

> . . . This learned African, Christian and Catholic, became a Montanist. Need we be surprised at the apostasy of Martyr and Ochin, since the Church has seen, after Tertullian, the fall of Origen, whose nobility, wisdom, continence, holiness of life, incomparable knowledge and rare eloquence were admired by those of his time and of all centuries after him? Spite destroyed Tertullian and pride ruined Origen, and the pleasures of the world these two of whom I am speaking. . . .[21]

Let us not forget that Origen was implicated, for centuries, in a wider process, of which he was only one of the star players. In this process, arguments in favor and indictments against were heard in turn according to the authors and sometimes both on the part of the same author. The *Planctus Origenis* suggested besides a link between the case of Origen and that of Samson and Solomon by having the unfortunate great man say after his fall: "O devil, what have you done to me? I once cried over Samson's mistake, but I have committed a worse one. I cried over the fall of Solomon, and I have fallen lower than he. . . ."[22] In 1609, the Jesuit Joannes de Pineda, in a book published in Lyons, formally examined the case of King Solomon;[23] this was in order finally to give him absolution; Solomon had sinned, but he had repented; he was saved. The advocate, not content with refuting hostile witnesses, also rejected the indecisive. He particularly disputed the testimony of the blessed Mechtilde, who believed she had seen in an ecstasy that the salvation of Solomon, like that of Origen and Trajan, was in doubt.[24]

---

[20] Petau's rival in patristics, Thomassin, who would prove rather severe with regard to Origen, would make no allusions to Epiphanius' account. The wholly doctrinal nature of his work did not lend itself to it.

[21] Rouen, 1618; l. 3, c. 5, 295.

[22] "O diabole, quid fecisti mihi? . . . Flebam aliquando super Samsonem: sed pejora perpessus sum. Flebam super Salomonem: et deterius cecidi. . . ." Baronius had quoted this passage from the *Lamentationes seu Paenitentia Origenis*: *Annales ecclésiastiques*, 3:24.

[23] Joannes de Pineda, S.J., *De rebus Salomonis regis* (Lyons, 1609), l. 8: "De extremis vitae et penitentiae gestis".

[24] L. 8, c. 1, sectio 2, n. 11. Cf. *Exégèse médiévale*, 1:287.

Soon, with Francesco Collius, member of the Congregation of Oblates of Saint Charles, the great penitentiary of the diocese of Milan, the dimensions of the process were going to take on a totally different scale. Collius published in 1622–1623 a large work, *De animabus paganorum.* Judging the fate of some famous pagans, he distributed salvation and damnation with authority, and if he hesitated over some of them, it was still, one might say, with the same assurance. Enoch and Melchizedek were saved; so were the Sibyls, Solon, Epictetus; the Queen of Sheba was, too; as for Anaxagoras, his fate had to be considered less certain; as for Orpheus, Socrates, Aristotle, they were excluded.[25] But the title of the work does not cover all its contents, for the second part, in his fourth book, treats of personages of the Old Law, beginning with Adam, in order finally to come, like Florimond de Raemond, to those two men so often associated: Origen and Tertullian. To settle the case of Origen takes Collius no less than seven chapters.[26]

From his adolescence, Origen appeared to be a saint. In his works, he often refuted the blasphemies of heretics. Numerous Fathers sang his praises; even his worst adversaries, like Theophilus, were nourished on him, they took delight in him. The Latins copy him as well as the Greeks. Yet, those who in these recent times have claimed, with Pico della Mirandola, Génébrard and Sixtus of Siena, that all the errors of his books were inserted into them by heretics have exaggerated: he expressed himself *prava et noxia dogmata.* It is also a fact that he did not obtain the martyr's crown. But how the snares of Satan made him stumble, how darkness chased Christian light from his mind, that is what is not equally clear to everyone. The *Paenitentia Origenis* is perhaps apocryphal. The account of his fall is read in Saint Epiphanius; Baronius believes it to be interpolated, but his reasons are not convincing; the silence of other authors can be explained very easily, and a rather clear allusion can also be detected in the synodal Letter of the Bishops of Egypt. In any case, the testimony of Jerome and of Vincent de Lérins shows that the origin of the fall was error in faith. Origen gravely erred; he committed the crime of heresy. As John Zonaras wrote, his pride led to blasphemy. He spread underhandedly his perverse doctrines, and he did not repent. Scandal came through him. He can in no way be absolved. Living and dead, he was anathematized. There is therefore

[25] Cf. Jean Daniélou, *Les Saint païens de l'Ancien Testament* (Ed. du Seuil, 1956), 12.

[26] Chapters 9 to 15.

every chance that he was damned. It was indeed he himself, his person and not only his books, that the Council of Constantinople declared condemned *in aeternum*. Anyone who would doubt this could not do so *sine flagitio*. "Suidas" and Nicephorus Callistus were right to call his doctrines rash and his death impious.[27]

One will note the new transformations undergone here by the legend, with the help of historical inaccuracies and oratorical generalities. Collius' work, according to Dupin,[28] was, properly speaking, only an intellectual game. Feller recognized much erudition in it, "but still more thoughtlessness and vanity".[29] It had, nonetheless, a certain success, since it was reprinted at least twice. This is not to say that he had won everyone's conviction. A little later, in 1628, the Jesuit Louis Richeome expressed a more modest opinion in a work where one would scarcely have thought to seek it, if one had not read his colleague Possevin: *L'Académie d'Honneur dressée par le Fils de Dieu au royaume de son Église, sur l'Humilité*. It is in section 27 that we find a eulogy connected with the mind of Caesar and with that of Origen. Richeome then warns his reader:

> . . . When he would have the mind and capacity of Caesar and Origen together, let him consider their fate, and he will see that his gifts will not keep him from being unhappy any more than they did those two. . . . For the first of these two excellent minds moans in hell and will do penance forever for the evil he committed by means of the fine gifts he had; and the other, through the pride of his noble mind, and other fine qualities, fell into several heresies, and it is not known if he abjured them with repentance before he died or if he is saved or damned.[30]

Richeome thus dropped the senseless fable. Like Possevin, he evokes the fall of Origen into heresy only with a view to drawing a lesson of humility from it. But the following year, here is another Jesuit, Father Étienne Binet, a prolific author, sometimes agreeable but not very serious—"distressing more than enlivening", Maurice Blondel pronounced with severity[31]—who published in French a whole treatise *Du salut d'Origène* (1629). He aimed it at the broad public of those

---

[27] "Ed. secunda, a multis mendis expurgata", Mediolani (1738), 259–87.

[28] *Bibliothèque ecclésiastique*, 17:109–11.

[29] 1858 edition, 325.

[30] Louis Richeome, *Oeuvres*, vol. 2 (Paris, 1628), 714.

[31] Letter to Henri Bremond, February 14, 1916. H. Bremond and M. Blondel, *Correspondance*, published by André Blanchet, vol. 2 (Aubier, 1971), 291. René Bady declares Binet's

who would soon be called "honest men". Perhaps the idea for it came to him following the reprinting that had just been made at Douai of the *Speculum majus* of Vincent de Beauvais (1624). Be that as it may, he exploited his predecessors without shame. Binet was scarcely less erudite than Collius (which does not mean that he wasted his time in reading Origen for himself); he was not more critical. He presupposes the "infallibly" acquired knowledge that the poor Alexandrian, "the Phoenix of Scholars and the Sun of the minds of his century", "poured out incense before idols; plunged by this crime into an abyss of sadness, he withdrew to Tyre, where he died. Some say that this was acknowledged by him at the end of his life, some say not." Would Origen not be "the Lucifer of the earth", as Lucifer was "the Origen of heaven"? Binet wants to make us hear the discordant voices that have not ceased to clash since the death of the great man. His book is presented as the analytical account of a trial court proceeding.

First parade by the exonerating witnesses: Jacques Merlin, Erasmus and the advocates: Génébrard, Pico della Mirandola, Saint Gregory the Wonderworker. Each goes to work with his discourse, setting forth reasons upon reasons for saving the "diamond of Theology". Jacques Merlin concludes his own by saying that "what Abraham was to the angels, Moses to men, Joseph to the Egyptians, Job to the suffering, Daniel to slaves, Origen was to the whole world. All my anger is caused by the fact that ungrateful Greece did not know the treasure that God had consigned to it; it has him, unfortunate, splashed, indeed, blackened with errors and outrages. . . ." Next comes Erasmus: "I could not", he declares in the course of an erudite deposition, "have such influence over my heart as to impose on it this law of believing such a man might fade and a Sun of the Church could be eclipsed." For "the learned Génébrard", if "some little ardor and human passion, having overheated him, tore from him a few propositions" that were less than correct, they "had since been drowned in a great torrent of tears", and if later a holy personage thought to see him in the flames of hell, "is this the first time that one has taken an illusion to be a vision?" Is it very certain, moreover, that this good hermit meant to speak of our

art of describing the wonders of nature to be "admirable" but recognizes that several of his writings "would lead one to think that devotion is only a better hygiene, something like the supreme art of happiness": *Humanisme chrétien dans les lettres françaises, 16–17ᵉ siècles* (Fayard, 1972), 95–96 and 110–11. In his *9ᵉ Provinciale*, Pascal criticizes Binet's book "De la marque de prédestination".

great Origen and not of some other, who was "in flames"?[32] Here, now, is Giovanni Pico: he concedes that "this great torrent of eloquence and doctrine made like other torrents, which in the midst of a great quantity of water, sometimes carry along some dirt", but he was at that time speaking only "dubitatively" and about things that the councils had not yet declared. Besides, if he truly sinned, he could do penance, and if the homily that attests this is apocryphal, the "fall" might very well also be, and so forth. As for the "vision" of which so much has been made, one can oppose to it that "of a great saint named Saint Mechtilde, to whom God revealed that he did not want the world to be certain about what finally became of Samson, Solomon and Origen, so that greater fear would be given to the strongest, the wisest and the most learned of the world, holding them in suspense in this uncertainty. . . ." Then the great Cardinal Baronius is introduced, who addresses a long harangue to the judges "in the name of Cardinal Bellarmine" and of all those who are against Origen. After the doctrinal grievances ("In order to spare his allegories, he ransacked earthly Paradise", and so forth), the matter of apostasy returns:

> If what Saint Epiphanius, and so many others, says had in fact turned out to be true, what means could there be of saving the folly of Origen and his extreme misfortune? During the time of the cruel persecution of Decius, or Severus, Origen suffered unbelievable torments, but, being reduced to such an extremity, that he must lose either his faith or his chastity, he preferred to lose his faith and to prostitute it than to defile the innocence of his body, and it is said that he threw two grains of incense before the idol and left Jesus Christ; if that is true, what ocean could wash away such a fault in such a man? . . .
>
> [It is not known] from any book or any authentic author that he did penance. . . . For, with respect to the last Sermon of which people talk and the treatise of his last regrets, these are pieces that Pope Gelasius declared to be truly apocryphal. . . . We must therefore believe that he fell in a condemned sense, that this crime clouded the eyes of the spirit, that this beautiful Sun of knowledge was eclipsed, and that his ambition plunged him into the abyss, preferring to perish than to retract and admit that Origen had made a mistake. . . .

The conclusion of the indictment: all that is said in defense of Origen "is a mediation for tender souls". He renounced his faith, incensed the

---

[32] We will find this distinction again later on.

idol, "that is only too beyond doubt". Nicephorus says that he died "unfortunately": Does that not mean "shamefully"? And again the stunning argument of the "vision": in a book quoted by the fifth general council, was it not related that a man "saw, as it were, a space of hell uncovered" and that he recognized there the various heretics, and among them Origen, "weighed down with horror, flames and confusion".[33]

We then hear the "Discourse of Mercy": Are Eusebius and Dionysius of Alexandria not worthy of more faith than Nicephorus? Is the vision of Saint Mechtilde not worth more than that of the man who supposedly saw Origen in hell? Is it not to misuse the council to change its anathema into damnation?, and so forth. But then we have Justice pleading, in his turn, in the opposite direction. It overwhelms "this unfortunate apostate", who, "in one morning reversed what he had done in fifty years" and whose virtues "were turned into vices", "worse than Judas, who recognized his fault". "I don't know", this Justice also says in fury, "if there has been a more disastrous fall since Lucifer. . . . Would it be nice to see that someone, in order to save Origen, wanted also to save Lucifer?" Thereupon Binet himself intervenes. Is it really certain, he dares to ask, that the unfortunate might not have repented? Baronius did not absolutely reject his *Planctus*, and Saint Jerome translated it; if this is not the very text of Origen's discourse, it is at least probable that there was one, perhaps even more intense, more worthy "of that incomparable mind and of that heart touched by a grief so sensitive and penetrating". Besides, one "would not willingly" doubt what is said by the serious Saint Epiphanius, so worthy of belief. Now, after having gone back over the scene of the apostasy, does not Epiphanius report that, having gone to hide his shame in Jerusalem, he was asked for a sermon, without his being able to escape? Having then opened the Bible, he read these words of Psalm (49:17): "Peccatori autem dixit Deus: Quare tu enarras justitiam meam? Odisti disciplinam et projecisti sermones retrorsum [But to the sinner God says: What right have you to recite my statutes. . . . For you hate discipline and you cast my words behind you]." And "as if these words had been a thunder clap, or as if he had been struck by a bolt from Heaven, he remained as if bewildered, for he could not add a word, but burst into sobs."

---

[33] The reader will be able to ascertain that Binet has not read Baronius any more closely than he has read Origen.

All that remains is the conclusion. Binet, however, cannot keep from introducing here a chapter on morals, in order to explain "how it comes about that the greatest minds of the world have often been the most wretched and the most lost": it is because they "know everything, except how to humble themselves". He is scarcely inclined to indulgence: "I seem", he says, "to see Origen in the solitude of Tyre: a haggard man, an empty dream, who takes pleasure in nothing, who amuses himself by concealing his errors, accusing everyone, mocking those who complain, getting angry at those who accuse him or want to put him back on the right road; writing against the bishops, fabricating heresies, doing evil deeds by the thousands, and being damned before dying." Nevertheless, our Binet does not want to render the sentence himself. After this parenthetical passage, he leads us back to the praetorium, where Justice and Mercy face each other again, this time in a closely written dialogue, while Truth gives the reply to both. None of the three places the fall into idolatry in doubt, nor the long series of errors that was the punishment for this initial weakness. "The whole thing consists in knowing" if the unfortunate Origen finally "cried for mercy from God". And as no one knows anything about that, here is the judgment of the Court; one recognizes the good heart of Father Binet in it:

> The matter will be appointed to God's judgment, and the definitive judgment will be reserved to him. Nevertheless, provisionally, and to Origen's profit, it has been said that, weighing everything in the balance, the evidence that saves him is stronger than that which damns him. . . .

Five hundred pages were necessary to obtain such a result. Huet was perhaps right to say that Binet sought the truth, not wanting to attribute anything too much to hate or to love,[34] and Bayle was no less right to say that he "does not dare to declare himself" for salvation "except in trembling".[35] But we are rather sensitive to the mixture of weightiness and triviality that characterizes such a work, to the futility of an undertaking similar to that of those writers of romance who seek to please the public while exploiting a fashionable theme. . . . Thanks to the final judgment, mercy and good sense triumph, but in the wake of what follies and sustained in what credulity? It is not surprising that

[34] *Origeniana* (PG 17, 1182 C).

[35] *Dictionnaire*, 3d ed., vol. 3 (1720), 2124.

Pascal chose this man as a target when writing his ninth provincial Letter. . . .[36]

III. *From the Calvinist Daillé to Le Nain de Tillemont*

The judgment pronounced, or rather contemplated, by Binet could not be definitive. The entire seventeenth century continued to take an interest in the salvation of Origen. In all camps, for and against, people became impassioned on the subject. All opinions were expressed. And there was no lack of sceptics to amuse themselves with it.

Two years after the Jesuit Binet, the Calvinist Jean Daillé (1594–1670) entered the lists, with his *Traicté de l'employ des Saincts Peres* (1631). His goal was to demonstrate that it is practically impossible to arbitrate the "differences of Religion" by means of the Fathers of the Church, since so many of the latter contradict each other and so many insoluble problems remain concerning their works. According to Bayle, this "trial shot" by a still young author "was a masterpiece".[1] The fact is that it aroused long controversies, it was reprinted in Latin translation in 1656 and John Keble thought he must still refute it in 1839, in one of the famous Oxford *Tracts*.[2] Daillé could not fail to meet Baronius on his path. He was at first indignant to see the great Catholic historian boldly affirming that texts are apocryphal as soon as he finds something in them that displeases him: this is the case when he claims that the passage from Epiphanius about the fall of Origen is an interpolation. In another place, however, Daillé treats the question on its own merits, in a way that seems more reasonable:

> What Epiphanius relates about his fall takes away nothing from the praise of this man. Even if things happened as Epiphanius says, there is no lack of examples of faithful men who succumbed to some grave temptation, as we see in the example of Peter. But also, to be completely open, Baronius' opinion pleases me: this whole story is untrue, invented by some jealous people who could not stand the glory of this great and admirable man. It

[36] On Binet, cf. Henri Bremond, *Histoire littéraire du sentiment religieux en France* . . . , vol. 1 (Paris: Bloud et Gay, 1923), 128–48.

[1] *Dictionnaire*, s.v. Daillé (vol. 2 [1730], 235–36). "There is a very strong chain of reasoning, which forms a moral demonstration, against those who would like to end the disputes of religion through the authority of the Fathers."

[2] "On the Mysticism Attributed to the Early Fathers of the Church"; it is no. 89 of the *Tracts for the Times*.

> could have been inserted fraudulently into Epiphanius' work, or rather, I think, might have been believed by Epiphanius, who would then have put it there himself in writing: this would be far from being the only case of an author who was mistaken; for even if he was a saint, he was also at times very credulous, as Petau asserts. . . .[3]

Let us not believe, however, that Daillé wanted in the final account to "save" Origen. He places him in the list of great heretics, and if he rejects the allegations of Saint Epiphanius, it is less to prove the Alexandrian scholar innocent than to reject his repentance for his errors. Besides, what interests him in all this is not so much that old story but the occasion it provides him for embarrassing his interlocutors of the Roman confession. We, indeed, see him nearly thirty years later, in 1660, at the time when a certain Mr. Cottibi, a minister in Poitiers, having converted to Catholicism, wrote to his consistory an explanatory letter in which he speaks of "Saint Origen". Daillé, charged with responding to him, is surprised. For merely having doubted the damnation of Origen, he observes, Giovanni Pico had been severely taken up by the masters in theology: "What would they not have done if he had placed him among the saints, as Mr. Cottibi has done?" Father Adam, a Jesuit, then came to the assistance of the converted pastor. In the style of the period, he reproached Daillé for his "masterful boldness, which is only a little swelling, and not knowledge and fullness": How dare he support the side of those who maintain that Origen was damned? "You ask me", Daillé immediately replies, "what reason I have for proving that this great man died without repentance, and quote me an old story to refute this opinion"; in reality, "God be pleased that no such unjust presumption ever entered my mind! . . . I have always admired this great and incomparable mind." All he wanted was to show how contrary to the style and laws of the Catholic Church the expression "Saint Origen" was. . . . In short, Origen was the pretext rather than the object of this quarrel, which always had need of fuel.[4]

The efforts, however timid, to prove Origen's innocence met with no more favor at all in the Catholic camp. Jean de Silhon says in his treatise: "Arsenic resembles sugar, and Origen was poisoned with it" (*De l'immortalité de l'âme* [1634]). In Florence, in 1639, appeared a treatise *De dogmatum Origenis cum philosophia Platonis comparatione*, by the

---

[3] *De usu Patrum*, 264–65.

[4] Cf. Bayle, *Dictionnaire*, s.v. Origen, new ed. (Paris: 1820), 11:245–49.

"theologian" Gaudentius Paganini. The author is content to comment on the principal features of the anathematizing of the fifth ecumenical council and to recall the "indignant" account of the "most holy Epiphanius". One might be surprised, he comes to observe, that men such as Didymus and John Chrysostom had taken up Origen's defense—but that would be to forget that in those times when persecution was rampant they did not have the leisure to give themselves over to an attentive reading of his works. Some might also maintain, according to the maxim of the legal experts, that no one could be condemned after his death: but the council is there to assure us of the contrary. During his lifetime, not all could be on guard in time against Origen's venom, because the latter had not ostensibly left the Church; he had nonetheless betrayed the Christian religion, through fear of punishment. He undoubtedly repented of it subsequently, he shed tears—but, *volens nolens*, he continued to fall into all kinds of errors and blasphemies, going to the point of teaching the worship of several gods, as the pagans do.[5] Some, in our own day, would like to prove him innocent. They do not recognize Justinian's right to have written against him; but did not Henry VIII write against Luther? If they had consented to read the dissertation of that emperor, they could only have declared him right, as the councils themselves have done. . . .

It would be difficult to push the contempt of history and absurdity farther. Paganini accomplished this tour de force by writing the thirty-seven chapters of his work without ever quoting a word from Origen. Let us nevertheless admire some of the legend's transformations: If the Alexandrian gave way at the time of persecution, this is no longer to preserve himself from the "Ethiopian" (at least that specification is not given): it is, more banally, through fear of punishment.

Paganini remarked in passing that there was a difference between the conduct of Origen and that of Tertullian. The former had not proclaimed his apostasy; the latter, on the contrary, had said farewell to the Catholics in order publicly to rejoin the camp of the Montanists, in such a way that no one could have been mistaken about it. This contrast, which is rather unfavorable to Origen, presupposed an analogy. The parallel between Origen and Tertullian was in fact commonplace, from that time on, in certain literature. The Jesuit theologian Jacques Gretser (1562–1625) had explained, in his learned treatise on canon

[5] An allusion to the "tritheism" reproached in the trinitarian doctrine of Origen.

law *De jure et more prohibendi livros malos* (1603), that, when it was a question of heresies long since dead and buried, there was scarcely any danger in reading the works that had proposed them.[6] Thus, he said, in virtue of an already long and deeply rooted custom, the writings of Origen and Tertullian are read everywhere and by all.[7] But the parallel was often more explicit and more precise. For Binet, Origen and Tertullian had been victims of the same evil, pride.[8] Starting from there, it was, for both of them, the same historic schema in three parts: a first period, Catholic and brilliant; a "fall" in mid-career; a final period lived in heresy and finished by a miserable end. One can see an echo here, from the preceding section, of Saint Francis de Sales and Collius of Milan. We will find another in the *Doctrine spirituelle* of Father Louis Lallemant, S.J. (1587–1635). This had to do with the gift of strength: "The occasion of a beautiful death", says Lallemant, "is so precious that no wise man must lose it when it presents itself. . . . What Origen and Tertullian would not be if, before their fall, they had found an occasion to die for Jesus Christ, to whom they had been faithful?"[9] Still another echo, amplified by the oratorical genius of Bossuet, in a 1665 sermon for the second Sunday in Advent, on the "divinity of Religion": "Heretics have spread confusion, the truth has remained pure. Schisms have torn the body of the Church, the truth has remained whole. Several have been seduced. . . . An Osius, an Origen, a Tertullian, so many others who seemed to be the support of the Church have fallen with great scandal: the truth has remained ever steadfast."[10]

[6] Cf. Bossuet, to Madame d'Albert, September 30, 1691: "The works of Origen have been rigorously prohibited in the past, because of his errors or those that had slipped into his books. Now that the matters in question then have been so clarified that there is no longer any danger in being mistaken about them, you can read him because of the piety that reigns in his works, nevertheless keeping in mind that he is an author whose authority is not equal to that of the other Fathers." *Oeuvres*, ed. F. Lachat, vol. 28 (1865), 37.

[7] Gretser was a humanist, scholar, polemicist. His bibliography contains 234 titles. *Opera omnia . . . aucta et illustrata . . .*, 17 vols. (Ratisbonne). The *De jure . . .* is in volume 13 (1739), c. 11: *De libris Marcelli Ancyrani et Origenis*, 42–43. In 1612, Gretser published a *Supplementum de more prohibendi, expurgandi et abolendi libros haereticos et noxios*.

[8] *Du salut d'Origène*, 403–4.

[9] Original text, ed. Aloys Pottier, S.J. (Paris: Téqui, 1936). Fourth principle, chap. 4, art. 6; 208–9.

[10] *Oeuvres*, ed. Guillaume (1885), 508. It was a Jesuit who came to the help of Osius, as others to the help of Origen: Michel-Joseph Maceda: *Hosius vere Hosius . . . hoc est Hosius vere innocens et sanctus* (Bologne, 1790).

It had eased Bossuet to know that the weakness of Osius had been that of a great old man with failing faculties, that Tertullian had become a Montanist with much show in the middle of his career, while the *Peri archôn*, whatever one thought of his doctrine,[11] was on the contrary a work of his youth[12] and that the heroic confession of Origen under Decius was much more belated: the legend of the "fall" inherited from Epiphanius, even when the concrete details of it were not retained, nevertheless compelled recognition of a parallel case. In current opinion, it would be carried on to the nineteenth century. We read from the pen of J. A. Lalanne, author of a work on the *Influence des Pères de l'Église sur l'éducation publique* (1850), this phrase that has shades of both romanticism and Prudhomme: "We must bow . . . before the names of Tertullian and Origen, with all the respect of which they are worthy, at the twofold title of genius and misfortune."[13] Msgr. Charles Freppel was to protest against this kind of pairing: "Origen", he wrote, "was not a mind of the same quality as Tertullian, and it is wrong to reproach these two natures that so little resemble each other."[14] But habits are not easily broken. We still find the very ones who would no longer admit anything of the legendary features or the prejudices that gave birth to it reviving the parallelism in one way or another. One name calls for the other. It is thus that Abbot Jean Steinmann still wrote, just several years ago, in his biography of *Tertullian*: "Having joined the Montanist mysticism cost Tertullian—like Origen—a halo

[11] Isidore of Seville expressed the common opinion when he had someone say to Origen, in the poem composed for his library:

> "Sola mihi casum Periarchon dicta dederunt:
> His me conjectum impia tela premunt."

Again one must observe that, while he was alive, the doctrinal authority of Origen was not at all attacked, rather, it never ceased to increase.

[12] The *Peri archôn*, "whose date is impossible to fix with certitude, must be one of the most ancient among the works of the great scholar". It was written certainly before 230 and "reasons are not lacking to believe that the years 212–215 were those of its composition": G. Bardy, DTC, vol. 11, col. 1501. (For Nautin: v. 229.) Origen was born around 183–186.

[13] P. 91.

[14] *Origène*, vol. 1 (1868), 19. Cf. p. 20: "When I see him, . . . after so many works and battles, appear, at the age of sixty-five years, before the court of persecutors and crown his vigorous old age with a brilliant confession of faith, with captivity and tortures suffered for the cause of Christ. . . ." Freppel no longer judges it necessary to make the least mention of the fable in order to refute it. Cf. 2:428–29. George Prestige, *Fathers and Heretics* (1948), 85: Origen belongs to a type of man totally different from that of Tertullian.

that the Church attributed without hesitation to Jerome."[15] We will see still other examples of this association later on.

Let us return to the course of the seventeenth century. The hostility of Jansenius (d. 1638) toward Origen is well known. He denounced the latter as an initiator not only of Pelagianism but of all the heresies that devastated the Church for more than three centuries. Without making any direct allusion to the legend of his fall, such as recounted according to Epiphanius, Jansenius gives the equivocal and significant title of *Lapsus Origenis* to the first of the chapters in which he criticizes his doctrine.[16] The great Arnauld himself was indignant at the thought that the Jesuits "have allowed two of their authors, to wit, Father Binet and Father Alvar,[17] to have published Apologies for Origen, who had so many times been 'condemned and anathematized' ".[18]

The Jesuit Corneille de la Pierre (1567–1637) would not have merited the indignation of Arnauld to the same degree. In his classes in exegesis, first at Louvain (1598–1616), then at the Roman College, he had had more than one occasion to encounter Origen. He seems to have given credence to the account of Saint Mechtilde, concluding with the uncertainty about his salvation.[19] Commenting on chapter 15 of Ecclesiasticus, he evokes his *lapsus* and the touching scene of his tears when speaking to the people at the invitation of the bishop of Jerusalem; yet he acknowledges that Baronius has placed the story in doubt, and he seeks a more certain example of repentance *certius exemplum* in the commentary of Saint Jerome on Isaiah.[20] As was his custom, he did only the work of a compiler here, without claiming to decide anything, and it was still a commonplace that he was transmitting, in any case, by declaring that if Origen was a great explorer of Scripture, nevertheless, "too confident in his valor and in his work, he

---

[15] *Tertullien*, ed. du chalet (Lyons, 1968), 291 (posthumous).

[16] *Augustinus* (1640), vol. 2, "Liber proemialis", c. 5, p. 5 A. Cf. vol. 1, l. 6, c. 6–19, 141–53; vol. 3, "Liber proemialis", c. 4.

[17] We have not been able to find a trace of this Alvar.

[18] *Oeuvres*, vol. 10 (1777), 707–8. Pascal did not share the sentiments of Arnauld on this point. In his seventeenth *Provinciale*, addressed to Father Annat, a Jesuit, without going into the basis for the debate over Origen's faith, he observes that neither Pico della Mirandola nor Génébrard nor Father Halloix (cf. below) failed to be good Catholics, bringing to bear another judgment about *the fact* of Origen's doctrines than the fifth general council (*Oeuvres*, ed. J. Chevalier [Pleiade], 877).

[19] *Commentaria* (Ed. Vivès), vol. 10, 498.

[20] *Commentaria*, vol. 9 (1866), 443.

fell into error through God's just judgment, and he teaches us through his misfortune not to harbor proud thoughts [*non alta sapere*]. . . ."[21]

Perhaps we will be allowed here, parenthetically, to make a place for the great Corneille, who in his tragedy *Théodore*, in 1645, set on stage the same case of conscience as legend attributed to Origen. Yet the hero of Corneille's drama is not the Alexandrian but the virgin Theodora, whose story Saint Ambrose had recounted in the second book of his treatise *De Virginibus*.[22] The dilemma with which the virgin is faced is the same as that of Origen: the judge forces her to choose between idolatry and unchastity. But she resolves it otherwise. She replies proudly to the judge that no corporal violence could force her to either kind of infidelity to her God:

> Whether you force my body into infamy
> Or my hand into incense for your impotent gods,
> I can preserve with a resolute soul
> A pure bride for an immaculate Bridegroom.[23]

We know how, thrown into a brothel, Theodora will leave it unscathed thanks to the ruse of a Christian soldier who exchanges clothes with her and how both will then obtain the palm of martyrdom.

Théodore was a disaster. In his *Examen*, Corneille himself agrees that to present on stage a virgin resolved to martyrdom was to condemn himself to giving a play without any action. He would not have been wrong, however, to protest against the fashionable sensitivities that averted one's gaze and to be astounded that "a story that constituted the most beautiful ornament of the second book of *Des Vierges* of Saint Ambrose was", according to them, "too licentious" to be represented.[24]

Soon after Binet and Corneille de la Pierre, another Jesuit would arise with a new apology for Origen. The latter was not an amateur like the first or a popularizer like the second. He was a true scholar, the

---

[21] *Commentaria*, vol. 13 (1866). *In 12 minores prophetas*, proemium, 235; etc. "Nimis ingenio et studio suo confisus in errores justo Dei . . . judicio prolapsus, suo malo nos docuit non altum sapere. . . ."

[22] L. 2, c. 4, n. 22 to 33. PL 16, 212–16. Cf. G. Couton, *Corneille* (Hatier, 1969), 117–21.

[23] Cf. Ambrose, op. cit., n. 24: "Sed nec virginis nomen agnoscitur, ubi virginitatis auctor negatur. . . . Tolerabilius est mentem virginis quam carnem habere" (PL 10, 213 B).

[24] To Voltaire, who had mockingly echoed the critics, Alfred de Vigny would reply: "Corneille is more true and more decent than Voltaire. . . . Only the body is violated, the soul is virgin." Cf. Émile Lauvrière, *Alfred de Vigny, sa vie et son oeuvre* (Grasset, 1945).

Belgian Pierre Halloix (1571–1656). He published at Liège, in 1648, a large volume, the third in a considerable work of Eastern patristics that remained unfinished:[25] *Origenes defensus, sive Origenis Adamantii presbyteri amatoris Jesu Vita, Virtutes, documenta. . . .* As an opening quotation, two maxims: "Virtuti comes Invidia" and "Nihil inventa ac defensa veritate dulcius". The work, dedicated to Pope Innocent X, is an outline of favorable testimony for our hero, coupled with a refutation by his enemies, ancient and modern. Two passages interest us. In the first, Halloix responds to those who claim that Origen supposedly sacrificed to idols: "Mera est fabula, pessime a pessimis hominibus confecta". His arguments, while not being new, are nonetheless sound.[26] He is less fortunate when, through fear of casting a slur on the memory of Epiphanius, he follows Baronius in considering this fable to be "impie ac sacrilege in sanctum Epiphanium intrusa". Farther on, he has a whole chapter "de salute et gloria Origenis". It is an accepted truth, he tells us, that three categories of faithful enjoy a particular halo:

> Aureolam Virgo, Martyr, fideique Magister
> Praeter communem dicuntur habere coronam.[27]

Now the great Origen, and he alone, has earned all three halos.[28]

For some polemical excesses, *Origenes defensus* was placed on the Index on March 12, 1655, *donec corrigatur.* But Halloix was to die the following year, without having had time to obtain his corrected edition.

Two years later, in 1658, in the notice to the reader of his edition of *Contra Celsum* and of the *Philokalia*, at Cambridge, William Spencer again quotes, according to Baronius, the "vision" recounted in the *Pré spirituel*—but in order to take up Origen's defense. In 1661, in his *Traité des hérésies* and in the *Dénombrement des hérésies* that accompanies it, Louis Abelly mentions Origen twice. Although he refers to Saint Epiphanius, he makes no direct allusion to the account of his apostasy, but, like so many others, he retains the general idea of a "fall", in punishment for his scholarly pride. "The whole Church", he con-

[25] *Antiquitates Ecclesiae orientalis* (Douai, 1638ff.). Halloix had published in 1622 a Saint Justin that the Bollandists would reproduce in their *Acta Sanctorum.*

[26] He points out, among others, the existence of an ancient martyrology that indicates to Alexander the names of several martyrs "converted by Origen".

[27] The Virgin, the Martyr, and the Teacher of the Faith / Are said to be crowned with a halo beyond the ordinary.

[28] *Origenes defensus*, 251–58 and 397–400.

cludes, "wept over the fall of Origen. . . . After having had the courage to want to expose himself to death for confessing the Name of Jesus Christ, he finally let himself be carried away by a presumption of his sufficiency, even into the abyss of Heresy". One will note the hesitant expression: "the courage to want to expose himself", which leaves a possible place for Saint Epiphanius' statement.[29]

We have now reached Daniel Huet (1690–1721), the celebrated author of *Origeniana* (1668), which is, Father Henri Crouzel tells us, "by far the most complete and most serious work that had been published about Origen up to this time".[30] Huet does not approve of the flagrant injustices of people like Luther and Théodore de Bèze, whom he contrasts with the relative moderation of the Centuriators of Magdeburg. If there are some, he declares, who want to treat Origen as a heretic, they must say as much for Irenaeus, Cyprian and many others. He rejects the "atrocious slander" spread by a certain number of Greek historians, notably Nicephorus. As a disciplined man of the Church, he is astounded that theologians had not taken into account the Decree of Gelasius declaring the *Paenitentia Origenis* to be apocryphal; he is astounded, as a prudent critic, that despite Erasmus' proof, historians persist in not recognizing the "ridiculous stupidity" of this statement of the case. With Petau, against Baronius and Halloix, he refuses to believe the disputed text by Epiphanius to be interpolated—and he uses this as an occasion for a sharp satire addressed to hypercritics ever ready to suppress whatever they find inconvenient in texts. . . .[31] Nor does he place much confidence in the perspicacity of the bishop of Salamis, who erred ("*hallucinatus est*") in placing his account in the time of Decius and who, in another work, relates the torments that Origen suffered under the persecution of this tyrant without making any allusion to the "Ethiopian". He reasonably sets forth all the reasons that demonstrate the extreme improbability of this "fall". And, despite everything, following Denis Petau to the end, he retains as historical Epiphanius' account, except to refer the facts to an earlier date,

[29] Cf. Spinoza.

[30] *Bibliographie critique d'Origène*, 115.

[31] *Origeniana*, l. 1, c. 4, n. 5: "Quaesivi sane multum ac diu, plusne perniciei in litteras an utilitatis critica ars intulerit. Quot enim sana et integra veterum scripta pervertit criticorum temeritas, dum quidquid minus mente perciperent, id ad arbitrium suum refingendi licentiam sibi fecerunt? . . ." (PG 17, 693 CD).

to the time of the Emperor Severus.[32] If, subsequently, Origen is seen to have been accepted benevolently by the Church, that must be explained by the indulgence and charity that the ancient Christians practiced in a sublime way with regard to those who had betrayed Christ through weakness. . . . Father Crouzel was decidedly right to warn us that, notwithstanding his distinguished merits, the learned bishop of Avranches reveals here and there "a certain obtuseness".[33]

We are going from paradox to paradox. Around the same time, an apparently much more obscure author, who has left no name in the history of criticism, proved himself wiser than Daniel Huet. The very year when the *Origeniana* was published, "Pierre Thomas du Fossé" undertook to write a *Histoire de Tertullien et d'Origène*, which he published ten years later under the pseudonym of Mister de la Motte (1675). This Thomas du Fossé had an alert sense of doctrinal development in the Church: "It was rather difficult", he observes, "in these early times, when truths were not yet clarified, for those who were writing not to fall into a few errors." To undertake at that time to comment on the Scriptures was "like engaging in a long voyage and undertaking to walk into a country whose roads remained nearly unknown until then. One must not judge these early times by those that followed them." Nevertheless, for him, Origen alone "surpassed all the Greeks and all the Latins"; but as a reward Origen found himself the object of a "more than raging jealousy", and so forth. The whole work tries to bring out not only the difference but the opposition between his case and that of Tertullian. For 763 pages, no allusion is made to the story about the Ethiopian. At the very end, on page 764, du Fossé simply tells us: "It would be shameful after that to come to a stop with an account recognized as fictitious by all the scholars,[34] touching the supposed fall of Origen during this persecution" of Decius. This account, he adds, "is not only without any probability and regarded as such by those who were most opposed to Origen", but "it also cancels itself out."[35]

[32] Under Decius, Huet maintains the firmness of Origen, "Obstante nimirum saevitia judicis, non Origenis perfidia, quominus martyrii coronam consequeretur" (PG 17, 690 B). Note the use of the word *perfidia* in its traditional sense (cf. H. de Lubac, *Exégèse médiévale*, 3:153–81).

[33] *Origeniana*, l. 1, c. 2, n. 13 (PG 17, 662–68); c. 4, n. 4–5 (689–93); l. 2, c. 21 (1180–82). *Origenianorum Appendix* (1280–81).

[34] Du Fossé exaggerates!

[35] Du Fossé, *Histoire de Tertullien*, particularly 452, 461, 510, 522, 764.

Is it solely critical flair, is it pure sympathy that explains this position? Another explanation is possible; let us say very probable. There is every chance that the modest Tillemont, who inspired and guided in an anonymous way more than one work of erudition, collaborated closely in the work of "Mister de la Motte". This hypothesis was formulated by Bruno Neveu.[36] There is, undoubtedly, no conclusive indication of it. But we know that Pierre-Thomas du Fossé (1634–1698), who was a student at Port-Royal, had had Tillemont as a fellow classmate and that he remained bound to him by a close friendship.[37] At the time when he was still treasurer at Rouen, this Norman found himself among those directed by Jean Guillebert, curate of Rouville, who was a disciple of Saint-Cyran.[38] It was he who, beginning in 1684, finished the Bible of Lemaître de Sacy, of whom he was also a close friend. He left long *Mémoires* for the benefit of the history of Port-Royal, which were (in part) published at Utrecht in 1739. As we see, his Jansenist connections were not to keep him from doing justice to Origen.

Tillemont, however—if it was indeed he who inspired the excellent Mister du Fossé—was not yet the victor. It is true that the *Grand dictionnaire historique* of Louis Moreri judges, in 1674, that "the most able critics doubt that this account, attributed to Saint Epiphanius, was by him, since in other places in his works, where he speaks about Origen, he says nothing about his so-called fall, nor do other Fathers, and in particular Saint Jerome, Theophilus of Alexandria and Vincent de Lérins, who wrote against Origen. . . . The apologists are not at all concerned about clearing him of this crime, with which he could not fail to have been reproached, if only he had been suspected of it." This was a return to the position of Baronius. But in reality, at this date, there was no agreement among scholars. Richard Simon seems to have wanted to stay outside the dispute. In a letter of July 20, 1683,[39] giving a few reflections about Origen, whom he admires in spite of

[36] *Un historien à l'école de Port-Royal* (La Haye, 1966), 155. Similarly: *Sébastien-Joseph du Cambout de Pontchâteau (1634–1690) et ses missions à Rome* . . . , ed. de Boccard (1969). Cf. A. Gazier, *Histoire générale du jansénisme* (Champion, 1922); 1:216, 221, 338; 2:34. Tillemont will quote du Fossé in his volume 8.

[37] Cf. Neveu, *Sébastien-Joseph*, 20. They lived close to Arnauld, Pontchâteau and Akakia. ("All together, we sing the Psalms, even while walking, during the night, in the forest. . . .")

[38] Jean Mesnard, *Pascal* (Hatier, 29).

[39] *Lettres choisies*, published by M. Bruzen la Martinière, 4 vols. (Amsterdam, 1730), 1:128–38, Letter 12 to Abbot G., from the Sorbonne house and society; 135–36.

his "allegories",[40] and passing in review the different editions of his works, he is content, on our subject, to note that Father Halloix "was wrong to consider the *Histoire des Hérésies* of Saint Epiphanius to be interpolated". In 1687, Jean Le Clerc (1651–1736), whose judgment of Origen—"more reading than judgment"[41]—applies rather well to himself, nevertheless rejects the twofold fable of the apostasy and the *Planctus*.[42] But two years later, the opinion tenaciously maintained by Petau and Huet received a new reinforcement, thanks to the Franciscan Antoine Pagi (1624–1699), who published in 1689 a monumental *Critìca historico-theologica in universos Annales . . . Baronii. . . .* Pagi presents a formal defense of Epiphanius' account. Did neither friends nor enemies, neither Christians nor pagans breathe a word of this story? But the explanation for this silence is quite natural. The adversaries, wholly occupied with refuting Origenian doctrines, disregarded this shameful story, or rather they thought it would be unjust and inhuman to recall a crime for which repentance had made amends. They would also have recognized that Origen, although he might have been prepared to sacrifice, did not do it by himself; the true instigators of the crime were those who seized him by the hands to make him throw incense on the altar. Certainly he nonetheless sinned gravely, for the mere fact of being a party, however slight, to an idolatrous act is a capital crime. Yet, it was impossible to accuse him of it without revealing thereby the extreme concern he had about chastity, something his enemies would not readily do. Hence their silence. As for Eusebius, undoubtedly he had already recounted, in his *Apologia* for Origen, many things that he would not want to repeat in his *Ecclesiastical History*, judging that they did not concern the universal Church. . . . Pagi even rejects the conjecture of his two "very learned" predecessors, who reported at the time of Severus what Epiphanius said had happened under Decius. Their arguments, by which they sought to preserve the historicity of the "fall", did not seem either necessary or convincing to him. Besides, Eusebius gives no hint that Origen had been disturbed under Severus, while he speaks of the torture he suffered under Decius: it was only at that time that the deplorable apostasy could have taken place.

"What, you do not know the Franciscan Father F. Pagi, who has just

[40] His works, he says, "contain inexhaustible depths of erudition" (128).

[41] *Bibliothèque ancienne et moderne*, vol. 1 (1714), 167.

[42] *Bibliothèque universelle et historique*, vol. 6 (Amsterdam, 1687); on Origen: 31–55.

given us a folio volume of criticism against Baronius? That is almost like asking who is Escobar." So Le Nain de Tillemont, writing to his friend Quesnel, expressed it. According to a contemporary, Tillemont was "one of the most precise critics" of his time. Renan would not be of that opinion. His writings, he would say, "are masterpieces of conscience, but the conscience is not critical"; and again, his criticism, "implacable and minute when it is a question of verifying the origin and value of sources, never dreams for an instant of questioning himself about the probability of the facts".[43] Without wondering if Renan always questioned himself about the probability of the pictures he traces for us, or even about his idea of probability and its presuppositions, we are able to verify that Tillemont, at least in the debate that concerns us, did know how to question himself and that his response is as pertinent as it is conscientious.

In the twenty-second of the *Notes sur Origène* contained in the third volume of the *Mémoire pour servir à l'histoire ecclésiastique des six premiers siècles*, published in 1693, Tillemont begins by sidestepping the false dilemma with which the readers of Epiphanius, divided into two opposing camps, remained completely enclosed:

> . . . Baronius believed this story so unlikely that he even wondered if this section might not have been added to Saint Epiphanius. But it is not necessary to resort to that. One need only have what this Saint says about Meletius and Arius to see that he sometimes based himself on very poor memories. This is why we know that several very judicious persons have believed that Saint Epiphanius did write what is found in his book but that he was mistaken through false rumors.

In short, this account "has all the appearance of a fable". As a good psychologist, with no illusions about human nature, Tillemont then does away with the reasons alleged by those who believed in the "fall" as explanation of the silence of Origen's enemies for more than two centuries:

> Saint Jerome was assuredly not for sparing him this fault because of any repentance that might have followed it, and Theophilus even less so. I strongly doubt that what Father Pagi says about this could satisfy those who are a little acquainted with the persons of whom he speaks. Even Vincent de Lérins would have spoken of this story; and there is no like-

[43] Cf. Neveu, *Un historien à l'école de Port-Royal* (Le Haye, 1966), VI, 28, 100.

lihood at all that Porphyry, who wanted, contrary to the truth, to snatch Ammonius from the Christians, would absolutely have ceded Origen to them.

Next comes a long explanation of a historical order to show that it is impossible to place the supposed deed, at whatever date at all, in the life of Origen and to reject the belated authority of Justinian and later Greek historians, "all great enemies of Origen".

Tillemont then feels the need to apologize. He has relegated this whole discussion to a note because the story coming from Epiphanius was little worthy, in itself, of consideration. But for him, that is already too much:

> We would not let this narration of Saint Epiphanius so detain us, and we would be content with that fable-like appearance that it has of itself, with the slight authority it draws from the one who first produced it, and with the judgment that many able and judicious people make of it today, if we did not see that Father Petau, Mr. Huet and Father Pagi had taken the trouble to support it, although the former is content to say that there is no proof that it is false. The judgment of these very considerable persons warrants at least that we not reject it without examining it with care. But we have not believed ourselves obliged to follow it, any more than Wettstein[44] did or others who have also written in this way after Mr. Huet and who have abandoned Saint Epiphanius.

Nothing more remains except for Tillemont, in a few words, to dispose of the fable of "repentance" after that of the "fall". After having observed that it is not known if the *Lamentum* had, in the mind of its author, any relation to the story of the apostasy, he assures us that "those who regard it as a work by Origen are laughable" and that "one would have to have scarcely any knowledge of Saint Jerome at all to believe that such barbarous Latin as that could possibly have come from him."[45]

[44] J. R. Wettstein, who published in 1673, in Basel, in Greek and Latin, several works of Origen, among which: the *Exhortatio ad martyrium*. Tillemont refers to page 100.

[45] Tillemont, *Notes sur Origène*, 766–69. In the body of the work, "Notice sur Origène", article 40, Tillemont declares that "as for what concerns his salvation, it is a point that is better left to the impenetrable judgments of God. It is certain only that the visions of those who imagined they saw him in hell do not put him there." There follows a very beautiful eulogy of Origen, accompanied by some regret that he had, despite his own warnings, granted too much "to human knowledge" and thus mixed "the idols of falsehood with the truths that the Word of God had taught him" (593–95; 2d ed. [1701]).

One might believe that the final period had been placed to this centuries-old dispute. Tillemont's treatise did in fact have a few echos, the principal one coming from the Protestant world. In his long *Histoire de l'Église depuis Jésus-Christ jusqu'à présent,* in the first volume (Rotterdam, 1699), Jacques Basnage, for whom "the crime of Origen was given too much credit", writes:

> I see learned men, who maintain that Origen made himself guilty of a crime that merited punishment by sacrificing to idols for fear of being violated by an Ethiopian. I acknowledge that Saint Epiphanius relates the deed, and I am not at all bold enough to erase this passage from the works of Saint Epiphanius and to say next that it was an enemy of Origen who added it. . . . I would rather remark that Saint Epiphanius there unearthed a fact . . . that had not been known by anyone. He was the first to speak of it, one hundred and fifty years after the death of this great man. Since he had a furious hatred for him, one can only wonder if he might not have believed this story without sufficient consideration, if he did not invent it himself. Saint Jerome and Saint Augustine . . . disgrace themselves by recording a fable that had no authority. It appears manifestly false if one examines the time at which Origen supposedly could have sinned in this way. . . .[46]

But in this same year, 1699, another ecclesiastical history appeared in Paris, this one in Latin, from the prolific pen of the Dominican Noël Alexandre.[47] One can read there, in volume six, a treatise *De moribus Origenis*, whose second *quaestio* treats *de negatione et thurificatione Origenis*. Alexandre maintains there the historicity of this *thurificatio*, contrary to the opinion of Baronius, by invoking the trinity of witnesses with whom we are familiar: Petau, Huet, Pagi. In the following treatise, he revives the inevitable question of "Origen's salvation", in order to conclude that this salvation is "doubtful" and to draw the usual lesson from it, in terms borrowed from an old author: "Grandis labyrinthus a diversis texitur de Samsone, Salomone, Origene an videlicet salvati sint, an non; quae quia sine periculo nesciuntur, nec Ecclesia certificata est de his, Domino totaliter committenda sunt."[48] Such are the

[46] Cf. 4, n. 5–6 (pp. 65–66).

[47] *Historia ecclesiastica veteris novique Testamenti*. . . . It is a reworking of the *Selecta historiae ecclesiasticae capita* (1677), following some criticism from a colleague from Louvain and from a Roman censor.

[48] *Historia* . . . , in the Lucques edition (1743), 3:762–64 and 775. The author quoted is "Wernerus Westphalus", whom Huet had already quoted. He refers to Werner Rolewinck,

positions of this historian who at Fleury joined in condemning "the excess of credulity" and whose colossal work has been described as not being distinguished by its critical soundness.[49]

Force of habit! It also hung over a little book, a model of obscurantist rhetoric, the *Histoire des mouvements arrivez dans l'Église au sujet d'Origène et de sa doctrine*, which appeared in 1700. Its author, Father Louis Doucin, of the Society of Jesus, finished it in 1696. He sees in Origen the author of a "prodigious number of heresies, none of which is not monstrous". Let us not believe for all that that Doucin wishes to crush the great man! The account he gives of his life has rather the tone of panegyric. The more he exalts his genius and his virtue, the more terrified he thinks the reader will be about his fall. Still, he presents the latter in the most benign way he can. It was in the year 250. The pagans had worked unceasingly to have this so reputed Christian scholar submitted to various combats, from which he came away with glory every time. "But finally an unforeseen temptation surprised him, and he succumbed to it." Baronius had been in doubt about it; but, our Doucin says without flinching, "what he alleges to the contrary has seemed so weak to the most celebrated writers of our century that the story has not at all suffered from it." And on to recount the story of the *thurificatio*, with some little amplifications and mitigations due perhaps to the extension of time drawn from the successors of Epiphanius.

> The judge, knowing how greatly he feared even the shadow of impurity, instead of intimidating him with the horror of torture, condemned him to be delivered at once to the vile passion of a Moor, at least unless he resolved to renounce Jesus Christ and to sacrifice to the idol, at whose feet he had been placed. —One can judge what impression was made on this chaste soul by the idea of so abominable a thing. . . . He was seen to grow pale at that very hour and to hesitate about what he was to reply. . . . As he deliberated, they promptly opened his hand and put incense into it.

He came to himself at that moment and tried to withdraw his hand. But, someone having adroitly pushed his arm from behind, made the incense fall on the charcoal, and then it was written that he had adored the gods. That was not basically true. But at that time, even having

---

the author of the *Fasciculus temporum*, of which Pico spoke in his *Apologia*.

[49] Émile Appolis, *Les Jansénistes espagnols* (Bordeaux: Sobodi, 1966), 24.

had the thought, having let it be perceived, was a great enough crime to cause the excommunication of Christians by the Church, at least for a considerable time. . . .

It was beginning with this, Doucin tells us, that people began to see at last the perversity of his doctrine, which had been, until then, the object of universal admiration. He nonetheless retained the esteem of the Christians he had formed and of numerous men of the Church. So, twenty years later, in 250, the "Ministers of Idolatry" were dead set against him in particular, but "nothing escaped him that was not worthy of a soldier of Jesus Christ." "Ever" since then "he was seen busy with holy things that marked an extraordinary zeal for the Church. But he did not think at all of making amends for the scandal caused by his errors through a precise abjuration. . . ."[50]

Doucin does not seem to perceive for an instant the absurdities and contradictions he piles up in his account. Such are therefore the insanities with which our French seventeenth century, the great century of historical criticism, closes on the subject of the life and death of Origen.[51] Bayle would be all too happy to gather them into the second edition of his *Dictionnaire*. One cannot read Origen, he writes, "without deploring the bizarre fate of the human spirit. . . . So many virtues, so much fine talent, motives so full of zeal, did not keep him from a heretical death or his memory from being held in abhorrence by an infinity of Christians."[52]

Tillemont had still not conquered.

[50] *Histoire*, 53–57 and 81–84, etc. Epiphanius said: "He raised his voice, saying that of the two things that were proposed to him, he preferred to sacrifice."

[51] It may be surprising to see that a historian such as Lucien Febvre, giving a bibliography on Origen in his *Origène et des Périers*, quotes only three names: J. Denis, E. de Faye and . . . Father Louis Doucin, S.J.! It is true that he gives a profusion of additional information, indicating the dates both of the permission of the Provincial and of the royal privilege, August 26 and October 28, 1696 (Paris: Droz, 1942), 137.

[52] *Dictionnaire historique et critique*, 4th ed. (Amsterdam-Leyden, 1730), 3:545–46: "Few people in communion with Rome dare doubt his eternal damnation." Cf. the 1820 edition, 11:244. Bayle also quotes some reflections of Doucin quoting Jerome and expressing the idea "that there was a branch of Spinozism in Origenism, to wit, the identity of all minds with the Divinity".

IV. From Bayle's Dictionary to Augustin Lémann

The eighteenth century, one suspects, took much less interest in Origen than its predecessor. If the history of Christian antiquity had remained timely for the general public and fashionable writers, Voltaire would not have failed to draw a few off-color jokes from Saint Epiphanius' page. Now he makes no allusion to it in either the *Essai sur les moeurs*, in which the name of the Alexandrian scarcely appears, or the *Dictionnaire philosophique*. Within the ecclesiastical world, however, habit still ruled the subject. They still continued to fight, not only for or against Origen, but more specifically, in his regard, for or against Epiphanius. Father Henri Crouzel points out in his *Bibliographie* two short writings that reject the fable. The first was an *Exercitatio historiae ecclesiasticae de lapsu Origenis* (1704): the author, Jean-Matthias Haas, presented it in 1704 in the form of a public dispute, "submitted to the calm discussion of scholars"; he concludes in favor of the falsity of the assertions of Saint Epiphanius, despite the numerous times they were repeated.[1] The second writing had a similar origin. It was the account of an academic dispute that took place on December 19, 1709, in Copenhagen between Matthias-Jacques Norup and Pierre Johannis, the one supporting the apostasy of Origen, the other making the improbability of it glaringly apparent.[2] We note, too, that Dom Auguste Calmet, who published in 1720 a *Dissertation* on the salvation of King Solomon,[3] did not take advantage of this to establish any parallel whatever, even in quick strokes, with the salvation of Origen: an author of the preceding centuries would not have let such an opportunity pass. Similarly, in the long account devoted to the life of Origen, in the second volume of his *Histoire générale des auteurs sacrés et ecclésiastiques*, Dom Remi Ceillier does not breathe a word of the legend; he restricts himself to quoting in a note the famous page from Epiphanius, with respect to the *Lamentum*, "which one rightly regards", he would say, "as the work of some ignorant impostor, who had a grudge against Origen's

[1] Crouzel, 129–30.

[2] Ibid., 132.

[3] *Dissertationes*, 2:178–92.

reputation".[4] Dom Ceillier no longer felt it necessary to proceed to a formal refutation.

Agreement, however, was still far from being unanimous. Witness Casimir Oudin (1638–1717), lexicographer, who was considered a scholar not without merit. To tell the truth, his work was one of compilation rather than of criticism. His commentaries and discourses on ancient writers of the Church appeared after his death in 1722. The first volume contains a *Dissertatio de vita, operibus, doctrina et morte Origenis Adamantii*.[5] The *thurificatio* is established at length in it, in opposition to Baronius, first, through the authority of Saint Epiphanius, *vir doctissimus*; second, through the treatise of the Emperor Justinian, which was approved at the fifth ecumenical council; third, through the account of Leontius (of Byzantium); fourth, through the philosopher Nemesius, who deplores, in a chapter of his treatise on the nature of man, that the case of Origen cannot be likened to that of the chaste Joseph and the chaste Suzanne; a final "proof" is drawn from the consensus of so many Greek historians: Nicetas Choniates, Anastasius Bibliothecarius, Zonaras, Glycas and finally Nicephorus Callistus. And, just as formerly Epiphanius had followed his diatribe with an interminable quotation from Methodius, our scholar ends his victorious dissertation by reproducing the pages in which Noël Alexandre had tried to respond to the objections of Baronius. He does not hide, moreover, his borrowings. The words with which he ends the last of his chapters on Origen are admirable in their candor: "Haec nos per compendium ex aliis, quid enim imposterum novi sub caelo dici potest?"[6]

Others seem to hesitate. They no longer dare decide, as Casimir Oudin did, for the historicity of the apostasy, but something in their tone is like a residual effect of it. "Let the example of this great man", writes Dom Bernard Maréchal in 1739, "make us tremble, and let his extraordinary deviations make us feel of what we ourselves are capable." We have there more than the acknowledgment of a few errors that escaped a great man: it is the implicit evocation of some tragic "fall" of an unspecified nature; more especially as, at the same time, Bernard Maréchal insists on explaining what were called the errors of

---

[4] Vol. 2 (1729), 584–782; cf. Crouzel, 138–39. New edition (Vivès, 1859), 2:199, note.

[5] *Commentarius de scriptoribus Ecclesiae antiquis . . . cum multis dissertationibus . . .* ; 3 vols. (vol. 2, cols. 231–66).

[6] Ibid.

Origen by the fact that "in those early centuries, dogmas were not clarified, settled and disencumbered as they have been since."[7]

But here it is in 1742 that we see the publication in Cologne of the first volume of the *Conférences ecclésiastiques, ou Dissertations sur les auteurs, les concils et la discipline des premiers siècles de l'Église.* It is a considerable, posthumous work by the famous Abbot Jacques Duguet. Its composition goes back to the years 1678 and 1679; they had been written for the conferences that Duguet regularly gave in Paris, at the Saint Magloire seminary. Later than the work of "Mister de la Motte", they are thus earlier, however, than that of Tillemont. The eleventh Dissertation, *Sur l'histoire d'Origène*, in its fourth paragraph, constitutes a correction that one should call definitive, if ignorance and credulity could ever be definitively overcome.

"It is not necessary to have read much of the Works of Saint Epiphanius", declares Duguet, "to be persuaded that he was inaccurate in reporting the facts, that he was too credulous and that, besides this, he had an extreme aversion to Origen." Everything shows "that he had not read this writer and that he had not taken the trouble to examine the easiest and best known thing in the world, that is, the number of Origen's writings and the actions of his life. Thus he saw evil without witness and without proof." There we are duly warned. And Duguet goes on: "He calls Origen vain, bold, rash, talkative and a great sayer of nothing. . . . He claims that he was not only heretical but the head of a party in revolt against the Church. . . . He made a crime of the most innocent things, and it was after having repeated his preface to the first Psalm, which is the most humble and most Christian that can be imagined, that he dares to write that he was a scatterbrain, a false sage, an evil oddity. . . ."

After this introduction, whose features are borrowed, without exaggeration, from the very text of Epiphanius, Duguet begins a critical examination of the famous account. First of all, he asks, "At what time did this supposed apostasy take place?" He demonstrates by the facts that it could not have been either under Severus or under Decius, or under Alexander Severus. Then he amasses the improbabilities that should be enough to make any sensible man put aside such a fable. Everything he sets forth had been published before; but he brings the arguments together into a solid group in firm and clear language:

[7] *Concordance des SS. Pères de l'Église . . .*, vol. 2 (Paris: 1739), 328 and 329.

> How is it possible that Demetrius knew nothing of Origen's fall, or that, having known of it, he did not reproach him for it?[8] . . . Why did he amuse himself by describing him as disobedient and presumptuous if he had been able to blacken him as an idolater? How in conscience could the bishops of Palestine, who were neighbors of Egypt and could scarcely have been unaware of Origen's fault, have received him with open arms, showered him with honor, and so on, listened to him as to their master? . . . And what shall we think of Saint Firmilian, who came to hear him . . . (and Gregory of Neocaesarea and Gregory of Nyssa, and so on). —Why did all the Churches in which Origen was known remain in communion with him? . . . Why did Eusebius not speak of so remarkable and public an incident . . . , or the martyr Pamphilius? . . . Why did Saint Jerome say in such uncertain terms that Origen was condemned only because he had too much knowledge and too much merit? By what accident did it happen that Saint Epiphanius alone knew something of which everyone before him and after him was unaware? For just as he had not followed any author of the third century, he was not followed by any in the fifth and sixth. How would Origen have dared write ardent and zealous letters in favor of martyrdom to various persons, after having been chased away from Alexandria, if he had been chased away for having offered incense to false divinities? . . .

To this emphatic argumentation, which was necessary not only in 1679 but also in 1742, Duguet joined several remarks about the *Libellus Poenitentiae*, whose author, according to all available evidence, must have been a Latin of the fifth century. About Saint Epiphanius, he concludes, having rid himself of the holy respect that had stopped Baronius as well as Petau: "This saint knew nothing about Origen, and he mixed everything up."[9]

Duguet was often, although wrongly, ranked among the Jansenist party. Yet, a friend of Arnauld and of Quesnel, he was among the "disciples of Saint Augustine". His admiration for Origen was all the more remarkable. It helped him undoubtedly to read Epiphanius and his followers with a critical eye, but without making him fall into the opposite blindnesses. A writer renowned for the purity and elegance of his style as well as for his doctrine on the understanding of Scripture, he was certainly widely read. Joined to that of Tillemont, his influence, for a time, got the better of the absurd legend. The latter was rejected,

---

[8] We know that Demetrius was at that time bishop of Alexandria.

[9] *Conférences ecclésiastiques*, 1:192–93.

for example by Abbot Pierre Tricalet, director of the seminary of Saint Nicolas du Chardonnet in Paris, whose *Bibliothèque portative des Pères de l'Église* was published, posthumously, in 1767.[10] It was similarly rejected by Nicolas-Sylvestre Bergier (1718–1790), in his *Dictionnaire de Théologie*, which appeared on the eve of the Revolution (1788–1789). Let us point out also the judgment of the German historian Johann Mosheim, who was known late in France in 1776,[11] as well as a curious treatise by another German, Marcellin Molkenbuhr. In this *Dissertatio critica*, published in Münster-en-Westphalie (1795), Molkenbuhr was wrong to throw into the same chapter, along with Epiphanius' stories, several better assured features of the history of Origen and to include among the apocrypha, along with the *Lamentum*, a whole lot of letters from Jerome, Rufinus, John of Jerusalem: which makes one doubt that this hypercritic had an accurate view when he refused to believe in either the *castratio* or the *thurificatio*.[12]

The reason was understood. In their "critical" monotony, treatises and discourses were no longer anything but school exercises, flying to the help of the victory won. . . . But in such domains, what victory is ever won? A seduced imagination does not surrender without going back. Historians and patristics scholars can finally see clearly: their conviction does not carry the consent of all. One of the final publications of the century that we must record is a very curious treatise in English, published in London in 1784. The anonymous author relates there "the conversion of a noble Frenchwoman of papist superstitions to the Reformed religion". By what secret logic does this work of edification come out with the account of Origen's apostasy and his repentance? Perhaps an attentive reading of the treatise would bring us some clarity on this subject; without doubt it is in virtue of the logic of contrast. It is still: "To which is added . . . Origen's *Lamentation*,

[10] On the "erroneous opinions" of Origen, Tricalet said: "He advances them only as opinions, doubting them and submitting them to the judgment of the reader. He first sets forth the Catholic Faith . . . : he treats the rest as problematical questions on which he proposes his thoughts with great modesty" (272). Cf. 268.

[11] *Histoire ecclésiastique ancienne et moderne*, translated from the second English edition, vol. 1 (1776), 554, note 67: "Epiphanius . . . wrote in the fourth century, but he lacked judgment and fidelity."

[12] "Dissertatio critica decima sexta, de Origene Adamantio, an is in idolatriam lapsus fuerit, seipsum castraverit, haereses docuerit. . . ." Cf. Crouzel, 103–4: "Uneven successes of radical criticism!"

for offering incense in an idol temple, after he was minister of the Gospel." It is the English translation of the *Planctus*.[13]

Just as the strange politics of the first Republic, according to Albert Sorel, only continued those of the Ancien Régime, or as the monarchical Restoration wanted to ignore the upheavals of the revolutionary period, Bergier's *Dictionnaire de Théologie* pursued its career for a long time without the long interim of 1789 to 1815 having been for its successive editors the occasion for any substantial updating. It is therefore not surprising that in 1826, then in 1840 and even in 1852, the article on Origen persisted in wisely refuting the account of Epiphanius: "Respectable personages have given credence to his account. But it is not believable that so courageous a man thus contradicted the lessons he had given to so many martyrs and that so many enemies who defamed him after his death made no mention of this odious accusation."[14] But was this truly only the echo of old controversies, no longer valid? Not completely, as we shall see.

In his *Études historiques*, Chateaubriand does not neglect Origen. He recognizes his genius; he knows that, through his influence, he worked "a multitude of conversions", that he was persecuted by pagan authorities and that "the people and the philosophers would have regarded the apostasy of this defender of the Church a great triumph (Oros. l. 7, c. 19)." He did not miss the opportunity to compare him to Abélard, while marking the differences to his advantage. But he also believes he knows something else; some vague memories, at the very least, floating around in his brain, and if his remark that Origen "had a weakness only for knowledge and virtue" does not presuppose any allusion to Epiphanius' account, he nonetheless goes on to this other: "His fault and his condemnation are well known."[15] Chateaubriand himself perhaps knew nothing about it, but he repeats the secular allusion whose source is the account of Epiphanius.

It is a strange thing to find that a remnant of the fable seems also to have inhabited the mind of the great Moehler. In a course on the history of the Church taught in 1835–1836, a rather summary course without great personality, and which he himself did not publish, one

[13] "The French convert, being a true relation of the happy conversion of a noble French lady from the errors and superstitions of Popery to the Reformed religion. . . . To which . . . ." Cf. Crouzel, 159.

[14] 1852 edition, 4:246; art. "Origène" in fine.

[15] Works of Chateaubriand, vol. 9, *Études historiques*, 1860 ed., 118 and 123.

in fact reads that Origen "at the end of his life was again received into the bosom of the Church":[16] as if some previous grave fall had had him excommunicated. It is again this fateful word "fall" that we read in the *Biographie universelle* of F. X. de Feller, in the article "*Origène*". The author of the article encountered it, he says, in "an ascetical theologian", whose name he does not give and whose opinion, moreover, he seems not to adopt himself. According to this theologian, "Origen's knowledge and precocious virtues, too admired and too exalted, the ill-considered actions of his father, who kissed the chest of his child with respect, the stir that his actions and books made in the world, the consideration to which the bishops gave witness in his regard, and so forth, swelled his head and prepared the way for the fall against which only humility and fear of the Lord can arm men who are illustrious through their gifts of nature and of grace."[17] No specifics are given about the nature or the date or the circumstances of this mysterious fall, but we know the original meaning of it. Around the same time, in 1840, another Englishman, anonymously, published a *Vie d'Origène*,[18] in which he "seems to accept certain assertions of Epiphanius"; but perhaps this is only a matter of the general thesis according to which, in the thinking of the Alexandrian, "Christianity has been contaminated by philosophy."[19]

Abbot A. Sevestre has another surprise in store for us. He is the author of a long study on Origen, published in 1855 in the fourth volume of the *Dictionnaire de Patrologie*, which forms the twenty-third volume of the *Nouvelle encyclopédie* of Migne. A new Merlin, Abbot Sevestre admires Origen unreservedly. Among all the Fathers, Doctors and Martyrs, he sees him "shine with a particular brilliance". No one can be permitted any more, he judges, "to raise the least doubt about the purity of the doctrines and the truth of the facts contained in his works"; in reading him, "one would be endlessly astonished at the depth of his perceptions, the elevation of his thoughts, the wisdom of his decisions about all the questions that were then stirring the nascent Church, if one did not recall that he was animated by the Spirit of God, which had been fully granted him in order to contribute to

[16] J. A. Moehler, *Histoire de l'Église*, trans. P. Bélet, vol. 1 (1868), 338.

[17] *Bibliographie universelle*, 1839 ed., 4:653, 2.

[18] *The Life of Origen* (London). "The Religious Tract Society".

[19] Crouzel, 183.

the foundation and the perpetuity of this Church. . . ." But it was as confessor of the faith that he was most admirable. Eusebius recounts how he suffered valiantly under Decius. Already in 204, he had given witness to Christ, in the course of the cruel persecution of Severus. Here, Abbot Sevestre runs into the account of Epiphanius.[20] Is he going to reject it? Not at all. He reproduces the first part of it word for word, which most of his predecessors had overlooked:

> Saint Epiphanius relates that one day the pagans of Alexandria seized him, and after having shaved him like the idolatrous sacrificers, they placed him at the door of the temple of Serapis, to distribute some palm branches to those arriving there. Far from letting himself be caught unawares or to show any hesitation, the young Origen took the branches and with a firm voice and with a tone full of courage, he cried out publicly: "Here you are! Take these palms, not as those of your idol, but as those of Jesus Christ!"

Thereupon Sevestre stops clean and passes immediately on to the episode of the castration. On the same page, in his account of one and the same figure, Saint Epiphanius is thus judged worthy of faith in what is for the glory of Origen and, for what would be to his shame, unworthy even of being pointed out or having a single word said in refutation.[21]

The indefatigable Abbot Migne was to undertake yet a "Third and final *Encyclopédie théologique*", which included a *Dictionnaire de l'histoire universelle de l'Église* in six volumes. The sixth volume, which is the fifty-sixth of the encyclopedia and which appeared in 1873, contains an article on "*Origène docteur de d'Église*", by L. F. Guérin. Of much more modest proportions than that of Abbot Sevestre, the article, however, does not fail to point out what Sevestre had omitted, but by trivializing the episode—perhaps through that kind of bourgeois modesty that characterized the period:

> It is claimed that, to get out of prison, he seemingly offered incense to the idol Serapis, in Alexandria, but one can believe that this was a lie forged by his enemies and reported without sufficient evidence by Epiphanius.[22]

---

[20] We see that Sevestre adopts the correction proposed by Petau, who deferred the scene from the time of Decius to that of Severus.

[21] A. Sevestre, cols. 204–339 (particularly 209 and 337).

[22] Cols. 524–32 (526).

Migne's great encyclopedias are buried in oblivion. The sole survivors are his two patrologies, Greek and Latin, rather convenient tools, although often mediocre and on the way to being replaced. Now, in 1858, volume 41 of the Greek patrology appeared, containing the works of Saint Epiphanius. The editor found nothing better, in order to comment on the all too famous page of the *Panarion* that relates the story of the *thurification*, than to reproduce in a series of notes the allegations of Denis Petau: Baronius had made a great mistake in parading his scepticism in the face of an account by the most ancient and serious author there could be; there is no reason either to suppose that the text is not by him or to place in doubt the fact that he reports. Despite the self-seeking silence of Eusebius, Origen's fall into idolatry is only too certain. If others do not make mention of it, it is only because they do not want to crush the memory of a man who had done penance or to let anyone believe that a personal animosity might inspire their condemnation of his errors.[23]

An interminable process, ever beginning again! It was therefore not against windmills that, the following year, in 1859, a German author, Balthasar Eberhard, took up the attack again by publishing the history of the anti-Origenist campaigns of Epiphanius, sifting out his principal accusations and trying to discern his motivations, conscious or unconscious.[24] Soon the historian Karl Joseph von Hefele, who wrote the article "*Origène*" for the *Dictionnaire encyclopédique de la théologie catholique* edited by Wetzer and Welte, could be content with these simple words: "Epiphanius is completely wrong to say that Origen fled [from Alexandria] because a little earlier he had proved weak in a persecution."[25] The French translation of this article is from 1864. The same year saw the publication in England of Newman's *Apologia*. We know the famous page where Newman recounts the admiration that seized him when he discovered the symbolism of the Alexandrian School and professes that there is a close union between the exegesis inspired by this symbolism and Catholic orthodoxy. Nevertheless, in a final chapter that sets forth the "Position of My Mind since 1845", Newman declares that he is certain that in the doctrinal disputes his adversaries were sometimes right against him. But he also says, distant

[23] Migne, PG 41, cols. 1070–74.

[24] *Die Betheiligung des Epiphanius am Streite über Origenes* (Trier [Lints], 1859).

[25] *Dictionnaire*, trans. J. Goschler, vol. 16 (1864), 415.

heir to a literary genre and faithful echo of a long and touching tradition: "I like the personality of Origen, and I cannot agree that so beautiful a soul be lost."[26]

The year 1865 offers us a paradoxical confrontation. The occasion was the death of Msgr. Gerbet (1798–1864), former disciple of Lamennais, who became bishop of Perpignan. The young Abbot Olympe Philippe Gerbet, responding to the book by Lamennais on *Les Affaires de Rome* (1836), in an article from the *Université catholique*,[27] had proclaimed in a pathetic way "the desire that God", he said, "might read also in the depth of our soul to give, if it be necessary, every drop of our blood to obtain from the fallen Tertullian the grace of a single tear". The allusion was natural. It is also found in a letter that Frédéric Ozanam addressed from Lyons on November 5 of that same year to his friend François Lallier: "Where are", he wonders, "the Ambroses, the Jeromes, the Augustines, who would come sit on the forsaken seat of Tertullian?"[28] It had been launched by the archbishop of Toulouse, Msgr. d'Astros, in 1834, in a pastoral letter that began the encyclical *Singular vox*.[29] Already in December 1831, in a confidential memorandum that Gregory XVI had requested from him, Don Baraldi, priest of Modène and friend of Lamennais, had written that he reminded him of Tertullian "by the strength of his dialectic and the boldness of his eloquence"; God willing, he went on, "that he might not have any other fatal resemblance to that hotheaded African!"[30] And Lamennais himself had, in 1808, in his *Réflexions sur l'état de l'Église*, traced a portrait of Tertullian that, in its anti-Jansenism, he applied to the great Arnauld, but that more than one reader had been tempted subsequently to apply to him.[31] But here is the paradox referred to. Thirty-three years

[26] *Apologia*, chap. 5. More than a century earlier, the Carthusian Bonaventure of Argonne had noted the "tenderness for Origen" of a certain number of apologists, *Histoire de la théologie*, a posthumous work published by Vincent Fassini, O.P. (Lucques, 1785). He himself had given in 1696 at Paris a treatise *De la lecture des Pères de l'Église* that was very favorable to Origen.

[27] Vol. 3, fasc. 1.

[28] *Lettres de Frédéric Ozanam*, 1, *Lettres de jeunesse* (Paris: Bloud et Gay, 1960), 240.

[29] D'Astros recalled the examples of Tertullian, Lucifer de Cagliari, Osius, Apollinaire of Laodicea. Cf. F. Duine, *Le Mennais* (Garnier, 1922), 195. Duine himself calls Lamennais "the Tertullian of the La Chênaie", 161. The same comparison had been made by Alexandre Dumas in his *Mémoires*, ed. Michel Lévy, vol. 8 (1863), 7.

[30] Cf. Paul Dudon, *Lamennais et le Saint-Siège* (Paris: Perrin, 1911), 136.

[31] "Tertullian also had some virtues; he was lost nevertheless because he lacked the most

after the response of Abbot Gerbet to Lamennais, on March 2, 1865, in the cathedral of Perpignan, the funeral oration for the bishop was given by Msgr. Berteaux, bishop of Tulle, who at that time was the most eloquent voice of the French episcopate. To celebrate the merits of the deceased, the orator could find nothing better than to compare him to the "great Origen". Now, a few weeks later, the successor to Gerbet at Perpignan, Msgr. Ramadié, took possession of his seat and in his turn eulogized his predecessor in the same cathedral. He recalled how, after the defection of Lamennais, the one who had first been his enthusiastic disciple had separated himself from him; here is where we see once again, but in another situation, Origen intervene:

> One day, the disciple and friend of a new Origen, he was too faithful to his master, but soon, like Dionysius of Alexandria, placing above the interest of the school and the rights of an intimate friendship the interest of truth and the rights of the Church, in order to remain faithful to the faith, he passed over his own heart; following again the traces of the holy patriarch of Alexandria, he refuted with learned pages the strayed philosopher and wept over his fall.[32]

Fall: the word must come. With respect to Lamennais, Gerbet had evoked Tertullian; his successor was to evoke Origen: Had these two great names not been long associated? But since, in the same Perpignan, and at the same time, to honor the memory of the same Gerbet, one bishop had wanted to see in him a new Origen, while for the other bishop this new Origen was the apostate Lamennais whom he had had the courage to leave, we must acknowledge that this is a fine contrast.

Yet, eloquence is not history. No historian could still be found today who would not only take seriously the stories of Epiphanius but also agree to refute them. We might think that the final blow was at last given them by Msgr. Louis Duchesne, in the second volume of his *Histoire ancienne de l'Église*. Duchesne is very careful not to make the least allusion to it in the chapter that deals with Origen. But when

---

necessary of all, humility. I cite Tertullian by preference, because there are some singular relations between him and the oracle of Jansenism, M. Arnauld. Both of an ardent, presumptuous, opinionated character, both full of genius, both having rendered religion eminent services, they let themselves be carried away—who would believe it of such great men?—by the passion of an imagination that forgot everything . . .", 1919 edition: *Réflexions sur l'état de l'Église . . . suivies de Mélanges religieux et philosophiques*, 22.

[32] Abbot de Ladoue, *Monseigneur Gerbet, sa vie, ses oeuvres et l'école menaisienne* (Paris, 1870) 3:379–80 (Berteaux) and 383–84 (Ramadié).

he comes to speak of Epiphanius, "simple and naïve man" and of his *Panarion*, he writes:

> He had been deluded into believing a lot about Origen, too. Although it would have been easy for him to find the real history of this personage in the writings of Pamphilius and Eusebius, he reports absurd legends to us about him. . . . He lost no occasion to charge at him, with a true rage.[33]

The question of Origen's salvation—or of his damnation—so often linked since antiquity to that of his apostasy and his repentance, nonetheless continues to haunt imaginations. Abbot Augustin Lémann, professor of Holy Scripture at the Theology Faculty at Lyons, had again raised it in 1885, in connection with a discourse given in Toulouse on March 7 on *Salomon et saint Thomas d'Aquin.* For each of these three great men, Samson, Origen and Solomon, he left the question open, as Étienne Binet had formerly done:

> One can only conjecture. Corneille La Pierre reports that Saint Mechtilde, in the year 1300, having asked the Lord about the eternal fate of Samson, Solomon and Origen, was given the reply that until the end of time there would be doubt about the eternal fate of Samson, so that men might fear to avenge themselves on their enemies; about the eternal fate of Solomon, so that men might tremble to abandon themselves to covetousness of the flesh; about the eternal fate of Origen, so that men might dread becoming proud of their knowledge.[34]

Saint Mechtilde had for some time seemed a bit forgotten in the matter. By associating, according to her, Origen with Samson and Solomon, Lémann revived an old classical theme, and one is all the less surprised by it since he was himself of the Jewish race, converted like his brother Joseph to Catholicism. Much closer to us, on February 28, 1959, Julien Green raised the question in his *Journal* and seemed to lean toward a pessimistic response. Only it was no longer with Solomon or Samson that he associated Origen, it was—as a substitute for Tertullian[35]—with Arius: "One can tremble to the very end. When one sees the

[33] *Histoire ancienne de l'Église*, vol. 2, 5th ed. (Fontemoing, 1911), 591–92.

[34] Speech at Saint-Sernin (for the feast of Saint Thomas Aquinas) (Toulouse, 1885), 24, note. Cf. Cornelius a Lapide, *In Ecclesiasticum*, c. 47, 22. Allusion to the opinion according to which Solomon supposedly wrote *Ecclesiasticus* in witness of his conversion.

[35] In his *Cours d'histoire ecclésiastique*, Abbot Rivaux had written of Lamennais: "We shall weep and learn at the tomb of the modern Tertullian": 6th ed. (Lyons, 1876), 3:510.

heights from which Arius and Origen fell—and what are we beside them?"[36]

Thus certain legends are transmitted from age to age. It seems that they are ineradicable. In Origen's case, ill will must have had at least something to do with it at the origin. But if one shrinks from bringing too black a judgment to bear on the human race, one could also think, and perhaps with even more probability, that men of dazzling genius have always struck the popular imagination. Hence the most extravagant explanations; such a person could have acquired his power or his knowledge only through some magic secrets, another only through a pact with the devil. . . . As for Origen, it could be that the story of the "Ethiopian" was not unrelated with that, better founded, of the voluntary castration, mixed with the memory of a trinitarian doctrine that brought him accusations of tritheism. . . . Whatever the case, we can conclude with that wise reflection of Bergier: "It is so true that a great reputation is often a very great misfortune!"[37]

Final Note

"Ethiopia" was not formerly, for the people of the Mediterranean basin, the country that we designate today by that name. The "Ethiopian" was a man of a dark and unexplored region, outside the frontiers of civilization, where an evil spirit blew. He was the "black man", inspiring repugnance and fear. The word that would correspond rather well with it, taking it (as it was at that time taken) in a pejorative sense and grafting onto it a symbolic and superstitious complex, would be the "Negro", itself the symbol of the devil. It was nearly in this way that the Romans and Carthaginians understood it in antiquity. (But they said rather: the "Egyptian".) This superstition was also imposed on the language of the early Christian centuries. Witness the *Pseudo-Barnabé*: "From fear that the Black might steal furtively among us, let us flee all vanity. . . . The road of the Black is tortuous and full of malediction" (IV, 10 and XX, 1).

Witness also the dream of Perpetua, in the *Passio sanctarum Perpetuae et Felicitatis*, c. 10: "Tandem pervenimus ad amphitheatrum . . . et mirabar

[36] Julien Green, *Vers l'invisible* (Plon, 1967), 90. The lesson, which is all that matters here, always remains opportune.

[37] *Dictionnaire de théologie*, 1856 ed., 4:246.

quod non mitterentur mihi bestiae. Et exivit contra me Aegyptius foedus specie . . . , pugnaturus mecum, . . . Et intellexi me non ad bestias, sed contra diabolum esse pugnaturam. . ."; cf. c. 18: "Illuxit dies victoriae illorum, et processerunt de carcere in amphitheatrum. . . . Perpetua psallebat, caput jam Aegyptii calcans. . . ." For Saint Epiphanius, *Panarion* (26, 16), the "Ethiopians" are "blackened with sin". In the sixth century, in his *Pré spirituel*, Jean Moschus would report the statements of a monk who, at the time that he was "a follower of Severus", furious at seeing his wife receive Communion as a Catholic, had torn from her mouth the sacred particle, which fell into the mud: "Two years later, I see an Ethiopian, clothed in rags, who says to me: I am the one who struck Jesus Christ on the cheek during the Passion; we have been condemned to the same punishment."[1] The same symbolism was perpetuated in alchemy. According to Marie-Louise von Franz, in her "edition, translation and commentary on an alchemical treatise attributed to Saint Thomas Aquinas",[2] "Ethiopia" is a frequent image for the alchemical *nigredo*, and it has a negative sense in most cases, as for *caput corvi* (crow's head). The author quotes a certain *Scriptum Alberti super arborem Aristotelis*: "One must purify the material and distill it, to the point that the black head, which resembles an Ethiopian, might be well washed and begin to grow white."

The same symbolism [is] in hagiography:[3] "A Neapolitan judge on familiar terms with the queen of Sicily had come to pay a visit to Brother Thomas in his cell at the monastery in Naples. Both went out to stroll to and fro on an embankment they had discovered from which they could contemplate the sea and the hedges. The judge perceived some kind of Negro, an Ethiopian, clothed in black, who was coming to prowl around Brother Thomas Aquinas, but Brother Thomas, his fist raised and threatening, advanced toward the Ethiopian, saying to him: 'How dare you still come to tempt me?' Frightened, the black devil, who was undoubtedly no other than the noonday devil, fled and disappeared." The account was drawn (but, if one dare say so, embellished) from Guillaume de Tocco, *Vita S. Thomae Aquinatis*, c. 55: "Inimicus . . . fuit visus in forma Aethiopis, cum ad praedicti Magistri

---

[1] Cf. *Sources chrétiennes* 12, 70–71.

[2] *Aurora consurgens* (Paris: La Fontaine de Pierre, 1982).

[3] Cf. L. H. Petitot, *Saint Thomas d'Aquin*: 2d ed. (Ed. de la Revue des Jeunes, 1923), 146–47.

cameram accessit, et Magister cum signo crucis opposito ipsum etiam clamando fugavit. Hoc vidit Judex Joannus de Blasio de Napoli, cum esset juvenis, et apparuit tanquam testis in processu canonizationis. . . . / Aliud prodigium ostensum in visione draconis, in forma Aethiopis ad indicium suae sanctitatis."[4] "Demon frequenter visus est in forma Aethiopis ipsum temptaturus ad cameram ejus accedere et magister ipsum signo crucis opposito et clamando fugere."[5]

In the *Noces Chymiques* of "Christian Rosenkreuz" (Jean-Valentin Andreae), a work published in 1616, it is a Moor who takes the place of the Ethiopian, or the Egyptian, in order to symbolize evil blackness. There is a more curious substitution, or rather equation, in Spinoza. In a letter to his friend Pierre Balling,[6] who imagined he heard, just after waking, the lamentations of his dead daughter, Spinoza relates to him that several times the image of a "black and dirty Brazilian" (which becomes without any explanation in the following phrase "the very image of the same Ethiopian") forced itself on him with intensity in the same circumstances. Justly intrigued by this transformation, at a space of two lines, from a Brazilian into an Ethiopian, Mme. Geneviève Brykman proposes a subtle explanation for it: this "image of the black and dirty Brazilian-Ethiopian" might be "the symbol for Spinoza's Jewishness", for that "misfortune of being a Jew . . . of which it was necessary to rid himself at all costs". On the other hand, "was the hatred of nations that pursued the Jews across the centuries not found equally crystallized in the Ethiopian; was it not very precisely the Spanish-Portuguese Inquisition about which Spinoza had heard endless talk as a child?"[7]

[4] Ed. Prümmer. Cf. the *Vita* of Pierre Calo, n. 26.

[5] Ed. Prümmer.

[6] Letter 17, *Oeuvres* (Pleiade, 1954), 1:115–16.

[7] *La Judaïté de Spinoza* (Vrin, 1972), 39–41.

II

TRIPARTITE ANTHROPOLOGY

1. Saint Paul: Body, Soul, Spirit

The distinction between a moral life and a properly spiritual life is frequently presented in the course of the Christian tradition in the form of a hierarchy. It is apt to be based on a tripartite anthropology, recognizable across the diversity of vocabularies and in very diverse cultural milieux. This tripartition is obviously not to be understood as implying three substances, or even three "faculties", in man: it is discerned rather as a threefold zone of activity, from the periphery to the center, or, to use a traditional and irreplaceable word, to the "heart".[1] It is opposed to a more current, bipartite anthropology, which seems to offer many thinkers, many "sages", whether Christian or not, a sufficient framework or support. It is opposed to that, or rather, as we shall see, it completes it.

In many authors, in many periods, this anthropology is connected explicitly to several texts in Scripture, Old and New Testament, and more particularly to a text from Saint Paul, quoted with predilection. When concluding his First Letter to the Thessalonians, the Apostle addressed a wish to them: "May the God of peace make you perfect and holy, and may your entire being, spirit, soul and body, be kept safe and blameless for the coming of our Lord Jesus Christ" (1 Th 5:23, Jerusalem Bible translation).[2] This verse has passed into certain liturgical texts: thus, in the *Liber mozarabicus sacramentorum* (Férotin,

---

[1] The "heart", one might say, "of the sixth beatitude": this word assumes an ontological meaning in order to designate the most radical and the most authentic reality of the human being. Cf. Roger Arnaldez, *Trois messages pour un seul Dieu* (Albin Michel, 1983), 62 and 64.

[2] The translation of L. Segond said similarly: "May the God of peace himself make us completely holy, and may your whole being, spirit, soul and body, be kept safe and without reproach until the coming of our Lord Jesus Christ!"

no. 18); and also in the Roman liturgy of today (*Lectio brevis* of Thursday Compline). Yet it seems to have embarrassed a number of modern commentators, who take pains, in various ways, as if it were an obligation for them, to take all significance away from it.

For some, it is only a formula that was current, commonplace, at that time, and there would be no point in seeking a precise meaning for it or in taking it into consideration in the exposition of Pauline doctrine. Such is the case with Ferdinand Prat, Martin Dibelius and George Findlay. Others make the observation that "it is the only place in the Letters where these three elements figure side by side"; such is the position of D. Buzy and Dewailly-Rigaux.[3] Still others tell us we would be wrong to believe "that this text implies a tripartite division in the Pauline anthropology"; so it is with W. David Stacey, who takes John A. T. Robinson as support for this observation. With prudence, Robinson only disputed the fact that in 1 Thessalonians 5:23, it is a matter of three "very distinct" elements; Paul's language, he observed, not without some plausibility, "is much too fluid for that".[4] Stacey concludes from this that in the Apostle's phrase, one need only retain the two words ὁλοτελεῖς (*per omnia*) and ὁλόκληρον (*integer*); these two words alone "indicate the true sense: Paul emphasizes the entirety of this preservation" that he wishes for his correspondents; "It is the whole man who is guarded; and spirit, soul and body simply underline the totality of this conception. . . . Man under each of his aspects, man in his totality, is to be guarded."[5] Stacey does not wonder (and it is the only thing that interests us here) why, in view of expressing this totality of man, Paul insists on enumerating three elements, or three "aspects", or, if you like, three terms, rather than two or four.

The note added to the text by the Jerusalem Bible constitutes a happy exception. Without doubt, it retains, by uniting them, the last two of the three considerations that we have just pointed out: "This is the only place where a tripartite division of man is mentioned in Paul, who, moreover, has no systematic and perfectly coherent 'anthropology' ";[6] which, taken literally, is incontestable. Only it does not stop there; it adds rather judiciously: "Besides the body and the soul, we see appear

---

[3] In the Pirot Bible, 12:169.

[4] Saint Paul, *Épîtres aux Thessaloniciens* (Ed. du Cerf, 1954), 52.

[5] Rev. W. David Stacey, M.A., *The Pauline View of Man* (London, 1956), 123.

[6] 1956 edition, p. 1562.

here the spirit, which can be either the divine principle of new life in Christ or, rather, the highest part of man, which is itself open to the Spirit", with a reference to Romans 5:5 and 1:9, where the reader will be able to find a mass of references, Pauline and other, whose eclecticism does not claim to take the place of commentary. Which shows at the very least that the wish of the Apostle for the Thessalonians, in its literal sense, was taken seriously: which constitutes at least a happy, if not the only, exception.

A more recent author, J. W. C. Wand, after having said: "There can be no doubt that Paul speaks from time to time of the body, soul and spirit, as if from his point of view psychology were based on a trichotomy", observes immediately that "at other times, however, he speaks in a more popular way of the soul and the body, in the way we do today."[7] A curious reflection for more than one reason, about which (taken in its French translation) we will make only two remarks: Paul does not have in mind, as the author seems at least to insinuate, a "psychological" trichotomy; and, on the other hand, contrary to what we read in Prat, Dibelius and others, here we see that it is no longer the trichotomy of the Letter to the Thessalonians but the simple soul-body dichotomy that is declared commonplace and "popular".

Still more recently, E. Schweizer went back to the idea of a popular, and consequently uninteresting, trichotomy: "In the famous passage from 1 Thessalonians 5:23, it is appropriate to understand *pneuma*, alongside *psyche* and *soma*, as an element of man above all in the sense of popular anthropology. The benediction formula is traditional, perhaps liturgical, and does not signify anything much about the notion of man in Paul. The combination may be chance, as in Deuteronomy 6:5."[8]

Different exegeses, which may contradict each other in detail, but which nearly all tend in the same direction.

It is not very difficult to detect the reasons for it. For some interpreters, it is above all, it seems, the desire not to find Saint Paul in opposition to "our classical doctrine", as D. Buzy (170) said, a doctrine

[7] *Ce que saint Paul a vraiment dit*, Banine trans. (Stock, 1970), 148. (Original English edition: London, 1968.)

[8] *"Esprit" dans le Nouveau Testament*, collective volume, "Esprit" (Geneva: Labor et Fides, 1971), 202 and note. (French translation of the article "Pneuma" of the *Dictionnaire biblique* of Kittel.) Eduard Schweizer refers to Martin Dibelius, *Thessaloniker*, 3d ed., and to John A. T. Robinson, *The Body* (1952), 27, note 2.

that counts only two elements in man: matter and spirit. Is this doctrine, which is guaranteed by the threefold heritage of Scholasticism, Cartesianism and, for France, the university spiritualism instituted by Victor Cousin, not imposed on every well-made mind? But, for the most part, another reason seems determinative. It is a kind of phobia that is quite widespread today: the phobia of "Platonism". Yet—and this is something that might seem strange—if the Pauline text makes us think of Plato, it is not always because we read him in the Letter to the Thessalonians: it is, in more than one case, because we find him quoted by Origen. Which accounts for the reflex action of distrust. Does not Scripture in fact have, for Origen, "like the human composite, a body, a soul and a spirit"? And is this distinction not "manifestly inspired by the trichotomy of Plato"?[9] It is in a similar way that an excellent historian of monastic life, Dom Adalbert de Vogüé, on the subject of Origen, evoked "the old Platonic trichotomy at first assumed by Saint Paul".[10] The Alexandrian, as everyone knows in advance, is a "Platonist"; but Saint Paul himself cannot be one! If, therefore, as Father Ferdinand Prat said, this Origenian trichotomy presupposes "a false psychology, since the soul and spirit of man are not distinct principles",[11] one can very well attribute this "false psychology" to Origen but not "accuse" Saint Paul of it, for the aforesaid trichotomy truly constitutes an item of indictment: Has not Saint Justin, too, been "accused" of distinguishing three elements in man?[12] It is therefore necessary that the same text, the same words not have at all the same meaning in the Apostle as they have in the Alexandrian, even if their primary source is common, or at least that, under the pen of the first of the two, they be only an ἅπαξ, common and unimportant.

The phobia of "Platonism", in any case, can be discovered in several of our exegetes.[13] Hence the veritable acrobatics in the TOB transla-

[9] Cf. Jean Mesnard (who in that intends only to repeat an apparently common opinion): "La Théorie des Figuratifs dans les pensées de Pascal", *Revue d'histoire de la philosophie et d'histoire générale des civilisations* (1943), 222.

[10] In *Théologie de la vie monastique*, "Theology" series, 49 (Aubier, 1962).

[11] *Origène* (Bloud et Gay), XVII. We know, on the other hand, that the two volumes of Father Prat on the theology of Saint Paul have long and justly been considered classics.

[12] The fact was recalled by Joseph Tixeront, *Histoire des dogmes*, vol. 1, 11th ed. (Gabalda, 1930), 258. Justin in fact says in chapter 10 of the *De resurrectione*: "The body is the house of the soul, the soul, that of the spirit." But it seems that this πνεῦμα is here the Spirit of God.

[13] It is through the effect of the same phobia that, in the recent translation of a liturgical text, the word "soul" is banished. *Et sanabitur anima mea* can certainly say "and my soul will

tion [*Traduction Oecumenique de la Bible*] of this Pauline verse and the explanations given in the end to justify it. The translation: "May the God of peace himself make you perfect and holy, and may your spirit, your soul and your body be kept perfectly safe in order to be blameless at the coming of our Lord Jesus Christ." The originality of this translation consists in the fact that the word ὁλόκληρον, which in Paul preceded the tripartite enumeration, is shifted so as to follow it and, in addition, transformed into an adverb, so that the two words that come next: αμέμπτως . . . τηρηθείη (in the singular, since the subject was ὁλόκληρον ὑμῶν) become (in the plural): "be kept perfectly safe in order to be blameless". To tell the truth, that does not change much, and cannot change much, in the obvious meaning of the text. The latter could be changed only by the, obviously impossible, suppression of one of the three terms of the enumeration. But this little ingenuity on the part of the translators allows them to introduce in a note a contorted exegesis with an intended goal about which they make no secret:

> Some understand: "May your entire being, that is, spirit, soul and body. . . ." This division of the human person into three elements would be that of Greek philosophy. It is not usual in Paul, and this verse, understood in this sense, would be a completely isolated text in the New Testament. In order to avoid this difficulty, others have understood the first term of the enumeration, "your spirit", to be the equivalent of "yourself"; they then translate: "may your whole person, soul and body", thus recovering the representation that Judaism and Paul had of the human person. We have rendered the sentence in a way that makes a simple enumeration of terms apparent, each of which can designate, for Paul, the entire man, whether it is a matter of *pneuma*, *psychè* or *soma*. There is no need at all, then, for an explanation borrowed from a Greek anthropology in three components, which, moreover, are never expressed with these three terms.[14]

One could not better display a stratagem. One could not be more subtle, more sophisticated, more inconsistent, too, but at the same time more honest, in the end more clear and, in the final proposition, more precise.

---

be healed". But "soul" would be a Platonic notion! . . . Jean Aucagne, "Traduction, Texte, Contexte", in *Annales de Lettres françaises* (Beyrouth, 1983), 16.

[14] TOB, 1973 edition (Ed. du Cerf).

But here is another strange thing. This unfortunate trichotomy, so suspect because of the "Platonist" Origen, this trichotomy that some would like to be able to forbid in reading Saint Paul for fear of having to admit that the Apostle, at least once, "Platonizes", this accursed trichotomy that some strive, for want of something better, to exorcise by making it commonplace, which one finds in Paul or in Origen or in anyone else, has nothing Platonic about it.

We can first of all take this on the word of some good exegetes, those at least who are not hypnotized by the First Letter of Paul to the Thessalonians. Do we not recognize, for example, the mark of Hellenic influence, and more precisely of Platonic opinion, on the *Book of Wisdom*, a little before the Christian era, in the fact that certain passages of this book enunciate or presuppose a bipartite division of the human composite, a division "more conformed to Greek customs than to Semitic"?[15] Do they not strive, with reason, moreover, to show that the recognized use of "Platonic doctrines about the distinction of body and soul" and about the immortality of the latter takes nothing away from the biblical foundation of a thought that is not that of a philosopher but that of a wise man of Israel, "nourished by the Old Testament"?[16]

If it happens that one has not read much of Plato, one can also go back to some authorities on him: what one finds in his work is totally different from what one finds in Saint Paul. There is a certain psychological trichotomy, in other words, a tripartite division of the soul: reasonable, irascible and concupiscible. So it is in the *Republic*, *Phaedrus* and *Timaeus*. According to *Phaedrus*, the θυμός and the ἐπιθυμητικόν are the two horses of the chariot led by the νοῦς. Origen, who is familiar with this division, is very careful not to make it his own; he observes, on the contrary, that it "is not confirmed by the authority of Holy Scripture" and, for this reason, on two occasions, he rejects it.[17] The translators of the TOB were very close to perceiving all that since at the end of their laborious explanations they finally tell us that Paul had undoubtedly borrowed nothing "from a three-part Greek anthropology", given the fact that the latter is never expressed in Pauline terms.

[15] C. Larcher, O.P., *Études sur le livre de la Sagesse* (1969), 278.

[16] Jerusalem Bible, 1004–5: Introduction to the Book of Wisdom (E. Osty).

[17] *Pèri archôn*, l. 3, c. 4, n. 1; GCS, 5, 264. *Contra Celsum*, l. 5, c. 47, *Sources chrétiennes* 147; cf. *Select. in Ps* 17, 29; PG 12, 1236 A. See Henri Crouzel, *Origène et la philosophie* (Aubier, 1962), 130.

But why then this fear, which has made them shrink from the simplest translation?

It is not correct, moreover, to say that the text of 1 Thessalonians is an isolated text in Scripture and in Paul himself. Undoubtedly it has been unduly compared to a verse from Deuteronomy: "You shall love Yahweh your God with all your heart, with all your soul, and with all your strength", to the sole end of insinuating that only the number three was here and there to be retained, as signifying simply a totality;[18] it is enough to read these two texts to see that they are not comparable. But, on the contrary, when the Letter to the Hebrews celebrates the Word of God, who "penetrates to the division of soul and spirit" (Heb 4:12), it is inspired without any doubt by an anthropology similar to that of Paul. And one can hardly maintain that the formula of the latter is a mere pleonasm, "for other passages show clearly that the Apostle, despite all the elasticity or 'fluidity' of his terminology, distinguishes clearly between the phenomena that indicate the body, soul and spirit."[19] He does so in the First Letter to the Corinthians, when twice he contrasts the unspiritual, or natural [*psychique*], man and the spiritual man.[20] W. David Stacey has maintained that these latter texts cannot correspond to that of the Letter to the Thessalonians; of the two conceptions in conflict, it would be necessary on the basis of all evidence to choose the one later in date, as expressing the mature thought of the Apostle:[21] the antagonism of natural and spiritual would be substituted for the hierarchical union of soul and spirit. But here again, the desire to eliminate or at least to neutralize a text deemed embarrassing seems to us to have led Dr. Stacey astray. It is very evident that the text of 1 Thessalonians is far from having the same significance as that of 1 Corinthians; that does not prevent the thought of Saint Paul from remaining coherent from one letter to another. The soul (the *psyche*) is never for its part the object, in itself, of a pejorative

[18] Dt 6:5. According to Stacey, *Pauline View*, 124. Robinson is right to say that Paul does not make a systematic dissection of the various elements of the personality (to be sure!); the true analogy with 1 Thessalonians would be found in Deuteronomy 6:5, in which a similar enumeration figures, in order to mark the totality of the human personality. Thus also, above, E. Schweizer.

[19] V. Warnach, article "Homme" in the *Encyclopédie de la Foi*, ed. H. Fries, vol. 2 (Ed. du Cerf, 1965), 253. Cf. 253–60.

[20] 1 Cor 2:14–15; 15:44–46. Cf. Jude 1:19.

[21] *Pauline View*, 124.

appreciation. If, in another context, he is severe or not very admiring of the man he calls "natural", it is insofar as the latter is *only* natural, insofar as he closes himself—or remains still provisionally closed[22]—to the Spirit of God, who would (or will) make of him a "spiritual" man, conferring on him thus his "fullness", as the Letter to the Ephesians will express it (5:18). The natural man of 1 Corinthians 2 can have a certain "human wisdom" that is not uniquely "carnal wisdom" (cf. 2 Cor 1:12), which does not lack all value but understands nothing "of the things of the Spirit of God": for him, they are "folly". To this "wise man", to this "cultivated man", to this "man of reason here below", the Apostle contrasts the "wisdom of God" manifested in Christ.[23]

It would be no more appropriate to bring out here the Pauline opposition, in a still more radical sense, between the flesh and the spirit. The carnal man is not the one who would stop, so to speak, at a first landing, that of the flesh, which is to say, in such a case, at things of the body, but the one who has fallen into evil. Body and flesh (it is really necessary to repeat this, since people still seem to be mistaken about this at times) are in no way synonymous or even comparable and do not belong to categories of the same order. In the thinking of Saint Paul, the "flesh" has "a close solidarity with sin"; it is this congenital weakness that makes the human soul fall into the slavery of sin. The "spirit", its antagonist, is "the state of freedom in which it blossoms when it has been faithful to the Spirit of God, who attracts it and comes to dwell within it". There is no question here of any gradation, but of opposition, pure and simple. Saint Paul does not speak there of any duality whatever in the structure of the human being, he does not correct a tripartite anthropology by another bipartite one. For him, flesh and spirit never designate two components of human nature—like body and soul would be—but always states—contrasted states—of the whole man.[24]

[22] The "worldly beings who have no spirit" of Jude 1:19 are of the first category, according to the portrait that is traced of it. One can also say that the whole of mankind, according to Paul, is included in it, following the picture of the first three chapters of the Letter to the Romans.

[23] In 1 Corinthians 15:44–46, the opposition between "natural" and "spiritual" is another, as the context suffices to show.

[24] Hans Urs von Balthasar, *Prayer*, trans. G. Harrison (San Francisco: Ignatius Press, 1986), 260. The human soul is the place of the struggle between the flesh and the spirit. Cf. Gala-

If one wants, therefore, to find a certain Greek antecedent of philosophical significance for the Pauline trichotomy, it would not be appropriate to look for it on Plato's side. It would rather be in Aristotle. The Stagirite in fact acknowledges in man, an animated body, the presence of a superior element, the spirit (νοῦς), the principle of intellectual life, immortal and divine. Nevertheless, the parallel takes a sharp turn: for there would be at least one major difference. While Aristotle spoke of a νοῦς, Paul speaks of a πνεῦμα. Now, as we know, the difference is not merely one of terminology. It is no longer a question of a simple nuance of thought. The substitution of one term for another was, besides, not made by Paul alone: it had already been carried out a little earlier by Philo. Friendly toward Hellenism, Philo "was imbued with the doctrine of the contemplative *nous*";[25] nevertheless, in the passages where he comments on the creation account, he does not speak of νοῦς but of πνεῦμα. God, he says, breathes into man a *pneuma*; not content with making him simply alive, composed of soul and body, he gave him part of his spirit; this is what Moses teaches by saying that he made him in his image. This *pneuma*, in man, is the principle of a higher life, the place of communication with God.[26] Now such is also one of the meanings of *pneuma* in Saint Paul. It is not in Greece that we must search for its origin but in the Bible.

Father Joseph Huby has said it in a few words, which more recent authors would benefit from rereading: In the Pauline verse, "famous because of the trichotomy spirit, soul, body, of the human composite, some thought to see a borrowing from Plato or Aristotle. Both do acknowledge, in fact, three principles in man; but if the latter two of those coincide with those[27] enumerated by Saint Paul, the first is differ-

---

tians 5, Romans 8: "The struggle that is to lead the disciple of Christ attacks what Saint Paul calls the "flesh" as the center of all violence: impurity, hate, discord, jealousy, transports, disputes, etc., and arouses the life according to the Spirit in charity, joy, peace, goodness, gentleness, self-mastery" (*Sources* [Fribourg, February 1987], 7–8).

[25] André-Jean Festugière, O.P., "La Division corps-âme-esprit de 1 Tess. 5, 23 et la philosophie grecque", in *Recherches de science religieuse* (1930). We are summarizing here the whole of this decisive and complete paper, which was reproduced by the author in *l'Idéal religieux des Grecs et l'Évangile* (Gabalda, 1932), 196–220.

[26] Philo, *Allégories des Lois*, I:12–13: "Quis rerum divinarum sit haeres. Quod deterior potiori. . . ." Texts in Festugière.

[27] In fact, the coincidence is only partial. The body, *sôma*, designates rather in Plato the carnal passions, and the soul, *psychè*, the good passions. With Aristotle, as we have said, the analogy would be closer.

ent. In Plato, it is the *nous*, the intellectual soul . . . , considered, moreover, by Aristotle as separable. Instead of νοῦς, Saint Paul puts spirit, or *pneuma*, here; with him as in Philo, this is a Semitic term, suggested by the account in Genesis (2:7), where it is said that God breathed into the nostrils of the man a breath of life. . . ."[28] The Pleiade Bible has taken the same explanation, which seems imperative to us. "Spirit, soul, body", recalls Michel Leturmy in a note to his translation, "such is, with the Semites, the most common division with respect to the human composite."[29] In a note to the translation of Matthew 6:25, the same author explains that the Greek ψυχή translates the Aramaean *näfshâ*, breath of the throat, animal life (the "soul"), through opposition to πνεῦμα, which translates the Aramaean *roûhâ*, divine respiration, breath of the nostrils (the "spirit"): see Genesis 2:7.[30]

We do not believe it would be enough, however, to trace the words of the Pauline triad simply to those of the Bible. The Apostle's anthropology is also based, in part, on his experience acquired from life in the Spirit of God. There are numerous commentators who, in consequence, consider the Pauline πνεῦμα to designate in reality, not something of man that would be higher than his soul, but the human soul insofar as it is informed by grace, participating, as the Second Letter of Peter (1:4) says, in an effective way in the divine nature, united to the very essence of God by the coming of the divine Spirit into it.[31] The ψυχή in this case would be not only "sensible life" but also the higher reality of man as man, that is, although Buzy translates it in an overly intellectualist language, "reason without grace".[32] This would be "the state of the specifically living being, which is inherent in man

[28] *Saint Paul, Épître aux Galates, épîtres aux Thessaloniciens,* "Verbum salutis" series, 14 (Beauchesne, 1946).

On the various meanings of πνεῦμα in Greek philosophy and Paul, cf. the explanation of Bernard Allo, O.P., commentary on the First Letter to the Corinthians (Gabalda), 91–112.

[29] *Bible de la Pléiade, Nouveau Testament* (1971), 689. Translation: "May the God of peace himself make you completely holy, and may your whole being, spirit, soul and body, be kept safe and blameless for the coming of our Lord Jesus Christ."

[30] Op. cit., 22. Cf. Jean Grosjean, 762, note to Hebrews 4:12: the separation of the soul and the spirit is an "Aramaean way of designating concretely the innermost point of man, according to the distinction (stressed by M. Jousse) between guttural breathing (soul) and nasal breathing (spirit)".

[31] Thus F. Amiot, *Saint Paul;* Verbum salutis series, 13 (1946), 351 and 352.

[32] D. Buzy, 170.

as such".[33] So too, schematically, Bonnetain: "The three terms come back to the following: grace, soul and body."[34] Father André-Jean Festugière is clearly opposed to this interpretation, which also proceeds in some from the fear of attributing to the Apostle an anthropology judged to be "Platonic". For him, the anthropology of Saint Paul is undoubtedly trichotomic; the *pneuma* in question in the wish addressed to the Thessalonians, as in the texts mentioned above from the First Letter to the Corinthians—and as, in addition, the Letter to the Hebrews speaks of it—is not the Holy Spirit, but actually a part of man: "the movement of the phrase, the two καί, the insistence on saying that we must be completely, in our whole being, under the divine safeguard" are the proof of it.[35] Besides, if this *pneuma* is not itself the divine life realized in man, it is indeed in him the center of the higher life: moral, religious, mystical; it is the "center of the Christian life", which is not a matter of feelings but of faith.[36]

Some hesitate to choose between these two contradictory interpretations, even if it means apparently contradicting themselves in their explanatory formulas. They are of the feeling that the thought of Paul is profound and complex; they would like to lose nothing of it but do not see well how to explain it in our language in a coherent fashion. Such is Father Joseph Huby, following the passage we have quoted: "For Paul, the *pneuma* is more precisely the spirit of man insofar as influenced, informed and heightened by divine grace"; it is the "principle of thinking, center of moral and religious life and summit of the soul. The original (biblical) concept of the *pneuma*, the human soul breathes from God, is magnificently deepened; the *pneuma* designates the reason informed by grace, man insofar as he becomes spirit, participating in the nature of God; through the spirit, the νοῦς becomes capable of conquering the flesh . . . , it is united to the very essence of God through the coming of the divine Spirit."[37] In this essay, somewhat awkward in its attempts at reconciliation, in which a fourth term (νοῦς) is introduced, we see to which side the author is leaning. We will say as much

[33] Stacey, *Pauline View*.

[34] Course taught at Saint-Sulpice (1939), 79.

[35] Festugière, "Division", 198–99.

[36] Ibid., 218. Cf. B. Allo, *Revue biblique*, 43 (1934), 341: The human *pneuma* in Paul depends no more on pagan mysticism than it does on Greek philosophy, and "there, where it is considered a constitutive, existential part of man, it is certainly not a fragment of God."

[37] Huby, *Saint Paul*.

of Max Alain Chevallier, who, with respect to 1 Corinthians 14:14–16, after having noted for us "the freely equivocal use of the word *pneuma* by Paul", seems to restrict immediately the significance of his observation by saying that this word "designates without describing it the inner man filled with the presence of God".[38] Karl Barth, in his *Dogmatics*, escapes such oscillations only thanks to his general doctrine, which prohibits him from "reifying" in a way, from giving a proper consistency to the human spirit considered in its relation to God. After having justly observed that the *ruah* of the Old Testament does not correspond to the πνεῦμα ἅγιον of the New,[39] but, insofar as a "anthropological notion", to the πνεῦμα of the address to the Thessalonians, Barth makes haste to add: "On the other hand, one cannot assert without reservation that the Old Testament and the New refer to a trichotomy of the human being. For both, the human being in himself is body and soul, earthly form and earthly life; but the body possesses a soul, and its earthly form is that of a living being, in the measure in which the human being receives the spirit and safeguards it." This spirit must, however, be conceived, "not as a property of man, but as a gratuitous gift", which at death must be returned to God and which persists, "which God withdraws from him or grants to him".[40] What must be maintained above all, according to Barth, is that man "is in no way 'related to God' (Gunkel); he has simply been awakened to his proper existence by the breath that God breathes into him and which allows him to breathe himself. What is he and what does he possess that he has not received and that does not differentiate him from God, since it is God who has created him?"[41]

The human *pneuma* of which Paul speaks would thus be both an element so little constitutive of his being that God can take it back from him and a created element that differentiates him from God. Such is the Barthian paradox. Without having to take him literally, perhaps

---

[38] *Esprit de Dieu, paroles d'hommes* (Delachaux et Niestlé, 1966).

[39] "The text of John 20:22, where it is said that Jesus breathes over his disciples, declaring these words: 'Receive the Holy Spirit', constitutes a going beyond Genesis 2:7, intended by the Evangelist."

[40] *Dogmatics*, French trans. vol. 3, t. 1 (Geneva, 1960), 266: "To die is to 'render one's spirit', as Luther translates inaccurately but correctly, in this perspective, the expression in Acts 5:5 and 10; 12:23. In dying, Jesus returns his spirit into the hands of his Father (Lk 23:46). In dying, Stephen prays that Jesus might receive his spirit (Acts 7:55)."

[41] Ibid., 260, see 262, the references he gives to Scripture.

we would have to unite ourselves with the "spirit" of it. Would it in fact be necessary to choose between two contradictory interpretations that confront each other or resign ourselves to a [false] harmonization that itself does not avoid contradiction? An expression used by Saint Paul himself, 1 Corinthians 2:11, could suggest an intermediate solution to us: "Who therefore among men knows the secrets of a man if not the spirit of the man which is in him (τὸ πνεῦμα τοῦ ἀνθρώπου, τὸ ἐν αὐτῷ)?" This *pneuma* is certainly not the Holy Spirit, since Paul adds: "Similarly, no one knows the secrets of God except the Spirit of God." Yet it does not appear completely like a constituent part of man as such, like the body or the soul: after having said "the spirit of the man", Paul corrects himself in a way to say: "the spirit who is in him", which marks a nuance of capital importance. Thus, what par excellence makes a man, what constitutes man in his worth among the beings of this world, much more, what makes him a being superior to the world, would be an element that, rather than being "of man", would be "in man". There is, it seems to us, in this Pauline πνεῦμα the same kind of ambiguity, notional because real, as in the divine "image" or divine "breath" of creation, such as Christian tradition interprets them. From one author to another, and sometimes in the same author, the same ambiguity will give place to oscillations, which will not go, however, to the point of compromising, before a rather recent date, the idea of a tripartite anthropology. We conclude, with a recent interpreter, that the Pauline concept of πνεῦμα is a concept "of which our modern anthropologies can absolutely not take account".[42]

[42] Chevallier, *Esprit de Dieu.* One cannot speak of incoherence, for if the vocabulary is not fixed, the variations of meaning are explained rather well by the different contexts. Paul's letters do not constitute a didactic treatise.

2. Patristic Tradition

I. *The First Two Centuries: Irenaeus*

It is a fact that Christian antiquity did not judge insignificant the Pauline verse about body, soul and spirit. Nevertheless, from one author to another, the interpretations differ, without always being in contradictory opposition to each other.

In his letter to the Philadelphians, Saint Ignatius of Antioch simply makes the Apostle's enumeration his own in judging that his correspondents, like the Ephesians and the Smyrnians, "will be honored by the Lord Jesus Christ, in whom they hope with flesh, soul and spirit (σαρκί, ψυχῇ, πνεύματι), in faith, charity and concord".[1] Athenagoras also distinguishes between soul and spirit; for him, the soul is placed between "the spirit of matter", which is to say "the flesh and blood", and the "heavenly spirit", which is "pure spirit", and it can, according to its choice, mix with one or become the other:

> The soul becomes passive when it receives the spirit of matter and is mixed with it, by looking below toward earthly things and, to speak in a general way, when it becomes only flesh and blood and ceases to be a pure spirit.[2]
>
> We believe that we will live another life, . . . heavenly and no longer earthly, if at least, close to God and with God, we have steadfast souls, mastering passion, and if we remain, not like bodies, but like a heavenly spirit. . . .[3]

In Tatian, also, the distinction seems clear, when he says: "We have knowledge of two sorts of spirits: one of them is called soul, the other is greater than the soul, it is the image and resemblance of God."[4] Only, subsequently, it is impossible to discern clearly if the spirit he distinguishes thus from the soul, and which he calls "divine", is not

---

[1] *Aux Philadelphiens*, c. 11, n. 2 (P. T. Camelot, *Sources chrétiennes*, 4th ed., 10:130–31).

[2] *Supplique*, c. 27, n. 1 (G. Bardy, *Sources chrétiennes* 3:144); . . . οὐκέτι πνεῦμα καθαρὸν γιγνομένη.

[3] Ibid., c. 31, n. 3 (157–58).

[4] *Discours aux Grecs*, c. 12, n. 1 (PG 6, 829 C).

simply the Spirit of God. The soul, he explains, is not immortal in and of itself; so, "if it remains by itself, it dies with the flesh. . . . But when it is united to the divine spirit (θεῖον), it does not lack for help, and it rises to where the spirit leads it. For the seat of the latter is above, while its origin is below. Now, in the beginning, the spirit was the guide of the soul; it abandoned it when it did not want to follow it. . . . Now the Spirit of God does not reside in all, but in some who live justly. . . . The souls who have obeyed wisdom have drawn the Spirit, who is closely related[5] to them (συγγενές). . . ."

Saint Irenaeus, then Origen, should make us pause a little longer because of the abundance of texts, their importance and their difficulty.[6]

It is in the fifth book of *Adversus Haereses* that Irenaeus gives us his views about anthropology. But his goal was not to write a clear and didactic exposition for the use of the historians who would pore over his text later on; it was to refute heretics who conceived of salvation for man only in "rejection of the flesh".[7] On the other hand, careful always to stick very close to Scripture, he lets himself be guided successively by the different texts he uses, which leads him to change more or less his perspective and his terminology in the course of his text.[8] Hence the difficulties for interpreters.

The first passage in which the distinction between the soul and the spirit is affirmed is of little interest to us, for it is there a question of an exposition of heretical doctrine.[9] In response, chapter 6, no. 1, is presented as an orthodox commentary on the Pauline texts:

> Through the hands of the Father, which is to say, by the Son and the Spirit, it is man, and not a part of man, who becomes the image and the resemblance of God. Now the soul and the spirit can be a part of man, but in no way man: the perfect man is a mixture and union of the soul who has received the Spirit of the Father and who has been mixed with the flesh modeled according to the image of God. . . .

[5] Tatian, *Ad Graecos*, c. 13, 2 (PG 6, 833 AB and 836 A).

[6] "The anthropology of Irenaeus", writes Dom Bernard Botte, "is not a learned anthropology" (BTAM, 10, 566). One can say as much for his whole theology. Which does not mean that it is without interest.

[7] More particularly, as we shall see, it passes from the perspective of 1 Corinthians 2:14–15 (opposition of the natural and the spiritual) to that, which is completely different, of 1 Thessalonians 5:23 (trichotomic gradation), the whole interfering with Genesis 1:26.

[8] *Adversus Haereses*, l. 5, c. 8, n. 1 (*Sources chrétiennes* 153:95).

[9] Ibid., l. 5, c. 4, n. 1: " . . . in saying what is vivified by the Father, this, whose duration

> Under the name of "perfect", the Apostle designates those who have received the Spirit of God. . . . He also calls them "spiritual"; they are spiritual through a participation of the Spirit, but not through a voiding and a suppression of the flesh. In fact, if one dismisses the substance of the flesh, that is, of the modeled work, in order to consider only what is properly spirit, such a thing is no longer the spiritual man but the Spirit of the man or the Spirit of God. By contrast, when this Spirit, in mixing with the soul, is united to the modeled work, thanks to this effusion of the Spirit, the spiritual and perfect man is achieved, and it is he himself who has been made in the image and resemblance of God. When, on the contrary, the Spirit is absent in the soul, such a man, remaining in all truth natural and carnal, will be imperfect, possessing indeed the image of God in the modeled work, but not having received the resemblance by means of the Spirit.[10]

From all the evidence, Irenaeus counts here three elements in man. But is it simply a matter of man or of the perfect man? Or rather, to speak without ambiguity, is it simply a question of the "perfect" man, which is to say, complete in his nature, or man divinized through the participation of the Spirit of God? Or indeed, does Irenaeus mix the two things? The text that follows will perhaps enlighten us:

> Modeled flesh alone is not the perfect man: it is only the body of man, thus one part of man. Neither is the soul alone man: it is only the soul of man, thus one part of man. Nor is the Spirit man: one gives it the name of Spirit, not that of man. It is the mixture and union of all these things that constitute the perfect man. And this is why the Apostle, in explaining himself, has clearly defined the perfect and spiritual man, beneficiary of salvation, when he says in this First Letter to the Thessalonians: "May the God of peace make you perfect and holy, so that you may be fully complete and so that your whole being—to wit, your Spirit, your soul and your body—may be preserved without reproach for the coming of the Lord Jesus."
>
> What motive did he have in asking that these three things, to wit, the soul, the body and the Spirit, be preserved whole for the coming of the Lord if he had not known that all three were to be restored and reunited and that there is for them but one and the same salvation? This is why he calls "fully complete" those who present these three things without reproach to the Lord. Thus those are perfect who, all at once, possess

is endless, is evident for everyone, to wit, the spirit, the soul and the other things of this kind . . ." (*Sources chrétiennes* 153:57).

[10] Ibid., l. 5, c. 6, n. 1 (153:75–77), translated by Adelin Rousseau.

> the Spirit of God, remaining always with them, and maintain themselves without reproach with respect to their souls and their bodies, which is to say, preserving faith toward God and keeping justice toward their neighbor.[11]

The hesitation remains. On the one hand, the Spirit constitutes with the soul one part of man; it is called the "Spirit of the man" and seems to be distinguished from the "Spirit of God"; it, in itself, does not constitute the man any more than the body or the soul does, but it is one of the three elements that constitute him; these three elements are also enumerated according to Saint Paul, who wishes them, all three, to be without reproach—a wish that would be irrelevant, even impertinent, in the case of the Spirit of God; finally, moreover, Irenaeus himself considers that they are all three to be "restored" and to be presented to the Lord. But, on the other hand, the soul receives "the Spirit of the Father"; the man is called "spiritual" insofar as he receives participation of the Spirit, and this participation makes him to be not only in the image but in the resemblance of God; finally, if this man is "perfect", it is because, in addition to the soul and the body, he "possesses the Spirit of God".[12] And these two series of affirmations are not found in different contexts, they are closely intermingled.

Yet, a little farther on, several passages come to support the second series:

> Those who possess the deposit of the Spirit and who . . . surrender themselves to the Spirit . . . , the Apostle rightly calls "spiritual", since the Spirit of God dwells in them: For spirits without bodies will never be spiritual men, but it is our substance—that is, the composite of soul and flesh—that, in receiving the Spirit of God, constitutes the spiritual man. . . .[13] The weakness of the flesh makes the power of the Spirit shine

---

[11] Ibid., 77–81. Like the translator, we always write Spirit with a capital, but without making too hasty a judgment about the precise meaning of the word: in any hypothesis, the dignity of this third principle merits a capital.

[12] Cf. Henri Rondet, *Le Péché originel dans la tradition patristique et théologique* (1967), 58: "Irenaeus linking up with Jewish anthropology. The soul of which he speaks is probably closer to the Hebrew *nephesch* than the Greek *psychè*, and it is in this sense that he says of it, in a text that has become a classic, that the perfect man is composed of a body, a soul and the Holy Spirit: *Adversus Haereses* 5, 9, 1 (Harvey, 2:342; PG 7, 1141 B). Cf. J. Lebreton, 2 (1928), 607.

[13] If we must believe the Latin version (and the Greek retroversion), Irenaeus takes "body" and "flesh" here as synonyms. The weakness of the flesh is not here, it seems, moral weakness (at least not at first); it is, if one can say so, ontological weakness. Cf. below, *Ad-*

> forth . . . , and it is of these two things that the living man is made: living due to the participation of the Spirit, man through the substance of the flesh. —Therefore, without the Spirit of God, the flesh is dead. . . .[14]
>
> The breath of life, which makes the natural man, is one thing, and the vivifying Spirit, which renders him spiritual, is another. The breath has been given indistinctly to all the people who inhabit the earth, while the Spirit has been given exclusively to those who trample down earthly covetous desires. . . .[15]
>
> "For the Spirit will come out around me, and it is I who made all breath" (Is 57:16). He ranks in a way the Spirit in a sphere apart, beside God, who, in the last days, spread it over mankind for adoption; but he situates the breath in the common sphere, among creatures, and he declares it something created. Now what has been created is different from the one who creates it. The breath is thus a temporary thing, while the Spirit is eternal. . . . After having enveloped man from within and without, he remains always with him and, henceforth, will never abandon him.[16]

One will note, however, that in these texts the perspective is no longer that of an anthropological analysis and that they are condemned by other biblical passages than the preceding. Moreover, as Irenaeus' principal objective just now was to claim for the body itself a salvation of which the heretics say it is incapable, his objective here is to show that this salvation, the definitive blossoming of the spiritual life whose seed is in each man, is the work of the Spirit of God in each man. In no passage is Irenaeus concerned to give us what we would call a philosophical anthropology. He does not go deeply into—to tell the truth, he does not even have in mind—the problem of the insertion of the Spirit of God in man. Despite the several expressions we have brought out, and several others as well, we believe that the Spirit of which he speaks is always the Spirit of God, even when he considers it in man. If, for example, it is said in 5, 6, 1 that the soul and the Spirit can be "one part of man", one can observe, with Dom Adelin Rousseau, that "*pars*" is in the singular. "Thus, although Irenaeus does not hesitate to see in the Spirit of God one of the three constitutive

versus Haereses, 5, 9, 1, where, if the two meanings of "flesh" succeed each other, it is the moral sense that carries it along.

[14] Ibid., l. 5, c. 8, n. 2; c. 9, n. 2–3 (pp. 588 and 592).

[15] Ibid., l. 5, c. 12, n. 2 (pp. 143 and 145). Cf. Gen 2:7 and 1 Cor 15:45.

[16] Ibid., 147–49. One should not dwell on: l. 5, c. 4, n. 1, which reports a remark made by the heretics (p. 57).

elements of the perfect man, he refuses, and for good reason, to make this Spirit a 'part' of the perfect man. . . ." A little farther on, it is said that the Spirit, like the soul and the body, is to be restored and saved, which seems strange if it is indeed a question of the Spirit of God; but, Dom Rousseau again comments, "what is to be saved is not the Spirit as such but the Holy Spirit insofar as communicated to man for his full achievement; in other words, the Spirit is less saved than it saves. . . ." These explanations are ingenious; they can seem a little subtle; they do not, however, in our opinion, falsify the general line of Irenaean thought. Perhaps it is only necessary to complete them by recognizing that the texts that are to be thus explained give witness to a rather clear tendency to conceive of man (even if it is a question of the "perfect man") according to the anthropological scheme suggested by the Apostle.[17]

If, therefore, the Spirit indeed designates for Irenaeus the Spirit of God, his very manner of considering this Spirit of God in man, and of seeing in it thus one of the three elements that combine to constitute the perfect man, poses an anthropological problem.[18] Just like the text of the First Letter to the Corinthians of which Irenaeus wants to give an account, it invites a resolution of this problem in the direction of a certain "trichotomy"—which Origen, more of a philosopher, will soon do. "The heretics", we read again in the fifth book of *Adversus Haereses*, ". . . do not understand that three things, as we have shown, constitute the perfect man: the flesh, the soul and the Spirit. One of them saves and forms, to wit, the Spirit; another is saved and formed, to wit, the flesh; another, finally, is between those two, to wit, the soul, which now follows the Spirit and takes its flight thanks

[17] Ibid., 5, 6, 1. Cf. *Sources chrétiennes* 152:228–29 and 233–34.

[18] On a point that does not inform his essential thesis, we hesitate to make our own an explanation by Dom Rousseau. According to him, the *substantia carnis* of 5, 6, 1 (p. 74, l. 21) would signify the flesh alone, and *spiritus hominis* (p. 76, l. 1) would signify the soul. But a little farther on, in 5, 9, 2, Irenaeus goes on to say: "The living man is made of these two things: living, due to the participation of the Spirit, man through the substance of the flesh" (p. 113, l. 38–40). This text is not annotated. If one understands it according to the explanation given for 5, 6, 1, and for other passages, would it not be necessary to conclude that, according to 5, 9, 2, man would have neither soul nor spirit? He would be, in his very perfection, composed of two single elements: the flesh alone (*substantia carnis*) and the Holy Spirit (*Spiritus*). On the "flesh" in the anthropology of Irenaeus, refer to the explanations of Hans Urs von Balthasar, *The Glory of the Lord: A Theological Aesthetics*, vol. 2 *Studies in Theological Style: Clerical Styles* (San Francisco: Ignatius Press, 1984) 62–67.

to him, now lets itself be persuaded by the flesh and falls into earthly desires."[19]

These explanations seem to us akin to those of Father Jean Meyendorff, with respect to man "composed of flesh, soul and Holy Spirit": "This view," he observes, "which sounds strangely pantheistic if one judges it according to later theological categories, shows in fact a dynamic concept of man that excludes the notion of 'pure nature'. Man is created so as to share the existence of God: this is what distinguishes him from the animal and is expressed in the biblical account of the creation of Adam "in the image of God".[20] As Pierre Boyer-Maurel also says,[21] if, for Irenaeus, a certain dichotomy "accounts for man fashioned in the image of God", it is nevertheless a trichotomy, "in which the breath only precedes the Spirit", who "accounts for the becoming of man, of that man who is created, by letting himself be created, throughout the divine Economy".

II. Origen

Irenaeus spoke particularly of the Spirit of God, even when that Spirit, shared, became, by consent of the soul, the spirit of man. Origen will speak more explicitly of the spirit of man, insofar as an opening to the Spirit of God. These are two inverse perspectives much rather than two adverse doctrines.[1]

One authority on Origen, Gustave Bardy, has, however, written that the tripartite division, "which is imposed on him, in a way, by several Scripture passages, plays no role in his teaching".[2] Another historian of ancient Christian doctrines, François Bonifas, had expressed a judgment in the contrary direction, but as little conformed to the reality; after having pointed out that "unsteadiness" of the Pauline terminology "makes it doubtful that the Apostle intended [in 1 Thessalonians

[19] *Adversus Haereses*, 5, 9, 1; *Sources chrétiennes* 153:107–9; cf. the commentary 152:249. Irenaeus mixes here the idea of the body, first element of human nature, with that of the flesh that is opposed to the Spirit.

[20] *Relativisme historique et autorité dans le dogme chrétien* (1969), 260.

[21] *La Génération divine selon saint Irénée*, chap. 1 (manuscript thesis).

[1] On the pneumatology of Origen and his trichotomic anthropology, see also H. de Lubac, *Histoire et Esprit* (Aubier, 1950), 150–58.

[2] *Dictionnaire de théologie catholique*, vol. 11, col. 1534; article "Origène". At least Bardy saw that the Pauline division was of biblical origin.

5:23] to make a scientific distinction", he went on, thinking essentially of Origen: "Yet the Fathers of the Church saw in the expressions of Saint Paul a rigorous division, in which they found once again that of their old mentor Plato."[3] Previously, J. Denis, while not mixing Plato up in the affair, had recognized in Origen the existence of trichotomic texts, but he saw in that only a foreign body in the midst of Origenian doctrine: "Generally speaking," he said, "the soul and the spirit are but one for Origen, and if he had not respected a division that came to him from Saint Paul, and which appears to have been adopted, generally, as much by the orthodox Fathers as by the heretic scholars, he would have suppressed one of the terms of this division and would thereby have been spared numerous contradictions."[4] The prejudice to which, in each of these three last cases, the historian is unconsciously giving way is not difficult to perceive. To overcome it would require an in-depth study. After the work by G. Verbeke on *L'Evolution de la doctrine du Pneuma du Stoïcisme à saint Augustin* (1945), the works of Henri Crouzel and Jacques Dupuis have brought us all desirable light on this point. "At times", Father Crouzel tells us, "Origen is a dichotomist, distinguishing the body and the soul following the Platonic custom.[5] But most of the time, he sees, according to Scripture, three elements in man: spirit, soul and body. He has recourse to this trichotomy when it is a matter of explaining his idea of man, and he states it each time he encounters in the texts an expression that suggests it: and this is so throughout his literary career."[6] But it is Father Jacques Dupuis who draws the matter into perfect clarity in his important monograph on *"L'Esprit de l'homme", étude sur l'anthropologie religieuse d'Origène.* For him, "There can be no doubt that the verse from Saint Paul is the immediate source of his anthropological trichotomy" (65). It is principally he that we will follow here.

"We often find it asserted in Scripture", says Origen, "that man is spirit, body and soul, and we have ourselves developed the subject at

[3] *Histoire des dogmes de l'Église chrétienne*, vol. 1 (Paris: Fischbacher, 1886), 312.

[4] *De la philosophie d'Origène* (1884), 237. One senses here the influence of the Cousinian spiritualism of our nineteenth century.

[5] Then one can find in him other kinds of distinctions, coming also from Greek philosophy, for example in *Contra Celsum*, l. 8, c. 60, speaking of God "whose power is different . . . in pouring out over men the benefits of the soul, the body, external goods" (P. Borret, vol. 4, *Sources chrétiennes*, 150 [1969]:313; cf. l. 1, c. 21; l. 6, c. 54; l. 8, c. 51).

[6] *Théologie de l'image de Dieu chez Origène* (Aubier, 1956), 130.

length."[7] In that as in other subjects, it is in fact the sacred text, most especially that of Saint Paul, that truly constitutes the framework for his thought.[8] And it is with reference to Scripture that he tries to define clearly the notion of the *Pneuma*. For him, the *Pneuma* is first of all the Divine Life in principle, but it is also the shared divine life: the creature itself becomes *pneuma*, in the measure that it possesses this life. Yet, it is a first kind of participation in the divine *Pneuma*, which does not yet allow it to be said that man has become *pneuma*; a participation that, without betraying Origen, we can already call natural, because it consists in an element that is an integral part of the nature of all men and that is precisely his *pneuma*: "The Spirit of God, even when it is present in us, is one thing, and the *pneuma* proper to every man, that which is in him, is something else. . . . The Apostle clearly affirms that this spirit (this *pneuma*) is different from the Spirit of God, even when the Holy Spirit is present in us, over and above the spirit of man that is in him."[9] The distinction could not be put more clearly. Origen asks again, in the same passage of the commentary on Saint Matthew: "Is the spirit of Elias the same as the Spirit of God who dwells in Elias? or, indeed, do we have two different things there?" And he replies: "The Apostle shows clearly that the Spirit of God, when he dwells in man, is distinct from the spirit of the man: 'The Spirit itself testifies to our spirit that we are children of God' (Rom 8:16), and in another place: 'No man knows what is in a man if not the spirit of the man who is in him; likewise, no one knows what is in God if not the Spirit of God' (1 Cor 2:11)."[10]

Origen indeed says, like Paul, *pneuma* and not *nous*. It is because they did not sufficiently distinguish between these two concepts that several have identified the *pneuma* of the anthropological trichotomy with the preexisting *nous* and have made it the higher (*intellectus*) part of the soul—unless, in order better to distinguish between *pneuma* and *psyche*, they reduced this latter to its sensible part. They then spoke

[7] *In Rom.* 1, 1, 18: "Frequenter in Scripturis invenimus, et a nobis saepe dissertum est, quod homo spiritus et corpus et anima esse dicatur" (PG, 14, 866, 2). Cf. *In Jo.*, vol. 32, 11 and 18 (PC 14, 790 A). *In Num.*, hom. 1, 7; *Peri archôn*, l. 3, c. 4, n. 1 and 4.

[8] G. Verbeke, *L'Evolution* (Paris-Louvain, 1945), 459; cf. 468. Jacques Dupuis, S.J., "*Esprit*" (DDB, 1967), 1 and 65.

[9] *In Matt.*, 13, 2. Klost. - B, GCS, 10, p. 180; PG 13, 1093 AB.

[10] Ibid. Cf. H. U. von Balthasar, *Origène, Esprit et Feu*, French trans., 1 (Cerf, 1959), 104–5.

of Origen's imprecisions, his unstable terminology, indeed of his inconsistency of thought and of his contradictions. This was from not having read him closely enough.[11] He distinguishes the spirit from the soul (and in this case he is not speaking of the *nous*) as clearly as he does the soul from the body, and he repeats at different times that "we are composed of a soul and a spirit": this is the case, it seems, in the third book of *Peri archôn*;[12] so too in the fourth book, in the famous theoretical parallel that he institutes between man and Scripture.[13] In the *Entretien avec Héraclite*, for the instruction of his august audience, he insists: "That man is a composite being, we know through Scripture. The Apostle in fact says: 'May God make you holy, spirit, soul and body', and so forth. This spirit is not the Holy Spirit, but one part of the human composite (μέρος τής τοῦ ἀνθρώπου συστάσεως), as the same Apostle teaches when he says: 'The Spirit gives witness to our spirit'. . . ."[14] In the commentary on the Letter to the Romans, he will also quote in support a text from Daniel;[15] here, he invokes as an example what happened at the death of Christ: having wanted to save all men, the Savior had taken body, soul and spirit; now "these three elements, during the Passion, were separated; at the time of the Resurrection they were reunited. During the Passion they were separated: How? The body, in the tomb; the soul, in hell; the spirit, he deposited it in the hands of the Father. . . ."[16]

This spirit of man, represented by the eagle in Ezekiel,[17] is placed above the soul.[18] But never, in the texts of the trichotomic series, does

[11] Cf. Dupuis, criticizing Verbeke, Denis, Méhat, Freppel, etc.; "*Esprit*", 11, and Henri Crouzel, *Introduction à Origène, Traité des principes*, 1 (*Sources chrétiennes*), 252.

[12] L. 3, c. 4, n. 1; GCS, 5, p. 263. We no longer have anything but Rufinus' translation: ". . . in nobis, id est hominibus, qui ex anima constamus et corpore ac spiritu vitali. . . ."

[13] L. 4, c. 2, 4: "Just as man is composed (συνέστηκεν) of body, soul and spirit (πνεύματος), in the same way was Holy Scripture given by God for the salvation of men." Ibid., 313.

[14] Ed. Jean Scherer, *Sources chrétiennes* 57 (1960): 68–70.

[15] *In Rom.*, 1, 10: "Deservit ergo Apostolus Deo, non in corpore, neque anima, sed in meliore sui parte, id est in spiritu. Haec enim tria esse in homine designat ad Thess. . . . Et Daniel dicit: 'Laudate, spiritus et animae justorum, Dominum' " (Dan 3:86). PG 14, 856 A. *In Matt.*, 13, 12.

[16] Ed. Scherer.

[17] *In Ezech.*, hom. 1, n. 16, GCS, 8, p. 340.

[18] Cf. Joseph Bonsirven, *L'Évangile de Paul* (Aubier, 1948), 281. "The Fathers of the Church will write: Man is composed of a body and a soul; the Christian is composed of a body, a soul and a spirit." This overall view, in general, is in any case not accurate as far as Origen is concerned.

Origen call it νοῦς—so that this could be a criterion for discerning the origin of certain passages given as Origenian but which are in reality from Evagrius.[19]

But how are we to understand this spirit which is "in us"?[20] What is its role? If we follow, again, the indications given by the Apostle, we will compare it to the moral conscience. "Our glory", says Paul, "is the testimony of our conscience" (2 Cor 1:12). The conscience always rejoices in what good I do; on the other hand, it can never be accused of doing evil, but, on the contrary, it remonstrates, it accuses the soul to which it is bound; this is a sovereign freedom; I therefore think that it is this very spirit that the Apostle tells us is with the soul, being associated with it like a pedagogue and a guide to teach it good, to chastise it and to reprimand it when it sins. It is this spirit of which the Apostle again says that "no one knows what the man is if not the spirit of the man who is in him"; it is the spirit of the conscience, also according to what Paul says: "The spirit himself gives witness to our spirit."[21]

We should not, however, in exalting the *pneuma*, excessively reduce its reality; if it is not a simple member of the human composite, neither is it the simple voice of the conscience. Inaccessible to evil,[22] placed in a way, as we have said, "above the soul" (ἀνωτέρω) as a "guide to virtue",[23] it is "much more divine than the soul and the body";[24] "belonging truly to man, it remains entirely in a participation of the Holy Spirit who gives himself to us; it is the point of contact between man and the divine *Pneuma* who inhabits him."[25] This is why it is al-

[19] H. Crouzel, "Recherches sur Origène et son influence", *Bulletin de litt. ecclésiastique* (1961), 111. Evagrius is closer to Plotinus: Crouzel, "L'Anthropologie d'Origène dans la perspective du combat spirituel", *Revue d'ascét. et de mystique* (1955), 364–65. Hans Urs von Balthasar, "Die Hiera des Evagrius", *Zeitschrift für Kathol. Theologie* 63 (1939).

[20] It will be noted that Origen several times makes the formula of Paul his own: "the spirit that is in man";—which he does not say for the body or the soul. Cf. Dupuis, "*Esprit*", 127: "The *pneuma* is part of the human composite, without doubt; it is not, however, properly speaking, man himself."

[21] *In Rom.*, l. 2, 10; PG 14, 893 AC. Cf. 2 Cor 1:12; 1 Cor 2:11; Rom 8:16.

[22] *In Jo.* vol. 32, 11: "The spirit of man that is in him cannot receive any evil" (PG 14, 789 A).

[23] *In Levit.*, hom. 2, n. 2: "Spiritus dux ejus (animae) est ad virtutem, si eum sequi velit." GCS, 6, p. 293.

[24] *In Jo.*, l. 2, 21 (15): ἐν τῷ τούτων θειοτέρῳ πνεύματι, GCS, 4, p. 78; PG 14, 152 A.

[25] Dupuis, "*Esprit*", 9. H. U. von Balthasar, "Le Mysterion d'Origène" *Recherches de science*

ways holy: it is holy by essence; not, of course, the "Holy Spirit", but, through participation, a "holy spirit":[26] "the seal of the Holy Spirit makes holy the spirit that is in us",[27] in each of us. Hence the paradox: the *pneuma*, in man, is holy, and it must become so; we must affirm at the same time the holiness of this *pneuma* and "the fortuitous character of a holy life".[28] If we seek to bring out the fundamental idea expressed (let us not say: sought, for Origen seems very much the master of his thought) in these texts and other similar ones, we could, without betraying it, express it thus: the *pneuma* that is "in man", in every man, assures a certain hidden transcendence of the man over himself, a certain opening, a certain received continuity between man and God. Not that there is the least identity of essence between the one and the other (like Irenaeus, like Clement, Origen is an implacable adversary of this pantheism of the pseudo-Gnostics); but it is, at the heart of man, the privileged place, always intact, of their encounter.

Would man, therefore, be after all impeccable? No. But the center of moral freedom and choice is not the *pneuma*. That is why we can say that for Origen the *pneuma*, "divine gift", is not, properly speaking, part of the personality.[29] The center of choice is the soul, in its higher part (νοῦς). The latter can be inclined, as Saint Paul says, on the side of the spirit or on the side of the "flesh" (which does not mean the body); which is to say that it is "capable of virtue and of vice".[30] When it is said that the flesh desires against the spirit and the spirit against the flesh, without any doubt the soul is posed between the two, as being able to acquiesce to the desires of the spirit (*si eum sequi velit*),[31] or let itself be led to carnal desires; in this latter case, it becomes with the flesh a single body of covetousness and of carnal appetite; in the former case, on the contrary, being associated with the spirit, it becomes a single spirit with it."[32] The spiritual man is the one in whom the

---

religieuse 26: 513–62; 27: 38–64: "The *pneuma* of man is described as a part that is coming to be added as a properly divine element to the psyche."

[26] *In Jo.*, vol. 20, 37 (29), and vol. 32, 18. GCS, 4, pp. 377 and 455. Cf. Dupuis, "*Esprit*", 99–103.

[27] "Fragment in Eph. 21" (on Eph 4:30). *Journal of Theological Studies*, 3:556.

[28] Dupuis, "*Esprit*", 143–46.

[29] Cf. H. Crouzel, *L'Image de Dieu*, 157.

[30] *In Jo.*, vol. 32, 11. PG 14, 789 A.

[31] *In Levit.*, hom. 2, 2; p. 293.

[32] *In Rom.*, l. 1, 18; PG 14, 866 A. Cf. *Sur la prière*, 9, 2.

spirit prevails;[33] the carnal man, he in whom the flesh prevails. The spirit itself, the *pneuma*, always remains holy; but, in each one, it can have vitality or torpor, flight or fall, flame or sluggishness.[34] This is why, paradoxically, Origen can affirm both, as we have said, that the *pneuma* is holy and that it must become so.[35]

Still following Paul, Origen also speaks of the "natural man", who is again neither carnal nor spiritual, and the explanation he gives in his respect manifests once again a paradoxical character, distinguished only with difficulty from that spirit (*pneuma*) that is in man without being uniquely of man and that becomes fully himself and fully completes man only in his participation in the Spirit of God: "The natural man does not understand what the law of God is, it is madness to him, but the spiritual judges all things" (1 Cor 2:14). We think that there is a reason why Paul omits the word "man" after "spiritual". For "the spiritual" is more than a man, he is superior to that humanity defined by the soul, the body or by the two together, and not by the spirit, which is more divine than these two elements and whose supernatural participation, once achieved, defines the spiritual. When the soul rises, follows the spirit and separates itself from the body, when it no longer even contents itself with following the spirit but remains in it (as this passages shows: "Toward you have I raised my soul", Ps 25:1), how would it not lose, so to speak, its own nature and not itself become spirit?"[36]

Toward the end of this text, a trace of the speculations of *Peri archôn* on the subject of the soul will be noted; but toned down by "so to speak". It is necessary to acknowledge, however, that from one work to the other, across the succession of dates and the varieties of subjects treated and literary genres, the points of view are so diverse that, in the words if not in the thought, the reader has some difficulty finding a perfect coherence among all the Origenian texts on the *pneuma*.

At death, all *pneuma* returns to God: this is what Ecclesiastes says.

---

[33] *In Jo.*, vol. 2, 21 (15). GCS. 4, p. 78; PG 14, 152 A.

[34] *In Isaiam*, hom. 6, 5; GCS, 8, p. 276. Cf. Dupuis, 126–47.

[35] "Fragment in Eph. 21", loc. cit. Cf. *Peri archôn*, l. 5, 5 (K., 5, 77; PG 11, 164 C; trans. von Balthasar, *Esprit et Feu*, 1, French trans. [1959], 1000): "The holiness in each creature is accidental; but what happens by accident is also apt to disappear." See von Balthasar, ibid., 97–98, for the summary of Origen's doctrine on this subject.

[36] *Sur la prière*, 9, 2; K. 1, 313; PG 11, 444 D. Cf. von Balthasar, *Esprit et Feu* 2 (1960), 174–75.

"Thus the *pneuma* of the just and that of the sinner have an identical destiny: both end at the Father."[37] But "it does not follow that saint and sinner share the same destiny. With the saint, the whole man enters into God; with the sinner, the *pneuma* returns to the Lord, the soul and body perish in Gehenna: hence the intrinsic tearing of the human being."[38] Like the remark by Father Crouzel, Origen is akin here to the thought of Saint Irenaeus, who said: "All those who are destined to life will be raised up with their bodies, their souls and their spirits . . . , those who have merited punishment will surrender their souls and their bodies to it, for, with them, they have strayed from divine grace."[39]

Later Christian tradition will not be as unfaithful to this conception of the *pneuma* as one might believe. It is found again in a series of intuitions, ideas and opinions of varied expression. This is, for example, the idea, dear to Ruysbroek, of a certain "deiformity" of the human being, of his higher, "superessential" life in God.[40] It is the obscure feeling that there exists in each of us, even the greatest sinner, a hidden room where no one but God can enter in, "that sacred point in us that says *Pater noster*", as Paul Claudel says magnificently in the famous "Cantique de Palmyre", and that cannot hide from love.[41] It is the intuition of a Georges Bernanos at the threshold of death, noting in his diary that "sin makes us live on the surface of ourselves" and that even when we offend God, "we never cease entirely to desire what He desires in the depths of the sanctuary of our soul".[42] There are similar traits in the work of Dostoyevsky; although they too can be rather equivocal (a novelist does not express himself like a theologian), they do not prevent him from glorifying personal freedom and proclaiming the necessity of uprooting evil in receiving "new birth". The Origenian doctrine of the *pneuma* also reverberates throughout

[37] Cf. *In Matt.*, series, 57; GCS, 11, p. 132. See above *Entretien avec Héraclide.*

[38] Dupuis, "*Esprit*", 149. Cf. *In Matt.*, series, 62, p. 144. *Fragm. in Matt.*, 382; 12, p. 163.

[39] Irenaeus, *Adversus Haereses*, l. 2, c. 54, in the Harvey edition, 1:380. Cf. Crouzel, *L'image de Dieu*, 65 and 133.

[40] Ruysbroek, *Le Miroir du salut éternel*, chaps. 9 and 16; *Oeuvres*, French trans., 1:87 and 123, etc.

[41] Paul Claudel, *Conversations dans le Loir-et-Cher*, Cant. de Palmyre, p. 19: "I have good news to tell you, and it is that . . . this whole aberration is not true! One need only close one's eyes to find our treasure again in the night . . . , to grant all its rights over us to this love from which we cannot hide in ourselves the juncture of vein and artery."

[42] January 23, 1948; etc. In Albert Béguin, *Bernanos par lui-même* (Seuil, 1954), 147.

the Bonaventurian tradition. In a totally different climate and without any need to search for a precise influence from one to the other, the very doctrine of Saint Thomas Aquinas would not be completely foreign to him. It questions neither the singularity of each human being nor the drama of existence nor the divine transcendence.[43]

NOTE

In his commentary on John 4:23–24, Origen defines "true adorers", first by the spirit, then in relation to the truth. He thus breaks down the dual Johannine formula and explains it term by term, drawing his inspiration again from Paul, who opposes spirit and flesh (Rom 8:9; Gal 5:6; 2 Cor 10:3). It is interesting to note that, in evoking Romans 8:9, Origen adds a μήκετι: those who are *no longer* in the flesh but in the "spirit". He thereby stresses the impact of the coming of Christ and of the gift of the Spirit—already evoked by Paul—which divide history into a before and an after. Origen does not work, therefore, only on words (flesh and spirit), but he is inspired by the Pauline thought in which these terms are not only anthropological but in which they evoke the impact that the history of salvation, the Incarnation and the gift of the Spirit have on man. It is the same with Galatians 5:16f. In verse 18, Paul in fact opposes the condition of man under the Spirit to that of this same man under the Law. As for the third evocation, it is a little different, Paul speaks there of his conduct, because some accuse him of acting according to the flesh, that is, of allowing himself to be guided by motives that are too human. (Jean-Michel Poffet, O.P., "Le Méthode exégétique d'Héracléon et d'Origène, commentateurs de Jean 4", *Jésus, la Samaritaine et les Samaritains* [Fribourg, Switzerland: Éditions Universitaires, 1985], 191.)

III. From Origen to Augustine

A few examples should be enough to show the continuity of this tripartite anthropology across the patristic age.

Cyril of Jerusalem addresses to the newly baptized the same wish that Paul did to the Thessalonians.[1] Gregory of Nyssa, in his treatise on the *Creation of Man*, practices a certain eclecticism. Following the

[43] Cf. Henri de Lubac, *Aspects du Bouddhisme*, 2, Amida (Seuil, 1955), 290–91. See also the curious symbolic text expressing the trichotomy in Origen, *In Joannem*, X, 11, 13, 19, 23: Capernaum = matter; Jerusalem = natural place; Temple = place of the spiritual.

[1] *Cinquième catéchèse mystagogique*, n. 23, in fine (*Sources chrétiennes* 126:174–75).

perspective that is naturally his own, since he compares the nature of man to that of the beings that surround him, and particularly of other living beings, he begins by distinguishing a threefold activity: merely vital (that of plants), sentient (that of beasts), rational: these are like three souls, or three substances, all three of which are found in man alone. The vocabulary is that of the philosophical κοινή of that period: the higher life of man is λογική, it is directed by the νοῦς, his nature is a νοερά φύσις. But this can also be understood, says Gregory, according to the words that the Apostle addressed to the Ephesians (*sic*). First of all, through a bold concordism, he places the body in an equivalence with the nutritive life, the soul with the sensate life, the spirit (πνεῦμα) with the intellectual life (νοερόν); then without further hesitation, and without seeming to perceive that he is changing the perspective, he finds once again the true Pauline thought, or at least comes close to it, by distinguishing life according to the flesh (σαρκική) from life according to the spirit (πνευματική), and by showing the soul in an intermediary situation, having to choose between vice and virtue.[2] Farther on, he will explain that only the soul endowed with reason, such as it is in man, fully merits this name of soul, in such a way that he would have rejected, it seems, any attempt at concordism between the νοῦς and the πνεῦμα.[3]

It is not Hellenism but, indeed, the Bible, that inspires the trichotomy of the Syrian tradition, such as we see it in this hymn of Saint Ephraim of Nisibis:

> For the soul is still more precious
> than the body.
> And the spirit is still more precious
> than the soul,
> And the Divinity
> more hidden than the spirit.
> The body will be clothed with the beauty of the soul
> when the end arrives.

[2] *De hominis opificio*, c. 8 (PG 44, 144–49); "We learn the same thing from the Apostle. . . ." And Gregory then returns to his first point of view, considering rational nature (λογική) superior to sensate nature and to simply vital nature, but including both in man.

[3] Ibid., c. 15 (PG 44, 176–77). The words here are: νοερὰ φύσις, λόγος, λογικός, διάνοια, νοῦς.

The soul will put on
  the beauty of the spirit.
The spirit will put on
  in its very image, the (divine) Majesty.
The body, on equal footing with the soul,
  will see itself elevated;
The soul, on equal footing with the spirit;
The spirit, at the height
  where the Majesty is. . . .[4]

In another, later Syrian text, the awkwardness of an attempt at harmonization between the three elements of man and the three Persons of the divine Trinity will be noted. Jacques d'Édesse (d. 708) writes in his *Explanation of the Mass*: "Sacred things are holy! The soul, the body and the reason are sanctified by three sacred things: by water, blood and spirit; and besides by the Father, the Son and the Spirit, and truly man does resemble God in virtue of this trinity of composition: the soul corresponds to the Father, the body to the corporeality of the Son, and the reason to the Holy Spirit. Thereby, man thus resembles God."[5] One can nevertheless wonder if the word translated by "reason" is not here the equivalent of *nous*, rather than of *pneuma*, and if the soul is not merely the sensate soul. The same doubt can be expressed with respect to a passage from the *Testament in Galilee of Our Lord Jesus Christ*, of which we have the text in Ethiopian: "Should the body be judged with the soul and the spirit? Will the body of every man be revived with his living soul and his spirit?"[6] We will find a similar hesitation in examining the Latin tradition, and perhaps one must say, in certain cases at least, it cannot be resolved.

Saint Ambrose writes, on the one hand: "Homo ex anima rationali constat et corpore",[7] but also, on the other hand: "Primum unusquisque homo est corporalis, secundo animalis, tertio spiritualis", and the parallel he institutes between these three elements and the three heavens to which Saint Paul alludes in the Second Letter to the

[4] *Hymnes sur le Paradis*, Hymn 9, strophes 20 and 21. *Sources chrétiennes* 137 (1968): 129.

[5] Cf. the German translation of the Syriac by Baumstark, in *Oriens christianus* (1905), 126.

[6] Edition and French translation by L. Guerrier, *Patrologie orientale*, vol. 9 (1913), 206 and 207 (nos. 33 and 35). The editor considers that the Ethiopian term translated by "spirit" means the *pneuma* (157).

[7] *De incarnationis dominicae sacramento*, c. 2, n. 11 (CSEL, 79; Faller, 8:229).

Corinthians does not enlighten us much about the meaning of this trichotomy.[8] Ambrose is not alone, in any case, in acknowledging it. We read in Gregory of Elvira: "Manifestum est enim tribus perfectum constare semimortalem hominem; id est, corpore et anima et spiritu."[9] And Augustine expresses himself in a similar way on several occasions.[10]

In reality, Augustine's vocabulary is rather evasive. The term *mens*, as we know, holds a privileged place in his work. In *De Trinitate*, he develops a distinction destined subsequently to become more rigid: that between *ratio inferior* and *ratio superior*. In commenting on Psalm 3, verse 4, "*et exaltans caput meum*", he explains that this "*caput animae*" is the "*spiritus*", or the "*mens*", and so on.[11] Certain texts, which have the appearance of explicit definitions, speak of two single elements as constitutive of man: "Homo enim constat ex corpore et spiritu."[12] "Nihil est in homine, quod ad ejus substantiam pertineat atque naturam, praeter corpus et animam; totus homo, hoc est, spiritus et caro."[13] Yet Augustine does not consider the two words *anima* and *spiritus* to be simply synonyms, although for brevity's sake he includes in only one of the two the complex meaning of both: "Nomen animae spiritus est, ab eo, quod spiritalis est; animae nomen est ab eo, quod corpus animet, hoc est vivificet."[14] From which we have a certain number of explicitly trichotomic texts, which are of great importance for a correct understanding of Augustinian anthropology, for it is on this trichotomy that Augustine bases his doctrine of the *memoria*,[15] and he gives it as essential to the Catholic Faith: "Si quis tenuerit catholicam fidem, ut totum hominem credat a Verbo Dei esse susceptum, id est, corpus, animam, spiritum. . . ."[16]

In the same *De fide et symbolo*, Augustine explains himself at somewhat greater length: "Et quoniam tria sunt quibus homo constat: spir-

[8] *De Paradiso*, c. 11, n. 53 (PL 14, 200 C).

[9] *Tractatus* 1 (Batiffol-Wilmart, 3).

[10] One will thus not say with François Bonifas, 1:314: "The Latin Fathers reject, in general, this distinction between the soul and the spirit."

[11] *In Psalm*. 3, n. 3 and 10. A number of indications will be found in William A. Schumacher, *Spiritus and Spiritualitas: A Study in the Sermons of Saint Augustine* (Mundelein, 1957).

[12] *Sermo* 128, n. 9 (PL 38, 717).

[13] *Sermo* 150, n. 5 (PL 37, 1887).

[14] *De natura et origine animae*, IV, 23, 37; CSEL 60, 417.

[15] See *Confessions*, bk. X, chap. X.

[16] *De Fide et symbolo*, c. 4, n. 8; PL 40, 193–94. B. Aug., 9, p. 36.

itus, anima et corpus, —quae rursus duo sunt, quia saepe anima simul cum spiritu nominatur; pars enim quaedam ejusdem rationalis, qua carent bestiae, spiritus dicitur, —principale nostrum spiritus est; deinde vita qua conjungimur corpori, anima dicitur; postremo ipsum corpus, quoniam visibile est, ultimum nostrum est. . . . Anima vero, cum carnalia bona appetit caro nominatur . . .";[17] we also quote several similar texts: "Ut totus homo sit spiritus et anima et corpus; sed aliquando duo ista simul nomine animae nuncupari. . . ."[18] "Propter spiritum et animam et corpus. . . ."[19] "Ad creaturae integritatem, id est, spiritum et animam et corpus: et illud quo intelligimus, et illud quo vivimus, et illud quo visibiles et contrectabiles sumus."[20]

In *De fide et symbolo*, at the same time as he distinguishes *anima* from *spiritus*, Augustine identifies *spiritus* and *mens*.[21] Likewise, too, he distinguishes the "*pars rationalis*" of the soul (which is thus no longer only the animator of the body as in animals) from the "*pars quae excellit, id est, ipsa mens*".[22] It is practically the last distinction expressed in *De Trinitate* by the seemingly equivalent words *ratio inferior* and *ratio superior*.[23]

In brief, the anthropological analyses of Saint Augustine are varied. H. I. Marrou has set up a table, which does not intend to be exhaustive,[24] and it must be noted besides that under the same word, under the same verbal distinction, it happens that Augustine places different realities. On the whole, less dependent on a literal interpretation of Scripture, and more particularly of Saint Paul, than Origen wished to be,[25] more inclined to express himself in a vocabulary borrowed in part from Neoplatonism, Augustine places under the word *spiritus* a reality that sometimes more closely resembles the *nous* . . . of Greek

---

[17] C. 10, n. 23; PL 40, 193–94. B. Aug., 9, p. 68. A rather embarrassed note by Rivière, p. 66: "A trichotomy that is rather verbal than real, no doubt in view of respecting the language of Scripture, which distinguishes sometimes between the soul and the spirit but which does not go so far as to separate them, since one and the same name 'often' covers them."

[18] *De natura et origine animae*, II, 2, 2. CSEL 60, 336–37.

[19] *De diversis quaestionibus* 83, q. 67, n. 5.

[20] *In Jo.*, 52, 11. CCL, 36, 450; PL 35, 1773.

[21] C. 4, n. 8: "rationali spiritu, quae mens etiam nominatur".

[22] *Quaest. div.* 83, q. 46.

[23] L. 12, 3, 3. *Contra Felicem Manichaeum*, c. 36. Cf. Jolivet, B. Aug., 17, pp. 786–87.

[24] "Le Dogme de la résurrection des corps et la théologie des valeurs humaines, selon l'enseignement de saint Augustin", *Revue des études augustiniennes* 12 (1966): 121.

[25] Despite the great influence of Paul, which he recognizes: *Confessions*, l. 7, 21.

philosophy than the *pneuma* of the sacred text. Yet, through the duality he recognizes within this *spiritus* (or this *ratio*, or this *mens*), he remains a faithful witness of the Christian tradition.

3. From Saint Augustine to Our Day

I. Medieval Spiritual Masters

In Augustine as in Origen (and as in the whole patristic tradition), the notions are fluid; the historian must strive to grasp the movement of their thought rather than to classify their concepts. Augustinian explanations, moreover, do not correspond point by point with Origenian analyses. The Christian spiritual masters of the Middle Ages will rather often be in this regard closer to Origen than to Augustine. In order not to interpret them in a simplistic way, it is necessary constantly to bring analogy into play. Perhaps even the undertaking to reunite them in a kind of continuous chain, extending to our time, is a little too reminiscent of concordism. Let us say, finally, that *spiritus* is not only designated or understood in various ways: with some, it splits, so that one has to deal rather with a quadripartite anthropology; one of the causes for this is the desire to make a place for the Platonian tradition of the intelligence, a tradition that is amalgamated somehow or other to the Pauline tradition. It is having made these remarks that we gather together the examples that follow.

For John Scotus, man is composed of three elements, but the third element, called in turn *animus*, *intellectus* or *mens*, resembles the νοῦς more than the πνεῦμα. We read in book 5 of *De divisione naturae*: "Totam humanam naturam, corpus videlicet et animam et intellectum" (PL 122, 910–11). But another text, in book 2, chapter 5, expresses a conception closer to the biblical conception: "Aciem mentis, qua illum [Deum] intelligimus et in qua maxime imago creatoris condita est" (PL 122, 531 c).[1]

The traditional trichotomy dominates the structure of Bernard's *Brevis Commentatio* on the Song of Songs (n. 1). In William of Saint Thierry, the third term, the "spirit", splits: either in order to grant a certain place

[1] Arno de Reichersberg, *Apologeticus*, specifies: "Anima, quae est potior pars hominis", ed. Wéribert, 57 and 63.

to the *nous*, to the *intellectus*, to rational understanding, or rather in order to detail the principal stages of the spiritual life. The *Letter to the Brethren at Mont Dieu*, that important text, distinguishes a *triplex status, animalis—rationalis—spiritualis*, which is to say, "those beginning", "those on the way" and "the perfect". The opposition between the flesh and the spirit is not denied, William will be able to remind those who, having begun to taste the sweetness of contemplation, might be tempted to neglect the permanent necessity of spiritual combat.[2] But rather than this dialectical opposition, the object of the *Letter* is to set forth a pedagogical ladder, which is, moreover, nonetheless Pauline in its inspiration. The beginners are still guided by an *animalis sensus* (this is the natural man of Saint Paul, which is not the carnal man); those on the way acquire a *rationalis scientia* (we observe here the care to integrate into the formation of the monk the whole cycle of human knowledge); and the perfect enjoy *spiritualis sapientia.*[3] In addition, these are not three, airtight categories or perfectly distinct and successive stages: just as there is passage from one to the other, there is immanence from one to the other. William remains faithful to the same schema in *Miroir de la foi,*[4] as well as in his commentaries on the Song of Songs: "tres status esse orantium vel orationum: animalem, rationalem, spiritualem".[5] In *De contemplando Deo*, a subdivision intervenes, between the *ratio*, the discursive faculty, and the *intellectus*, which does not seem to be at this point the equivalent of the *spiritus* (l. 4).

Isaac of Stella speaks in nearly the same way, in a language, however, that has more of an intellectualist ring to it, in distinguishing the understanding from the reason, which abstracts the forms of the sensate, *vis animae qua immediate supponitur Deo.*[6] We have the feeling that this second-generation Cistercian was familiar with Scholasticism.

---

[2] *Expositio altera in Cant.*: "Ideo, post manifestatam puritatis vitam, post apertam januam contemplativae libertatis, subjungit et dicit: 'Equitatui meo in curribus Pharaonis assimilavi te, o anima mea.' Etsi sis amica, et quantumvis amica, tamen scias adhuc et equitandum tibi et currendum esse, laborandumque ac pugnandum. . . ."

[3] L. 1, c. 5 and 12; PL 184, 315 CD, 330 C. *Epist.* 352; PL 183, 352–53. The stress placed on the pedagogical point of view comes from (among others) Origen, whom William had read at Signy.

[4] *Aenigma fidei*; PL 180, 404–5.

[5] *In Cantica*, n. 11; M. M. Davy, 40. Cf. Louis Bouyer, *La Spiritualité de Citeaux* (1955), 120–24.

[6] *Epistola de anima*; PL 1480 AB, 1884 A, 1888 B. Cf. 1885 2: "Rationem vero superat intellectus, ordine et virtute, sicut aerem firmamentum."

Hugh of Saint Victor is closer than Isaac to Bernard and William of Saint Thierry. According to him, the eye of the *flesh* (which is to say, here, the body) sees the world and what it contains; the eye of the *reason* sees the soul and what it contains; but the eye of *contemplation* penetrates to the innermost depths of man and above man. This eye of contemplation belongs to those who possess the spirit of God.[7] In Achard of Saint-Victor, the order of the last two elements, or of the last two stages, seems reversed; he treats *de discretione animae, spiritus et mentis*, *mens* was, as another author of the twelfth century says, *quasi quoddam divinitatis insigne.*[8] (But this is hardly a question of vocabulary alone.)

Whatever might be the distinctions and subdistinctions, orientations, inflections and differences in vocabulary, it can be said of all these spiritual masters of the Middle Ages, as well as of many of those who will follow, that they took up the essential chorus of the Pauline and patristic trichotomy and that most even attribute extreme importance to it, as Sandaeus, a seventeenth-century authority, was to remark:

> Magni aestimant Mystici nonnulli, et putant maxime necessariam ad suam Theologiam ac perfectionem, divisionem inter spiritum et animam.[9]

This is also true of Bonaventure: "Habet enim anima tres potentias: animalem, intellectualem, divinam, secundum triplicem oculum, carnis, rationis, contemplationis".[10] We recognize the schema of William of Saint Thierry and Hugh of Saint Victor.[11] For Thomas Gallus, closer in this regard to Isaac of Stella, "reason feels, the intelligence sees."[12] Johannes Tauler, in several of his sermons, teaches that "man is, so to speak, composed of three men" and that one must distinguish in him first of all an "external man" or "animal man", then a "reasonable man", finally a "higher man, wholly inner and hidden", that "noble

[7] *In Hier.* (PL 175, 976 AB). Cf. René Roques, *Connaissance de Dieu et théologie symbolique d'après l'In Hierarchiam caelestem Dyonisii de Hugues de Saint-Victor* (Recherches de philosophie 3–4, "De la connaissance de Dieu", 219).

[8] Cf. Jean Châtillon, *Théologie, spiritualité et métaphysique dans l'oeuvre oratoire d'Achard de Saint-Victor* (Vrin, 1969), 129–35.

[9] Page 332.

[10] *In Hexaëmeron*, collatio 5, n. 24 (Opera, Quaracchi, 5:358 a). "Primus viget, secundus caligat, tertius excaecatus est."

[11] For Saint Thomas Aquinas, see below, the chapter on the Catholic Synthesis.

[12] Quoted by Robert Javelet, *Intelligence et amour chez les auteurs du XIIe siècle*, RAM, 37 (1961), 280.

and deiform" man, "made in the image of God".[13] The mystical theology of Harphius (Henry Herp) also says that "the soul is, according to Scripture, divided into three parts . . .",[14] and the appeal to Scripture, despite the appearance, is justified. For our authors, in fact, the adding of a supplementary term to the Pauline enumeration does not derive from the fact that they would abandon Paul in favor of Plato, but from the fact that they are concerned besides about a theory of knowledge, which Paul did not at all have in view in his address to the Thessalonians. Yet *La Perle évangélique* leads us to a tripartite schema, the body being understood, as in Paul; but at base, the difference from the medieval authors we have just enumerated is hardly perceptible:

> Each man seems almost to represent three men: according to the body, he is bestial; according to the soul, he is reasonable and intellectual; and according to the spirit, or the naked essence of the soul where God dwells, he is deiform. . . .[15]
>
> This very noble portion of the soul . . . , some call *mens*, insofar as it continually breathes after God and is, as it were, a largely deiform or divine thing and the image of God in man. It is something divine in being, as it were, flooded with God and united to him. It is also called the point and the summit of the spirit, because God, without intermission, shines in the latter like a mirror. It is also, according to what the good Father Ruysbroek says, the highest part of the soul. . . . It is also called the sparkle of the soul, because it is in God what the sparkle is in fire. . . .
>
> In the first [unity or union], we are superessential and deiform, and in the second, spiritual and internal, and in the third, active and moral. . . .[16]

The foregoing is the text of a compiler, from which one must not ask too great a coherence in terminology or too great a unity in point of view. If we now appeal to a theologian who was the adversary of the

[13] *Sermons*, Hugueny trans., 3:51, 87, 130–31.

[14] Cf. Louis Cognet, *Introduction aux mystiques rhéno-flamands*, 298–300.

[15] As we see, the "soul" is in a way divided: it is once again the classic distinction between the *ratio* and the *intellectus*.

[16] Quoted by L. Cognet, *Introduction* 317–32. The first edition of *La Perle* is from 1535; the Latin translation is from 1545; the French translation from 1608, by Dom Beaucousin. Cf. J. P. Van Schoote, S.J., *La Perle évangélique*; RAM, 37 (1961), 297–99. Other texts in Louis Cognet, *Histoire de la spiritualité moderne* (Aubier), 43 and 46: "Even God is the life of the spirit, and the spirit the life of the soul, and God is always in the spirit, which is the image of God in the soul" (l. 1, chap. 14). According to the body, man is bestial; according to the soul it is reasonable and intellectual; according to the spirit, or the pure essence of the soul where God dwells, it is deiform (l. 1, chap. 5).

mystical school represented by Tauler, Harphius and *La Perle évangélique*, and who refers to more reliable authors, such as Augustine, "Bernard" and Hugh, he will give us the same essential distinctions:

> Tres cognoscendi modi sunt, quorum unus animalis dicitur, utens maxime oculo carnis; alius rationalis, utens plus oculo rationis; tertius spiritualis, utens oculo contemplationis, sicut distinxerunt divini homines tres oculos et tres vivendi modos.[17]

Louis de Blois, finally, in the *Institution spirituelle*, perseveres in bringing out this "depth of the soul" that, under different names, always corresponds to the "Pauline *pneuma*" and that will not find a place in the late Scholastic anthropologies or in most modern anthropologies:

> God who, to tell the truth, is everywhere, dwells in the spirit of man and in the simple depth or inner sanctuary of the soul in a particular manner. He dwells there in his own image and never absents himself.[18]
>
> This depth, naked and stripped of any image, is raised above all creatures . . . , it transcends time and place, and through a kind of perpetual adhesion, remains united to God in his principle. It is, however, in us by essence, for the abyss and depth of the soul are essence. . . .
>
> The soul . . . possesses a certain supernatural unity of spirit, in which it dwells as in its own habitation, and it is carried away into the divine essence even to this supreme unity in which the Father, Son and Holy Spirit are in the simplicity of the divine essence itself. . . .[19]

Assuredly, these speculations about the divine essence—even if they maintain a trinitarian affirmation—and about the essence of man presuppose a long evolution of thought that, in one sense, distances us greatly from Saint Paul. But, across languages, theories and, as one never stops saying today, cultural contexts that differ greatly, to be sure, it is possible to discern a fundamental continuity.

This continuity will not be broken by the period called the Renaissance.

---

[17] References to Augustine, *De vera religione*, 3, 3 and 26, 69; "Bernard", *Epistola ad Fratres de Monte Dei*.

[18] *L'Instruction spirituelle*, chap. 3.

[19] Ibid., chap. 12. Texts in Cognet, 50, 51, 52.

II. *Saint Thomas Aquinas in Tradition*[1]

I

In the spiritual history of mankind, the three domains constituted by what one can designate under the three denominations of religion, morality and mysticism are often presented as independent or even opposed to each other. The alliance or the mutual penetration between mysticism and morality does not appear achieved in and of itself any more than that between morality and religion. Yet one could not conclude that such an alliance, or such a mutual penetration, is an artificial and wholly contingent phenomenon. In opposition to an empiricism that disintegrates everything without explaining anything, we will say, rather, that it responds, if not to the demands, at least to the profound wish of nature. But nature itself has taken time in finding itself.

In fact, we note that it has not fully found itself outside the Christian revelation. The union of the three aforementioned elements, religion,[2] morality and mysticism, does not reach its fullness, it does not become harmonious and indissoluble in principle, except in the tradition coming from the Gospel. There, and most specifically in the Catholic form of this tradition, it does not appear as a secondary fact, obtained by convergence subsequent to various gropings, but as an original and essential fact. Religion, morality and mysticism manifest themselves there "in a reciprocal envelopment". Between these three, both an attraction and a tension exist that could be the source of many vital problems, but there is objectively neither separation, exclusion nor conflict: for "the Deity, while transcending being, the true and the good, contains them formally."[3]

This is why, in particular, in the Catholic tradition—lived and re-

---

[1] This study appeared in the *Bulletin de littérature ecclésiastique* (Toulouse, 1975), 81–90. We reproduce it just as it is, with the introduction and conclusion that sum up the unpublished chapters published here.

[2] Faith is obviously included in "religion", when it is a question of Christianity. From the historical point of view, which is ours here, we have not had to consider a dissociation that is not observed anywhere, up to a recent period, in the Christian tradition. Likewise, we speak of "morality", and not of "ethics", a word that seems today to be favored by many, because it is the word "morality" that predominates in the texts.

[3] Joseph de Finance, *Existence et liberté* (1955), 352.

flected—"reasonable" life and "spiritual" life, or life "according to the spirit", penetrate each other without being identified with each other,[4] and *morality penetrates the mystical life to the end.* Pseudo-Gnosticism relegated the rewarding of good and punishing of evil, those pillars of the "Demiurge", to the lower level of "exoteric" faith; the great tradition, on the contrary, maintains this moral aspect "at the heart of the revelation of the Father through the unique Son".[5] "It is not", says Saint Justin, for example, "because of his [natural] affinity with God or because he is spirit like him that man sees God: it is because he is virtuous and just."[6] In his *Psychologie des mystiques*, Joseph Maréchal noted this essential characteristic: Mystical ascent, he explains, does not erase "any specific trait of the common Christian life".[7] In other words, the Christian virtues, proposed for the practice of all, are not simply means of freeing oneself; their exercise is not simply something transitory: in their substance, they are already something of the end itself. This is what Saint Ambrose was able to explain wonderfully in a brief sentence in his commentary on Saint Luke, with respect to the Beatitudes: "Sicut enim spei nostrae octava perfectio est, ita octava summa virtutum est."[8] And this is what Saint Augustine repeated in similar terms, speaking of adhesion to God, the blessed life and eternal wisdom: "Una ibi virtus erit, et idipsum erit virtus praemiumque virtutis."[9]

In a remarkable thesis, Pierre Nemeshegyi has posed the same problem with respect to Origen: "To place Being and moral Goodness in equation; to place this moral Goodness in God formally, and as characterizing the final ground of his Being—is this not to be condemned to enclosing all spiritual life in an anti-mystical moralism? The Good is a transcendental. But is it, formally, what we understand by "moral Good"? Or is there not a deepening of this moral Goodness, which would reestablish the possibility of an innermost mystical depth?" And Nemeshegyi concludes: "In fact, in Origen's conception, moralism and

---

[4] William of Saint Thierry, *Lettre aux Frères du Mont-Dieu*, l. 1, c. 5: "Perfectio vero hominis rationalis, initium est hominis spiritualis" (PL 184, 316 B).

[5] H. Cornélis and A. Léonard, *La Gnose éternelle* (1959), 74.

[6] *Dialogue avec Tryphon*.

[7] *Pschologie des Mystiques*, 1 (1924), 15.

[8] *In Lucam*, l. 5, n. 49 (ed. G. Tissot, *Sources chrétiennes*, 45:201).

[9] *Epist.* 155, c. 3, n. 12 (PL 33, 671).

mysticism are one and the same thing."[10] Saint Gregory the Great, often so close to Origen, will unite good sense to spiritual fervor in order to remind contemplatives that if they want to be faithful to the Gospels and to advance on the true way, they must take care to scorn the humble precepts of morality and to seek to understand them in a more sublime sense.[11]

The medieval spiritual masters will take up again these thoughts of Origen, Ambrose, Augustine and Gregory. Expressing ourselves in the customary categories of their exegesis, which the Middle Ages systematized, we will say that for them "anagogy" achieves the final perfection both of "allegory" and of "tropology" (of dogma and of morality).[12] Of all authentically Catholic mysticism, one could declare what one historian said of Saint Bernard, by allusion to the traditional interpretation of the "Books of Solomon": for each of them as for him, "the moral school of Ecclesiasticus and Proverbs, the necessary preliminary for the mystical school of the *Song of Songs*, is a school whose doors are never closed behind us."[13]

This "spiritual" equilibrium has at times seemed threatened, in one direction or another. Some spiritual scholars have seemed to want to transcend purely and simply the sphere of morality and reason. This is what causes Evagrius, not without reason, to be judged severely at times; it is what Ruysbroek reproaches in the false mystics of his time; it is one of the points that the bull *In agro* of John XXII criticizes in Meister Eckhart. Whatever may have been true in each of these cases, the thing that interests us here is the norm that inspired such criticisms. While following Saint Paul in distinguishing the "soul" from the "spirit" (not, moreover, as two substances nor even as two "faculties"), one always refuses to separate them, as if the penetration into the higher zone of the "spirit" must make us reject as no longer valid the operations of the inferior zone of the "soul". But the hierarchical distinction is maintained, which is to say that the mystical life is not for all that reduced to the plane of simple morality. A text from Saint Teresa is very enlightening here: the saint observes that the "center of

---

[10] *La Paternité de Dieu chez Origène* (1956). Cf. W. Völker, *Das Volkommenheitsideal des Origenes* (1931), 100.

[11] *In Ezechielem*, l. 1, homily 10, n. 1 (PL 76, 886 C).

[12] Cf. Henri de Lubac, *Exégèse médiévale*, 2:632.

[13] Rev. Watkin Williams, *L'Aspect éthique du mysticisme de saint Bernard dans Saint Bernard et son temps*, 2 (1929), 312.

the soul'', or the "spirit of the soul'', is a "difficult thing to express, and even to believe'':

> Certain interior effects give the certitude that there is, in certain respects, a very real difference between the soul and the spirit. Although in reality they are but one, we sometimes perceive a division between them that is so delicate that it seems the one functions in one way, and the other in another. . . . There are so many things in our innermost depths, and things so subtle, that it would be boldness on my part to undertake to explain them. We will understand all that in the other life, if God . . . deigns to admit us to the dwelling where we will have understanding of all these secrets.[14]

Yet the equilibrium can be upset in the opposite direction from that for which Evagrius and Meister Eckhart were reproached. This has been true periodically for anti-mystical scholars or simply anti-mystics, against whom, periodically, too, protests are raised. With them, it is not the "soul'' that is forgotten or scorned, in the name of the superior "spirit''; it is the "spirit'' that is ignored, misunderstood, in the name of a truncated moral wisdom. But with any of the great scholars of the Catholic tradition, we do not have to register any such misunderstanding. This is what we would wish to demonstrate here, with respect to Saint Thomas Aquinas, and more particularly with respect to the *Summa theologica*.

II

From first appearances, one might be brought to believe that Saint Thomas, in the *Summa*, is one of those scholars who upset the equilibrium in the second direction. But in reality he did nothing of the sort. His doctrine, in the *Summa theologica*, contains in fact the equivalent of what others have expressed through the distinction of soul and spirit, understood as the distinction of a moral region and a mystical region. If one does not observe this right at the beginning, it is because Saint Thomas expresses himself in different words.

It could be written that in his doctrine "all the problems that the spiritual life and its evolution pose return in this *consideratio moralis*, which has but one object: man in progress toward his blessed des-

[14] *The Interior Castle*, seventh mansion, chap. 1 in *Collected Works of St. Teresa of Avila*, 2 (Washington, D.C.: Institute of Carmelite Studies, 1980), 432.

tiny."[15] The thing is incontestable. Still, it might be useful to specify how. No more in Saint Thomas than in others is the union of the two moral and spiritual (or "mystical") elements a confusion or a reduction pure and simple from the mystical to the moral. The synthesis is not a unification in the exclusive favor of one of the two. Of course, one could judge that the Thomist anthropology, by its Aristotelian roots, favors the originality of the mystical life less than others. And like the virtue of "religion", the theological virtues seem at first glance mixed in a long list of "virtues" within the second part of the *Summa*. It is appropriate, nevertheless, to remark, before seeing things at closer range, that only a later usage gives this second part the name "moral". After having, in the first part, considered God as the universal cause, Saint Thomas considers him now as end; after the divine model, he clings to his image; after the departure of God from all things, he envisages the return of all things to God. Now—this is the important point for our subject—this itinerary of return comprises several stages.

It is true that the prologue to the *Secunda secundae* speaks of *scientia moralis*, of *materia moralis*, and that all seems, right at first, to be reduced to the *consideratio virtutum*. But let us look a little closer. In this same prologue, as in the articles that follow, Saint Thomas nonetheless distinguishes, from the *virtutes morales* not only the *virtutes theologicae* but also the *virtutes intellectuales*, which are, along with prudence, wisdom, understanding and knowledge, closely connected to the gifts of the Holy Spirit of the same name. Moreover, after having exhausted the plan he had outlined for "omitting nothing of moral things" by studying successively the virtues and the vices that are opposed to them, he considers, in a kind of extension, a series of new questions, related first of all to "prophecy", to "rapture" and other gratuitous gifts, then to the "contemplative life"; a series he attaches, a little artificially, one must admit, to the section on the different states of life.

This artifice has sometimes embarrassed commentators, who do not always understand the articulations that the plan of the *Summa* comprises here. Thus we have Father M. D. Chenu, who has the "treatise on the states of life" begin at question 183, starting from where "the spiritual life is linked to social functions".[16] The thing seems in fact

[15] *Initiation théologique*, 3 (1952), 1224.

[16] *Introduction à l'étude de saint Thomas d'Aquin* (Paris, 1950), 276.

rather logical. Yet, Saint Thomas himself said, in his little introduction to question 171, "*De prophetia*":

> Postquam dictum est de singulis virtutibus et vitiis, quae pertinent ad omnium hominum conditiones et status, nunc considerandum est de his quae specialiter ad aliquos homines pertinent.

So Father Antoine Lemonnyer had adopted a different solution from that of Father Chenu. He saw in questions 171 to 198, concerning the gratuitous gifts, a kind of parenthesis and made the final treatise of the *Secunda secundae* begin from question 179, which is to say, from the "contemplative life": he gave a certain unity to this final treatise thanks to this single yet twofold title: "Human Life, Its Forms and Its States".[17]

The divisions adopted respectively by Father Chenu and Father Lemonnyer both have their probability, and both can be supported. In fact, however, as Father Chenu remarked, Saint Thomas treats the states of life properly only beginning with question 183, entitled: "De officiis et statibus hominum in generali". But already before that, questions 171 to 182 form a whole, very distinct from the preceding questions, in which we have the equivalent of a little treatise on mysticism.

Even if he did not treat explicitly at that time the relations between active life and contemplative life,[18] the place accorded by Saint Thomas to this latter in his general plan would thus authorize us to distinguish it from the domain of morality. He himself, besides, tells us so in proper terms: "The moral virtues are not a constitutive element of the contemplative life";[19] in fact, "they are ordained to action."[20] Now, action is inferior to contemplation. The latter is "*simpliciter melior*".[21] Action

[17] *Saint Thomas*, edition of the Revue des Jeunes.

[18] On these relations between the two "lives", a certain ambiguity always remains in the thought of Saint Thomas, from the fact that, like many other witnesses of the Christian tradition, he considers action and contemplation, both together or side by side, as what we call morality and mysticism, and as two "states" or two different "professions" or two kinds of activity, so to speak, to which one cannot give oneself at the same time (one cannot sing the office in choir and preach or fulfill other duties of charity at the same time). Cf. q. 182, a. 3: "Sic manifestum est quod vita activa impedit contemplativam, inquantum impossibile est quod aliquis simul occupetur circa exteriores actiones et divinae contemplationi vacet."

[19] *Secunda secundae*, q. 180, a. 2: "Essentialiter quidem virtutes morales non pertinent ad vitam contemplativam."

[20] Q. 181, a. 1: "ordinantur ad operandum".

[21] Q. 182, a. 4: "Secundum suam naturam . . . vita contemplativa est prior quam activa, inquantum prioribus et melioribus insistit . . ."; q. 1: "simpliciter melior est quam activa".

prepares for contemplation by winning the soul, through the external exercise of the virtues, the necessary "preliminary dispositions", by disciplining the passions and by submitting them to the reason.[22] Contemplation is the act of the "higher reason", which is to the inferior reason, following an old biblical and Philonic symbolism revived and slightly transformed,[23] as the man is to the woman.[24] It is ordained to "perfect love", and, as Saint Gregory taught, while the active life is synonymous with service, the contemplative life is synonymous with freedom.[25] As Aristotle had already affirmed—but we know with what freedom Saint Thomas changed and transformed the thought of the philosopher even while he invoked him as an authority[26]—it is a life above the human condition[27] and is made to last always.[28]

No more than any other of the great witnesses of the Christian tradition did Saint Thomas reduce the spiritual life to the exercise of morality or spiritual understanding to rationality. Father Pierre Rousselot, too neglected today (at least in France), demonstrated this well by placing in evidence the distinction between *intellectus* and *ratio*, a fundamental distinction with numerous consequences.[29] —But neither does he separate them: on the one hand, as an authentic heir of the Fathers, he integrates the virtuous life into eternal life, by saying: "Uniuscujusque perfectio, nihil aliud est quam participatio divinae similitudinis."[30] And, on the other hand, he knows that, in the earthly condi-

[22] Q. 180, a. 2: "Dispositive autem virtutes morales pertinent ad vitam contemplativam . . ."; q. 182, a. 3: "quantum ad hoc quod interiores animae passiones componit et ordinat . . . vita activa adjuvat ad contemplationem." Q. 182, a. 4, ad 2 m.

[23] Cf. M. D. Chenu, *Introduction à l'étude de saint Thomas d'Aquin* (1950), 134–35; cf. 159.

[24] Q. 182, a. 4: "Ratio enim superior, quae contemplationi deputatur, comparatur ad inferiorem, quae deputatur actioni, sicut vir ad mulierem, quae est per virum regenda, sicut Augustinus dicit, De Trinitate, 1, 12, c. 12." On this distinction in Saint Augustine: R. Jolivet, *Bibl. aug.*, 17:786–87; see also *Contra Felicem manichaeum*, c. 36, n. 41. And Saint Thomas, *De Veritate*, q. 15.

[25] Q. 180, a. 1 and 7. Q. 182, a. 1, ad 2 m: "Vita contemplativa in quadam animi libertate consistit. . . . Et hoc quod Gregorius dicit super Ezechielem" (Hom. 3), "quod activa vita servitus, contemplativa autem libertas vocatur."

[26] Cf. Henri de Lubac, *Le Mystère du surnaturel*, 193–96.

[27] Q. 180, a. 8, obj. 3. It will also be noted that the Nicomachean Ethics places the dianoetic virtues above the ethical virtues. Cf. q. 182, a. 1: "Vita contemplativa est secundum divina; vita autem activa est secundum humana."

[28] Q. 180, a. 8.

[29] *L'Intellectualisme de saint Thomas* (1908).

[30] *In Joannem*, c. 17, lectio 3, n. 1. Cf. *De Veritate*, q. 12.

tion, external action, which is first of all the virtuous life, must itself proceed from contemplation.

The comparison with the Plotinian philosophy, or with the "agnostics", can in this regard be very enlightening because of the apparent proximity of the doctrines:

> In a parallel way, one would find in Christianity [says Jean Trouillard on this subject] a going beyond ethics by the theological virtues and the gifts of the Holy Spirit. The Christian life consists in divinization, not in ascesis. Yet the role of the will seems much more considerable in Christians than in the Plotinians, not only in charity but also in faith, which is itself presented as a duty. Theologians do not ordinarily situate the theological virtues on the other side of the decisions of the faculties or on this side of the constituted values. This is what must not be forgotten when faced with the use of the Neoplatonic doctrine of virtues attempted by Christian authors, in particular by Saint Thomas (1a, 2ae, q. 61, a. 5).[31]

And again, Maurice de Gandillac:

> Plotinus . . . harshly criticizes the Gnostics who believe that by "raising oneself near to God on wings of a dream" (2, 9, 9), one escapes the human condition. According to the fragments of Heracles (Legrand, 315), Moses, the author of the Law, . . . belongs to the "natural" world. Superior to pure matter, however, he ignores the spirit. By proscribing, by judging, by punishing, he fulfills an inferior ministry, and the "perfect" are in no way subject to his commandments. Pure at the beginning, they are saved without exercise, as without repentance and without pardon. This presumption will be the common gospel for all the sectarians who . . . across the Middle Ages will preach a "going beyond the ethical".[32]

We should not let the differences in emphasis from one author to another or from one school to another hide from us, therefore, the consistent thought of the Christian tradition. Already, in someone like Origen, the union is achieved between "a resolutely contemplative religious ideal and a passionately active life".[33] For Saint Gregory the Great, to whom Thomas Aquinas refers, the whole spiritual life is subject to a rhythm, and "true perfection begins to mature only in the dif-

[31] Jean Trouillard, *La Purification plotinienne* (1955), 193. See also Plotinus: "There is ἀρετή virtue in the soul but not in the spirit or beyond" (I, 2, 3, 31; Trouillard, 138); and again: "Man does not seek to be exempt from fault but to be God" (I, 2, 6, 2; Trouillard, 189).

[32] Maurice de Gandillac, *La Sagesse de Plotin* (1952), 82–83.

[33] Henri Crouzel, in *Théologie de la vie monastique*, 18.

ficulties and obstacles of the active life".[34] Medieval monasticism did not scorn Martha in the name of Mary, it maintained that action must be joined to contemplation, or the "practice" to the "theory", a little like love of neighbor to the love of God.[35] The two inseparable aspects of the Christian doctrine on this subject will once again be expressed very well in the reflections of John Henry Newman, still an Anglican, preaching on "evangelical sanctity the completion of natural virtue". Newman in fact shows in this sermon that there is "an essential resemblance between the spiritual man and the virtuous man", following the words of Saint Paul: "The fruit of the Spirit is in all goodness and righteousness and truth"—while drawing the attention of his listeners to "the point of difference between them; viz. that the Christian graces are far superior in rank and dignity to the moral virtues".[36] Moral perfection and holiness, virtuous life and mystical life are distinct, they are hierarchical: but at the same time they are united in charity, *forma virtutum, vinculum perfectionis*.

III. Renaissance and Reformation

Nicholas of Cusa takes up the Pauline trichotomy again, in the same terms as the Apostle. He places it in correspondence with, on the one hand, a cosmic trichotomy and, on the other hand, what is perhaps unexpected, the three Persons of the Trinity. He uses Saint Augustine as his authority for both these correspondences.

We read in fact in one of his Sermons: "In homine sunt spiritus, anima et corpus, sicut in mundo elementalia, vitalia et intellectualia";[1] and in his opuscule the *Beryl*, he distinguishes "three modes of know-

[34] L. Weber, quoted by Robert Gillet, O.S.B., in *Théologie de la vie monastique*, 350. Cf. Saint Gregory, *In Ezechielem*, 2, hom. 7, n. 12 (PL 76, 1020). This is what can justify the title of *Moralia in Job* (if one takes *Moralia* in the modern sense), for a work that is as much mystical as moral. On Augustine and Gregory see Edward Cuthbert Butler, *Western Mysticism* (1926).

[35] Cf. Jacques Fontaine, in *Théologie de la vie monastique*, 363. Dom Jean Leclercq, *Études sur le vocabulaire monastique du Moyen Age* (1961), 110–15.

[36] Third University Sermon (March 6, 1831), no. 3. In a similar way, no longer considering man but God, Father Louis Bouyer evokes the biblical notion of the holiness of God, "which certainly does not reduce it to morality but which, on the contrary, raises the most demanding justice at the very heart of the 'sacred', to the point of making the two notions radically inseparable": *Du Protestantisme à l'Église* (1954).

[1] *Opera* (Basel, 1565), 472. *Excitationum*, l. 5.

ledge: the sensate, the intellectual and the intelligential", which, he says, correspond, according to Saint Augustine, to the three "heavens".[2] That was the cosmic analogy. And for the trinitarian analogy, set forth in the work *De Concordantia catholica*:

> Unde homo, secundum Augustinum Super symbolo (40, 193–94), ad instar Trinitatis imaginem gerens, ex spiritu et anima et corpore constitutus exsistit. Spiritus autem est superior, nobilior et altior intellectualis personae Patris figuram repraesentans, et corpus personam Filii, et anima quasi utriusque naturam participans, ab utroque procedens personam Spiritus sancti.[3]

Taking up his position, like Nicholas of Cusa, from the point of view of knowledge, Marsilio Ficino distinguishes the *sensus*, the *ratio* and the *intellectus*. We recognize in that the heritage of the great Scholasticism. In a similar manner, in the prologue of his *Heptaplus*, Giovanni Pico della Mirandola distinguishes the vital instinct, discursive and practical knowledge and the contemplative faculty.[4] More important is the twofold witness, here in agreement, of Erasmus and Luther.

In his famous *Enchiridion militis christiani*, Erasmus, who takes his inspiration directly from Saint Paul, "ends finally in a tripartite anthropology, which finds its completion in the gift of the Spirit".[5] After having, in chapters 4 and 5, spoken of man such as Plato describes him, first according to the *Timaeus*, then according to the *Phaedo*, *Phaedrus* and the *Republic*, and recalled his distinction of the soul as reasonable, irascible and concupiscible, Erasmus describes in chapter 6 the Pauline opposition between the flesh and the spirit; then he comes, in chap-

[2] *De Beryllo*, c. 5, cf. Augustine, *De Genesi ad litteram*, l. 1, c. 9. The correspondence is not obvious!

[3] *De concordantia catholica*, l. 1, c. 2; ed. G. Kallen (1964), 45–46. Nicholas goes on: "Et sic homo se secundum spiritum intellectivum subiciens et credens in Christum, quod ipse sit via, veritas et vita, de Ecclesia dicitur, licet nondum spiritus subjecerit sibi animam nec per animam corpus. Unde ad hoc, ut homo bene divinae Trinitati configuretur ad percipiendam illam vitalem concordantiam, oportet spiritum esse perfectum, sc., ut per fidem, spem et caritatem se jungat Spiritui divino tanquam vitae et veritati. Oportet animam esse perfectam, ut spiritui oboediat, cui saepe non natura, sed consuetudine peccandi resistit, et tunc animalis homo non percipit, quae sunt Spiritus Dei. Et sic, quando anima oboedit spiritui et spiritus Christo, non est desperandum corpus etiam naturae restitui propriae per resurrectionem, ut totus homo spiritualis Deo uniatur. . . ." Cf. ibid., 35: "Hoc generali ordine trinitatis gestant cuncta creata."

[4] Ed. Garin.

[5] F. Wendel, RH Ph. R. (1968), 82, considering E. W. Kobls, *Die Theologie des Erasmus* (1966).

ter 7, to the trichotomy of 1 Thessalonians, which he comments on with reference to Origen. "He does not hide", observes Charles Béné, "his pleasure in setting forth this theory: 'Libet et Origenicam hominis sectionem breviter referre.'" He sees it based as well on Isaiah (29:9) and on Daniel (3:86), so he adopts it in order to make it intervene "as a definitive stage after the analyses of pagan philosophers", to serve "as an introduction to the great rules of Christianity".[6] With Origen, he sees in the soul this "median part" of the human being, which can swing either to the side of the flesh or to the side of the spirit.[7] In the *Methodus* or *Ratio verae theologiae*, a similar text recalls our trichotomy indirectly: "Nec omnis affectus hominis est caro, sed est qui dicitur anima et qui dicitur spiritus, quo nitimur ad honesta."[8] But it is particularly in the controversy with Luther about free will that Erasmus opposes to the exclusivism of his adversary, hypnotized by the sole dialectic of the flesh and the spirit, the divine pedagogy explained by Origen according to the Pauline schema.

Luther himself, paradoxically, had provided a commentary in his own manner, with respect to the first words of the *Magnificat* (1520), on the text of 1 Thessalonians, and his manner did not differ perceptibly from so many of the others we have seen:

> "My soul glorifies the Lord". . . . Scripture divides man into three parts, when Paul says, at the end of 1 Thessalonians: "May God . . . make you holy through and through, in such a way that all your spirit and your soul and your body. . . ." And each of these parts—like the entire man—is equally divided in another way concerning, not nature, but quality. In other words, nature has three parts: spirit, soul and body, all three of which can be good or bad. . . . The first part, the spirit, is the highest, the most profound, the most noble part of man; it is what makes him capable of grasping imperceptible, invisible and eternal things. In brief, it is the house where faith and the word of God dwell. . . . The second part, the soul, is exactly the same spirit according to nature, but accomplishes a different function. It is the spirit insofar as it animates the body and acts

[6] Charles Béné, *Érasme et saint Augustin*, the influence of Saint Augustine on the humanism of Erasmus (Geneva: Droz, 1969), 140–41.

[7] Erasmus, *Enchiridion militis christiani*, Introduction and translation by A. J. Festugière (Vrin, 1971), 123–26.

[8] *Methodus*, ed. Holborne (Munich, 1933); cf. 150–62. On the *Ratio verae theologiae* (1518), cf. Georges Chantraine, *"Mystère" et "Philosophie du Christ" selon Érasme* (Namur-Gembloux, 1971).

> through it. . . . Its proper role consists in grasping . . . the things that reason can know and probe. . . .[9]

As for the third term, the body, its function is to "act" and to "put into practice the knowledge of the soul and the faith of the spirit". As Maurice de Gandillac observes, here, the body has nothing to do with "mire". And by adopting such a tripartition of the human being (which is not at all to be understood, we repeat, as a division of three "faculties"), Luther envisages the human subject, as Saint Paul and, after him, the whole of Christian tradition have done, "in a perspective that is more biblical than Greek".[10] The relative assimilation that he works between the soul and the spirit is the echo of a common Scholasticism and the fruit of an inflection toward the point of view of knowledge, which was not that of Saint Paul in his address to the Thessalonians but in no way contradicts it. Of these two characteristics, the preceding centuries have already brought us many an example.[11]

Like his predecessors, Luther thus maintains the threefold gradation, which he also develops through a traditional image:

> We will give a simile for that, drawn from Scripture. Moses made a tabernacle with three different edifices. The first edifice was called *sanctum sanctorum*: it was the dwelling of God, and there was no light from within. The other, *sanctum*, contained a chandelier with seven branches and lights. The third was called *atrium*, the parvis; it was located in the open air, in the light of the sun. This figure depicts the Christian. His spirit is *sanctum sanctorum*, the dwelling of God in the night (stripped of light) of faith, for he believes what he neither sees nor senses nor understands. His soul is the *sanctum*: there are found the seven lights, to wit, all kinds of understanding, discernment, science and knowledge of corporal and visible things. His body is *atrium*: it is manifest for all, in such a way that one can see what he does and how he lives.[12]

It is necessary, however, to recognize that this trichotomy did not have for Luther an importance comparable to his dialectical opposition between the flesh and the spirit. In Saint Paul, from before the com-

[9] Cf. the explanations given by Maurice de Gandillac, in *Histoire de la philosophie*, 2 (Gallimard, Pléiade, 1973), 203.

[10] Cf. ibid., 203–4.

[11] See also, for example, *La Perle évangélique*, l. 1, c. 46: the spirit is "the highest part of the soul", etc.

[12] *Oeuvres*, French trans., 2 (Geneva, 1963), 21–22. In 1521.

mentary on the *Magnificat*, he had been selective; the lessons on the Letter to the Romans (1515–1516) were already setting up an opposition between the flesh and the spirit without anthropological reference to any subject whatever,[13] and later, in his controversy with Erasmus, he was to prove all the more hostile to the anthropology drawn from 1 Thessalonians 5 by his adversary, whom the latter, guided by Origen, used to weaken his dialectic. He writes in *De servo arbitrio*:

> I am well aware of Origen's fable about the threefold affection of man: of flesh, soul, and spirit,[14] the soul holding the middle between the flesh and the spirit and able to turn either toward the one or toward the other. But this is dreaming; he says them but does not prove them at all. Saint Paul calls flesh everything that is without spirit, as we have demonstrated.[15]

Luther does not formally contradict here what he had said in the commentary on the *Magnificat*. What he reproaches in Origen, as in Erasmus, is believing in free will. But this preoccupation leads him to falsify their anthropology and thereby to forget or to misunderstand the Pauline verse that he had first interpreted correctly. To which, in his enormous second *Hyperaspistes*, Erasmus will reply several times over that the tripartition of 1 Thessalonians 5, even if counterparts are

---

[13] Cf. Jared Wicks, *Man Yearning for Grace, Luther's Early Spiritual Teaching* (Wiesbaden: Franz Steiner Verlag, 1969; Institut d'histoire européenne de Mainz, dir. J. Lortz, no. 56): "A second anthropological problem arises from Luther's exclusive use of the dualism *caro/spiritus* in the *Lecture on Romans*. He speaks only of the two opposed powers struggling for dominance in a human life. Luther did not make it clear that there is a human subject who is decisively qualified either by his nonagreement with the Spirit or by his surrender to the flesh. In the terminology of the *Dictates*, who is it that takes to himself God's judgment so as to justify God in his words and bring the Gospel from being 'ostensively and doctrinally' judgment and justice to be fully this in the life and self-awareness of the Christian? In the language of the *Lectures on Romans*, who lusts with self-seeking or who serves willingly with and under God's grace? It is not enough to say the flesh lusts and the spirit loves, for this can go on independently of our choice and willingness. —This is not an artificial problem. . . ."

[14] This is a gross error about Origen's thought, as can be readily perceived. Luther confuses the anthropological trichotomy with a threefold "affection" or orientation of man; as if "body" and "flesh" were synonymous.

[15] *Traité du serf arbitre*, trans. Denis de Rougement (Paris, Geneva, 1936), 308–9. The translator writes in a note: "Origen sets forth a 'tripartite' psychology that one finds again, in varied forms, in different earlier and later Gnostics and philosophers and up to the modern period (in several theoreticians of German romanticism and in certain theologians)", 349. These remarks are an accumulation of confused errors. To enumerate "body, soul, spirit" is not to enunciate a tripartite psychology—and if Origen had done so, Saint Paul would have done so before him; he would be equally responsible for the "agnostic" errors and should be counted as the first ancestor, in the Christian era, of the theoreticians of German romanticism. . . .

found in the philosophers, is proper to Saint Paul. The philosophers, in fact, do not usually call the highest part of the human being *spiritus* (*pneuma*), but *mens* or *ratio*; and what Paul understands by *spiritus* is not any *ratio* whatever, but the *ratio* already inspired by grace. That, he concludes, is what Luther does not want to recognize. As often happens, the discussion in which Erasmus finds himself involved leads him himself to a partially inaccurate interpretation of Saint Paul's text by making him attribute to the "spirit" what Paul says of "the spiritual man". Yet it remains true that he had first analyzed perfectly the address of the Apostle to the Thessalonians, and Luther had at first done the same.[16]

Lutheran mysticism, at least in the rather unorthodox Sébastien Frank (1499–1542), nonetheless recognizes the three elements of which man is composed: body, soul and spirit. Frank sees in the soul the personal and free being capable of orienting himself in one direction or in the other; he sees in the spirit the inner Word, or God present at the heart of every man, enlightening him through his Word and inclining his will through his Spirit.[17]

The same traditional distinctions, originating in Saint Paul, are found in the humanists of the sixteenth century of mystical tendency. For a Paracelsus (1493–1541), since man is a microcosm, he must unite within himself the three constitutive parts or elements corresponding to the three stages of the universe: material world, astral world, Divinity[18] (an idea of Nicholas of Cusa, although distorted, is recognizable in this). Cornelius Agrippa, in his *De occulta philosophia*, tried to unite the Platonic traditions to Moses and to Saint Paul:

> Plotinus itaque et Platonici omnes post Trismegistum similiter tria ponunt in homine, quae vocant supremum, infimum et medium. Supremum est illud divinum, quam mentem, sive portionem superiorem, sive intellectum illustratum vocant. Moses in Genesi vocat ipsum spiraculum vitarum, a Deo vid., vel a Spiritu ejus in nos spiratum. Infimum est sensitiva anima, quam etiam idolum dicunt, Paulus Apostolus animalem hominem nuncupat. Medium est spiritus rationalis utraque connectens

---

[16] *Hyperaspistes*, II. *Opera omnia*, LB, vol. 5, 19, 1460 A, 1464 AC, 1497 C. Cf. 1458 F. On the passage corresponding to the *De servo arbitrio*, see the curious note in LF. 218, note 1.

[17] Cf. Doris Rieber, Bibliothèque d'Humanisme et Renaissance, 21 (1959), 191. In Frank the explanation presupposes a modalist theology.

[18] *Philosophia sagax*. Cf. Alexandre Koyré, *Mystiques, spirituels, alchimistes du XVIe siècle allemand* (1955), 52.

> extrema atque ligans, vid. animam animalem cum mente, et utriusque sapiens naturam extremorum. . . .[19]

Guillaume Postel, as original as ever, at least in expression, distinguishes in man the *anima*, the *animus* and the *mens*.[20] It was undoubtedly following him, four years later, that Charles Toutain wrote, in his tragedy *Agamemnon*:

> Three natures in us, which all talk with each other
> Excite our life and keep it alive:
> The Spirit, the Soul, and Animus. And one being taken away,
> Suddenly all life together would depart.[21]

The Anglican Lancelot Andrewes (1555–1626) expresses himself in a similar way in his devotions:

> Into Thy hands, O Lord, I commend myself,
> my spirit, soul, and body. . . .[22]

IV. The Modern Period

Saint Francis de Sales will open this period for us. His *Traité de l'amour de Dieu* [*Treatise on the Love of God*] reproduces the Pauline doctrine to perfection. After having explained that "we have three kinds of loving actions: spiritual, reasonable and sensual", Francis de Sales observes that "the powers of the sensory part, which are or must be the servants of the spirit, ask, seek and take what has been rejected by the reason, . . . dishonoring . . . the purity of the intention of their master who is the spirit; and in the measure that the soul is converted to such gross and sensate unions, it is diverted from the delicate, intellectual and cordial union." Thus, by the same movement as we find in Saint Paul, the way is sketched to the opposition of the flesh to the spirit. Like many

[19] L. 3, c. 36. *De homine quomodo creatus ad imaginem Dei*. Text in *Archivio di filosofia* (1955), 140.

[20] *Les Très Merveilleuses Victoires des Femmes du Nouveau Monde* (1553).

[21] In 1557, cf. Lucien Febvre, *Le Problème de l'incroyance au XVIe siècle*, 203. For Postel, the Spirit illumines the *animus* and the *mens* illumines the *anima*.

[22] *The Devotions of Bishop Andrewes*, "Order of Evening Prayer", "Commendation" in *Prayers, Verses and Devotions* by John Henry Newman (San Francisco: Ignatius Press, 1989), 17.

in the Middle Ages, Francis de Sales, following Saint Augustine, also distinguishes "two portions of the soul, the inferior and the superior", the inferior being that which discourses on the basis of the experience of the senses, while the superior, founded "on the discernment and judgment of the spirit, . . . is commonly called the spirit and mental part of the soul"; in this "superior portion" he also distinguishes "two kinds of light", a natural one and a supernatural one, and so forth. This whole apparatus of precisions, which aims at integrating, as we have already seen in others, the "degrees of knowing" within the spiritual movement, is not without interest; but it is in some ways only a flowering from the basic trichotomy.[1]

It is this same trichotomy that we find again, as might be expected, in a philosopher attentive to the spiritual life, such as Maine de Biran. We know the place that the doctrine of the "three lives" holds in Biran: animal life, human life and divine life, particularly in the reflections of his *Journal intime*.[2] Jules Lachelier also adopts it, but perhaps by diminishing it, in his desire to work a kind of synthesis between Maine de Biran and Kant, when he explains the three components of existence: sensibility, understanding and reason.[3] We detect also an indication of the very strong mystical tendencies in Joseph de Maistre in this affirmation from the *Éclaircissements sur les sacrifices*: "The animal has received only a soul; to us were given a soul and a spirit."[4]

One might be tempted to seek a distant analogy with Saint Paul in the Kierkegaardian theory of the three spheres (rather than stages) of existence: aesthetic, ethical, religious. If that analogy is an illusion, other thoughts of Kierkegaard are right in finding their place here: "It is impossible to treat of sin in any of the sciences that ordinarily speak of it, because all are occupied with what is psychological in our nature, while sin is a determination of the spirit"; and again: "The spirit intervening, psychology is impotent. So good, as its name indicates,

---

[1] *Traité de l'amour de Dieu*, l. 1, chaps. 10 and 11. Ed. André Ravier (Gallimard, Pléiade), 379–89.

[2] *Journal intime*. . . . Cf. Gaston Fessard, *La Méthode de réflexion chez Maine de Biran*, Cahiers de la Nouvelle Journée, 39 (Bloud et Gay, 1938), 125–47: "La Dernière synthèse". Henri Gouhier, *Maine de Biran* (Seuil, 1970), 148.

[3] Jules Lachelier, *Cours de psychologie de l'École normale supérieure*. From Lachelier again, these words quoted by Aimé [André] Forest: "It seems to me that whoever says soul, life, beauty, says something purely spiritual and escapes, at least in substance, all the determinations that are the sole object of understanding." Forest, *L'Avènement de l'âme*, 24 (see below).

[4] Chap. 1. Cf. *Sur les délais de la justice divine*, chaps. 46 and 47.

is occupied with the soul. It sees everything from outside; the spirit itself is lived only from within. . . . Seen from outside, an act is always determined, and for all that the object of psychology. But. . . ."[5]

One might also be tempted to evoke here the Blondelian distinction between "noetic" and "pneumatic". This would not be completely wrong. But Blondel places these two kinds of thought in correlation rather than inviting us to rise from one to the other. He does not thereby have in mind a relation of the *psyche* to the *pneuma*, but rather a division of the function within the spirit. Despite the word "noetic", this is not the *nous* but rather the *logos*, which would be, according to him, the partner of the *pneuma*;[6] and the dialectic of the noetic and the pneumatic is in play at every step, so to speak, of the development of thought and life in this conception: the first, the concrete principle of universality, being the factor of objectivization and unifying force, while, conversely, the second, the concrete principle of singularity, is the diversifying element and subjective function.[7] Both, at the same level, are thus essentially complementary. Blondel held to his distinction; he often took up the study of it. He wrote in 1907 in one of his personal notebooks: "Think out the discovery of the two thoughts."[8] Now, in 1909, he wrote again: "The two thoughts. Ah! how they are always in me, tending to supplant each other, while it is necessary to reconcile them, hierarchize them, make them differently but equally serve the divine work of final and total reintegration."[9] This word "hierarchize" must be understood as demanding a reciprocal hierarchization.[10] It does not necessarily follow, however, that any

[5] Cf. Johannes Hohlenberg, *L'Oeuvre de Sören Kierkegaard*, trans. P. H. Tisseau (Albin Michel, 1960), 75 and 83. Page 75: "Man, says Kierkegaard, is a synthesis of soul and body. But a synthesis is inconceivable without a third part where the two factors meet and unite. This third part is the spirit. . . ."

[6] On the relation of the *logos* and the *pneuma*, see the reflections of Jean Meyendorff, in *Istina* (1969), 262.

[7] Numerous texts, *La Pensée*, vol. 1 (PUF, 1934), etc. Refer to the study by A. de Jan and A. Chapelle, "La Noétique et le pneumatique chez Maurice Blondel, un essai de définition", *Revue philosophique de Louvain*, 59 (1961), 600–630. Cf. Étienne Borne, *Passion de la Vérité*, 82–83.

[8] *Carnets intimes*, 2:157.

[9] Cf. Maurice Blondel and Auguste Valensin, *Correspondance*, 2:30–32. Jacques Paliard, "L'Idée de lien dans la philosophie de Maurice Blondel", in *Études philosophiques* (1950), 57–60; ibid., "Maurice Blondel ou le dépassement chrétien" (1950), 275–96.

[10] A parallel example of "horizontal" trichotomy, that is, of a distinction, within the spiritual being itself, of a threefold function, copied from trinitarian theology (in which the

analogy with the Pauline trichotomy, any echo of the "three lives" of Biran are absent from the Blondelian work. Blondel was too penetrated with the thought of Saint Paul and Saint Bernard, he was too closely interested in mysticism, he was too familiar with the spiritual authors of the Christian tradition to let us believe in such an absence without a fuller examination. But the fact that his dialectic of the noetic and the pneumatic, which is fundamental in his philosophy, does not turn explicitly into a hierarchy of the soul and spirit or of the discursive reason and mystical intuition (although he obviously knew of this distinction as well as that between the understanding and higher intelligence),[11] is not a negligible indication. Blondel maintained a prudent attitude in the face of natural mysticism, just as, on the other hand, he remained prudent in the face of facile personalisms.

In the Russian theologian Sergius Bulgakov, the Pauline distinction between the soul and the spirit is placed in powerful relief. It assumes a mystical aspect that is more emphasized than in the Apostle, or at least it proceeds from a base of natural mysticism that, despite the reference to the famous discourse at Athens, does not seem to correspond perfectly to its more complex notion of the spirit:

> Although it is a creature, a certain eternity of creation, a certain non-creation, are proper to the spirit. . . . Spiritual existence is rooted in the eternity of God, the created spirit itself is similarly eternal and uncreated. Cf. Acts 17:28.

It is true that Bulgakov can also invoke the authority of the Greek Fathers: Had Saint Cyril of Alexandria not written that "the image of

---

three Persons are equal among themselves), is offered us by John Scotus Erigena, in whom we find the following table:

Mens	—*peritia*	—*disciplina*
Ousia		—*logos*
Nous	—*energeia*	—*dianoia*

to which correspond:

Essentia	—*virtus*	—*operatio*
Intellectus	—*ratio*	—*sensus interior*

Cf. René Roques, *Remarques sur la signification de Jean Scot Érigène* (Rome: Lateran, 1967), 71.

[11] He knew and admired the thesis of Father Pierre Rousselot on *L'Intellectualisme de saint Thomas* (1908), whose fundamental idea consists precisely in the distinction between the *ratio* and the *intellectus*—but at the same time he criticized the intellectualist conception, according to which this distinction was understood.

the divine nature was imprinted in man by the infusion of the Holy Spirit''?[12] The importance of his anthropological theory derives in any case from the fact that it is from this that he explains the mystery of the Incarnation:

> The postulate of the divine Incarnation is a certain original identity between the divine I and the I of man, an identity that does not abrogate their essential distinction. . . . The human hypostatic spirit . . . draws its divine and uncreated origin from the "breath of God''. . . . Through his spirit, man communicates with the divine substance and he is fit to be "divinized''. . . . Man is . . . god-man by predestination, potentially, through his formal structure. At the same time he is flesh, . . . through an "animated'' body, he sums up the entire world. . . . Man is made of an uncreated divine spirit, hypostasized by the I of the *creature*, and of a soul and of a body created from the psycho-somatic being.[13]

Bulgakov insists. The very idea of divinity by predestination seems too weak to him. He corrects himself almost immediately: "Not only is man theanthropic by predestination but also the Logos is the eternal God-Man, insofar as the first Image of the created man. . . . This is why the hypostasis of the Logos, the heavenly Man, could itself become the hypostasis of created man and make of the latter the authentic God-man, by achieving its eternal theanthropy.'' The conclusion is nonetheless fundamentally in keeping with the spirit of Christian faith: "Man is already the form, ready for the authentic theanthropy that he is not capable of achieving himself, but in view of which he was created and called. The divine Incarnation is not at all a catastrophe for the human essence or some violation; on the contrary, it is an accomplishment.''[14]

This leads us far from the narrow anthropological dualism that triumphed in modern Scholasticism as well as in the university philosophy springing from Cartesianism. "Saint Paul'', noted R. M. Albarès,[15] "had distinguished three orders: the carnal, the intellectual

---

[12] *De adoratione*, 9, D.

[13] *Du Verbe incarné* (*Agnus Dei*), translated from Russian by Constantin Andronikof (Aubier, 1943), 10 and 113.

[14] Ibid., 114 and 116. Let us retain these two observations from the same author: "Spirituality raises the feeling of connection with the natural world, but it also gives the sense of depth proper to the spirit'' (12); and: "The image and resemblance between them are like the foundation and the end, the given and the proposed, the alpha and the omega'' (71), which is the most classic patristic doctrine.

[15] *L'Aventure intellectuelle du XXe siècle*, 2d ed. (1959), 47.

and the spiritual.[16] The Cartesian dualism had fused together the intellectual and the spiritual, and rationalism had gradually reduced the spirit thus created to being only an intellect without transcendence, without dynamism or immortality, destined only to understand and to organize the world." On the other hand, for all sorts of reasons that we do not at all have to seek here, but in particular because of a certain poverty in its common philosophy, Christian thought did not seem able to fill the void thus created in man. It must not, therefore, be surprising that the inevitable reaction was produced in para-Christian forms. "If a scholar", André Préaux recently wrote,[17] "encounters the old doctrine that man is composed of a body, a soul and a spirit, he has scruples about considering it, for what do 'soul' and 'spirit' mean. . . . Unfortunately, in a society where science is the supreme authority, this silence is equivalent to a negation. What dissolves the errors and complexes, what protects against neuroses and fantasies, is precisely that which is silently and discreetly dismissed."

The same year as André Préaux, and reacting like him, Gabriel Germain took support from Saint Teresa to remind us of the unrecognized depths of the life of the spirit:

> Above the understanding, below the ordinary conscience and what fills it, *exists* a sheet of peace and light. . . . Whoever approaches it can have no more doubt of it. Anyone who has not sought it has no right to judge it.
>
> Saint Teresa expresses the same reality in very different terms. Now no one had taught her this, nor had anyone prepared her for such an experience. This agreement over the centuries and doctrines reassures me more than anything. She writes in the book of the *Mansions* (seventh Mansion, chapter 1): "Interior things are seen that show in a sure way that there is, beneath a certain relationship, an obvious difference between the soul and the spirit, although they are but a single thing. . . ."[18]

Likewise, again, situating his own thought in relation to the "noosphere" of Teilhard de Chardin and in relation to the "collective unconscious" of Jung:

> The noosphere, in the philosophy of Teilhard de Chardin, appears to be like a mental view, a conclusion. This is because its very name evokes an

---

[16] He should say: the compound.

[17] "Le Vide et le néant", in *Le Vide*, Hermès, 6 (1969), 95.

[18] *Le Regard intérieur* (Seuil, 1969), 116.

> intellectual activity, the subtlest but, whether exploratory or constructive, directed according to logical norms.[19] What I could call (but I will keep myself from doing so) pneumatosphere, let us say: the spiritual ocean, is the object of experience. By other paths, to other ends, it is the same reality, I suppose, that Jung attained and which he called the collective unconscious. But these two terms restrict the origin and meaning of it. . . .[20]

With Jung, in fact, we penetrate but we remain within what is psychological. The life of the spirit, in the Spirit, is wholly different. A certain Calvinist dryness, a phobia about mysticism and all "interiority" conspire at times, along with rationalism and contemporary positivism of all forms, to brush this life in the Spirit aside. But in a quite natural way, the Lutheran Paul Tillich, who was interested in ontology, in the history of religions, in mysticism as well as in biblical history, brings the Pauline tripartition up to date again:

> There is no religious statement on man and his destiny without a judgment on the relation between different elements that are combined and opposed in the life of man. These elements have been variously described as being his body, his soul and his spirit. . . .[21]

The exegetes in contemporary Catholicism seem no more disposed than most of the theologians to return the Pauline verse to a place of honor and draw its consequences. It is toward the writers that we must turn to perceive an echo of it, in free expression. Although this expression is truly, we believe, faithful to the doctrine of the *Pneuma* and to its authentic development, it is not certain that Saint Paul would have recognized his thought at first glance. "I have good news to announce to you", says Paul Claudel in the "Cantique de Palmyre", "—it is another within the depths of you who has the word. . . . I have good news to announce to you. . . . You need only close your eyes to find your treasure in the night. . . . There are many souls, but there is not one of them with whom I am not in communion through this sacred point in us that says *Pater noster*."[22] And Georges Bernanos, in his di-

---

[19] That is perfectly accurate. But the author could have found the analysis of this spiritual ocean he sought to grasp in the "divine milieu" of which Teilhard speaks; this divine milieu is the object of experience, and the (spiritual) experience of which does not depend on intellectual constructions about the noosphere.

[20] Germain, *Regard intérieur*, 257.

[21] *La Dimension oubliée*, trans. Henri Rochais (DDB, 1965), 103–4; cf. 113.

[22] *Conversations dans le Loir-et-Cher* (Gallimard, 1935), 117–19.

ary: "His will is ours, and when we revolt against it, it is only at the price of an uprooting of our whole inner being. . . . Our will has been united to his since the beginning of the world. . . . What sweetness to think that even while offending him, we never cease completely to desire what he desires at the depths of the Sanctuary of the soul!"[23] A wonderful conjunction of Claudel and Bernanos!

The reader will have noted, in Claudel's text, the word "soul". An inversion of vocabulary is in fact produced. The "spirit" having become, in the modern leveling dichotomy, the immediate correlative of the body, it is the "soul" that has taken its place, in those who have not taken part in this leveling. We are familiar, again in Claudel, with the parabola of *animus* and *anima*. The word "soul", in the same sense, compels recognition with greater strength in order to escape the scientistic totalitarianism that reigns abusively in the name of the "human sciences". "In the measure in which they are scientific," wrote Henri Gouhier in 1973, "the sciences of man can consider man only by selecting points of view under which it is possible to treat him objectively. It is obviously not a question for the philosopher to ignore the various forms of sociology, psychology, ethnology, neurology, and so forth: he must simply wonder if the sciences of man, added up, constitute a science of man."[24] And man, simply as such, man who cannot renounce the call he hears in the depths of himself, refuses to let himself suffocate. He rehabilitates the word "soul" as the most fitting to express what philosophers and men of science are too often skilled at eliminating through preterition or through negation. The soul then becomes almost the synonym for the *pneuma* of Saint Paul and Origen. The passage from Henri Gouhier that we have just quoted figures in a preface to *L'Avènement de l'âme* by Aimé [André] Forest, a work, he says, that "finds its timeliness in its apparent obsolescence". The author of the work and that of its preface both evoke on this subject the "three lives" of Maine de Biran. André Forest also recalls these words of Henri Bergson: "By calling a certain assurance of facile intelligibility an idea and a certain uneasiness of life the soul, an invincible current brings modern philosophy to elevate the soul above the idea." Modern philosophy, as a whole, has not followed the path on which Bergson

[23] Tunisia, January 23, 1948. Cf. Albert Béguin, *Bernanos par lui-même* (Seuil, 1954), 146–47 (see above).

[24] Preface to Aimé [André] Forest, *L'Avènement de l'âme* (Beauchesne, 1973), 11.

thought he saw it engaged. Gabriel Marcel, however, among others, wanted to preserve this word "soul" and to keep "the fullness of its meaning". Charles du Bos, in search of traces of God in us, asked: "Who will leave us a journal of the dilation of the soul?" What André Forest wants is to help us discover or to rediscover a certain "inner unity", a certain "pure source", and each of the chapters of his work traces an avenue toward an encounter with this. "The discovery of the soul", he tells us, "is the development of a spiritual philosophy. . . . The soul is the advent of presence and grace raised above the world of nature and objectivity."[25]

The same fundamental reaction, the same sudden start, or, if you wish, the same awakening, five years later in a much younger author, whose nostalgia, if this is what it is, cannot be that for the past but that which springs from a new reflection, this time against the oppression of a thought reduced to its politico-social components, the final end of scientistic intelligence. In his essay on *Job, ou l'excès du mal*, Philippe Nemo insists on this same word "soul" in order to recall man to himself and to his essential problem. . . .[26]

Across the numerous changes in vocabulary, the complications introduced by theoreticians eager for analysis, across, too, the unceasing variations in points of view, the tripartite anthropology, whose expression is found in Saint Paul, has consistently furnished, in the tradition of the Church, a basis for spiritual doctrine and life.

[25] Ibid., 15, 16, 25, etc. P. 188, A. Forest quotes Maine de Biran, who had already written in his *Journal*, June 5, 1815: "One can find another soul at the depth of this soul that one is analyzing or that one paints from outside."

[26] Grasset, 1978.

4. The Spirit

I. The Place of Mysticism

As we have already been able to perceive, these various distinctions are far from always being covered perfectly either from one author to another or even, as in the case of Augustine, in the work of the same author. C. R. Doddau's remark on the subject of the ancient Greeks applies here: "One must undoubtedly agree that the average man of the fifth century (and this is true in all periods) possessed a very complicated psychological vocabulary."[1]

The Pauline tripartition has nonetheless remained the constant basis serving to support the spiritual doctrines of the Christian tradition.

Commenting on Pseudo-Dionysius, Saint Maximus the Confessor defined man by this threefold pair of epithets: "Supermundialis et spiritualis—circummundialis, animalis—mundialis, carnalis."[2] The author of the celebrated *Philokalia*, Saint Nikodemos of the Holy Mountain (748–809) will explain that the "Jesus Prayer" brings into operation the three powers of the soul: the intellect (*nous*), the discursive reason (*logos*), the will or spirit (*thélēsis, pneuma*), in the action of the soul alone, by which, uniting in itself, the soul is made fit to be united to God.[3] But perhaps that is a matter, rather, of a "horizontal" trichotomy, of three functions or three activities proper to the higher part of the spirit.

With more than one spiritual writer of the Latin Middle Ages, one should speak of four elements rather than of three in their analysis of man—even without considering other complications, many subtle subdivisions, an echo of Scholasticism, dear to a certain number, subdivisions destined either to establish agreement between authors or to

---

[1] *Les Grecs et l'Irrationnel*, trans. M. Gilson (1965), 138.

[2] *Opera S. Dionysii*, ed. Cordier (1634).

[3] In Louis Bouyer, *La Spiritualité orthodoxe. . . .* (Aubier, 1965), 64. The reversal of meaning, or of value, will be noted between the two terms "soul" and "spirit" in a rather large number of authors; notably Henri Bremond, Paul Claudel, and more recently Aimé [André] Forest, *L'Avènement de l'âme*. But the soul is no longer the simple *psyche*, and the spirit that it transcends is not the *pneuma*.

detail the stages of spiritual itineraries. As, for example, this schema traced by Isaac of Stella in his *Epistola de anima*: "Animae in mundo sui corporis peregrinanti quinque sunt ad sapientiam progressus: sensus—imaginatio—ratio—intellectus—intelligentia."[4] Two different modes will be noted, both inspired by Saint Augustine, in the expression of tripartism: for some, it is: *corpus, anima, spiritus*;[5] for others: *corpus, ratio, mens*. Hence, to accord these two modes, the quadripartite division: *corpus—anima—ratio inferior—ratio superior sive mens*. We know the ground gained in the Middle Ages by that Augustinian subdivision of the *ratio inferior* and the *ratio superior*.[6] What will correspond to this in Saint Thomas Aquinas will be particularly the distinction between the *ratio* and the *intellectus* recently brought out by Pierre Rousselot.[7] This would also be the place to mention the Franciscan doctrine of the two faces of the soul, which is of Neoplatonic origin, coming through the twofold channel of Augustine and the Arabs[8]—but that, like, moreover, the Thomist distinction of the *intellectus* and the *ratio*, is an essentially "scientific" (philosophical) theory, having little relation to the spiritual life. The explanation of the latter is founded rather on the doctrine of the twofold *ratio*, lower and higher, which corresponds to action and contemplation. But then a new subdivision is introduced: the *ratio superior*, the place of contemplation, assimilated to the *intellectus*, becomes the higher part or function of the *mens* and receives names such as *acies mentis*, *oculus cordis*, and so forth.

Whatever might be the various complications and the varieties in the names, "all the great Christian mystics are in agreement in considering the human soul as a complex reality, presenting regions and stages. . . .

---

[4] PL 194, 1880 AB.

[5] With respect to *spiritus*, we read in the *Sententiae Anselmi* (twelfth century): "Hence, in our Scriptures, rather often the charity that God has for us and that which we have for God are called by the same word *spiritus*." Cf. Robert Javelet (140): "It is a fact that for a number of spiritual men, *spiritus* is both divine and human, one of those places of 'concatenation' of which we spoke with respect to Isaac of Stella. *Spiritus* is the *mens*, burning with divine charity, the divinized summit of being, suited to the *unitas spiritus*—and the very Person of the Holy Spirit. It is no longer a question of a psychological triad but of a trichotomy whose third term is ambiguous, whether of man or of God, certainly of God in man."

[6] Cf. Étienne Gilson, *La Philosophie de saint Bonaventure*, 363–64.

[7] *L'Intellectualisme de saint Thomas*, 1st ed. (Alcan, 1908; Sorbonne thesis). See also M. D. Chenu, *Introduction à l'étude de S. Th. d'Aquin* (Vrin, 1950), 134–35 and 153.

[8] J. Rohmer, "Sur la doctrine franciscaine des deux faces de l'âme", *Archives d'histoire doctrinale et littéraire du Moyen Age* (1927), 73–77, quoting Jean de la Rochelle, Dominicus Gumdissalinus, both Algazel and Avicenne.

All are also in agreement in admitting that, among these various regions, there is a privileged one, that where God dwells in a particular manner. . . ."[9] "There is a spiritual life when a relationship with God exists",[10] and there is a secret point in man that is the permanent place of that relationship, of that possible encounter, because it is already, and always has been, the place of the divine presence: that *pneuma* of Paul, commented on by Origen, that "sacred point in us that says *Pater noster*" of the "Cantique de Palmyre".[11]

So we see that the philosophers and theologians, more concerned about rationality than mysticism, tend to reduce (even in their historical studies) the trichotomy to a dichotomy—while, on the contrary, the spiritual masters tend to bring out the trichotomy. They readily glorify the *spiritus*, not only above the *anima* but above the *ratio*, whether theoretical or practical. It is instructive to compare in this regard the Abélardian writing *Ysagoge in theologiam* with the commentary on the Song of Songs by William of Saint Thierry. For the first: "Duo haec nomina, sc. spiritus et anima, non magnam habent in significatione discrepantiam".[12] The second, on the contrary, strongly emphasizes the hierarchical distinction of three orders: "animal", "rational" and "spiritual".[13]

To keep to the general schema that results from the text of Saint Paul —a schema that itself in fact includes many nuances and, as we have seen, many interpretations—morality will therefore be the act of the soul, mysticism the act of the spirit. "The body", says Evagrius Ponticus, "has bread for nourishment, the soul has virtue, the understanding has spiritual prayer."[14] Morality, whose object is virtue, is the πρᾶξις, and the life of the spirit is contemplation, the θεωρία. The first is ordained to the second, as the soul is ordained to the spirit: "Strive", says Cassian, reporting the statements of Abbot Nesteros, "to acquire in the first place a complete possession of moral discipline (πρακτική), for without that you cannot obtain contemplative purity (θεωρητική)."[15]

---

[9] Louis Cognet, *Les Problèmes de la spiritualité* (1967), 51–52.

[10] Ibid., 13.

[11] See above, 143, 175.

[12] *Ysagoge* . . . , c. 3. Ed. Landgraf, 157.

[13] See above, 151.

[14] *Traité de la prière*, 101.

[15] Fourteenth conference.

For Gregory of Nyssa, virtue is "the forecourt of the Temple".[16] Origen had said before them: "According to the doctrine of the very wise Solomon, he who wishes to acquire wisdom must begin by studying morality"; it is in fact "good conduct" that prepares one to receive the visits of the Logos, and when one is solidly exercised in it, then one will be able "to pass from moral things to mystical understanding".[17] In his treatise addressed "To the Brethren at Mont Dieu", which remains one of the fundamental texts of Christian spirituality, William of Saint Thierry traces a similar route for those who want to give themselves over to the perfect life, and, for the final stage, his program is even one of a boldness that some could misunderstand (it is true that it is addressed to a Carthusian monastery): "It is for others", he tells them, "to serve God; it is for you to cling to him. It is for others to believe in God, to know that he exists, to love him and revere him; it is for you to taste him, to understand him, to know him, to enjoy him."[18] The same doctrine is set forth, as it had been earlier with Origen, in parallel with the doctrine of the threefold biblical sense, by another writer of the twelfth century, Godefroi d'Admont:

> Sicut triplex est visio, corporis, spiritus et mentis, ita triplex etiam sensus est in scripturis sanctis: litteralis, spiritalis, intellectualis. Litteralem atque spiritalem sensus egregius ipse Doctor gentium tunc transcenderat, et usque ad tertium coelum, intellectualem scilicet sensum, gloriose conscenderat, quando toto cordis intellectu ita coelestibus est conjunctus, quod utrum in corpore, an extra corpus esset, se nescire asseruit.[19]

The same fundamental schema is found again in the great representatives of what one often calls, with a term that can lend to confusion, "intellectualist mysticism", which is to say, with the Rheno-Flemish mystics of the fourteenth and fifteenth centuries. The same schema, although with differences in terminology and in a sometimes different climate of thought, particularly in Meister Eckhart.

Ruysbroek "assigns to the spirit a threefold role. First of all a vital

[16] Hans Urs von Balthasar, *Presence and Thought* (San Francisco: Ignatius Press, 1995), 129.

[17] *In Cant.*, prologue. *In Numer.*, hom. 7, n. 1. *In Ezech.*, hom. 7, n. 10, etc.

[18] *Ad Fratres de Monte Dei*, c. 2, n. 5: "Aliorum est enim Deo servire, vestrum est adhaerere. Aliorum est Deum credere, scire, amare et revereri: vestrum est sapere, intelligere, cognoscere, frui" (PL 184, 300 C).

[19] PL 174, 999.

role, in which it animates the body; then an intellectual role that is manifested by thought; finally a role of higher spiritual activity, in which it becomes the principle of unification of the whole inner life and in which it is mixed with the very essence of the soul."[20] Hence, for example, in the *Livre des sept clôtures*, the definition of the seventh enclosure, "which surpasses all the others": "simple beatitude beyond all holy life and practice of the virtues".[21] Likewise, in the *Miroir du salut éternel*, in which the higher degree is only divided: after "the virtuous life, which dies to sin and grows in virtues", comes the state where "all ownership of the will dies": then the spirit is made fully free through its union to the Spirit of God, even to the point of the "living life" (*levende leven*) that blossoms, which is all "hidden in God and in the substance of our soul".[22] Ruysbroek takes up again here an expression long since current, which he could have read in Saint Bernard (*vivida vita et vitalis*),[23] William of Saint Thierry (*vita vivens*)[24] or Thomas de Froidmont (*vita vitalis*).[25]

The same gradation is found in Tauler, based on the same traditional "ternary schema". Tauler distinguishes in man "three things: one clings to nature in flesh and blood; the other is the reason; the third is an essence of the pure soul and without mixture". This is what he expresses again "in the symbolism of the three men, which correspond to the sensate life, the intellectual life and the spiritual life in the sense of union with God".[26] This "third man", this "essence of the pure soul", is what Tauler often calls the *gemuete*, a word that Father Étienne Huguény translates as "deep-seated will" and Louis Cognet prefers to call "deep instinct"; it is the "depths" of being to which, says Tauler, the "divine ground" alone corresponds: *abyssus abyssum invocat*; it imprints on our nature "an eternal and deep-seated tendency

---

[20] Louis Cognet, *Introduction aux mystiques rhéno-flamands*, 260.

[21] Chap. 16, *Oeuvres . . .*, 1:183.

[22] Chaps. 2, 3 and 17.

[23] *In Psalm. Qui inhabitat*, sermon 17, n. 1; PL 183, 250.

[24] PL 184, 353 B.

[25] PL 184, 1301 C.

[26] Cognet, *Introduction*, 126–31. This division, in the opinion of Cognet, "is in no way Thomist, and it is through a rather unconvincing but veritable tour de force that he [Huguény] has tried to lead back to it. Its Platonic ancestry is obvious, and one could put side by side the views of Tauler and those of Origen (Weilner); yet it is particularly with Eckhart that the relationship is striking". For Eckhart, see above. The whole relationship with Saint Thomas is not, however, absent: see above.

to return to its origin", a tendency that "persists even in the damned, because it is linked to the very essence of the soul".[27] Tauler's preaching rests on this structure. The abnegation to which he invites his listeners is not only the liberation from sensible appetites; it goes beyond simple morality: it is a profound attitude that "flows from the growing experience of God"; mystical passivity, succeeding the activity of the virtuous life; "inner recollection", above the exercise of the virtues and reason as well as that of the senses.[28] "It is necessary that, after having overcome the senses, the reason be freed from itself, renounce itself, so as to be transformed into pure and simple spirit."[29] Then the Kingdom of God is established. And Tauler repeats, so as to make himself well understood: "This Kingdom is established in its own manner, in the innermost part of the spirit, as soon as man, through all his exercise, has absorbed the exterior man in the inner and reasonable man and as soon as the man of sense and of reasonable power are entirely absorbed into the more interior man, in the hidden ground of the spirit, where the true image of God dwells, and as soon as he flees into this divine ground, into which man, from all eternity, is found in his uncreated state."[30]

The relationship of Tauler to Eckhart is obvious. In one as in the other, the distinction of the soul and the spirit (of the psyche and the πνεῦμα), colored by Platonic exemplarism, is affirmed everywhere. Eckhart enunciates it with reference to Saint Augustine. "According to Augustine," he says "our intellectual element divides itself into two parts: through the one, we are oriented intellectually toward an intellectual grasp of knowledge that our cognitive faculty receives from outside; the other, to use the very words of Augustine, manifests itself at the deepest center of our spirit ('*abditum mentis*')."[31] It is this center that particularly interested, that fascinated Eckhart, this place "where no image enters or leaves, but where there is only God himself". "The

---

[27] Texts and commentaries in Cognet, ibid., particularly pp. 127–28, 134. "This deep instinct . . . always contemplates God, the soul enjoys it without interruption." These should, once again, be compared with the recent texts of authors like Paul Claudel and Georges Bernanos.

[28] Sermon 13, n. 1. *Sermons of Tauler*, by Hugueny, Théry and Colin, 1:278–80.

[29] Sermon 4. Ibid., 196. Cf. fragment of sermon 3 on the Epiphany, 278–80.

[30] Quoted by Cognet, *Introduction*, 137–38.

[31] Quoted by Cognet, ibid., 22, who points out an analogy with the distinction of the two, agent and possible, intellects.

soul", he also said, "has two eyes: the inner one and the other, outer one; the inner eye of the soul is that by which it contemplates being and receives it directly from God."[32] What differentiates him from Origen and Augustine, Bernard and William of Saint Thierry, is the "uncreated" character that he attributes to this "inner eye", or to this "*abditum mentis*". The disquieting feature of his mysticism consists in this, a feature that will be less emphasized in Tauler and even in Henry Suso, although the latter speaks also of the ground of the spirit as "eternal".[33]

Follower and compiler, Harphius (Henry Herp) will symbolize the "three kinds of life" emanating from the three parts of man in the three biblical figures of Leah, Rachel and Mary Magdalen;[34] and he works at length to describe the *mens*, or the *apex mentis*, the *spiritus*, or the *interior sinus mentis*, which is to say, still that *pneuma* by which the zone of rational and moral activity is transcended:

> Dicitur etiam [anima] quandoque mens, quae sc. ipsis viribus interior est et supereminet; quia vires in mente sicut in origine sua sunt counitae; ex qua sc. effluunt ut radii ex solari rota, et in quam refluunt. Et est illud centrum in anima, in quo vera Trinitatis imago relucet: et tam nobile, quod nullum ibi nomen proprie convenit, licet in multis nominibus circumlocutive manifestatur. Haec est igitur mens, vel apex mentis, aut centrum ipsius animae; ut feliciter renovetur, ipsae vires quae dicuntur spiritus ad interiorem sinum mentis sunt reflectendae, et mens ipsa ad intimum suum regerenda, sc. in Deum ibidem suaviter recubantem. . . .[35]

Warning us that this higher part of man cannot be appropriately designated by any name, and multiplying the formulas himself by which one must indeed try even to speak of it, Harphius invites us not to stress, whatever the interest of the other part might be, the variations in vocabulary from one author to another or from one period to another, which could hide from us the continuity of a tradition that, in essentials, is very firm.

---

[32] Quoted by Cognet, ibid., 76. Cf. 78 and 79, quotation from a sermon of doubtful authenticity: "At this depth . . . a profound silence reigns, for neither creature nor image reaches there. . . ."

[33] "The supreme and superessential being", writes Henry Suso, "has ennobled man by giving him the light of his eternal deity, and that is this image of God imprinted in the *gemuete* of the spirit, which, too, is eternal." Cognet, who quotes this text, observes also that Suso's anthropology is rather imprecise: ibid., 193–94.

[34] *Miroir de la perfection*, cf. Cognet, ibid., 303–4.

[35] Book 2, p. 5 (Cologne, 1611), 639–40.

Saint Catherine of Genoa offers us a similar schema; very classically, she distinguishes body, soul and spirit, the latter being designated in itself by the word *mente* and, when it is animated by infused love, by the word *spirito*; in this latter case, the *spirito* is finally identified with infused Love, which is God. Since the Saint is less concerned to give us a theoretical course in anthropology, even spiritual, than to describe the spiritual life itself, we can understand that from her pen *mente* is rare and *spirito* frequent.[36] On the other hand, following the example of many other mystics, she loves to detail the stages of ascent: "When God", she says, "addresses his first call to us, he gives us at first the instinct for virtues; later, he urges us to perfection; then, through infused grace, he leads us to the annihilation of ourselves; finally, to true transformation."[37] Saint Teresa and Saint John of the Cross likewise know that there exists a life higher than the exercise of the virtues, when they celebrate "freedom of spirit",[38] "holy freedom of spirit",[39] and Saint Teresa observes in her *Interior Castle* that "certain interior effects give certitude that there is in us, in certain relations, a very real difference between the soul and the spirit".[40] We also quote as an example Fénelon, who, in commenting on Cassian, finds himself, at the same time, summing up the whole mystical tradition: "Although we judge the other virtues to be necessary and useful, we believe, however, we should place them only at the second degree, because one seeks them all only in view of this one thing of which Jesus Christ says: 'Martha, Martha, you trouble yourself about many things, there is only one thing necessary.' He placed the sovereign good, not in work, although laudable and abundant in fruit, but in contemplation that is truly simple and one. He declares that little is necessary for this perfect beatitude that contemplation is."[41] And a little farther on, in the same writing: "There is thus a state where this appropriation of virtues is no longer opportune."[42]

---

[36] Compare this with Saint Irenaeus, who has a similar motive speaking of the Holy Spirit in preference to the *pneuma* of man (see above).

[37] *Oeuvres*, new ed. (1926), 57.

[38] Saint John of the Cross, *Dark Night of the Soul*, chap. 23.

[39] Saint Teresa, *Way of Perfection*, chap. 10.

[40] Seventh Mansion, chap. 1.

[41] On the authority of Cassian, 7.

[42] Ibid., n. 15. See also Saint Francis de Sales, *Treatise on the Love of God*, bk. 1, 12 (*Oeuvres* [1894], 4:67ff.).

The great Protestant spiritual master Gerhard Tersteegen (1697–1769) professes the same doctrine: "There must necessarily be in us a capacity to recognize God and spiritual things in an essential and present way. And that exists in the pure Reason [*Vernunft*], which has been given us closed and unused until God gives us the understanding by which we know the very Truth so intimately and essentially that we are ourselves drawn into the true God."[43]

If a certain number of authors, in the course of this long tradition that we have just examined, seem also to distinguish, as it were, two elements above the *psyche*, while Saint Paul saw only the *pneuma* above it, this is usually, as we could ascertain from some of the examples cited, because they mean by *psyche* only the animal soul, animater of the body and seat of sensation, or rather because they want to assure a seat for "objective" knowledge and profane culture. For Paul, on the contrary, and more explicitly for Origen, the soul is the very seat of the personality, the reasoning and self-willed being, which judges and freely determines itself. It is the place of decision. According to the orientation taken by the soul, the human being will become "carnal" or "spiritual" (*pneumatikos*). As opposed as he might be to free will, Luther himself saw very clearly that the Pauline *psychè* of 1 Thessalonians 5 was much more than the principle "that animates the body and acts through it". In an article in the *Revue thomiste* (1971), Father P. R. Régamey, O.P., is perfectly in keeping with the traditional line when he distinguishes (497) these three degrees: psychosomatic complex—rational function of abstraction and discourse—primacy of spirit in its greatest purity. And what, in the theoretical order, is the "rational function" corresponds, in the practical order, to what we could call, in a rather restrictive sense, the "moral function". Saint Paul also invites us not to confuse this moral function with the properly spiritual life, which raises man above himself, when he places above the exercise of active benevolence and of all virtue this reality of another order, a gift of God, which is Charity (1 Cor 13:3). Dietrich Bonhoeffer was also faithful to the tradition that originated in the Apostle when he exhorted the Christians over whom he had responsibility not to confuse,

[43] Quoted by Louis Bouyer, *La Spiritualité orthodoxe et la spiritualité protestante et anglicane* (Aubier, 1965), 268. This *Vernunft*, translated here by "pure Reason", must not make one think of Kant; it is the "reason" of Eckhart (which in others is called *intellectus*); it is both, indistinctly, the *pneuma* of Origen and the *nous* of Evagrius; it is also the "fine point of the soul" of Saint Francis de Sales.

in their assemblies, "spiritual community with mystical overheating" (cf. A. Dumas, 64). "The great theme of community life is the revival of the very Pauline distinction between the natural, eager, equivocal, nostalgic, desiring, in a word: idealistic, and the spiritual, respectful, enlightened, serving, knowing, in a word: realist" (ibid., 145). "The one", Bonhoeffer also says, "who does not let Christ be a path toward the other falls into natural chattering, which kills the spiritual word. . . . Prayer is the salutary limit to desires of immediate effusiveness. . . . Community life is communion through spiritual mediation and non-confusion in the natural immediacy" (146–47).

II. Morality Integrated into Mysticism

In Christianity itself, it is characteristic of the Catholic Church to assure the equilibrium between the three components (religion, morality and mysticism), an equilibrium necessary to the integrity of the human being. Faithful in everything to her spirit of synthesis, she maintains all three in solidarity, without ever letting any one of the three be lacking or eclipse the others or be devalued, in the humblest forms of spiritual life any more than in the highest. To take a very simple example, when Fénelon exclaims, in his *Traité de l'existence et des attributs de Dieu*: "My length of life is but a perpetual extinction",[1] these words, to be well understood, must be taken at once morally, religiously and mystically.

The various Protestant confessions place more emphasis on contrasts and clashes, as has often been remarked. J. A. Moehler wrote in the last century, in his *Symbolique*, with respect to morality and religion: "In the eyes of Catholics, religiosity and morality, if we may be permitted to use these two terms, are united by their essence and are both eternal. According to the Protestants, on the other hand, there is no relationship between these two things, for one is of an eternal price and the other is of only passing value. Luther insists in many places on this difference. . . ."[2] There would be many nuances besides to note here, but in this essay on typology we must keep to the most general characteristics.[3] In Calvinism, mysticism is the object of mistrust, or even

[1] *Treatise*, 2d part, chap. 6, art. 2. See the commentary given by Father François Varillon, *Fénelon* (Seuil, 1954), introduction, 2.

[2] *La Symbolique*, French trans., 1:246.

[3] See several explanations in our study on *Mystique et Mystère*.

reprobation.[4] We also know the abyss, in Luther, that separates ethics and faith. As a result of this, there is a tendency with Lutheran mystics —to say nothing of Luther himself and of Lutheranism in general—to depreciate all moral activity, as constituting on man's part an affirmation of self that, far from bringing him closer to God, distances him, and to recognize a value in religious life only in an abandonment close to quietism;[5] a depreciation of morality that goes hand in hand with that of reason and that of freedom—we recently read from a Protestant pen an article on morality considered solely as "cultural reality". Such an attitude, to take it simply as such, could also facilitate invaluable analyses in many regards, such as the analysis of the "levels of life" in Kierkegaard or that of the "sacred" in Rudolf Otto. But these analyses do not always stop at posing formal distinctions. Thus, in order to bring out more clearly the specificity of the category of the sacred or of the religious, Otto cuts the latter off from morality; he is not content with showing that, on the level of history or psychology, these two orders are often separated in fact; he is well on his way to a separation by right.[6] As a repercussion, when morality reclaims its place, in other authors of Protestant inspiration, it sometimes absorbs religion and dries up mysticism by incarcerating all spiritual life "within the limits of reason".

In reality, however—that is to say, by right, in the nature of things —on the one hand, "the sacred is not reabsorbed into moral value, the religious transcends the ethical", but, on the other hand, it does not merely accommodate morality and mysticism: it remolds them, so to speak, by installing them in its heart. Religion, morality and mysticism "appear in a reciprocal envelopment"; there exists between the three both an attraction and a tension, which will be the source of many vital problems, but there is objectively neither separation nor exclusion nor

---

[4] Hence certain consequences even in exegesis, notably in the conception of the relation between the two Testaments. Cf. our *Exégèse médiévale* and chapter 4 of *La Postérité spirituelle de Joachim de Flore*.

[5] See, for example, Valentin Weigel, *Dialogus de christianismo*. Cf. Alexandre Koyré, *Un Mystique protestant, Maître Valentin Weigel* (1930), 8. On mysticism in the Protestant confessions, see the works of Hasso Jaeger.

[6] Cf. Jean de Menasce, O.P., *L'Expérience de l'Esprit dans la mystique chrétienne* (Eranos Jahrbuch, 1945, vol. 13 [1946], 371–72, note 2): by separating "religious" from "moral", Otto "must necessarily integrate it into an order that, whatever his intentions might have been, could only be aesthetic". This particular consequence does not seem fatal to us; but the cut nonetheless seems as detrimental to us as to Father de Menasce.

conflict: for "the Deity, while transcending being, truth and the good, contains them formally."[7] This is why, in particular, in Catholicism, just as the reasonable life and life according to the spirit penetrate each other,[8] *morality impregnates the mystical life to the end*. "Through it, the good rewarded and the bad punished, these pillars of the revelation of the Demiurge, degraded by Gnosticism to a lower level than exoteric faith, regain their place at the heart of the revelation of the Father through the only Son."[9] Hence, Saint Justin, in his *Dialogue*: "It is not because of his affinity with God, or because he is spirit like him, that man sees God: it is because he is virtuous and just."[10] And Father Jean Rigoleuc on spiritual persons: "All their reason, and the lights they receive by it, are given to them only so that they might be perfected in these virtues."[11] "The mystical ascent" does not efface "from common Christian life any specific trait".[12] The Christian virtues are not merely means of freeing oneself from the world: in their substance, they are the end itself; the promised beatitude is not made of different material. This is what Saint Ambrose expresses admirably in a brief sentence from his commentary on Saint Luke, with respect to the beatitudes: "Sicut enim speri nostrae octava perfectio est, ita octava summa virtutum est."[13]

Pierre Nemeshegyi poses the same problem with respect to Origen: "To place Being and moral Goodness in equation; to place this moral Goodness in God formally, and as characterizing the final ground of his Being—is this not to be condemned to enclosing all spiritual life in an anti-mystical moralism? The Good is a transcendental. But is it, formally, what we understand by 'moral Good'? Or is there not a deepening of this moral Goodness, which would reestablish the possibility of an innermost mystical depth?"[14] Again with respect to Origen,

[7] Joseph de Finance, S.J., *Existence et liberté* (1955), 352.

[8] Cf. William of Saint Thierry, *Ep. ad Fratres de Monte Dei*, l. 1, c. 5: "Perfectio vera hominis rationalis initium est hominis spiritualis" (PL 184, 316 B).

[9] H. Cornélis and A. Léonard, *La Gnose éternelle* (1959), 74.

[10] Justin, *Dialogue*.

[11] *Heures spirituelles*, ed. A. Hamon (1961), 288.

[12] Joseph Maréchal, S.J., *Psychologie des Mystiques*, 1:15.

[13] *In Luc.*, l. 5, n. 49 (ed. G. Tissot, *Sources chrétiennes* 45:201). Henri de Lubac, *Catholicisme*, 170; *Exégèse médiévale*. Compare with Spinoza, *Éthique*, l. 4, 38–39: "Beatitude is not the reward for virtue but virtue itself." And cf. *Proudhon et le christianisme*, 278–79.

[14] Pierre Nemeshegyi, S.J., *La Paternité de Dieu chez Origène* (1956), typed thesis, p. 218, note 2.

W. Völker remarks: "We observe . . . a hesitation very characteristic of Origen's turn of spirit . . . and which one finds again in a nearly identical way in Philo: side by side, and sometimes even the mutual penetration, of moralism and mysticism."[15] And Nemeshegyi concludes: " 'Moralism' and 'mysticism' are in fact one and the same thing in Origen's conception."[16] Origen himself specifies, in his argument against Celsus: "God is not merely 'the Good', as all the Platonists say, he is 'the Righteous'."[17] Saint Gregory the Great also reminds us, with his usual good sense, always linked with spiritual fervor:

> Solent quidam, scripta sacri eloquii legentes, cum sublimiores sententias ejus penetrant, minora mandata quae infirmioribus data sunt, tumenti sensu despicere, et ea velle in alium intellectum permutare. Qui, si recte in eo alta intelligerent, mandata quoque minima despectui non haberent, qui divina praecepta sic in quibusdam loquuntur magnis, ut tamen in quibusdam congruant parvulis, qui per incrementa intelligentiae quasi quibusdam passibus mentis crescant, atque ad majora intelligenda perveniant.[18]

Saint Augustine had said the same, in a very Origenian shortcut, in speaking of eternal life: "Una ibi virtus erit, et idipsum erit virtus praemiumque virtutis."[19] Picking up again Saint Ambrose's turn of phrase, Alexander Neckham, cosmologist of the twelfth century, explains that the octave of the beatitude brings the perfection of its consonance to the septenary of the virtues, as in our material universe the eighth sphere, including the whole universe, brings its conclusion to the harmony of the heavens.[20] Let us say, in the categories of medieval exegesis, that anagogy achieves perfection both of allegory and of tropology. Thus one should say of all Catholic mysticism what one historian says of Saint Bernard, through allusion to the traditional in-

---

[15] W. Völker, *Das Volmkomenheitsideal des Origines* (1931), 100.

[16] Nemeshegyi, *Paternité*, 218, note 2; cf. W. Völker, 334.

[17] *Contra Celsum*, 3, 70 (vol. 1, 262, 24–27); cf. 6, 62: ἔστι γὰρ ἀυτῷ ἀρετή (vol. 2, 132, 26). *Selecta in Num.* (PG 12, 578). *In Joannem*, passim, etc. Already Gromarius, *Origenes* (1837): " 'Die Idee' von Gott, die Idee des absolut Seyenden, der, als solcher, der Eine, Gute und Gerechte ist."

[18] *In Ezechielem*, l. 1, hom. 10, n. 1 (PL 76, 886 C).

[19] *Epist.*, 155, c. 13, n. 12 (PL 33, 671).

[20] *De natura rerum*, l. 1, c. 15, 54–55: "Septenarius virtutum perfectam non reddit consonantiam, antequam ad octavam beatitudinis aeternae perveniatur." Ed. Wright, 545. Read the sentences that precede this. Cf. *Exégèse médiévale*, 2:632. Cf. Rupert, *In Matt.* 4 (PL 168, 1389 C); Gerhoh, *Libellus de ord. donorum* (*Opera inedita*, 1:98).

terpretation of the "Books of Solomon" and of their progressive sequence; for each of them, as for him, "the moral school of Ecclesiasticus and Proverbs, a necessary preliminary for the mystical school of the *Song of Songs*, is a school whose doors are never closed behind us."[21] And, reciprocally, in fulfilling the precept of the Lord, one merits not only the eternal dwelling, one does not merely prepare for it: one is already building, Saint Hildegarde tells us, the tower of the heavenly Jerusalem.[22]

It would be good to return to the celebrated *Golden Epistle*, in which William of Saint Thierry, the friend of Saint Bernard, condenses for the brothers of the Carthusian monastery of Mont Dieu the essence of Christian anthropology and spirituality, such as the most common Catholic tradition understands them. William puts, first of all, the sublime ideal of the contemplative in abrupt terms and with an appearance of separation, of complete transcendence from one degree to another, which could be surprising:

> You have not only pledged complete holiness, but the perfection of all holiness and the height of all perfection. It is not your business to languish in the practice of ordinary precepts, or to devote yourself only to that which God commands, but to aim at what he wishes, in the search for his good, agreeable and perfect will. It is for others to serve God, it is for you to cling to him. Faith in God, knowledge, love and reverence are for others. For you, taste, understanding, knowledge, enjoyment. A high vocation, an arduous task. . . .[23]

Farther on, William takes up again the distinction of the three states, or three degrees, which is reminiscent of the free fashion of the Pauline trichotomy:

> The state of beginners can be called "animal"; that of progressers, "rational"; that of the perfect, "spiritual". . . . The first state attends to the body; the second is busy with the reasoning soul; the third finds its rest only in God. . . .[24]

---

[21] Rev. Watkin Williams, "L'Aspect éthique du mysticisme de saint Bernard", in *Saint Bernard et son temps*, 2 (1929), 312.

[22] Hildegarde, *Epist.* 10 (PL 197, 162 D).

[23] *Lettre aux Frères du Mont-Dieu*, ed. and trans. Jean Déchanet (*Sources chrétiennes* 223 [1975]; nn. 15–16). The second part of this text has sometimes been quoted separately, which adds to the "separatist" character of it and also seriously falsifies its meaning.

[24] Ibid., n. 41 and 44; pp. 177 and 179. Cf. n. 197, p. 307.

These kinds of schemas are several times accompanied by appeals to humility, which should form the common and unalterable basis for all disciples of Christ, at whatever degree they find themselves in their spiritual ascent.[25] Several points of resemblance to Saint Paul are still to be noted: the distinction between *anima* and *animus*, which corresponds closely to that between the *psyche* and the *pneuma*;[26] the reference to the discourse at Athens[27] (Acts 17:27–28); the definition of the spiritual man as the one whose spirit is informed by the Spirit of love;[28] the indication of the end as being "the unity of spirit" with God:

> There is also another resemblance to God . . . so particular that it is no longer given the name of resemblance but that of unity of spirit. It is when man becomes a single thing, a single spirit with God, not only through the unity of a single will but also through some truer expression of a virtue that is no longer capable . . . of willing anything else. . . .
>
> Once conformed to wisdom, the reason [= reasoning soul] puts [everything] to profit . . . and hastens to spring toward freedom of spirit, toward unity, so well that the faithful man becomes, as has often been stated, one single spirit with God.[29]

Freedom of spirit, unity with God: we know the abuses that such formulas have frequently covered throughout twenty centuries of history.[30] We know, too, how the fear of these abuses have made a number of timorous souls avoid them; how, still more, the bourgeois, individualist incomprehension of the last century banished them, and how they seemed suspect to many who thought they were judging in the name of pure Catholic orthodoxy.[31] Within the context of that spiritual masterpiece, the *Letter to the Brothers of Mont Dieu*, these expressions can be accepted in all their power, in the same sense that they have in Scripture. And the keeping of a moral life integrated into a mystical life is also explicitly recognized here: besides the word "virtue", which figures in the same text we have just quoted on "the unity of spirit"

---

[25] Ibid., n. 15, 17–20, 190, 296; pp. 155, 157–61, 299, 383.

[26] Ibid., n. 198, pp. 307–9.

[27] Ibid., n. 207–8, pp. 313–15. Cf. Augustine, *De Trinitate*, l. 14, 12, 16 (PL 42, 1048).

[28] William of Saint Thierry, *Lettre*, n. 249 n.; pp. 343ff.

[29] Ibid., nn. 261–63 and 286–89; pp. 353–55 and 373–77.

[30] Cf. *La Postérité spirituelle de Joachim de Flore*.

[31] Hence, again recently, the quarrel sought by some theologians with Father Teilhard de Chardin, although the latter has repeatedly explained himself perfectly. It is nevertheless permitted, he said one day, to think that in company with Saint Paul!

with God, other texts recall it with insistence. They speak "in praise of virtue, the daughter of reason, but even more of grace",[32] they show it, not surpassed by, but assumed into spiritual perfection; the latter is achieved "when the soul encompasses all the virtues in itself, not as elements borrowed from somewhere else but as quasi-natural products of its being, according to that resemblance to God by which it is the whole of what is". Mystical unity with God is wholly impregnated with morality because it is the perfect adherence to Him who is not only the Righteous but, in the most concrete and singular sense, the Good.[33]

This Catholic equilibrium was undoubtedly already jeopardized in a great spiritual master who is not at all to be confused with the false spirituals to whom we have alluded. Evagrius was considered a disciple of Origen; but, in this, an unfaithful disciple. Despite the appearances of several expressions, the same criticism could not be made of a Tauler or a Ruysbroek: they condemn without equivocation the mystical claims that think to hold themselves above morality and reason, beyond affirmations of the faith. The case of Meister Eckhart is perhaps more disputable, but it is right to dissociate the profound intention of this great thinker and this great mystic from some paradoxical expressions held to be condemnable by the bull *In agro*. *La Perle évangélique*, following Eckhart and several others, seems to place "the spirit" in contact with the divine Unity "above the multiplicity of the Persons":[34] a grave problem, which we will not take up here but which, for a Christian, governs the judgment to be passed on mysticism in its relation to the primary mystery of his faith.[35] To stay with the relation between mysticism and morality, let us say that one is happy to find a fine example of equilibrium in an author carried in other respects to many unilateral excesses. This refers to George Tyrrell, who wrote in a fine passage from *Christianity at the Cross-roads*:

> [The apocalyptic Kingdom of heaven] is the fruit and reward of the moral life, but is a supermoral life—the continuation of that divine and spiritual life which, under present contingencies, manifests itself principally

---

[32] William of Saint Thierry, *Lettre*, no. 227: "Quid est virtus? Filia rationis est, sed magis gratiae. Vis enim quaedam est ex natura; ut autem virtus sit, habet ex gratia", 326–27.

[33] Ibid., no. 276; pp. 365–67. Origen can be recognized here (cf. above).

[34] J. P. Van Schoote, "*La Perle évangélique*", in *Revue d'ascétique et de mystique* 37 (1961), 299.

[35] Several brief indications in our study on *Mystique et Mystère*.

> by morality . . . and, above all, in religion and conscious union with God. But [in the Kingdom] the contingencies, that now call for the moral struggle with all its pain and suffering, shall be done away.[36]

We will end by quoting a more authoritative witness, the great Saint Teresa, who unites the soul and spirit of which Saint Paul spoke as much as she distinguishes them with him, by observing that "the center of the soul", or the "spirit of the soul", is a difficult thing to express and even to believe:

> Certain interior effects give the certitude that there is, under certain relations, a very real difference between the soul and the spirit. Although in reality they are but one, we sometimes perceive a division between them that is so delicate that it seems that the one functions in one way and the other in another. . . . There are so many things in our innermost depths, and things so subtle, that it would be boldness on my part to undertake to explain them. We will understand all that in the other life, if God . . . deigns to admit us to the dwelling where we will have understanding of all these secrets.[37]

III. Conclusions

Optimi corruption, pessima. One should not at all conclude from this, as some authors, particularly in Protestantism, have done, that mysticism should be condemned.[1] Nevertheless, even without considering the case of the aberrations we have just seen, certain precautions should be taken in order not to jeopardize the spiritual equilibrium. Just as it is necessary to reject an anthropology that, refusing man any higher faculty, stifles the spirit in him—which is what all positivisms, all rationalisms and all psychologisms do—so it is necessary to guard against reducing theoretical or practical reason in it by failing to recognize its transcendence in relation to the sensible order and its participation in the absolute. "The mind", writes Hans Urs von Balthasar,[2] "destroys

---

[36] *Christianity at the Cross-roads* (London: George Allen and Unwin, 1909), 93.

[37] *Interior Castle*, Seventh Mansion, chap. 1. *Collected Works*, 2:432. Cf. 437: "This center of our soul, or this spirit. . . ." See also chapters 2 and 3.

[1] Thus, to cite only one old example, E. A. Borger, *Disputatio de mysticismo* (1820), 235: "Sic rationem concludo, quantum nunc mysticismum religioni, tantum virtuti noxium esse." To understand this diagnostic, one must, it is true, refer to the "mysticism" of the period.

[2] *God Question and Modern Man*, trans. Hilda Graef (New York: Seabury Press, 1958), 51.

itself and crumbles if it splits into an inferior and a superior mind, an autonomously functioning reason (*Verstand*) and a *ratio* (*Vernunft*) that is reserved for special philosophical and religious purposes." Then the risk of a short-circuit appears, from "infantile naturalism" to high spirituality; from alienating exteriority to "divine" magnetization; from the "caves of the unconscious" to the "birth" from above; from the "possessive I" that is "radical servitude" to "disinterested" love.

Charles du Bos was not lacking in clearsightedness the day he noted in his *Journal* "the necessity from an ethical point of view of guarding oneself against mysticism".[3] In the same sense, he wrote one day to Father Auguste Valensin:

> Since the end of July 1927, God, in his goodness, has recalled me to Himself, I have happened to suffer in the face of a certain unformulated—and at times even formulated—disdain that believers, who are advanced, moreover, in spiritual ways and even mystics, witness or at least seem to witness toward the moral order as such. If one admits (and I admit it very strongly) that ethics are only the narthex of religious truth, nevertheless there exist natures (to the number of which I belong) who venerate the narthex all the more as it helps to introduce them into the sanctuary, and the more their religious life deepens, the more faithful their gratitude becomes. . . .[4]

Du Bos had noted in his *Journal*, on January 11, 1925, "the necessity of guarding against mysticism", and, on January 18, 1929, analyzing himself:

> Basically, it is always a question with me of an offensive directed by the *moral* against the *religious*: because, as my Journal often notes, the moral being is primary with me; in the period when the plane of temperament is transcended, the form that temptation then takes is a moral form, summed up in the question of my right to religious life. Yes, that is indeed it; and my effort now must be, not only to adhere to God, but to consider that from the instant I do what I must on the plane of living, I adhere to him de facto. . . .[5]

[3] *Journal*, 2:234, January 11, 1925.

[4] In Auguste Valensin, *Textes et documents inédits* (Aubier, 1961), 206–7.

[5] *Journal*, 4:23. It has little importance for us here that du Bos says indistinctly "mysticism" and "religion". He gives "religion" its highest sense, which includes mystical interiority. He wrote before the time when many no longer admitted the term religion except in an inferior, indeed caricatural, meaning.

Du Bos' reflection, as we see, was not unilateral, although he emphasizes the moral, which he judges to be dangerously disregarded (what would he not say thirty or forty years later!). In return, Emmanuel Mounier was no less right to bring out the complementary truth in recalling that "morality has no other end but the spirituality of which it keeps house"; when one isolates it and clings to it, he explains, one kills it; it is replaced by moralism,[6] the enemy of mysticism as well as of religion. History in fact shows that the abandonment of mysticism in the name of any form whatever of moralism has never been, at best, anything but a stage in spiritual development, in view of a less confused mysticism. "As it is nearly inevitable, in philosophy, to pass through a phase of idealism, so it is inevitable to pass through a phase of intellectualism in morality; inevitable and good." But on condition that one does not cling to it. A deeper understanding knows that it is not knowledge that saves man from sin, and it will always ask: "Who, for example, is the one more free of appearances—a Spinoza, who, in observing actions or sentiments that the common men call sin, explains them through a defect in knowledge—or a Surin, who proclaims that to the degree that one does not see sins even in one's inadvertencies and first movements, to that degree one will not weep over one's vanities as sacrileges, one will "never get to the root"?[7] Both have cut through appearances (not always the same ones); both, in their order, are right. But, basically, how much more is this true of Surin! And if the intellectual criticism worked by a Spinozist is not coupled with a spiritual deepening, how his clearsightedness ends in blaming it! The world, Bergson said very justly, has much to learn from the great mystics.[8]

Likewise one is right not to consent to letting the understanding be classed among the provisional values, to be reduced to the rank of "naturalism", that is, close to animality. Perhaps the word "soul", so far from being univocal,[9] used in the tripartite division of man, is not without some danger in this regard. But this is not a sufficient motive

[6] *Traité du caractère*, 734.

[7] Surin, Letter to Father d'Attichy, 1631, *Lettres*, ed. Cavallera, 1:19.

[8] Cf. Isaac Benrubi, *Souvenirs sur Henri Bergson* (Neuchâtel, 1942), 43. But perhaps Bergson himself did not succeed in assigning a place to morality between social pressure and the beyond of morality.

[9] Think, for example, of the pair *animus-anima* (as in the celebrated parabola of Claudel) and, in the inverse sense, of the pair *anima-spiritus*.

for rejecting the very idea of this tripartite division, such as some, as we have seen above, were led to do. Even Sandaeus himself, an apologist and theoretician of mysticism, while noting that a number of mystics judge recourse to this division indispensable, declared that there could be room to debate this.[10] Sandaeus was thereby echoing a fear or a mistrust frequently shown in the most brutal fashion by Schoolmen in the face of all mystical thought; we know how sharp the dispute was, even within the Catholic Church, throughout the seventeenth century.[11] Since then, through their efforts to minimize the text of Saint Paul on which the distinction is based, others witness a discomfort if not a similar hostility. The mystical tradition of the great Church, however, offers them desirable assurances: thus with Tauler, transforming the way one views the classical terms of the division. He is thereby going parallel to the doctrinal tradition such as it is expressed in a Saint Augustine, for example, or a Saint Thomas. The rather pusillanimous minds to which we are alluding do not give enough consideration to the fact that, in wanting to save the absolute of morality and reason, they risk failing to recognize the gifts of the Spirit and lowering the mystical life. Stifled, unrecognized in its authentic forms, the latter, in despair, is then in danger of developing on the margins of all rational and moral norms. A certain intellectualism—very poorly named—is a worthy counterpart of moralism, and as pernicious.

To return to this latter, we can think that the general use, in the ecclesiastical vocabulary of the modern Christian West, of the term "director of conscience", to the detriment of the traditional terms "spiritual father" or *spiritus moderator*,[12] is the sign of an inflation of pure morality, tending to casuistry, or lends itself to falling into psychologism (while

[10] Sandaeus, 333: "An ait omnino extra controversiam divisio mysticorum inter animam et spiritum? —Resp: negative. . . ."

[11] In his *Réfutation du Quiétisme*, Nicole said: "The essence of the Christian life consists in doing good and avoiding evil." And Jean de Silhon, in a letter to Coëffetau (1627): "The true religion is none other than to live according to Reason, and the most pleasing sacrifice one can make God is the practice of the moral virtues." In *Les problèmes de la spiritualité* (1967), 80, Louis Cognet writes that for many authors of the sixteenth and seventeenth centuries, Charron, Lemoine, Binet, etc., "in the end, the ideal of Christian virtue is nothing more than the ideal of the honest man, on the purely human plane." For others, on the contrary, in the twentieth century, the necessary effort of morality and of ascesis is classified "under the general and contemptuous title of moralism", and one then assigns it "a very secondary place in relation to the primary end of Christianity".

[12] Roman Office for August 21, sixth lesson, feast of Saint Jeanne de Chantal.

waiting for psychiatry), to the detriment of the attention paid to things of the spirit, which is to say, to the relation to God. "Have we not seen people", wrote René Guénon, "who, when it is a question of 'spiritual master', go so far as to translate it 'director of conscience'?"[13] It is possible to agree with his remark without sharing the least part of his own notion of "spiritual master", or, more precisely, his doctrine of the spirit. Still another sign of the small esteem given to things of the spirit, and first of all of an inadequate understanding of them, is manifested in the designation "intellectualism", which is too easily attributed today to the whole doctrine of contemplation. There is, of course, a philosophical contemplation. There is a Greek intellectualism that is expressed in an ideal of contemplation. We discern some traces of it in the history of Christian thought and life; but these are only traces—and all are not, moreover, blameworthy.[14] As it has done for many other concepts, Christianity has modified this; at the same time as it took on its permanent values, it profoundly transformed it. How is it that even Christian historians have perceived so little of this? One can, indeed, if one wishes, reject the word, in seeking another that lends less to equivocation; but it should not be necessary at the same time to reject the doctrine that the Christian centuries had included within it; it should not be necessary to depreciate what is the very basis of the best spiritual tradition at the heart of Christianity. This would be at the same stroke to depreciate the order of the theological virtues, in direct contradiction to Scripture itself. The supremely active Father Teilhard de Chardin did not fall into such contempt; he forcefully maintained the primacy of contemplation, in which he could recognize the superior form of action, that which an activist will never achieve.[15] The transformations and progress achieved in the course of history, the entrance into an age dominated by the technical, the development of the "human sciences" that tend to assimilate man to

[13] "Guru and upaguru" in *Études traditionelles* (January–February 1948), 9.

[14] Cf. Gabriel Marcel, *Etre et Avoir* (Aubier, 1935), 277: "The old idea . . . according to which contemplation is the highest activity is a completely lost idea. . . . Moralism, in all its forms, with the belief in the nearly exclusive value of works, has certainly contributed in large measure to throwing discredit on the contemplative virtues."

[15] See, for example, *Le Milieu divin*, 166–68, where contemplation and purity coincide; or *Énergie spirituelle de la souffrance* (1950), where immobile and contemplative suffering become the "supremely active principle of universal humanization and divinization", in union with "the prodigious spiritual energetics born on the Cross". *Oeuvres*, 7 (Seuil, 1963), 255–57.

the object of the sciences of nature, will change nothing: not only the high mystical life but already the whole spiritual life, while taking the greatest consideration of morality and including morality (as well as of rational activity), comprises, along with varied nuances according to the case, something beyond morality taken in the human sense of the word, something beyond all that we commonly call action, because it always comprises something beyond man.

That is what signifies the great traditional theme of Martha and Mary, based on the Gospel. It will always remain true. "In his duabus mulieribus duas istas esse figuratas, praesentem et futuram, latoriosam et quietam, temporalem et aeternam."[16] And of these two realities, the second is already present, as an active anticipation, at the heart of the man en route toward his divine destiny.

Finally, the maintenance of the distinction between the zone of the natural [*psychisme*] and that of the spiritual is of a major importance for maintaining in their just place, within the limits of their competence, all the kinds of psychology. It opposes "the dissolving psychoanalytical confusion of natural and spiritual".[17] If stopping one's aim at the "rational" and the "moral" was often the great temptation, and if this temptation remains, what is to be even more greatly feared today is stopping at the "natural [*psychique*]". One of Teilhard's weaknesses, which was benign, to tell the truth, because he thought above all to dissipate the illusion of a materialistic monism, was a certain confusion of vocabulary between spiritual and natural: in the *Phénomène humain* (which does not claim to be a treatise on spirituality), he happens to speak at will of "spiritual energy" or of "natural energy". —But, "the spirit intervening, psychology is powerless. It sees everything from outside, although the spirit is lived only from within"; it sees uniquely "that part of the natural life that the spirit has not touched and which, consequently, unfolds in the unconscious".[18]

Without doubt it is only through our participation in the mystery of the trinitarian Life that we are to become fully capable of going beyond

---

[16] Saint Augustine, *sermo* 27, "De verbis Domini".

[17] Jacques-Albert Cuttat, *La Rencontre des religions*, 2 (Aubier, 1957), 40.

[18] Johannes Hohlenberg, *L'Oeuvre de Sören Kierkegaard*, French trans. (1960), 82 and 83. Cf. Pierre Emmanuel, *Le Monde est intérieur* (Seuil, 1967), 282: "Protagonist, that is what [the poet] is in the natural order; that is what the religious is in the spiritual order." Pierre Emmanuel, *Baudelaire* (1967), 38: "More than mystical and spiritual, Baudelaire's conscience is magic and natural." Cf. 113.

this psychological vision that can indeed scrutinize certain "depths" but to which this other depth is not accessible, this depth which is human transcendence, this otherwise mysterious zone where the impulse toward God is situated, the encounter with God.

> There is in us a certain root that plunges into the depths of the Trinity. We are these complex beings who exist on successive levels, on an animal and biological level, on an intellectual and human level and on an ultimate level in those very abysses that are those of the life of God and those of the Trinity. This is why we have the right to say that Christianity is an integral humanism, which is to say, which develops man on all the levels of his experience. We must always be in defiance of all the attempts to reduce the space in which our existence moves. We breathe fully in the measure to which we do not let ourselves be enclosed in the prison of the rational and psychological world but to which a part of us emerges into these great spaces that are those of the Trinity. And this is what creates the incomparable joy of existence in Christianity.[19]

Pertinent remarks of great importance in ecclesiology as well as in the liturgy, more timely today than ever. The distinctions recalled by Dietrich Bonhoeffer and by Father P. R. Régamey, based, like those of so many others, on the Pauline anthropology of the First Letter to the Thessalonians, are at once, for every member of the Church, an appeal to the highest spiritual life and a warning against its counterfeits.

---

[19] Jean Daniélou, *Mythes païens, mystère chrétien* (Fayard, 1966), 103.

EPILOGUE TO PART ONE

The Light of Christ

"If you believe", we are told, "in the divinity of the Christian religion, it is because you are ignorant about all the conditions that marked its beginning and growth. The comparative history of religions has made enough progress so that henceforth it is no longer possible to speak of a 'Christian miracle' coming to break the thread of human religious acts. There is nothing in it that is not explained in the way everything is explained. Of course some points still remain obscure, certain influences remain unperceived. The task of historians has not yet been accomplished. One can also recognize that several of them have been a little too quick in thinking to detect, here or there, analogies or relationships, and their intemperance was capable of provoking a prudent reaction in some scholars anxious for a more rigorous method. But the general orientation of science is nonetheless certain, and its result is nonetheless assured. Every day leads to a new light, uncovering some new connection, and here and now we see clearly enough to be able to affirm that Christianity is a human phenomenon, very human, deeply rooted in the earth of history, where it has drawn all the essence from which its marvelous vigor is nourished."

An objection that insinuates itself under a thousand forms, with respect to a thousand problems. A stronger objection, in many eyes, than all those of dialectics, because, without fighting, it claims to explain. Believers are upset by it. Men of good will, whom Christianity attracts and who already believe they see God's work in it, find themselves stopped in their tracks by it: they fear to commit themselves thoroughly to what is perhaps only the work of man. If it were a question only of a milieu providentially prepared to favor the birth and rise

Affrontements mystiques, T.C. (1949), 185–213.

of the religion of Christ—Jewish Messianism, Stoic universalism, the organization of the Diaspora, the Roman peace . . . —this ensemble of fortuitous conditions could indeed account for its concrete possibility, but it would definitely not for all that cancel out the miracle of its existence. A favorable atmosphere has never sufficed to explain the fact of a birth. One would have to be completely incapable of perceiving religious values to be tempted to explain the apparition and success of Christianity solely by a series of external circumstances, as important and as favorable as one supposes them to be. Better known, the information that history brings in this order can therefore only add to the admiration that already seized the Fathers, such as Saint Leo exclaiming before his Roman listeners: "Numerous States have been united into a single Empire, so that the ways necessary for the preaching of the Gospel might be ready!"[1] Admiration that was also Pascal's: "How beautiful it is to see through the eyes of faith Darius and Cyrus, Alexander, the Romans, Pompey, Herod act, without knowing it, for the triumph of the Gospel!" and who a short time earlier had had this sung to Péguy:

"The steps of the legions had marched for Him. . . ."[2]

But history seems to show us much more today. Much more even than a subjective preparation of souls, suffocating in paganism, thirsty for salvation. One by one, all the elements of which Christianity is made: the conceptions it presupposes, the notions it sets in motion,

---

[1] *Sermon* 82, c. 2: "Ut autem hujus inenarrabilis gratiae per totum mundum diffunderetur effectus, Romanum regnum divina Providentia praeparavit; cujus ad eos limites incrementa perducta sunt, quibus cunctarum undique gentium vicina et contigua esset universitas. Dispositio namque divinitus operi maxime congruebat, ut multa regna uno confoederarentur imperio, et cito pervios haberet populos praedicatio generalis, quos unius teneret regimen civitatis" (PL 54, 423 B). "So that the effects of this indescribable grace might spread across the entire world, divine Providence has prepared the kingdom of Rome, whose extensive frontiers came to touch all the other nations. It was in fact fitting to the highest degree for the work God was proposing that a great number of kingdoms be associated in a single empire, and that in this way preaching rapidly reached all the peoples already united by the laws of a single city."

Cf. Origen, *Contra Celsum*, l. II, c. 30. Erasmus, *Antibarbarorum*, l. 1: "Omnia ethnicorum fortiter facta, scite dicta, ingeniose cogitata, industrie tradita, suae Reipublicae praeparaverat Christus."

[2] *Eve.*

. . . The steps of Darius had marched for him,
It is he they were awaiting in the heart of Persia.
And the steps of Alexander had marched for him
From the paternal palace to the banks of the Euphrates.

its worship practices, the forms of its institutions, the prescriptions of its morality: all are identified, classified, ranked in their place along continuous series. Not a dogma, not a feature of discipline or of liturgy that does not have its history—a history that always includes a first, pre-Christian period. All that had been amalgamated in it is returned to its origin, and soon it seems that nothing of its own remains. How dare we still, in the face of these facts, a great number of which at least are solidly established, speak of a religion given from heaven, of divine revelation? How, consequently, dare we speak of "transcendence", of supernatural, absolute, definitive truth? Everything that is born and grows according to the common law is transformed and also perishes according to the common law. As imposing as it seems, Christianity will not escape it. Even more, perhaps, than the defeats to which it has submitted in the course of these recent centuries, the history of its origins warns us of its inevitable decline. It is no longer for us the unique exception, the extraordinary thing that it seemed to be for so long a time. It can no longer be loyally preserved from universal evolution. Whether the brilliant flash projected by religion ever since humanity existed is a false flash or an authentic light is of little importance here: in the case of Christianity, one thought to see a unique star appear abruptly in the heaven of religions and miraculously hang there; but a more experienced look discerns that it, too, was only for a moment, welded to the others, passing like the others, in this long, luminous trail. . . .

Yet the illusion, if such it be, has existed. It still persists with many, who are not at all ignorant people. This, too, is a fact that must be taken into consideration. One should not reply without further examination that the same is true for all religion. Contrary to almost all the

---

The dreams of Plato had marched for him
From the dungeon of Socrates to the prisons of Sicily.
The ideal suns for him alone had shone,
And for him alone sang the giant Aeschylus.

The rules of Aristotle had marched for him.
From the horse of Alexander to the Scholastic rules.
And for him the asceticism and the rule had shone
From the rules of Epicurus to the monastic rules.

He was going to inherit all human effort. . . .

others, without excepting even Judaism, Christianity appeared in the middle of a historic period. Its legend, if there is a legend, is contemporaneous with its existence. What a difference there is, in this regard, for example, with its great rival Buddhism![3] Why, then, contrary to so many human phenomena, is it presented in so tenacious a way as being absolutely exceptional? Is ignorance about its true origins enough to explain this illusion in its regard, or might it not be, rather, the very true perception of its transcendence that veiled by its brilliant flash certain features of its human history? The hypothesis at least deserves consideration. It is not without analogies. Many men think themselves free in actions where without doubt they are not at all, or with a freedom that is not at all real. Is this illusion completely explained by a myopia that prevents them from perceiving the bonds of determinism, or does it too not come from an obscure but truthful perception? Rather than a total illusion, is it not a simple error of localization? An error attesting to an awkwardness in analysis, a scientific inferiority, but without any damage to the essential truth.

Now it happens, too, that one badly localizes the transcendence that one recognizes in Christianity, setting it up in positions from which the experienced historian will have no trouble dislodging it. This is why, in a more or less explicit way, one conceives of it then above all as a solution of continuity. To suppose such a transcendence possible, a transcendence whose true name would be "exteriority", is not the act of Christianity. What would remain, for example, of the thought of Saint Paul—who nevertheless so dominated the thoughts of his century—if one cut it from the thousand roots that, in fact, attached it to the earth of Tarsus and Jerusalem? How can a single one of its essential points be analyzed without constant reference not only to the history of the Hebrew people but also to Greek civilization, to Eastern mysticism, to the Roman Empire? This would be an imaginary transcendence, pure chimera, linked to a no less chimerical ideal of revelation. The reality that it would effect, if this were possible, would not be superhuman but inhuman. Far from being sublimated by it, it would only be impoverished, dried up.

[3] Anyone who would like to measure the difference in historical situation from one religion to another need only read, for example, with regard to any history of Christian origins or of any serious introduction to the New Testament, the memoir that Abbot Étienne Lamotte has recently devoted to the legend of Buddha in the *Revue d l'histoire des Religions*, 134 (1948), 37–71.

It would find the path neither of our spirit nor of our heart. Artificial, superficial, and not at all supernatural. Such as those devout people of whom Péguy speaks, who, because they do not have the strength to be of nature imagine that they are of grace: in reality, dried fruits. But there is another transcendence, a true transcendence, of which the first was only, at best, the naïve transcription. An intrinsic transcendence, in virtue of which a given reality, considered as synthesis, in what comprises its own being, surpasses essentially the realities of the same kind that surround it, whatever might be the community of elements that it informs along with theirs; whatever might be, too, the ties of origin that render these different elements solidary. Any true synthesis is always more than synthesis. A certain recasting that is much more than a new combination, a certain "revival from within" transforms everything. It is, in a phenomenal continuity, the passage to a new, higher, incomparable order.[4]

Now, for anyone who can see—but which of us can flatter himself that he always can, once and for all?—the intrinsic transcendence of Christianity is obvious. It alone counts, and a direct look, well aimed, is enough to establish it. The unbeliever does not have to overcome historical continuities, nor does the believer have to refuse to see them. A priori, they must be. Scholars dedicated to discovering these continuities are not at all devoting themselves to a vain task. They can indeed often be mistaken (certainly, they do not fail to be so!) or give in to the temptation of confused conjectures: the hypothesis that guides them is nonetheless sound. The fragility of certain constructions does not at all prevent the firmness of their foundations. Besides, in research that some would hold to be sacrilege, science is after all only exploiting the Pauline idea of the "fullness of time". It is uniting in a way with the thought of the Fathers of the Church, so anxious to bring out the "evangelical preparations" in order to spare Christianity the appearance of a "sudden improvisation": "Nihil putem a Deo subitum, quia nihil a

[4] Cf. Sertillanges, *l'Idée de création et ses retentissements en philosophie*, 153–54: "It is a rather widespread error, but an error all the same, to believe that continuity and transcendence are opposed to each other, as if in the analysis of a single phenomenon the one were exclusive of the other. The truth is that continuity and transcendence are on two different planes and do not impede each other in any way. A ray of sun that strikes water does not prevent it from running, and the current does not prevent the shining of the sun. —That is true of absolute transcendence, as in the case of creation, and of relative transcendence, where general nature can suffice. . . ."

Deo non dispositum."[5] It agrees with the reflection of the philosopher who, considering the Christian event, refuses, by very reason of its unparalleled proportions, to attribute an accidental character to it.[6]

But, in what touches the very basis of religion, these continuities are only appearance. Yes, in one sense, Christianity is human, *completely human.* We can, we must speak of its birth. If the words it uses are necessarily borrowed, then it is unavoidable that the concepts are too. And how would man tell himself the truth, even divinely revealed truth, except by using concepts? There is no revelation except supernatural "in the pure state". How would God give himself to man if he remained a stranger to him? And how would his Word penetrate him if it were not also to become a human word? The messages of Saint Paul or Saint John are already "theologies", and the very consciousness of Christ is the consciousness of the Word *made flesh.* But a less rudimentary psychology has shown us that the concepts themselves are, in their multiplicity, far from expressing the whole of a doctrine: for they are, within the spirit, the part closest to matter. With how much greater reason, if it is a question of an object that is not only doctrine but first of all reality! By what makes it itself, by its original essence, which consists neither in words nor in concepts and which the whole *sum* of words and concepts is never capable of translating adequately, Christianity is divine, *completely divine.* Through the close texture of relationships of ideas and beliefs, without break, without tear, a new spirit—the Spirit himself—has passed. He has stolen in with gentleness, and he has burst in with power. He has penetrated human history, and all has been transformed. The face of the earth has been renewed by it. This was a new *Fiat,* a true creation: "Emitte Spiritum tuum et creabuntur, et renovabis faciem terrae."[7] The Spirit of Christ has founded a wholly new thing, the religion of Christ, and this religion of Christ, for which all human history had prepared, for which all human thought had slowly woven the fabric, suddenly rises up, in the midst of men, "sine patre, sine matre, sine genealogia". Pure creation, pure miracle. There we have this "new" idea, which, Jules Lachelier said, "is born from nothing, like a world".

---

[5] Tertullian, *Adversum Marcionem,* l. III, c. 2.

[6] Cf. Henri Bergson, *Les Deux Sources de la morale et de la religion,* 231: "The abrupt leap, which was definitive, was not at all accidental."

[7] "Send forth your Spirit, and they shall be created, and you will renew the face of the earth" (Liturgy).

What new ideas, though, that do not come from us ourselves! The inventions of man enrich humanity, discovering in the soul some nuance unperceived until then, but always leaving it to its essential finitude—to its incurable decay. Once past the first amazement, the ironic and despairing refrain of Ecclesiastes is heard again. The circle, enlarged or shifted, closes again. On the contrary, with a leap, the Christian Idea transports us beyond our limits. It breaks this circle within which all our progress had been condemned in advance to fit. Such was the thought, at its appearance, breaking the circle of animal transformations. It is born in its own time, it has its marked place within the progress of life, and nevertheless what it brings is much more than progress. From the time it emerges, a new kingdom has begun: the human kingdom. So the preaching of Jesus marks the advent of the Kingdom of God.[8] For how many of the sentences of the Sermon on the Mount would we not find analogies in the Jewish Bible or in the teaching of the rabbis? The One who pronounces it speaks nonetheless as man had never spoken—as man would never speak.[9] The Gospel inaugurates the time of grace. It is a wholly new order that begins, "a new order of love in the universe".[10] A dike has been broken, which lets the flow of Love pass through. Now, it would be as vain to dream of a reality more divine than Love than to imagine a reality more spiritual than Thought. The transcendence of Christianity is thus not only relative to such and such an earlier achievement. It is not only something original, something superior, a provisional novelty, clearing the way for some ulterior invention destined to go beyond it. It is an absolute transcendence. "Omnem novitatem attulit."[11]

Péguy has also sung it:

> He was going to inherit a world already made,
> And yet he was going to remake it entirely. . . .

Of course, the order of charity is not revealed, any more than is the

---

[8] C. Péguy, "L'Argent", suite. *Oeuvres*, XIV:196.

[9] There are excellent reflections on this subject in G. Kittel, *Die Probleme des pälastinischen Spaetjudentums und das Urchristentum* (1926), 88–140: "Das religionsvergleichendo Problem".

[10] Bérulle, *Élévation à Dieu sur sainte Madeleine*, c. 1 (Migne ed., col. 536).

[11] Saint Irenaeus, *Adversus Haereses*, l. 4, c. 34, n. I (PG 7, 1083). "He brought something entirely new." On the Christian idea of love: Yves de Montcheuil, "Le 'Ressentiment' dans la vie morale et religieuse", in *Mélanges théologiques*, 192–209; and "Une Philosophie du devoir", ibid., 235–39, 251–57.

order of the spirit, in all its fullness or in all its depth, to that observation from outside that constitutes the work of the pure historian. But if their inner essence still escapes observation, would the simple sight of their effect not already arouse the sense of their incomparable greatness? We know the repercussions, observable to the naturalist not blinded by an overly narrow concept of science, produced in the universe by the apparition of thought: the paradoxical properties of the "human phenomenon", its extraordinary power for expansion and concentration, out of proportion with the weak morphological originality of man, presuppose a presence of which the naturalist can only catch a glimpse, but they set him on the way that must normally lead him to go beyond his science to discover in truth the human kingdom.[12] The repercussions produced in humanity by the advent of Christianity are no less prodigious: the human spirit immeasurably increased, an unparalleled moral fruitfulness, a society tirelessly at work for an ideal of justice and unity, and so forth. These features are accessible to the historian who knows how to step back a pace. Nevertheless, let us recognize, just as reflection alone, properly speaking, can reveal thought to itself, so too only a process of a religious order can disclose the absolute superiority—which is to say properly, the transcendence—of Christianity. Like the divinity of Christ itself, the *definitive* newness of the Christian principle can be perceived only by the eyes of faith. It is here that the advantage of the simple believer over the man of science and of life over technique shines forth. For the anthropologist who systematically denies himself any inner reflection on the lived thought, as well as the historian of religions who does not consent to regard Christianity from within and to begin to live it at least through a basic attitude of real sympathy, will never understand anything about the true object of their learned studies. If their science itself does not lead them to the final affirmations, it must at least set them on the path. But if they wish to trust solely in it to the end, surrendering their conscience as men into the hands of their intelligence as specialists, the greater the latter will be and the more it will risk misleading them.

"The history of the formation of ideas", said Amiel, "is what makes the spirit free."[13] Beneath the ideas that it organizes and transforms, let

---

[12] Pierre Teilhard de Chardin, "Le Phénomène humain", in *Revue des questions scientifiques* (1930), 390–406.

[13] Schérer ed., vol. 2 (9th ed., 1905), 199.

us know how to discern the Christian Idea. This Idea has no history: this is what must make the spirit submit to it.

A great Deed was done for the world twenty centuries ago: the Deed of Charity.[14] Right at first, men's habits of thought were not any more overturned by it than were empires. Was an obscure variety of Jewish "Messianists" worth even a glance? The grain of wheat sown by Christ remained buried in little upper rooms that counted for nothing in the history of the world. Christianity itself would wait five hundred years to found retrospectively the "Christian era", and it would take another five hundred years for full Christian practice to become widespread.[15] The first disciples of Jesus still dreamed of the Kingdom of David their father; they went up to the Temple, as was their custom, with a fervor that was only increased. Having contemplated the Deed that had been done before them, they must nevertheless have had the feeling of an unparalleled newness. The testimony of it appears everywhere in their rare writings: "New teaching, new covenant, new commandment, new name, new song, new man, new life, second genesis of the world."[16] Such a feeling did not mislead them. They were not in danger, those who had seen, who had heard, those who had touched, of taking the Christian Mystery to be a more or less spontaneous mixture of the Jewish Messianism exalted by Jesus and cult forms then in vogue in the Hellenized East—any more than Christian dogma was in danger of appearing to their successors of the great patristic period as a learned product of the Bible and Greek philosophy. This chemistry of impotent historians could not have been created by them. They knew, from an immediate source, that they were dealing with something very different. They sensed the unity of what myopic analysts

[14] Cf. Isaiah 53:1:

> Who has believed what we have announced?
> Who has been able to discern the Deed of Yahweh?

[15] We know that the initiative came from Dionysus the Lesser, monk and priest of Rome, Scythian by origin (d. 540). The usage took root thanks to the *De ratione temporum* of Bede and was not truly widespread for another thousand years.

[16] Cf. Léonce de Grandmaison, *Jésus-Christ,* 2:24–25, and L. Cerfaux, *La Première Communauté chrétienne à Jérusalem*: "A joy of spiritual essence (ἀγαλλιασις) raises the young community. This joy comes from the Spirit, from the tension of souls, from the certitude one has of belonging to a new world." *Ephemerides theologicae lovanienses* (1939), 30. Amphilocus, *Sermon pour le samedi saint*: ὢ καινῶν καὶ παραδόξων πραγμάτων (O things new and paradoxical!) (PG 39, 89 D).

think to understand by decomposing it. This is because the principle of synthesis was in them, living and active. It is because, living this dogma themselves before drawing up the inventory of it, adoring this mystery before translating it, they penetrated its spiritual meaning.

In addition, their testimony is for us more than a guarantee. It constitutes a call. If that call is at first necessary for us, we do not have to hold to it. "Now", said the inhabitants of Sichar to the woman who had led them to Christ, "it is no longer because of what you have said to us that we believe, for we have heard him himself and we know that he is truly the Savior of the world."[17] For twenty centuries, the witness of the first generation of believers is preserved intact, because it always remains a living witness: *abyssus abyssum invocat* [deep calls to deep]. Why should we be riveted to history? The Spirit still gives witness to our spirit.[18] The Kingdom of God is still in the midst of us. "The Gospel of Jesus Christ, Son of God", which was heard for the first time in Galilee, under Herod, during the fifteenth year of Tiberius Caesar, at the time of the High Priests Annas and Caiaphas, still resounds today, and if the forms of its preaching are different, it is the same Voice that proclaims it. Like the creative Deed, which does not cease to maintain being and life everywhere, the Deed of Charity is pursued over the world. The second Genesis, henceforth as permanent as the first and, like it, infinitely fruitful. The Church, Bride of Christ, continues the work of her Bridegroom. We have only to contemplate her—not from outside, in her sole visible organization, with its human characteristics, which are often too human, perhaps with its defects, not even in the works of its scholars, always unequal to their task and whose insufficiency can be so painful[19]—especially when they themselves do not seem to feel it—but in her inner life, in her ideal, in her belief, in her

[17] Jn 4:42.

[18] Rom 8:16.

[19] It is a wonder, said Origen, to see Christianity spread so quickly despite the persecutions: and he added: "et eo maxime mirum est, quod ne doctores quidem ipsi vel satis idonei sunt, vel satis plures." *Peri archôn.*, l. 4, c. 1, n. 2 (Koetschau, 295). In all centuries great believers have stressed this paradox of the Church, this contrast between her human miseries and the splendor of her divine role, which reveals the Bride of Christ in her. As, for example, Saint Bernard, *In Cantica*, sermo 27, n. 14: "O humilitas, o sublimitas! Et tabernaculum Cedar, et sanctuarium Dei; et terrenum habitaculum, et caeleste palatium; et domus lutea, et aula regia; et corpus mortis, et templum lucis; et despectio denique superbis, et sponsa Christi! Nigra est, sed formosa, filiae Hierusalem, quam etsi labor et dolor longi exsilii decolorat, species tamen caelestis exornat, exornant pelles Salomonis . . ." (PL 183, 920 D).

secret fidelity, in the purity of her zeal, in the marvelous fruits of holy joy that she makes ripen in the depths of human hearts. In all that the "world" does not perceive. Then the light shines, then the Truth bears witness to itself: *veritas index sui*. No need for laborious comparisons or of an erudite return to the past. The clearsightedness of a limpid look is preferable here to all the sharp perspicacities of criticism. This is because the miracle is endlessly produced before our eyes. Today as formerly, by virtue of Christianity, "all things are becoming new." Even—Saint Augustine had already noted it—the more time advances, the more privileged is our situation as witness. The mystical Christ, in the measure he increases, better reveals his power. To the signs of it that already multiply, still others will be added when his message has truly reached the most distant peoples. Today we only begin to see all the fullness of the Deed that renewed the world. The sudden clarity of the first days has become a great, luminous path, which grows with the centuries.

. . . This great Deed of Love, Jesus, it is You, Yourself. Perceptible to man, humble, dying in a corner of Judea, oh!, yes, You are man! Flower of Jesse, You are indeed the fruit of our earth. Born of a woman, truly formed from her substance. You are not some sort of phantom come down from the clouds of heaven. You are deeply rooted in our earth.[20] But in You, Jesus, as in no other child of our race, God showed himself. You were not merely His messenger, You are His living and substantial appearance. Through You, He has not only spoken. Or rather His language is an action, His word is a deed: it is You Yourself. *Splendor, Verbum et imago Patris*. You, Jesus, on your Cross, the act uniting earth to heaven.[21]

---

[20] Fulgentius of Ruspe, *De incarnatione Filii Dei*, c. 13: "Qui nisi homo ex homine fieret, naturae nostrae particeps non fuisset" (If he were not man, born of man, he was not a participant in our nature") (PL 65, 581). Gregory the Great, *In Ezechielem*, l. 2, Hom. I, n. 4: "Creator etenim noster, quia pro nobis incarnatus est, fructus terrae factus est nobis" (For our Creator, by the fact of his Incarnation, became for us the fruit of the earth") (PL 76, 938).

[21] If it is true that the whole activity of Christ reveals it, can one not, however, think that through the Cross alone incarnate Charity is wholly revealed? This language alone communicates to us, along with the experience of Love, the knowledge of its conditions. Without it, then, who among men would truly be able to understand the Gospel? "What makes us believe", says Pascal, "is the Cross." Cf. the discourse of Peter, in the (apocryphal) *Acts* of Peter, c. 38: "It is fitting to cling to the Cross of the Christ who is the Word heard, unique

In You, God still shows Himself, and in your holy Church. In your best disciples, He still shines, so well that one cannot mistake it. For it is You who live in them. Have we not all known someone in whom a divine flame burned, which they had lit at your hearth alone? Their silent testimony is all the more persuasive. *Non eloquimur magna, sed vivimus.*[22] "As for me," said Gerbet, "I lend an ear to the sounds that holy souls make with greater respect than to the voice of genius."[23] What a great wise man concludes after long studies and profound meditations in favor of your divinity: that encourages me, but scarcely moves me forward. But that a Francis of Assisi, that being so obviously predestined to make a ray of eternity shine over our earth, makes himself your absolute disciple; that he loves You, adores You, annihilating himself before You; that he is ambitious only to place his steps in your steps and to live from You by reproducing each of your features, that he wants always to be only your humble *repetitor*;[24] that not for a moment does he entertain the idea of engaging in a personal way, of trying another experience, of adding at least something to your message: this humble and total will to imitate—*Christo totus concrucifixus et configuratus* —in the face of your sovereign independence: such literalness in such an effusion of the Spirit; such contrast in a similar holiness. . . . The more I reflect on it, the stronger the argument seems to me.[25]

After that, what do the difficulties matter in which my reason gets tangled? Or rather, how could it be that so lofty an object would not

---

and alone, of whom the Spirit says: What then is Christ, if not the Word, the echo of God? So, the Word, that will be the part disciplined by the Cross . . ." (Vouaux, 449).

[22] "We do not offer great words, but we live": Minucius Felix, *Octavius*, c. 38, n. 6 (PL 3, 357 A). Similar declarations with Saint Cyprian and Saint Anthony according to Saint Athanasius. Cf. J. A. Moehler, *Athanase le Grand*, French Trans., II:102.

[23] Olympe Phillipe Gerbet, *Le Dogme générateur de la piété catholique*, c. VIII.

[24] Saint Bonaventure, *Itinerarium mentis in Deum*, prologue, 1 (Quaracchi, V:295).

[25] Renan calls Saint Francis of Assisi: "the second Christ of the Middle Ages". In one sense, there is nothing more fundamentally false, and the expression gives the impression of blasphemy. "The glorious lord Saint Francis", we read in the beginning of the *Fioretti*, "was, in all the acts of his life, similar to the Blessed Christ." Similar, but like a copy is to the model, dependent on Christ in everything and proclaiming him. "His most decided intention," says Thomas de Celano, "his most ardent desire, his supreme goal was to observe in everything and always the Holy Gospel, and to follow the doctrine and the traces of our Lord Jesus Christ perfectly, by keeping it with all vigilance, all his zeal, the whole application of his spirit and all the fervor of his heart. Thanks to assiduous meditation, he always had his words in his memory, and a very penetrating contemplation kept his works continually before his eyes. I consider the blessed Francis to be like a very holy mirror of the holiness of the Master and an image of his perfection" (I, 84, and II, 26).

put it to flight? If You have come to unveil a new kingdom and a new existence to me, how should I not consent to letting myself be removed from my usual surroundings? Is it not normal that I have to abandon my usual modes of thought?[26] Your word upsets my instinctive logic, it overturns all my arrangements of ideas; it shatters my concepts. This is the price for the liberation of my understanding. Yet, little by little, in mystery, a new equilibrium is established. Under the secret action of your Spirit, faith is able to find its exact expressions, which protect it against the ever-reborn assaults of a reason too little converted. This was not without a long and arduous work. To define your twofold nature, as for all that is worth the effort of our understanding, it takes time, reflection, groping, disputes, materials from all sources. A long and perilous journey! A complicated, winding history, strewn with a thousand contingencies. An often tragic history—a wonderful history![27] It was through the adventurous concepts of thinkers that Catholic Christology ended in rejoining the first intuition of faith.

More than any other, because it is at the center of all, the definition in which the result of this labor is found today is imperfect. An inevitable and blessed imperfection! Not accidental but essential, necessary so that humble astonishment before the mystery may subsist in the precision of belief and in the firmness of adherence. . . . But already, Jesus, your very first disciples, when they loved You above all and when they left all to follow You, when they gave You all without thinking thereby to take anything from God, when they contemplated You seated at the right hand of the Father, when they called

[26] Cf. Saint Augustine, *In Joannem*, tract. I, n. 10: "Ne vile aliquid putes, quale consuevisti cogitare, cum verba humana soleres audire . . ." (PL 35, 1384).

[27] Paul Claudel evoked it in a page from the *L'Épée et le Miroir* (64–65): "When, in the church of my village, I hear the *Credo*, one article after the other, delivered by the unpolished voice of the cantor to which the naïve yapping of the little girls respond, I quiver with an inner enthusiasm, it seems to me that I am present at the creation of the world. Each of these formulas, each of these forms imprinted on eternal truth, I know what it has cost, at the price of what convulsions, of what injury to heaven and earth, of what torrents of blood, of what efforts, of what birth of understanding and of what effusions of grace, they have come to light. I see these great continents emerge and take form before me, one after the other, I see humanity at work, which, finally, succeeds in tearing from the heart the definitive nomination. It is like a cathedral that is at once immobile and in motion, with all its pillars, from the porch to the choir. Jesus 'passes by in doing good', but he has left behind him, like a procession of witnesses, one after another, 'these words that do not pass away'."

You the one Lord, proclaiming that all had been renewed by You and that all knees must bend before You, your disciples believed in You. Extraordinary, impossible faith—and yet authenticated beyond doubt. A scandal as grave for the historian as the dogma itself for the thinker. For, though not being absolutely the same as ours, the difficulties for a Saint Peter or a Saint Paul in believing were no less strong. Nor were those of their successors, the Origens and the Cyrils, the Ambroses and the Augustines. Modern man flatters himself when he judges that the Copernican revolution or the Kantian revolution dug out a new hiatus between his thought and the thought of the Ancients. It was as hard to believe then as it is today! It was hard, for a Jewish monotheist —"Listen, Israel! Your God is one!"—to believe in the divinity of a man.[28] It was hard to believe in the crucifixion of the Son of God.[29] It was hard for a reasonable man, who had been able to see up close the Son of Man in his humiliation, to believe in the resurrected Christ, and in all these histories "that do not allow themselves to be allegorized. . . ."[30]

"A scandal for the Greeks and folly for the Jews!" Our Fathers passed beyond; their faith conquered all the obstacles. What they were capable of, we ourselves will be capable of, and if we do not make ourselves unworthy of them, the reasons that quickened them will not be less strong for us. Their attitude will thus be ours. We could not transcend it, but neither could we restrict it without denying your message at the same stroke, Jesus. For it is no more possible to abstract You from this message than it is possible to abstract God from Yourself. On what would we base the demands of your Law if we began by failing to recognize the Demand of your Person? Who would guarantee us the

---

[28] This is the fact with which criticism collides and that inspires M. Couchoud with the desperate and fantastic solution familiar to us. Cf. Jean Steinmann, in Chaine-Grousset, *Littéraire religieuse* (1949), 339: "If there ever was a people not ready to deify a man, it was indeed the Jewish people, where the very name of Yahweh had become unpronounceable. For the first Judeo-Christians to recognize in their Master the Son of God, the greatest psychological revolution of history was necessary, brought about by the teaching and the miracles of Jesus."

[29] Cf. Clement of Alexandria, *Stromata*, l. I, chap. XVIII, n. 57: "They find it fanciful, in their illusion of wisdom, that God should speak through the mouth of a man born of man; —that he had a son—and, to add insult to injury, that this son had known suffering."

[30] In addition to the scandal of the Athenians at the preaching of Paul, recall the numerous declarations of Celsus, Sallust the Philosopher, Julian. . . . See also, for example, Gregory of Nyssa, *Discours catéchétique*, c. 11, 15, 16, etc.

hope of the Kingdom if we were not to recognize the King of it? Does everything in You not tell us that You are Yourself the Kingdom, as You are the Truth and the Life?[31] So, from the beginning, the *religion of Jesus*, which is the ideal of love, was indivisibly the *religion of Christ*, that is, the cult of incarnate Love. It is folly to want to dissociate them, and to believe that the first would survive the ruin of the second. The religion of which Jesus is the subject and norm is gradually achieved in us only through the religion of which Christ is the object. Moreover, it is blindness not to recognize their identity: it is to tear the seamless robe that the Gospel presents to us, and it is not to see the metaphysical significance of Love.

Evangelium Christi—Evangelium de Christo: a modern, scarcely more subtle form of the old antithesis between practice and dogma.[32] But in maintaining, contrary to those who set them in opposition, that there is an essential relation between them, we do not mean simply that one must observe dogma as a means for assuring practice. Their ties are intrinsic,[33] and the necessity of their agreement is only one consequence. On the one hand, "practice" can be correctly defined only by dogma, from it alone does it receive its meaning and spirit; and, on the other hand, in one sense, it already contains everything in itself, for it is summed up in charity, which is the spiritual being in act.

God is Love, and in a great feat of Love he came to take up man, sinner and miserable. Man and God embraced each other in Christ.

[31] Origen, *In Matt.*, vol. XIV, n. 7: "He himself is the king of heaven; and since he is wisdom itself, and justice itself, and truth itself, is he not also, in a parallel way, the kingdom itself (ἡ αὐτοβασιλεια)?" (PG 13, 1197 B). Cf. *Contra Celsum*, l. VI, and Ambrose, *In Luc.* (PL 15, 1722–23).

[32] An antithesis developed by Lessing, and followed by Johann Herder. This latter writes, in his *Idées sur la philosophie de l'Histoire de l'humanité* (trans. Edgar Quinet [1834], III:206): "Your religion, which is to say, your living charity, your love of man. Religion, in you, which is to say an unreflecting worship for your Person and for your Cross." He adds: "[This worship], your soul, full of the future, had rather foreseen it, and it would be an injury to your name to dwell on so much impure mud descended from your clear source." Again, it should at least be necessary to explain the immediate outburst of so much "impure mud".

[33] It is not, in fact, a matter of the observation of a law that would find its justification in a doctrine, or at least it is only a first, wholly external aspect of reality. It is a matter of a spiritual life that makes the Mystery of Christ real in each Christian, member of the Body of Christ.

The unique intellectual fecundity of this Deed: it is specifically pregnant with all Christian dogmatics, so that the latter must be called, strictly, revealed. No more, in fact, than one could dissociate the revealed truths from the very Person of the Revealer could one conceive a just and complete idea of the transcendent newness of Christianity if one did not see that in this Person of Christ, such as the Apostles already show him to us and such as the Church never ceases to contemplate and reproduce him, the reality of Charity and the truth of Dogma are indissolubly united, Charity constituting the reality of this Dogma, as this Dogma itself constitutes the truth of this Charity.[34]

As for the intellectual elaboration from which the dogma in its second state results, which is to say, in that abstract and learned formulation that multiplies it in distinct enunciations, wholly guided by the Spirit of Truth as it is, it nevertheless remains a human operation. The materials it employs, just like those that entered into the first, spontaneous expression of faith, are human materials. They can thus serve them, too, in the real (though always inadequate) transmission of divine truth only in the measure to which they are *related to the Whole of Dogma.*[35] In the measure to which, on the contrary, they are considered each in isolation, the formulas cease to bear witness to the divinity of their origin; they lose the best of their meaning, ceasing to have relation to divine charity, such as it appeared to us in Christ. For our faith is one,

[34] It does not seem, then, that one must distinguish in Christianity, in the Bergsonian sense of these words—however that may be in Bergson's thought itself, which is not here in question—as a twofold element: the "dynamic" element, which would consist essentially in the Life of Charity, and the "static" element represented by dogmas as well as by rites—even if it entails adding that both, equally divine in their origin, lend themselves to a mutual support. Some apologists have, we believe, taken the wrong road, or at least have remained on the surface of things, by striving to justify a static element *by itself.* It would be appropriate, rather, to show that such an element is static only in appearance, that it represents an intellectual condensation and, as it were, a "precipitate" of the dynamic element, its refraction across the human understanding, so that it constitutes the precise and indispensable expression of it. (This is, one could say, the whole difference of the *dogma of myth.*) In short, although an appreciable part of "static" elements enter historically into the work of elaboration and formulation of our dogmas, elements for which it will always be permissible to indicate the human provenance and to discuss the absolute value, the Dogma itself, far from being explained entirely by such elements, always transcends it by using them and transforming them. If it is the perfect norm of the whole spiritual life, it is because authentic spiritual life is nothing other than Dogma in act, in the image of the Life that manifested itself in Christ.

[35] For some complementary explanations, cf. *Recherches de science religieuse* (January–March 1948): "Le Problème du développement du dogme".

and it is wholly summed up in You, O Jesus.[36] You are the center and the bond of all its "articles". All its expressions, all its developments are only so many means of understanding You better and of situating ourselves better before You. This is why the historians who, instead of considering Christianity in its living unity—which one can do fully only if one lives it oneself—always scrutinize its elements only by taking them one after the other, as a series of detached pieces, resist any possibility of understanding it. The essence escapes them. They do not find the soul at the end of their scalpel. In Christianity, they find nothing divine, not seeing Christ in it.

How true it is, therefore, to say that if dogma is necessary for the maintenance of practice, the role of practice is nonetheless essential for maintaining the reality of dogma intact! We now discover the whole meaning of such an axiom. Without the truth of dogma—although there may be some good "unfaithful"—one will only have an apparent practice; but, on the other hand, without the reality of practice—although there may be some bad Christians—one will no longer have anything but an apparent dogma. On the one hand, a charity that is less than genuine; on the other, a superstitious belief or a verbal orthodoxy, an "orthology" without any real content. This is because, if the articles of faith are numbered, the Object of Faith is marvelously one. If the former are formed of abstract propositions, the Latter is marvelously Living! And just as, according to the old Scholastic theory, all physicochemical bodies, once assimilated by the human organism, are directly informed by the soul, so that there is no longer either carbon or oxygen, and so forth, but only human matter: so with all the elements, religious or profane in origin, that enter into the Christian synthesis. Constructed completely, in one sense, with human materials, the dogmatic formulas nevertheless express divine truth. Elaborated by men, they channel a part of divine revelation. But this is on condition, once again, that one always relates them to that same revelation, to the living Center, to the divine Center from which all radiates and to which all must lead us: to Jesus Christ. Jesus Christ, the personal manifestation of Charity. Jesus Christ, in whom are all the treasures of wisdom and knowledge because in him dwells the fullness of the Divinity. Jesus Christ, Word of the Father, who speaks him and gives him entirely. There is no absolute newness, no revelation properly speaking, no true

---

[36] Cf. Saint Bonaventure, *Breviloquium*, l. v, c. 8.

transcendence outside of the unique reality of his Person. We must always return to the words of Saint Irenaeus: "Omnem novitatem attulit, semetipsum afferens."[37]

Jesus, I believe in You. I confess that You are God. You are for us the whole Mystery of God.[38] What other definition of God would we seek than that given by your Apostle? And was it not in contemplating You that he found it? God is Love. This single word contains an unfathomable mystery, which I adore. But through You this mystery illumines our night already. For Love has done a great deed, and this Deed of Love, the Love made visible to our eyes, perceptible to hearts of flesh, effective and saving Love, is You Yourself! It is God made man, it is the Incarnation of God.

We stammer as we can. Our formulas are insufficient. Necessary to shield the treasure of our faith, their form nevertheless troubles us. But your true adorers, O Jesus, haven't You Yourself said, are not those who put their trust in frail words: they are those who understand your feat and who, sustained by You—for that costs more than blood—strive to reproduce it.

An absolute feat: nothing has any value except through charity. Charity demands all, assumes all. Charity judges all.

An efficacious feat: through this "divine strength" already recognized by the Apostle Paul,[39] he uproots us from our egotism, he *opens*

---

[37] "He has brought total newness by bringing himself": *Adversus Haereses*, loc. cit. Cf. Yves de Montcheuil, *Leçons sur le Christ*, 184–85.

[38] Cf. Saint Augustine, *Epist.* 187, n. 34: "Non est enim aliud Dei mysterium, nisi Christus" (PL 33, 845).

[39] Rom 1:16; 1 Cor 2:4. Cf. Clement of Alexandria, *Stromata*, l. 1, c. 20 (Stählin, 62–64). Origen, *Contra Celsum*, preface, and l. 1, c. 46, 47 and 62 (Koetschau, 51–55, 96–97, 113–14).

One risks minimizing revelation if one does not see that it is at the same time redemption, personal transformation, efficacious grace. It is by this efficaciousness that the Fathers judged above all the divinity of Christianity. They emphasize rather complacently—and at times excessively—the comparisons that could be made between its dogmas and the doctrines of philosophers. Cyril of Alexandria enjoys finding points of contact between the trinitarian dogma and the philosophy of Plotinus; likewise Saint Augustine. The same attitude in Theodoret, Gregory Nazianzen, already in Justin and Eusebius, etc. As for Saint Gregory of Nyssa, who, moreover, is not fond of profane philosophy, that "sterile woman", he expresses himself on the Trinity in terms that, to take them literally, would create a syncretism: "The authority of unique sovereignty is not divided into a parcelling out of different divinities, and, on the other hand, the doctrine is not confused with Jewish belief; but the truth holds the middle between the two conceptions, it purges each of these schools of its errors us, takes us, raises us, makes us capable of adopting the contours of it in our turn. He eradicates the old man and implants the new man. *Operatorius sermo Christi.*[40]

A finally definitive feat. Whatever might be the future progress of our race, whatever the enlargement of its knowledge or the refinement of its ideal, we will not be taken unawares. The coming of Christ has marked the fullness of time. No fullness, no depth will ever exhaust the Deed of Calvary.[41]

That is why, peaceful about the past. we also look to the future without fear. "Quid amplius reservandum, cum amplius nihil sit plenitudine perfectionis?"[42] Sure that our faith will never mislead us, we go ahead of the excavations of history and the research of science. Ahead, too, of human progress—and we know too well that all progress of

---

and draws from each what good it includes" (*Discours catéchétique*, c. 3, n. 2: Méridier, 21). Cf. Gregory Nazianzen, *Discours* 38, c. 8 (PG 36, 319); Maximus the Confessor, *Exposition de l'oraison dominicale* (PG 90, 892 A–D), etc. (Besides, this syncretistic appearance is superficial. There is in Gregory of Nyssa a profound sense of orthodoxy, a dogmatic intransigence, a consciousness of the incommensurate distance between Christianity and paganism, which comes to the fore everywhere; for example, *Contra Eunomium*, l. VIII: to compromise, with Eunomius, the eternity of the Logos is, however one quibbles, to work the reversal of Christianity and the return to the worship of idols: PG 45, 772B.)

The point of view of modern apologists is quite different, perhaps too different. Would it not sometimes be too intellectualist? By means of considering Christianity as a doctrine that, taken exclusively as such, should witness to its transcendence, does one not risk removing its higher character? Its victorious efficaciousness is not a superadded note. Cf. Origen, *In Joannem*, XIII, 3: "If one lets oneself be taken by a theory, one always finds oneself again faced with the same difficulties; but I, Jesus, I possess a word that makes a potion of life spring up in the one who receives my teaching" (PG 14, 404); Gregory of Nyssa, *Contra Eunomium*, l. II; "τὴν τῶν μυστικῶν συμβόλων τε καὶ ἐθῶν κοινωνίαν, ἐν οἷς ὁ χριστιανισμὸς τήν ἰσχὺν ἔχει" (the communion of mysteries and customs in which Christianity has its strength) (PG 45, 880 BC).

[40] It must be added, if that were not already to introduce us to another subject: a universal gesture. "Agnus occisus ab origine mundi. Christus illuminat omnem hominem."

[41] Cf. P. Lachière-Rey, *Le Moi, le Monde et Dieu*, last chapter, in fine: "Transposing thus what M. Brunschvicg writes of the inner unity to the conscience, we will say that, beyond the reciprocity of the love between God and man, there is nothing, not because one has been incapable of finding anything but because there is in fact nothing to seek. The ascendant dialectic is terminated and the spirit gives witness to itself of this conclusion."

[42] Saint Ambrose, *De fide*, 1, III, c. 12, n. 102 (PL 16, 610 A). "How could something greater be held in reserve, considering that there is nothing greater than perfection in its fullness?"

The very ones who want to attack the Christian ideal directly do not dare to do so fully; they must begin by distorting it and reducing it to something else. Such is, we know, the case with Nietzsche.

the world will not obtain the least beginning of salvation! Ahead of the new values to which history gives birth through its crises. Man can vary and perfect his culture without end. He can discover and exploit new potentialities in it. The very Universe can grow immeasurably, and distant stars can one day reveal a humanity more numerous, more civilized—more miserable—than our own: the Deed of Christ would still take it in. It embraces all worlds, just as it shines above time. For all equally, for each one of us and at all times, for those who believe in man and for those who despair of him, its rays are those of Eternal Life.

"He has come, the Christ of God, the Leader of the Promises! And without any doubt he has been, he alone, to the exclusion of all those who preceded him—and I have the audacity to say, he is to the exclusion of all those who follow him—the one awaited by the Nations."[43]

[43] Origen, *Contra Celsum*, l. 1, c. 59.

PART TWO

Disputed Questions and Resistance to Nazism

III

DISPUTED THEOLOGICAL QUESTIONS AND ANTICIPATIONS OF VATICAN II

1. Internal Causes of the Weakening and Disappearance of the Sense of the Sacred

If I were not afraid of failing in respect to the Bishop of Tarentaise, I would say that he has become, in a way, a devil's advocate for you —an advocate of numerous devils—by exposing before your eyes the various systems whose seductive glamor has separated so many men from the Church and from the sole authentic source of the Sacred. My own role is more horrible: it is almost that of the devil himself: it is the role of the biblical Satan, who is presented as the "accuser", as the malicious analyst of the faults of the just. I must indeed play this role, since it has been imposed on me. Yet I would hope that it be in a spirit totally different from diabolical, and I hope that none of you will mistake it. What are our responsibilities, we Catholics, especially we priests, theologians, pastors, preachers, "men of the Church", in this loss of the sense of the sacred that we note in our people of France?

Such a subject is risky. To treat it sincerely and with any chance of profit, it is best not to water it down. An examination of conscience is in great danger of being useless if it is not, at least in some regards, disagreeable. We should not, however, confuse it with a venture in disparagement. A list of deficiencies is not a caricature even though

Bulletin des aumôniers catholiques. Chantiers de la jeunesse, 31 (August 1942). Cf. *Résistance chrétienne à l'antisémitisme*, 116 [English translation: *Christian Resistance to Anti-Semitism* (San Francisco: Ignatius Press, 1990), 110ff.].

it is not at all a complete portrait. I believe it necessary to present these remarks right at the beginning, not as a measure of oratorical precaution but out of concern for truth. If we were here to trace an historical picture, many other traits would have to be brought out and emphasized besides those that I am going to indicate, traits that would be wholly to the credit of our contemporary Catholicism; perhaps it is even the reality of the progress accomplished that makes us more clearsighted and more demanding. Many encouraging signs could also be discerned: I would have to tell you, for example, that in the little town where I happened to be last week on Easter Sunday, a town that has not grown very much in population over the last century, there were thirty people in 1842 receiving Easter Communion, while there were nearly seven hundred in 1942! But the very laws of my subject oblige me to reflect on a sad fact that, as an overall phenomenon, is unfortunately only all too real and to dwell almost solely on the inner deficiencies that are, at least partially, the cause of it.

We are therefore going to examine some of these deficiencies. Others undoubtedly could have been noted and the subject taken in a more concrete way. If I take my point of view from within theology, it is not only, at least I hope, because of a professional idiosyncrasy, as Father Forestier just said; it is in order to be in less danger of remaining at the level of symptoms. Besides, I am sure you will be able to excuse what will nevertheless be a little too abstract in what this report has to offer. I will not speak of that broad subject of the personal formation of the priest. Neither will there be one word in allusion to the *Chantiers*: I did not want to feign before you a concrete experience I do not possess. After considering four deficiencies in our theological work, we will quickly point out several consequences and will make an effort, in concluding, to situate ourselves at the very center of religion.

If our people of France—and by that I do not mean only what are termed the working classes, or the masses—have lost in so large a proportion the sense of the Sacred, is it not first of all because we have not known how to maintain it in them, to protect it against other influences? Much more, is it not because we have more or less lost this sense ourselves? For the demarcation here is not absolutely to be made between "believers" and "unbelievers" in the common sense of those words. This "frightful lack of the sacred" in which Péguy saw the mark of our modern world (at times with an excess in expressions that is in keeping with the laws of prophetic language) also prevails within the "believing" and "practicing" world, within the ecclesiastical world as well. If we seek to discern its causes, four remarks can be made, which we will rank by order of growing interiority.

1. There is an easily observable contrast in many men between their secular knowledge and their religious instruction; the former is that of a grown man, who has studied for a long time, who has specialized in some professional skill, who knows life, who is cultivated; the second has remained that of a child, wholly elementary, rudimentary, a mixture of childish imagination, poorly assimilated abstract notions, scraps of vague and disconnected teachings gathered by chance from existence. The disproportion is such that it often ends in an abandonment of faith. Without doubt, it will always be true that the "spirit of childhood" is a marvelous grace, and one should always repeat with the Gospel that the Kingdom of heaven is for children and for those who resemble them; but childishness is not the spirit of childhood, spiritual candor is something totally different from intellectual default, and Saint Paul must also be heard when he says: "Evacuavi quae erant parvuli." This access to manhood, to the maturity of the believing intelligence, is too often what is not produced.

Now what is true of too many individuals was also true for a whole succession of generations. In several points of doctrine where science and faith encounter each other, while the first was developed, the second was too easily content with a few representations that might well be called childish. From which proceeded a series of conflicts, more or less open or latent, exploited by unbelief. The classic example is that of the origins of the world, of life and especially of man. It could be said in general that, for a long time and still today, the problem of human origins seems to involve a totally different solution depending on whether one asks scholars or Catholic theologians in general. Father A. D. Sertillanges, like many others, noted this recently in his work *Dieu ou rien*. This dualism has penetrated everywhere. The little child of ten is confused by it, pulled as he is between the teaching of his schoolteacher and that of his priest, unable to reconcile his schoolbook with his catechism. You know the page by Péguy, in *Notre jeunesse*, on the two contradictory metaphysics that the secular masters of his primary school and the catechisms of Saint-Aignan's parish poured into him. He received them both "with the same faith, the same seriousness, the innocence of childhood. He loved them with the same heart." But not all children have the "innocence"—or the prophetic intuition—that permitted the little Péguy to receive them together.

If theology is, in part, the result of an encounter between a given of faith, which is immutable, and a given of science, which is changeable, there is no cause to be alarmed at seeing it, at certain moments, slightly maladjusted and its equilibrium, as it were, breaking down. But the situation can become serious when this theology, in the person of its principal representatives, neglects to undertake the work of clarification that proves to be necessary. Consult certain theological treatises signed by particularly authoritative names, and you will understand what I mean. Then, each is left on his own; each, among those who sense the difficulties of the situation, tries to escape from it at his own risk. Hence the confused, incomplete theories, which fail to satisfy the mind, or even suspect theories, more or less dropping the eternal substance of dogma along with the cover of obsolete representations. The fault is often that of an indifference on the part of theologians who, refusing to face squarely the problems they nevertheless have a mission in the Church to study, too easily take to be firmness and vigilance what could well be, rather, routine and laziness.

Today, for example, when the essential doctrine of the unity of the human race is attacked, mocked by racism, do we not sometimes experience a pang of anguish when we see it so weakly defended?

These remarks could be extended to a large part of biblical history. How much time was needed for a reasonable critic to gain acceptance! What facts advanced or maintained without serious examination, for fear of seeming to "deny the supernatural"! What chronological assumptions imposed in the name of a "tradition" that, even if respectable, had nothing to do with divine Tradition! Yet, the sense eventually dawned that there were some thorny problems there that were not yet settled. From then on, in practice, there was silence, the renunciation of knowing and using the Bible. This Old Testament, which once formed the very basis of religious teaching (as the long series of "prophecies" on Holy Saturday still gives witness), this "holy history", which was then learned by everyone, this repository of so many beautiful narratives and expressive figures, is scarcely taught any more, is scarcely ever preached any more. Many theologians themselves forego acquiring a deeper knowledge of it, considering it an obscure domain, reserved for the exploration by a few, rare specialists. So the

Bible tended to become principally a source for rationalist objections to which the apologist had to respond.

There is no need to speak ill of the apologist. His work was always necessary, and it is to him that theology owes at least the beginning of much of its progress. But his task is not easy, particularly when the principles that guide him are ruinous. I can only allude here in passing to that concordist apologetic that reigned—let us rather say raged—throughout the nineteenth century and of which many minds are still not completely free today. What effort has been spent to make some particular letter of the biblical account "agree" with the "latest state" of science! Under the appearance of triumph, the process had something sheepish about it, and the effort was always in vain, always to be begun again, because the accord was always established with yesterday's scientific theory, or day-before-yesterday's. Above all, this predominance of a wholly external apologetic involved an atmosphere of combat, and, to fight on terrain where one's defeat was assured, any effort at doctrinal penetration was left aside. One no longer had the time, nor in a way the idea, to study the Bible religiously. One got out of the habit of drawing from this incomparable reservoir of the Sacred.

2. If we penetrate now to the interior of doctrine, one thing cannot fail to strike us. To anyone who glances over the theological literature of these past centuries, who consults the plan of the manuals in use and their tables of contents, it quickly becomes apparent that the proportions of the doctrinal edifice are at times poorly balanced: certain parts are hypertrophied; others, on the other hand, are greatly reduced. Why? Because the expositions depend closely on the doctrinal battles that fired particular periods: and thus so many treatises on actual grace. Because the dominant concern is less to seek an understanding of faith, to be nourished on mystery, than to respond to and oppose heresies. Here, too, a polemical concern has outpaced the concern to build a complete and truly positive doctrine.

"Positive": Has the very meaning of this word been lost? When one spoke in the past of "positive Doctors", such as Saint Ignatius Loyola in one of his "Rules for Thinking with the Church", we understood by that the great men of the Christian past who had built doctrine in a positive way, in contrast to those who had principally engaged in disputation; whereas since then, the name of "positive theology" has been conferred on the certainly very useful but still preparatory work that consists of studying historically the documents, inspired or not, that tradition hands over to us.

Of course, there is no reason to reject all controversy or to fail to recognize its providential usefulness. When error is dangerous, it would be treason to look the other way in order to devote oneself to speculation that could be called disinterested. The development of dogma, moreover, has always been a function of heresies: *Oportet haereses esse.* But the defense of attacked truths need not make us forget the rest or even lead us to mistrust it. Have we not seen, since the [First] Vatican Council, a certain number of bishops reject the use of the term *corpus mysticum* and by that very fact oppose what the Council found of interest in the doctrine of the Mystical Body, because, in the course of the preceding centuries, Protestants had made use of it? That is only one very small example. But other, more considerable ones could be cited. I will merely point out two of them.

Our treatise on the Church, such as it is taught today nearly everywhere, is constituted almost solely by opposition, on the one hand, to the doctrines of imperial and royal jurists and, on the other hand, to Gallican and Protestant doctrines. Hence we have long developments, which are of course accurate but at times unilateral, on the rights of ecclesiastical authority in confrontation with civil authority, then on the prerogatives of the hierarchy and particularly of the papacy. Hence, in consequence, the obliteration of the mystical point of view; and then, when one feels the need to give some importance to this point of view again, the painful feeling that one is dealing with two parts that one has no idea how to reconcile. How much more balanced, more synthetic, was the doctrine of someone like Saint Thomas! Father Yves Congar has just shown us this in a recent work, *Esquisses du mystère de l'Église*, in which he himself proposes to us a theology that is more serene, more concerned to make the most of the whole treasure of revelation than to oppose some particular error.

And how many of the faithful know the significance of the very name "Catholic", which is ours? For the great majority, it is only a label. For others, a little better instructed, it is a word that serves to distinguish them from other Christians, Protestants or "Orthodox". Very rare are those who know its etymology, the use that the Fathers have made of it, the permanent witness it bears to the universality of the Church in all her forms. Does this single detail of vocabulary not explain well the deviations and perversions of faith in our generation?

Our theology of the Eucharist would give rise to similar remarks. It was created particularly in opposition to Berengar, then against the Protestants. The idea of the "real presence" dominates nearly all of it, and the explanations on this subject are of a more "scientific" than religious nature. Is there not something excessive in this? We find almost nothing in our books about the place of the Eucharist in the overall economy of the Christian Mystery, on its spiritual meaning and its essential fruit, which is the unity of the Church, on this crowning that it brings to any religious effort of man, as Msgr. Terrier has recently reminded us. How the very explicit riches of Tradition are thus practically lost for most priests and, a fortiori, for the great majority of the Christian people!

The deficiency I am analyzing at this moment could be symbolized by saying that our theology is copied too closely from a collection such as Denzinger's *Enchiridion* (which is otherwise excellent in its class). Simply the mere fact of taking such a collection more or less as one's foundation, even if against all possibility it were perfect and complete, would be debatable: for the doctrine of the Church extends far beyond what has been defined, put into formulas, promulgated by the competent authority during the course of the centuries according to the occasion. But besides, how the equilibrium of the parts is compromised in this collection! How false the perspectives are at times! Right at the beginning, if the completely essential texts are excepted, a choice is made, by the force of circumstances, among the enormous mass of documents; then this choice, again by the force of circumstances, is here and there tendentious. For example, some long excerpts are quoted from the encyclical *Providentissimus* of Leo XIII on Sacred Scripture: now one does not find in it one line from the passage concerning the spiritual sense of the Bible, which is nevertheless so important both from the point of view of tradition as well as from the point of view of the Christian interpretation of the Scriptures. The choices are not alone in being tendentious: the emphases and the table of contents are as well. Current theology is not so much modeled on its sources, it is rather these sources that are chosen, interpreted, commented upon according to the need and the partialities of current theology.

Through this second deficiency, our doctrine gets weighed down with occasional developments that, for having been too dependent on a precise actuality, quickly grow old and become a kind of dead weight. It loses its radiance, it loses its fullness, it loses its nourishing quality. It loses, let us add—and this will introduce us to the two other considerations that remain to be covered—it loses its religious and sacred value.

3. During the same period of about three centuries that has just elapsed, there is one point of our theology that has not failed to contribute in its way to the loss of the feeling of the Sacred in many minds, even when the latter did not absolutely break away from all faith. It was less a matter of a theory, moreover, than of a habit of thought, of a psychological insistence that forced and falsified it. It was our conception, which is wholly modern as well as apparently clear and convenient, of a duality going so far as to be a kind of separation between nature and the supernatural. This conception, thank God, has been receding for some time now already. It can be explained historically. It was worked out in order to react against some errors, such as Baianism, that tended toward a confusion of the two orders, natural and supernatural. It was nonetheless something entirely modern, which had never in the least degree been canonized and against which all Tradition rises up. For the Fathers of the Church, man, created in the image of God, that is to say, with those divine prerogatives of reason, freedom, immortality and dominion by right over nature, was made in view of his resemblance to God, who is the perfection of this image, which is to say, that he was destined to live eternally in God, to enter into the inner movement of the trinitarian Life and to bring all creation along with him. Just as for Saint Thomas, there is in human nature as such, because it is spiritual, a desire, a natural appetite, a sign of an ontological ordination, which could not remain ever unsatisfied without the work of the Creator having failed and which could be satisfied in no way but through the very vision of God, face to face. (If there are some possible divergences in interpretation with respect to some detail or other, Saint Thomas' principal lines of thought are nonetheless certain.) This doctrine, moreover, is not only Thomist; it is also that of Saint Bonaventure, and it was for a long time, in its essence, common to all the Schools. One could say that the unanimous Tradition, for fifteen centuries, is summed up on this important subject by this famous exclamation of Saint Augustine,

which should be taken in its reflexive and ontological sense: "Lord, you have made us for yourself, and our heart is restless until it rests in you."

There is thus an absolute distinction, a radical heterogeneity between nature and the supernatural, and it is good to stress this first in order to avoid certain deadly and sacrilegious confusions. But that does not prevent there from being an intimate relation between them, an ordination, a finality. Nature was made for the supernatural, and, without having any right over it, nature is not explained without it. As a result, the whole natural order, not only in man but in the destiny of man, is already penetrated by something supernatural that shapes and attracts it. When it is absent, this absence is still a kind of presence. In other words, which we can take here to be nearly equivalent, it is undoubtedly very true that we must distinguish in things in general and in human life a twofold zone: the zone of the "secular" and the zone of the "sacred"; it is very true that certain things that we know and use, certain activities that we deploy, are, considered in themselves, purely secular. But we must add that this is, in one sense, an abstraction. For in concrete reality, nothing is purely "in itself". All, in one measure and for reasons that can vary much but that are never negligible, all is sacred by destination and must therefore begin by being so through participation.

All—which is to say, first of all, obviously, our fellow men, who are not, even among the reasonable animals (classed "according to their species"), merely our collaborators or our instruments for purely human tasks, but spiritual beings, made like us for God alone; and, as miserable, as closed, as dull as they may seem to us, at the very depths of each of them still burns at least a sacred spark, and all these sparks are destined to be joined for a salvation that God wishes to be fraternal. All—which is to say as well, all nature, which is not only the prey of our reason or the place of our material action or the great storehouse for our subsistence or the enchantment of our aesthetical sense, but also and especially the infinitely vast and diverse symbol across which the Face of God is mysteriously reflected. A man is religious to the very degree that he recognizes everywhere these reflections of the divine Face, that is, that he lives in a sacred atmosphere.

Now as a result of the dualism into which, in the recent past, we have too often allowed ourselves to be led, men, taking us at our word, have brushed aside all the supernatural, that is, in practice, all the sacred

—for, if some of them still spoke of a "natural religion", this religion had a strangely secular appearance. They relegated this supernatural to some distant corner where it could only remain sterile. They exiled it to a separate province, which they willingly abandoned to us, leaving it to die little by little under our care.

And during this time they set about to organize the world, this world that was for them the only truly real one, the only living one, the world of things and men, the world of nature and the world of business, the world of culture and that of the city. They explored it, or they built it, outside any Christian influence, in a wholly secular spirit—while waiting for others, at a subsequent time, rediscovering in the depths of themselves this thirst for the sacred that can never remain for long without making itself felt, to seek to recover the sacred in this world itself, and even in its grossest elements, as if in its source (and it is against this new danger that we must fight today, it is against this temptation that we must sometimes protect ourselves). Through a tragic misunderstanding, we more or less fall in with this game. There was, as it were, an unconscious conspiracy between the movement that led to laicism and a certain theology, and while the supernatural found itself exiled and proscribed, it happened that some among us thought that the supernatural was placed outside the reach of nature, in the domain where it was to reign. . . .[1]

Now, basically, this world is not by itself either sacred or secular, for it receives its significance only through man. It can become one or the other according to the way in which man behaves in its regard. This world is for man like a first and immense sacrament, the great natural sacrament that was, in the state of innocence, to lead us as if effortlessly to the unique Source of all that is sacred, which is to say, to God, and which even now, in our state as redeemed sinners, is to rediscover all its meaning and all its sacral value thanks to another great sacrament, more mysterious still and more intimate, more intrinsically sacred: the supernatural sacrament, the wholly divine mystery

---

[1] Cf. Gustave Thibon, *L'Échelle de Jacob*, 9–10: "Too often, Christians, instead of impregnating the world with God, restrict themselves to superimposing God on the world, and, as a result of this split between the secular and the sacred, the things of heaven, deprived of concrete ties, slide over the surface of formalism or of dreams, while the things of the earth, cut off from their eternal source, find themselves handed over to all the ravages of corruption and anarchy. Nature and grace must now acknowledge each other in our hearts, a place must be made for God, who is everywhere. . . ."

in which all the others are summed up: *Sacramentum Christi, Mysterium Christi.*[2]

4. Now we will enter completely into the interior, into the sanctuary, and we will approach the most delicate point. There, where it would not suffer from the three deficiencies we have just seen, is it not true that the general appearance of our theology, and in consequence of our preaching, to the degree in which it is doctrinal, has a too often rationalist appearance?

I am not speaking, of course, about doctrine: it is only a question of atmosphere, of spirit. I am not discussing theses, I am simply observing those of whom it is said that they "know their theology". The expression can assuredly be taken in a good sense, but it happens to stress a failing, whether intentionally or not. If we believe ourselves to be among them, perhaps then we stroll about theology somewhat as if in a museum of which we are the curators, a museum where we have inventoried, arranged and labeled everything; we know how to define all the terms, we have an answer for all objections, we supply the desired distinctions at just the right moment. Everything in it is obscure for the secular, but for us, everything is clear, everything is explained. If there is still a mystery, at least we know exactly where it is to be placed, and we point to this precisely defined site. We are conscious of being specialists in knowing what common Christians do not, as the specialist in chemistry or in trigonometry knows what common students do not.

Thus, for us, theology is a science a bit like the others, with this sole essential difference: its first principles were received through revelation instead of having been acquired through experience or through the work of reason. But this difference itself is, after all, extrinsic. How little mysterious, then, is this very word "revelation" for us: God has spoken: What could be simpler? He said this and this and also this: that is clear. Consequently, one can deduce from that this and this and also this. Scripture, Tradition are only points of departure: their contribution is at times judged to be a bit rudimentary, without anyone daring to say it too loudly. It is necessary to push "farther" than this revealed given. If doctrine increases in a way with the centuries, all is still explained wonderfully well: a major part faith, a minor part

[2] Cf. Jean Daniélou, *Le Signe du Temple, ou de la présence de Dieu* (Gallimard, 1942).

reason bring about a theological conclusion. The theologians lay in a stock of them, and they hand them over to the Magisterium, which will solemnly define those it judges appropriate according to the need. They are the proprietors of sacred doctrine. An elementary catechism teaches the rudiments, then there are more and more complete expositions at greater and greater depth, up to the large theological treatise, which comprises the science in its entirety.

Lord, Lord! There we have what men make of your Mystery! There we have how the best-intentioned and at times the most intelligent among them treat your Word! As if the revelation that, in your love, you have made of yourself were reduced in fact, as if it could be reduced to some series of statements! And as if we could "push farther" than this revelation! What presumptuousness! And what naïveté! How much more honest and more profound was the attitude of so many of the Ancients who, even though they were doing doctrinal work, feared to apply too secular a reason to your sacred teachings, just as one feared to lay hands on the Holy Ark! Saint Hilary in antiquity, William of Saint Thierry in the Middle Ages, and how many others, cursed the heretics who forced them to such a work. And it was in the same spirit that Pascal wrote one day: "The miserable ones, who oblige me to speak of the very depth of religion!"

Let a sacred silence contemplate this mystery!

It is true that this must be in fact only a first sentiment, for man must overcome this scruple in order to devote himself with confidence to the understanding of his faith, without fear of using, in their turn, the most rigorous methods. But it is still necessary that this be done in a spirit not only of humble respect but of contemplation and prayer; in a spirit of adoration. Not in a spirit of polemics or ratiocination. Not with the sufficiency of the expert or the lack of deference of the sacristan. It is necessary for the feeling of Mystery, which is one of the principal forms of sacred feeling, to persist and be ever more profound insofar as one examines it.

We believe we preserve it sufficiently through a distinction we have made habitual: that of the *est* and the *quomodo*. A legitimate distinction, certainly, but one that lends itself to abuse. In fact, it happens that we thought we conceived the object of the mystery clearly and were merely unable to understand how it could be. For example, when we ponder the eucharistic presence, we easily believe that this concept of the "real presence" offers nothing obscure or mysterious in itself, but that the manner in which this presence is produced is totally miraculous and that it is impossible for the reason to understand how it can be achieved. We do not see well enough that it would be necessary first of all and always to say to ourselves, after all the proposed explanations: What is the real presence? Or: What is the Man-God? Or again: What is the Church?, and so on. Not, certainly, in a spirit of scepticism but in an ever-new amazement of the spirit and with this conviction that we always have to seek to understand it better, but that these various subjects, which are *mysteries*, always go beyond our intelligence and that we will see all the more that they surpass us the greater our effort to understand them becomes. Whereas this "how" of mystery, distinguished by the object itself, is reduced in the final analysis to some problem of a scientific or metaphysical order, and the admission of the ignorance in which we remain with respect to it is then only the recognition of an enigma: an admission of a curious question to which the reason has not managed to respond, it does not generate a feeling of the sacred.

How, above all—and here once again it is myself I am questioning before you—how do we treat the first and final object of our faith, which is God? Is it always with that sacred respect that his greatness and his mystery must engender? Do we have a deep enough feeling that here it is not a question of an object like the others? Do we sufficiently realize his transcendence, in theory and in practice? It has been necessary for a century, in opposition to all the forms of agnosticism, to speak with a renewed insistence of his rational demonstration. Has this necessary insistence not occasioned a certain rationalism? Does it not seem sometimes, in the same way in which our whole "theodicy" unfolds, that our God is (if I may be permitted to couple these two words in such a monstrous way) a secular God? What dryness, so unattractive and poorly conformed to the secret expectation of man, in these books about God that we propose to the unbeliever (I am not examining their intellectual value here)! Whether it is a question of enormous volumes or, on the contrary, brief summaries, how little rooted their contents are in the human experience and how little they communicate the feeling of the divine mystery!

Here, I recall a little story. It was in school. In the playground, a child made fun of the sermon he had just had to put up with. A poor sermon, like so many others. Wanting to say something about God, the preacher had drenched his young audience with a flood of a mixture of abstract and devout formulas, producing the most ridiculous effect on those whose minds had not gone completely off to sleep. . . . The superintendent, who was a man of God, called the scoffer and, rather than giving him a good scolding, asked him kindly: "Have you considered that there is nothing more difficult than to speak about God?" The child was not stupid. He reflected, and this incident was for him like a first awareness of the mystery, of the twofold mystery that each person carries within himself: the mystery of man and God. The sacred had penetrated his life, and in its purest form.

Whether they are of a rather scientific order or even (and these are the most serious) of a particularly spiritual order, the deficiencies we have just examined have greatly weakened the radiance of our faith and have prevented us from fighting effectively, through a powerful witness, against so many external causes that are working to diminish or falsify or corrupt or completely deaden the sense of the sacred. In an age of scientific civilization, in fact, religion cannot remain naïve in everything without the risk of being considered childish; it is necessary that it appear, not within, but beyond the zones given over to the exploration of the critical mind.

In the face of powerful movements that present themselves as totalitarian conceptions of the world and systems of life, what action can be based on a doctrine whose statements too often remain abstract, tied to ancient controversies, fragmentary, inorganic, without internal fullness? Is a theory that tends to separate the supernatural from nature a suitable instrument for penetrating the whole reality and life of the authentically sacred? Is it not in danger, on the contrary, of favoring or promoting confusions that place the whole of Christianity in question? Finally, in a shriveled, rationalized world, how will we make the sense of this Sacred spring up anew if we have let ourselves be contaminated by this world to the point of participating, even if only in small amounts, in its shriveling rationalism?

All the more since such deficiencies do not remain isolated in the mind. They bear fruit in practice (or, if you prefer, they are the theoretical expression of an interior attitude that is also translated into the domain of action). To describe these fruits, it would be necessary to make a kind of history of religious life in the course of recent centuries. I will not even make a vague attempt at this. But, before concluding, I will merely draw your attention quickly to three points, which touch on numerous manifestations of Christian life within the Church and which seem to me to be important.

In the first place, it is certain that a religion "within the limits of reason", as Kant said, is inviable. A doctrine without mystery, a moralism deprived of any mystical element, cannot satisfy a soul that has, despite everything, remained religious. If therefore the sense of mystery and the sense of the sacred come to be lacking, something else would have to be found to replace them. These are often found, it seems to me, in a certain sentimentalism, which is characterized notably by *the abuse of devotions*.

Abuse, because these devotions are then less the overflowing of an inner life than a parasitic excrescence; because they are by that very fact poorly founded in doctrine, even when they are not based on superstition; and because they develop a certain superficial form of piety that is to the detriment of the virtue of religion (devotions contrary to devotion). It is easier to give oneself to tender sentiments and multiple practices than to deepen in oneself the sources of respect, of submission, of adoration that true love presupposes. This failing arises in worship when the essential lines of the liturgy are as if swamped or monopolized by secondary details, when the ritual of the sacraments (baptism, confirmation, anointing) is scarcely understood by most of the people and scarcely opens them at all to mystery, when preaching seems to play an ornamental role in ceremonies, a little like the organs, green plants, tapestries, lights and verger, when an opulent or shoddy luxury replaces the beauty that would spring from a praying people. Much has already been done to rediscover the Mystery of Christ in its sobriety and seriousness at the altar; much more, however, remains to be done.

In the second place, and in consequence, the opinion has spread, in many of our countrymen perhaps more than in other countries, that *religion*, that is, in practice, Christianity, *is the affair of women and children.* A relatively recent prejudice. Let us consider our seventeenth century and the number of religious geniuses that it produced among men, and not only among priests, for one of the greatest of them was Pascal. On the threshold of the century, Saint Francis de Sales dedicated to his Philothea the *Introduction to the Devout Life*, but the *Treatise on the Love of God* he addressed to his Theotimus. And, at the very end of the century, that great director of consciences, Fénelon, directed a whole elite of eminent men. In between, there was, for example, the story of Port-Royal. Many laymen, at that time, were actively interested in dogma, in the liturgy, in asceticism; they knew the Christian past, they read the Fathers of the Church. For some of them, the mysteries of religion were "terrible mysteries", which is not perhaps an excellent definition: but which is not as perversely Jansenist as has sometimes been said, for this word "terrible" is a translation of *tremendum*, which is a traditional word and designates at least one of the characteristics of the sacred; which shows, in any case, that these men had a profound and serious idea of their religion. In the nineteenth century, on the other hand, the Catholic renaissance became sentimental and feminine. Religiosity outstripped religion. It was the period of romanticism. The beautiful, the very beautiful verse of Lamartine: "Happy the man to whom God gives a holy Mother!" is like a slope at the base of which one perceives more than one indulgent sneer, a smile that is sometimes nervous. Proudhon will have no difficulty letting his wife keep a crucifix in her room and will have his children baptized; Renan will say: "Christianity satisfied everything in me except my reason", and so forth. As was said in the preceding century: "Religion is necessary for the people", now they began to say: "Religion is necessary for women."

In the third place, finally, it seems that in the Church we are a little too quickly discouraged, not certainly from giving faith to these men who considered that religion was not made for them, but from giving them that fullness and keenness of religious sentiment that constitutes the sense of the sacred. All has often taken place as if the normal domain of man, even the believing man, were the secular domain; as if it were understood in advance that, in order to interest men seriously, it was necessary to speak to them of other things besides religion itself. Other things that were often excellent, indeed, necessary, but that were found to be a pretext for avoiding the essential.

Was this a simple tactic? Or was it an insufficiency in ourselves? In our ecclesiastical literature, between the abstract theology, or the spirituality for specialists, and the at times mediocre quality of popularized piety, where, for a long time now, has been the place of religion itself, simple, concrete, human, virile, profound religion? On the one hand, we had a hypertrophy of piety particularly for the use of women, and, on the other hand, we created, for example, a social morality or other, more indifferent things. Now, it is very certain that religion must inform everything, penetrate everything, that all the activities of man must be Christianized, that it is therefore necessary to broach, in our teaching and in our day-to-day apostolate, all sorts of subjects that do not seem to be purely religious; but the phenomenon I am trying, a bit awkwardly, to grasp here was very different. It can be connected to the inclination toward politics: the latter certainly constituted, for one segment of the clergy, an habitual temptation. It could only have protected itself fully from this if its thinking had been more firmly established in the heart of religion, whereas it was established, on the contrary, in a climate as unfavorable as possible to the flowering of the sense of the sacred. But I can only touch in passing on this subject of politics and clericalism, which would require a separate study.[3] You are familiar with the page from Péguy, which is always instructive, even if we consider it not to be entirely equitable in its generalized form:

> How is it that we have always had, even with our old parish priests, even with those we loved like sons, only a rather hesitant relationship and a certain feeling of defensiveness? That is one of those secrets of the heart where one would find the most profound explanations. We no longer believe a word of what our old masters said; and our masters have kept our whole heart, a maintenance, a complete openness of trust. We believe entirely what our old priests said (I do not dare say more than they themselves believed, because it is never necessary to say what one thinks), and our old priests certainly had our heart; they were such fine men, so good, so devoted, but they never had that peculiar kind of total openness of trust from us that we gave *de plano* and so liberally to our lay masters, and that we have kept wholly for them.
>
> This is not the place to go deeply into this secret. That would require a dialogue, even several, and I am not saying that I will write them. It is the very problem of the temporary dechristianization of France. There must be some reason why, in the country of Saint Louis and Joan of Arc, in the city of Saint Geneviève, when one begins to speak of Christianity, everyone thinks it refers to MacMahon, and when one is preparing to speak of the Christian order, everyone thinks it refers to the sixteenth of May. . . .[4]

There are many other traits still to be noted, some perhaps more important than those I have retained. But this is enough, if not too much, criticism. Through seeing the shortcomings, we risk letting ourselves get depressed, and I already have a feeling of remorse over the task

---

[3] Cf. Joseph Lecler, "Qu'est-ce que le cléricalisme?", in *Construire*, 7 (1942).

[4] *L'Argent*, in *Oeuvres complètes*, 3:411–12.

accomplished before you. In conclusion, is it necessary to propose a few remedies? After all that has already been said, I would like to stress this. The essential remedy, basically the only remedy, is nowhere but in the lived understanding of the twofold character of Christian and priest, which is to say, in a more complete, ever-renewed restoration of the sense of the sacred in all its authentic tenor in a way that avoids the twofold peril of slipping into the secular and of a sacrilegious surrender to a "sacred" usurper.

The Sacred, for us, is Christ, God and Man. God, he infinitely surpasses us in his Mystery: he is Transcendent, the object of sovereign respect and adoration. Man-God, he opens to us his Mystery, he reveals to us that God is Love, he introduces the creature to the interior of this Mystery of love. Is the sacred untouchable? Yes, certainly, and yet we touch it. Is the grandeur inaccessible? Yes, and yet we are raised up to him; he is that *tremendum*, the object of a religious fear? Yes, and yet he draws us to himself by opening his Heart to us. Against the background of biblical revelation, where God manifests himself particularly in his greatness, the Gospel shows him to us in his Goodness. May this twofold and unique revelation show through us, may it be translated into our gestures of prayer and into our fraternal gestures, that in the whole life of the priest, the consecrated man, men may perceive a mystery and that they may understand that this mystery is, in the final analysis, a mystery of love.

2. "Catholic Action"
Positions, June 12, 1943

There can be no doubt about the basic answer to the question you pose. Even if the discussion of it were entirely unrestricted for a Catholic, it is far too certain that Catholic Action represents an immense gain, in the life of the Church in our age, for anyone to consider for an instant renouncing it. In any case, there could only be a question of carrying results beyond what it has already attained, not of returning to a point short of that. Moreover, it seems no less clear to me that this is just as the youth of the Church understand it. Do we not in fact read in the article to which you allude: "At most, we would like to avoid resting too comfortably on attainments, to lead to the discovery of complementary objectives, so that the creative impulse might not fall back before the whole task is accomplished."

The spirit of Catholic Action is the very spirit of the Church, first of all because it is authentically a spirit of the Church. Its method of

---

Positions was the weekly founded by Roger Radisson in 1942, after the disappearance of Stanislas Fumet's *Temps nouveau.* (Cf. *Églises et chrétiens dans la Seconde Guerre mondiale*, vol. 2, *La France* [1978]. Actes du Colloque de Lyon, Presses universitaires de Lyon, 1982: Renée Bédarida, "Roger Radisson et l'Hebdomadaire *Positions*", 1942–1944, 421–41.) *Positions* ended on July 29, 1944, with its eighty-first issue. "Roger Radisson, arrested by the Gestapo, imprisoned at Fort Montluc, was subjected to torture. On August 20, 1944, at Saint-Genis-Laval, he fell under German bullets" (ibid., 441).

On this occasion, cf. the letter of Cardinal Gerlier, which he himself carried personally and read to Commander Knap, on August 22, 1944, on his return from Saint-Genis-Laval:

"I have the painful duty of bringing you, along with the expression of the indignation I experienced in the face of a spectacle that words cannot portray, a solemn protest against the abominable cruelty of the execution carried out there on August 20 and that unfortunately continues to be carried out against many others.

"I have seen, in the course of my life, many horrible spectacles. I have never seen any that revolted me as much as that which I viewed there a short while ago. . . .

"I cannot believe that your human heart would not shudder like mine and those of all the witnesses of these horrors shuddered.

"I am convinced that you yourself are not aware of the refinement of savagery that marked that atrocious execution, but I do not hesitate to declare that those who bear the responsibility for it are forever dishonored in the eyes of humanity.

"May God deign to pardon them!"

(Note by Cardinal de Lubac, 1989.)

a specialized apostolate responds and will respond for a long time to come, if not always, to practical necessities. It is true that this method is only one means and that it is in fact desirable that, throughout their movement, militants and leaders be able to glimpse and desire the end, which is the spiritual unity of all believers in the one Church; they must tend to form with everyone "but one soul" in a single body, the Body of Christ. But precisely the different movements of Catholic Action are in their way the different members of this one Body, and reacting against this differentiation of members would not be to advance the work of real unity but, on the contrary, to retard and perhaps to compromise it. We would be in danger then of obtaining, at best, only a formal unity, a worthy counterpart of that formal freedom in which a certain liberalism has long thrived with what has been justly designated today an unconsciousness or hypocrisy.

Yet, is it not to be feared that these movements of Catholic Action, through their very specialization, might lead to making too great a place for temporal action, thereby losing to some small degree sight of the Church herself? I do not deny that many delicate problems are posed here, problems that are difficult to resolve in practice and for which, as well, an ideal solution is undoubtedly impossible. But do we believe that ecclesial unity, and first of all that of the parish, could ever be real and living if it operated only on an abstractly spiritual level? Does the history of parishes not show us that, at the time of their prosperity, they were a center of social as well as religious activity? (Cf. the pastoral letter of Msgr. Terrier, *Positions* [1943], 41.) And, except for the case of a very small minority, do we believe, moreover, that a temporal action that is both powerful and well directed could be led by Catholics left entirely to their individual initiative? In the majority of cases, it is outside the Church and her doctrine that they will go to seek their inspiration.

Of course, Catholic Action cannot take the place of temporal institutions, and certain contingencies can nevertheless make the creation of such institutions by Catholics necessary, or at the very least desirable. In failing to recognize this need on principle, Catholic Action would tend to separate religion from real life, contrary to its spirit; by claiming to suffice, it would temporalize itself excessively and would be on its way down the slope of a certain clericalism, no less contrary to its spirit. But it is one thing to monopolize the temporal and something else again to inspire it through an action that inserts the religious into the social.

What remains true is that Catholic Action must know how to criticize itself in its accomplishment, in its own name. An effort of this kind, if carried out in the desired conditions of calm and sincerity, is always fruitful. So we will be grateful to the Youth of the Church for urging us to do so.

Like everything that is excellent in principle, Catholic Action naturally risks growing dull by the sole fact that it endures and risks losing something of its original *élan*; its methods risk changing into process; by inflating its manpower without enough discernment, by accepting on too large a scale faithful who are too "habitual" and insufficiently spiritual, it could lose its *élan* and let the political, in the broadest sense of the word, gradually predominate over the apostolate. The danger of clericalism is not excluded either, something that could discourage initiatives and keep away the strongest personalities. If questions of good external order and the concerns of human prudence were to take precedence over necessary commitments, it would totally lose its vitality, along with its *raison d'être*. Finally, we must take care that an action that is not disinterested in the social consequences of the gospel remain faithful to the evangelical inspiration, so as not to fall into a dream of eudemonism or into a kind of social humanism in which imagination plays the greatest part and which would tend to confuse "Christian social order" with the Kingdom of God.

But, if it is important to keep an eye open for these dangers, it is nonetheless important to discern with care in what spirit more or less explicit criticisms of Catholic Action are made. Some attack real or possible distortions in the name of the Christian ideal conceived in all its uncompromising rigor and aim only at promoting greater perfection; some others, on the contrary, beyond these same distortions, which it is not always a matter of denying, might well be attacking Christianity itself. So, a discernment of spirits is imperative here as the most urgent task.

3. Against Vain Impatience

The race of minor prophets sprouts many a descendent today. There is no need to complain of this. We should even congratulate ourselves, if they can refrain from completely rejecting the parallel heritage of the Wisdom literature.

They tend to see things in black. This is not at all a crime: it is a law of the genre. A comforting impression emanates from their very groans and their ironies. The list is already long of these pamphlets whose occasionally juvenile excesses, partialities, indeed blunders, have been unfailingly brought to light; and the suspect inclinations of their authors have at times been shown. I prefer to observe the family likeness they offer, despite everything, to writings and subjects of a more serious tone. In a satirical fashion (and this is only a borrowed fashion), they echo so many cries of alarm issuing from the hearts of the apostles! They join in the concerns of the Hierarchy. Now this is what reassures me. This anguish, this anxious search, this ever-wakeful thought, this realistic, unrelenting self-criticism, this swelling number of "experiences": these are not the signs of a religion that is dying or of a faith that is growing dim. How much more dangerous would be a euphoria that sinks little by little into its dream! How much more alarming, that self-satisfaction that no longer allows any reaction, any reform, any salutary invention! The Holy Spirit is protecting us from this today more than in other periods. All Christians of good will are shaken from their sleep. Everywhere in the Church, at all degrees, in all circles, there is a sharp, painful, sudden awareness of both the misery of a world that is becoming paganized and of our own multiple deficiencies, we who are the messengers of its salvation.

An uncomfortable, perhaps perilous situation, but healthy and stimulating. There is no doubt that we have entered a crisis. How could the religious man not suffer at least the repercussions of our disordered age? How could he not be sensitive, if only obscurely, to the storms

---

Response to an inquiry by *Esprit*: "Monde moderne, monde chrétien", *Esprit*, 125 (August-September 1946), 285–88. Cf. *Mémoire sur l'occasion de mes écrits* (Namur: Culture et Verité, 1989), 242 (English trans.: *At the Service of the Church* [San Francisco: Ignatius Press, 1993]) (read: 1946, not 1947).

that still threaten? With some, everything seems to have been placed in question, from the methods of action to the forms of thought. They question themselves about the value, the authenticity, the profit of all the pieces of which the old religious instrument is, so to speak, composed. They denounce the worn wheels, the loose springs. They measure its maladjustment. Who would be surprised that there might be in all that more than one illusion to the contrary, that, in the diagnosis of evil as well as in the choice of remedy, some errors or lack of moderation might have slipped in? A just intuition of new needs can be accompanied by too narrow a knowledge and some illusion. But, once again, all that, taken together, is a sign of life. The current agitation does not have to do with Christianity itself: it has to do with the multiple conditions that must allow them to animate everything. The very thing that could be interpreted as a danger or a symptom of disintegration can, if it receives the required direction in time, contribute to the renewal that is being prepared.

History can instruct us here. Our world is more unaccustomed to Christianity now than it was fifty or a hundred years ago (which does not mean to say its customs were more Christian then). But is Christianity in a recession? That would be a wrong conclusion. In many respects, the situation seems better. We would no longer find, I believe, the same number of omens as there were around 1830 predicting Christianity's immediate demise, omens that were apparently well placed and worth being listened to. If it occupies less surface space today, it is taken more seriously. Intellectually and socially, in fact, there is no doubt that it has progressed greatly—I mean in the awareness of its followers, helping in a way toward a reconquest of itself, to the degree that it stops looking like a thing of the past. More than in other times, it thereby becomes present to the world again. I know all that can be said to the contrary. I, like everyone else, see very well the misunderstandings, the obstacles; I suffer from them along with all the disciples of Christ. But my judgment is not shaken by them. For, as it is currently lived by a growing number of faithful, Christianity has what it takes to reduce these misunderstandings, to overcome these obstacles. I am thinking in particular of that rise in young men, forming neither a school nor a party, of virile and considered faith, open and firm. . . . Contact has again been made, in depth. If the great breakthrough has not been made—and there is no need to expect it tomorrow—it is at least going well.

Let us not dream, moreover, of an easy presence, of a world where one can be a Christian without any rupture. The religion of Christ is, like its Founder, a sign of contradiction. It is never triumphant, and if it happens to seem to be so, the appearance is perhaps never more misleading than in this case. It is not giving way to eloquence or a romantic sentiment but in order to enunciate a law of its nature that we repeat Pascal's words on Christianity: it, like Christ, must be in agony until the end of the world.

Yet, new Sons of Thunder, some grow impatient. They would like it to be, they say, more effective—although with another kind of efficacy than the fire of heaven! I have difficulty understanding this complaint or this regret. Is it a question (in the broadest sense) of a political effectiveness? But first of all, where, in the past one or two hundred years, not to go back any farther, do we see Christianity called to preside over earthly affairs? Where do we see the century, in its principal representatives, ask it for its Lights? Has the conduct of societies or states been committed to it, even for a time? Christians as a whole, both governing and governed, have on this point followed in the wake of the world, in such a way that, if one were to reproach them, it would not be so much for impotence as for resignation. How, consequently, would the handful of those who did not accept such a state of things not often have proved timid or inexperienced? One must much rather wonder at the fact that, against winds and tides, what has been called Catholic social action has achieved a work of doctrine and of penetration whose fruits are not negligible. And if one wants a more specific example of efficacy, who could argue with the fact that the resistance of the Christian conscience throughout the entire world, beginning with Germany, was one of the determining factors that brought about the downfall of nazism, that dehumanizing machine of our species?

But without failing to recognize the urgency of the problems of the city or the irreplaceable part Christianity brings to their solution, how can we forget that Christianity's intention is to resolve a higher and more extensive, more constant and more complete problem? Presupposing—and we are unfortunately far from it!—so perfect a social operation, which is to say, an order as human as possible, its work would not, so to speak, have begun. On the other hand, if it sought temporal effectiveness above all, even the latter would not be given it; and if it expected, in order to accomplish the work of salvation in the midst of the world, that temporal conditions might be better in the end, it would be unfaithful to its mission, which is to save, not a future humanity that is only a myth, but all of humanity, in the concrete men of each generation. If, therefore, we can and sometimes must be severe with those who bear the name of Christian—with ourselves—it is still necessary that our severity not mistake its object. . . .

Only here do we approach what is essential. But how can we express this essential? We others, said an old apologist, at a time when the Christian community was composed of scarcely more than poor, unlettered men, without any influence over the institutions of the Empire, "we others, we speak little, but we live." These words always remain true. Christian vitality is much less dependent in any period on all that is debated and takes place on the world scene than one is led to believe. Beneath the political agitations, the swirl of opinion, the currents of ideas and the controversies, escaping the auscultations and the inquiries, a life is maintained, is transmitted, which it is nearly impossible to judge from outside. My conviction, based on obviously too brief an experience, is that in our days, in many members of the Church, this life—a life given by God, a life of faith, of hope and of charity—is of a depth, a purity, a vigor very rarely attained.

4. The Problem of the Development of Dogma

I

When Father M. Tuyaerts published his *Étude théologique sur l'évolution du dogme* in 1919, he ran into the liveliest resistance at the very heart of the School. This is in fact because this *enfant terrible* of intellectualism was making an all-out attack! His victims were not only heterodox thinkers, modernists, superficially analyzed, or even Catholic authors such as Blondel and Newman. They also included two theologians who had just treated the question *ex professo* with more authority: Fathers Léonce de Grandmaison and Ambroise Gardeil. And these polemical excesses were engendered directly by the excess of the doctrinal position. Reducing straight off the vast and complex problem of development to the classical problem of "theological conclusions", Father Tuyaerts brought it the narrowest and also the most generous solution. His doctrine is summed up in these two theses: all theological conclusions, and only they, are definable: in other words, they are so as such. "The limit of theological conclusions", he wrote, for example, "is also the limit of the evolution of dogma"; the latter, considered from an objective or subjective point of view, is in any case "of a purely logical or dialectical order". It follows that "the doctrine of nearly all the articles of the Summa" was "fit to constitute new dogmas" and that the twenty-four "Thomist" theses, while being "of a philosophical

---

Recherches de science religieuse, 35:130–60, with an unpublished appendix from 1955: "From the Vatican Council to the Development of Dogma".

"In 1948, I also published in *Recherches* a 'Bulletin' that surveyed the principal current theories concerning the *development of dogma*, reviewing them one by one. I took Newman's principles as my basis. For the very conception of the 'bulletin', I was inspired by those once published by Father de Grandmaison in that journal, which he had founded, and I would have liked to be able to set up a team of specialists, whose respective reports would have consisted of, not a mere series of reviews, but a clarification, through the examination of a select number of recent studies, of a real and central problem concerning their discipline" (*Mémoire sur l'occasion de mes écrits* [Namur: Culture et Verité, 1989], 65; English trans.: *At the Service of the Church* [San Francisco: Ignatius Press, 1989], 64).

order", were nonetheless "at the same time of a revealed order", while, on the contrary, no proposition could ever be defined by the Church or considered as revealed that had not appeared rigorously proved from its premises.[1]

The work, as we have said, was generally poorly received.[2] To tell the truth, it was scarcely taken seriously. Either one or the other of his two theses was judged prohibitive. Thus, Father Gardeil reproached his colleague from Louvain first of all for having extended "indefinitely the domain of the definable"; he asked for some distinction between conclusions and conclusions; he refused to hold as an object of dogmatic definition those that included a premise of reason and, without denying, far from it, what he called the "homogeneity as such" of theology with revelation, he had the wisdom not to attribute to it an "absolute homogeneity". Next—and it is particularly this second point that interests us here—he no less refused to admit that a dialectical operation was ever sufficient to effect development, or even that it was necessary. "That the divine action", he wrote, "cannot be analyzed by us with certitude is without doubt what disorients a dialectician, but it is not what surprises a believer, for whom Christianity is not necessarily a religion of syllogisms and who finds that, by right, divine intervention is far more homogeneous with the demonstration of the object of faith than dialectic." And here is how he summed up his judgment: "Too narrow, too inclined to measure the divine word (which has been given us, after all, to lead us to heaven) according to the sole demands of a reasoning that is given us to instruct us about the earth, too generous with regard to logic and not enough with regard to the freedom of divine initiatives and the unknown ways and means of men that divine Providence employs, in the conduct of its dogma as in the world, so this exposition seems to us." In brief, he concludes, not without irony, "it is a fine case of theologism."[3]

After, just as before, the daring and unfortunate essay by Father Tuyaerts, the work that Father Ambroise Gardeil published in 1908

---

[1] M. M. Tuyaerts, O.P., *L'Évolution du dogme. Étude théologique* (Louvain, 1919); cf. 192, 214, 201, 206, etc., 236: "The nature of dogma and that of our mind make possible only one single process in dogmatic evolution: the dialectic process, or the process of reasoning."

[2] Cf. H. Riedinger, *Revue pratique d'apologétique*, 34 (1922), 689–91; J. Rivière, *Revue des sciences religieuses*, 2 (1922), 186–88.

[3] A. Gardeil, "Bulletin d'introduction à la théologie", *Revue des sciences philosophiques et théologiques*, 9 (1920), 658, and 11 (1922), 689.

on *Le Donné révélé et la théologie* continued to be received with favor in the most classical circles. No one was surprised to find there a series of well-marked distinctions between dogma and theology, and, within theology itself, between theological knowledge and theological system. Nor was anyone surprised to read there that "there are some theological conclusions of the first order that are not dogmas", while certain others, "only probable from the point of view of logical appearances, have given rise to definitions". It was not considered strange that the true field where definitions are prepared was not "the purely dialectical field" but "that of the living and social faith of the Church", and of "the Church as a whole, teaching and taught". There was no difficulty in admitting that the principle of differentiation between purely theological assertions and definable truths was, "by social order and basic value, supernatural".[4]

The same was true for Father Léonce de Grandmaison. The latter "will defend himself very well all alone", Father Gardeil had said. He did not even need to defend himself. The series of articles he had devoted in 1908 in the *Revue pratique d'apologétique*[5] to the development of dogma continue to be a light for many. All the problems, to be sure, were not resolved in it: Who would flatter himself as having resolved everything? Would such a claim even have meaning? But it was admirable in its balance, in the psychological acuteness, the sure knowledge of facts and traditional doctrines and, in the most noble meaning of the term, the ecclesiastical sense that made his work one of the most outstanding and most effective in the battle against modernism. Soon after his death, in 1927, when there was interest in gathering together some of the articles he had written over a period of some thirty years, this series formed the largest part of the collection entitled *Le Dogme chrétien: sa nature, ses formules, son développement.* Now Father de Grandmaison, too, was far from thinking that it was enough for an assertion to be correctly deduced from a given of faith in order to be established in dogma; he tended rather to believe that its very

[4] A. Gardeil, *Le Donné révélé et la théologie* (Paris, 1909), 174 and 179–80. In his work *Critique et catholique*, 2 (Paris, 1914), Father Étienne Hugueny adopted the same position as Father Gardeil; 49: "The rigorous deductions of synthesis or of logical analysis are not the sole means the Church has to disengage a dogmatic teaching from the explicitly revealed propositions in which it was only sketched out. . . ."

[5] "Le Développement du dogme chrétien", *Revue pratique d'apologétigue*, 6 (May to July 1908).

character as conclusion, if it had required "a logical discourse going beyond a simple expression of terms", prohibited it from ever being so,[6] and of the contrary opinion he believed he could write, since he would encounter so few voices in disagreement around him at that time, "This opinion, generally abandoned . . . , does not seem ever to have been revived." But, he adds—and this was the point dear to his heart—"the question remains entirely that of knowing whether the Church could recognize and proclaim a revealed truth in areas where all our reasoning, all our investigations would arrive only at a theological conclusion, *or even less*." Responding in the affirmative, he gave the following explanation:

> This authority to go beyond in certain cases, on the irreducible evidence of a systematic exposition, the natural scope of the historical and logical "discourse" that prepares the definition; this superior gift of intuition that makes the Church clearly aware of truths that no demonstrative argumentation has shown obviously present in the deposit of revelation; this kind of prophetic instinct that gradually inclines the ecclesiastical Magisterium in the direction of an analogy, of an agreement of faith, of a warm propensity of the Christian people, and then makes it find the necessary distinctions and the triumphant responses—this is the work of the Holy Spirit in the Church, the accomplishment of the promises of the Master, the driving force of dogmatic development.[7]

---

[6] Such was also the teaching of Father Schultes, O.P., a teaching condensed in his *Introductio in Historiam dogmatum* (Paris, 1922); cf. 195: "Conclusiones theologicae quoad se, id est doctrinae virtualiter tantum revelatae, tanquam dogma definiri nequeunt." It is true that the author greatly expanded the field of "conclusiones theologicae quoad nos tantum", judged by him as alone definable. Cf. *R.S.P.T.*, 14 (1925), 301, and 15 (1956), 593–94.

[7] L. de Grandmaison, *Le Dogme chrétien* (Paris, 1928), 251–52, 255, 262–63; cf. 264: "There is no need to seek some exact proportion between the dogmatic definitions and the inquiries made, the motives alleged by those who, in the name of God, pronounce them. . . . The reasons alleged . . . are so little the measure of this infallibility that the theologians admit the possibility of an error in the grounds expressed for a definition of faith."

In opposition to the tendency that was to be affirmed so immoderately in Father Tuyaerts, Father de Grandmaison had, as early as 1898, distinguished dogmatic definitions from the "concepts of human philosophy that surround [them], like an atmosphere, and without being necessarily implicated in it". "The dogmatic concept", he added, "has an absolute value: the terms participate in it only on precarious grounds. Necessary in order to clothe the thought, they do not embody it to the point of being but one with it: without betraying it, they translate it." He admitted that many theologians had "often attached to dogma philosophical concepts that were very distinct from it and made these share in its stability", etc. "L'Élasticité des formules dogmatiques", *Études*, 76 (1898); an article included in *Le Dogme chrétien*, 18, 29 and 40. No one we know of has ever seriously suspected insidious modernism in these ever-timely remarks of good sense. No more than in the similar remarks by

By expressing himself in this way, Father de Grandmaison did not have the sense that he was expressing an opinion that was in any way new, and without a doubt none of his readers thought so either. It was thought that his own originality consisted much more in a happy balance of gifts and abilities, as well as in a certain concrete and spiritual manner of treating his subject, than in any capacity for invention or systematization. In fact, in the passages we have just quoted, he was repeating an explanation that Father J. V. Bainvel had pointed out shortly before, with respect to the Immaculate Conception. Father Bainvel had invited his readers to admire in the history of dogma "the great independence" of the Holy See "with regard to scholars" as well as the capacity for a certain "secret instinct" on the part of the faithful, "which is basically the Catholic sense". He was not proved wrong in opposing it to theology, but, after having recalled the resistance coming from the latter, "it is a wonder", he had stated, "that the idea had made its way despite everything, had conquered the scholars, had become the explicit faith of the Church; this is one of the most beautiful and most touching cases of piety, I do not say . . . triumphing over science, but going before science, stimulating science, enlightening science, finally leading science to ratify the intuitions of love and piety." After which, seeking to keep a little more closely to the "higher criterion" to which the Church refers when proceeding to a definition, he had discerned only one thing: the very "thought" of the Church, her "conscience".[8]

"Conscience of the Church": this expression that we have encountered from the pen of Father de Grandmaison, which had already come from that of Father Bainvel, Father Pinard[9] and Father Lebreton,[10] was also used by Father Gardeil when, looking for what can make the theological conclusion a definable truth, he saw this truth in certain cases "showing solidarity, in the conscience of the Church, with the object

Father Portalié: "When the Church borrows images, metaphors, expressions or even theories from philosophy, she in no way defines because of that the system itself from which these formulas are borrowed: an extreme circumspection is necessary, in these cases, in order to distinguish the dogmatic idea clothed in a philosophical envelope, unless the philosophy that has furnished the formula or image is to some small degree sanctioned by the faith." "Le Dogme et l'histoire", *Bulletin de littérature ecclésiastique* (1904), 136–37.

[8] J. V. Bainvel, "Histoire d'un dogme", *Études*, 101 (1904), 617, 620–21, 623–24, 625.

[9] *Dictionnaire apologétique*, s.v. *Dogme*, 1, col. 1169.

[10] *L'Encyclique et la théologie moderniste* (1908), 36–37.

of faith, to the point of becoming received, I was going to say believed, theology".[11]

In perhaps less fortunate vocabulary, and perhaps by making too great a distinction at times between two processes that always more or less penetrate each other without ever meeting, another theologian, Father Marin Sola, expressed his opinion in the same direction. Father Sola was a "strong champion of the speculative evolution of dogma"; he did not grudge theological conclusions their part; without going to the final excesses of Father Tuyaerts, he maintained the definability of "all the strict conclusions of the *Summa theologiae*" and of the quasi-totality "of the propositions of the Thomist Syllabus of Pius X". Yet neither did he hesitate at all to recognize as well what he called a "vital way", or an "affective way". The Church, he proclaimed, is not more bound to the reasoning of theologians than to the sentiment of the faithful, being their mistress in everything; but, assisted by the Holy Spirit, she uses both equally as instruments. "Doctrinal vigor" is developed, therefore, as much and even more by the vital way than by the logical way, through the knowledge of saints than through that of the learned, and when the first is strong enough, the second can be bypassed: the "sense of the faith" carries it. And Father Marin Sola specifically reproached Father Tuyaerts for having in the matter of dogmatic development "attributed everything to reasoning and little or nothing to the sense of the faith, which has as much and more importance than reasoning".[12]

Father Grandmaison gave too much consideration to the study of contemporary authors and the examination of their problems always to obtain the full sympathy of the pure "Scholastics", some of whom seem to take pleasure in locking theology into a well-bolted ghetto. With some of them, Father Bainvel could pass for one of those "eclectics" who are too inclined to see the relativity of systems, whose finesse one appreciates but about whom one declares that "there is nothing definite in them." Father Gardeil himself, in his rather heavy robustness, had perhaps something too personal to appeal equally to everyone. But in Father Marin Sola, everyone agreed they recognized a Thomist without compromise. He had first developed his thought in a long series

[11] A. Gardeil, *Le Donné révélé et la théologie*, 180.

[12] Marin Sola, O.P., *L'Évolution homogène du dogme catholique*, French trans., 2d ed. (Fribourg, 1924), 2:57; 1:280 and 368, etc.

of articles in the *Ciencia tomista*;[13] the monumental work in which he took it up once again (soon followed by a French translation) formed the first volume of the *Bibliothèque des Thomistes espagnols*, dedicated "to the Angelic Doctor" for the sixth centenary of his canonization; and one need only read the reviews of the principal theological journals to learn of the favor, indeed, the enthusiasm with which it was received. Father Gardeil is not alone in rejoicing to rediscover in his Spanish colleague the same path by which he had tried, he says, to clear a passage. In the *Revue thomiste*, from the pen of Father Pègues, the approval is without reservation: everything is demonstrated, he tells us, "with a profusion of authoritative proofs, theological reason, historical facts, which leave the mind in a kind of amazement".[14]

Thus, in this question of dogmatic development, despite one discordant voice that excited only universal disapproval, agreement might seem total among theologians on the point that could be called capital, whatever might be the profound divergences dividing them in many other regards. This agreement was maintained during the following years, and almost on the eve of the last war, in 1937, an issue of the *Angelicum* brought us from the University of which it is the organ a perfectly concordant echo. In a very remarkable article, which we would still have occasion to quote, Father Simonin, after having noted that "the new definitions like the old ones have to do essentially with a mystery", concluded that "the passage from one to the other cannot be the fact of a perfect clarity that would itself solicit the mind's adherence". Certain more explicit formulas can well come to be imposed insofar as checkmating a threatening heresy; but "on the contrary, the direct passage from the old formulas to the definitions that explain them, if one excepts the case of a deferent submission to the decisions of the Magisterium, remains a difficult step, uncertain in its result, which a thousand particular circumstances can make strangely problematical." And Father Simonin saw his assertions confirmed by the practice of the Church. If the latter, in fact, "proceeds against the heretics, she does so in the name of her sovereign authority, in virtue of the divine assistance that is promised her in that event; she does

---

[13] From 1911 to 1919.

[14] T. M. Pègues, "L'Évolution homogène des Dogmes", *Revue thomiste*, 7 (1924), 57–67. A. Gardeil, "Bulletin d'introduction à la théologie", *R.S.P.T.*, 9 (1920), 661–62, and 13 (1914), 587–88.

not hope to administer a formal demonstration of their errors, a subtle mind always being able to dispute the value of any reasoning."[15]

Under these conditions, the volume of the *Gregorianum* for the year 1940—which was able to reach France only during 1946—had a surprise in store for us. It contained an article entitled: "What Is Theology? Reflections on a Controversy", an article by Father C. Boyer. We read there the following page, where, in expressions that are a little less abrupt but basically without appreciable difference, the very thought of Father Tuyaerts is revived:

> I do not see that one can deny the logical connection, which not only exists in itself but which can be traced by our means of investigation, between the progressive precision of dogma and the greatest indefiniteness of origins. The development of a truth can only follow a logic, and this path, at least at the point of arrival, must be perceptible. Appealing to life and, in a way, to the irrational—*quoad nos*—seems to us to be a concession to certain contemporary philosophies. And in fact, if we take the example of the dogmas that are least explicit in the sources, such as that of the Immaculate Conception of Mary, we see quite sufficiently how it derives from the *proto-evangelium* [proto-Gospel] of the greatness of the Mother of God and of that of Christ: "*propter honorem Domini*", and this could be seen before the approval of the Magisterium.
>
> In the end, it is true, the Magisterium had to intervene; but, as we see in the bull *Ineffabilis*, by sanctioning itself the theological speculation on these themes that contained implicitly the truth defined today. The Church, assisted by the Holy Spirit, places her authority on the side of true logic.
>
> If it were otherwise, it would not be of development that we would have to speak, when a dogma is defined, but of radical innovation and creation. How could we say that revelation was closed at the death of the last of the apostles if a subsequent belief were not connected to it by a truly rational and logical bond?[16]

Father Boyer does not profess the first of the two theses that we distinguished in Father Tuyaerts. Without absolutely dismissing it, he leaves it out of consideration and refuses to enter into the details of the quarrel concerning the theological conclusions that are definable

[15] H. D. Simonin, O.P., "'Implicite' et 'explicite' dans le développement du dogme", *Angelicum*, 14 (1937), 134–35.

[16] C. Boyer, S.J., "Qu'est-ce que la théologie? Réflexions sur une controverse", *Gregorianum*, 21 (1940), 264–65.

and those that are not.[17] We will similarly leave out of consideration the particular points of the controversy with respect to which he took up his pen. But it is obvious that the reflections we have just read are not opposed to any particular opinion of Mr. Draguet, Father Charlier, Father Bonnefoy or anyone else. Undoubtedly, whatever might be the modesty of the expressions used, they are presented to us as an appeal to classical truths, linked to orthodoxy, rather than as a personal hypothesis; but they nonetheless take the position against what well seemed until then to be the *consensus* of theologians. Do they not risk authorizing the hazardous thesis against which those theologians had unanimously reacted?

Now they seem to us to be the sign of a new state of mind, which is tending, here and there, to spread and which does not proceed, we believe, without danger. That is why, without being content with the testimony in the contrary direction gathered from theologians of the earlier age, we believe it to be useful to institute a brief examination of this thesis. The argument of authority, such as results from the preceding, can be all the less adequate here, since the theologians we have quoted are far from having all assured the soundness of their opinion by expressing it in a coherent whole.

II

Basically, we believe we can note an initial misunderstanding in the very position of the problem and in the way of approaching it. If there is a legitimate development, we are told, on the basis of the object of faith explicitly revealed, this development can take place only by way of analysis or of logical deduction.[18] Without necessarily attributing to all theological conclusions the dignity of definable truths, therefore, one nevertheless is reasoning from the outset as if the *whole* problem of dogmatic development were reduced to this problem of theological

[17] Ibid., 259: "It is one question to know if the theological conclusions engage the faith and can be the faith, 'definable', and it is another question, our own, to know if they are legitimate and certain." And 262: "Whether that is enough for the conclusions obtained ever to be terms of divine faith is, I repeat, another problem. . . ." Consequently this kind of conclusion seems to the author not only legitimate and certain (which we admit as much as he) but absolutely necessary in all cases for dogmatic development.

[18] We recognize here the equivalent of the words used by others: formal implicit and virtual implicit; or again: a conclusion *quoad nos tantum* and a conclusion *quoad se*.

conclusions, in the most precise sense of the term. But is reducing the former to the latter in this way not to reduce it unduly to the dimensions of a much more restricted question? By what right do we declare, so to speak, a priori and presuppose as if established in advance that the development of dogma is entirely circumscribed within these narrow limits? Is this not because we are used to seeing in it only the problem of the conditions of definability of new formulas, which is most important but not the whole of it? Yet a mere glance at the history of twenty Christian centuries should be enough to show this: even to presuppose that, in fact, no definition of faith could ever take place without the guarantee of the aforesaid natural perception of a logical connection, the development that meets our eyes is very far from being reduced to the history of consequences drawn by theologians reasoning from certain principles of faith, whatever way we understand them and whatever value we attribute to them. If, even before seeking to resolve a problem, one made the effort to observe and describe what in fact the problem will consist of, one would unfailingly take this into account: the phenomenon in question is far more complex. It also, and above all, results from the penetration of Christian reality across the universe of human thoughts and from the battle engaged by faith with all kinds of elements of the natural order. There where we seem to discern only a linear movement, by way of consequence, the reality shows us a perpetual reaction to surrounding assumptions, by way of defense, elimination, selection, transformation, assimilation. This is what Father de Grandmaison expressed very well when he wrote: "The theological problems directly raised by the activity of the human mind seeking to penetrate, to organize, to defend its beliefs, to define it according to its other knowledge; these very problems, implied by new and variously resolved difficulties of ecclesiastical practice; the changes that have occurred in human institutions, sciences and philosophies; the profound instincts and heartfelt intuitions of piety—all these elements at once have a part in this great movement."[19]

One could already say, keeping to the analogy of human truths, that in their development, the essential thing does not consist in a proliferation of particular formulas and, so to speak, in an indefinite filtering of conclusions on the basis of their premises.[20] It is much more in a

[19] L. de Grandmaison, *Le Dogme chrétien*, 241–42.

[20] In his *Introduction à l'étude de la théologie*, M. G. Rabeau wrote: "We know well enough

renovation of the problems, in a new way of considering certain eternal givens, which the human glance cannot embrace at once in all their aspects; hence this other consequence: that such a development is never progress pure and simple, but that all gain includes its revenge. . . . But the very principle of the analogy is challenged here, or at least one cannot admit it without some serious correctives. One is right to think, in fact, that it is far too much to lower the horizon of supernatural truth, to transpose the whole "dogmatic fact of development onto the plane of the logical process proper to the human mind". Father Simonin had already observed this in the article in *Angelicum* that we quoted above: "A simple appeal to the processes according to which the human mind establishes a conclusion on the basis of rational principles or penetrates more profoundly a truth that it has acquired solely by the strength of its nature could never furnish an adequate knowledge of the very particular phenomenon that it is a question of studying."[21] Now such is, nevertheless, the postulate that serves as the basis for the thesis we are discussing.

It is this twofold narrowness (reduction of the fact of development to the mechanism of theological conclusions, reduction of the problem of development to a problem of pure human logic) that gives some the illusion of having here the authority of Saint Thomas Aquinas for them. Father Boyer makes a great case of a text from the Summa, where Saint Thomas, he tells us, expresses himself thus: "Ex articulis fidei haec doctrina [theology] ad alia argumentatur. . . . Ex eis procedit ad aliud ostendendum."[22] But whatever might be the precise meaning of these affirmations (we will return to them), why think that they would contain the whole secret of the question we are considering? It would be better to recognize that neither at this point nor else-

---

that theologians like to draw consequences *ad infinitum* from principles, and they have often been reproached for this, as if what is the glory of the mathematician were the shame of the theologian" (Paris, 1926; 222). But theology is not mathematics; and neither is philosophy. Besides, many theologians have not fallen into such a mistake. We do admit, however, that there was a temptation for them in this at the time when the idea of theology that one of them (A. Vacant) expressed in the following sentence was prevalent among them: "To deduce from truths, revealed to men and for men *ex revelatione publica*, the greatest number of consequences that they contain, that is the goal and the essential task of the theologian." A concept justly criticized by Fathers M. R. Gagnebet (*Revue thomiste*, 44 [1938], 240, note) and M. D. Chenu (*La Théologie comme science au treizième siècle*, 2d ed. [1943], 91, note).

[21] Simonin, "'Implicite'", 130.

[22] Boyer, "Qu'est-ce que la théologie?", 259–61. Cf. 1a, q. 1, a. 8.

where[23] did Saint Thomas consider the fact of the development of dogma; nowhere did he present "any explicit doctrine" for it, and if one can find strewn about in his work a few principles capable of shedding light on this subject, nothing authorizes us to think that it might be above all in this article of the Summa; a fortiori, that this article might contain the principle of an adequate solution to the problem.

Besides, we must add that such an illusion is possible only because one attributes first of all to this article, in the most literal explanation, a meaning that is not its own. Saint Thomas does not treat theological conclusions there, but he speaks of the link to be established between certain articles of faith, serving as principles, and other truths of the faith, equally explicit, that can be connected to them as consequences. To be convinced of this, one need only read the entire sentence from which Father Boyer excerpted one line: "Haec doctrina non argumentatur ad sua principia probanda, quae sunt articuli fidei; sed ex eis procedit ad aliquid aliud probandum, sicut Apostolus, 1 Cor., XV, ex resurrectione Christi argumentatur ad resurrectionem communem probandam."[24] The example supplied is doubly clear, since it has to do with a truth recorded both in Scripture and in the Creed.[25] The matter, taken in its major principles, is so obvious that one could say it has won over in recent times all those concerned with it. The authority of Melchior Cano and John of Saint Thomas could not prevail against the evidence. Already, in support of his opinion, which tended

[23] Nor elsewhere, contrary to those who believed they could use for this purpose the Thomist doctrine concerning the progress of the faith in the Old Testament (2a, 2ae, q. 1, a. 7, etc.). Cf. H. D. Simonin, "La Théologie thomiste de la foi et le développement du Dogme", *Revue thomiste*, 18 (1935), 537: "The theology of Saint Thomas, such as he historically formulated it, presents no explicit doctrine dealing with the development of dogma and does not even consider, in its whole, the fact of the development of Christian dogma." It is much rather, as we know, of a certain regression that we would have to speak, according to one or two texts, if one wished to press them: 2a, 2ae, q. 1, a. 7, ad 4m; cf. q. 174, a. 6.

[24] Saint Thomas here follows Saint Augustine, *De doctrina christiana*, l. 2, c. 31, n. 49 (PL 34, 58). He returns more than once to the same example; *In Sent.*, prologus, a. 5, ad 4m; *In 3 Sent.*, d. 23, q. 2, a. 1, ad 4m; d. 25, q. 2, a. 2, sol. 1, ad 5m; *De veritate*, q. 14, a. 2, ad 9 m.

[25] This argument, observes Father Bonnefoy, *La Nature de la théologie selon saint Thomas d'Aquin* (Paris-Bruges [1939], 51), "presents that rare particularity of placing in connection two truths, direct objects of faith, and of being itself revealed". There is nothing at all to be surprised about in this, if it is true that in this article of the *Summa*, Saint Thomas is speaking above all of Scripture (cf. ibid., 23). —Undoubtedly one could say that, if Saint Thomas does not include the theological conclusion here, it is only because it is outside his perspectives. But the fact that he does not speak of it and does not think of it is enough to make it impossible to quote him in its favor.

to restrict the area of definable conclusions, Father Schultes had remarked that the old theologians, like Saint Thomas, divided revealed truths into articles of faith and other truths, formally revealed, too, but not expressed in the Creed.[26] Since then, following analyses by Fathers Bonnefoy and Charlier, Father Gagnebet has concurred with this interpretation, while opposing other views held by these two theologians. Noting this particularly significant agreement, Father Congar soon adopted the same position.[27] Father Chenu, who, along with his mentor Father Gardeil, had at first maintained a contrary position, was shortly after converted to it as well.[28] Finally, more recently, we have seen Father Labourdette implicitly concede the accuracy of it.[29] One wonders why Father Boyer insists on reproducing an interpretation abandoned by everyone. He thinks to find in it, it is true, a support

---

[26] Cf. A. Gardeil, *R.S.P.T.*, 11 (1922), 688.

[27] M. J. Congar, *Bulletin thomiste*, 5 (1938), 500: "With Father Gagnebet and Father Charlier, we are in agreement in saying that it is to add to the thought of Saint Thomas to assign as an object to theology the deduction of *new* conclusions on the basis of revealed truths, with the aid of principles of reason. We have seen that for Saint Thomas, the scientific quality of theology is not acquired from the deduction of *new* truths but from the rational construction of the Christian teaching through an attachment of truths—conclusions to some truths—principles." Cf. *D.T.C.*, s.v. *Théologie*, 15, col. 380. —Cf. M. R. Gagnebet, "La Nature de la théologie spéculative", *Revue thomiste*, 44 (1938), 229–40, commenting on Ia, q. 1, a. 8; p. 234: "Such are the principles of theological knowledge. To these are attached, through causal connections, the rest of the revealed given. The essential role of theological reasoning is to find this connection between the diverse parts of the divine teaching." And 239: "In no sense will it be true to make the knowledge of these conclusions the end of theological labor. . . ."

[28] M. D. Chenu, O.P., *La Théologie comme science au treizième siècle*, 2d ed. (1943), 9: "They had once given in to a rather unwieldy interpretation of the deductive function in theological reason and marked its role in abrupt formulas, inclining in this direction the line of Saint Thomas' thought, which was in truth more flexible, as much for the transposition of the concept of science into sacred doctrine as for the variety of functions of the reason; deduction certainly has a scientific quality in theology, it is not the principal operation or the most worthy, in *intellectus fidei*. It is necessary here, we believe, to resist the logic of Cano, who determined too inflexible an exegesis." The first edition of the work thus criticized had appeared in 1927 in the *Archives d'histoire doctrinale et littéraire du moyen âge*, vol. 1.

[29] M. Labourdette, O.P., "La Théologie intelligence de la Foi", *Revue thomiste*, 46 (1946), 37: These truths that the theological demonstration attaches to earlier certitudes were perhaps already revealed in themselves; but, as the object of faith, they were not at all held in virtue of the connection grasped by the intelligence." The author adds a few lines farther on: "But in other cases, the enunciated thus attached through a middle term, necessary to a truth of faith, was in no way revealed itself . . ."; a complementary assertion, the truth of which we will not, moreover, contest, either in itself or insofar as conformed to the thought and practice of Saint Thomas. A good clarification of this whole question in R. Guelluy, *Philosophie et théologie chez Guillaume d'Ockham*, 40–42 and 53–54.

for his theory. But does this theory stand up, at least, to the test of facts?

Here, we admit our embarrassment. Logical rigor is one thing, its appreciation is another. How, with any chance of success, can we decide between two groups of theologians, some of whom, in the presence of argumentation, speak of expediency, analogies, considerations proper to incline the mind, while the others speak in its regard of rigorous reasoning and strict, scientific, fully convincing deduction? Now such is the case for the example to which most of our authors refer in this case: the dogma of the Immaculate Conception. Fathers Bainvel, de Grandmaison, Hugueny[30] decide on one side; Fathers Schultes, Marin Sola, Boyer, on the other.[31] An admirable thing, a change of camp fails to be produced. Father Gardeil, who counted himself at first among the former, hurling a kind of defiance at Father Marin Sola,[32] seemed almost to yield to the demonstration he had thus provoked. But this was only an appearance: the agreement was one of pure courtesy: "His deduction", he concluded, "is among the most probable."[33] It was indeed a matter of probability! Did Father Boyer himself, on the whole, feel completely assured? "We can see very sufficiently", he tells us "how [this dogma] derives from the *proto-evangelium*. . . ." Yes, we all admit that. "We see very sufficiently", provided that we adopt certain Christian value judgments, that we reason according to the analogy

[30] Cf. É. Hugueny, O.P., "La Tradition", *R.S.P.T.*, 6 (1912), 222: "The rigorous deductions of synthesis or of logical analysis are not the sole means the Church has to disengage a dogmatic teaching from the explicitly revealed propositions in which it was only sketched out. Certain propositions can be conceived in terms susceptible of a more or less extensive or comprehensive interpretation. It will sometimes rest with the heart of catholicity, with piety enlightened by the life of the Spirit, rather than with theological reason, to seek and find the formula that will determine correctly the meaning of revelation, when there will be a need for it to prevent the work of speculative thought from attacking the integrity of intuitive knowledge. This is the case with the Immaculate Conception." A position similar to that of M. R. Draguet, "L'Évolution des dogmes", in *Apologétique* (1937), 1186–87. And already of Father Pinard, col. 1174.

[31] To take literally certain expressions of M. G. Rabeau, one might believe that he would be ranked in the second group; but, if one judges by other, more explicit passages, this would be an error. Compare *Introduction à l'étude de la théologie*, 284–86 and 226–29. See also Gardeil, *R.S.P.T.*, 15 (1926), 594.

[32] "Let Father Marin Sola show us the dogma of the Immaculate Conception, since he holds it, being deduced through a conceptual reasoning from the dogma of the divine maternity": *R.S.P.T.*, 11 (1922), 689. Cf. Marin Sola, *L'Évolution homogène*, 1:322–31 (and, on the Assumption, 2:37–38). Similarly, Tuyaerts, *L'Évolution du dogme*, 53–54 and 187–89.

[33] *R.S.P.T.*, 13 (1924), 586–87.

of faith, and particularly after the event, when we are guided by the unanimous Christian sentiment, itself canonized by the decision of the infallible Magisterium; when we have thereby attained the certitude that none of the objections raised is valid and that no other will ever be presented. . . . We see very sufficiently: Is this to say, as it was first declared to us, that we maintain, from the point of view of human logic alone, a rigorous demonstration? Is it to say also that it is upon this demonstration, recognized as indispensable, that the Magisterium has made its pronouncement, and that, in pronouncing, it has, so to speak, only guaranteed by its authority the value of a logical operation? Far from it! Here, too, Father de Grandmaison seems to have, in his moderation, dealt more justly:

> There were texts, theological reasons, expediencies in particular, and a profound instinct of the Christian people *for*, texts and theological reasons apparently *against* the dogma; humanly, the solution was undetermined, or only probable, let us say, infinitely probable, in the affirmative sense. But the Church knows, better than the beloved disciple, how to recognize her Lord, she has the power to discern the voice of her Bridegroom there where the human ear perceives only a weak or indistinct echo.[34]

But, indeed, even when one managed to convince the most exacting minds of the perfect rational evidence of the Immaculate Conception on the basis of the primary givens of revelation, it would not follow that this would also be true, or particularly that it must always be true, in fact and by right, for all the dogmatic formulas of the present or of the future. One must resign oneself to this. As for us, our faith rather rejoices in it. For, poorly conformed to the facts, imprudent, the theory we are discussing seems to us, besides, less apt to respect the perfect independence of the teaching Church in her dogmatic judgments. Without doubt, theologians have a role to play, and a very important one. The Church is served by them; she is attentive to their opinions; but she is never content simply to record these opinions. While consulting theologians, she examines them, she judges them. She is not bound by the reasons they bring to her. In whatever direction she decides, she does not mean, moreover, to make a pronouncement on the value of these reasons. What she seeks to find is not if such a proposition is or is not correctly deduced but if such an assertion is or is not contained in her faith. On that, it seems to us the agreement should be unanimous.

[34] *Le Dogme chrétien*, 259–60.

But for that, let us repeat the expression, the Church interrogates her conscience. She has conducted her inquiry before theologians as before scholars; she does not hold the work of either one or the other to be negligible. But between the results of this twofold work and her decision itself, there is not simply a certain disproportion: there is a passage from one plane to another. The latter is in no way the effect of the former. Consequently the Church has no more need, for example, in favor of the Immaculate Conception, to receive a true "proof" by means of a theological conclusion than she has need to receive from scholars an irrefutable historical attestation of the belief of the faithful in this truth since the beginning.[35]

An excessive zeal in this regard does not seem, moreover, to her taste. Reread the constitution *De fide catholica* of the [First] Vatican Council. One will certainly not find there a declaration sufficient to invalidate the point at issue; but one could nevertheless not fail to recognize there "a manifest tendency to exclude from the control of natural reason the stages of dogmatic progress achieved in the Church":[36]

> Neque enim fidei doctrina quam Deus revelavit, velut philosophicum inventum proposita est humanis ingeniis perficienda; sed tanquam divinum depositum Christi sponsae tradita, fideliter custodienda et infallibiliter declaranda.[37]

Without doubt, the principal idea here is that revealed doctrine is not incomplete as are human doctrines at their beginning, and that it is thus not susceptible of a true progress *simpliciter*. On which no disagreement is possible. But does it not also result from this text that, if nevertheless the revealed doctrine proves to be susceptible of a certain development, the latter could not have taken place through paths that were identical to that which affects human doctrines? An invaluable piece of information, on which it would prove of interest to reflect. Will it be enough, in order to comply with it, to say that the theologian who works toward an explanation of the revealed deposit always works only in a Christian climate, that the suggestions that come to

[35] Similar reflections could be made on the subject of the interpretation of the Bible—a subject so close to our own. The Church does not teach us that the Bible is always clear, even with the knowledge of the most experienced exegete.

[36] H. D. Simonin, *Angelicum*, 14 (1937), 132–33.

[37] *Vaticanum, Constitutio dogmatica de fide catholica, caput IV, De fide et ratione*, Denz.-Bannw.-Umberg, edition 24–25, no. 1800.

him from the collective belief and from his own spirit of faith make him intuit, so to speak, that he must carry the effort of his analysis in a certain direction, or, on the contrary, that a certain path that he had tried to enter is only a dead-end? He would thus perpetually receive "confirmations", similar to those confirmations that the light of Christian revelation brings to the philosopher himself, without troubling the rational purity of his thought?[38] Such an explanation, already too minimalist, we believe, for theological work taken altogether, letting us see poorly how a man without faith could not, strictly, make good theology,[39] seems to us more insupportable still in the case of dogmatic development. It can clarify some particular step of it. But it is not enough to take into account the fact that this development has, as a whole, "a totally different nature from the progress that is accomplished in opinions and in the human sciences", according to the expression of Msgr. Ginoulhiac,[40] or according to the expression of Cardinal Franzelin, of the fact that the human element itself which prepares a new definition of faith "deducitur per supernaturalem gubernationem Spiritus Sancti".[41] Does it give enough room to a certain logic of Christian judgment? Does it sufficiently take into account the intrinsically supernatural and mysterious character of revealed truth?

In fact, it is not enough to say once and for all as a matter of duty that we have not found this truth by ourselves, that our reason was incapable of attaining it, that it was given us through divine revelation, in order to behave with it then as we would with any other truth whatever. It always remains a mystery for us. Our natural observation will

---

[38] Even on the level of philosophy, if all were reduced to these kinds of "confirmations", there would be many "Christian philosophers", as has been remarked, but not a "Christian philosophy".

[39] Cf. the excellent reflections of Father M. D. Chenu, in his preface to the new edition of Gardeil, *Le Donné révélé* (1923), xi: "The man who has no faith cannot do theology. Of course not; nor even the faithful, if he did not understand that these articles of faith from which he starts are, in all the force of the word, *principles* in this scientific elaboration and that his first work is to absorb the whole content of it, to be filled with the spirit of it, religiously, in lively faith, in contemplation, so that the divine reality is made his own in truth in his understanding." "Principles", in this sense, which is to say much more than "premises".

[40] Ginoulhiac, *Histoire du dogme catholique*, 2d ed., 1:xxvii.

[41] Johannes Franzelin, *De divina Traditione et Scriptura*, 4th ed. (1896), 279. Cf. 277. And yet it could have been written of Franzelin himself that he conveyed "in perhaps too exclusive a manner the logical side of dogmatic expansion": Pinard, col. 1126. A similar remark in E. Hocedez, *Histoire de la théologie au dix-neuvième siècle*, vol. 3 (1947), 165.

never embrace it as it does all the others. Our natural logic is not going to be able to display itself in everything in its regard as it does with the objects of our reason. Not having *conceived* it, not having formed it in ourselves, we will never be the masters of it. To tell the truth, we do not possess it: it possesses us. We do not measure it: we are measured by it. We seek to penetrate into its understanding, and we do in fact reach it: the mystery is incomprehensible, it is not unintelligible. But the more we reach, the more we sense at the same time that this truth surpasses us, that it overflows us and disconcerts us.[42] Each light acquired with respect to it is the cause of a new and more profound obscurity. The exercise of reason is stimulated by it, but it must in the final analysis admit to failing: *nam qui pervenire praesumit, non quaesita reperit, sed in inquisitione deficit.*[43] Antinomies loom everywhere, and always, to be faithful, we must begin again to hold in the night "the two ends of the chain". No mystery is a simple truth, and if we become attached with too narrow an attention to one of its aspects in order to establish the main part of it, we risk ending in many an absurdity or many a heresy. A mystery can never be, in a way, handled in the way a natural truth can; we will never have the right to apply the laws of our human logic to it univocally, without precautions and correctives. We are obliged perpetually to revise our concepts in order to adapt them to its normative truth. What am I saying? It shatters them. History offers famous examples of this. In their dogmatic use, the concepts of nature and of person are not those a purely natural philosophy has elaborated. And who will express all the intellectual repercussions of the revelation of God as Love? So, we indeed come to show that there is no contradiction in dogma—or rather (for that is already saying too

[42] "It is very true", writes Father Boyer, "Qu'est-ce que la théologie?", 258, "that the reason, left to itself, does not know that God is in three persons. But when it learns this from faith, it knows it; it knows neither why nor how; but it is sure that this is so." Without doubt. So, indeed, it is not a question here of certitude or lack of certitude. But the ignorance of "why" and particularly of "how" does not seem to retain Father Boyer's attention; as if this "why" and particularly this "how" did not affect anything in the nature of the "this is so", as if one could without difficulty separate them from it, in order to be concerned only with reasoning according to the rules of logic on the basis of "this is so" alone. . . . So he reasons as if there were nothing more mysterious in the divine truth once revealed; revealed truth, but from then on grasped, possessed by the mind like any truth the mind would have found; truth whose virtualities are explorable by the natural reason for the same reason as those of these found truths.

[43] Saint Leo, *In nativitate Domini sermo* 9 (PL 54, 226).

much) to show that one cannot establish that there is any contradiction in it; but that is still a wholly negative stage, and, from the point of view of pure logic, we do not go beyond this stage. So, it is usually the same for the consequences that, *sedulo, pie et sobrie*, we draw from it. These consequences can be conformed to the laws of logic (and, if the Church approves them, if she comes to canonize them, we will receive the assurance of it). This is a necessary guarantee, for we have no more right to talk nonsense in theology than elsewhere; but this guarantee is not always sufficient, for there can be in the truth we have served in principle certain elements that have escaped us; or, if you prefer, we have been able to inflict on the given of faith some abusive simplification in order to accommodate it to this major role in our reasoning. This is obvious in the case where mystery is expressed in still very concrete, vivid terms: we know, for example, what deceptive theories have resulted from all those who, reading in Scripture and in the traditional teaching that Christ had redeemed us, wondered to whom this *redemption* had been paid. But it is just as true for certain dogmas of more abstract formulation. Jesus Christ is truly God and truly man: Is one going to conclude from this that he has a human personality? The conclusion might appear unavoidable at first. Today, the case can seem a little embarrassing to us; we find it very simple to explain that since personality is not a constitutive element of nature, it is possible to possess human nature in fullness without, however, being a human person; that an absolutely perfect human nature cannot be its own master but can be possessed by a divine person. Undoubtedly. But this is only apparently what we are reasoning here according to a purely human logic. For, in reality, we are, in a way, making use of a system of concepts and distinctions that are effects of the action of the mystery. This is the exigency of the dogma of the unity of Christ, a religious exigency, perceived religiously, which has forced the intelligence to discoveries that it now uses in its elaboration of the dogma. This elaboration can therefore well assume a logical form: it is nonetheless a demonstration after the fact; an effect much more than a cause or even than a means of invention or of inventory of the dogmatic truth expressed as a conclusion. A rational organization that we need not scorn, which responds to a profound need of our mind and which contributes to that "apology for dogma" that the believer owes to himself before owing it to others; an organization that can be different from and much more than the perception of an expediential link between two truths; but an organization that is only subsequent, thanks to derived means. Other supernatural means, other criteria are at first necessary for a truth to be perceived in a new way, with the assurance that it is a revealed truth.

III

But we hear the objection. It is found formulated on the very page we were quoting: "How could one say that revelation was closed at the death of the last apostles if a later believer were not connected to it by a truly rational and logical bond?" It would then be necessary to speak, not of development, "but of radical innovation and creation". Such was already the objection of Father Tuyaerts against Father Gardeil and Father de Grandmaison. "If the human mind," he said, "reasoning on the basis of the revealed given, can arrive only at what is less even than a theological conclusion, how could the Church, which is to say, the men who exercise the Magisterium, arrive at a revealed truth, a dogma, without the help of a new revelation?" And again: (It is said that) "the Church can, in certain cases, discover what is impossible for the human mind to discover; in other cases, she can discover with certitude what the human mind can discover only with probability. To arrive at that, there is no other means possible than divine revelation, since it is indeed a question here of the manifestation of a truth that is unknown and unknowable for us by our natural means although already assisted by revelation, a manifestation that essentially constitutes divine revelation. The assistance of the Holy Spirit thus understood would necessarily be transformed into revelation."[44]

The concern from which this objection proceeds is legitimate. All truth has been given us by Christ and in Christ, and revelation, according to the traditional formula recalled by a proposition of the decree *Lamentabili*,[45] was closed at the death of the last apostles—of the last of his witnesses. We all believe it along with Saint Irenaeus: "It is not permissible to say, as some dare to, that the apostles preached before having perfect knowledge. . . . For after our Lord was resurrected from the dead and they received the power of the Holy Spirit coming

[44] Tuyaerts *L'Évolution du dogme*, 84 and 173–74. Cf. 191–92.

[45] *Propositio* 21: "Revelatio, objectum fidei catholicae constituens, non fuit cum Apostolis completa" (DZ., no. 2021).

from above, they were filled with everything and their knowledge was perfect."[46] The objection is nevertheless unacceptable, and the fears of Father Boyer on this subject do not appear to be better founded than those of Father Tuyaerts: "God can enlighten the Church on a point contained virtually within the deposit without revealing new truths to her."[47] Subjective illumination and objective revelation are two different things, and we do not see why one truth would not also be very much contained within a first, since the means of extracting it might be of one nature or another. For those for whom the "logical" means is not adequate do not believe that this is in virtue of a lesser capacity for this truth in the original, but it is, they think, because of the supernatural and mysterious character of the latter, which does not offer the same grasp to the work of human logic. They are not content with "less than a theological conclusion": they want a link that is, not looser, but of a different nature. The objection, therefore, is ineffective.

Or rather, we recognize, it expresses a real difficulty; a basic difficulty, the examination of which is imperative for everyone, whatever might be the mode one admits for development. Whether this mode, in fact, be purely logical or not, whether it be purely natural or not, it is nonetheless true in any hypothesis that, if one speaks of development, it is since a truth appears that was not at first perceived; it is thus that it presents itself, at a given moment, as new. Now it is not enough, to be reassured, to say, as we are often content to do: "This truth is not new *in itself*, since it was really contained in the original; it is only new *in relation to us*; what has progressed is therefore not the dogma itself, it is only the knowledge that we have of it." Nor is it enough, at least it seems to us, to specify that the "advance" that has occurred from the original state of the doctrine to its present state is limited "solely to the order of knowledge, revelation being considered as a quantity adequately circumscribed and integrally furnished to the

[46] Irenaeus, *Adversus Haereses*, l. 3, c. 1, n. 1: "Nec enim fas est dicere quoniam ante praedicaverunt (Apostoli) quam perfectam haberent agnitionem, sicut quidam audent dicere, gloriantes emendatores se esse Apostolorum. Postea enim quam surrexit Dominus noster a mortuis, et induti sunt supervenientis Spiritus sancti virtutem ex alto, de omnibus adimpleti sunt, et habuerunt perfectam cognitionem." Irenaeus invoked his principle against those who claimed to correct the apostolic teaching; he did the same against those who claimed to add to it.

[47] A. Riedinger, *Revue pratique d'apologétique*, 34 (1922), 690, note 2.

Church at her origin".[48] For such a response to be fully intelligible, it would in fact be necessary for us to be able to give a real meaning to the idea of a truth at once revealed and remaining nevertheless, as it were, "in itself", not perceived by the intelligence; to the idea of a dogma subsistent in itself, independent of the knowledge of the one to whom it was communicated. (Since if one replied that this dogma does not subsist "in itself", but that it was implicitly contained in the dogma of which the faithful already have explicit knowledge, this reply would not refer us back to the initial difficulty.) Besides, under the circumstances, "it is not a question of the truth in itself, an abstraction made of the intelligence that knows, but indeed of the dogma such as it is known: this dogma is unchangeable. The entire revelation, such as it is known, or the knowledge of revelation, is therefore, in one sense, unchangeable."[49]—And yet, one must also speak, in another sense—*secundum quid*—of progressive knowledge! Once again, I say it for everyone: partisans of a "rational" development or of a "vital" development, no one escapes this first aporia. Perhaps the fully satisfying solution escapes us all equally: theological problems offer us other examples of this, and there should not be anything in that to trouble us. But what we believe we see is that this aporia is inevitably transformed into an invincible objection against those who insist on a wholly logical development, because they have removed in advance, through their very conception of the revealed deposit, any means of overcoming it.

The difficulty, let us note, has not at all remained unperceived by a theologian such as Father Marin Sola. He felt, indeed, that dogmatic progress, such as he himself explained it, was "not simply subjective", but that it had necessarily a certain objective character, since it took place "through the elucidation of new objective aspects . . . not at first brought out". He did not see how one could deny that the new definitions "complete, even perfect revelation, since they explain it with the aid of new concepts".[50] Let us say, in different language, that in such a domain, the distinction between subjective and objective is not entirely acceptable: that there is an objectivity of the subjective order, because the objective order of revelation is in close correlation with

[48] Draguet, "L'Évolution des dogmes", 1177–78.

[49] P. Claeys-Boouaert, mimeographed course (Louvain).

[50] Cf. Gardeil, *R.S.P.T.*, 9 (1920), 661.

it. Consequently Father Marin Sola was not afraid to acknowledge that the idea of a passage from the virtual to the formal in knowledge was equivalent to the idea of a "mediate revelation". This is what disturbed him, and with good reason. And it is what made him consider a corrective to his theory indispensable.

A corrective, in truth, so enormous that it constitutes—how has this not been more generally noted?[51]—an admission of defeat. His entire construction, he recognizes, is of value only from the second Christian generation on. It would be impossible to maintain in proper form with the necessary part of immutability unless by professing that the apostles had the formal, explicit knowledge of all the dogmatic truths put into words today or which will be from here to the end of time:

> When we seek to know if there has been progress or evolution of dogma . . . it is a mistake to consider the state in which these dogmas were found in the idea of God or in that of the apostles. With regard to the divine or even the apostolic intelligence, the words formal and virtual, mediate and immediate, implicit and explicit, are here absolutely stripped of meaning. In God and even in the apostles, all was not only formal and immediate but also explicit; since then, the question of progress is no longer posed.[52]

A frank and unequivocal declaration. It is in founding himself on such a principle that Father Marin Sola presupposes as the most natural thing in the world that the apostles would very well have been able to teach their successors about truths such as the Immaculate Conception or any other similar ones.[53] But is there need to insist on the extreme improbability, to say nothing more, of such an hypothesis? How could the apostles have merely expressed to themselves truths whose formulation presupposes in some cases all sorts of notions and habits of subsequent thought? How then could we explain their refusal to transmit them, or their negligence in doing so? Or, if they did do so, what are we to think of that flood of forgetfulness in which the second Christian generation was suddenly engulfed? At least the intrepidity of the logic of the author of this strange conception has been generally recognized. It is this that urges him on, starting with the idea he developed of revelation and of knowledge of the revealed.

---

[51] The thing has, however, been brought out by Draguet, "L'Évolution des dogmes", 1178–80.

[52] Marin Sola, *L'Évolution homogène*, 1:59; cf. 57, 301, note.

[53] Ibid., 2:38.

If others who share this idea with him do not follow him to that point, it is perhaps only because they are less fearless. Their hesitation, their withdrawal is wholly to the credit of their historical sense. But how then do they face the difficulty from which Father Marin Sola had thus extricated himself? How do they account for what Father Pinard recently called very justly the "fullness of the apostolic times"?[54] How do they explain, otherwise than through the verbal distinction whose insufficiency we have demonstrated, that dogmatic development is not really a progress of revelation?

That is the core of the problem. This is what Father Hugueny had seen well when he wrote that "to understand the laws and the character" of development, it was essential to have "an accurate idea of the fact of revelation that has given the world the supernatural truth whose treasure Catholic tradition protects and makes fruitful".[55] Now we are not saying that most of the theologians who have discussed this problem were forming an inaccurate idea of revelation, but we must note that they were too often content in its regard with quick and superficial views. The situation had scarcely changed in this respect since the time when Father Lebreton complained of it, in the article he devoted in 1911 to the work of Father Louis Billot, upon his elevation to the cardinalate. "Classical theologians", he said there, strongly systematized certain parts of the dogmatic: as, for example, the fine constructions of Father Billot on the Trinity, the incarnate Word, grace . . . ; but they have moved too far away from the "fundamental concepts of revelation and faith".[56] If they have analyzed profoundly some particular content or other of the faith, they have given too little examination to the large formal categories.

Hence the insufficiency of many a study on dogmatic development. Hence, with several theologians, this postulate "according to which revelation would be reduced to a certain number of formulas, absolute in their error, univocal in their elements, proper, in a word, to playing before the mind the role of first principles" or of major premises.[57]

[54] Pinard, col. 1157.

[55] É. Hugueny, *Critique et catholique*, vol. 2 (Paris, 1914), 37.

[56] J. Lebreton, "Son Éminence le cardinal Billot", *Études*, 129 (1911), 521 and 522.

[57] J. Rivière, *Revue des sciences religieuses*, 2 (1922), 187. In a form more respectful of history, this is a concept not sufficiently different from what we find in Draguet, "L'Évolution des dogmes", 1177: "When [the Church] professes that the age of revelations closed with the apostles, she simply means to affirm that all the principles of Christianity were fixed at

Such was the postulate from which Father Tuyaerts spoke. He himself declared that his study rested entirely "on the definition of dogma, which is nothing else but a truth revealed by God and defined by the Church"; and, from the fact that this dogma "is a logical reality adapted to our human intelligence", he concluded, as we have seen, that "it could evolve only with the aid of a logical process, the only thing our mind can use."[58] This was, as one might say, to put the cart before the horse. This was at least to confuse two very different states of the revealed reality, according as one considers it at its source, at its first moment, or later, in the formulas gradually worked out in the course of the centuries and sanctioned one after the other by the Magisterium. This was not to see that this same word "dogma" is susceptible to two meanings that are, without a doubt, closely interdependent but nevertheless distinct and that, to take it in the second of these meanings, it is legitimate to speak not only of its development but, first of all, of its formation.[59] How can we start from a notion of dogma insofar as "defined by the Church", whereas it is precisely a question of explaining and justifying the facts that will bring forward the successive definitions? But the confusion was not only of a historical order; it touched on doctrine. For, as we are going to see, the content of revelation, to take it in its original form and in its subsistent integrality, is neither accurately nor sufficiently designated as a series of statements.

Undoubtedly we would encounter few theologians who would maintain *ex professo* Father Tuyaerts' error (which was also, on this point, that of Father Marin Sola) without bringing at least some nuances to it. But the analytic deficiency that we have just recalled, following Father Lebreton, makes some adopt an attitude that is practically analogous. Considering the "new methodology" of Mr. Draguet and Father Charlier, Father Boyer writes that, according to them, "the revealed given is not to be considered first of all as a system of propositions."[60] But, I do believe, not according to Father Boyer either! Why give oneself

---

the death of the last apostle." It would be necessary, we believe, to specify at the very least that this word "principles" is not taken absolutely in the same sense as when human knowledge is in question.

[58] Tuyaerts, *L'Évolution du dogme*, 251; cf. 34.

[59] On the role of dogma insofar as resulting from an "abstract formulation" and its relation to the original faith, it would be profitable to reread the fine pages of Father Léonce de Grandmaison, *Jésus-Christ*, 2:213–17.

[60] Boyer, "Qu'est-ce que la Théologie?", 262.

the appearance of contesting such evidence? The original adherence to Christ was a "wholly concrete and wholly living perception", and numerous dogmas remained at first "latent in the richness of this first perception".[61] Even the texts that are presented to us with striking clarity that would later have formulas of faith are caught up in a whole large context within which alone they are handed on to us and from which alone they receive the fullness of their meaning: a context of thoughts and realities, a "concrete synthesis", a "living organism"[62] from which it is we who disengage them. Our effort at analysis tends, on the one hand, to consider only the strictly intellectual aspect of the reality first given, then to make a series of divisions, finally to obtain as many distinct objects as will be our different "dogmas". Such an operation is legitimate: *abstrahere non est mentiri*. It is even necessary; our intelligence cannot bypass it, and it was already accomplished well before there were "professors of religion" in the Church, professional theologians similar to those of today. It began, one could say, with revelation itself. The apostles were already catechists, and our "New Testament" contains several passages that are true formularies of faith. But it would no longer be legitimate to fail to recognize that, if the apostles were already catechists, they were, more fundamentally, witnesses (both, moreover, indissolubly). It would be to forget the long work to which we have devoted ourselves since their testimony and to place the result of our analysis and of our abstractions, as justified as it might be, *in place* of the reality on which they are exercised. For this result does not cover it and will never be able to cover it completely, but it must, on the contrary, always be inscribed in it. It would not be legitimate to believe, in consequence, that revelation has been made to us without any intrinsic link with the one and total reality of Christ, which it has given to us as a simple collection of formulas, in a series of propositions detached from that unique mystery and thereby separated from each other, like "major premises", wholly ready for our future reasoning.

Here again, here above all perhaps, one must distrust human analogies. The case of revealed Truth is unique. This is what "logicists" as well as "vitalists" seem to us not always to have considered sufficiently in this question of development. So the scheme of the syllogistic con-

[61] J. Lebreton, *L'Encyclique et la théologie moderniste*, 36.

[62] J. Lebreton, *Histoire du dogme de la Trinité*, vol. 1, 6th ed., 256.

clusion is in danger of leading the former astray just as the metaphor of the seed has at times led the latter astray. The original state of doctrine is not a "rudimentary" state—except always, of course, *secundum quid*—and if it is true that in the human order "nothing great has great beginnings",[63] this is not true of the Christian newness—although the criteria of its greatness are not the criteria of human greatness. This newness is reducible neither to "principles" nor to a "seed". In reality, concretely, what is first and that from which one must start without ever leaving it—what is first and last—is the redemptive Action; it is the gift that God makes us of himself in his Son; it is the definitive accomplishment of that great design hidden in himself since the beginning and now revealed: "Our gratuitous vocation to eternal life through Christ and in Christ, or, in other words, Christ, the fullness of God's gift and the unique source for men of eternal salvation."[64] And it is at the same time the revelation of all that. For it is all that which, in Jesus Christ, is revealed to us. It is all that which, at first undivided, forms the total Object, the incredibly rich Object of revelation. We can call it, to use an equivalent expression, "the Whole of Dogma". And this "Whole of Dogma" is, as its name indicates, not susceptible to any increase. It, too, like the Whole of the redemptive Action, is at once first and last. It is unsurpassable.

Under its form of action and under its form of revelation, as reality and as the object of faith, this unique and total Thing carries one and the same name in Scripture and in Christian Tradition: it is *mystery*. It is already a first abstraction, therefore, to separate completely the gift and the revelation of the gift, the redemptive action and the knowledge of redemption, the mystery as act and the mystery as proposed to faith. It is a second abstraction to separate from this total revelation or this "Whole of Dogma" certain particular truths, enunciated in separate propositions, which will concern respectively the Trinity, the incarnate Word, baptism, grace, and so on. Legitimate and necessary abstractions, we repeat—for the mind can only preserve the total truth

[63] Joseph de Maistre, *Du principe générateur des constitutions politiques*, no. 23. He adds: "One will not find in the history of all the centuries a single exception to this law." Yes, a single one: and it is precisely the history of Christian revelation (although, in more than one aspect, there is an analogy).

[64] Joseph Huby, "La Connaissance de foi dans saint Jean", in *Le Discours après la Cène*, 153. Cf. Augustin, *Épist.* 187, no. 34: "Non est enim aliud Dei mysterium, nisi Christus" (PL 33, 845).

by actively exercising itself on it and according to its own laws—but on condition that we be aware of it and that we not fail to understand the concrete "Whole" whose contents we will never exhaust.

Now this concrete "Whole" is not proposed to our intelligence alone. We sometimes reason as if revelation had come simply to add a few bits of knowledge, higher or more hidden, to that which man already possessed or that he could at least possess by the fact of his reason. He knew, for example, that God is one: he will henceforth know besides that God is also Trinity. This way of seeing is superficial. The irruption of the Spirit of Christ is something quite different! Revelation, in fact, is at the same time a call: the call to the Kingdom, which is not open to man without a "conversion", which is to say, an inner transformation and, as it were, a recasting not only of will but of being itself. Then the entrance into another existence is produced.[65] It is a new creation, which resounds in one's entire awareness: it upsets the original equilibrium, it modifies the orientation of it, it opens up unsuspected depths in it. Eyes open anew on a new world. The community of a new life allows the giving of a meaning, its whole meaning to the divine object of faith.

There we have, very quickly sketched, the fact that should be described at length, by taking it first, so to speak, on a historical level, in order then to deepen its nature, by striving to let nothing of its very rich and yet unique complexity be lost. There we have the reality that should serve as our foundation if we want to work out a theory on dogmatic development. We would undoubtedly realize, even though it is possible to give great emphasis to this development—as the facts of Christian history oblige us to do—without risking an attack on this original truth, that in Jesus Christ all has been both given and revealed to us at one stroke; and that, in consequence, all the explanations to come, whatever might be their tenor and whatever might be their mode, will never be anything but coins in more distinct parts of a treasure already possessed in its entirety; that all was already really, actually contained in a higher state of awareness and not only in "principles" and "premises". We are not even beginning to undertake such a work. We have not wanted to propose any theory—and we know in advance that any theory will be weak in places. The preceding characteristics are suggestions at the most. They draw attention to a large fact, without

[65] Romano Guardini shows it admirably in several passages of *The Lord*.

wishing also to interpret it. But we will note, in concluding, that it is on this path that some theologians who have given us the most satisfactory view of development are engaged. Such is Father Lebreton, recalling at the outset of his large work on the *Histoire du dogme de la Trinité* a truth that is so simple but weighty with consequence: that the point of departure and the very substance of dogma is "less a teaching than a person" and that "Jesus, for Christians, is the very object of faith".[66] So, too, Father Hugueny, showing how "the intellectual progress of Christianity is only a work of slow integration in discursive thought of what has existed in its entirety in the intuitive thought of its founders."[67] And finally, so too, Father Simonin, devoting himself to finding in the Thomist theory of faith the idea of the organic character of the revealed deposit. It is this deposit, he explains, that one must grasp in its unity, in its substance, in its profound orientation; it is on the basis of it and not abstract and explicit propositions that we must see the development take place. Then we will understand that, contrary to one current affirmation, which is at the source of the difficulties we have shown, the "implicit" is not contained in the "explicit" as such. It is, from the beginning, the "explicit" that is contained in the "implicit", "in the definable fringe of the mystery".[68]

---

[66] *Histoire du dogme de la Trinité*, 1, preface, 6th ed., xv; cf. 541.

[67] *Critique et catholique*, vol. 2 (1914), 47. Cf. 46–47: "When we speak of development of the knowledge of supernatural facts (which constitute revelation), it is necessary to distinguish between knowledge and knowledge, between intuition, experiential but also total knowledge of the concrete reality in all its efficacy, and the discursive thought, the speculative analysis, the rational dissection of the different concepts with which we try to decompose into very explicit ideas, better proportioned to our natural knowledge, the impression that the supernatural fact manifested by revelation and accepted by faith has produced on our consciousness. . . . The knowledge of the incarnate Word, which the apostles had derived in their intimate relations with Jesus before his Passion and after his Resurrection, is wholly different from that which the theologian finds in the study of a treatise on the Incarnation. . . ."

[68] "La Théologie thomiste et le développement du Dogme", *Revue thomiste*, 18 (1937), 552; " 'Implicite' et 'explicite' dans le développement du dogme", 139, 143. Cf. *De veritate*, q. 14, a. 11: "Implicitum proprie dicitur esse illud in quo quasi in uno multa continentur. . . ."

The work by Father O. Faller, which has just come to us, *De priorum saeculorum silentio circa Assumptionem B. Mariae Virginis* (*Analecta greogoriana*, 1946), seems to us to make the reflection proposed in this Bulletin even more timely. The conceptions of the author on the development of dogma lead him to formulate a series of arguments that he presents with insistence as being, not expediential arguments, but rigorously necessary reasonings, but which without doubt very few of his readers will judge so. So, on page 127, in capitals:

"Filius Dei, humana natura ex Mariae carne assumpta, ineffabili unitate cum matre con-

The page of the *Gregorianum* quoted above gives evidence of the fear that, if one does not adopt in everything the position that it maintains, one would find oneself carried along into a kind of vitalism and irrationalism, which would be a regrettable "concession to certain contemporary philosophies". That such a danger exists, that the history of ideas gives witness to it, we will not argue. But let us be careful: this would not at all be to avoid it; it would be, on the contrary, to aggravate it by letting one believe that there is no other way to avoid it than that of a pseudo-rationalism that is as little satisfactory for the reason as it is for faith. No more than one would give proof of "firmness" in "the interpretation of sources" by forcing the texts in order still to find "the belief today *just as it was* in the past" would one give proof of intellectual rigor by declaring reasonings to be always and necessarily rigorous, when they often are not so and have no need at all to be so, because one at first imagined a theory in the name of which they must be so. We believe we can discern in such a demand a certain stiffening that resembles pragmatism more than true intellectualism. And the concern for a too human security that it denotes, this need to enclose the whole life of the Church in a system of strictly rational control, seems to us neither sufficiently conformed to what we glimpse of the flexibility of God's ways nor sufficiently respectful of the action of the Holy Spirit in the Christian intelligence. It may be that some particular one of the more moderate, and in our opinion more clearsighted, theologians whom we have quoted has sometimes, in his language, been influenced by a certain "vitalism": the danger would be minimal

---

junctus, matris honorem tutatur, cum legem a se latam, honorandi matrem, ipse impleat. (Cf. Mt 5:17; Lk 2:51, Job 19:26ff.)

"Jam vero corruptio in morte non est honor, sed pars condemnationis ob peccatum originale. (Cf. Gen 3:19.)

"Ergo Filius Dei et Mariae non permisit corruptionem matris in morte."

In addition, the only text quoted by Father Faller in his introduction in support of his idea of development—that very one we have just criticized—is a text of Saint Ambrose, *In Luc*, l. 6, n. 105 (PL 15, 1697). But the misinterpretation is obvious. When Saint Ambrose writes: "Non in principiis perfecta quaeruntur, sed de principiis ad ea quae perfecta sunt pervenitur", he in no way has in view the state of Christian doctrine at its beginning and in its subsequent progress; he is treating the pedagogy of conversion: "Lege sermonem Apostoli apud Athenienses habitum, qui si a primo destruere voluisset caeremonias idolorum, sermonem ejus aures gentilium respuissent. . . ." (Paul is thus speaking to them at first of God the Creator, then he refutes idolatry, then he comes from that to Christ, but without unveiling yet either his divinity or his virginal birth.) "Qui enim tractat, debet audientium considerare personas, ne prius irrideatur quam audiatur. . . ."

if it is true that he was only thus expressing the traditional belief, in terms on which an era has set its mark and which are, moreover, not without scriptural foundation. Several of these theologians, in any case, have not ceased to maintain the cause of the intelligence in all that is legitimately its own. They have led, from the first, an effective battle against modernism. If, in order to do so, they did not believe they should adopt the system that is proposed to us today as indispensable, it is perhaps because their knowledge of Christian Tradition was more complete, their idea of reason more demanding and their respect for mystery more consistent.[69]

Appendix: From the Vatican Council to the Development of Dogma

(Unpublished text from 1955)

Father Guérard des Lauriers wishes to remind me (*Revue thomiste* [1955], 490, note 2) of a text from the [First] Vatican Council saying that "a certain understanding of the mysteries can be obtained: either through analogy or through the links that exist either between the mysteries reciprocally or between the mysteries and the ultimate end of man." This text is very dear to me. I have had occasion to quote it myself, from the time of my first publication (*NRTh*, [1930], 366). I have often been inspired by it since then. It is impossible for me to say in what way the words for which the Reverend Father reproaches me would be in opposition to it. "We come . . . to show that one cannot establish that there is any contradiction in it [= in dogma]; but that is still a wholly negative stage, and, from the point of view of pure logic, we do not go beyond this stage" (*RSR* [1948], 148). These words do not enunciate an idea that is even slightly personal: it is a truism, recalling that one cannot prove *positively* through pure reason the possibility of the mystery: would my contradictor wish to undertake to make this proof, for example, for the dogma of the Trinity, or for that of the Incarnation? or, indeed, would he not rather quickly confuse demonstration and understanding? I do not even see in what way my truism

[69] These pages had already been drafted when another article by Father Boyer (*Gregorianum*, 1947) reached us, an article devoted to our *Surnaturel*, in which several of the problems raised here were indirectly touched upon. We hope to be able to return to this later.

would have any relation to the subject of the conciliar text. Finally, if the reader refers to the article in which this figures in passing, he will see there, as in another publication, that I was prompted to give very great emphasis to the *quaedam intelligentia* of which the Council speaks.

On the other hand, Father Guérard des Lauriers does not seem to have seen that the Council speaks of the mysteries taught by the Church, consequently of truths already known, not of truths that, by hypothesis, are still implicit. Even in this hypothesis (which is perforce that of all work on dogmatic development), I grant the reason a very large part in the explanation of these truths. I only maintain, along with Father Simonin, for example (*Angelicum* [1937], 130), that "a simple appeal to the processes according to which the human mind establishes a conclusion on the basis of rational principles, where a truth that it has acquired solely by force of its nature penetrates most deeply, will never to be able to provide an adequate knowledge of the very particular phenomenon that it is a question of studying." I maintain that if development can be made in certain cases by way of a rigorous logical conclusion, it is not necessarily always so—which does not, moreover, signify that the theologian might not bring many "theological reasons", many "expedient arguments" . . . (*RSR* [1948], 143–49).[70] It is not up to me or Father Guérard des Lauriers whether or not this

[70] Father H. D. Simonin went, it seems, a little farther, when he spoke of a "radical opposition between the progress of the sciences and dogmatic development", of a "manifest tendency" of the Vatican Council "to exclude from the control of natural reason the stages of the dogmatic progress accomplished in the Church", when he added that "just as the human reason is not the norm for the adherence of faith, it is not the norm for its progress", that the passage of old truths to new "cannot be the fact of perfect evidence"; that "in all dogmatic progress . . . , the direct passage from old formulas to the definitions that explain them, if one excepts the case of a deferent submission to the decisions of the Magisterium, remains a difficult step, uncertain in its result, which a thousand particular circumstances can make strangely problematical". He did not fail to understand, for all that, that "the Church has often sanctioned" statements that the work of theologians "had managed to deduce from the principles of the faith." "In this privileged case," he specified, "it is licit to speak of a positive connection, perceptible at least for the theologian, thanks to which a more or less rigorous demonstration permits one to pass to the revealed deposit through some assertions that the latter virtually contained, in the way in which any conclusion is logically implied in the understanding of its premises. . . . But one maintains that the conclusion established, insofar as it is thus deduced, rises strictly from the domain of theological *knowledge*, without belonging, on its own authority, to that of faith. In fact, the adherence that is given to it is directly motivated by an intellectual evidence, the fruit of human inference, it cannot be equivalent to an affirmation of the faith that is founded on the testimony of the word of God . . ." (loc. cit., *Strena Garrigou-Lagrange*). These final particulars were also ours (144–45).

thesis is traditional. To cite once again only one author, whose memory is particularly venerated, this was, without any possible argument, the thesis of Father de Grandmaison, whose study on the development of dogma, abundantly quoted by me on this precise point, has always served me as a model of balance and of theological soundness. I would assume that he, like so many others, knew and respected the Vatican Council.

5. The Mystery of the Supernatural

I

Quicumque studio antiquioris philosophiae christianae ex ipsis fontibus operam dedit, non potuit non animadvertere discrimen illud, quod inter Doctores Scholae antiquioris et modernae in aliquibus conceptibus et doctrinis, haud parvi nonnumquam momenti, intercedit. Quod discrimen, generatim, progressu scientiae faciliter explicatur: in quibusdam

---

Recherches de science religieuse (1949), 80–121.

A little prior to Father de Lubac's banishment from teaching and the publication of the encyclical *Humani generis*, this article develops the conclusion of the historical studies gathered together in *Surnaturel* (on the composition of this work, see K. Neufeld and Michel Sales, *Bibliographie H. de Lubac: 1925–1974* [Einsiedeln: Johannes Verlag, 1974], 64). Contrary to a tenacious legend that continues to circulate, even within the theological circles of the Society of Jesus, the encyclical of Pius XII, far from condemning the views set forth here, ratified them by repeating on its own account one key sentence from this article. Here is what Cardinal de Lubac wrote on this subject in his *Entretiens autour de Vatican II*, 13–14.

"As for the Encyclical, it was—not very generally as a whole, but on a few precise points—very different from what some had anticipated: it even caused in them some disappointments that I need not explain here. 'Disappointment' is, moreover, an understatement: as one good, very learned theologian recorded at the time, it was 'a boomerang' for them. (The details of this story would be very picturesque.) In what concerns me, one can, if one wishes, pick out two allusions in *Humani generis*. Pius XII expressed in passing his fear that suspect doctrines were spreading secretly: I have no reason to take that as referring to me, and I have good reason to think that, as for the Pope, at that date, the fear did not concern me either. The second allusion relates to the supernatural: far from containing any blame or any reservation in my regard, it borrows a phrase from me to express the true doctrine, and it is not by chance that it avoids any mention of the famous "pure nature" that a number of highly placed theologians were accusing me of misunderstanding and which they wanted to have canonized. Yet criticism lasted for some time yet and became even more violent. Some of my Superiors insisted on making Pius XII aware of this situation; they did so through the intermediary of Father Bea, his very good friend. The Pope immediately had Father Bea address a letter to me whose every word he dictated: it thanked me for the work accomplished up until then and encouraged me to pursue 'with much confidence' a work 'which promised much fruit for the Church'. Quite the contrary of a reproach. I have never had to make, either in writing or even orally, either in public or in private, the least particular act of submission or retraction on any point. And when I resumed my teaching, it was on my own accord; discreetly consulted by my Dean, the Congregation of Seminaries and Universities, from whom I took my orders, was even surprised that I had interrupted it for some time."

tamen casibus aliam explicationem, ab extrinseco petitam, postulare videtur.[1]

This is what Father Edmund Elter had to say a few years ago, on a subject close to ours, since it was a matter of opposing the old school to the relatively new one on the idea of beatitude. As he made us

---

This article from 1949, considerably developed, was to become the work of the same title, *Le Mystère du surnaturel*, Theology series, 64 (Paris: Aubier, 1965), 301 pp. On the question of the supernatural, see also in *Entretiens autour de Vatican II*, 11–12, 27–32.

The article in *Recherches de science religieuse* that we publish here was, however, withdrawn, along with several other books or articles by Fathers de Lubac and Father Y. de Montcheuil, H. Bouillard, J. Daniélou and J. M. Leblond, from the libraries of the Scholasticates and houses of the Third Year of the Society of Jesus all over the world. The letter from the Father General of the Society and the list of works will be found in the *Acta Praepositi Generalis* (1950, vol. 11, fasc. 6 [Rome, 1951], 882–83). See *Mémoire sur l'occasion de mes écrits* (Namur: Culture et Vérité, 1989), 75 [English trans.: *At the Service of the Church* (San Francisco: Ignatius Press, 1993), 74; hereafter the page references to this translation will be given in brackets following the page reference to the French edition].

In his *Mémoire sur l'occasion de mes écrits*, H. de Lubac provides numerous pieces of information and documents about the origin, genesis, stakes, reception, consequences and disappointments earned him by his historical studies on the supernatural. It was Father Joseph Huby to whom, if not the inspiration, at least the first confirmation goes back (33 [35]), and these works, published without raising any objection beginning in 1931 (cf. 21–22 [25–26]) would become, fifteen years later, the catalyst for the most absurd suspicions and the occasion for the mythical Fourvière "affair" and for the "new theology". Here are the numerous passages where all this is dealt with: 33–35 [34–37] (final editing and publication of *Surnaturel*), 59 [59] (oppositions to *Surnaturel* recorded by Father de Lubac in a journal of 485 manuscript pages), 63 [62] (the editorial direction of *Recherches de science religieuse* is taken away from Father de Lubac), 63–64 [62–63] (the 1949 article on "Le Mystère du surnaturel" in relation to *Surnaturel*), 72 [71] ("Le Mystère du surnaturel" quoted in *Humani generis*), 75 [74] (this article is withdrawn from the libraries of formation of the Society of Jesus), 124–32 [123–30] (the fresh attacks, supplementary material, stakes and works created by Father de Lubac after 1960), 161 [157] (extensions to the second part of *Surnaturel* in the Italian edition), 189–92 [183–88] (Father de Lubac's debt with regard to M. Blondel, whom he had read in 1921, and correspondence with Blondel), 202–3 [199–200] (the historical aim of *Surnaturel*), 203–26 [200–223] (reactions to *Surnaturel*, followed by the text of the principal reviews of the work since its publication), 249–51 [245–47] (important letter), 294–309 [290–309] (documents and information on the period following publication of *Humani generis*, 352–55 [352–59]).

Acceding to the insistence of several friends with good advice, Father de Lubac kept on the "Fourvière affair" a file of 1610 pages of notes, correspondence and various documents, a copy of which he deposited in the archives of the Church of France after his accession to the Cardinalate.

[1] "Anyone who has studied ancient Christian philosophy in its original sources cannot help but note the difference—often of considerable importance—between ancient and modern authorities in some of their ideas and teachings. This difference can for the most part be readily explained by development of the knowledge (of the subject matter). In some cases, however, one must seek another explanation outside [the subject matter]." Edmund

see, it is possible to quote many other examples of theological theories which, after having achieved unanimity in at least one part of the Church, subsequently found themselves in decline, or deserved to. In the explanation of the relations between Church and State, did not the so-called theory of "direct authority" reign for several centuries, notwithstanding strong opposition? Yet what theologian today would want to see it revived? It was not only abandoned in fact: the official teaching of the papacy decided against it. We would bet, nevertheless, that if it could still find defenders today, they would not fail to read it in the famous bull *Unam Sanctam* or use Bellarmine's misfortune as an argument. With respect to the Redemption, the author of a series of good historical works, Canon J. Rivière, recently appealed to "the law of development" in order to demonstrate that, if the dogma itself obviously remained unchanged, "theological reflection was slowly working to translate [it] into less and less inadequate concepts."[2] In other words, a linear theological development had necessarily to result, through a certain progress, in the theory set forth by the author. Scarcely a few years have passed, and here we are invited on various sides, and not without reason, to return to the very rich givens of Christian antiquity, which the "development" of this modern theory had been wrong to expel. Undoubtedly, neither the Molinist system of the *scientia media* nor the contrary explanation that could be attached to the name of Bañez ever won over more than one part of the school; but, at least, both together rallied nearly the whole of it. Now there are many today, in increasing numbers, from both opposing camps, who judge that it would be better to hold a simpler, less anthropomorphic as well as older view. Father Sertillanges won numerous followers in this regard.[3] Is it necessary to go on to recall the *Mysterium fidei* of Father de la Taille, which can be considered an attempt to eliminate overly complicated systems developed since the sixteenth century around the Sacrifice of the Mass? One need not subscribe to all the theses of this long treatise in order to consider it a salutary work. Finally, not to mention other examples, are we not witnessing a similar movement with respect to

---

Elter, S.J., "De naturali hominis beatitudine ad mentem Scholae antiquioris" in *Gregorianum*, 4 (1928), 269.

[2] J. Rivière, *Le Dogme de la Rédemption au début du Moyen Age*, 256.

[3] Cf. Antonin D. Sertillanges, *Saint Thomas d'Aquin*, 1, 3d ed. (1922), 259–68. See also Maurice de la Taille, "Sur diverses classifications de la science divine", *Recherches de science religieuse*, 13 (1922), 7–23.

the very notion of theology? For several centuries—precisely or very nearly those in which the idea of "pure nature" prevailed—theologians agreed rather generally in thinking that their discipline was essentially a science of "conclusions"; that it had less to do with penetrating to the innermost part of the revealed object in order to acquire some "intelligence" of it than, on the basis of it, to draw more numerous but also of necessity more distant consequences. Now, despite the considerable differences that set them in opposition to each other, even in what concerns their method, the theologians of today seem to be more and more in agreement in rejecting such a concept, which they regard as unfortunate.[4]

What has happened to other theories could well happen to the theory of "pure nature". It is true that it has reigned nearly uncontested within the school for a rather long time. Let us nevertheless note that, put back into the twenty centuries of Catholic tradition, this time must appear short. Let us also note that the theory never penetrated Eastern theology. Such an absence has never been seriously considered a doctrinal obstacle to union. It is explained by the fact that the ancient Greek tradition did not include any similar idea. Now it is our belief that the same is true for the Latin tradition up to a very late period. Without doubt, the structure of the new theory more or less flowed back over the interpretation of ancient texts.[5] That is also a rather natural phenomenon. Moreover, if some, renouncing an overly arbitrary historical concordism, willingly abandon Saint Augustine as less explicit or less "distinct" in this regard, many still believe they find authority for it in Saint Thomas Aquinas. But, to tell the truth, it seems, from certain signs, that they are less and less sure of this,[6] and good

---

[4] In his introduction to *Symbolique*, J. A. Moehler made some similar reflections for Protestants. "Why then", he wrote, "do Protestants want so very much to attribute to the universal Church the particular opinions of her members, as if such and such a scholar had given her existence? . . . It would be absurd to confuse them with the doctrine of the Church. It can even happen that, during a certain period, some particular system may obtain rather general assent without, however, ever being considered an integral part of dogma . . ." (French trans., 44–45).

[5] For example, in what concerns the texts in which Saint Thomas speaks of a twofold beatitude. Cf. "Duplex hominis beatitudo", *Recherches de science religieuse*, 35 (1948), 290–99.

[6] In any case, many gave up using his authority to shield the dualist system that denied any properly natural desire for the supernatural, a system that not long ago people still thought to find easily in him, or even seeing in his work the explicit affirmation of the possibility of a purely natural order, in the modern sense of the expression. The analyses from the *Bulletin*

historians contest it.[7] This is a point that, we believe, cannot fail to be seen with increasing clarity as the number of historical works grows.

In this last case, as in several of those we mentioned above, the return to simplicity would thus coincide with a return to antiquity. A return to simplicity: complications are not always equivalent with progress of thought, far from it.[8] No more in theology than elsewhere is there need to reject systematically any analysis, any precision, any distinction that the necessity to avoid error or the spontaneous movement of the spirit comes to make necessary. But one must also admit that very often the strength of the doctrine and its very depth are more diminished than increased by a certain lack of sobriety. The indefinite proliferation of concepts is not always without danger. In theology as in philosophy, it can become indispensable to undertake from time to time that "reducing diet" of which Léon Brunschvicg once spoke. A return, by that very fact, to antiquity: which does not mean a return to a "rudimentary" or "undifferentiated" doctrinal state. It is great naïveté to represent the movement of ideas through the centuries, and especially in theology, as being only a long passage from implicit to explicit, or from confused to distinct, up to a certain privileged state that will be declared the definitive end of this evolution, unless one prefers to leave the route indefinitely open. As if an author, although less distinct perhaps in relation to one who comes after, if one takes one's position from the point of view of this latter, could not, on the contrary, be much more so from the perspective of his own problems! These are, in a science whose nature should have better preserved it from such invasions, echoes—though undoubtedly unconscious echoes—of those doctrines of progress that appealed so greatly to the age that preceded us. Neither the bourgeois of Louis Philippe, who thought they had closed the era of the Revolution, nor the intellectuals of the beginning of this century, who smiled at the perspectives of an indef-

thomiste and the *Bulletin de théologie ancienne et médiévale* have done much, in recent times, to lead to a better historical understanding of Saint Thomas' thought.

[7] See, for example, Edgar de Bruyne, *Saint Thomas d'Aquin* (1928), 97. (The author, departing from modern presuppositions, sees there, moreover, a "blemish" in the work of Saint Thomas.) Proceeding from more precise analyses, Henri Bouillard, *Conversion et grâce chez saint Thomas d'Aquin* (1944), 77–82; Henri Rondet, "Nature et surnaturel dans la théologie de saint Thomas d'Aquin", *Recherches de science religieuse*, 33 (1947), 56–91.

[8] Cf. Saint Augustine, *In Psalmum* 4, n. 9: "Non enim multiplicatio semper ubertatem significat."

inite progress once opened by Condorcet, could be models for us. As we know: the Church, guardian of revealed truth, assures us in every century of the pure and integral maintenance of the truth; with more or less success, the effort of every century also contributes to bring out the importance of this sacred deposit; dogma itself is called to profit from it, in certain explanations that the ecclesiastical Magisterium will perhaps solemnly ratify.[9] Not everything, however, in the results of this theological labor is always equally sound. All is not equally destined to endure forever. We do not share the superstitious attachment that some theologians seem to have for the "modern" as such (whatever the exact definition they may give it). We do not think it is enough, in order to get rid of doctrines that have long been traditional, to apply names to them such as "archaic conceptions" or "obsolete theories".[10] We do not believe that a happy fate predestines us to think everything in a less "inadequate" way solely because we were born later. We do not deny progress, even theological progress: we simply do not believe that this progress is total, or that it must always be affirmed a priori. πάντα δὲ δοκιμάζετε, τὸ καλὸν κατέχετε (1 Thes 5:21).

In the present case, which concerns the doctrine of the supernatural, is it, as some think, a return to Augustinianism that is at issue? Yes and no. On the one hand, this "Augustinianism" is also that of all the great Scholastics of the thirteenth century as well as that of Saint Augustine himself, and we would not want to lose the benefit of their clarifications. There is also, as we have said, the fact of the Greek tradition. It is not tied to the thought of the Doctor of Hippo in what must be exclusive to that thought, and the example of Saint Thomas Aquinas shows that it can well be accommodated to an Aristotelianism transformed by the principles that are at the basis of all Christian philosophy. On the other hand, Saint Augustine and a number of his disciples habitually mixed two problems that we have since learned to distinguish better—and which the Greek doctors in the line of Irenaeus already distinguished better—the problem of the final end and that of man's initial equipment in view of his progress toward salvation.[11] Whence

[9] On the role of theologians in the development of dogma, I have proposed a few suggestions in a recent "Bulletin" in *Recherches de science religieuse*, 35 (1948).

[10] Cf. Rivière, *Dogme . . . au début du Moyen Age*, 252; *Le Dogme de la Rédemption dans la théologie contemporaine*, 130, 222, 235, 245, 249.

[11] In the twofold Baianist and Jansenist controversy, we know that, beyond the problem of sin and its consequences, it was the second of these questions that was directly at issue, the

some misunderstandings whose trace can be observed throughout fifteen centuries of history. Finally, the return to the essence of an earlier position should never be a pure and simple reconstitution. Such archaism is always mistaken. It does not contain any less illusion, though in the opposite direction, than the ideas of linear progress. Neither the Greek Fathers nor Saint Augustine nor Saint Thomas nor many others could pose to themselves all the problems that the dogmatic given raises and will always raise in the human mind in the same way we are obliged, without placing the least personal factor in it, to pose them to ourselves today. In this sense, it is true to say that one never retraces one's steps. One never turns back the course of time. (Our faith is not old: it is eternal and ever new.) If there is thus no need, at least as it seems to us, to change the idea that the ancients have transmitted to us about our basic relation to our supernatural end, an effort nonetheless certainly has to be provided to show us more clearly, according to the current needs of our mind, with respect to difficulties to which the development of thought has given rise or whose illumination it has at least modified, how this master idea is in perfect harmony with the demands of faith.

Perhaps this effort should consist particularly, in relation to Augustinianism, in better assuring the real consistency of the natural order in all its degrees as well as in better distinguishing this natural order from the order of sin. With respect to Thomism, it might consist in showing more explicitly that the kind of continuity shown in summary by the axiom *Gratia perficit naturam*[12] does not exclude, from another point of view, the total transcendence and heterogeneity of the supernatural; for "the dogmatic quarrels since the Reformation have made us more attentive to all the difficulties of the subject."[13] Perhaps there would even be a need to go so far as to disclose in the finite being, as it were, two antagonistic tendencies, equally radical, so that the passage to the

first intervening only in an indirect fashion. Invaluable information could have been found in this regard in Saint Thomas, *De Veritate*, q. 18, a. 1, ad 5, 6 and 7: "Homo factus erat ad videndum Deum non in principio, sed in ultimo suae perfectionis. . . ."

[12] After having noted in certain formulas of Saint Thomas some "delicate nuances full of thought", Father G. de Broglie added very justly: "They show to what degree grace was for him a completion given to nature in the same sense as his active inclinations had already outlined": in *Archives de philosophie*, 3:222, note. In the same sense, Étienne Gilson, *Le Thomisme*, 5th ed. (1945), 495–96.

[13] A. Motte, O.P., in *Bulletin thomiste*, 3 (1933), 674.

supernatural order, even for an innocent nature, could never be accomplished without a kind of death.[14] Let us say clearly, in any case: to renounce the modern hypothesis of "pure nature" could not be a way of diminishing, even to the least degree, the idea of the supernatural, of making the latter, so to speak, "less supernatural". Some have at times rather inaccurate ideas on this subject. The most separable realities are not, however, necessarily those that are the most strongly distinguished from each other. Union and differentiation are much rather two things that grow at the same pace. If we will be permitted a comparison—which we will bring to bear only on this one point—Scholasticism admits that matter does not and cannot have any existence independent of form: Does that mean that matter has in itself some resemblance with the form, that it is, so to speak, cut from the same cloth, or that it must be understood as an already inchoative form? As everyone knows, the conclusion to be drawn is just the opposite. The fact that nature is not conceived as an order able to come definitively to an end upon itself, but as having a supernatural finality, does not mean as a further consequence that it already has the least positively supernatural element in itself or as part of its property. Nor does it mean that nature is without proper consistency. A similar comparison, which should be pushed no more than the first, will help us perhaps to take this into account. If we consider the doctrine of Platonic or Cartesian inspiration that makes the body and the spirit two substances and the doctrine of Aristotelian and Thomist inspiration that sees man as substantially one being, we find that it is not the first that best assures corporal values their rightful place and best resists the pressure of false spiritualisms, in conformity with revelation itself: it is incontestably the second.

Consistency of nature, heterogeneity of this nature in relation to the supernatural: let us not be too quick to believe we have placed these two things *in tuto* because we have formed once and for all the hypothesis of a possible universe in which nature would supposedly have known its complete development and its "proportioned" end without ever having raised above itself. Is this not somewhat the same here as in the subject of the so-called doctrines of "tolerance"? There is, as we know, an attitude that consists in easing one's conscience by affirming an intransigent "thesis", in order then to give way to all

[14] The idea is sketched on a fine page by Father D'Arcy, *La Double nature de l'amour*, French trans. (1948), 196–97.

accommodations, indeed, to all abandonments under the cover of the "hypothesis". All is maintained, and perhaps exaggerated, "by right": all is compromised "in fact". Similarly, it is possible to insist very much on the idea of a possible order of "pure nature" and all at once, in the actual order of reality, to crush this poor existing nature under the pressure of a poorly understood supernatural. The position that one would apparently make for it "by right" is thus ruined "in fact". Only consistency "in point of fact", however, the consistency of our effective nature, in *this* creation of God, would interest us.

Perhaps, in affirming the possible dissociation of the two orders, natural and supernatural, a dissociation such as the first being sufficient in everything, one is still more liable to lose the profound sense of their "infinite qualitative difference". If one wants this concept of a "pure nature" to be anything more than a big X that responds to nothing in the spirit and is henceforth no longer of any help for thought, it is difficult, in fact, to press it at all without being led to transfer to it more and more, one after another, all the attributes and all the privileges which our present humanity enjoys in its relation to God. The supernatural order thus loses its unique greatness. In the end it constitutes nothing more than a kind of double in relation to the natural order. This is, beyond doubt, the path on which, through the very logic of its position of departure, one whole segment of modern theology appears to have committed itself. Nature and the supernatural find themselves in a way juxtaposed and, whatever one may say, enclosed in one and the same genre, of which they constitute, as it were, two species. Too separate to be truly differentiated, they develop on two parallel, fatally homogeneous planes. Prayer, love, grace, faith, virtues, all are reintegrated into the "purely natural" order that one imagines. Henceforth, everything is thus conceived in double parts—everything up to the "immediate vision" and the "possession" of God![15] And the only intelligible difference drawn between one series and the other consists

[15] In proposing his hypothesis of an "immediate natural vision of God" (cf. *Surnaturel*, 439–47), Father Pedro Descoqs did not express *extra chorum* some bizarre idea about which there was great need to insist: he carried a whole current to its culminating point. The idea had, moreover, been launched as early as the sixteenth century, and Suarez felt obliged to refute it: *De ultimo fine hominis*, disput. 16, section 1, n. 5 (Vivès, 4:152; cf. 145); one might judge that he was thereby fighting against the logic of his own position. Father E. Peillaube, S.M., following Sylvester Maurus and Gotti, also spoke of the "natural possession of God": *La Destinée humaine* (1930), 56.

in the epithet joined to them respectively, the one being the so-called "natural" and the other "supernatural". Is one not then in full nominalism, not to say in full psittacism? For if one resists this path and if one allows oneself to be carried along by the opposite logic, one ends in supposing a being who is sufficient to himself, who does not pray, who does not abandon himself to any Providence, who stands before God in a jealous autonomy, who undertakes no relation of love with him. Any idea of gratuity is banished from this "purely natural" world inhabited by this being. Can we say that such a picture agrees with the idea we have—whether through pure reason or through revelation is of little importance—of the one true God?

Without doubt, we are pushing things here to the extreme in either direction. We do not claim that any theologian professes them reflexively to this point. But if we wanted to clarify a little the idea that is vaguely formed of a "pure nature", we would really have trouble not falling actually into one or the other of these too opposite excesses. Or else, we repeat, we would then have nothing but an hypothesis devoid of content, and the absence of any perceptible link between this X and our actual nature would render the use of it completely sterile.

Under these conditions, is it not simpler to return, as we propose, to the position of the Ancients, who were not burdened by such an hypothesis? We would, of course, have to show—as is proper in any case, and without, moreover, claiming to elucidate fully what touches on mystery—how the total gratuity of the Gift of God—of that Gift of God that is nothing but God—can be introduced. This is what we have endeavored to do in a quick sketch placed at the conclusion of our *historical studies* in *Surnaturel.* The explanation has seemed satisfactory to more than one theologian. A certain number tell us of their positive agreement. Few precise objections, referring to what we have actually written, have been presented to us. As for the disparaging remarks and distortions of which our text has at times been the object, we will hope that they will be so obvious to the attentive reader that he will have no difficulty in noting them. Without repeating, therefore, what we have already said, we would like now, *in pace catholica pacifico studio,*[16] and, as the Ancients also said, γυμναστικῶς, to urge research on a little more. And it is to this end that we will pose to the partisans of "pure

[16] Cf. Saint Augustine, *De Trinitate,* l. 2, n. 16 (PL XLII, 855).

nature", by reason of a subsidiary argument, this simple question: Do you think that your hypothesis, supposing it solid and without difficulties, is useful for the end that we are all proposing?

II

The question is important. In fact, the principal motive that has pushed modern theology to forge its hypothesis of "pure nature" and to place it at the base of all its speculation on the final end—we see this very well, for example, in Bellarmine[17]—was the concern to assure, against the modern deviations of Augustinianism, the full gratuity of the supernatural gift. It did succeed in practice. One can nevertheless wonder if a more exacting reflection would not find some fault in the theory from this very point of view. This would not be the only example, in the history of theology, of a theory that, in practice, attained its end but did not succeed in satisfying the mind and spirit in everything. It can thus be asked: Considering a way of looking at the matter that can no longer be in all respects that of the theologians of the sixteenth or the seventeenth century, is the theory worked out by the latter sufficient to assure the dogma of the total gratuity of the supernatural? Is it truly suited for it? Without making concessions to philosophical modes, without becoming an adherent of any new system of thought, one cannot prevent the work of the times from being accomplished. One cannot, if one uses one's mind—and theology requires that one make use of it—refuse to respond to the real problems in the form in which they present themselves. These variations in the problematic are not our doing: they are imposed on us. To recognize them does not involve any complicity with the mind of the times or any relativism as far as doctrine itself is concerned, and they must be taken into consideration if one wants to say anything that actually matters.[18] Let us therefore pose the question.

It is said that a world could have existed in which man, without

[17] Cf. Henri Rondet, "L'Idée de la nature pure au seizième siècle", *Recherches de science religieuse*, 35 (1948), 481.

[18] Such a step is, on the contrary, explained only by a concern for timeless truth, absolute truth. As for knowing whether we will attain the latter in everything, in our human theories, better than our ancestors or than our successors, that is another affair. The act of doubting it deserves the name of modesty rather than the too scholarly one of relativism.

prejudice perhaps to another desire, had restricted his reasonable ambitions to some inferior beatitude. But that being said, one is, indeed, obliged to concede that in our actual world, in fact, the ambitions of man cannot be so limited. Then this word "ambitions" is undoubtedly no longer suitable—but neither is that word "limits". In me, a real, personal human being, in *my* concrete nature, the "desire to see God" could not be eternally frustrated without essential suffering. Is this not the very definition of the "punishment of the damned"? And consequently, it seems, the good and just God could not frustrate me in this way if it were not I who, by my own fault, freely turned away from him. The infinite seriousness of this desire placed in me by my Creator constitutes the infinite seriousness of the drama of human existence. It is of little importance that, in the actual circumstances of this existence, it is not objectively perceived in all its force: it will be so in any case when my entire being will have become flesh, when my nature will appear to me such as it is in its innermost depths. This is because this desire does not come to me from any perhaps modifiable particularity of my individual being or from some historical contingency to more or less transitory effects. It is in me from the fact of my belonging by nature to actual humanity. For my finality, of which this desire is the expression, comes to me from my nature. And I do not have any other real end, that is to say, any other end actually assigned to my nature, except to "see God".

It remains to be shown, therefore, how the supernatural is gratuitous not only in relation to a hypothetical human nature, or even in relation to human nature in general, outside of any achievement of this nature, but how it is also and precisely so in relation to the concrete men that we are, in relation to all those who make up this present humanity, or this "historical nature", as is sometimes said. It remains to be shown that it is totally gratuitous for me. Without which, nothing has yet been done. For my situation in relation to my final end is no longer exactly the same as the situation of the nature about which one first argued. For example, when a Saint Irenaeus proclaims: "God shows himself to men when he wishes, to those he wishes, as he wishes", we do not understand his thought at all unless we apply it immediately to these men that we are today, to all the men of *this* world, and first of all to our first father. In other words, the true problem, if there is one, is posed for the being whose finality is already supernatural, since such is our case. It is presented to the being for whom the "vision of God" marks not only a possible end but the end which, to judge it in human terms, must be. (From the moment I exist, in fact, all indetermination is lifted, and whatever may have been "before", no other end is henceforth possible for me except that which is now inscribed in my nature and for which, by that very fact, I carry within me, consciously or not, the natural desire. If I lack that, I lack everything.) Such a being does not have only "*a* natural desire" to see God, but the desire to see God is "the desire of his nature".[19] We must, therefore, show how, for this very being, there is no real "requirement" for such an end, in the sense in which this word justly causes scandal. Whether or not one has first made the hypothesis of a "pure nature", one cannot be dispensed from considering this new aspect of the problem.

This is because, in fact, in order to maintain the gratuity of the supernatural through recourse to another possible finality, it would not be enough to say (as we have just seen) that, in another order of things, the same human nature could have been constituted with this other finality. This would not be going into the matter deeply enough. We should still have to be able to say that of the same humanity, of the same human being, finally of the same me. Now, on reflection, this is what makes no sense. For, in posing another order of things, one poses at the same stroke, whether one wishes to or not, another humanity, another human being and, if one could say so, another me. In this purely natural world that one imagines or affirms to be possible, "my nature", it is said, would have found its place. Let us admit that—although it is not at all as sure as one believes. But in any case, this would not be the same "I". You can put into this hypothetical world a man as perfectly similar to me as you wish: you have not put "me" into it. Between this man who, by hypothesis, is not destined to see God and the man who I am in reality, between this futuristic possibility and this living being there is still only a wholly ideal, wholly abstract identity. Perhaps even that is already to concede too much. For the difference between the one and the other does not affect only individuality but nature itself. How could we conclude, therefore, on the basis of the situation of the former, in favor of the gratuity of the gift made to the man who I am? Yet, let us repeat, it is uniquely in relation to me, in

[19] Let us observe in passing that many of the exegeses that water down "natural desire" in Saint Thomas would be weakened if their authors noted that Saint Thomas does not say only *desiderium naturale* but also *desiderium naturae*.

relation to us all, that, in the final analysis, this question of gratuity is posed.[20]

In other words, if I am to be able to say without equivocation that God gives himself to me, that he shows himself to me freely, in all independence, it is necessary for the supernatural to appear gratuitous not only in relation to a generic, abstract and unrealized nature but in relation to the concrete nature in which I participate here and now. It is thus within the existing world, which is to say, within a world of supernatural finality that is, not possible, but existing, that I must find (to the degree possible for human intelligence) an explanation of the gratuity of the supernatural, without having recourse to any supposition whatever that makes me leave this world. Now this is what the hypothesis of "pure nature" does not succeed in doing. For it does not in fact show, as one seems to believe and as it should, in the logic of the theory, that I could have had another more humble, wholly "natural" destiny. It only shows, still presupposing it to be reasonable, that in another universe another being than I, possessing a nature analogous to mine, would have had this more humble destiny. But, once again, what does this other being have to do with me? What do I have to do with it? In order to assure me that I could actually have had this more humble destiny, one would have to be able to show it to me, if only for an instant, inscribed in me, in fact, in my concrete nature. Now this is what, by hypothesis, is impossible. My destiny is an ontological thing, which I cannot change as an object changes in destination. It is therefore necessary to seek some other way to assure the required gratuity.

Perhaps someone will say that this reasoning is inspired by a nominalism that denies any specific reality to nature by wanting to see only the concrete me. This would be difficult to understand. It is not at all a

[20] The objection would be particularly strong against the thesis that denies any "natural desire" properly speaking in the state of pure nature. If, in fact, in this state, the view of God in itself does not inspire "any curiosity" in the mind, either the ordination to this view, arising in another state, will not be experienced by him as a benefit (any more than the best meal would be by someone who has no appetite), or, in order for the appetite to come along with the ordination, the mind in question will have to be profoundly transformed. And then (not to speak of the very dangerous empiricism that such a conception of the mind presupposes), if it was already clear that there was not, from one state to another, an identity of subject, it is clear now that there is not even an identity of "nature" any more. What does the hypothesis of "pure nature" do for me under these conditions? In what way can it serve to resolve the problem posed?

question of making a pure abstraction of human nature. I must recognize that I participate, the individual I, in the same nature as Socrates, for example, or as some primitive man or as any other real or realizable man in this world. Humanity is a reality. Human nature is a reality. But this is, at least in part, precisely because, if we all participate in it, we all have the same essential finality. If one speaks to me of another nature hypothetically realizable with another finality in another universe, I no longer feel anything but a purely abstract link with it, whatever traits of resemblance with our own one might confer on it, perhaps arbitrarily besides. I cannot draw the consequence we are seeking from this abstract link.

This inability of the theory of "pure nature" to play to the end the role for which it was imagined is increasingly apparent, it seems, the more the idea of the person emerges, under the influence of Christianity and to the degree a more concrete ontology tends to be constituted. But we are not mistaken about it. This is not essentially a new view. It is, rather, a return to the point of view of ancient tradition. In patristic thought and particularly in Saint Augustine, we do not encounter this opposition between an "essential", abstract order, which would be an order "by right", and a "historical", concrete order, which would be the order "in fact", an opposition that holds so central a place in modern explanations. The essence itself is historical in it, and history, in this sense, is essential to it. Certain Fathers are not devoid, as is sometimes said, of any truly metaphysical thought because they do not speculate about an abstraction without any connection to the effective realization of natures. We do not do justice to a Saint Augustine if we see in his analyses of the human mind or the human soul only the working of his gifts as a marvelous psychologist. As for Saint Thomas Aquinas, despite the undeniably more abstract turn of his thought, it is basically the same for him. When he deals with problems relating to our final end, he always does so both by analyzing the essence of the created spirit and by remaining within our universe whose finality is supernatural. Not having encountered in this regard the difficulties that were subsequently raised, he does not treat in detail the problem of gratuity: the philosophers he had to combat imposed another task on him. But when he does treat it, he does not call finality itself into question. There is every reason to think that, confronted with this problem, he would have judged mere words and of no importance any solution that had recourse to the hypothesis of a "pure nature", which is to say, to the hypothesis of another man and another universe.[21]

The solution to the problem of the gratuity of the supernatural, if sought on this path of another possible finality, could thus be given only in the following manner. It would be necessary to mark in the very course of my actual and personal existence, or at least—if one considers less the individuals themselves than the humanity of which they are a part and which makes them interdependent in their destiny—in the very course of the actual existence of our race, a particular instant when God would intervene, either in order to assign me an end left in suspense up until then or in order to change the end that he had first of all assigned me. An absurd double hypothesis, of a radical extrinsicism, destructive either of the idea of nature or of the idea of finality, if it is not of both at once. Neither the epic of the world nor the drama of my destiny can admit of such a claim. These suppositions are, moreover, at least apparently rejected by the universally admitted axiom, according to which the state of pure nature has never existed in fact, even for only an instant. Yet they are impossible to escape from the moment one posed in principle that an end is gratuitous, for a determined being, only if another end were objectively possible for it: that is to say, "pure nature" has been made the indispensable and unique guarantor of the gratuity of the supernatural.

In fact, the theory of "pure nature" was born and developed in an intellectual milieu in which the notion of finality had been diminished. What this theory presupposed at its beginning, although not always explicitly, was that, before the grace of baptism or some other such substitute grace, all men, in our same world—if one disregards original sin and its consequences—were in the state of pure nature. Finality was thus considered only as a rather extrinsic thing: not a destiny inscribed in the very structure of the being and which, ontologically, he cannot avoid, but a destination received more or less from outside and after the fact.[22] That is why they did not see any obstacle to having a supernat-

[21] For Saint Thomas, the end of the created spirit "in any hypothesis is God himself, which is to say, the supernatural". Perhaps it is not merely a chance coincidence if, in this same period where we have shown the invasion of the system of pure nature in theology, the process unfolds in philosophy that will end in what Étienne Gilson calls a de-existentialized essence and if, as a result, these Scholastics of Wolffian inspiration are very far from authentic Thomism. Cf. Étienne Gilson, *L'Être et l'essence*, 176, note.

[22] And even that was made possible, it seems, only because of an initial ambiguity: the

ural beatitude come to be "superadded" to an essentially natural beatitude. In connection with Cajetan, who was one of the initiators of this theory (for it was not constituted all in one day), they spoke of "historical nature". Now this "historical nature", along with the desire to see God that accompanies it, included, according to Cajetan, let us recall, the positive revelation and objective knowledge of certain supernatural effects.[23] Other theologians, since then, have understood the matter in this way. Some, it seems, still understand it in this way today. When they say with all the others that the state of "pure nature" has, in fact, never existed, we see from then on in what an attenuated sense or, to put it better, transformed sense it is advisable to take their affirmation. For them, the final destination of the universe can be changed in the course of time, without anything being changed in the structure of that universe or in the essence of the beings who comprise it. This paradox has been maintained by certain commentators of Saint Thomas.[24] One learned historian of Thomist thought could write in this regard: "One could not dream of a more categorical reversal inflicted by commentators on the thought of the Master."[25] We know in fact to what extent, in the latter, finality is an intrinsic thing, affecting the depths of being. We also know that, for him, one single change in the natures that comprise the universe was enough for one to be dealing with another

---

expression *pura natura* (or, at first, analogous expressions, such as *pura naturalia*) had for a long time designated only a certain state of nature deprived of supernatural gifts, without implicating its finality or its subsequent history.

[23] Cf. *In Primam*, q. 12, a. 1: "Novit quosdam effectus, puta gratiae et gloriae, quorum causa est Deus ut Deus est in se absolute, non ut universale agens. Notis autem effectibus, naturale est cuilibet intellectuali desiderare notitiam causae. Et propterea desiderium visionis divinae, etsi non sit naturale intellectui creato absolute, est tamen naturale ei supposita revelatione talium effectuum." *In Secundam Secundae*, q. 3, a. 8: "Author tractat de homine ut theologus. . . . Et sic, licet homini absolute non insit naturale hujusmodi desiderium, est tamen naturale homini ordinato a divina providentia in illam patriam . . . quia indictum est naturaliter ut viso effectu, desideremus nosse quid est causa, quicquid sit illa." Cf. John of Saint Thomas, *Cursus theologicus*, disput. 12, a. 3, n. 6: "Cajetanus . . . id explicat de homine supposita aliqua notitia fidei seu rerum supernaturalium, non ex solis naturalibus considerato" (2:140).

[24] Thus Billuart and Gotti; Réginald P. Garrigou-Lagrange, *Le Sens du mystère*, part 2, chap. 2, 190 and 192. Billuart: "Nullam habet (visio Dei intuitiva) connexionem cum causa aut effectu naturali, ex cujus cognitione mens ascendat ad illam indagandam aut demonstrandam, ita ut, si non existeret aut non foret possibilis ista visio, res omnes naturales forent nihilominus eodem modo quo nunc sunt."

[25] A. Motte, O.P., in *Bulletin thomiste*, 4:577.

universe.[26] For us, it will suffice to say here that, if such a conception is alone truly consistent, once the premises that we criticized have been posed, it seems to us in itself unintelligible. Undoubtedly one can well admit that the supernatural finality of our universe has no direct relation, for example, with the laws of physics or chemistry; so that, if by some impossible hypothesis this universe found itself suddenly deprived of any supernatural finality, these laws would remain what they are. But can one maintain that it would be the same for man, in the roots of his intellectual and moral life? And, even to suppose that so radical a change at work in man did not have to have repercussions on the material universe or on the knowledge that man acquired of it, would such a change not be enough to make him, at least, this particular man, no longer absolutely the same?[27] And how, on the other hand, can we admit in the Creator this recasting of his work? If he truly destines man to see him, what meaning can there be in this idea that he destines him to do so only after a certain moment?

Either, then, the idea of a "pure nature" is to be conceived within our actual world (but then it leads us into absurdity) or it is to be referred to another universe (and then it appears incapable of the service expected of it). But, whether one adopts it or not, if one succeeded in showing directly—as one must do somehow—that the supernatural end cannot in any case be the object of an exigency, even for the being who could not have any other, then there would no longer be any need to appeal to this in direct consideration of a purely natural order. We have just seen that this consideration was insufficient. Now it would no longer even be necessary. By trying to show, without leaving by means of any abstract fiction the limits of our world such as God made it and which is the only one we know, that the Gift that God offers us of himself is and can be only totally gratuitous, with no higher gratuity imaginable, we believe we have followed the only efficacious path— on which others could progress with greater success. It seems to us also that it was the principal path opened up by tradition. If we have succeeded in our intention, without however obliging anyone to reject any idea of "pure nature", we will have reinforced this fragile rampart

[26] Cf. *Prima*, q. 25, a. 6, ad 3m: "Posset tamen Deus alias res facere, vel alias addere istis rebus factis, et esset aliud universum melius."

[27] Otherwise, if I can thus receive a new finality at will, it is necessary to admit the reign of the arbitrary in everything and to suppress any idea of nature and reason.

of a bastion that seems to us more sound for the common defense of a Truth prior and superior to all our theories. If, however, some felt it impossible to save this divine Truth without having recourse still to "pure nature", we would be the first to say that they not only have the right to maintain it, they do not have the right to abandon it.

III

"Well and good!", one will say. "But we do not take these last words as a concession for some. We take them as the acknowledgment of a necessity imperative for all. For, after all your reasoning, it nonetheless remains that if the end to which God guides our world today is for its part wholly gratuitous, it is because another world could have existed, which would not have been guided to this end. How can we conceive of things otherwise? There is no gratuitous gift if it cannot be denied. When the old clergyman of France voted his 'gratuitous gift' to the king, in keeping with a custom from which he could not escape, he knew well that the adjective had become deceptive. When I make a gift to someone, if it is not possible for me to be dispensed from making it, this would not truly be a gift, and to the degree that conformity was solicited from me, it is a gift only in an improper sense. Nothing will prevail over the good sense of this view. And that is why the idea of 'pure nature' will always be indispensable for giving an account of the supernatural."

A view with good sense, certainly, and on its surface, we would not think to contradict it. But a very superficial analogy when we think of the unique and mysterious Object who solicits our reflections. The Gift of God to his creature, this Gift who is he himself, likened to the gift that one man makes to another man! It will not be to rush into rash subtleties to submit this analogy to criticism for a few moments. We will do so by taking our bearings from another analogy: that of the first gift God made us by giving us being. For there is a real parallelism, as we will see, between this first gift of creation and the second gift, completely distinct from it: the ontological call to deification, which will make man "a new creature".

In order to represent to myself these two radical benefits from God toward me, benefits that both logically precede in me any offer of grace to my free will, I proceed in fact according to the analogy of the gift received from a man through a man. Of necessity, I must represent myself to myself first of all as preexisting, as the subject of attribution or rather of reception of these two successive benefits. I thus declare in the first place: "God has given me being"; then, the second benefit: "On this being that he has given me, God has imprinted a supernatural finality; he has made resound in my nature a call to see him." Thus, inevitably, I seem to precede my being, and my being in its turn seems to precede its finality. That is an unavoidable process of dissociation and exposition, given the nature of human intelligence, which is always, at least at first, *intellectus dividens*. It is impossible to exempt myself from it if I want to form a correct, although still very inadequate, idea of the twofold initial benefit for which I am indebted to God. The first of these two formulas: "God has given me being" expresses in its way a total contingency, the radical distance that exists between my essence and my existence. In a parallel way, the second formula: "God has imprinted on my being a supernatural finality" expresses in its way the total gratuity of the supernatural gift, the radical distance that exists between my natural being and my supernatural end, in other words, between my condition as creature and my divine filiation.

Yet, no more than we can exempt ourselves from proceeding in this way can we then remain there. It is clear, in fact, on the one hand, that I did not preexist my creation, in order then to receive in it a being that would pass in some way from the hands of God into mine, like the gift that a child receives from the hands of its parents. Taken literally, univocally, the first of our two formulas therefore provides no meaning. It is contradictory. It does not express truly—it does not express *sufficiently*—the radical gift of being that God gave me (here, however, I fall back into that unavoidable language) in creating me. For this gift is wholly within me, and nothing of what I am is without it. It is for me incomparably more *gift* than all external, superadded gifts that can then be made by men. If I want to remedy a little the weakness of my language without risking the impossible effort to correct it thoroughly, I should thus say that, through creation, God has given me to myself.[28]

[28] We could have reasoned on the basis of still another example. When Saint Robert Bellarmine says, in one of his sermons: "Infra lunam . . . nihil est nisi mortale et caducum, praeter animos generi hominum Dei munere datos" (*Conciones de quatuor novissimis*, concio 4; *Opera*, 9:447), he speaks like everyone else, and no believer will contest the truth of what he says. It is nonetheless true that mankind did not exist at first—even in a logical instant—in order then to receive the spirit from the hands of God as a gift.

Now the same remarks are imperative, *mutatis mutandis*, with respect to the second formula, relating to the benefit of the supernatural finality. This formula, too, presupposes the analogy of a human gift, as if God were before me in the manner of another man, although infinitely better and more powerful than any other; as if his situation with respect to me were wholly exterior, allowing him, too, to make me only a gift, a wholly exterior gift. But I cannot stop at such a representation here any more than I could a few minutes ago. The analogy of the human gift does not suffice; any more than the analogy of human testimony, for example, could give an account of divine faith. It is a necessary springboard, but one which is justified only by the impulse that it permits and which is soon brushed aside. It lacks that element of interiority—one could just as well say transcendence—an attribute of the Creator God who "is more interior to me than I am to myself". To criticize the original analogy is therefore not at all equivalent to placing in doubt or merely diminishing the value of the idea of the gift or of that of the testimony. Quite the contrary: the divine testimony is incomparably superior to any human testimony, and the divine gift likewise. Which does not signify simply that this testimony is stronger or that this gift is more magnificent. By this way of speaking we will still not be leaving the human order. The human analogy would not be truly criticized. It signifies that this testimony is more truly testimony, that this gift is more truly gift, in an eminent sense. The formal idea of gift, like that of testimony, is verified in God in his relation to us in a higher, infinitely higher fashion—and particularly if we recall that the gift of God is God himself—than that which is accessible to our experience from human relations.

In short, from the time I say "I" exist, I have my being; and from the time I exist, from the time I have my being, I am finalized. It is impossible actually to dissociate these three elements in order to divide them into three times between which one would have to conceive of a twofold hiatus. Strictly speaking, these formulas: "God has gratuitously given me being" and: "God has gratuitously imprinted on my being a supernatural finality" are thus not acceptable. So we must, at a second moment, criticize them, after having necessarily posed them at a first moment. Let us note one thing well, however. In criticizing them, we are not, properly speaking, dismissing them as false. We are not replacing them with contradictory statements. We will show that they can be pronounced only by posing first of all a fictitious subject, which is something entirely different. We do not deny, therefore, the reality that they affirm: we deny merely their imaginative presupposition. Neither in the one case nor in the other does the negation have to do with the gratuity, first or second, of God's Gift. Quite the contrary, the criticism instituted permits us at least to glimpse in this Gift of God a twofold miracle of gratuity whose power no analogy drawn from human gifts can express.

The phase of negation succeeding a first phase of affirmation was therefore negative only in appearance. It was not so in reality any more than "negative theology" is a negation of God. If the latter is, on the contrary, opposed in the extreme to atheism, the former will likewise be opposed in the extreme to naturalism. Afterward just as before, we can continue to say that if God had wanted, he could have not given us being, and that he could have not called this being that he gave us to see him. For if this language is inadequate, it is not at all because of the sovereign freedom it recognizes in God: if, for the reason we have just seen, it must be criticized, it nonetheless translates in its own way a very just and important truth, while the contrary proposition would suggest a twofold error. We know, both through what God is and through what the creature is, that it could not be otherwise. God could not be constrained by anything, either from outside or from within himself, to give me being. Neither could he be constrained by anything to imprint in my being a supernatural finality. And if it is true that in God all is identified in a perfect simplicity, at the very least through relation to me, I must carefully distinguish and always maintain a twofold gratuity, a twofold divine gift, and therefore, if one may say so, a twofold divine freedom. There are here, as it were, two successive planes, like two landings without any communication from the bottom one to the one above. A twofold ontological passage, doubly impassable to the creature without the twofold initiative that arouses and calls him. No more than creation itself is the necessary consequence of something that preceded it, then, is the supernatural gift a simple *sequela creationis*. Between the existent nature and the supernatural to which God destines it, the distance is as great, the abyss is as profound, the heterogeneity is as radical as between nonbeing and being. The *donum perfectum*, to go back to the traditional words borrowed from the Letter of Saint James, is transcendent in relation to the *datum optimum*. It is "of another, supernatural order". It is, properly speaking, as Scripture says, a new creation, and without common measure with the first creation. The only one who can doubt it is he who, like Baius,[29] does not conceive at some point that this gift constitutes for nature a real *sublimation*, a real *exaltation* above itself, in brief, a real *deification*. It is not the supernatural that is explained by nature, at least as postulated by it: it is nature that is explained, to the eyes of faith, by the supernatural, as willed for it. Considered in itself, statically, so to speak, or again, "in its kind", my nature is only what it is: there is not, let us repeat, the least supernatural element in it. But no more than one would be justified in considering, except in a manner of speaking, an actual subject prior to its position in being through the creative act could one actually consider this nature prior to seeing its supernatural finality inscribed on it. Thus it is not in any case nature that of itself calls the supernatural: it is the supernatural, if one can say so, that arouses nature before summoning it to receive it.[30] If, then, one next comes to say that a purely natural end is impossible for this nature, this could always be only *ex suppositione*. And in that way we will find ourselves rejoining the champions of "pure nature" in what motivated their theory.

On another point, however, we continue to be separated from them —at least from some of them. In fact, there is nature and nature. If, as opposed to the supernatural order, the being of the angel and that of man, such as they result simply from their creation, must be called natural, if there is thus an angelic nature and a human nature, in another sense, spirit is opposed to nature. Spiritual beings are not natural beings (*entia naturalia*), that is to say, they have certain prerogatives that, making them in the image of God, make them at the same stroke higher than any order of the cosmos. This important distinction is not

[29] This is what results from his own protests against the wording of several propositions condemned by Saint Pius V. For him, the supernatural gift did not have as an end "a new spiritual creation", but it was still linked to the decree "whose effect was the production of natural divine works". (We borrow these expressions from Father. F. X. Jansen, *Baïus et la baïanisme, étude théologique, Museum Lessianum* [1927], 128.)

[30] It seems to us that all this could be summed up in the very brief, very plain Thomist formula: "Non est aliquid naturae, sed naturae finis." One could also say: Nothing would be more false than to maintain that there was nothing more, after all, in our divine vocation than the creative act; but quite the contrary, it is true to assure that there is nothing less in the creative act than this divine vocation. But vocation is not yet realization. As ontological, so to speak, as its effect might be, the call to union is not yet union. In other words, the priority of the supernatural in the order of intention—*prius intenditur deiformis quam homo*—does not mean that created nature is to the slightest degree in continuity with the supernatural in the order of execution.

an invention of modern philosophy; it is everywhere in Christian antiquity,[31] it is also everywhere in the great Scholastics, notably in Saint Bonaventure[32] and Saint Thomas.[33] One can say that was already being prepared in Aristotle, through the famous aphorism: "Any soul is not nature."[34] The laws that obtain within the cosmos, and which consequently govern "natural beings", cannot, therefore, be applied without transposition to human nature, if one considers in the latter not only what makes of it an animal species of superior degree but that by which it is spirit. Now this is what those who were at the origin of the theory of "pure nature" did not consider sufficiently. The same oversight is still observed today with a certain number of their heirs. Hence their habit of thinking strictly of the relation of the spiritual creature to God by means of analogies drawn from what happens within nature, in the sense that we have just specified. Thus one comes to lay down as law that all being must have its connatural end, proportioned to its nature and of the same order as it. But what one thus takes to be a universal principle is true precisely only within nature, or the cosmos, from which one has defined it by induction. When one applies it in the case of the spiritual creature, one in reality is only reasoning by analogy. Now, here, the analogy does not hold true precisely because it is the property of this spiritual creature not to have its destiny circumscribed within the cosmos. The spiritual creature has a direct relation to God that comes to it from its origin. And that changes everything. From that, with it, comes this kind of lopsidedness, this mysterious limp that is not that of sin but, more radically, that of an animal that is spirit, of a creature who, strangely, touches God. At once "nothingness" and "image". Thus the laws of the "dynamism proper to the spirit" are not calculated on the laws of the "*dynamism of natural forms*".[35] It would thus be vain to repeat in endless forms the argument expressed, for

[31] Father A. M. Festugières, O.P., has shown how the idea of created πνεῦμα was original in Christianity: cf. "La Trichotomie de 1 Thess. v. 23 et la philosophie grecque", *Recherches de science religieuse*, 20 (1930), 385–415.

[32] *In 2 Sent.*, d. 29, a. 1, q. 2, ad 4m.

[33] See, among many other texts, *Secunda Secundae*, q. 2, a. 3: "Sola autem natura rationalis creata. . . . Natura autem rationalis. . . ." Cf. *In Boet. de Trin.*, q. 6, a. 4, ad 5m.

[34] Aristotle, *Parties des animaux*, l. 1, 641 b, 9 (that is: "the intellectual soul is not nature"). The positive side of Aristotle's teaching is, moreover, too far here from the truth brought out by Christian philosophy for there to be any need to force a comparison.

[35] We are borrowing these expressions from Father Joseph de Finance, *Être et agir dans la philosophie de saint Thomas*, 339–40.

example, in this phrase from Cajetan: "Si astra haberent vim progressivam, natura dedisset eis organa opportuna";[36] one would be saying nothing that holds true for the spirit. Whether explicitly, as in this text, or, as in others, veiled beneath more abstract forms,[37] the analogy must be challenged. *Dicendum, quod non est simile.*

Thus, in the final analysis, it is a twofold imagination whose spirit must be liberated: that which conceived of God as a man, that which conceived of man as a "natural being". What could have been considered conditions of thought in this problem of the supernatural were only first conditions of representation, analogies that are still coarse and in need of criticism. From then on, if this criticism appears justified, we must enter resolutely into that "negative phase" indicated a moment ago. We will not find, undoubtedly, a position of complete repose there. For this will be the beginning of a reflection that is destined to have no end.[38] The human intelligence is made in such a way that, if it has the power to criticize its own representations, it does not have an equal power to replace them. It succeeds in detecting everything inadequate in them: it is precisely in this that its greatness shines forth. But it will never possess the adequate formula that would put an end to its search. That is why it can seem to the intelligence that through this work of criticism it is carrying out a negative work. At the very least, it seems, through a series of overly subtle steps, to be compromising the truth of which it had had at first an assured, total

[36] Cajetan, *In Primam*, q. 12, a. 1, following Aristotle, lib. 2 *de Caelo*. Suarez quotes and approves it, *De ultimo fine hominis*, dissert. 16, sec. 1, n. 11, 4:154; cf. disput. 15, sec. 2, n. 6: "Omnes aliae naturae possunt assequi suos fines naturales per media consentanea naturae: cur ergo natura humana erit in hoc pejoris conditionis?" (148), etc. Saint Thomas never ceased to fight against this false analogy. Similarly, the theologians of the French school (who were naturally farther from it, since they used, in general, less physical analogy). By prevailing later in the Thomist school, it led the theologians of this school more than once to positions diametrically contrary to those of their master.

[37] This is what is at the source of Suarez' reasoning, repeated everywhere: "Repugnantia est, quod finis supernaturalis quoad consecutionem sit naturalis quoad appetitionem: cum appetitus naturalis non fundetur nisi in naturali potestate" (*De gratia*, proleg. 4, c. 1, n. 8, 7:181); cf. *De ultimo fine hominis*, disput. 15, sec. 2, n. 5–6, 4:147–48; disput. 16, sec. 1, n. 10, 153). Or John of Saint Thomas, *Cursus theologicus*, disput. 12, a. 3, n. 8, Solesmes, 2:141. Or again, Father C. Boyer, in *Gregorianum* (1937), 300–301, which contradicts all the old school.

[38] Such is the frequent teaching of the Fathers, notably Saint Augustine and Saint Leo. We know the wonderful formulas of the latter. The one who stops is not at the end, he has fallen on the way. Cf. Origen, *Peri archôn*, l. 1, 4, 4: "Sed rursum in hoc humana intelligentia hebetatur" (Koetschau ed., 66).

perception, although the expression that was given of it was, as it well knew, only roughly approximate. With its anthropomorphisms, in its imaginative conceptions, it at least enclosed a certain truth. It held it *in tuto*. Now is this very truth not going to be called into question?

Such is the objection—or rather such is the instinctive fear—that any attempt at real reflection always awakens. The life of the spirit, like that of the body, is inevitably the source of "unease". The dead alone are in *complete repose*. The intelligence is thus in dread of itself. It fears generating its own bewilderment. That, in the present case, the fear is unfounded is what seems clear to us. What is at issue here is, in fact, an "understanding of the faith", which always presupposes at its foundation the given of faith itself and which never ceases to be regulated according to it. It does not even seek to go beyond it. We must repeat: it does not at all seek to possess it more fully. Faith has its own light, which can be superior in the understanding of the simple believer to that in the best theologian. The effort of the intelligence can aim only at better understanding reflexively the given of faith, which, moreover, has indeed its price and which corresponds as well to a necessity. For this twofold reason, it is fully justified. But it develops wholly, let us repeat, within this given, and each of its stages is always measured in its results strictly on the basis of this given.

All minds, however, do not experience equally the need for such an effort. It is nonetheless very often necessary for them, on the level where their natural speculation usually moves, for dogmas to be given a certain coherent view, more systematized than the teaching of the Church, which renders these dogmas more assimilable to them and which prevents ever-possible deviations. Whence the permanent usefulness of theories that are constructed, through the arrangement of concepts, within common sense, starting with uncriticized representations. Their intellectual value can be weak. To admit them is not, however, pure pragmatism, since they are useful, not for any end whatsoever, but *for the maintenance of a truth*. At the end of this study, we call to mind one case of this kind by citing the theory of the *scientia media*: it remains a necessary support for those who need to conceive of the relations between grace and human freedom as an organized system and who could not otherwise preserve the idea of freedom.[39] A similar

[39] Father Auguste Valensin has justified this kind of thought intellectually by pushing it to

example could be found in the theory that goes farther than that of Saint Anselm, which pits justice and mercy in a struggle against each other in the heart of God, and in still other theories. . . .

A reflection more concerned for the truth, as theology must strive to be, could not be content with theories of this kind. This is not because it seeks to push them farther: on the contrary, through a regressive movement, it returns to their presuppositions in order to purify them of anything imaginative that might have entered in, or anything still unworthy of the divine Object they wish to express. It does not, moreover, produce any wavering in the mind. Remaining in submission to this divine Object, it is not without firm roots or precise references, it does not cease to be securely oriented. Its "uneasiness", conformed to the human condition and to the life of faith, is healthy. It knows, however, in advance that it will never end in another theory that is finally complete and fully satisfying. Such a culmination is neither of earth nor of heaven. All Tradition cries it out to us: it is one of the forms of the fruitfulness of Mystery which an unstoppable movement engenders in the thought of man. To be afraid of it would be to lack faith. The believing intelligence gives itself without fear to its work, knowing well that this work, far from ever placing in question the truth first held of the Mystery, tends only to show it to be ever more profound and more wonderful.

IV

This mystery of the supernatural, which is the mystery of our divine destiny, appears somewhat like the form within which all the other mysteries of Revelation will come to be inscribed. Numerous are the aspects under which it can be considered. Numerous are the problems that it poses to the mind. The old Scholasticism applied itself in particular to elucidating the consequences of the fact that a created intelligence, thus finite, is called to see God directly, such as he is in himself. "Nulla creata substantia potest sua naturali virtute pervenire

---

its extreme in one paragraph of his little work: *Autour de ma foi* (1948), 114–16. Let us observe, however, that such theories, while they serve to maintain a truth on which attention is fixed, generally thereby compromise a complementary truth, which it is sometimes no less important to hold. We know well enough the weak point in Molinism. I tried to show, in *Surnaturel*, how the theory of "pure nature" had, fatally, "cleared the ground".

ad videndum Deum per essentiam."[40] To see God "face to face", to know him "as he knows himself", to enter with him thereby into a reciprocity of love: How is that possible? Henceforth, another problem increasingly compels attention. If it is true that this view of God is nevertheless our effective destiny, it is thus the Good par excellence toward which, in one way or another, the desire of our nature tends: How, then, can it be wholly gratuitous? Another antinomy, added to the first. We are creature, and we will see God. The desire to see him is in us, it is we ourselves, and it will be fulfilled only through pure kindness. Such antinomies do not surprise us. They arise from any mystery. "Faith is always agreement of two opposed truths."

"There are a great number of truths of the faith and morality", Pascal also said, "which seem contradictory and which all subsist in a wonderful order." Heretics, "not being able to conceive of the relation of two opposed truths, and believing that the admission of one involves the exclusion of the other, devote themselves to the one, they exclude the other, and think that we, on the contrary. . . ."[41] In speaking thus, Pascal was not only developing a theme familiar to the writers of Port-Royal. He was expressing a thought belonging to all traditional times, whose value had already been demonstrated by the orthodox adversaries of Marcion. It has also very often been noted that the various Protestantisms were religions of antitheses: the Catholic fullness always offers a synthetic character. But it is not a synthesis effected humanly. It is not possessed in the light of reason but believed first of all in the night of faith. A synthesis, then, but, for our natural understanding, an antinomic synthesis. This must also be said of each of the mysteries as well as of their relations with each other, in particular, or of their agreement with rational truths. "Make us return to you, Yahweh, and we will return", is written in Lamentations (5:21), and in Zechariah: "Return to me, and I will return to you" (1:3); and there we have what furnished the argument to the Pelagian heresy as well as to the opposite heresy; but the Church retains both texts and quotes them together in her councils.[42] If the Word is engendered, how can he be eternal? And if he is dependent on the Father, how can he be his equal? There

[40] Saint Thomas, *Contra Gentiles*, l. 3, c. 52.

[41] Pascal, *Pensées*. Cf. Joseph Lortz, *Pour un dialogue interconfessionnel*, thesis 18; French trans. in *Document* (1948), 291.

[42] Cf. Council of Trent, session 6, chap. 5.

we have the Arians triumphant twice over. But even before examining anything, Hilary replied to them that it is better to hold to the divine Word than to reasonings of human astuteness. The eternal birth of the Word, like his quality as Son at once equal and submissive, are for him mysteries; he is not surprised that he does not straight off possess the key to them in his reason.[43] After having long meditated already on the union of grace and freedom, after having given explanations for it which are still beacons of light for us, Saint Augustine nonetheless wrote: "Quaestio ista . . . ita est ad discernendum difficilis, ut quando defenditur liberum arbitrium, negari gratia Dei videatur; quando autem asseritur Dei gratia, liberum arbitrium putetur auferri";[44] and who is the theologian, however assured he may be of his system, who must not repeat such an admission on his own account? We find a similar statement in Origen. It is with respect to another problem: God, it was said, must be creator and all-powerful from all eternity, and yet we could not admit that there is a creature coeternal with God. But the occasion is not of much importance, nor the solution provided. What interests us is the universal importance of the remark that it inspires, on the subject of the combat that is engaged within the mind: "Cum ergo inter se humanarum cogitationum atque intellectuum pugna sit, rationibus utrobique validissimis occurrentibus ac repugnantibus, et contemplantis sensum in partem suam quamque torquentibus. . . ."[45]

All cases are obviously not the same. It can sometimes be that the dogmatic given, obliging the reason to an effort of verification of itself, thus frees it from illusions and prejudices that are not at all rational. It can also be that the indirect consequences of revelation on human experience provoke indirectly the formation of new concepts, thanks to which the contradictions one first came up against will be dissipated. But these explanations, even though they have their role to play, are insufficient to account for the most important cases. The sole adequate response consists in an appeal to the very idea of mystery, an idea that is perfectly acceptable from the moment the idea of a personal and transcendent God is admitted. The truth received from him about him

[43] Saint Hilary, *De Trinitate*, l. xi, c. 12; l. xii, c. 18 and 26–31. Cf. Pierre Smulders, *La Doctrine trinitaire de saint Hilaire de Poitiers* (Rome, 1946), 173 and 178–80.

[44] *De gratia Christi*, c. 47, n. 52.

[45] *De principiis*, l. 1, c. 4, n. 4 (Koetschau ed.), 67.

has to escape our grasp. It must offer this character of higher synthesis whose final link escapes us. A philosophy of pure understanding is obscured by it, but not a philosophy that sees in the human intelligence both this absolute of power that makes it pronounce the true and this abyss of obscurity in which its twofold condition as carnal creature retains it. "Or else, or else", always declares the understanding, which is made the measure of all and confuses its limits with the limits of being. "Contradiction does not revolt you enough", wrote Renouvier to Secrétan, with respect to problems that were not concerned with Revelation itself but with the very being of God. And Secrétan replied to him: "You scorn synthesis too much. . . . Contradictions whose terms are necessary undoubtedly lead to the discovery of a lacuna in our effective knowledge or in our possible knowledge. . . . The really irreducible contradictions mark the limit of our understanding."[46] This was to repeat in its turn the doctrine whose perhaps strongest and most paradoxical expression is found in Nicholas of Cusa: "I experience how necessary it is that I enter into obscurity, that I admit the coincidence of contraries, which goes beyond the capacity of my reason, and that I seek the truth in which the impossibility appears. . . . I have found the place where you will be found unveiled, O my God, surrounded by the coincidence of contradictories: it is the wall of the Paradise you inhabit, and one will penetrate it only after having conquered the reason that guards its door."[47]

Secrétan and Nicholas of Cusa were partly right. They were right to reject "that intransigent conceptualism whose law seems at times to want to dictate to the intellect of God himself".[48] They both admit only too quickly that the contradiction is irreducible for us. In reality, the defeat required of the reason can also be its enlargement. And, as we have seen, if our knowledge is incurably deficient, it at least has this mysterious power of criticizing itself. The results that it obtains thereby can well be negative: they are enough to raise the scandal of contradiction. But they are not at all equivalent to a positive solution, in the clarity of which the mind would have only to repose. Father Sertillanges has explained this very well with respect to human action

[46] Charles Renouvier, April 13, 1869. Charles Secrétan, July 15, 1869, and April 26, 1873. (*Correspondance*, 22, 24, 93; cf. 127.)

[47] Vansteenberghe trans., *Autour de la docte ignorance*, 40.

[48] Cf. É. Gilson, *L'Être et l'essence*, 160.

that we affirm to be free even though in total dependence on God. Once it is understood, he says, that God "is first, but *separate* first", "no objection can be made any more, and the joint possibility of the relative and the absolute remains intact." But, he immediately adds, "it is not necessary to conclude that we claim it to be *established*. To establish in a positive way the joint possibility of the relative and the absolute, it would be necessary to define both; now both are indefinable. . . . While God remains inaccessible in himself, the intersection of his being with ours, of his action with ours, remains no less inaccessible."[49]

When it is between two truths of the faith that positive conciliation is not visible, the choice of one of the two to the exclusion of the other constitutes, properly speaking, heresy. We have a series of classical examples of this in the great trinitarian and christological heresies. Those are extreme cases. Without leaving the bounds of orthodoxy, a theology overly concerned about tangible conciliations and definitive explanations always risks compromising the balance of the synthesis by taking away something of its weight from one of the affirmations clung to. Such are those systems which, in order to make the Trinity in divine unity more acceptable to the understanding, reduce to the extreme the category of relation that is used to picture the Persons, speak of the "extreme poverty" of personal being and declare in consequence that the three Divine Persons are "as little distinct as possible from each other". Or those other systems that, in order better to assure the divinity of Christ, minimize the consequence of his Incarnation, so that it is his human reality that is compromised. A modalist or unitarian tendency, a monophysitic or docetic tendency, due, like the inverse tendencies, to a concern that is overly impatient for a positive conciliation between the contrasting elements of the mystery.[50] Fruits of a theology of understanding that refuses to be transcended. It is solely from this formal point of view that we are considering them here. In other cases, only one of the two truths present is a dogma, properly speaking, although both form, as it were, an undivided heritage of Christian thought. Henceforth the temptation is stronger, in order to obtain at little cost the peace sought by the mind, to eliminate or at

[49] Antonin D. Sertillanges, *Saint Thomas d'Aquin*, vol. 1, 3d ed. (1922), 266–67.

[50] It is also very difficult, let us recognize, to escape it completely. The absolutely perfect balance is ordinarily superficial and even risks being only verbal.

the very least to weaken the truth that seems to be antagonistic. This is what has happened, we believe, in the question of the supernatural, with the second problem that we distinguished a moment ago. Theologians ran into an apparent opposition between the essential destiny of man and the gratuity of that destiny. Moved by the desire for an easy solution, on the plane of understanding, they let themselves be guided by analogies drawn from human relations or even from the material world. On this level, all conciliation required a sacrifice. It could not be a question of sacrificing the gratuity. So it was the essentiality that fell. The result was "pure nature", set up in a system.

Thus, what should have stimulated thought like a problem made it draw back like a scandal. They attended to the most urgent thing, to what seemed the surest thing, and dogmatic truth now seems fully possessed in peace. But they did not take care, through this manner of maintaining the gratuity of the supernatural order, not to retreat in their understanding of it. They made of it something quite accidental and, let us say, superficial, a superstructure which man, it would seem, could very well have done without. And they did not even obtain thereby that peace they so desired. For, obtained at so cheap a price, appeasement of the mind is artificial. Soon reason has its revenge by declaring that, under these conditions, the supernatural is only a chimera and of no further interest. It is very well for some theologians to blind themselves to the consequences of the premises that they themselves have posed: "separated philosophy" and "separated theology" are in close correlation, in history as in logic.[51] But, on its side, faith is not long in protesting against a method that mutilates the heritage of tradition. All tradition, in fact (we are taking the word here in the broad sense), since Saint Irenaeus, passing through Saint Augustine and Saint Thomas as well as Saint Bonaventure, hands on to us both of these two truths: man can live only by the sight of God, and this sight of God depends absolutely on the divine good pleasure. Do we have the right to drop one of these two truths, even with the intention of holding on to the other more securely? After a long eclipse, many have realized this in the end. They have also understood the objection to the thousand different forms that a dualist theology had encouraged. This is what has given rise, for several decades, to these theories that have yet again made a

[51] That is one of the deepest roots of modern secularization. Cf. L. Malevez, "L'Esprit et le désir de voir Dieu", in *NRTh* (1947), 28.

place for "natural desire". They mark an unquestionable progress, in the effort of thought as well as in the return to theological tradition. But often the same timidity of method still inspires them, the same impatient concern to eliminate all paradox from the human reality and to reach a positive result that is entirely clear to the understanding, so that the "natural desire" they wanted to reestablish is bent into a vague "inclination",[52] a "wish", a "platonic wish", unfit for the service that it must render.[53] Wouldn't it be better "to hold both ends of the chain" even if one still did not glimpse any solution?

One can do more, as we have shown. One can ascend to the harmony of an opposition one has risen above. Here, however, an objection must still be considered. The desire for the supernatural, as natural and serious as it may be, is not in any case what determines the effective gift of it on God's part. Between these two terms, the relation can only be inverse: it is the will of the donor that awakens the desire in the one that it wants to reach. This point is beyond contestation. If it is well understood, it is enough to avoid any suspicion of naturalism. It nonetheless remains true, one will say, that such a desire becomes the sign not only of a possible gift but of a certain gift. On the basis of the knowledge acquired of this desire, is one not thenceforth right to conclude in favor of the effective reality of the gift? Will man not thus succeed through his natural reason to know that he is made for the vision of God? The objection thus depends, as we see, no longer on the gratuity of the divine offer, but on the mysterious character of the dogma that teaches us about this offer. One is reminded of the discussion that was raised recently about the "mystery of our supernatural elevation".[54] Father G. de Broglie had no difficulty in showing that he was right in thinking that the natural reason can recognize in us a "radical aptitude for supernatural felicity": for this power is not that of knowing either the essence of such a felicity or the fact of our

[52] Even from the sole point of view of language, it does not seem justified to want to sum up the doctrine of Saint Thomas in this word, which he never uses in the very numerous texts concerning the subject, although he knows and uses it otherwise.

[53] This timidity is shown again in the exegesis of Saint Thomas, whose famous principle "Desiderium naturale nequit esse inane" is often interpreted as remaining in the sphere of possibles, although in reality the reasoning that Saint Thomas founds on it "concludes in favor, not of the mere possibility of the intuitive vision, but of its reality" (J. de Blic, *Mélanges de science religieuse* [1947], 97).

[54] Cf. *NRTh* (1937, 1938 and 1939). P. Descoqs, *Le Mystère de notre élévation surnaturelle* (1938).

actual call to enjoy it. It would be different on this last point if it were necessary to combine the hypothesis we are considering with that of Father Broglie. But is the desire for the beatific vision, in its whole nature and its whole strength, knowable by the reason alone? That is what we do not believe. It happens rather frequently that one reasons as if the whole mystery were on the side of God, while nothing in man escapes the grasp of reason. Our whole nature is supposedly, at least by right, transparent to us. That is some illusion. One doctrine dear to the Fathers of the Church was that man is in the image of God not only through his intelligence, his freedom, his immortality, his dominion over nature, but also and especially, in the final analysis, through what is incomprehensible in him.[55] Certain abysses of his nature opened slightly only on impact with Revelation. By revealing himself to us, Bérulle said, God "has revealed us to ourselves". All light on God is a light on man. It is in perceiving the divine holiness and divine love that we become aware of our sin.[56]

It is through the promise that is made to us of the face-to-face Vision that we learn to know our desire in truth. Of course these two cases are far from being comparable in everything. In the first, we are in full reality religious, and the correlation is immediate. In the second, a reflection of metaphysical appearance brings out what implies the revealed object. Consequently the desire of the mind, which does not fall into the field of empirical psychology, is no longer deduced on the basis of purely rational premises. Not that it is a question of total innovation, in no way foreshadowed or prepared. What human doctrines could not be evoked in which this desire would show through! But Revelation alone permits one to interpret it correctly. It is Revelation, too, that will definitively judge these doctrines, that will condemn ὕβρις, will measure its divergences, will sift out the soul of truth from it. The desire to see God, the desire for union with God: these two ends meet outside of Christianity and independently of it. But what equivocations in each of them! We can discern very well, for example in the mystical aspirations of which history offers us such lofty models, a witness in favor of the destiny for which God has made us. But this

[55] Among twenty others, Saint Augustine, *De symbolo*, l. 2 (PL XL, 628).

[56] Cf. Gabriel Marcel, *Journal métaphysique*, III: "One could say that what we are directly aware of is not, is not yet, sin. . . . It seems to me that the reality of my sin flows into my consciousness only insofar as I awake to the infinite love of which I am the object" (*Fontaine*, April 1946, 594 and 600). Cf. also Origen, *In Isaiam*, h. 4, 2.

is on the condition that we interpret them in the light of our faith. To take them strictly, particularly in the doctrines that comment on them and systematize them, we would be as fully justified in denouncing in them what is often the perfect antithesis of Christian salvation. The "eternal life" proclaimed by Jesus Christ consists in the view of the "one true God". Completing and transforming our idea of God, it is not possible that Revelation would not at the same stroke complete and transform our idea of man—and our idea of his desire. In making us know the God of love, the personal and trinitarian God, the creative and saving God, it changes everything.[57]

Here a whole new cycle of problems is unveiled before our eyes which is impossible to approach within the limits of this article. But we wish to conclude at least by recalling once again this revelation of Love—not only of the love of God but of the God who is Love.

"God is simply the Lord, there is nothing, consequently, that stands before him or from which something like a 'Destiny' would result for him. He is also the Master of himself, there is thus no 'pressure of being' in him that he would be interiorly constrained to follow. God is absolutely free. . . . But he loves truly and actually."[58] He is Love.

So the relation between man and God could never be conceived, basically, as governed by any natural law or any necessity whatever, either internal or external. Everything, in the Gift that God wishes to make of himself and, consequently, in the desire that results from it in our nature, is explained by Love.

This is not a Good that, by its nature, is necessarily distributed: it is a personal Love, it is Love in person which, freely, arouses the being to whom he wishes to give himself. "Nothing limits the sovereign independence of the God who gives himself";[59] no exigency of any order compels him. But also, as Father Leopold Malevez wrote at the end

[57] When a Saint Augustine, for example (following Origen), says that the Platonists have well conceived the end of man, which is the vision of God, and that they have only misunderstood the means, to wit, the mediation of the incarnate Word, will we reproach him for attributing to natural intelligence the knowledge of a supernatural mystery? We will rather say that he himself would have agreed, if he had analyzed his own thought more reflexively, that this knowledge of the last end by the Platonists was only distantly analogous. Does he not define knowledge of the true God by the experience of *caritas*, and does he not say that the miracle of the beatific vision is *videntem videre*? "Nobis autem promittitur", he adds, "visio Dei viventis, et videntis."

[58] Romano Guardini, *Le Sérieux de l'amour divin*, in *Dieu vivant*, cahier 11, pp. 24 and 25.

[59] *Surnaturel*, conclusion, in fine, 494.

of an article whose favorable consideration we especially appreciated, "the stage of pure nature is unfailingly transcended by the fullness of creative Love."[60]

[60] "L'Esprit et le désir do voir Dieu", 31, in fine. If it is not possible for me to subscribe to all the interpretations proposed in this article, at least I am happy to be able to retain the final suggestion. Since these pages were written, I have read the important review that Dom M. Cappuyns made of my work *Surnaturel* in the *Bulletin de théologie ancienne et médiévale* (October 1947, n. 924, 251–54). I have noted with joy that Dom Cappuyns approves the whole essence of my historical positions, notably the interpretations that I proposed of the doctrine of Saint Thomas. I dare to hope that his authority in the matter, long since established, will dissipate, better than my own explanations, most of the objections that have been addressed to me. If some difficulties remain, they will, I believe, for the same reason, compel the attention of any mind concerned with traditional thought, and besides, such difficulties will never be lacking, if it is true that any solution gives birth to new problems. The truth of faith does not cease to maintain and orient the movement of the spirit.

6. The Doctrine of Father Lebreton on Revelation and Dogma according to His Anti-Modernist Writings

Preliminary Note

The controversies to which allusions are made several times in the course of these pages have given rise since that time to numerous works, clarified by the publication of various previously unpublished texts, notably of corre-

---

Unpublished text. Cf. H. de Lubac, *La Révélation divine*, 3d ed. (Paris: Cerf, 1983), 88. On Father Jules Lebreton (1873–1956), see the account by Joseph Lecler, S.J., in *Catholicisme.*

After Father Lebreton's death, his archives were confided to Father Robert Rouquette so that he might write a work about his life and works. The latter was not able to acquit himself of the task that had been confided to him and that would remain undone. Father de Lubac frequently visited Father Lebreton in the last years of his life, and the latter had made him a number of confidences. In his *Entretiens autour de Vatican II*, he briefly called to mind the absurd limits to which the mythical affair of a pseudo-"Fourvière school" had been able to go: "Is it necessary to recall again", he writes, "that, in the vast proceeding based on assumptions, not facts, that was instituted against it, Fourvière was becoming a gigantic monster? The Paris-based 'Études', where Father René d'Ouince reigned so mildly, was absorbed by it. It even extended to the whole Assistancy of France. Men who had left Fourvière long before or who had without a doubt never even set foot there and had maintained no sustained correspondence with it, such as the venerable Father Lebreton, dean of the Theology Faculty of Paris, were ranked under its banner. Father Lebreton's courageous anti-Modernist writings from around 1910, after having won for him the deeply moved thanks of Saint Pius X, were raked over the coals by new censors and came (an incredible thing) to enlarge the Fourvière file" (ibid., 97). The censors in question (Jesuits in this case) were the ones who [at that time] forbade the publication of the text that we are publishing here. Cf. the letter of H. de Lubac to Auguste Valensin of September 1, 1951: "I had sent to Rome (on the urgent invitation of the Father Assistant) a little article on Father Lebreton, almost wholly comprised of long quotations from the latter, accompanied by a letter congratulating me for my accuracy, and approved by the provincial censor. The article ended by recalling how Pius X had insisted on congratulating Father Lebreton for having saved the Church from the Modernist peril. The Jesuit censors in Rome now declare that the Doctrine of this article is false, Modernist, contrary to the Vatican Council, to the encyclical *Humani generis*, etc. They attribute to me errors that are so great, and so obviously absent from my text (or rather from the texts quoted from Father Lebreton) that it is rather amusing. . . . But this incident shows me that 'Rome' is not relenting in an a priori in my regard. It is because of this that I am relating this to you."

In the "Mélanges Jules Lebreton", Father de Lubac could give only a very short article spondence. Our sole aim here was to clarify the thought of Father Lebreton himself and, thereby, to do honor to his memory. Since the 1950s, during which this work was written, and even more especially since the beginning of this century, many historical and theological perspectives have been renewed. Research has progressed on the numerous points broached here. (On some points, too, oversight of earlier research has not always been without damaging effect.) So we must ask the reader not to lose sight of the dates indicated here. All serious theology includes a historical dimension. This dimension enters into other effects, permits it to be nourished on writings already old and even more or less "surpassed", which, for a mind immersed in the immediate, might not seem to respond to its problems. We believe that Father Lebreton's work, on the contrary, could still be profitable for many, if it were better known.

When Father Jules Lebreton (1873–1956) was called, when still at a young age, to the Theology Faculty of the *Institut catholique* of Paris, more than half a century ago, the Modernist crisis was reaching its keenest point. At the end of two years devoted to teaching dogma, the chair of Christian Origins was offered to him. Despite some opposition, which was not hidden from him, which he felt very keenly

---

entitled "A propos de la formule: *diversi, sed non adversi*" (cf. *Recherches de science religieuse*, 39–40 [1951–1952], 27–40).

On the courageous attitude of Father Lebreton during the Occupation, see also Gabriel Marcel-Gaston Fessard, *Correspondance 1934–1971* (Paris: Beauchesne, 1985), 299.

In his *Mémoire sur l'occasion de mes écrits* (Namur: Culture et Vérité, 1989), 74 [English trans., *At the Service of the Church* (San Francisco: Ignatius Press, 1993), 72f.], Father de Lubac gives the following additional information:

"The Father General reminded sternly that everything written by me, on any subject, had to be submitted beforehand to a censor in Rome. Now I had taken as a spiritual adviser, in Paris, Father Jules Lebreton, who had a short time before defended me energetically in the *Surnaturel* battle. As I knew his work well and as I was much interested in the work he had done before 1914, together with Father de Grandmaison, I composed in 1951 a brief study on his anti-Modernist writings, for which Pius X had been anxious to express his personal gratitude. That, it seemed, was solid ground. I submitted my work to Father Lebreton, he approved it by a letter dated May 7, 1951, and, after approval by the censors of my Province, I sent the manuscript to Rome: the writing was not only rejected but reproved as Modernist. Two other attempts, after modifications, explanations and competent recommendations, were to be likewise turned down. After Father Lebreton's death, which occurred unexpectedly in 1953, *Recherches* wanted to publish an homage to his memory: they ran into the same refusal. The faction that was at that time triumphant, overstepping all limits both in the ideas as well as in the arbitrariness of its power, was hostile to the spirit of Fathers de Grandmaison and Lebreton, whom I had always been taught in the Society to consider as the best of masters."

Then follows (74–75 [73]) the rediscovered rough draft of a projected letter to the Father General of the Society on this subject.

and which gave him a foreboding of a painful hostility at the very heart of the *Institut*, he accepted it. It was an intrepid decision, which threw him, who was so peaceable, into all-out combat. He knew it. He wanted it, for he had assessed the danger that, even from within, was threatening the whole Church at that time. Before the supreme authority had clearly denounced it in all its dimensions, without any impetus but that of his faith, he intended to face it. This chair was like an advance post, which permitted him to be thoroughly engaged.

He was sustained in his resolution as in his labor by an uninterrupted exchange with his colleague Father Léonce de Grandmaison (1868–1929), scarcely older than he, who was at the time professor of fundamental theology in the scholasticate at Ore Place (Hastings)[1] and who was soon (1908) to come rejoin him in Paris, at the head of the *Études* house. Both thus began a harsh battle, very little in accord with their inner tendencies; a battle whose hard vicissitudes they could not foresee, and on a field they were not free to choose or to delimit.[2] Both had, moreover, a concern to free themselves as quickly and as completely as possible from an often deceptive controversy and from an apologetic that had to be perpetually resumed, so as to forestall the evil by a positive work and by a better organization of work. For they felt only too keenly the doctrinal insufficiencies that never ceased to provoke deviations and stiffening in a fatal circle. It was this common concern that would give birth, in 1910, to the *Recherches de science religieuse*, of which they were the founders and then the successive editors for nearly forty years.[3] Both, however, knowing that the Church

[1] In 1907, for example, troubled by Tyrrell's article "Théologomène", which was in answer to an article by Father Lebreton published in the February issue of *Revue pratique d'apologétique*, Father Lebreton had recourse to his friend: "He reread Tyrrell's paper several times and annotated it page by page; I still have in front of me the long note he sent me; with much perspicacity he grasped the elusive thought of the author and, on the most serious points, stressed its failure. . . ." *Le Père Léonce de Grandmaison* (1932), 168.

[2] Father de Grandmaison had published as early as 1898, in *Études*, two articles that attracted immediate attention on "L'Élasticité des formules de foi, ses causes et ses limites [The elasticity of the formulas of faith, its causes and its limits]". He had just published, in the *Bulletin de littérature ecclésiastique* of Toulouse: "Qu'es-ce qu'un dogme?" He was preparing to give the *Revue pratique d'apologétique* a series of studies on "Le Développement du dogme chrétien". These different works were gathered together in a volume, after his death, under the care of Father Joseph Huby: *Le Dogme chrétien, sa nature, ses formules, son développement*, 2d ed. (1928).

[3] Father Pierre Rousselot (d. 1915) was editorial secretary. "The spirit that will animate us", said the preliminary article, "is a spirit of active submission to the teachings authorized

was not dealing with a mere "school heresy", with an easily remedied awkwardness of language or even of thought, but indeed with a "fundamental criticism of dogma",[4] pursued the battle step by step for as long as was necessary for the defense of the threatened faith. Those who reread today their writings from this early period, prior to the great works that established their mastery, admire the fact that they conducted it with so much courage and lucidity. With so much moderation, too, let us say immediately, and so much discernment—which earned them both much suspicion. With such nobility of views, such balance, such a sense of Christian tradition, so delicate a concern not to compromise what was essential by debatable side-issues, such detachment, finally, from what might have been their own ideas. And, without ceasing to pursue at the same time, and to encourage in those younger than they, a work of research no less indispensable. A rare spectacle, how invaluable an example! An episode too little remembered today but well worth being retained with honor in a history of the Church and of Christian thought.

I will not give an account, even in summary, of those distressing polemics, about which Father Lebreton often spoke with me, any more than I will go very deeply into the problems themselves that were debated in them. We would merely like to recall a few of the explanations that they led Father Lebreton to provide, touching on the ideas of revelation, dogma and theology. In fact, his articles of that time, scattered throughout various journals for a dozen years, have never been collected. Now they nevertheless constitute one of the essential works of Father Lebreton. Their historical importance was great. Moreover, although always occasional, at times nearly improvised and most often engaged in the everyday life of the controversy, they contain a number of pages whose importance goes beyond the occasion and the controversy, and, although not forming a complete body of doctrine and, to tell the truth, a little outdated, they offer many teachings that would always be useful to gather together.

---

by the Catholic Church and, at the same time, of precise fidelity to good scientific methods." *Recherches*, thanks be to God, has always maintained this spirit. Cf. Jean Levie, S.J., *La Bible, parole humaine et message de Dieu* (1958), 57: It "has always kept, in the course of its history, up to this day, the openness of spirit and loftiness of views of its two founders."

[4] *L'Encyclique et la théologie moderniste* (1908), foreword and p. 5. This is what was sometimes called, after the title of an article by R. J. Campbell, the "new theology". Cf. *Études*, 113:504–5. The very old expression frequently came up in the polemics of that period.

In the 1911 article in *Études* where he commented on the recent promotion of Cardinal Louis Billot, Father Lebreton noted with frankness that the theologians of our century do not always bring solutions that sufficiently illuminate "the problems posed on so many sides and with so much anxiety on dogma, revelation, faith and, in a word, on the origin and value of religious knowledge". He regretted to find their response generally so summary, so schematic, so poor in experience; he did not hide his suffering at seeing them apparently so little preoccupied "with unraveling the difficulties such as they appear to so many souls, who are caught up in them and bruised by them". Writing in the journal of the French Jesuits in order to salute the elevation to the cardinalate of a compatriot and colleague who had given eminent service and who was then, moreover, at the height of his doctrinal reputation in the Church and of his favor with the Holy See, he did not believe himself obliged, he, the young Parisian professor, to assume the tone of a panegyric. He wrote a "critical study". Of course he did his best to emphasize the qualities and merits of the Roman theologian; he was happy to do so and he did it generously. But he did not abdicate his freedom of judgment. Coming, for example, to compare Billot to Franzelin, he recognized in him "more penetration and depth" in the metaphysical interpretation of dogma, but he affirmed, on the other hand, that his predecessor, "having made a more personal and more complete study of tradition", had been able to give to his treatises "greater foundation and a fuller doctrine". Neither did he have any scruples about going on to express regret that so eminent a master, on the other hand, had been unable to discern the urgency of applying his reflection seriously to the "fundamental concepts of revelation and faith". Supported by an experience already serious and bitter, which he would have liked to share with all those in his profession, he added: "Does one not have the right and the duty to wonder, here too, if the problem is correctly posed, or if the school problems have not changed the terms of it? And even if one does not pose this question spontaneously to oneself, it is impossible to remain deaf to so many voices that suggest it, or rather, make it imperative."[5]

These last words, and even some of those we quoted earlier, refer us to a period of crisis from which our own, as one will readily agree, differs profoundly. So profoundly that, when it happens that a few

[5] "S. Em. le Cardinal Billot", *Études*, 129 (1911), 522.

survivors of these times past see and interpret things of our times by referring instinctively to the tempest that shook their early youth, they seem a little like ghosts from a strange world. In the misleading calm that marked the last years of the liberal period, before the era of catastrophes, of social agitation and spiritual upheavals opened by the war of 1914, minds flew into passion, both over the question of biblical exegesis and over problems of knowledge that seemed at times to call all beliefs into question, indeed, definitively to ruin all beliefs at their foundation. New solutions were sought, which were only mirages. Many were the victims of this collective dizziness. Today, the Church is always in the midst of combats. We are again in a time of crisis—but how dissimilar! The difficulties, the temptations, the anguish of new generations are not less than those of yesterday or before; neither are their illusions—but they are different. Catholic exegesis has accomplished immense progress; it pursues its path briskly, in a climate of confidence then unknown. Philosophical fashions have changed very much. The problems of pure thought no longer trouble many minds among the young clergy. Perhaps they do not occupy them enough. Nevertheless, on the level of technical research, it must indeed be admitted that the deficiency pointed out formerly by Father Lebreton remains in rather large part. In this regard, the situation that he described has not changed as much as it was hoped. But perhaps precisely, thanks to efforts such as his, we are now in circumstances that will permit us to attend to it in peace.

Father Lebreton, from the very beginning, ran into the Modernist idea of revelation: not, as the entire tradition of the Church proclaims it, the supernatural communication or manifestation of truth, but "the exaltation or excitation of the religious sense", "urged forward by the religious feeling that, at certain moments, coincides, so to speak, with the depths of the subconscious, and where the believer recognizes a divine touch". "Emotion", "impulse" experienced directly by each individual, for himself and for him alone; provoking through a spontaneous reaction "an imaginative or intellectual representation" of which it is indeed the origin but not the norm, and which depends entirely in its content on the personal formation and the social milieu of each. Such representation cannot therefore have any other value but that of a passing utility; under a coating of symbols that may remain the same, it will vary from one individual to another, from one milieu to another, and especially from one century to another, with an unlimited plasticity; it is always justified only by the services it renders to each for the present needs of his conscience, or to the overall Church for her maintenance in time.[6] Under these conditions, it is clear that there is no more place for an infallible dogmatic authority than for an absolute truth; it is clear, too, that if the Church can always be regarded as "a benevolent institution", "she is no longer the Body of Christ."

We recognize in this that mixture of immanentism and pragmatism that constituted, if not always the doctrine, at least the tendency or mentality of Modernism. Now this is not, repeats Father Lebreton, the traditional idea. Such is not the sole, authentic Christian notion. In all reality, our faith proclaims it: "God has spoken to men, and men have recognized his voice." The object of revelation is certainly not an abstract truth, but it has no less value as truth, properly speaking, and the dogma to which the believer submits himself is believed "on the testimony of God". It thus compels the recognition of the intelligence, which is the faculty of the true. Without doubt, the Catholic knows well "that the formulas themselves that the Church proposes to him are very inadequate with respect to their object"[7]—which means that they are imperfect but not that they are inaccurate—for he is himself on the way, not at the end. Along with the whole Church, he is on "pilgrimage". He lives under the rule of time, not of eternity; under the rule of obscure faith, not of vision.[8] To these formulas, to these statements, he nevertheless clings "with all his soul, knowing that they alone infallibly illuminate his path to God. To the degree he advances on that path, he feels that he draws near the light, and this credo, which is so simple and, for the unbeliever, so poor, appears to him richer in truth and life every day." "He does not stop at the symbolic images

[6] Father Lebreton quotes this sentence from the *Programma dei Modernisti*, 90: "The formulas of the past and those of the future have been and will also be legitimate provided that they faithfully respect the needs of the evangelical religion, eager to find in a reflective thought the instruments of its preservation." *L'Encyclique*, 41.

[7] Cf. Léonce de Grandmaison, 282: "Words are important here only to the degree in which their meaning, actually received, expresses sufficiently a truth that precedes them, surpasses them and will always transcend them."

[8] Cf. E. Portalié, S.J., *Bulletin* (1904), 121: "To adhere to the formula as such, it is said, would be to adhere to its unavoidable imperfections, to proclaim it adequate. —But in no way!" R. Garrigou-Lagrange, *Se Sens commun*, 3d ed. (1922), 358: The concepts that the Church uses to express her dogmas, "obviously inadequate, can always be made more precise, they will never be outdated".

that it encloses;[9] neither does he bind his faith to more or less passing human systems, which some of its declarations call to mind; he goes straight to the meaning that the Church has given once and for all to her formulas and which her authorized teaching makes known to him. He regards this adherence to dogmas . . . as necessary to salvation." Finally, and, by that very fact, contrary to the Modernist, the Catholic, "trusting the promises of Christ and submissive to his orders, knows that in listening to the teaching of the Pope, he is listening to the teaching of Christ, and that in scorning the teaching of the Pope, he would be scorning the teaching of Christ". In Christ and in his Vicar, he perceives "the same accent of sovereign authority and inner persuasion".[10]

In truth, noted Father Lebreton, these are not only two particular ideas in confrontation; they are indeed "two contradictory conceptions of Christianity: the Catholic conception and the Modernist conception". The whole faith is at stake.[11]

Truth of the object revealed by God and of the affirmation that concerns it, immutability of the meaning that the believer attaches to it under the infallible authority of the Church: no explanation of any order, historical, psychological, sociological or metaphysical, can shake the rock. No "equivocal" or "fleeting interpretation" is acceptable.[12] As Father de Grandmaison had written in 1898, the formulas of faith "have a certain, absolute, objective meaning, independent of ephemeral systems, a meaning that cannot be changed without reducing the entire Christian tradition to an empty catalogue".[13] Father Lebreton, in his turn, repeated it, with the same moderation, but also with the same precise insistence, which had become necessary. A "living" Credo, he says, is not a "flexible" Credo.[14] We have received our faith from God himself. It participates in the absolute of God and can be affected by neither our individual limitations nor our collective evolutions nor our caprices nor our subjective needs:

---

[9] Here Father Lebreton cites the article of the Creed concerning the "descent into hell", which habitually entered into the controversies: "The Catholic is not obliged to believe that hell is under the earth and that our Lord descended there."

[10] "La Controverse moderniste", *RPA*, 6:635 (July 15, 1908).

[11] *L'Encyclique*, 26–32 and 50–51. Cf. *Études*, 113 (1907), 507–16.

[12] *L'Encyclique*, 69. *Études*, 113:522.

[13] *L'Encyclique*, 17.

[14] Ibid., 44.

> We are told that the dogmatic formulas are benevolent and protective; but how? It is not, I think, as magical formulas, through the material pronunciation of syllables; it is thus through the meaning that they carry, through the judgment they transmit, and, if one claims that this intellectual judgment has no value as absolute truth, by what right does one impose the declaration of it?
>
> . . . If Christ is not God, according to the proper and natural meaning of this formula, neither does the Church have the right to impose it on me, nor do I have the right to repeat it; it would be a tyranny, on the one hand, and a lie on the other.[15]

Let us understand well, however, this idea of revelation. The Word that God addresses to men is not in itself a perceptible phenomenon —though, clearly, there are many elements of the sensible order in the whole complex of facts across which this Word is said to us. It must not be conceived *from any point* according to the analogy of a human word.[16] The correction that was indispensable does not intend at all to authorize such a simplism; to be effective, it is even necessary that it break away from it. It is to this that Father Lebreton next applies himself.

To found the faith of the apostles, he says, the effusion of the Spirit was necessary: "No external manifestation could suffice for it; it was necessary that, from within, God himself spoke and made his voice recognized."[17] "Consequently, we do not intend . . . to reduce revelation to a perceptible phenomenon; it is to the soul and in the soul that God speaks. This inner word is sometimes accompanied by external signs, but the very essence of revelation consists in psychological illumination and not in vision or corporal hearing."[18] "This doctrine",

---

[15] Ibid., 61–62. "L'Étude historique des origines chrétiennes", *RPA*, 5 (1907–1908), 311: "The dogmas of the faith are not probabilities that we risk affirming because we need them: they are truths about which we have not the least doubt."

[16] Cf. the title given recently by Father Joseph Levie to his work on Holy Scripture: *Le Bible parole humaine et message de Dieu*. Cf. C. H. Dodd, *The Bible To-day* (Cambridge: University Press, 1956), 104: " 'The Word of God.' The expression is obviously a metaphor; for a word, properly speaking, is the product of certain physiological processes which we cannot attribute to the Eternal."

[17] "La Révélation du Fils de Dieu", *Études*, 114 (1908), 794.

[18] Of course, on the other hand, no "psychological illumination" is revelation, and Father Lebreton is not unaware of this. It is, moreover, necessary to take the epithet "psychology" here only in opposition to that of "corporal". Another term would undoubtedly be chosen today. On divine illumination in the act of faith: Matthias J. Scheeben, *Nature et grâce*, French trans. by B. Fraigneau-Julien (1957), 239–43.

Lebreton adds, "is traditional in the Church; our adversaries often misunderstand it and fight against phantoms." And he refers to Saint Thomas, quoting and commenting on the words of Saint Augustine: "Cognitio prophetica maxime ad mentem pertinet."[19]

In fact, says Saint Thomas, in divine revelation, the sensible element, or element of "representation", is comparable to that which exists in all human teaching; what is specific in it, what constitutes its essential element, is the "inner illumination"—along with, of course, a content of truth—which belongs to the "judgment".[20] If this very wise and incontestable remark of the great doctor had retained more attention, Father Victor White, O.P., would not still have been obliged in 1949 to complain in his turn, and how justly, about the "legend" that attributes to Thomism and, because of the claims of some who represented it very poorly, practically to the teaching of the Catholic Church, a coarse and wholly material idea of revelation.[21]

The facts of the Gospel corroborate this remark. Or rather, before any critical reflection, they compel recognition of it, and even when he makes no explicit reference to them, one senses that Father Lebreton has offered them to the attention of the spirit. No more than the doctrine of scriptural inspiration can be constructed a priori, without considering biblical facts and texts, can the doctrine of revelation be established without reference to the history of this revelation, such as God has created it. Pure speculation on "essences" considering only the nature of human intelligence in the face of the omnipotence of

---

[19] Loc. cit., 507. *L'Encyclique*, 27–28. Saint Augustine, *De Genesi ad litteram*, l. XII, c. 9, n. 20: ". . . unde apparet magis ad mentem pertinere prophetiam quam ad istum spiritum, qui modo quodam proprio vocatur spiritus, vis animae quaedam mente inferior, ubi corporalium rerum similitudines exprimentur . . ." (PL 34, 461). Augustine is referring to Saint Paul, 1 Cor 14:15. On the *Locutio Dei* to the soul, cf. the analyses of Saint Gregory, *Moralia in Job*, l. XXVIII, c. 1 (PL 76, 447–52).

[20] *Secunda secundae*, c. 173, a. 2: ". . . Per bonum autem prophetiae confertur aliquid humanae menti, supra id quod pertinet ad naturalem facultatem . . . quantum ad judicium, per influxum luminis intellectualis, et quantum ad acceptionem seu repraesentationem rerum, quae fit per aliquas species; et quantum ad hoc secundum: potest assimilari doctrina humana revelationi propheticae, non autem quantum ad primum; homo etiam suo discipulo repraesentat aliquas res per signa locutionum, non autem potest interius illuminare, sicut facit Deus. . . ."

[21] Victor White, O.P., "Le Concept de la révélation chez saint Thomas", *L'Année théologique* (1950), fasc. 1–2; the article appeared first in *Dominican Studies*, 1 (1949). Cf. p. 2, with respect to explanations from a handbook on revelation: "There we have very poor nourishment for one who is thirsty to learn how, in his concrete reality, God speaks, teaches, illumines, reveals. . . ." Cf. Noël, O.P., in *Oeuvres complètes de Jean Tauler*, 4 (1911), 347, note.

God would not of necessity engender error, but it would in any case lead only to useless generalities. It is therefore necessary to observe how God wished to reveal himself, how, as the Letter to the Hebrews expresses it, "after having at other times, in many and various ways, spoken to our fathers through the prophets", he has finally "spoken [to us] through his Son".[22] We must see how the Son has spoken to us.

Now we must note that the revelatory mission of Jesus Christ to men did not consist uniquely (very far from it) in a certain number of oral teachings, in a series of declarations that would be repeated by his apostles. At the same time as they received the mission to "teach", the apostles were constituted—they themselves proclaim it, and with his own watchword—the "witnesses" of the Word made flesh.[23] Neither of these two aspects must be left in shadow, and they must not be dissociated. The teaching itself of the apostles does not reproduce merely the words of Jesus: for a very large part, it is also the fruit of their reflection, guided by the Spirit, on his being and on his role. That is true to the fullest extent and is seen with clarity in the case of Saint Paul: Jesus is, so to speak, the living Text for which his Apostle writes the commentary. As for the message of Jesus himself, it is not that of any messenger whatever, no more than he himself is any *legatus divinus* whatever. This message concerns essentially his person. But also, more precisely, as Father de Grandmaison writes in a phrase that Father Lebreton insisted on quoting: "The originality of the Gospel on this point consists justly in the close union—going, in large part, all the way to identification—of the person with the message."[24] The person of Jesus is not revealed uniquely by means of formulas that he himself taught to his apostles. Once again, very far from it! It is that, in his very being, he is Word: *Logos, Verbum*. "He is the substantial Revelation."[25] "He is the Revelation of God subsisting in a created being."[26] "He is the great Mystery of divine Piety mani-

[22] Heb 1:1. Cf. J. Lebreton, *Lumen Christi* (1947), 26, on Christianity: "It is a history at the same time as it is a doctrine."

[23] Acts 1:8. Cf. Lk 1:2. Father Georges H. Tavard will say more strictly: "The substance of Revelation has not consisted in the teaching of a doctrine: it was the coming of a Presence among men." *Écriture ou Église?* (1963), 16.

[24] *Jésus-Christ*, 2:6. Father Lebreton quotes this text in *Le Père Léonce de Grandmaison* (1932), 154, note.

[25] Romano Guardini, *Prières*, French trans., 37.

[26] I. H. Dalmais, O.P., *Le Mystère, Le Maison-Dieu*, 14, 76. Cf. 77.

fested in the flesh.[27] "Revelat [Filius Patrem], per hoc quo Ipse intellegitur."[28]

All these affirmations concur with that of Saint John, on which Father Lebreton comments. "No one", proclaims Saint John, "has seen God; the only Son, who is in the bosom of the Father, has made him known to us."[29] He has related it to us in his unique way, "as he alone", says Lebreton, "could do": "still more than by his teaching, Jesus manifests to men the divine life and its secrets by his appearance on earth." He does so above all "through the manifestation of his person".[30] For he is himself in person—this is the paradox and this is the basis of our faith—"the Truth and the Life".

This person is coming to insert himself, in the most real manner, into the fabric of our human history. He shows himself, he speaks, he acts, he radiates, he draws along[31]—and the Father who is in heaven, who is the Father of Jesus, enlightens those who do not avoid his half-open mystery. Jesus is born, he lives on earth, man in the midst of men, he teaches, he forms disciples, he rules nature, he remits sins, he dies in order to affirm and accomplish his mission, he is resurrected, he shows himself again in fleeting appearances, he finally returns to heaven; and the Holy Spirit, who is the Spirit of Jesus, sent by him, bears testimony to him so that he may be fully recognized by his own. Under the action of this twofold, combined light, that from without and that from within, they believe. They believe, and they are the first to formulate their faith. It springs from their hearts and from their lips; it is expressed, as it well must be, in human words—some pronounced first by Jesus himself, others found by them, whether by the fact of a wholly spontaneous impulse or by that of a mature reflection.

---

[27] 1 Tim 3:15–16.

[28] Origen, *Peri archôn*, l. 1, c. 2, n. 6 (Koetschau ed., 36).

[29] Jn 1:18.

[30] J. Lebreton, *Le Dieu vivant* (1919), 17–18. Cf. Joseph Holzner, *Paul de Tarse*, French trans. (1951), 86: "The Gospel taken as a whole did not only teach; it also, and much more, acted. Its words were followed by the death of the Cross, the Resurrection, the descent of the Spirit and the dogmatic interpretation of these facts by the apostles. It is in these realities that Christianity's center of gravity is found and not in the Sermon on the Mount or in the parables." Perhaps the choice of this expression "center of gravity", however, could be debated.

[31] Cf. Saint Jerome, *In Matt.*, l. 1, c. 9, on Mt 9:9–13: "Fulgor ipse et majestas divinitatis occultae, quae etiam in humana facie relucebat, ex primo ad se videntes trahere poterat aspectu."

In its substance,[32] this faith is real adherence to a Reality; it is the "wholly concrete and wholly living perception"[33] of a Fact—and it is at the same time the impulse of a personal commitment to a Person. It is not the simple knowledge or the simple affirmation of an impersonal truth. Fruit of a direct illumination—Jesus himself says: of a revelation of the Father. Recognition of the reality of the incarnate Word, comprising a certain relation of a personal kind with him. Faith, in the proper sense, in the Christian sense of the term, and not solely belief in a certain number of truths taught by him,[34] one or the other of which might eventually concern him.[35] *Credo in Jesum Christum*. Now this faith is no less "intellectual", it is no less charged with "truth" than the sole assent of the intelligence to a purely abstract teaching would be. Quite the contrary. This personal and concrete adherence is an integral part of this assent, of which it is, as it were, the source and of which it remains the soul. The one and the other, far from opposing or excluding each other, integrate the one Christian faith: for precisely, as we have said, the incarnate Word is in the midst of us, *the Truth in Person*.[36] This is what Saint Irenaeus was vigorously explaining as early as the second century, that witness of Christ whom Father Lebreton never ceased to consult with predilection in his subsequent works. According to Irenaeus, "the apostles and the Church give witness, by their teaching, to the Truth that is Christ, and it is this thesis that is the rule of faith and the Christian attitude. For Irenaeus, the truth is not a system, however well arranged and seductive it might be—to believe

[32] It is we who add, after Saint Thomas, the words: "in its substance", in order to indicate a nuance of thought that Father Lebreton, without having explained it in this passage, obviously did not fail to understand. For in the successive enunciation of each of the "articles", faith, insofar as distinguished from "substance", should be defined rather differently. Cf. below.

[33] *Encyclique*, 36. *Histoire du dogme de la Trinité*, 2 (1938), 5–6. A "concrete perception", Father H. M. Féret, O.P., will likewise write with respect to the faith of Saint Paul in the Resurrection of Jesus: *Le Mystère de la mort et sa célébration* (1951), 86. Cf. Holzner, *Paul de Tarse*, 63.

[34] It is clear that this does not mean that faith is not founded on the testimony of God; this was not the problem being considered by Father Lebreton. It merely wishes to specify, after that, that the faith of the first disciples was addressed indeed to him, to his person.

[35] One should refer here to the analyses of Saint Augustine on the *credere in Christum* and of Saint Thomas on the *credere in Deum*. Cf. *Méditation sur l'Église*, chap. 1, 3d ed. (1954), 21–28 [English trans.: *The Splendor of the Church* (San Francisco: Ignatius Press, 1986), 28–37]. Cf. likewise Saint Anselm and Saint Bernard.

[36] Jn 14:6.

this is the error of the Pseudo-Gnostics; it is in the theandric Person of Christ, whom the apostles saw, with whom they lived, whom they touched with their hands. . . ."[37] "Veritas ergo Dominus noster existens: Ego sum veritas et vita."[38]

A historian of Christian origins, Father Lebreton would often have occasion to return to this idea, let us say rather, to this important statement of fact. He was not tempted to give in to the tendency that was once more or less that of Judeo-Christians. In Jesus of Nazareth, he sees, of course, the "didascalia", or the "prophet"; but he sees at the same time much more. He likes to recall the very clear texts from the New Testament that are normative here. This is Jesus Christ saying to Philip, on the last night of his mortal life: "He who sees me, sees my Father."[39] This is Saint Peter, when a replacement is being elected for Judas, wanting this new Apostle to have been an eyewitness to the life and Resurrection of the Lord.[40] It is Saint Paul, evoking for the Corinthians the glory that shown on the Face of Christ,[41] or again, writing to Titus: "Apparuit benignitas et humanitas Salvatoris nostri Dei [When the goodness and loving kindness of God our Savior appeared . . .]."[42] It is the very solemn beginning of the First Letter of Saint John: "What was from the beginning, what we have heard, what we have seen with our eyes, what we have contemplated and what our hands have touched concerning the Word of Life—and the Life was made manifest, and we give witness to it, and we proclaim to you this eternal Life, which was with the Father and was made manifest to us —what we have seen and heard, we proclaim to you as well."[43] It is above all, it is quite in the first place, the confession of Simon Peter

[37] H. Holstein, S.J., "La Tradition des Apôtres chez saint Irénée", *RSR*, 36 (1949), 249.

[38] Saint Irenaeus, *Adversus Haereses*, l. 3, c. 5, n. 1, ed. P. Sagnard. *Sources chrétiennes*, 34 (1952), 120. Cf. William of Saint Thierry, *Speculum fidei*, following Saint Augustine: "Omnia enim facta Verbi verba nobis sunt, in quibus nobis loquitur, semetipsum indicans nobis in factis suis bene intellectis" (PL 180, 386 D).

[39] Jn 14:9.

[40] Acts 1:21–22. J. Lebreton, "L'Étude des origines chrétiennes", *RPA*, 5:298–99.

[41] 2 Cor 4:4–6. Cf. J. Lebreton, "La Révélation du mystère de la Sainte Trinité", *La Vie spirituelle* (June 1946), 769. Many were conquered by "the divine light that enlightened the humanity of Christ"; p. 765: undoubtedly the apostles did not "thoroughly enter into the blessed vision that, already here below, the Son had of his Father, [but] they were at least enlightened by reflections of this vision of the Lord at the same time as they were instructed by his teaching."

[42] Titus 3:4. J. Lebreton, *Le Pére de Grandmaison*, 154.

[43] Jn 1:1–3, *L'Étude des origines*, 299.

on the road to Caesarea. To the question of the Master: "Vos autem, quem me esse dicitis? [And you, who do you say that I am?]", Peter replies: "Tu es Christus, Filius Dei vivi [You are Christ, the Son of the living God]." And Christ resumes: "Beatus es, Simon Bar Jona, quia caro et sanguis non revelavit tibi, sed Pater meus, qui in caelis est [Blessed are you, Simon Bar Jona, for flesh and blood have not revealed this to you, but my Father, who is in heaven]."[44] After having thus recalled this initial dialogue, which is at the determining origin of all our professions of faith, in using the same terms of the Gospel, Father Lebreton makes an observation that others, long ago, had already made.[45] Jesus, he says, "does not at all dictate to his apostles their profession of faith, he leads them to it; he brings about the awakening of the soul."[46] He questions, and Peter replies.[47] The first "formula of faith" comes from the first believer.[48]

This account makes us grasp well how the faith of the apostles, which is to say, the "faith of the Church", is neither a "blind impulse", as resulted from extreme Modernism, nor the communication of a kind of "infused theology", as some accused orthodoxy of believing. Once again, Father Lebreton notes, repeating a word used by Saint Thomas:

---

[44] Mt 16:13–17. "Catholicisme", *RPA*, 4 (1907), 541. *L'Étude des origines*, 300, cf. *Histoire du dogme de la Trinité*, 1, 6th ed. (1927), 295.

[45] Cf. Paschasius Radbertus, *In Matt.*, l. XI, c. 24: "Et nusquam invenies Dominum in Scripturis hoc ipso sermone usum, ut diceret: 'ego sum Christus'. Sufficiebat enim suis ostendere doctrinis et miraculis quo Ipse esset, quia opus Patris in eo erat, et sermo doctrinae quem docebat, et virtus clamans: 'ego sum Christus', ultra quam si mille voces eum clamarent. Et ideo, nescio si invenires dixisse; sed per opera Patris se exhibuit, et per doctrinam pietatis; quam pseudochristi non habentes, repromittebant se vocibus esse, quod non erant" (PL 120, 800 BC).

[46] "La Révélation du Fils de Dieu", *Études*, 114 (1908), 736: "Christ is content to question, to bring about the awakening of the soul, the decisive action comes from the Father who speaks to the heart."

[47] The role of Christ, Claudel will say very well (*L'Épée et le miroir*, 35–36), "is not to furnish a ready-made truth, it is to elicit it, to call it forth from this depth of the human creature that is prior to the morning".

[48] As Father V. White ("Concept de la révélation", 5) will write in a manner that is perhaps slightly paradoxical but suited to illuminating this important point, while commenting on Saint Thomas: "For Saint Thomas, revelation is truly the word of God, while the *articulus fidei* is essentially the word of man: the word of man responding, however, *in faith* to the word of God; this is precisely its name: an article *of faith*, not immediately and directly an article *of revelation*. It is absolutely infallible because it is pronounced *quasi ex persona totius Ecclesiae*; but in itself, it is neither inspired nor revealed." It is not Jesus, for example, who gives himself the name of Logos. But Saint Thomas' remark is true a fortiori and is fully applicable when it is a question of words and "articles" that are not explicitly scriptural.

it is truly a "perception"[49] born of a revelation of the Father.[50] "Jesus, through his response, establishes the divine origin of it."[51] In order to be made more explicit in the mind of the one who is its beneficiary, it undoubtedly clothes itself in concepts, "expressions and images that are familiar to that mind; but, more powerful than they, it reacts on them and transforms them."[52] Thus a "religious knowledge that proceeds directly from revelation" is constituted, "a natural and spontaneous expression of a belief, of an adherence of the mind to a revealed reality".[53] An initial and indissoluble synthesis, the work of both God and man—but the work of man in total dependence on the work of God—in the image of its Object, in which God and man are indissolubly united. A judgment of faith, a humanly formulated divine truth. Father Leopold Malevez would say later in a similar manner, in speaking of the whole of revelation deposited by God in the memory of the Church: "If it is not Christ, it is at least the refraction of him, divinely guaranteed, in our mind, the intelligible image sketched by the Holy Spirit in the heart of Christians; this is enough to warrant its sharing with Christ the designation of revelation and even of word."[54]

A brief explanation must still be brought forward here, so that we do not misunderstand the thought of Father Lebreton by mistaking first of all the precise problem he was treating, a problem imposed on him by the state of the controversy. Do not a number of misunderstandings between author and reader stem from the fact that the reader is seeking in what he reads the response to a problem that is no longer exactly the one to which the author was seeking to respond in what he wrote? Father Lebreton was not considering the problem of faith in itself, nor in all its extent. Neither was he studying the case which, while the most current, is nonetheless the most derivative: the case

[49] *Secunda secundae*, q. 171, a. 1, ad 4m: "In prophetia requiritur quod intentio mentis elevetur ad percipienda divina. . . . Sic igitur ad prophetiam requiritur inspiratio quantum ad mentis elevationem; . . . revelatio autem quantum ad ipsam perceptionem divinorum; in quo perficitur prophetia. . . ."

[50] "Catholicisme", 41. Cf. *L'Encyclique*, 36.

[51] *Le Dieu vivant*, 101. Cf. Saint Hilary, *In Matt.*, c. XVI: "Quia Dei Filium in homine vidisset. Beatus hic est, qui ultra hominum oculos intendisse et vidisse laudatus est. . . . Dei Filium caelestis Patris revelatione conspiciens. . . ."

[52] "Catholicisme", 45.

[53] *L'Encyclique*, 36.

[54] "Révélation et témoignage", *Mélanges de science religieuse* (1949).

of the individual who hears the preaching of the Church. Taking the problem to its roots, and examining it as a function of the problem of revelation, he studied solely, as he had to do, the most privileged case of all, that of the first response made to the revelation of the God-made-man. He had, therefore, to define the faith of the apostles, through the testimony of which, up to the end of time, all Christian generations will believe in Jesus Christ. Now obviously Peter did not believe on the basis of Peter's testimony. He did not come to ask the Church for faith, as the neophyte presenting himself for baptism does today. He did not consult her Magisterium. . . . He was himself, and he always remains in his successors, as Saint Hilary says, with respect precisely to his confession of faith on the road to Caesarea, "felix Ecclesiae fundamentum".[55] Our own faith, the faith of every believer who learns from the ecclesiastical Magisterium the truths in which he must believe, arises in the first place under completely different circumstances. The order of factors is, so to speak, reversed there.

It is in receiving the truths taught by the Church, those truths that are presented to him, under a necessarily abstract and impersonal form, even somewhat like a catalogue and in their state of final clarification, that the understanding of the convert or that of the catechized child adheres to the divine Truth. It receives communication with the unique Mystery of Christ by subscribing to a certain number of "dogmas" that are, as it were, various members of this one Body (the twelve "articles" of the *Credo*). That is an obvious fact. We should only be careful not to forget that our submission to the Magisterium, if it is truly what it should be, does not remain wholly extrinsic. It works in us a real participation in the faith of the Church herself, in continuity with that of the apostles. There is thus, of course, an undeniable diversity in the empirical circumstances, in the external process: Saint Irenaeus had a very vivid awareness of this, he saw so well how unique the case offered by the apostles was that he did not want to speak of their "faith", since he could not resign himself to use the same word both for them and for us.[56] This diversity is enough to make the analysis effectuated

[55] Saint Hilary, *In Matt.*, c. XVI.

[56] The apostles give birth to faith in those they evangelize in the name of Christ; they distribute to believers the Spirit they have received from the Lord. *Démonstration*, c. 41. Cf. D. E. Lanne, "Le Ministère apostolique dans l'oeuvre de saint Irénée", *Irenikon* (1952), 121. I have explained the above myself in *Méditation sur l'Église*, chap. 1 [English trans.: *The Splendor of the Church* (San Francisco: Ignatius Press, 1986), chap. 1].

by Father Lebreton inapplicable as such to us. Yet, it does not prevent a profound identity. To speak like the ancients, the believing soul is always, in the very measure of its faith, "*anima ecclesiastica*".[57] There is only one, single faith.[58]

After the Resurrection, after Pentecost, the faith of the apostles attained its full force and possessed its whole content. Already a number of "dogmas", although not yet put into words by the first Christian generations, were found "latent in the wealth of this first perception".[59] Here, we feel, Father Lebreton has weighed his words; he does not say that these dogmas were contained "implicitly" in some "major premises": not, undoubtedly, that such an assertion would have seemed inaccurate to him; but he would have judged it much too partial, not rendering full account either of the first state of the faith or of the processes of its subsequent development. Little by little, he continues, from this inclusive wealth, a number of particular "dogmas" would, so to speak, be extracted, placed in as many distinct declarations of it. "The Church, enlightened by the Holy Spirit", would gradually become "more clearly aware of the truths" that, from the beginning, "she had carried within her".[60] But she would not, for all that, add anything to it.

In fact, as we have seen, from the very first, faith had been translated into certain "declarations"—some of which had been gathered from the very mouth of Jesus and others called forth by him. The twofold reflection of Saint Paul and Saint John had soon contributed to enrich and refine them. Subsequently, although it was no longer a matter henceforth of revelation, the declarations continued to multiply, following the very laws of human intelligence and under the impulse

[57] Cf. *Méditation sur l'Église*, 3d ed., 33–35 [English trans.: 42–44].

[58] Diversity and unity are well marked, for example, in Pierre de Celle, *Mosaici tabernaculi mystica et moralis expositio*, l. 1: "Disquire profunda fidei nostrae mysteria. . . . Dico autem, de fide Ecclesiae, non de fide unius fidelis personae, —quanquam et totum credat quicumque est in Ecclesia, quod credit tota ipsa Ecclesia" (PL 202, 1052 AB).

[59] *Encyclique*, 36.

[60] Ibid., 36–37. Cf. L. de Grandmaison, 259–64. Yves Congar, O.P., "Le Purgatoire", in *Le Mystère de la mort* (1951), 280, 287, 326. Pie Regamey, O.P., *Les Plus beaux textes sur la Vierge Marie* (1942), 41: "The life of the Church through the course of the centuries, animated by the Holy Spirit, becoming aware—I repeat these words, which are the proper words—of her faith." Already Father J. V. Bainvel ("L'Histoire d'un dogme", *Études*, 101 [1904], 631): The Church "possesses [the revealed truth] by a kind of direct intuition, like we possess our ideas."

of all kinds of historical necessities.[61] A divinely instituted authority rules their meaning and use. All believers to come will be instructed by them; all should submit their understanding to some of them—those whom the authority of the Church, herself obeying what she has received, will have definitively sanctioned in an unconditional way. The historical root of the Christian faith is not, however, in this multiplicity: this multiplicity is for us today, and it will be subsequently for each of the generations that follow us, the pedagogical beginning, the social guarantee as well as the permanent condition of it.[62] Nor do we have there the whole exercise of that faith: even a sincere and firm adherence to all the formulas of faith still mark only a first degree in the life that must be that of the believer; it is not yet that *sanctae fidei plenitudo* toward which it must tend and whose perfection belongs only to the Church herself. Finally, neither do we have there the heart of the faith: the *articuli fidei*, considered in their multiplicity, which makes them in a way external to each other, are not, *as such*, that "substance of the faith": they become effectively so in the principle that binds them. Saint John of the Cross, whom Father Lebreton studied a great deal, compared this "substance" to the "crystal fountain" whose "silver waves" are the articles.[63] The declarations, by their very nature, are an objectivization of the impersonal mode of faith that, in its deep intentionality, is personal adherence to Christ and, through Christ, to God.

It follows from all this that dogmatic progress, whose rectitude is guaranteed by the assistance of the Spirit which Christ promised to his Church, is of a different order from the progress that one notes in the history of the ancient people of God. It is not a progressive revelation. These two ideas of assistance (including infallibility) and revelation must be carefully and profoundly distinguished.[64] With Christ, in fact,

[61] Saint Thomas, *Secunda secundae*, q. 1, a. 7: "Quantum ad explicationem crevit numerus articulorum." That is, moreover, an obvious fact.

[62] *Dogme et critique*, cf. note 77.

[63] *Spiritual Canticle*, strophe 12.

[64] The traditional doctrine on this subject has been clearly set forth by Fénelon in his *Instruction pastorale* of March 3, 1705: "There is an essential difference, which any true theologian sees at a glance, between the immediate revelation of God himself and the infallible declaration of . . . the Church. There is an essential difference between the inspiration of the sacred writers to whom the immediate revelation was made and the simple special assistance that was promised to the Church in order to preserve her from error, when she judges texts to be orthodox or heretical. The Church is specially assisted by the Holy Spirit,

in Christ, all has been given to us. In him we have all revelation as well as all redemption. This is why a traditional axiom, expressing a truth of the Catholic faith,[65] tells us that "revelation was closed at the death of the apostles", which is to say, of those who were constituted witnesses of the Epiphany of God in Christ. Or again, following an expression of Saint Irenaeus, dear to Father Lebreton: "Christus . . . omnem novitatem attulit, semetipsum afferens."[66] Henceforth, nothing more that is in fact new is to be expected. The deposit is living, certainly it is fruitful, but it is indeed a deposit. The Church has the guardianship of it, and it is on it that she fixes her eyes in order to judge at all, in whatever century of her history she may be. No theory of "development" should ever forget this essential principle. This is what Father Lebreton recalled in opposition to a very unilateral and distorting interpretation of Newman's celebrated theory. In the face of a recent mentality that tends to confuse dogmatic progress with a kind of natural progress in human things, it is no less important to recall it today.

Besides, to consider, for an instant, only the human intellectual mechanism by which the later work of dogmatic clarification is carried out —whatever might be the occasion and the stimuli, which are by nature very varied—one should recognize that it does not differ essentially from that which gave birth to the first declarations on the lips of Peter and his companions. The structure and the natural laws of the human mind are always the same; supernatural revelation has not suppressed them. A simple "assistance", carried out by the Magisterium, in order to avoid any error in definitive choices, has succeeded to the positive inspiration of the early times, whose fruits are preserved in the writings of the "New Testament". But it is indeed always a matter of "elaboration". The Church, says Father Lebreton, "works out [*élabore*] her formulas of faith".[67] Now this work necessitates the active interven-

---

and, through that assistance, she is infallible in order to guard the deposit; but she is not at all inspired, like the sacred writers; she does not at all receive, as they did, an immediate revelation. To confuse such different things is to confuse the primary elements of theology. . . ."

[65] See, for example, J. V. Bainvel, *De magisterio vivo et traditione* (1905), 125–27.

[66] *Adversus Haereses*, l. 4, c. 34, n. 1 (PG 7, 1083). Cf. Saint John of the Cross, *Ascent of Mount Carmel*, book 2, chaps. 20–22.

[67] *Le Dieu vivant*, p. 13: "From the beginning, it is around this central dogma [of the Trinity] that she [the Church] elaborated her formulas of faith."

tion of the human intelligence; it presupposes the use and often the recasting of human concepts.

Thus gradually a whole is formed that is always being increased with clear, irreversible formulas, of precise meaning, proposed for the adherence of all. In their particular tenor, they represent, as is patently obvious, a second state of the faith. For many formulas, for the most part, this is true even chronologically, since they were found only well after the time of the apostles, to the degree necessary for maintaining the rectitude of the faith, and were often received only subsequent to many vicissitudes. For all, this is true in a radical sense, since none of them has, as they say, "fallen from heaven" ready-made.[68] No one, however, has the right to consider them optional or secondary.[69] No one has the right—or, to tell the truth, the power—to situate himself in his thinking in a century prior to the one in which the voice of the teaching Church resounds for him. No one has the right, either, at any time whatsoever, to declare closed the list of dogmatic declarations. This would be to deny the fecundity of dogma and to limit in advance the exercise of the ecclesiastical Magisterium. On the other hand, if, as time progresses, believers can enumerate a greater number of declarations, that assuredly represents a gain for them; much more, even assuming that it is not indispensable for them in order to prevent or reject certain definite errors, such an increase is still a necessity for them. Our understanding can preserve what it possesses only by making it fructify. To preserve the initial treasure such as it is, it is necessary to preserve it in its assimilating power.

The wholly static permanence of this treasure in its first state is impossible: it would in reality be only a deterioration, a loss. Thoughts

[68] V. White, "Concept de la révélation", p. 5: "A tendency seems to exist in a certain recent Catholic theology—implicit and only half-conscious—to want the *articulus fidei*, defined dogma, nearly to supplant the primary revelation from which it derives and on which it is based, to treat dogma as if it were, in fact, itself revelation or at the very least revealed. I do not want to imply that theologians of the stature of Father X or Father Y are ever guilty of such a solecism, but it seems to me that the preoccupation with the validity of dogma leads to a certain lack of consideration for the process of revelation and the events on which it itself depends and is liable to stop research and theological curiosity about the true bases of dogma, about the nature of the vision and apostolic witness on which faith and dogma also depend. Only there can we find an explanation for that curious legend . . . , to wit, that the Thomist clings to the idea that revelation is comprised uniquely of affirmations of truth, fallen, so to speak, from heaven. . . ."

[69] Cf. the fine text of Saint Hilary, *Collectanaea anti-ariana*, Feder ed., 102.

are not stones, even precious stones.[70] Yet the greater number of dogmas or *particular truths* that believers hold and enunciate today does not mean that they possess, properly speaking, more divine *truth* than did the believers who lived before them. The progress from which they benefit is never only a progress *secundum quid*. Their understanding is not in a more perfect relation with the Truth who is Christ; it has not received any supplement to the Word of the one Logos. Like Father de Grandmaison,[71] Father Lebreton was fond of repeating this. It was in no way, to their eyes, the expression of a more or less optional theological thesis. With good reason, both judged such an affirmation paramount. It is impossible, in fact, to oppose it without placing oneself, however subtle one proves to be, outside the great traditional current[72] and without entering on the path that leads to a confusion of dogmatic progress with a kind of continued revelation: a danger that is not more imaginary today than it was during the period of Father Lebreton. The faith of the early Christians, the faith of the apostles of Jesus was surely less "differentiated" than ours; but who does not see that it would be at the least rather improper to say that it was more "rudimentary" or more unformed? Who would seriously wish to call "the fullness of the apostolic times" into doubt?[73] The Christian Mystery is always total,

---

[70] Cf. H. Urs von Balthasar, "Tâche de la théologie", in *Théologie de l'histoire*, French trans. by R. Givord (1955), 162, with respect to theology: "Whoever would wish . . . to transmit the treasures of theology almost like workers throwing quarry stones from hand to hand in the hope that they would thus be damaged as little as possible, altered as little as possible, would be the victim of a profound illusion. Quite simply because thoughts are not rocks; even more, because, since Easter morning, a fight has flared up between the rock and the spirit."

[71] *Le Dogme chrétien*, 261: after a new dogmatic definition, "There is not more truth to be believed, although there are more dogmas to be believed." This text will be quoted and approved by Father Clément Dillenschneider (*Le Sens de le foi* [1954], 370). Cf. John Walsh, S.J., *De Grandmaison and Gardeil: Their Ideas on Dogmatic Development* (Rome, 1950).

[72] Already, on the apostles, Saint Irenaeus, to whom Father Lebreton particularly liked to refer. H. Holstein, "La Tradition des Apôtres chez saint Irénée", *RSR*, 36 (1949), 232: "Their knowledge is so perfect that no one could surpass it, and to want to attain it is one of those ridiculous pretensions discrediting, straight out, those who raise it."

[73] We are borrowing this fine expression from Father Pinard, himself the echo of the whole Catholic tradition, article "Dogme", *Dict. apologétique de la foi catholique*, by A. d'Alès, vol. 1, col. 1157. Cf. L. de Grandmaison, *Le Dogme chrétien*, 264: "To be more amply formulated, more clearly defined in detail, our knowledge of dogma will neither transcend nor ever equal the direct, living, infused knowledge that the first disciples had, the 'ministers of the word'." J. V. Bainvel, *De magisterio vivo*, 138–39. Cf. H. Holstein, *La Tradition dans l'Église* (1960), 225, note: "A more distinct knowledge of the 'articles of the faith' is not a more profound 'understanding' of the revealed given."

and from the beginning it was revealed and believed wholly. The multiplication of declarations that arise in the course of time is in more than one regard a necessity; but it adds nothing, let us repeat, to the deposit of faith. It assures the integrity and efficacy of it; it averts incorrect interpretations; it makes the fruitfulness of it manifest. But the Object of faith is indivisible, and where the faith is authentic, it can be neither augmented nor diminished. As one commentator of Newman, having become the student and then the colleague of Father Lebreton, would write in a page alluding to some Newman texts whose close inspiration one senses in Father Lebreton: "It is the living reality and a reality of the mystery of God revealed in Jesus Christ", a reality that the formulas of faith "encircle on all sides, without ever being able to exhaust it or even less to divide it".[74] Christ is the Mystery in person, and "one does not go beyond the Mystery of Christ."[75] His affirmation is always "unique". "Jesus is the divine Word, the first and the last":[76] "Unus est Christus, et una tantum summa."[77]

Besides—this is again a remark of Father Lebreton, destined to ward off a certain Modernist objection—all these formulas of our faith, those bequeathed to us by the apostolic age as well as those that were worked out only later, can seem "poor". They are so, in one sense: it is necessary to recognize this, if one thinks of the nature of the realities they

[74] Louis Bouyer, *Newman, sa vie, sa spiritualité* (1952), 239. Cf. 288ff. See John Henry Newman's profound page, n. 23, pp. 243–44; again, n. 28, pp. 347–48. And Msgr. Charles Journet, *Esquisse du développement du dogme marial* (1954), 26, 28, 72, 75.

[75] A. Liège, O.P., "La Foi" in *Initiation théologique*, 3 (1952), 491; and 494: "Across the multiplicity of declarations that the Magisterium of the Church has had to set up, in order to affirm the whole world of the faith, the believer will be able to link up with the living and personal unity of the ever-unique affirmation of the Mystery; the end of the act of faith is not declarations but the Reality of Jesus Christ. It is to be feared that the incontestable pedagogical advantage of the symbolical or catechetical type of expositions of the faith may at times end in a loss of that living and personal unity of the object of faith. This would be remedied, in part, if one took care to give God or Christ as the subject for all the analytical propositions of doctrine. Like the Apostles' Creed, which declares the *actions* of God for the salvation of the world and not concepts objectifying these actions (for example: Jesus Christ became man, and not: the Incarnation). The Christian faith is thus an affirmation of reality. . . . So this act must adopt the structures of the objective affirmation of the human spirit. . . ." See also Dom Odo Casel, *Le Mystère du culte dans le christianisme*, trans. J. Hild, "Lex orandi" series (1946), 17 and 138.

[76] L. de Grandmaison, *Jésus-Christ*, 1:166.

[77] Saint Bonaventure, *Breviloquium*, l. 5, c. 7, Quaracchi, 5:261. Cf. Journet, *Esquisse*, 59. Hugh of Saint Victor: "Materia divinae Scripturae est verbum incarnatum cum omnibus sacramentis suis" (PL 175, 24).

translate. They must indeed be "poor" in order to reach our poverty. God always takes us where we are—in order to lead us to him. "Nevertheless, this poverty of the official formula should not at all make us fail to recognize its social role and its necessity; it is a link that connects us to the past and allows us to attain, through and under the dead letter, the life of the Spirit in the Church. . . ."[78] And undoubtedly, if one places oneself for a moment, with Father Lebreton himself, in a subjective—which does not mean subjectivist—point of view, which is to say, if one studies the life of faith in the believing soul, it would be true to say that "the more the faith penetrates the soul, the more inexpressible it becomes"; but that in no way prevents the formula that the Catholic *Credo* imposes from remaining always, in all truth, "its norm and its rule".[79]

It is still necessary to know how to interpret this formula, so as to recognize without error, without overestimation as well as without minimism, "the meaning that the Church attaches to the dogma". Minimism would be fatal, destroying the dogma's value as truth; but an undue overestimation of the formula, of its meaning and its role, by preventing the perception of its place in relation to the whole, would be as well a perversion of the dogmatic truth itself. A withdrawal into the formula would be the death of the impulse of faith.[80] Pushed to its limit, we would have nothing but an ideology, said to be revealed.

All sorts of delicate problems are posed on this subject—doubly delicate since they touch on both the life of the spirit and the mystery of faith. Many are problems of a technical nature, whose very terms, it must be noted, elude certain minds. A slightly implicit intransigence or

[78] "Dogme et critique", *RPA*, 4:204.

[79] Ibid.

[80] Cf. Karl Rahner, *Écrits théologiques*, 1:115–16, *Problèmes actuels de christologie*, trans. Michel Rondet: "The whole revealed truth of God is truly an opening on the infinite and the beginning of the unlimited, because it is given us as the route that leads us and the force that impels us toward an immediate community with God. The clearest and most explicit terminology, the holiest formula, the most classical expression of the secular reflection of the praying, thinking and fighting Church on the mysteries of God live precisely from the fact that they are the beginning and not the end, a means and not the goal. They are *a* truth that frees one for *the* ever-higher truth. . . . Whoever takes seriously the 'historicity' of human truth (in which the truth of God is incarnated in his revelation) knows well that it permits one to justify neither the negation of a formula in its excess nor the petrified preservation of human knowledge. . . ."

a suspicious turn of mind incline one to become impatient with them. Yet their examination, technically indispensable, could harm neither the rectitude nor the simplicity of the faith, neither its balance nor its depth, in the one who wishes to be faithful, on all levels, to the delicate demands of the true. Such was Father Lebreton, and this is why he did not turn away from these problems, although he could not broach them all nor treat them always in depth. Besides, sensitive to the dangers that their examination aroused around him, he could not resign himself to the disastrous attitude of those who refused even to see them posed.

There are, first of all, the problems of history, for there is often need to appeal to the "historical givens in order to decide the value of the terms".[81] We know what Father Lebreton's work was to be in this historical domain. His *Histoire du dogme de la Trinité*, although he was not able to pursue it beyond the end of the second century, remains one of the great theological works of our time.[82] The idea seems quite natural to us: he, along with several others, however, had to fight to gain acceptance for it. He succeeded, thanks to a doctrinal balance that always kept him not only from excesses and mistaken ideas but from an historicist narrowness.[83] At first very hesitant, Cardinal Billot was won over by it. It was, however, a problem of a different kind, calling the very idea of dogma into question, that was at the base of the controversies in which Father Lebreton found himself involved. At issue was a criticism of dogma by certain parties that went to the point of declaring it unacceptable in its traditional meaning. This dogma was represented as claiming to be "a revealed theology", as it were, a "rudimentary theology, developed by an infallible ecclesiastical dialectic",

[81] *Dogme et critique*, 203–4.

[82] Cardinal Louis Billot wrote one day, a little belatedly, to Father Lebreton: "You have made me understand one thing that had never entered my mind, to wit, what one can draw from *historical theology*, from the point of view that alone must interest us, after all, that of the ever more profound penetration of the truths that it pleased God our Lord to reveal to us. . . . I was imbued with the prejudice that that was only an instrument of demolition rather than edification. I have now shaken off that prejudice, and it is to you that I owe this." An invaluable admission, and one that lets us glimpse the difficulties which Father Lebreton, and several others with him, encountered *from both sides*.

[83] Cf. J. Lebreton, "Mgr. Batiffol serviteur et historien de l'Église", the *Correspondant* (February 10, 1929), 386–87: "In theology, history does not suffice in everything, philology even less; it is dangerous to cling to the program that we recalled above: nothing but facts, nothing but texts." In the discussions of 1903–1905, on the tradition and historical value of dogmas, Father Lebreton was in sympathy with Maurice Blondel, contrary to Pierre Batiffol.

which ended in canonizing all kinds of systematic speculations that were in fact purely human.

Father Lebreton declares that he "completely declines responsibility" for such a caricature, certain repudiations of which were justified but which itself could also to a certain point be justified (this, to be fair, must be recognized) by certain expositions that were at the least awkward or by certain exaggerations owing to polemics—indeed, at times, to a sectarian intemperance. Not that he is lacking in regard for the fruits of theological activity. This believer, this historian, is a theologian at heart. But he reacts against the confusion. He does so with courage, knowing that not everyone in the Church would be equally grateful to him for it. He does so with special clarity when he judges the stakes to be more serious. He understands well, he says, that no one "confiscates dogmatic truth for the benefit of his school". Grave words, carefully weighed. To his eyes, two fundamental affirmations are to be placed here at the same time; these two affirmations are complementary; they are interdependent, and if the first is "a point of faith", the second is in his eyes equally certain. On the one hand, in its very precision, "the meaning given by the Church to her dogmas is definitive and irrevocable"; on the other hand, and for that very reason, "dogma is not at all formulated in technical language by scholars, for their exclusive use, it is written in the common language by Christians for all mankind", and one must always, in the final analysis, take the formulation of it "in its common and obvious sense".[84]

Here, we admit, one is tempted to be surprised. In fact, for some formulations at the very least, an initial inquiry gives a contrary impression. In relation to them, such expressions as "common language" or "common sense" give a paradoxical impression. Father Lebreton is not unaware of it. He knows enough history, particularly that of doctrinal controversies and councils, not to give a naïve meaning to his affirmations. Perhaps he could have chosen a better word. In any case, let us not stumble over one word. Our author has been specific enough about his thought. Let us therefore try to understand it by continuing to listen to what he himself says:

"If we confine ourselves to the letter of several dogmatic defini-

[84] "Catholicisme", 528–29, 533, 540. Is there any need to add that this does not mean that the meaning of the formula is "left to the choice of the common people", as one theologian thought to read!

tions," he observes, along with everyone else, "it seems that a whole metaphysics is involved in them; there is a question of form, of matter, of substance, of hypostasis. . . ." Is that not already true of the first in date, that of Nicaea, with its "consubstantial"? But, to take another example, often brought forward in objection, is the term "transubstantial", used by the Council of Trent, not the very type of technical terms? Does it not seem unavoidably to "link at the same time our faith and our reason to the Scholastic categories of substance and accident and thereby to the whole philosophy attached to them"?[85]

Now here is the reply. Let us not dissociate any element of it. "As false as it might be", the impression that Father Lebreton has just described is nonetheless, he observes, "very widespread, and the apologist has no more right to disregard it than the theologian". Yet, it must be possible to clear it up without sacrificing anything of historical accuracy or doctrinal rigor, provided that one have recourse to the most attentive observation. It is in fact, he thinks, only a matter of an appearance, and one that "does not support examination". This is because, to maintain such a thesis successfully, it would not be enough, as some are content with, "to note in conciliar definitions some words of peripatetic [or Platonic or other] origin". . . . It would still be necessary to establish that these words, once incorporated into these definitions, retained the "specific value that they had in the system" from which they were borrowed. Now, "this is what cannot be proved." For, starting from the moment when such words are assumed by dogmatic language, in view of a more rigorous formulation that allows one to block the way to certain errors, they escape the systematic context from which they drew their origin, or from which they had received their special meaning. They have allowed explanations that the concrete situation rendered opportune, indeed, in certain cases, urgent; explanations that remain *forever acquired*. But they have not, for all that, linked divine truth to human constructions.[86] The system has been placed at the service of the faith; but it has not entered into it; it has not been joined to it; it has faded away before it. Thus we see, for example, a Bossuet, in his

[85] Ibid., 533. *Dogme et critique*, 194.

[86] Cf. L. de Grandmaison, *Bulletin de littérature ecclésiastique* (1905), 191–92. John Meyendorff, *L'Église orthodoxe, hier et aujourd'hui* (1966), 67: "In the confessions of faith destined to define the orthodox dogma with regard to reformed theology, the term μετουσίωσις, *transsubstantiatio*, is used, but with the express reservation that it does not presuppose the adoption of the Church of the Aristotelian philosophy on form and matter."

Declaratio fidei orthodoxae—this is still Father Lebreton who is speaking, choosing by design an example that might be judged extreme—comment on the Council of Trent relating to transubstantiation, without one being able to note in his text the least trace "of the theory of substance and accident". Yet no one has ever claimed that Bossuet was a "concessionist" and, for the sake of peace, weakened the rigor of conciliar definitions.[87]

The same is true, Lebreton adds, of several other definitions that concern the sacraments. They were "enunciated in terms of the theory of matter and form". It would nevertheless be more than abusive, it would be completely erroneous to claim that the Catholic is "obliged", in order to submit to it, to adhere to Aristotle's physics.[88] In fact, while the Church borrows certain terms from philosophical or theological systems, she does not employ them in the rigor of their technical sense and consequently does not at all imprison our faith in a systematic construction.[89] That is a statement that any observer of good faith can make, and one that becomes all the more obvious as one becomes more familiar with the details of the history of conciliar assemblies and with ecclesiastical tradition.

One is therefore right, concludes Father Lebreton, to maintain it with assurance: the formulas that the Church proposes to our faith are no more "school theses" than they are mere "prophetic visions" or mere pragmatic declarations. Between these two reefs, Catholic truth clears a straight path. It rejects the dilemma. Dogmatic propositions are "manifestations of revealed truths, enunciated in simply human language, and, in consequence, in need of interpretation." Even when their origin is obviously learned; ordinarily, one will never find, if one really wishes to look closely, "under the technical form, anything but the religious truth accessible to all and independent of any system". As we see, Father Lebreton is not afraid of repeating himself, but it is each time in order to add a nuance to his thought. He does not mean to insinuate here that the intellectual value of dogmatic truth thus un-

---

[87] *Dogme et critique*, 194 and 195: "Catholicisme", 533, note; 534 quotation from Bossuet, *Declaratio*, c. 3, p. 3. Several Protestants in fact accused Bossuet of watering down Catholic doctrine in his desire to attract their coreligionists; but the Church did make such a reproach of him.

[88] *L'Encyclique*, 42–43.

[89] Ibid., 42, note, with quotations from Johannes Franzelin. One is referred for details to the still classical work by Pierre Pourrat, *Le Théologie sacramentaire*.

derstood would be less. Quite the contrary! To believe so would make it necessary to develop a very particular and very narrow idea of intelligence.

The technical use of the intelligence is something completely necessary, and, historian that Father Lebreton is, he knows well, besides, the whole part that has returned to it in the preparation of conciliar definitions. The human intelligence is naturally metaphysical. A certain technical intellectualism would be very naïve in its pride if it came to think that a technician's intelligence finds access to higher regions of the being that are closed to common intelligence, and this kind of intellectualism would at the same time be very suspect if it consented to recognize intellectuality in the given of faith only insofar as it was, so to speak, assumed into a philosophical systematization. Father Lebreton is here in perfect agreement in advance with Étienne Gilson, who was to write nearly twenty years later: "That the Christian faith has . . . experienced the need to borrow vocabulary and concepts from philosophers in order to define and express its content is what the history of dogmas makes manifest and what no one tries to dispute"; but it does not at all follow that it must be depicted as "a faith ashamed at feeling inconceivable, going modestly to seek from philosophers the means of formulating itself".[90] Moreover, the more one studies history, the more one notes everywhere in this regard "on the part of the Church the same reserve, the same concern to maintain dogma outside of and above systematic constructions"[91] (the history of the last two ecumenical councils, in particular, make this fact very obvious). It can happen that theologians, with a zeal that is insufficiently mortified and insufficiently aware of their "proper meaning", imply something else. But their unfounded or excessive assertions also have the serious disadvantage of "representing traditional doctrine as an intolerable yoke for the spirit". Their own excess, which is in reality a deviation, provokes in others an "extremist reaction"—and then, under the influence of this reaction "which is judged necessary", there is even the danger of a loss of faith.[92]

[90] *Le Thomisme*, preface to the third edition (1925).

[91] *Dogme et critique*, 195 and 196. "Catholicisme", 528. Cf. C. M. Travers. O.P., *La Valeur sociale de la liturgie d'après saint Thomas d'Aquin* (1954), 195, note 1: "The Church has canonized the formula (attributing matter and form to the sacraments)", but matter and form "must be understood in the conciliar texts according to common sense".

[92] "Catholicisme", 535 and 540. One constantly senses in Father Lebreton this concern

As we have said, far from being inspired by a more or less laxist or minimizing tendency, far from compromising the intellectuality of dogma, such explanations are, in the eyes of Father Lebreton, in close correlation with the immediate demands of faith. They want to save the transcendence of it. Without doubt, they come to be clothed in a slightly unilateral character because of the point of view that is imposed by the objection they must face. Complementary insights and other nuances would be found in the writings of Father de Grandmaison, which are, sometimes at least, more independent of controversy.[93] But this would always be on the basis of the same basic doctrine. For Father de Grandmaison also declares, for example, that "the formulas of the Council of Chalcedon and of previous and subsequent synods must not lead us astray"; he protests against those who speak in their regard "of philosophical intrusion, of human opinions incorporated into dogma"; he shows that it is not there a question, as had been written, "of a Christology born under the influence of Greek philosophical ideas, which it has become impossible for us to share".[94] For him, of course, the historical reality is the reverse. He explicitly distinguishes, in fact, between a "proper meaning" and a "technical meaning", the former not necessarily carrying along the latter, and he, too, observes the concern of the Church "not to press the technical meaning of expressions that sum up the overall whole of philosophical speculations"; she "accepts them", he says, "or imposes them only in their general sense, and purified of systematic conceptions that have been, as it were, encrusted in them".[95] He also holds it to be a "grave error" to confuse "dogma, properly speaking, the object of faith that must be preserved, defended and elucidated, but to which nothing could be added with-

---

not to let himself, so to speak, be maneuvered by an adversary whose game would consist in presenting first an exaggerated and caricatured image of what he was undertaking to refute. Cf. *L'Encyclique*, 3: "One cannot let it be thought on all sides, by our adversaries and by our friends, that all sincere work of history and exegesis is hereafter condemned by the pope." Cf. on the distinction between dogma and theology: Yves Congar, *DTC*, vol. 15, col. 440. Lucio da Veiga Coutinho, "Tradition et histoire dans la controverse moderniste" (*Analecta gregoriana*, vol. 73 [1954]), 79, note. 4: "As Congar remarked, one of the misfortunes of the Modernists (especially Tyrrell) was that they did not know how to distinguish theology from dogma."

[93] This is what we find in *Le Dogme chrétien*, 30, 36, 51–52, 77–78, 282–84.

[94] *Jésus-Christ*, 2:214–17. The quotation is from Father Friedrich Loofs, *What Is the Truth about Jesus Christ?*

[95] "Qu'est-ce qu'un dogme?", *Bulletin*, 191–92.

out a criminal offense, with the periphery of explanations, deductions and speculations that constitutes" theology and apologetics.[96] He also notes that, "depending on whether it is a question of dogma or of theology, properly speaking", "the conduct of the ecclesiastical Magisterium is very different."[97] He cites in the same sense the very clear declarations of several other theologians such as Father E. Portalié[98] and Father Ambroise Gardeil.[99] Finally, certain, with good reason, that they are all merely expressing a fundamental truth, which a failure to recognize had once again been revealed as harmful, he concludes that "this distinction is as old as reflective Christian thought".[100]

Yet, if Father Lebreton puts particular stress on this, it is not solely with an apologetic intent. Nor is it only because it seems to him necessary to bring forward more information on a delicate point that is in danger of being misunderstood—and events proved to him that it is in fact sometimes misunderstood. The "grave error", the "veritable attack" that he denounces in union with Father de Grandmaison, has for him the effect of a sacrilege. This is why he returns again to the point that is dear to his heart, in order to treat it in itself, without any

---

[96] "M. Pierre Lasserre et 'la jeunesse d'Ernest Renan' ", *Études*, 184 (1925), 538. Cf. Bruno de Solages, "Le Procès de la Scolastique", *Revue thomiste* (1927), 332.

[97] "Qu'est-ce qu'un dogme?", 191.

[98] "Le Dogme et l'histoire", *Bulletin* (1904), 136: "When the Church borrows images, metaphors, expressions or even theories from philosophy, she does not at all define for all that the system from which these formulas are borrowed; extreme circumspection is necessary, in those cases, in order to disentangle the dogmatic idea clothed in a philosophical envelope, without the philosophy that furnished the formula or image being in the least degree sanctioned by the faith. . . ." We see that Father Portalié used in passing the old image of clothing, which is worn and banal, inadequate but innocent; many others likewise used it. We do not know why, suddenly, several years ago, a few theologians thought to discern in this image abysses of dogmatic perversion.

[99] *Le Donné révélé et la théologie*, 112: "There is no dependency on the part of dogma vis-à-vis the systematizations analyzed by a philosophy, even if it is, I have no difficulty saying, the philosophy of being . . ."; cf. 109–14. J. M. Perrin, O.P., introduction to Simone Weil, *Attente de Dieu*, 17: "I often had to strive to show her the distance between the faith revealed by God and theologies, no matter how authorized they were."

[100] The same essential idea will be emphasized, in 1954, by Father Louis Bouyer, *Du Protestantisme à l'Église*, 231: "While the 'definitions' of the Catholic faith, even when achieved with the resources of a theological school marked by a certain place and a certain period, impose on the faithful only truths that go beyond those particularities and, consequently, leave the most diverse schools perfectly free to subsist in the Church, these [Reformed] 'confessions', which were nothing but efforts to impose in all its detail a more and more particularized view of Christianity, have had as a foreseeable consequence the very rupture of the reformed 'Church' that they were aiming to unify."

more allusions to the disputes that had first provoked the examination of it. "This independence of human systems", he writes, "is required by the most essential characteristics of dogmatic truth: it is unchangeable, and its fate cannot be linked to that of human philosophies; it is universal and cannot be reserved to one School of thinkers; it is more profoundly penetrated by those whose soul is purest, most detached from the world, most united to Christ, not by those whose mind is the most penetrating and the most educated."[101] More simply still, and in a word that says everything, if one really wishes to reflect on it humbly, dogmatic truth is *revealed*. Now, "if properly systematic notions are formally and explicitly contained in the dogmas that God has revealed to us, they carry along with them the whole system of which they are an integral part. Being linked necessarily to the overall whole, and at least partially controlling it, is in fact the peculiarity of a systematic conception. What becomes, in this hypothesis, of that definition of the Vatican Council: the doctrine of faith that God has revealed to us has not at all been proposed to the human mind as a philosophical invention, in order to be perfected by it?"[102] Finally, if it is true that this revealed truth is supernatural, eminently transcendent, it follows that the dogmas that express it to us "do not come to be inserted like theorems in the sequence of our human systems: they dominate them like facts."[103]

---

[101] *Dogme et critique*, 197. Compare Father Benoit, O.P., "Un Adversaire du christianisme au IIIe siècle, Porphyre", *Revue biblique* (1947), 571: "We do not wish in any way to minimize here the essential doctrinal element in Christianity; we wish on the contrary to mark how much it remains transcendent in respect to our human, contingent sciences and receives from this fact a universal value. The steps by which God has acted for us and spoken in our language are full of an extremely rich actuality, but one which has nothing in it of human science, because it surpasses reason and comes from above. And this is why this revelation is, in its essence, transcendent and universal, why it accommodates all sorts of philosophical and theological constructions but never allows itself to be enclosed by them. History gives proof of it. . . ."

[102] "La Connaissance de foi", *Études*, 117 (1908), 744. Compare again L. Bouyer, in *La Vie intellectuelle*, February 1950, 249, on the theologians who seem to want to lead men from outside into an "invincible prejudice that Catholic thought is only a substitution of philosophy for the Gospel".

[103] *Dogme et critique*, 197. In *Études*, 104 (1905), 172, "L'Explication morale des dogmes", Father Portalié wrote: "Dogma . . . is presented almost like the declaration of a fact from which it is possible to construct many different theories but which all theory must take into account. . . ."

This is not at all to say, of course, that the doctrine revealed by God remains in us "without contact with human philosophy". Far from it. Father Lebreton now goes on to apply himself to bringing out a certain number of consequences of the principles that he has set, consequences that also constitute a complementary aspect of them.

First of all, it is all too clear that divine truth, by its sole presence, dismisses many systems, many ideas whose tenor is incompatible with it. The notion of truth has had as a necessary correlative that of error, and the adherence to the true leads to the rejection of the false. That is understood as much for exegesis or history as it is for metaphysics.[104] But let us not dwell on these truisms. It is important to remark besides, if we do not want to reduce that doctrine revealed by God to an overly human plane, that it therefore rejects error "by affirming facts, not by constructing theories".[105] It does not at all provide any systematic interpretation for these facts that it affirms. They are. It is for the intelligence to come into agreement with them, to change its ways as need be, in its spontaneous conceptions or in its learned constructions, in order to be able to receive them. The adherence that they demand is unconditional. They do not adapt themselves to our human systems: it is for these systems to adapt themselves to them.[106]

Notwithstanding the negative turn it necessarily takes in our language, this character of dogmatic facts must not be understood as a kind of deficit. It is, quite the contrary, a matter of extraordinary, eminently active and positive strength. In the understanding of the believer, the *Credo* is the master. An absolute master, a demanding master, but also a powerful master, an operative master. When the given of faith comes to penetrate a human intelligence, it always encounters there, in a state that is more or less naïve and spontaneous or technical and

[104] *Dogme et critique*, 221.

[105] Compare again, Father Benoit, "Un Adversaire", 570: "The message of Christ was not one philosophical preaching after many others. God did not propose to us in his person a new gnosis, contingent like all the others. He posed a fact: the entitative renewal of fallen human nature, carried out in the Person of Jesus. . . ." And L. Bouyer, "Le Baptême et le mystère de Pâques", *La Maison Dieu*, 2:51: The baptismal initiation "must be an initiation to the faith conceived above all, not as the knowledge of notions, but as the recognition of the divine fact of God's intervention in this world for the salvation of man".

[106] Cf. William of Saint Thierry, *Aenigma fidei*: "Cum ergo hujusmodi aliquid admittitur, non tam ipsum quam quid de ipso ratio fidei efficere velit attendatur; nec rationibus seu ratiocinationibus hominum subjiciamus causam fidei nostrae, sed omnia illi serviant ubi oportet, non se ingerant plus quam oportet" (PL 180, 419 C; cf. 428–29).

reflective, "a thousand concepts of a natural order", which themselves gravitate around "several main ideas, which govern the intellectual and moral life in each soul".[107] In a certain, variable, measure, it rests on these; but it also always collides with them. A battle then ensues, a battle at times long and tragic; a battle whose principal vicissitudes are retraced for the collective conscience by the history of dogmas. Merely refer to the *Histoire du dogme de la Trinité*: Will Hellenism absorb the Christian innovation, or will the Christian innovation succeed in taking root? Will it be victorious in the end, after having assimilated for its own benefit the natural resources that Hellenism would offer it? What dangers of suffocation, in the first centuries, from the quarters of a proliferating "Pseudo-Gnosticism", then from Arianism! Always, finally—not, unfortunately, in all individual consciences, but in the great Church assisted by the Holy Spirit—faith triumphs. Then only—to revive an old traditional image that Saint Thomas retained—the foreign captive becomes a servant and even a spouse. Then only a new equilibrium is established that must always be actively maintained. Thus wrote Father Théodore de Régnon several years earlier, a theologian whose thought certainly marked that of Father Lebreton,[108] "the mystery shatters all the rational frameworks", justified or not on the natural level, "in which we seek to enclose it".[109] It does not timidly beg for a place beside, or even "above", acquired conceptions: it does not at all hesitate to overturn them. In order to serve as expression for it, the most essential notions, those that could be called basic categories, will have to be elaborated anew and often allow themselves to be profoundly transformed. Let one reflect, for example, on the action exercised by Christianity over ideas such as those of nature and person, or over that of love. . . .[110] For "Christianity is not an element of social construction like we encounter in the inert rock and brick of all architects' fantasies. It constructs, like life does, through fermentation,

[107] *La Connaissance de foi*, 744.

[108] "This much misunderstood master, whose name should be placed beside those great initiators Moehler and Scheeben": Father Irénée Vallery-Radot, *La Mission de Dom Vital Lehodey* (1956), 43.

[109] *Études sur le mystère de la Sainte Trinité*, 3d series, 1 (1898), 43.

[110] Whence, too, "a decisive semantic evolution [brought about by revelation]. B. B. Waifield observes that, thanks to the language of the New Testament, a complete revolution has been worked in the terminology of love": C. Spicq, O.P., *Agapè*, 1955, XII. One should also measure the newness of the expression: *Credo in Deum*, and all that it implies.

through a bubbling, a seething that is produced in our life and in our human ideas by this seed that is foreign to it." It was Paul Claudel who expressed himself in this way, in a letter to André Gide, on January 15, 1910.[111] The perfect harmony of his thought with that of Father Lebreton in his articles of 1907 and 1908 is admirable—although apparently there was no dependence whatever of the one in relation to the other.

In the individual soul, Father Lebreton goes on, "if faith is truly alive, it tends in its turn to invade the soul, to fill it, to direct it", and all the while receiving in its expression the stamp of the ideas that it finds installed there already; far from being warped by these ideas, it "transforms" them and "elevates" them by its contact. Not one single exception, he affirms, will be found to this law.[112] In that way, a "perpetual transfer of old words to new meanings" is produced in the course of the history of the Church, thanks to that continued and effective effort of assimilation;[113] that, of course, is not within the faith![114] but for the passage to the order of faith. There again, Father Lebreton, who is at the same time a good observer of historical givens, proves to be a faithful interpreter of doctrinal tradition in his analyses. William of Saint Thierry, for example, had explained well this indispensable recasting of human concepts, instruments forged by common reason for designating common objects, for their singular, paradoxical, unforeseeable application to revealed truth: "Hujusmodi enim cum sint communis rationis instrumenta circa res communes, cum in causa fidei assumuntur, nonnisi scandala sunt, si non rationi fidei fideliter

---

[111] *Correspondance de Paul Claudel et d'André Gide*, 117.

[112] *La Connaissance de foi*, 744–46. *Histoire du dogme de la Trinité*, 1:XVI: "It is impossible to find in the Christian faith a single concept that has not been transformed and elevated by its contact." Cf. *La Sainte Trinité et la vie surnaturelle*, by a Carthusian (1948), 32–33: "We must, in order to accept this new and properly divine science, break the categories of our natural intelligence. It is in this sense, perhaps, that the prophet glimpses the science of God invading the earth like the all-powerful tide of a new ocean, making rivers overflow, spilling over dams, inundating plains and covering mountains. *Repleta est terra scientia Domini sicut aquae maris operientes* (Is 11:9)."

[113] The expression is from Father M. D. Chenu, O.P., *Introduction à l'étude de saint Thomas d'Aquin* (1950), 96. Cf. already L. de Grandmaison, *Études*, 184:538: "The attributes given to the Word are going to be modeled on the common faith of the Church and not vice versa."

[114] There, on the contrary, as William of Saint Thierry says, *Aenigma fidei*, all becomes *sine immutatione sensuum antiquorum* (PL 180, 410 C).

coaptentur."[115] Saint Thomas Aquinas, in turn, makes the same remark by using an image that is as traditional as it is energetic: the miracle of Cana is forever reproduced, water is always being changed into wine.[116] Or, if one wishes another image, also drawn from the Gospels, new wine is always bursting the old wineskins. In fact and by right, faith is first.

Father Lebreton himself developed at length another example, borrowed from certain aspects of dogma and from the theology of the Trinity. When, in books five to seven of *De Trinitate*, Saint Augustine brings out, on the basis of revelation, the notion of subsistent relation, he does not apply from outside a philosophical concept *ne varietur* that would serve him as norm and criterion for judging the revealed given, or as a mold for modeling it. It is just the opposite that happens: the revelation of the mystery of the Trinity "gives to the notion of relation a new and transcendent meaning that it had not had up until then; the old concept is usable only because it is the sign of a reality that surpasses it". The same thing occurs in the second part of *De Trinitate*. "In the light of dogma, Augustine discovers that the soul is in spiritual relation, one in the trinity of terms that it unites and to which it is identified by turns. This time again, the interrelationship of powers illuminates dogma only because it is first illuminated by it and because it remains inadequate for it."[117] William of Saint Thierry made similar reflections with respect to the two ideas of number and person, in their application to the trinitarian formula.[118] Father Lebreton considers the

---

[115] *Aenigma fidei* (PL 180, 409 D).

[116] Saint Thomas, *In Boethium de Trinitate*, q. 2, a. 3, ad 5m: "Quando alterum duorum transit in naturam alterius, non reputatur mixtum, sed quando utrumque a sua natura alteratur. Unde illi qui utuntur philosophicis documentis in sacra Scriptura redigenda in obsequium fidei, non miscent aquam vino, sed convertunt aquam in vinum." Cf. the body of the article, commenting on 2 Corinthians 10:5. This same word *convertere, conversio*, has long been traditional for the entrance of profane wisdom into the Christian synthesis. We find it in Rabanus Maurus, Rupert de Deutz, etc.

[117] Pierre Agaësse, S.J., introduction to *De Trinitate*, l. 8–15, *Oeuvres de saint Augustine*, 16 (1955), 14–15.

[118] *Aenigma fidei* (PL 180, 410–19). Cf. col. 426 D and 427 A–B: "Quicumque notitiam aliquam Trinitatis seu rerum divinarum investigans per signa verborum, labyrinthum divinae revelationis ingreditur, non scrutator majestatis opprimendus a gloria, sed pauper spiritu, cui proxime semper est misericordia, scire debet alium esse ordinem discendi in rebus humanis, propter quas significandas cuncta quaecumque sunt verba reperta sunt, alium in divinis, quibus significandis nulla prorsus verba idonea sunt. . . . Quae quamdiu ad profectum cognitionis Dei nos adjuvant, quantum nos verba adjuvare possunt, veneranda et am-

history of trinitarian theology in all its consequences in order to come to a similar conclusion. This is a page of the study he devoted in 1908 to the knowledge of faith:

> We can still distinguish today, in the theology of the Trinity, some conceptions that have become very coherent among themselves but that betray diverse origins: the Son is the Word uttered by the Father, the exemplar for creatures, the law of the world; these different theses only go to develop givens of the faith; but they have developed them first with the help of different conceptions. The earliest Fathers, especially the apologists, on whom the stoic influence was most pronounced, freely apply to the Word the stoic conception of the logos law of the universe; the Alexandrians particularly develop the exemplarism; the analogy of the mental word will receive its full value only from the psychological analyses of Saint Augustine, and particularly from the theory of intellection systematized by Saint Thomas. The historian has no difficulty distinguishing these various sources; and yet the theologian notes today neither contradiction nor disparity between these notions; quite the contrary, the filiation appears necessarily linked to diction, and from the fact that the Son is Word, it follows that he is exemplar and law of the world.
>
> But we understand that, if these various conceptions today blend so harmoniously, it is because they have been elaborated by Christian theology and corrected according to the revelation to which they have been applied: for the stoics, the law of the world is its soul, an impersonal force that is not distinguished from it; for the Christians, it is a person distinct from the world, who creates and governs it. Neoplatonists represent the ideal world as the work or emanation of the supreme God, an intermediary between him and the sensible world; Christians confess that the Word is the Son of God, consubstantial with the Father. These examples could be multiplied; we would ascertain, across the whole history of theology, this vigor of the Christian idea, which, far from letting itself be distorted by so many different conceptions, transforms them by assimilating them. It is not surprising, therefore, that some systems very antipathetic to Christian dogma, if considered in their whole—stoic monism, for example—have nevertheless been able to deliver some useful element to Christian theology. . . .[119]

plectenda nobis sunt; ubi vero deficiunt verba, sicut verba, cum gratia ejus qui nominatur et benedictione pertranseunda sunt." We cite this text because, even beyond an agreement in thought, it seems to us to manifest a perfect community of spirit with Father Lebreton. For the commentary on *Aenigma fidei*, cf. Louis Bouyer, *La Spiritualité de Citeaux* (1955), particularly 141.

[119] *La Connaissance de foi*, 748–49.

These last considerations in large part go beyond the case of dogmatic formula. They even go beyond somewhat the case of theological activity, which is always the architect—often very technical architect—of dogma considered in the precision achieved in its formulas. They also concern, in all its fullness, the intellectual fecundity of revelation. They bring out the law of all Christian thought. They thereby lead us to understand better how this thought, while using—under the required conditions—philosophical systems, "is exclusively enslaved to none of them".[120] This observation by Father Lebreton, which he bases again on history, is of great importance in theology. It would remain true even if one did not admit the distinction, which is, however, indispensable in our opinion, between theology in general and theological systems. Let us suppose, indeed, a theology that uses, in fact, only one single philosophical system and that tends to be expressed wholly within that system's framework, with a formal rigor that is as thorough as possible: if that theology remains faithful to its divine sources, it of necessity introduces into that system a principle that reshapes it and, in a way, recreates it; so well that the most systematic theology never appears to be the application pure and simple of a wholly preformed system for the organization of the revealed given. The theologian does not bring to his task "notions already learnedly worked out through abstraction and reasoning, like stones cut to the plan of the architect, brought to the site all ready to be put in place and determining in advance the whole design of the construction".[121]

Yet, even if the work of recasting the human elements has been sufficiently accomplished, the theologian worthy of this name—the ideal theologian, the theologian according to the heart of Father Lebreton—never takes pleasure in his system as if it had brought him the final word of truth. He does not cling to it in an exclusive way or, above all, with the same kind of fervor he places in his adherence to the divine Word himself. With all the more reason will he avoid, in his manner of speaking, all that would seem to attribute a kind of subsequent

[120] Art. cit., 747.

[121] P. 744. The most important and most classic case is that of Aristotelianism. There is no point in recalling in detail the profound transformations that it underwent in the thought of Saint Thomas Aquinas, in order to become suited to the organic exposition of Christian truths, and first of all the truths of natural philosophy in relation with them. To take only two examples, we know that Saint Thomas did not find in Aristotle the *forma excedens* or what É. Gilson calls "the metaphysics of the Exodus".

perfection to it. He will always distinguish with care the three very diverse levels of dogma, theology in general and system. So, as strongly as he may hold to this latter—and he may be right in holding to it—he will guard against overestimating its value and role. And he will do so not only, of course, in the judgments he brings to bear and in his manner of appreciating the orthodoxy of others, but also even in his most personal and innermost life. He will never give the impression of holding to it as much or more than to faith itself, because, in all truth, he will not make an idol of it. Father Lebreton explains this to us in a page where he was able to communicate something of his believing and praying soul as well as of his theological thought. The whole of it must be quoted:

> Dogma is a divine message, and it makes us participate in divine knowledge, it makes us see religious truths from within, as God sees them. Now, if there is a mode of knowledge that carries the imprint of our human infirmity, it is the system. In speaking so, I do not intend to depreciate it, still less to condemn it: it is a very imperfect and at times dangerous instrument; but often, it is the only one that we have at hand, and, well handled, it can render us good service: not being angels, we are often reduced to supplying through constructions the intuitions we lack and to striving to enclose within our logical network the being that we cannot penetrate; still it is true that, even in its successful results, the system, more than any other mode of knowledge, betrays the native weaknesses of our reason: it grasps things only by fragments and from outside. Consequently, as experience teaches theologians, properly systematic conceptions, even those that are dearest to their mind, scarcely penetrate their religious life and poorly nourish their piety; by instinct, their soul refers, in prayer, to those simple views of faith that they have in common with all the faithful. I am not saying that their scientific effort is without profit for their spiritual life; quite the contrary, it must be recognized, as Saint Teresa liked to repeat, that theology can be a help to contemplation, in what it gives to the soul of the most lofty ideas of God and of the mysteries; but these ideas themselves do not belong as such to the system that bears them; in order to nourish the soul, they must be detached from it like a ripe fruit. Religious knowledge, born of faith, penetrates the soul like the voice of God, recollected and profound; systematic knowledge does not have this accent at all: it is human discourse, which resounds and stirs at the farthest point of our mind; it absorbs all our attention there, but it does not penetrate into that inner sanctuary of the soul where God resides.[122]

[122] *La Connaissance de foi*, 743.

Anyone who would not consider as completely the same the relation between the two kinds of knowledge that coexist in the theologian, or who would desire a bit more complete analysis of that "religious knowledge" evoked by contrast with the "system", or, again, who would not reject so freely the help that could be afforded by the effort of theological thought to sustain the impulse of prayer and to refer the soul to the "simple views of faith", that very one could not fail to be sensitive to such a tone. However little experience he has of the life of faith, he could not fail, I believe, to agree at least with the overall idea that this text seeks to bring out.[123] "Regnum Dei in simplicitate fidei est."[124] He will most certainly derive a safeguard against a certain kind of pride, sufficiency or illusion that lies in wait for the professional theologian.[125] And he will repeat, with Dom André Louf, that "the distance that the theologian maintains vis-à-vis a system, even if his own, so as to judge it in the light of the one faith is a condition of any healthy and fruitful theology."[126]

But a final precision must still be brought forward, which shows the unavoidable limit of any theological system existing in fact—and probably also the congenital limit of any system. It is in his article on Cardinal Billot that Father Lebreton is led to explain this.

Insofar as theology is organized more strictly, in a more "scientific" effort, insofar as it tends, in its own line, to a more consummate systematic perfection, it is without doubt fatal for it to leave outside of

[123] Here again, we will note the affinity of spirit with William of Saint Thierry, *Speculum fidei*: "Fidei puritatem non assequitur nisi vera et profunda humilitas cordis, et devotio pia, et pervigilis instantis orationis. . . ." To have an in-depth share in the truth revealed by the Father, it is necessary to be among the "simplices filii Dei, spiritu ferventes"; those "non in silentio suo hebetes aestimandi sunt, sed in eo quod acceperunt singulariter sapientes"; if one has done scholarly theological work, it should at least be necessary that "fervor naturalis rationalitatis, operante gratia, vertatur in fervorem amoris" (PL 180, 378, 380 D).

[124] Saint Ambroise, *De fide ad Gratianum*, l. 1, c. 5, n. 42. Again William of Saint Thierry, *Aenigma fidei* (PL 180, 407–8).

[125] Bossuet expresses a similar thought in the *Second traité* of *L'Instruction sur les états d'oraison*, chap. 18, with respect to what he calls the prayer of faith: "One is, in a way, in this prayer, whether one uses discourse or not, from the time one believes that one no longer has need of it and rests only on faith. A sublime theologian, who knows all the proofs of the faith that one can have, is nonetheless in the prayer of faith because he makes it his sole support, just as the smallest in the Kingdom of heaven do before God. *He leaves aside* his theology, which is necessary to him only for others, and, for himself, he is reduced like a child to faith and to his catechism." Levesque ed. (1897), 49.

[126] André Louf, on the *De Gratia* of Saint Hilary (1956).

its grasp any part of the concrete richness conveyed from century to century by the one and multiform tradition of the Church. How could it embrace the whole infinity of the mystery at once? How could it make the most of all its aspects at once? So the theologian must avoid like a trap the temptation to enclose his whole theological thought in his system. No great theologian has ever done that. For the same reason, one must not expect that any state ever achieved by theological speculation, as satisfying as it might be, will in some way annul the previous states. The finest progress is never without a counterpart. The gain is never total. It cannot be. It must not be. History, in any case, verifies these views. One cannot put together, for example, in order to organize them into a single logical and definitive whole, the combined riches of Augustinian thought and Thomist thought; such an operation cannot even be achieved for the thought of Saint Paul and that of Saint John. Father Lebreton notes in general that the Fathers of the Church "formerly gave a profound interpretation of the Christian mystery, and it cannot be said that the fullness of their doctrine was transmitted integrally into the medieval tradition"[127]—although the latter had retained much more than was perceived by a number of disciples and later commentators, who were subject to other influences. Father Lebreton's remark in any case means neither that the Middle Ages did not record a certain progress in more than one regard nor that there should have been a return, pure and simple, even in a limited domain, to the thought of the ancient Fathers. But what we have acquired since then will never excuse us from placing ourselves endlessly in their School.[128] They must be for us something very different from witness-mouthpieces of an embryonic state of dogmatics or of the "prehistory of theology", and we must not draw a few arguments from their works only in order to support our theses; we must receive

[127] *S. Em. le cardinal Billot*, 523. Cf. P. Rousselot, *RSR* (1914), 64, with respect to the article "Foi" by Father Saint Harent in the *DTC*: "The rich scriptural and patristic treasures, which the Vatican Council did not exhaust and which contain such magnificent doctrinal reserves for present and pressing needs, seemed to interest the author only to the degree in which modern Scholasticism has utilized them."

[128] Cf. Dom Besse, *Le cardinal Pie*, 6: "The writings of the Fathers were, after the Bible, his favorite reading. . . . He excelled in setting their most luminous testimony into the exposition of his own doctrine. Not content with seeking from their pen arguments to support his words, he used them to educate himself about the doctrinal inspirations that characterize them, and, by nourishing himself on their literature, he assimilated their genius. In that, he walked in the steps of Bossuet." It does not matter here that the praise was a bit hyperbolic.

doctrinal inspiration from them: "Patristic theology does not serve only to prove dogmas but also to clarify them."[129] In brief, whatever might be the progress achieved, in the elaboration of theology as in that of dogma, it is always the total tradition that a true theologian must be concerned to explore.

Nothing would be more erroneous than to interpret such reflections as the mark of a certain, even relative disfavor with regard to Scholasticism or of less esteem with regard to the progress that theology has accomplished in the course of the centuries. They are aimed only at the narrowness, negligence, disdain, illusions and—why not say it? This is not an unheard-of hypothesis—the ignorance that would prevent the theologian from accomplishing his task in an appropriate way. At the time when he recorded them, Father Lebreton had, moreover, given sufficient proof. We know that he was one of the restorers of Thomism within his Order—and that did not at all proceed without resistance at the time: younger ones than he have still experienced this. He does not fear, however, to add, in a kind of dream of the future, one of those dreams that are necessary to encourage oneself to work and to keep thought alive, even though past experience as well as reflection on the laws of the human spirit seem very much to show that they could never be more than half-realized, if that: "There can be no doubt that the theology of Saint Thomas gives our teaching the principal theses that assure its rectitude and determine its orientation; but it also seems that, since the ancient monuments of our tradition are now incomparably better known than they could have been in the thirteenth century, the ambition of a theologian should be to gather all the truths contained in these venerable doctrines and to integrate them into a more comprehensive synthesis. . . ."[130]

---

[129] *S. Em. le cardinal Billot*, 523. One can compare this page with a paragraph from the encyclical *Humani generis* of Pius XII (1950), which recalls once again the importance of the study of sources, notably patristic sources, for a certain theology that tends to be too forgetful of them. For example, as Father Karl Rahner writes (*Écrits théologiques*, French trans., 1 [1959], 110): "The Greek concept of the Trinity must be taken seriously by all theology, for reasons that rest on the authority of Scripture."

[130] *S. Em. le cardinal Billot*, 523. Father Auguste Valensin wrote of Father Lebreton to Maurice Blondel, June 27, 1907: "I believe there are few Thomists as authentic as he who are capable, in these difficult moments, of leading as he has a discussion to the profit of charity and light."

As we said at the beginning: Father Lebreton's teaching on these matters always remained fragmentary and occasional. The analogous texts that could be gleaned in later works would add nothing essential to it. They would merely show a continuity of views that is a sign to us of its reflective soundness. The uninterrupted study of dogmatic history, over the course of a long life, would only confirm, as a whole, positions chosen with such a concern for traditional reality consulted in all these aspects. But the examination solely of these writings that could be called youthful, in which such lofty problems are broached under circumstances that might seem so little favorable, already leaves the mind generally satisfied by the honesty of the analysis as well as by the firmness of a kind of higher good sense, more invaluable than certain flaunted technicalities, overly subtle cleverness or overly abstract strictness—or stiffness—in others.

It would assuredly be possible to practice picking out a few deficiencies in it. Traces here and there give one the sense of a necessarily hasty drafting: it was not a question of works ripening at leisure! Their author knew this only too well, and he excused himself by "the urgency of the work".[131] One could criticize certain rather loose expressions in it, debate perhaps one or another secondary idea. In such studies, the objection is not pursued in all its possible entrenchments. The imperative correction is effected, with perfect vigor and sureness, but the rational justifications of this correction are sometimes only outlined. One friend, a demanding philosopher, Father Auguste Valensin, wrote this to Father Lebreton in 1907. We have his reply:

> For the *via media* between systematic knowledge and prophetism, I have guided myself as I have been able to, with the help above all of the theological givens. My response would without any doubt have been more complete and more interesting if I had insisted more on the psychological aspect of the problem.[132] I have not done so for the following reasons: first, I have preferred to remain on sure ground and where I did not have to fear any surprise by the adversary. . . . Second, in such material, I believe historical faith alone can tell us to what point systems enter into dogmatic formulas; it seems to me impossible

[131] *L'Encyclique*, foreword: "The urgency of the work will, I hope, be my excuse; at a time of acute conflicts one is not very concerned with doing a definitive work; it is enough to do loyal and Christian work."

[132] Psychological, in contrast to historical and theological. It would be better, I believe, to say: "noetic".

to give a better overall solution than by the historical study of particular cases. . . .[133]

Father Lebreton's correspondent did not confess to being fully satisfied. The problem raised about the nature of revealed knowledge, he wondered, is so fundamental a problem "that it seems to me to place in question the instructive value of the historical givens themselves". To know in depth if the conciliar affirmations "propose a truth or if they merely support one of them", and what kind of truth they support, he judged that it was impossible to keep to the *sole* point of view of historical theology and that it was necessary to make a larger appeal to psychology and to the philosophy of language "as well as to the metaphysics of knowledge". Rationally, he was not mistaken. One can add that the defensive point of view to which urgency drove the theologian did not permit him that resumption of research in company with the other which alone, brought to a successful conclusion, is ordinarily completely persuasive. Father Lebreton, thus, did not go to the bottom of everything—although, even on the plane where he did not want to let the debate be restricted, he brought light. But this was not his principal object. He intended above all to dissipate ambiguities, those ambiguities by means of which, in troubled periods, deadly error is introduced without being perceived in a number of minds that would have been horrified if they had seen it exposed. He wanted to show the true meaning of Catholic Tradition, in such a way as to oblige anyone who had departed from it either to return to it or to recognize at last that he was no longer seeking his orientation from it. While others shut their eyes to the real difficulties, he was willing to consider them seriously. He well knew, nevertheless, that he could not exhaust, on the occasion of one pressing controversy, infinitely complex problems, the examination of which would be poorly adapted to a feverish atmosphere—and this is why we will not ask him for a complete theory of the understanding of the faith or of the life and advance of truth in the believing soul. But he wanted to be, and he truly was—and this is more important than anything else, this was the urgent need of the Church—a man of Tradition.

---

[133] Letter from Father Auguste Valensin to Father Lebreton, July 7, 1907. Father Valensin and Father de Grandmaison both had furnished Father Lebreton with a few reflections written to aid him in his response to the article: "Théologisme". Cf. J. Lebreton, *Le Père Léonce de Grandmaison*, 168.

Since then, the fever has subsided—or has been relit in other hearths. Even in the examination of the same problems, other aspects have compelled attention. The theologian of today would have to bring them out in an occasional effort to bring balance. It would be contrary to the spirit of Father Lebreton, as to the very letter of his thought, to claim that one need only reproduce some particular thing, in any of his formulas, following unchanged proportions, in order to respond to difficulties or to prevent dangers that are no longer exactly the same. His real agreement with the most recent documents of the ecclesiastical Magisterium would also have to be made manifest. As for particular details of expression, a refinement would be useful. That is a necessity that time imposes on the work of all theologians, or rather on all those whom time does not dismiss to nothingness. Perhaps the analogous relation that Father Lebreton placed between dogma and theological speculation, on the one hand, facts and scientific theories, on the other, as enlightening as it might be from the angle he was considering, could not be exploited in depth without disadvantages. Perhaps, too, in the overriding concern to respond to the Modernist grievance of "theologism", a grievance that was justified by all-too-real abuse, the apologist has seemed to diminish somewhat the significance of theological work or has not always succeeded fully in overcoming the antinomies that he found at his point of departure. Perhaps, finally, a rather artificial conception of "system" and a rather extrinsic conception of the intelligence in the believer who is at the same time a theologian enters into the exercise of theological thought and that of the life of faith. Perhaps. . . . But the very ones who, from around 1908 on, made one or another of these remarks recognized at the same time that Father Lebreton's effort had not at all been without profit. Between the opposite poles of error, he had helped the truth to rise. At the end of a half-century, we see it better still. In all its substance, his work appears to us to be ratified by the proof of time. Father Clément Dillenschneider recently cited Father Lebreton among the theologians of whom one can and must say that, for their doctrine of revelation, of the faith of the faithful and of dogmatic development, "the apostolic constitution *Munificentissimus* certainly does not prove them wrong."[134] Many works,

[134] *Le Sens de la foi et le progrès dogmatique du mystère marial* (Rome, 1954), 372; cf. 364. Reviewing the work in the *Revue thomiste* (1954), 650, Father M. J. Nicolas, O.P., writes: "The author's manner of seeing presupposes, it seems to us, that divine revelation was made, not

published in the course of the past fifty years, could also go to confirm Father Lebreton's thought in its principal outlines, while bringing it those nuances or complements that human imperfection always summons. More than one consequence, finally, could be drawn from that thought that would be useful in orienting more than one recent debate. We are thinking in particular of the tendency, already manifest in the writings analyzed here, that constantly pushes Father Lebreton to reject a certain arrogant and pernicious distinction between *majores* and *minores* in the midst of the Church in order to emphasize, on the contrary, all the true intellectuality and profound rectitude that can be found in spontaneous faith, in its least "scientifically elaborated" expression.[135] Following the very wish he expressed, one could also be inspired by him to state certain points even more precisely, such as the relations between the immutability of dogma and its progress, those between revelation and the formula of faith,[136] those between witness and teaching,[137] those between the faith of the Church and the faith of each of the faithful. . . . But rather than try to do so, I will prefer to note in closing the depth of the spirit of faith and Catholic sentiment that animates this whole effort of thought.

Reconsidering the Modernist period at a later date, again following Father de Grandmaison, Father Lebreton quoted a fine text by Saint Vincent de Lérins, applying it to those who had had to, and knew how to, make the sacrifice in themselves that the encyclical *Pascendi* demanded of them. They had to be those true Catholics, he said along

in the form of principles, from which conclusions can be deduced, but in the form of a concrete and living given from which there is occasion to draw principles and formulas, but without any pretense of exhausting the meaning in them of what God has revealed." Assuredly, and that applies as well to the writings of Father Lebreton. But how could there be another "manner of seeing", in essence, the historical "form" of revelation? Rather than a theory, is this not an affirmation that anyone can still easily make by opening the "New Testament"? On the other hand, what theologian would dare to claim to "exhaust" in a few principles, conclusions or other formulas "the meaning of what God has revealed"?

[135] In *L'Encyclique*, 56, Father Lebreton quotes these words of Saint Paulinus of Nola, epist. 23, n. 25: "De omnium fidelium ore pendeamus, quia in omnem fidelem Spiritus Dei spirat" (PL 61, 281).

[136] One would thus react against the tendency criticized by Father V. White "to want the *articulus fidei*, defined dogma, nearly to supplant the primary revelation" ("Concept de la révélation", 5).

[137] This final point is treated by L. Malevez, S.J., *Révélation et témoignage*, 217–32; more recently and from a historical point of view by André Rétif, S.J., *Foi au Christ et mission* (1953), c. 2, 33–35.

with the ancient author, they had to be those men "who love the Truth of God and the Church, which is the Body of Christ; who can prefer nothing to the divine religion and to the Catholic faith—neither the authority of man, whoever he might be, nor his friendship nor his talent nor his eloquence nor his philosophy—who scorn all that in order to cling to the faith and remain inviolably faithful to it."[138] He knew such men. He esteemed them among all. He had taken up his pen above all to enlighten them. He explained to them "the price of faith".[139] More than one of them had confided to him their inner debates—for they sensed that he was more desirous of helping his neighbor in secret than in triumphing over him in public. Even with the ones he had to combat, he was able, like Father de Grandmaison again, although in a slightly different style, to imprint a tone of nobility and sympathy on the controversy. Like him, he sought as much as possible "a common base", a *locus catholicus* permitting a first agreement from which the discussion could be pursued in a climate of peace.[140]

Can there be, he also said, more than a day's misunderstanding, born of human obscurities and which the Light of God will dissipate tomorrow, "between two Christians sincerely discussing their faith"?[141] So Christian a disposition, so far removed from any sectarianism as well as from any intellectual sufficiency, so contrary to that of "integrism, with its excesses and its treachery", would engender in him more clear-sightedness than other, unfortunately more current, attitudes would. Joined to the awareness of the theologian's responsibilities, it would also at times produce a perplexity in his soul. He could not help making a confession, at times, to his reader. "The questions to be debated" in the crisis in which he is intervening "are the most vital in religion; one discusses them only with trembling, because one fears that a poorly directed blow might wound some conscience to the quick. . . ."[142] And again: "When one writes for souls whose faith is at stake, the problem

[138] Saint Vincent de Lérins, *Commonitorium*, c. 20 (PL 50, 605). Father de Grandmaison also liked this text: J. Lebreton, *Le Père Léonce de Grandmaison*, 169. Cf. *Études*, 117:305. Reminder of the Church as the Body of Christ: *L'Encyclique*, 516.

[139] Title of a later article, 1932, on the *Mémoires* of Alfred Loisy, which remains in manuscript form.

[140] Cf. L. de Grandmaison, "Qu'es-ce qu'un dogme?" (1906), 22.

[141] *Dogme et critique*, 221. Cf. the fine text by Saint Augustine, epist. 238, quoted by Father de Grandmaison on a similar occasion; ibid., 329.

[142] *Le Père Léonce de Grandmaison*, 187. *L'Encyclique*, 1–2.

often becomes full of anguish; minister of Christ and responsible for his doctrine, one is afraid of either betraying the integral truth through accommodation or of compromising the divine authority through human systems; guide of souls, one fears either to impoverish in them the Christian faith from which they must live or to render it intolerable to them through unjustified demands."[143]

Happy, despite these anguishes, is the theologian who, in times of crisis, understands his role in this way. Happy in this very anxiety, in this perplexity that also guards him from the opposite but equally formidable excesses. Happy, despite the mistrust and the hostility that his attitude almost definitely earns him,[144] the one who achieves in so measured a balance the type of the man of the Church. Happy he of whom it can be said that he seeks neither the success of his own ideas, even when he cannot abstain from committing himself completely to the fight, nor the advantage of an official ratification, nor the applause of the violent, but solely the service of the divine Truth, of that Truth who is the Life in souls. Father Lebreton had the joy of being received one day by Saint Pius X. He himself told us about it, adding that this old memory still illuminated his existence. This was following some of the articles that we have just analyzed. The principal one among them had been printed in a booklet and translated into Italian.[145] The Father of all the faithful, having wanted to read this text himself, had then insisted on expressing his deeply moved gratitude to the author,

[143] "Chronique de théologie", *RPA*, 3 (1907), 543.

[144] When the article by Father Lebreton on "La Controverse moderniste" appeared in *RPA* (July 15, 1908), the *Critique du libéralisme*, an incompetent but powerful integrist journal, declared that it experienced "some astonishment and a slight feeling of uneasiness" (1:138–39); etc. Father Auguste Valensin wrote to Maurice Blondel on April 5, 1908: "Many will not pardon him . . . for not having designated and pursued with eloquence men whom we would have been much grieved to see confused with Modernists. His efforts have earned him only troubles. . . ." In the very course of this battle, after Father Lucien Laberthonnière had criticized with his customary liveliness several of Father Lebreton's positions, some thought to see in his intervention a maneuver destined to ruin Lebreton's moral authority in the *Institut catholique*. But Laberthonnière insisted on separating himself publicly from integrists of all sides: "Let no one imagine that, in speaking in turn of theologism, rationalism and agnosticism, I am coming here to designate Father Lebreton as guilty of these 'heresies'. No, of course not, and may God preserve me from it! . . ." (*Annales de philosophie chrétienne* [August 10, 1908]). Cf. Blondel-Valensin, *Correspondance*, 2:13–22.

[145] Translation by L. Zarantonello (Vicenza, 1908). The same study is reproduced in the *Dictionnaire apologétique*, s.v. "Modernisme", vol. 3, cols. 665–95. No theologian would dare face publicly the absurdity of uttering reservations about the orthodoxy of this and related writings of Father Lebreton.

in the name of the Church herself, for having effectively protected the faith of all in the battle against Modernism.[146] Yet, as precious as such a reward might be to the good servant of the Holy Father, it was not essential. Other witnesses, more humble, more hidden, were able to express the benefit of an action that had not wished to be brilliant swordplay or a battle of influence but which had received all its weight from the very weight of the commitment linking the man, in faith, to Jesus Christ, his Lord and his God.[147]

[146] "The Modernist errors had been disavowed and condemned by the blessed Pope in the pastoral letter *Pascendi*. I had repeated the teaching of the Holy Father in a booklet that was a commentary on it. Pius X knew this booklet: his first words, in receiving me, were a fatherly thank you: 'My Father,' he said to me, 'I thank you for what you have done to defend the faith of Holy Church.' "

[147] Cf. J. Lebreton, "Foi dogmatique et religion mystique", *Études*, 230 (1937), 206–7. We will say of Father Lebreton what has been written of Father de Grandmaison—what is appropriate to say of both of them together: "It is fitting that the host of Christians should know and venerate his name." Father Pierre Debongnie, "Un coeur de prêtre, le P. Léonce de Grandmaison", in *La Voix du Rédempteur* (1928), 196.

IV

CHRISTIAN RESISTANCE TO NAZISM AND TO ANTI-SEMITISM

1. The Theological Foundation of the Missions (1941 and 1946)

First Lecture
Overall Exposition

Why the missions? If we reflect on it, the sole fact that such a question has been posed already constitutes a paradox and almost a scandal. That chairs for missiology are founded in our Catholic universities or within our missionary institutes, that "weeks" or congresses for missionary studies are organized, for the purpose of recording experiences in mission lands, confronting them, interpreting them, refining methods, equipping future apostles, and so forth—the advantages of these are obvious; let us say even more: to the degree that missions

The substance of this short treatise is composed of two lectures given in January 1941 in the chair of the missions founded by the Propagation of the Faith at the Catholic Faculties of Lyons. The first of these two lectures was reproduced in the Journal of the *Union missionnaire du clergé* (January–April 1941). As for the second, the reader will have no difficulty understanding that the very circumstances that gave it a character of urgency prevented it at the same stroke from being published. Now that publication has become possible, we have not believed it necessary to modify either its form or its tone. A few notes have merely been added (H. de Lubac, April 5, 1945).

"In my naïveté", Father de Lubac would further specify in *Résistance chrétienne à l'antisémitisme*, "I still believed at that time that I was expressing the common sentiment of a very large part, if not all, of French Catholicism. I will also admit that if I had been able to foresee in concrete terms what was going to take place in the course of the following four years, I too would have undoubtedly been afraid and 'given way by a timid flight'" (24–25 [English trans.: *Christian Resistance to Anti-Semitism* (San Francisco: Ignatius Press, 1990), 25]). See also *Mémoire sur l'occasion de mes écrits* (Namur: Culture et Verité, 1989), 41 (January 1941) (English trans.: *At the Service of the Church* [San Francisco: Ignatius Press, 1993], 42–43).

develop, such a genre of teaching is all the more imperative. Numerous initiatives have responded to this need, which has been stressed by our recent popes. That publications of all kinds, learned and popular, strive as well to interest the Catholic public in the work of the missions, that suitable preaching is used to awaken their zeal by recalling the duty of all the baptized toward those of their brothers who have not received the Good News, this too is self-evident. But that it might be necessary to undertake a new work outside the classical structures of theology or catechetics; that it might be necessary, through a kind of "wing" added on to the great, wholly constituted edifice of Catholic doctrine, still to construct a "theology" or "dogmatic of the missions", as we have seen it being done nearly everywhere in the Church these past twenty years, that is what is strange. Insofar as missionary work is an essential and central thing, it seems that it should be impossible to speak of the Church, even in the most rudimentary way, without going into the missions in her very definition.[1]

It is nevertheless a fact that many Catholics are uninformed about the missions; that numerous works treat the Church in a learned way without even broaching the missionary problem and that theological treatises themselves are almost silent on this subject—and if I say "almost", it is a euphemism. . . . Consequently, since necessity obliges it, nothing is more justified, in fact, than to seek as if from outside, through special instruction, a response that has been demanded in vain from overall expositions of religion. Let us merely specify immediately that this special instruction could not pretend to explore new terrain: it can consist only in a reminder of some very simple truths, it can only lead us to the primary elements of Christianity, to the very center of our faith.

So, what is the theological foundation of the missionary work of the Church? Or, more simply: Why the missions?

One response is obvious, which, in a sense, suffices for all: it will be the subject of the first part of this lecture. We will not then have to go beyond it or even to complete it, but only to make an effort to understand it and, modestly, to justify it: such will be the effort of our second part.

---

[1] Cf. Pierre Charles, *Dossiers de l'action missionnaire*, 2d ed., 1:34: "The missionary dogmatic is nothing more, nothing less, than the theology of the expansion of the visible Church."

I

The Church's missions fulfill one of Christ's orders.

After his Resurrection, Jesus, Saint Matthew tells us, had kept a rendez-vous with his disciples on a mountain in Galilee. Approaching them, he spoke to them thus: "All authority has been given me in heaven and on earth. Go, therefore, teaching all nations, baptizing them in the name of the Father and of the Son and of the Holy Spirit, teaching them to observe all that I have commanded you."[2] Nearly the same scene occurs at the end of Saint Mark, where the words of Jesus immediately precede the Ascension: "Go through all the world and preach the gospel to every creature."[3] Saint John gives the cenacle as the framework for the same conversation, on the evening of the first Sunday: having wished peace to his disciples who had gathered together, behind closed doors, for fear of the Jews, Jesus adds these solemn words: "As my Father has sent me, so I send you"; then, breathing over them, he says to them: "Receive the Holy Spirit; those whose sins you forgive, they will be forgiven of them. . . ."[4]

These texts, let us note, are the foundation charter of the Church. Previously, there had been distant preparations; there had been the day-to-day education of the chosen apostles; there had been the proclamation and the promise: "I say to you that you are Peter, and on this rock I will build my Church, and the powers of hell will not prevail against her"; there had been the mystical birth on Calvary, when, from the pierced side of Jesus, water and blood flowed out, symbols of the sacraments and of vivifying grace. . . . Now, it is the express foundation. Now these same texts are also the foundation charter of the missions. It is by sending them to preach the gospel to every creature that Jesus hands over to his apostles his divine powers. Missionary work will therefore not be a superogatory work, it will not be as if on the periphery of the Church's activity: it is her primary work, it constitutes a part of her essential activity. Without a play on words, it is *her mission*: "Ecce, ego mitto vos." In the person of the Twelve, the Church is *sent*. This is what an Instruction addressed on December 8, 1929, for

[2] Mt 28:16–20.

[3] Mk 16:15. Cf. Acts 1:7 and Lk 24:27.

[4] Jn 20:19–23; cf. 17:18: "As you have sent me into the world, I also send them into the world."

the Congregation of the Propaganda to all mission Superiors recalled: "The Church, which has received the mandate of her divine Founder, . . . continues the mission of Christ on earth—*ipsius in terris consequitur missionem*—not seeking anything but to lead the whole human race to the knowledge of Christ and to lead it, through the observation of the evangelical law, to heavenly glory."

Now this goal has not yet been attained. How far we are from it, even today! Insofar as it has not been fully accomplished, Christ's order thus still resounds with as pressing an urgency as ever in the consciousness of the Church. It merges, for her, with her *raison d'être*. The Church is essentially missionary because what we call her *missions* are nothing but the primary means by which she accomplishes her *mission*. She is therefore not only missionary in some of her members, charged with a specialized function. She is so in all her members, jointly responsible for a common growth. She is so especially in her entire hierarchy, in her bishops and in her supreme pastor. It was to all his reunited apostles that the Savior delegated the mission that he had received from his Father: it is the whole episcopal body, successor of the apostolic college, that is jointly responsible for it today. Pius XI stressed this recently in his encyclical *Rerum Ecclesiae*, addressing all his brothers in the episcopate: each of them not only has charge of the diocese that is particularly confided to him, but, called into union with all the other bishops to govern the Church of God, participating with them in solicitude for all the churches, he must never cease to hear the call that goes up from pagan lands and souls and contribute, for his part, to responding to it.[5]

"Go, teach all nations": these words have launched the Church, for twenty centuries, onto all the routes across the vast world. Without more reflection than Peter dashing over the water before his master, she goes. She claims neither reasons nor guarantees. How would she contest an order from which she draws her very existence? Besides, whether these words were pronounced under the circumstances related by Saint Matthew or whether they must rather be understood as a styl-

[5] Cf. *Acta S. Congregationis de Propaganda Fide* (1622), and *Constitutis Gregorii PP. XV* (June 22, 1622), *Collectanea S. Congregationis de Propaganda Fide* (1893), 1 and 3. "The bishops", says Bossuet, "altogether have but one single flock, each one of whom leads a part that is inseparable from the whole: in such a way that in truth all the bishops belong to the whole and to unity, and they are divided up only for facility of application" (*Oraison funèbre de François Bourgoing* [1661]).

ized memorial of the highest instructions left by the resurrected Lord; whether they are simply the direct echo of his teaching or whether the experience of the first years in Palestine and Syria were necessary so that this teaching, clearly understood at last, could thus be gathered into a formula, as some historians say and as the very account of the Acts seems to suggest: in any case, the essential fact is incontestable. The Church became aware of herself only by waking to the missionary duty that her Founder had traced for her,[6] and it was at first by this duty that she explained herself in her own eyes.

She was prepared for it by the prophets and by the whole history of Israel such as the Holy Books, read and commented on in its assemblies, unfolded it to her. The extraordinary understanding that she possessed from the beginning of this extraordinary history is one of the greatest spectacles offered to the historian; and despite all that is arbitrary, strange or antiquated in the exegetical methods that we see used by the Christians of that era, from Saint Paul or Saint Matthew up to Saint Justin or Origen, in the course of their controversies with the Judaism of their time, we must recognize that they have seen correctly. They are only capitalizing, with varying degrees of success, on an extraordinary intuition, the very one of the Church. The latter, with an infallible gaze, is penetrating to the heart of a reality whose meaning henceforth escapes the blindfolded eyes of the Synagogue. Succeeding the patriarchs and the prophets, she knows herself to be the heir of the Chosen People and of its hopes. She knows herself, as Saint Paul says, to be the true Israel, Israel according to the spirit, because she alone, thanks to the spiritual revolution of the gospel, can bring to a conclusion the work for which Yahweh had raised up Israel. So that, supposing that Jesus had not formally given the watchword that we have seen, she would have known just as well that this was her task, the magnificent and necessary task for which she alone in the world was suited.

The missionary idea in Israel did not arise in a single stroke. It had first been necessary for the God of the patriarchs and of Moses to be universally recognized for centuries as unique and for the exclusive cult of which it was always jealous to become, in its adorers, strictly monotheistic. "You will adore only me alone. Listen, Israel, your God

[6] L. de Grandmaison, "L'Expansion du christianisme d'après M. Harnack", *Études*, 96: 470–71.

is one!" If the monotheistic principle is already contained in the monolatric order, it did not appear there immediately. And, once formulated,[7] it did not produce all its consequences immediately. The conviction that the God of Israel was the one true God of all the earth did not lead right away to the conclusion that this God had to be known and adored by all peoples. A day came, however, when the Jews found themselves faced with this problem, with apparently contradictory givens: Yahweh, the one God, is the God of all; he is, however, nonetheless the particular God of Israel; his worship remains linked to the observation of the Torah and to the service of the Temple in Jerusalem, where he has established his dwelling.

Two types of solutions were then adopted, of which the Bible has preserved many a trace for us.

Some cherished a hope that was as simplistic as radical. Since the divinities of the nations were only vain idols or evil powers, they would vanish, it was thought, before Yahweh, and those who served them would one day be exterminated.[8] Then Yahweh would reign alone, and his people would possess the earth. That would be Israel's great revenge. Others, animated by a less fierce sentiment, reconciled their national particularism more successfully with the awe-inspiring perspective that their faith opened to them; they hoped that a day would come when the pagans, conquered, would be converted to Yahweh, less by an attraction of the heart than by being forced to admit his power:

> And the glory of Yahweh will be revealed
> and all flesh without exception will see it.[9]

Then all will go up to Jerusalem to pay tribute, humanity being organized around Israel as if around a caste of priests for the praise

---

[7] For example, Isaiah, chapters 44 and 45, etc.

[8] Is 30:27–33. The Rabbot Midrash, on Song of Songs 7:4, will say: "Often it is said that the pagan nations would be entirely destroyed once the Messianic Kingdom opened. The world was created for Israel, in such a way that, at the end, the other people will be burned and annihilated."

[9] Is 40:5. Cf. Ps 46:11:

> Be still and know that I am God:
> I rule over the nations, I rule over the earth.

Cf. Sir 36:1–5.

of Yahweh and the service of his people. Such is, for example, the vision by which one prophet from the time of the Exile strengthens his oppressed brothers:

> Barbarians will appear and pasture your flocks,
> foreigners will be your laborers, your vinedressers;
>
> And you, you will be called priests of Yahweh,
> men will name you ministers of our God.
>
> You will eat the substance of the nations,
> you will be glorious with their magnificence.[10]

The extermination or subjection of the pagans:[11] this first type of solution was nevertheless not the only one. Some Israelites did not place boundaries on the generosity of their God or restrictions on their hope. These were undoubtedly a very small number, but through them the Spirit passed. They were par excellence those men whom Saint Augustine was to call: men living under the Old Testament but not of the Old Testament; proclaimers of the New Testament in the midst of the Old: "homines in Vetere Testamento, non autem de Vetere Testamento. . . ."[12] This summit of prophecy appears to us particularly in the second part of the book of Isaiah, which has been called the Book of the Consolation of Israel. Its author does not promise to the exiled and battered people a brutal revenge; rather he shows Yahweh's solicitude extending to the sons of the foreigner:

---

[10] Is 61:6. Likewise, 60:1ff.; verses 10:11:

> The sons of the foreigner will build up your walls,
> their kings will be your servants. . . .
> And your gates will always be open,
> they will be closed neither day nor night,
> To lead to you the wealth of the nations,
> and their kings at the head of the caravans.

(Father Albert Condamin gives these chapters 60 and 61 as being from the second Isaiah himself because the situation is well adapted to the time of Exile.)

[11] See also, for example, Ezekiel 28:21–22; Micah 7:15–17; or Zechariah 14:12–19, where the universalist perspective appears as much like a punishment for the Gentiles as like a blessing; for them, it is a question of servitude rather than liberation. And Psalm 47:4:

> Yahweh subjugates peoples to us,
> he places the nations under our feet. . . .

[12] *Sur l'épître aux galates*, no. 43.

I will bring them to my holy mountain,
  I will make them joyful in my house of prayer;
Their holocausts will be acceptable on my altar,
  for my house will be called:
The house of prayer for all peoples.[13]

Yet, in this same second part, among all the poems relating to the Servant of Yahweh, arise poems in which Jewish universalism becomes missionary. In the person of this mysterious Servant, Israel no longer waits in inactivity for the day when the entire earth will know its God, but it becomes aware of the mission dispensed to it to work toward the coming of that day:

Listen to me, O coastlands,
  and hearken you distant peoples!
Yahweh has called me from my birth,
  from my mother's womb he has named my name.

He has said to me:

It is too little that you should be my Servant
  to reestablish the tribes of Jacob
  and restore the preserved of Israel;
I will make you a Light of the nations,
  to carry my salvation
  to the ends of the world![14]

The Servant of Yahweh is therefore not only the suffering Just One, Redeemer of his people: he is at the same time the one who proclaims everywhere the Law of Yahweh; he is the one sent, the missionary:

---

[13] Is 56:6–7; 54:2: "The tents of Israel will expand. . . ." Cf. P. Barba, *La Doctrine missionnaire d'Isaïe et sa destinée* (supplement to the *Union missionnaire du clergé* [July 1936]).

[14] Is 49:1 and 6. And 42:1–4:

Here is my Servant whom I uphold,
my chosen one in whom my soul is pleased.
I have put my spirit into him,
he will show the Law to the nations. . . .

He will faithfully show the Law,
he will not tire or grow weary,
Until he has established it on earth,
and the Isles wait for his doctrine.

Be attentive, people, to my voice;
nations, lend me your ear!
For from me will come doctrine,
my Law will be the light of the peoples.

My justice approaches, my salvation comes,
my arm will be justice for the peoples,
It is I whom the Isles await,
it is in my arm that they hope.[15]

What is this Servant? Is he a particular man? Is he the personification of Israel? We know the discussions of the exegetes, the multiplicity of solutions proposed. At one time it seems clear that it refers to an individual, and at others it is the people itself that seems definitely designated. Perhaps it is good that a certain ambiguity remains, perhaps this very ambiguity has a profound significance: How could the prophetic Spirit have separated Christ from his Church?

The same universalism whose inspiration stirs the book of Isaiah appears in more than one psalm:

I will sing praises to you among the peoples, O Adonai,
I will sing praises to you among the nations!

I will recall your name in all the ages,
and the peoples will praise you forever![16]

And during the time that followed the Exile, the great fact of the Dispersion of Israel in the midst of the nations is interpreted by some as a providential fact, permitting the Chosen People to accomplish its missionary vocation. It is understood in this way by the author of the Book of Tobit, who sums up his teaching in the song that he places on the lips of the old Tobit after the disappearance of the angel Raphael:

You are great, Lord, in eternity,
and your reign extends to all the centuries. . . .

[15] Is 51:4–5.

[16] 57:10; 45:18. Cf. 47:2.

All you peoples, clap your hands,
celebrate Yahweh with shouts of joy!

Cf. Joseph Schmidt, *l'Idée missionnaire dans le psautier*, supplement to the *Union missionnaire du clergé* (July 1934).

Celebrate the Lord, children of Israel,
  and praise him before the nations,
For he has scattered you among the nations that do not
    know him
  so that you might recount his marvels and so that you
    might make known to them
  that there is no other all-powerful God but him alone.[17]

Yet, on the other hand, the Sinai covenant remained, inviolable, along with the Law and its thousand observances, and the more time that advanced, the more rigorous became the measures of protection and isolation of the holy people. "I have separated you from the peoples so that you might be mine!": this order from Leviticus (20:26) is reinforced, from the time of the Exile, by the group of Ezekiel and his disciples. It was reinforced again, upon return to the holy land, by Nehemiah and by Esdras. Thanks to the persevering work of the scribes, the holy people was not only separated; it was, so to speak, sequestered, like the Holy of Holies of the reconstructed Temple. It was just as true in the Dispersion as on the soil of the homeland: "The Jews", says Haman to his sovereign Ahasuerus in the little book of Esther, "are a nation living apart among others, and their laws differ from the laws of all other nations."[18] The attempt at the Hellenization of Palestine, under Antiochus Epiphanius, provoked an even stronger reaction: it was from this time that, along with the revolt of the Maccabees, the constitution of the Hassidic faction dates, a faction which would become famous under the name of Pharisees, which is to say, the "separated".

Thus the Jewish people, with its twofold treasure: its worship, always more national, and its God, always more universal, became a living contradiction. It was not simply a question of two currents confronting each other, between which it would be permissible to choose. The conflict was more internal. This whole religion was summed up in two demands that seemed incompatible. How could it renounce its universal mission, which was its whole reason for being and which alone explained it to itself? But how could it devote itself to it without

[17] Tob 13:1–4.

[18] Est 3:8. And the letter of Pseudo-Aristaeus (second century B.C.): "Our law-giver, instructed in all things by God, has enclosed us within inviolable barriers and within walls of iron, so that in nothing we mix with other nations, we keep body and soul pure."

denying itself, since its structure was so rigorously and narrowly determined? No child of Israel could forget the words of Deuteronomy: "Yahweh has chosen you for himself to be a particular people among all the nations that are on the surface of the earth."[19]

Hence an inextricable situation. To get out of it, some sought refuge in a solution of despair: without abandoning in principle the great views of the future bequeathed by the prophets, they left it to God alone to take care of achieving them; the conversion of the Gentiles and the Messianic peace by which it would be followed would be the work of a miracle by Yahweh, in the day of his power: this is the solution that can be called eschatological.[20] Others, animated by true zeal but hindered by the rigors of the Law, could only meagerly open the door of the Kingdom halfway to those they converted—the "proselytes", those who "feared God": a bastard compromise that, despite what they said, constituted a regression. Others, finally, transforming their theocracy into an arrogant "nomocracy",[21] no longer thought of anything but making the Law a definitive "fence" that would no longer merely protect Israel but also reject forever the scorned Gentiles. Such was the celebrated Akiba, commenting on the verse from the Song of Songs "My beloved is white and red":

> When they hear these praises, the peoples of the world say to the Israelites: We want to go with you, we want to seek him with you. But the Israelites reply to them: You have no part with him; my beloved belongs to me, and I to him.[22]

By this third solution, which prevailed increasingly with a number of its representatives, Israel renounced its mission, it closed its ear to the call from above. It was definitively twisted, it seems, by this aggravated, defensive reflex.

---

[19] Dt 14:2.

[20] For example, in Psalm 86:9–10:

> All the nations that you have made will come
> to lie prostrate before you, Lord,
> and give glory to your name.
> For you are great and you work wonders:
> you alone are God!

[21] Joseph Bonsirven, *Sur les ruines du Temple*, 142.

[22] On this attitude of one part of the Jewish nation, there are indications in M. J. Lagrange, *Le Missionnaire chez les Juifs* and *Le Judaïsme avant Jésus-Christ.*

Its whole history ends therefore in an impasse. If we forget for a moment that Christianity is going to come out of it, Judaism of the first century appears to us, according to an expression of Alfred Loisy, like "a singular religion that can no longer be that of one nation and that cannot be that of the world".[23] No means for Israel to be faithful both to its vocation and to its being, no means of surviving without losing its reason for living—unless through a transformation of its whole self, through an extraordinary and unforeseeable change, through a death according to the letter for a rebirth according to the spirit. Now, that very thing had been proclaimed. The message of it has been confided to the most interior and tender of the prophets, Jeremiah:

> See, the days are coming, declares Yahweh,
> when I will make with the House of Israel and the House of Judah
> a new covenant;
> Not like the covenant I made with their fathers
> on the day when I took them by the hand
> to lead them out of the land of Egypt. . . .
>
> But here is what the covenant will be
> that I will make with the House of Israel
> when those days have come, declares Yahweh:
> I will place my Law within them,
> and in their hearts will I write it,
> And I will be their God,
> and they will be my people! . . .[24]

It is from this passage, quoted at length by the Letter to the Hebrews,[25] that the term "New Testament" originates. A wonderful anticipation! Such was in fact to be the work of the Messiah.[26] So it was not without a profound feeling of its vital need and of the meaning of its history that, as the "fullness of time" approached, Palestinian Judaism was centered in the expectation of the promised Messiah. The voice of the prophets had long since ceased to resound, and yet never

[23] See also J. Bonsirven, *Le Judaïsme palestinien au temps de Jésus-Christ*, 1:71–72.

[24] Jer 31:31–33.

[25] Heb 8:8–12.

[26] See Louis Richard, *Israël et le Christ, dans Israël et la foi chrétienne* (Paris-Fribourg: Luf, 1942), 83–119. "A conflict between the letter and the spirit; a conflict between the sacred particularism and the universal vocation; it is one and the same drama, which attains its supreme crisis at the time when Christ comes to fulfill the Promise. . . ."

more than at the beginning of the Christian era had the liberator of Israel been anticipated.

This anticipation itself was full of new contradictions, and one can say that it, even much more than our present faith, took place, according to the words of the Apostle, "per speculum et in aenigmate". So it is not surprising that, when the Messiah finally appeared, many of his own did not recognize him: having themselves become that "nation without understanding" of which Deuteronomy spoke.[27] But, for the little flock, docile to the illuminations of the Spirit, the horizon that had seemed closed was torn open: Jesus does not come to destroy but to complete; he comes to fulfill all hopes, to remove all contradictions. Beyond Moses, he accomplishes the promise once made to Abraham: "All the families of the earth will be blessed in you."[28] The old Simeon can sing in his joy: "Lumen ad revelationem gentium, et gloriam plebis tuae Israël [A light for the revelation of the Gentiles and the glory of your people Israel]." For, heir of Israel, Jesus transforms it into the Church.[29]

When, having returned to his Father, the resurrected Christ sends his apostles, as we saw at the beginning, to preach the gospel to every creature, he is thus only clarifying the meaning of his whole work, expressing a conclusion that is self-evident. When he speaks as the Son of God, he speaks at the same time as the son of Israel. He confides to his disciples the mission he received from his Father and that which he inherited from his people. Since he is son of missionary Israel, the Church that he founds to continue Israel can only be missionary.

Missionary Church, Catholic Church, this is in fact all one thing. One characteristic of the true Church, catholicity is not properly speaking a thing, an objective given, a reality that is in some way material and tangible. At least it was not so at first. It is still only very slightly so today, and it will perhaps never be so fully, if it is true, as a number of theologians have thought, that the "torch of the gospel, which

---

[27] Dt 32:21; cf. Rom 10:19.

[28] Gen 12:3.

[29] M. Isidore Lévi (*Revue des études juives*, 41:7) attributes to Saint Paul the "stroke of genius" of a rupture with the Law. Father Lagrange responds justly, *Le Judaïsme avant Jésus-Christ*, 272: "Saint Paul's stroke of genius could be produced only as a result of a new fact: the coming of the Messiah. No genius, whatever it might be, could force Judaism to break with the Torah revealed by God, with the intent to give satisfaction to human aspirations if, beforehand, God's intervention had not been noted."

must go around the universe", illumines new regions only by letting those that it had first visited fall back into shadow.[30] But whatever might perhaps be too confident in this hypothesis, it is certain that catholicity is not only an empirical fact. It is an essential attribute and not a superadded accident. It is above all a fact of consciousness. It is an idea and it is a force. It is an ambition and it is a necessity. The Church is catholic because, knowing herself to be universal by right, she wants to become so in fact. Her catholicity is her vocation, which is mingled with her being. She has been aware of this vocation from the first day; she will remain faithful to this vocation until the last day. The rest, the alternatives of success and failures, advance and retreat, do not always depend on her, and her nature could not be affected by them. But insofar as she has not attained the dimension of the world, she cries out through the mouth of the Prophet: "Angustus est mihi locus, fac mihi locum ut inhabitem [This place is too narrow for me; make room for me to dwell in]" (Is 49:20).

It is Saint Gregory of Nyssa who assures us of it,[31] and all the Fathers say it to us with him. For them, the Church can only be coextensive with the *oikoumenè*. Now, this is not simply because the *oikoumenè* was then a synonym for the Roman Empire. Despite the illusions that several of them entertained on the subject of the actual extension of Christian preaching,[32] and despite the rhetoric which they too often devote to celebrate its triumphs, they cannot ignore the fact that paganism remains intact in certain regions. In expressions such as "per orbem terrae Ecclesiae latitudo diffusae", Origen is proclaiming a necessity, proceeding from the idea that he forms of the Church, rather than pronouncing a judgment of fact.[33] Saint Augustine himself knows that the Ethiopians, for example, have not yet received the gospel, and the same is true, in Africa, for innumerable barbaric nations, "barbarae innumerabiles gentes".[34] So, when he argues against the Donatists that

[30] Fénelon uses the idea in his famous Sermon for the feast of the Epiphany: "The river of grace, it is true, is not dried up; but often, in order to water new lands, it diverts its course and leaves only dry sand in the old canal. Faith has not died out, I admit; but it is not bound to any of the places it illumines; it leaves behind it a frightful night for those who have scorned the day, and it carries rays of light to purer eyes." Cf. Amos 9:7.

[31] Discourse on the baptism of Christ (PG 46, 577). Cf. Is 49:20.

[32] Summary of their opinions in Charles, *Dossiers de l'action missionnaire*, 37–40.

[33] Second homily on Genesis, n. 5. Origen knew how to see the real situation: cf. *In Matthaeum series*, 39.

[34] *In Psalmum* 71, nn. 11–12; *Epistula* 197, n. 4; 199, n. 46.

their church is not catholic, what he reproaches them for is not at all so much the small extent of their territory as their claim to be satisfied with it, to have confined the church to it without concern for other peoples, and to settle all problems among themselves, *inter Afros*. What, on the other hand, he admires and loves in the *Catholica* is the fact that, without ever agreeing to restrict herself to any one place, she goes "from East to West", "from sea to sea", to sing over the entire universe the ever-new song of universal charity.[35] She perceives the call of those "isles" that the Prophet once evoked, and she knows that it is she who has the mission to respond to it. For she applies to herself what the prophets proclaimed. Everywhere she reads herself in their oracles. It often requires an effort to find Christ there, so wrapped in mystery is his divine Person, but as for her, she recognizes herself there clearly,[36] and to the degree that her mission is accomplished, she is aware that the prophecy is also accomplished.

Dynamic catholicity and missionary impulse: there is no difference between the two. Or, if one insists on finding one, let us say that this catholicity implies that impulse, that this catholicity is its authentic and sincere self only if it is extended in that impulse, in order to take form, insofar as God makes it effective, in a realized catholicity.

II

Why the missions? It seems to me that we already hold the essential answer in the threefold form it can assume. Because it is the will of Christ. A will formulated by his own mouth as a precept to his apostles. A will already expressed in the whole of Scripture, through prophecies, in the long history of the proclamation and formation of the Church. A will, finally, inscribed in the very structure of this Church and in the consciousness that she has always had of herself.

To tell the truth, we will add nothing to this answer. Once theology has made every effort to grasp as fully as possible the object proposed by God to our faith, by as precise and as thorough a reading as possible of the great book of revelation, it does not have to push beyond. Such

[35] *In Psalmum* 149, n. 7. *In Psalmum* 57, n. 6: the movement of the Church is not one of turning in but of extension: "Huc veni, huc veni [say the Donatists]. Ecce Ecclesia per omnes gentes, incipientibus ab Hierusalem. Non dico: huc veni, ipsa ad te venit." Already Optatus of Milevis, *De schismate Donatistarum*, 1–2, c. 1.

[36] Augustine, *In Psalmum* 30, *sermo* 2, nn. 8–9; etc.

a pretension would be as absurd as it is sacrilegious. But nothing is more traditional, on the other hand, than for it to seek to understand this object, to clarify it better, to determine its *raison d'être*, to justify itself, in a way, by proceeding according to the analogy of faith. Is this not the method recommended again by the Vatican Council when it exhorted us to study the bonds that unite the different mysteries so as to understand their whole better? This is what we are going to try briefly to do, by asking ourselves why Christ wanted his Church to be missionary, or, in other words, what motives are at the basis of the work of the missions.

For this, we can use as our point of departure a remark made by Pius XI in the encyclical *Rerum Ecclesiae*. "To live in the fold of Christ", says the Pope, "without having any concern for those who stand miserably outside would be so contrary to the charity that we must have toward God and toward all men that it is pointless to make a long demonstration of it. God's love, which imposes itself on us as a duty, requires in fact that . . . we increase the number of those who know him and adore him in spirit and truth. . . . And can we give witness to our neighbor of a greater charity than by drawing him out of the shadows of superstition and by instructing him in the true faith of Christ?"

Thus, whether one takes up one's position from God's point of view or from man's point of view, the same duty of charity ordains missionary work just as it governs the whole apostolate. Besides, the glory of God and the salvation of man are two goals that are actually but one, according to the beautiful expression of Saint Irenaeus often recalled in recent times: "Gloria Dei, vivens homo." It will be enough for us, then, to ask ourselves at first what the exact relation is between the missions and this salvation or this life of man.

Now two responses present themselves, two responses that apparently clash, between which it seems that one might have to choose. Are the missions necessary in order to make salvation possible for the pagan, or merely to make it less difficult for him? Is it essentially a question of wrenching him from hell or of providing him with more numerous and more powerful means of grace? A more "rigorist" solution and a more "laxist" solution, between which many hesitate, fearing, on the one hand, to be too hard on those to whom the Good News has not been proclaimed, or, on the other hand, to diminish the urgency of missionary activity and thereby to extinguish the ardor of those who must leave everything in order to go to the Gentiles. The problem is, in fact, extreme, for both solutions raise inextricable difficulties.

On the one hand, it is not legitimate to found zeal on false reasons. Now it is false to say that, without a missionary, the "pagan" would be irrevocably given up to hell. We all know by experience what force "social pressure" exerts on the mind as well as on the will, in such a way that societies in which evil seems to us to reign in frightening proportions perhaps do not count many individuals who are gravely responsible in the eyes of God. In particular, it is not only permitted us, it is imperative for us to believe that the light of the Word illumines all men coming into this world and that, in a thousand anonymous forms, the grace of Christ can be everywhere at work. Do we know by what secret paths the man of good will can, across the aberrations received from his environment, slip into the harbor where God leads him? If we must maintain that the infidel is outside the normal conditions of salvation, it is in order to add immediately that divine power is above these conditions. Once it is not a question of appealing to considerations that might seem the most telling to us, personally, but of regulating our thought according to the teachings of the Church, we must then reject the "rigorist" solution.[37]

Will this be to profess that the end of the missions is simply to facilitate salvation for the infidel? But this solution makes the inverse mistake of implying, if not in what it actually declares at least through what it passes over in silence, that Christianity might not be absolutely necessary: as if Christianity did not always bring to everyone something for which there is no substitute as well as something which the world cannot do without. . . . In still another way, such an explanation is "laxist" in that it presupposes that the Christian could be content with less of an effort than the infidel: as if the evangelical parables did not warn us that each is to be judged according to the gifts he has received, and that from the one who has more light and strength, more will be demanded. Does the relative indulgence professed with regard to the infidel not cover a more dangerous indulgence with regard to the Christian himself, urging him in a way to be content, in a false

[37] See Louis Capéran, *Le Problème du salut des infidèles, essai historique, et essai théologique*, new ed., 2 vol. (Toulouse, 1934). By the same author: "La Mission de l'Église et les missions dans le plan providentiel du salut", *Union missionnaire du clergé de France* (October and December 1945). See also Alexandre Durand, S.J., *Le Problème théologique des missions*, "Le Témoignage chrétien" series (1942).

security, with a third-rate Christianity? One thinks of the invectives of Pascal—not totally unjust, it must be admitted—against those theologians who place the benefit of Christian revelation in the fact that, in the final analysis, it dispenses us from loving God. . . .[38]

Rigorism or laxity: How are we to escape this dilemma? If we remain locked into it, we have without a doubt let some error slip surreptitiously into the very givens of the problem. We must then go back to the point of departure and revise these givens. First of all, is the notion of salvation that is at their foundation any good? Is this notion not basically entirely negative? It makes salvation consist in the attainment of a certain level—the same for all—by which one escapes damnation, and in consequence it sees above all in Christianity a privileged means of attaining this level. But is it not proper, rather, to reverse the terms and to model our idea of salvation on the idea of Christianity? If, then, we believe that Christianity is first of all a law of love and that, in consequence, the salvation that it brings to the world, the realization of this law of love, is an essentially positive reality, another way is open to us. We could then say, borrowing an expression from Canon Glorieux, that, for the infidel in general, the missions are not so much a matter of life and death as of the fullness of life.[39]

Such an expression, I know, has been criticized. Certainly it is incomplete: and, indeed, its author has not at all claimed to enclose the whole theology of the missions within it. But, if understood well, it seems irreproachable. In the perspective we have just indicated, the evangelization of the pagans does not become for all that less essential, for the fullness in question here, far from constituting a kind of addition or luxury, must be considered the very essence of salvation. Let us say, then, if one wishes, that this fullness of life can itself become, in a sense, a question of life and death. In such a perspective, the conversion of the infidel to Christianity, just like the conversion of many a baptized who is at first unaware of his baptism, must not only permit him to attain more easily a certain frontier line: it must place him in a position to exercise an ever more excellent act. Christianity brings with it possibilities but also, at the same stroke, new obligations and

---

[38] Cf. Yves de Montcheuil, *Problèmes de vie spirituelle* (1945), 67 and 209–12.

[39] P. Glorieux, *De la nécessité des missions, ou du problème du salut des infidèles*, supplement to *Missionnaire du clergé* (January 1933). By the same author: *Rapport au Congrès de l'Union missionnaire du clergé* (Strasbourg, 1933).

responsibilities,[40] and the more the truth of its mysteries is imposed on the meditation of a soul, the more the salvation of that soul sees its level in a way raised.

Far from discouraging the zeal of the missionary, these considerations seem well suited to inflaming it. "Gloria Dei, vivens homo. . . ." Without doubt, many great missionaries, in the first ranks of which is Saint Francis Xavier, believed in a quasi-exclusive rule of the devil over pagan souls, and their apostolic ardor utilized this belief; but it was only their theology that had dictated it to them. In fact, we see many others, such as Matteo Ricci, on the other hand, generously open heaven to infidels.[41] All of them, basically, were moved by the same motive, and it is true to say of all of them that, the more they admired the richness and the beauty of the souls that God allotted them, the more they burned with the desire to communicate to them the Light of Christ, the beginning for these souls of an unsuspected ascension.

The revision that we have undertaken is not yet finished. Perhaps it would be fitting to criticize more radically or to go more thoroughly into the initial givens of the problem. In the text from which we took our point of departure, Pius XI spoke of the missions as a duty of charity. But if charity, as he reminded us at the same time, is the essential obligation of the Christian, if no one is a Christian except on the condition that he exercise it, who does not see that the missionary duty, a duty of charity toward God and toward neighbor, also includes, as it were, a duty toward oneself? So that it should not be necessary, in order to lay the foundations for it, to make an explicit appeal to the

[40] Why, a few pusillanimous spirits will perhaps then ask, trouble good faith, aggravate responsibilities, create formidable risks? Cf. Rom 7:7: "Peccatum non cognovi nisi per legem, nam concupiscentiam nesciebam, nisi lex diceret: non concupisces. Occasione autem accepta, peccatum per mandatum operatum est in me omnem concupiscentiam." A question similar to that which would ask God why he made us free, or why all children do not die at a young age, etc. A lack of confidence in God, who thus offers the corresponding strength along with light: if the Mosaic law, considered in its providential role, was nevertheless a benefit, how much more the law of grace! And who could maintain that the risks are not worth the difficulty of it? The missionary, like the educator, imitates God, who, in creating us, puts us in peril. Besides, such fears, supposing that they were in any way founded, could not stop a work otherwise necessary.

[41] He wrote, with respect to the Chinese: "We can hope of the divine mercy that many of their ancient sages were saved by observing the natural law with the assistance that God, in his goodness, will have given them. Idols then entered into that kingdom, but we know that they are little respected there; some even accord them no esteem." Henri Bernard, *Le Père Matthieu Ricci et la société chinoise de son temps, 1552–1610*, 1 (1937), 334.

need in which the infidel finds himself or to talk at length about the degree of urgency or about the precise nature of that need. Not that all the children of the Church must effectively devote themselves to the specific form of the missionary apostolate: that is self-evident. What is true of the Christian as such applies in very unequal degrees and in very diverse forms in concrete reality. . . . But if the gifts and calls of the Spirit are diverse, the Spirit himself is one, and the submission to this Spirit of love, without any consideration of utility or finality, orders the Church to conduct her missionary activity.

The Church is the body of charity on earth.[42] She is the living bond of those whom this divine flame burns. Her sole end is to maintain it and make it always go up more purely to heaven. But one does not possess charity if one does not want to spread it universally. It cannot be a good that one wishes to enjoy for oneself alone or a growth whose limitation one could in any way accept. No closed hearth could delude itself into thinking that it was conserving its warmth. The desire to spread everywhere in order to ignite everywhere the fire of divine charity, such is, then, the essential stimulus of the life of the Church, and the Christian feels this desire born and growing within him to the degree that he participates more in this life, to the degree that it is less he that lives but the Church and, through the Church, Christ who loves, wills and lives in him. The Church, then, lives only in a spirit of universality; in other words, she lives only as missionary. She does not begin through being realized on one point of the globe in order to want *then* to spread elsewhere; she could not have any existence outside her will to conquer all. If she did not try to be everywhere, she would not be anywhere. The fire does not start out being in order then to begin consuming. To be, for it, is to consume, and when it has ceased to do so, that is, ceased to win, it is dead.

This necessity within the Church has found its magnificent expression in these words of Saint Paul: "Si evangelizavero, non est mihi gloria: necessitas mihi incumbit; vae enim mihi si non evangelizavero [If I preach the gospel, that gives me no ground for boasting. For necessity is laid upon me. Woe to me if I do not preach the gospel!]."[43] An unconditional necessity, an obligation without counterpart. The impulse

---

[42] The following paragraphs were inspired by an unpublished work by Father de Montcheuil: *Quelques notes sur la raison d'être des missions.*

[43] 1 Cor 9:16.

comes from within. A call is heard also from outside, but it is not this call that determines it. "Vae mihi si non evangelizavero": mysterious and profound words. If I cease to evangelize, it is because charity has subsided in me. If I no longer experience the need to communicate the flame, it is because it no longer burns in me. But it should not, for all that, be said that missionary activity so understood is fed by an egoistical source. The Christian does not use the infidel he converts in order to realize himself, in the way an ascetic would by giving his belongings to the poor for the sole purpose of freeing himself. He does not maintain charity within himself on condition of the gift he makes to the other, like a reward he would obtain from this gift. His life is this gift itself, because to give is to participate in the divine Life, which is Gift. There is no duality in that, no self-absorption. The Christian offers his individuality to the divine charity so that it might be grafted onto it and so that it might live by it. He offers it as wood is offered to the flame so that it might burn.

At the same time as it is thus disinterested, the missionary attitude of the Christian is humble. Knowing that he possesses his treasure only in the act of giving, he knows that he needs the one to whom he gives. The richness that he seems to dispense to him does not have its source in him, but the apostle and the convert both receive it together from a common source.[44] God offers us access to life only by asking us to make the effort—each in our own singular way—to introduce our brothers to it, and we have truly received nothing unless we have tried to give it. In choosing us, God did not choose us over against others or to the exclusion of others but for others. When Israel resolutely turned in on itself, it ceased to be the Chosen People. There would not be on earth a single Christian life if there were not in at least one heart a desire for the conversion of all men, and a desire ready to be translated into action. In brief, in missionary activity, what is at issue is not merely the extension of the Church but her very existence.

We thus rediscover, through the analysis of charity, what history had taught us a while back about the nature of the Church. We could not

[44] Hence the inanity of the objection often made to Christian charity, for example in G. Guy-Grand, introduction to Proudhon, *De la justice dans la Révolution et dans l'Église*, 149–50: "When, by hypothesis, the gratuity is entire, what a terrible temptation of pride as well as of humility. To tell oneself that one rules one's equals from the full height of one's disinterestedness, that one gives them everything without asking anything of them, really to reflect on it, what an affirmation of power, or what possibility for contempt!"

conceive of it for an instant without a desire for universal conversion. Charity, in fact, respects neither person, race nor nation. It wants to embrace all. So, each time that a new human group is revealed differentiated either by its position in space or by its ethnic composition or its civilization, a mission is spontaneously organized with respect to it. The Spirit chooses apostles and urges them toward these new lands. It does not matter that the task is not finished elsewhere: charity does not tolerate slowness. No possible worksite is left unopened. If the missions proceeded from a considered plan of systematic conquest, such behavior would be poorly understood. But in its desire for universal expansion, nothing discourages or limits charity. Its progress is not at all cleverly methodical—although it knows how to put method at the service of its action. It goes just as well to people in decline, people who are finished, as to those who have a future before them. It certainly wants there to be a particular interest in centers of influence, such as Saint Francis Xavier seeking to convert the Chinese in order to have through them more of a hold on the Japanese. But Xavier had not shown any less zeal for the poor Paravas: people with brilliant destinies attracted no more charity than the others.

In summary, since divine charity is unable to exist without seeking to be everywhere, the Christian—let us say with the ancients, the *homo ecclesiasticus*, which is to say the man in whom the consciousness of the Church is incarnated in fullness—seeks to spread it everywhere. He knows that he possesses it only to the degree in which he seeks to spread it. The infallible sign, but also the only sign, that he has been touched by it is the fact that it leads him into its current. If the fire that Christ came to ignite has touched certain points of our globe first, it is because it was indeed necessary to approach it at one point, just as one sets a fire at one determined place. But this is in order to spread from there in all directions. Its nature is to burn everything. Or, if another comparison is wished, no more than one asks the living why he lives does one ask the Church why she is missionary. Or rather, one could well ask it of her, and she will be well able to reply by furnishing reasons, the very ones we have seen; but the final reason goes beyond these particular reasons, of which, for herself, the Church has no need. Insofar as she is not everywhere, her missionary activity is her life.[45]

[45] As we see, to found the missionary duty on the idea of charity is a very different thing from assigning to it, as one's sole motive, pity toward the infidel.

The preceding considerations, by which we have tried to clarify somewhat the fact of the missions by indicating its nature and its *raison d'être*, leave us with the feeling that they have in the process let fall the greatest part of the wealth that revelation had deposited in our hands. So it is with any effort at theological elaboration. A rational effort in which too much of the human enters in for divine truth not to seem reduced. How much theology is far from being really coextensive with its object! A task to which one must nevertheless devote oneself, because it is the law of our being. But let us at least know not to attribute to our theory and hypotheses an importance they do not have, let us be able to recognize that they have in particular the purpose of avoiding inaccurate representations, and that in order to rediscover the substance of doctrine and in order to nourish our spirits, it is important to return endlessly to the concrete sources of faith. So indeed, in leading us to the essential idea of Christianity, which is charity, our reflections have led us by the same stroke to the nature of the Church, messenger and organizer of this charity. They thus unite with the ecclesial perspective to which the direct examination of Scripture and Tradition had already directed us. And it is again this same idea of the Church that is now going to compel our attention if we seek, in conclusion, no longer so much the reasons or motives for missionary activity as its proper object, or the precise and immediate end at which it aims; if we ask ourselves, in other words, once we have admitted that it is a necessary work, in what, *hic et nunc*, it precisely consists.

Here again, we are tempted to be content with a first response, as apparently obvious as it is simple: Is the end of the missions not the conversion of infidel souls, in view finally of their salvation? Let us not introduce into our inquiry vain disputes of an overly finicky Scholasticism. It is perfectly just to say in general that the missions tend to procure the conversion and, in the final result, the salvation of souls, and no one will be surprised that the prayer of the Mass for the propagation of the faith begins by an invocation to God, who wants all men to be saved. The formula, then, can be retained: but on condition, we

---

In a parallel way, it could be, considering charity and religion as two particular virtues, that one should assign missionary activity to the latter rather than to the former, and it might have been useful to specify that in order to redress certain inaccurate ideas about the missions. It nonetheless remains true that, if charity is not just one virtue among others, if it is at the center of the Church's life as her soul, one is right to explain that life and its principal manifestations by means of it.

will specify, that this "salvation" be conceived, as we said above, in a positive way (let us say, then: salvation and sanctification); on condition that this "soul" be taken as a spiritual category rather than as a metaphysical category and that it not designate some kind of entity that would leave all corporal values outside of salvation; on condition that this "salvation of the soul" be considered, not in an individualistic way, but in its relation to a collective salvation;[46] on condition, finally, that it be a question less, as we have seen, of an end considered as extrinsic to the Church than of the end where her spontaneous activity is to lead.

But, if the formula is acceptable, it remains very general: for it is equally true of any apostolic activity. It is not specific, then, to the missions as such. The latter would normally have accomplished their task well before all men were converted! The nature of the missions is to bring the essential means of salvation to men who do not yet have them at their disposition. Now, these means are summed up in one single one: the visible presence of the Church in the midst of men. We conclude that the proper object of the missions is to bring to men this visible presence, that is to say, to found or, as the liturgy expresses it, to plant the Church in all the lands where she is not yet established: "*plantaverunt Ecclesiam*", is said of the first apostles. The Church, with the seven sources of life from her sacraments, with her works of teaching and mercy, with her faith, her hope and her charity, with her worship, her ceremonies, her perpetual sacrifice, with her traditional forms of religious life and her organized laity, with her priesthood and all her hierarchy.

"To plant the Church": after having encountered some resistance, perhaps, here and there, it seems that this formula has ended in winning over all theologians.[47] They have understood, in fact, that it is not opposed, on the same plane, to the larger formula of "conversion" or "salvation of souls", but that it better marks, within the goal of any apostolate, the particular goal of the missionary apostolate. One sentence from the encyclical *Rerum Ecclesiae*, moreover, brings out very

[46] We have left nearly entirely aside here this important point of view, which can be found developed in *Catholicisme*, chapter 7: "Le Salue par l'Église" [English trans.: *Catholicism* (San Francisco: Ignatius Press, 1988), chap. 7: "Salvation through the Church"].

[47] This result is due in large part to the numerous missiological writings of P. Charles, a certain number of which are collected in *Missiologie*, 1 (1939). Cf. Msgr. Bruno de Solages, *Pour rebâtir une chrétienté*, 148–52.

well this continuity between the two formulas: "The Church", declares Pius XI, "has the unique mission of leading all men to participate in the salvation of the Redemption while extending the Kingdom of Christ to the entire world."

But this "Kingdom of Christ", which is here synonymous with the Church, can itself be understood in two senses. The Church is a means, the great means of salvation, and she is also herself an end, the supreme end of creation. She is a visible and transitory body, and she is the Body of Christ, mysterious and eternal. Just as Christ is the way that leads to life but also the life itself in which this way ends, so, too, is the Church, according to the aspect under which one considers her: way of salvation, she is also the end; she is that spiritual unity in which the reality of salvation consists. Just as, in the first sense, she was once announced by the prophets, as we have briefly seen just now, so she is nonetheless present, in the second sense, in the heart of the Old Testament. She is there at first under the already very spiritual image of a reconciliation of enemy peoples under the protection of Yahweh, henceforth recognized as the Father of all. This is the marvelous vision described by the nineteenth chapter of Isaiah. Many historians hesitate or even refuse to attribute this to the prophet Isaiah himself, since its breadth renders it so anachronistic; one can, however, observe that the second chapter, describing the peace of Messianic times, had already proposed a similar view.[48] Whatever may be the case, let us reread that sublime page:

> In that day there will be a road
> from Egypt to Assyria;
> The Assyrian will go into Egypt,
> and the Egyptian into Assyria:

[48] 2:2–5:

> In the days to come
> the mountain of the House of Yahweh
> will be established at the summit of the mountains . . .
> and all nations will flow to it. . . .
> They will beat their swords into plowshares,
> and their spears into pruning hooks.
> No nation will lift the sword against the other,
> they will not make war any more.
>
> House of Jacob, come,
> let us walk in the light of Yahweh!

Egyptians and Assyrians will be united
in serving Yahweh.

In that day Israel will be a third
with Egypt and Assyria,
like a blessing in the middle of the earth.
Yahweh's blessing of the hosts that says:
Bless my people of Egypt,
Assyria, work of my hands,
and Israel my heritage![49]

In this same sense again, the Church appears in the Bible in the form of the figure of Israel, and it is thus that even in its national particularism, the Chosen People are presented as a symbolic anticipation, as the sacrament of that heavenly City in which the Church is to end. On the day of Yahweh, Jerusalem, long humiliated, will be lifted up in glory, all its dispersed children will be gathered within her walls, and it will draw to her all the treasures of the earth in order to make them serve in the worship of its God. This very specifically Israelite dream, which could so easily be made to convey a heavily carnal sound, is precisely the one at which the Church rejoices on the day of her betrothals, on the feast of the Epiphany. It is here that she glimpses her own destiny:

Arise! be radiant! for your light is rising,
the glory of Yahweh is dawning upon you,
While darkness extends over the earth
and shadows over the peoples.

Here is the dawning of Yahweh over you,
His glory is made manifest over you;
And the nations walk in your light,
the kings in the brightness of your dawning.

Lift your eyes, look around you:
they all gather together and come to you;
Your sons arrive from afar,
they lead your daughters by carrying them.

When you see that, you will be radiant,
your heart will thrill and grow large;

[49] Is 19:23–25; see also 11:13. Cf. the 3d Sibyl.

For toward you will flow the treasures of the sea,
the wealth of the nations will come to you.

A multitude of camels will invade you,
and dromedaries from Midian and Ephah;
All these throngs will arrive from Saba:
they carry gold and incense,
they proclaim the glories of Yahweh. . . .

Who are these that fly like a cloud,
like doves to their cotes?
Yes, the ships are assembling for you,
and the vessels of Tarshish are coming first,

To lead from afar your children,
with their gold and their silver,
For the name of Yahweh your God,
for the Holy One of Israel who glorifies you![50]

Peace and the embrace of all peoples! The glory of the Holy City! Are we not in a full-fledged dream, a utopia? Is it not the hard reality, the terrible and ever-recurring reality of war, that of the ruin of the homeland and of the dispersion of its captive children, that has given rise, in contrast, to these sweet and brilliant chimeras in the minds of the seers of Israel? Yes, without doubt. But the visions of these seers are not at all like other visions. A divine force, coming from a distant future, makes them rise to the horizons of the soul while waiting to make them effective. Is their real perspective, at least, not purely eschatological? Yes again. But the Church is already, here below, in mystery, the figure of that final and transcendent reality; the Church, who gathers human beings into the unity of her body; the Church, the true Jerusalem, within whom all creation of man must find its place in order to be transfigured there:

Urbs Hierusalem beata, dicta pacis visio,
Quae construitur in celis, vivis ex lapidibus. . . .[51]

---

[50] Is 60:1–9. Cf. Micah 4:1–2.

[51] First form of the hymn of the Dedication (seventh century). Fifth strophe:

Angularis fundamentum lapis Christus missus est,
Qui parietum compage in utroque nectitur,
Quem Sion sancta suscepit, in quo credens parmanent.

There is no work more necessary or greater than to work, through all the chaos and all the heartbreak of this world, to construct this City.[52] Such is the *mission* of the Church. Such is the work of her *missions*.

Second Lecture
Reply to Objections

The missionary Church obeys Christ's order with the boldness of faith. The latter is indispensable to her, much more than it was to Peter throwing back his nets after the efforts of a fruitless night. For such an order is, from many sides, disconcerting. Whatever one might say at times, it is not so natural to man to seek to spread his religious convictions everywhere, even if they are loftier and sounder. In fact, not all religions are missionary. Actually very few of them are. The religion of the ancient Greeks was not; the Hindu religions are not. Hellenism and Hinduism did indeed conquer vast territories: but their extension was not the product of religious proselytism, it merely accompanied the progress of a higher form of civilization. Other cults, such as Manicheism and, to a certain degree, Mazdeism and several Greco-Roman mystery cults were missionary. And today, Islam and Buddhism (particularly in its Mahayanist form) are missionary. Islam manifests a prodigious power of expansion; Buddhism, older, perhaps

Cf. the article by Pierre Paris on this hymn in the *Bulletin Joseph Lotte* (February 1939).

[52] This is what Saint Bernard recalled to his son and father Eugene III by disturbing his conscience on the subject of the missions to the infidels: "The Gentiles! What will you respond to me about them? Or rather, if you question the above, what does the consideration respond to you? What were they thinking of, those of your predecessors who set boundaries to the gospel, who suspended the word of truth when there were still infidels? Yes, why has this 'swiftly running word' been stopped (Ps 147:15)? Who was the first to hold back its beneficent progress? As for your predecessors, perhaps some unknown reason or necessity made us an obstacle to their desire. . . . But we, what excuse do we have for doing nothing? In virtue of what assurance, in virtue of what conviction do we fail to introduce Christ to those who do not have him? Is it not unjust on our part to hold back the truth of God in this way (Rom 1:18)? And yet, it is indeed necessary that one day the communion of peoples be achieved. Do we expect faith to fall to them from heaven? . . ." *De la considération*, l. 3, nn. 3 and 4; Senlis trans. (Alger, 1944) (Pierre Dalloz [Grenoble, 1945]), 116–17. —The translation of the final words: "quandoque perveniat plenitudo gentium" is perhaps a little forced. But this does bring out well the relationship between the Bernardine definition and that which, five centuries later, the Jesuit Manuel Diaz would give: "We came from Europe to this end of the world in order to unite ourselves with the Chinese gentiles and to make with them one and the same body of Christianity" (Letter to the provincial of the Dominicans of Manila, June 26, 1639).

more dated, offers in its long history wonderful examples of disinterested preaching. Christianity alone, however, is integrally missionary, because it alone achieves all the conditions of a true universalism.

The obstacles it encounters are nonetheless formidable. Now these are not only external difficulties, resistance that, while suited to discourage its zeal in practical ways, could not make it doubt itself and the full justification of its ambition. There are also objections that, creeping into the heart of the doctrine, attack the very source of the missions. As if to dry up this source more surely, the most serious of them directly challenge the principle of Christian universalism. Some are of a theological order; others are of a moral or social order; others, finally, appeal to considerations of general philosophy, making history, psychology and even biology come to the rescue. . . . It is important to be familiar with the principal ones. . . . After having reviewed some of them in the first part of this lecture, we will devote the entire second part, not certainly to the strongest, but to the most current and the most virulent. If the pure exposition of doctrine has seemed to float a bit in the clouds, the exposition of objections will lead us back to earth. Undoubtedly we will have to note that the vapors it exhales when the Spirit abandons it have less consistency than our would-be clouds.

I

The theological objections arose particularly in the sixteenth century, and they were radical. We find them set forth in the two great leaders of the Reformation, Luther and Calvin. Is there any need to say that we will not recall them in a spirit of polemics? Lutherans as well as Calvinists have, since then, recovered the Christian tradition on the missionary duty with enough eagerness for there to be no longer a question of anything on our part but emulation of them.[1] Their historians, moreover, are the first to recognize the deficiencies that we must note on this point in the first generations of the Reformation.[2]

---

[1] The journal *Missionnaires de la Compagnie de Jésus* has devoted a special issue (November–December 1944) to the "Protestant Missions". The text of this issue, joined to that of the January 1944 issue on "The Missions and Christian Unity" was published in a booklet of 64 pages (Le Puy: Xavier Mappus, 1945).

[2] Georges Goyau, "L'Idée missionnaire dans le protestantisme et dans le catholicisme aux XVIe et XVIIe siècles", *L'Église en marche*, 1st series (1928), 89–124. François Rousseau, *L'Idée missionnaire aux XVIe et XVIIe siècles* (1930), 17–24. Auguste Lecerf, "Calvin et les

While Erasmus, in the name of Christian humanism, preached in 1535 a new crusade, as it were, for the benefit of the pagan peoples whose vast number had been almost suddenly revealed by recent discoveries,[3] Luther refused to do so, alleging three precise reasons. There was first of all on his part a historical prejudice: Christ's order, which he did not contest, had been accomplished by the end of the first century, and, in consequence, the special powers that the apostles had received in order to accomplish it had, by that very fact, expired. There was next a theological postulate: in Luther's eyes, the Turks—meaning Muslims—were specially charged by God to be the scourge of Christianity: it would thus have been contrary to the view of Providence to seek to convert them; as for the Jews and pagans, both had fallen through their own fault into the power of the devil: there was no point in drawing them back out of it. These two reasons were confirmed by an apocalyptic vision: the end of the world was near, it was perhaps going to occur in 1558; there could no longer be a question of launching great undertakings but only of waiting for Christ.

Calvin, whose cooler head was more open to certain historical proofs, did not fail to admit that there were "antipodes and other very distant peoples" who had never been able to receive the Christian preaching; but he judged that to go to them, it was necessary to await the hour when God himself would give the order, reestablishing the extraordinary functions of the apostles and evangelists, long since disappeared from the Church.

This position of Calvin, as strange as it might seem to us,[4] was nevertheless less implacable than Luther's. So this explains why his disciples returned more quickly to a sounder doctrine. In the middle of the seventeenth century, official Lutheranism insisted on the ideas of its founder, despite the repeated appeals of Leibniz. Gerhard reinforced those ideas by explaining, for example, that the inhabitants of Mexico were guilty of having rejected the gospel which the Ethiopians had once preached to them; Ursinus judged that one must not throw the mysteries of God as food to these dogs, to these pigs that the pagans

Missions", in *Les Précurseurs de l'idée missionnaire en France* (1928). J. Pannier, *L'Église réformée de Paris sous Louis XIII* (1922). Maurice Leenhardt, "Les Missions protestantes françaises", in *Protestantisme français*, "Présences" series (1945), 372–405.

[3] *Ecclesiastes sive concionator evangelicus*.

[4] On reflection it is less surprising: the *Docete omnes gentes* could no more, in itself, be addressed to the successors of the apostles than the *Tu es Petrus* to the successors of Peter.

are; the theology Faculty of Wittemberg declared that if a prince established the Church in pagan territories subject to him, this could be only a wholly secular act, in virtue of the juridical principle *cujus regio, ejus religio*. . . . On the other hand, more accessible to the influences of Catholic theology and of the missions themselves, the Dutch Calvinists were soon numerous in demanding back the institution of a Christian mission. The movement spread next into France, and we can say the cause was definitively won, at least in principle, starting in 1667, by Charles Drelincourt, pastor of Charenton.[5]

The state of mind of the first Reformers is explained in part by a state of mind prior to the Reformation. We know the contradictions of all kinds encountered by Blessed Ramon Lull in his at once bizarre and inspired propaganda in favor of the missions. In one of his poems, Lull had a hermit object to him:

> Ramon, when God wants the conversion of the world
> His Spirit will spread the torrent of wisdom
> And will give the knowledge of language to his servants;
> As in the times of the apostles, so will he do again. . . .[6]

Beyond the theological reasons put forward by Luther or Calvin, it is undoubtedly also necessary to take into account other causes, stemming from circumstances. The Reformation fought for a long time for its establishment in Europe, and the lands where it was first established were not then powerful colonizers.[7] A certain withdrawal can, moreover, be considered conformed to the needs of the work of reformation: "Before thinking to win the world", should the Church not

[5] A first attempt, as early as the sixteenth century, must be pointed out. Leenhardt, "Missions", 372–73: "Circumstances, from the beginning of the Reformation, were not favorable to the Huguenots. But these were the ones, nevertheless, who, in Protestant history, attempted the first missionary undertaking. Forced to emigrate, they sought to colonize the lands of the New World. But they did not separate from this concern that of giving witness to the pagans, the Indians. Under the patronage of that father of colonization, Admiral Coligny, a group of Huguenots left for Brazil; pastors accompanied them 'to attract the savages to the knowledge of salvation'. The leader of this group, through weakness of spirit or felony, we do not know, failed in his duty, betrayed his companions and promoted Catholicism and persecution in Buenos Aires. Pastors and colonists had the choice of fleeing to France or of dying as martyrs, not by the pagans but by intolerance." The affair was recounted by one of the Huguenots who returned to France (1578).

[6] Pierre Charles, *Missiologie*, 1:133.

[7] "Petite histoire des missions chrétiennes", by a layman, *Société des missions évangéliques* (1929), 63–64.

"think to save her own soul"? Before any effort at expansion, was it not fitting to assure first of all "the purity of the gospel"? Whatever these illusions may have been, some of which endured for a long time,[8] it is clear that the objections formulated by the first Protestant generations present scarcely more than a historical interest.

Perhaps the same is not completely true of another objection, more restrained, to tell the truth, which has made its way, in recent centuries, to Catholic theologians as well. Negligible in itself, it must nevertheless be pointed out because of its connection with a state of mind that is itself still only all too current. It concerns the idea that there are people who are cursed, whom it would be perfectly useless to want to evangelize.[9] The identity of these peoples, their geographical situation, the nature of the curse whose weight they bear comprise numerous variants. Let us merely say, without pausing at the colorful absurdity from which we could make an ample harvest here, that it is in general the Negro race that is the subject of this theory, which believes it finds its foundation in the curses of Noah against Ham and Canaan, reported in the ninth chapter of Genesis.

In reality, what we have here is a misinterpretation to which a thousand ethnographical or historical fantasies on the descendants of Ham have come to be added. And, too, such a prejudice was foreign to Christian antiquity. Many a witness of that period proves to us that blacks were very highly esteemed. Even in the sixteenth century, at the time of theological disputes relative to the slavery of blacks, no allusion was made to an anathema that would legitimate this slavery; under Jules II, a Congolese, the very son of the king, was made apostolic protonotary, and the matter was taken to be quite natural.[10] At the

[8] It is thus that Alexandre Vinet, raised in Protestant orthodoxy, first judged severely the attempts made by his coreligionists to carry the gospel to the pagans. Cf. J. D. Benoît, "Le Double visage de Vinet", *Revue d'histoire et de philosophie religieuses* (1941), 117. Similar illusions in Anglicanism. In 1793, Bishop Horsley declared to the House of Lords: "Even if it were even possible, which I deny, there would be no obligation for us Christians to try to convert the natives of India; the order of our Savior to his apostles to go out over the world was not addressed to us." And in 1814, there was such opposition to the nomination of a bishop for Calcutta that Middleton had to be consecrated secretly in the palace of Lambeth. (Coolen, *Anglicanisme d'aujourd'hui*, 89.)

[9] Pierre Charles, "Les Noirs, fils de Cham le Maudit", *NRTh* (1928); "Peuples maudits", *Dossiers de l'Action missionnaire*, no. 52; Raoul Allier, *Le Race nègre et la malédiction de Cham* (1930).

[10] It is through an error (an error in which his father, King Alphonse, already shared) that he is at times made out to be a bishop. Cf. Charles, *Dossiers*, 285.

end of the eighteenth century, Bergier's *Dictionnaire théologique* rejected the idea of the anathema as a ridiculous fancy. Heir of old rabbinical speculations, this legend seems to have been taken in first in Holland, by a few Protestant authors, who based it on a poorly understood text by Luther. It was then that it spread into circles where slavery was practiced, which had an interest in taking hold of it and spreading it. It is more paradoxical that it would find entry into Catholicism: it is, however, a fact that it experienced an enthusiastic reception there, both at first in some Jansenist circles around the end of the Great Century,[11] and then particularly during the last century.[12] The disillusionments that experience brought after the naïve theories of the eighteenth century about the "noble savage", the ruin of theological studies following the French Revolution, the success of the traditionalist school, which had to find this explanation by the Bible congenial, put into favor an insane doctrine, contrary, moreover, to the first principles of the faith.

The famous Antonio Vieira, S.J., said to his compatriots, in the sermon preached on Epiphany in 1661 in the royal chapel of Lisbon: "The nations are more or less black or more or less white according as they are more or less close or more or less distanced from the sun; and could there be anything more unreasonable than to imagine that I, I must be your master because I was born farther from the sun and that *you* must be my slave because you were born closer?" *Sermons*, Poiret trans., new ed., 1 (1869), 302.

[11] Cf. the *Lettre d'une personne de piété sur un écrit des Jésuites contre la censure de quelques propositions de leurs Pères Le Comte, Le Gobien. . . .* (1701), 13–14.

According to certain Jesuits, it was Ham, the second son of Noah, who had first come to China; according to others, it was Zoroaster, king of the Bactrians, who had founded the Chinese Empire. But, in the eyes of Navarette, the two opinions were not contradictory, for this Zoroaster, inventor of magic, was no other than Ham. . . . Thus, concludes the author of the *Lettre*, we see the Jesuits "change the curse to a blessing in favor of Ham and his posterity. This nation cursed by God through the mouth of Noah became the nation most constantly favored by God himself. The blindness of the human mind goes to that extent when God abandons him to himself in order to punish him for his pride." Cf. 36–37.

[12] See, for example, the *Lettre du capucin Zénobe, préfet apostolique du Congo, au Préfet de la Propagande*, December 23, 1894: "I do not believe I am mistaken in saying that the character of the Negroes will always be an incomprehensible mystery, so much so that we will never succeed in discovering their origin and in recognizing in it a kind of curse to which they are subject. If the curse of Noah falls on all descendants of Ham, and if the Negroes are the descendants of Ham, the whole mystery is cleared up, but this point cannot be clarified except by books of science and in a favorable climate. It seems to me that this would be a thing glorious to God and useful to souls, if the Sacred Congregation confided to experts the examination of these two questions . . ." (quoted by P. Charles, supplement to *L'Union missionnaire du clergé de France* [July 1932], 146).

Cf. the Chevalier de Paravey, in the *Annales de philosophie chrétienne*, 42 (1851), 23: "These Negroes, who undoubtedly descend from the common father of men but whom a divine punishment has degraded. . . ." See also Msgr. Alexandre Le Roy, *Les Pygmées* (1931).

Without wishing to enter into the secrets of consciences, secrets that belong to God, the Church teaches that there are no cursed souls and that everything must be tried for the salvation of every man up to his final moment. With how much more reason are there not cursed peoples! One could not admit this, even in watered-down forms, without wounding Christianity at its very heart.

On the other side of the horizon voices are raised giving witness to very different concerns. Some protest in the name of respect for souls, to whom an indiscreet propaganda would do violence; they rebel against this fanaticism that wants to impose its own belief; to Catholic proselytism they oppose at need, along with a Count de Keyserling, the indulgent and mild Buddhist benevolence, which never hurries conversions but knows how to wait patiently for a spontaneous maturation to be achieved in the end.[13] Others draw attention to the social dangers that missionary activity often presents. Social structures are a delicate thing, which a change risks overthrowing: Have we not thus seen anarchy, disorder and demoralization result at times from massive conversions? Or rather, if it was a question of individual cases, did not life become impossible for the new converts, cast by that very fact outside all the frameworks that sustained their existence? Two types of objections about which there is undoubtedly insufficient space to dwell at length, for they do not touch the root of our problem. They merely raise a thousand questions about apostolic practice, whose delicacy and complexity we have no desire to contest. The work of the missions is by no means an easy undertaking! The missionary can accept the counsels of prudence and discretion that are generously lavished upon him. Most of the time he is the first to see the difficulties that are pointed out to him. He knows that true zeal, always respectful of consciences, must become all the more delicate the more the souls he approaches are shaped by a refined culture, and must be all the more careful not to shake anything prematurely in the social edifice the more primitive the form of the society in question, or the more closely the structure is bound to religion itself,[14] as is the case for the

[13] *Journal de voyage d'un philosophe.*

[14] Cf. M. Sohier, *Treizième semaine de missiologie* (1935), 113 and 115–16: "The abolition of a custom that was unimportant in appearance often has consequences, incidents, whose depth we do not sufficiently realize. . . . Certain customs are so intimately linked to the whole of the indigenous organization that to suppress them hastily would shake the entire edifice: this is the work, not of years, but of five years and sometimes of centuries. To have

Islamic countries. He knows, too, that the apparent strangeness of a custom, or its distance from our Western customs, is not a sufficient reason to condemn it. But he also has cause to think that those who grow impatient with a zeal they judge to be aggressive perhaps lack a little warmth in their love of truth as also in their love of neighbor, and that they are not completely right in claiming Buddhism as their authority, for its benevolence has been coupled with an ardent missionary spirit.[15] He would also like to be sure that the prudent warnings against social upheavals never proceed from a desire to maintain certain populations in a more complete subjection. With good cause, Raoul Allier spoke of "the nearly revolutionary importance of conversion" in many lands.[16] There must not be an object of fear in this for us. If it is necessary to avoid certain abrupt changes that destroy without reconstructing, leaving beings helpless, it is normal, it is good for Christianity to carry its fruits into the domain of laws as well as into that of customs.[17]

More fundamental, against the very idea of mission, is the following objection, according to which the destiny of Christianity, the religion of Europe, would be inexorably linked to the destiny of Europe itself. I borrow the expression of it from a little book by Jean Schlumberger, *Sur les frontières religieuses*:

---

prohibited slavery or polygamy, from one day to the next, without the necessary transitions, would have been to throw to the ground the whole economic structure and family life of the black society. And their progressive suppression is without danger only if it is fortified by a real knowledge of the difficulty to be overcome."

Raoul Allier, *La Psychologie de la conversion chez les non-civilisés*, 2:307: "[If the mission] brought about the pure and simple legal abolition of slavery, it would risk leading to a sudden disorganization of the social classes, an unleashing of antagonistic passions and perhaps a true catastrophe."

[15] What is generally called Buddhist charity does not merely include the *maitri* (benevolence) and *karuna* (pity) but also, especially in the Great Vehicle, the *Dana* (gift), of which the best kind is the "gift of religion". It is in this sense that Sakyamuni proclaims, in chapter 27 of the *Lotus of the Good Law*: "I am the Master of the Great Alms" (Burnouf trans., 287).

[16] Allier, *Psychologie*, 2:325. See also, 308, on the Negro slaves of the Antilles: "These miserable ones, whom the White mistreats like vile objects, learn that, by the same right as all men, they are the children of God, loved by him, sought by him in their misery, invited by him to the privilege of his communion. They experience a need, at first vague, then more and more specific, they whom the world scorns, to respect themselves, to make themselves respectable, at least in their own eyes. . . ." And 332, 347–48, etc.

[17] For a concrete examination of some of these problems, precise indications will be found in the two works by Joseph Wilbois: *Le Cameroun* (1934); and *L'Action sociale en pays de mission* (1938).

> It will indeed be necessary for Christianity to recognize in the end that it cannot undermine certain great religions like Islam or Hinduism. It makes appreciable progress only where Christian populations are established and thrust the aborigines aside. On the only terrain where it might still hope for such conquests, black Africa, it is reduced to leading an unequal fight against Islam, which is much more capable of adapting itself to primitive peoples without being degraded. Everywhere, on the surface of the globe, the division into zones of influence has been made, positions have been taken. . . . Each of the great religions into which the world is divided has proved capable of developments, variations, refinements and even affectations that allow it to shelter all kinds of spirits. The dreamer as well as the practical man, the mystic as well as the moralist, the sensual as well as the ascetic find ways of settling down in it. There undoubtedly exist in Buddhism and in Islam all the doctrines and sects corresponding to the various nuances of Christian religiosity. To leave one system of belief in order to enter into another is to change one's civilization much more than to change one's religion. It will indeed be necessary for Christianity to end by accepting this obvious fact, that it is tied to a culture and to modes of thought that are not universal.[18]

To tell the truth, this "obvious fact" hardly disturbs a believer, for he knows, he experiences that his faith is something different, that it is essentially different from what it seems to be to someone who observes its manifestations from outside. It is nonetheless true that many appearances, either in Christianity itself, such as it is thought and lived, or in its history and in its effort at conquest, give at first glance great weight to the objection. Especially since it proceeds from a way of thinking that, without reflecting on it, Catholics have shared, and sometimes still share, with a number of unbelievers. Not so long ago—but it is true that so many things have changed since then—one of the greatest historians of the Church, Msgr. Louis Duchesne, wrote: "The religion of Jesus Christ, being the only true religion, is destined to become the religion of mankind. Nevertheless, because of its long and close union with the civilization of Europe, it seems that its spread might have to progress at the same pace as the conquests of that civilization."[19] Moreover, some time prior to that, in his intransi-

[18] Published first in the *Nouvelle revue française* (October 1934), 550–52. Numerous similar judgments in the nineteenth century, after the discovery of Buddhism in the works of Eugène Burnouf. See also P. L. Couchoud, *Jésus le dieu fait homme* (1937), conclusion.

[19] *Les Origines chrétiennes* (mimeographed lecture).

gent love for the Roman liturgy, Dom Prosper Guéranger was led to profess a still more narrow principle. In his opinion, the unity of the Church could be realized only in a true uniformity, and he conceived a reunion of the Christian Churches only through a conversion of all dissident churches to Latinism. Outside of that, according to him, there was no means of "sealing the brotherhood". He even decided, imposing his views on the Church with as little modesty as historical sense, that such had always been "the policy of the Roman Pontiffs"; and this "policy" scarcely cost him, he was so persuaded that outside Latinism all was or could be only "bastard Christianity", impotence and ugliness. . . .[20]

Who today does not see the fatal danger of such illusions? From the day when, with eyes opened onto an enlarged universe, one perceives that latinity, or the Greco-Roman culture, represents only one of the successes of human effort—even if it is for us the most perfect and only livable one—does this discovery not go to affect our idea of Catholicism, in which we will now be tempted to see but one of the religious forms that humanity has given itself? And if, in a period of conquering optimism, in which Europe believed itself certain to dominate the world through its culture as much as through its weapons, it was accepted without reservation that the fate of Europe and the fate of Christianity were connected, is there not a danger that, in a movement of disillusioned withdrawal, some will continue to link the fate of Christianity with that of a Europe whose decline they believe they perceive, undoubtedly prematurely? Thus, after having thought they could westernize the Orient without difficulty, some began to declare that it was necessary to renounce as a chimera the plan to Christianize it. "The East is the East", they repeated, "the West is the West—and Christianity is a thing of the West." A new form, on a much larger scale, of the first objection addressed to the Catholic missions, when

[20] *Institutions liturgiques*, 2d ed., 2:657–58, 668–69, 671. Likewise, 3:500–501, "Lettre à Mgr. l'archevêque de Reims sur le Droit de la Liturgie": "I well know that the variety of ecclesiastical usages introduces harmonies into the general plan; that it is written that the robe of Europe is diversified in its colors; but what is to be said? because, on the general plane of being, the power of God has been able to arrange in a marvelous concert the light and shadows, the monsters and perfect beings, . . . does it follow that the monsters must be applauded for not being perfect? . . ." As we have no difficulty in seeing, the principle at play in such declarations goes well beyond the question of the appearance to be given a few ceremonies or the language to be employed in offices. . . .

pagan wise men, like Celsus,[21] or Porphyry,[22] laughed at the mad claim flaunted by Christians, those new barbarians, to unite all men in one and the same faith. To each people its gods. To each civilization its great religious system. The rest is a chimera. . . .

One has already accomplished a great deal by not giving rise to the objection in the exposition one makes of the doctrine or in one's way of acting. It belongs to the power of the Holy Spirit to overcome it by showing in point of fact that all cultures can be Christianized, just as it has long since been shown in point of fact that people whom everything divided could be united in the worship of the one God. Will we add that, beneath all the diversities of superstructures that the centuries have built, there is in human nature a common base and, as it were, a common platform, where Christianity must find its foundation? Such an assertion is susceptible to many meanings, more than one of which admits of difficulties. At one time great appeal was made to a base of "primitive revelation", which it was a matter of rediscovering everywhere by purifying it of its scales: an ingenious theory, which overflowed in torrents of digressions, in the fine day of traditionalism. Since then, one seems to count rather on a base of "natural religion", which must exist in any being participating in human nature and of whose conclusion Christianity presents itself as the extension. But from the time one wishes to be a little more specific about this so-called "natural religion", does it not appear to be rather a residue? Is it not above all what remains of a long Christian inheritance in beings from which Christianity itself has been withdrawn? The history of religions inclines us to think that human nature, taken concretely, never remains identical to itself and that, if always and everywhere it proves to be religious, not only is that religion never "purely natural", but, like the nature it expresses, it is particularized in a series of forms that are heterogenous to each other even in their roots. But, across so radical an objective diversity, and without being solidified into conceptions or identical systems, one and the same current seeks to spring up, one and the same aspiration arises that is discernible to the one who observes it in the divine light:

Mens non omnibus una, nec diversa tamen.

---

[21] Origen, *Contra Celsum*, l. 8, c. 72; l. 5, c. 37–40.

[22] *Ad Marcellam*, 15.

A multiform and dynamic unity which only a Christian is in a good position to observe because only Christianity gives meaning to it. Let us say, then, borrowing the language of the Bible and the Fathers of the Church, that any soul is naturally Christian, not because it possesses already an equivalent or, as it were, a first stage of Christianity, but because the image of God shines in the depths of this soul; or rather, because it is itself that image, and because, burning to be reunited with its Model, it can be so only through Christ.[23]

If Christianity must be the religion of the world, if it is truly supernatural and transcendent to any human effort, it then follows that it must gather into its midst all the diversity of this effort. This is one of the essential views that preside over the missionary impulse of the Church. The Church knows that she herself, far from representing one small fragment of this effort, has the mission of embracing it wholly, of purifying it, vivifying it, deepening it, and finally of bringing it to a successful conclusion, thanks to the divine revelation of which she has the deposit.[24] The universal mission par excellence, which she accomplishes not only through a feeling of justice toward all who merit life but also in the conviction that all races, all centuries, all centers of culture have played their part in bringing out the full value of her own treasure. "Scripture will be fully understood", a young Chinese said to me one day just after his baptism, "when it has been translated, read, meditated upon, in all the languages of the earth." He himself, who had wanted to receive the name of John to give witness of his veneration for the author of the Fourth Gospel, showed by his example alone how men coming to Christ from distant regions—and I do not take this word region solely in its geographical sense—can reveal certain

[23] Everywhere man is both more and less than this "natural" man that is imagined with more or less confusion. Man is both "fallen" and "called". This theological principle takes into account the aspirations of man and his powerlessness as well as his aberrations; it takes into consideration his essential inner lack of balance, observable in the history of humanity as well as in individual life. Christianity does not come to "add" something to human religions, except as one adds the solution to the problem or the end to the course. Outside it, religion always appears more or less primitive in its idea and perverted in its act; the religious effort of man (to judge objectively) miscarries because it is false. Christianity comes to redress it, to purify it, to transform it in order to make it come to a successful end; so that it is the religion, the one which effectively binds man to God.

[24] This refers not only to the effort of culture but to the religious effort itself. This is what separates the Catholic thesis from the thesis inspired by Barthian theology. Cf. Jean de Menasce (below, Appendix), pp. 423–27.

delicacies of Christian feeling whose nuance was without precedent until then. For her fullness and for her harmony, the Church needs the contributions of the entire world. Her missions tend to prepare, in all possible measure, profoundly indigenous churches, for only such churches are capable, through their personal reactions, to enrich the Christian heritage by participating actively in Christian life: "living churches", and not mere "spiritual colonies".[25] Christian universalism is thus not amorphous and undifferentiated; it is even less so to the degree that the unity it spreads is more profound, being more supernatural, and it would be to misunderstand its character thoroughly to see in it a kind of cosmopolitanism with a religious hue. Two reasons make of it something quite different from cosmopolitanism: it is differentiated and, at the same time, it is centered; divinely centered, humanly differentiated; two complementary and intertwined notes, like nature and grace. . . .

Of course, only those who have acquired a long, personal experience of concrete situations can determine with competence and security the application of these principles. In the face of the objections that unbelief makes to the mission of the Church, they must nonetheless be recalled in their full force and in all their clarity. The consequences that follow are immense, in the order of thought as well as in that of action,[26] and

[25] To study this problem on the basis of a concrete example, it would be fruitful to refer to the very fine work by Robert Ricard, *Le "Conquête spirituelle" du Mexique, essai sur l'apostolat et les méthodes missionnaires des Ordres Mendiants en Nouvelle-Espagne de 1523–24 à 1572* (Paris: Institut d'ethnologie: 1933).

[26] It is the whole question of "adaptation" that would have to be studied here. It is not, moreover, a matter of adapting Christianity but a matter of each civilization, each people, adapting itself to Christianity in its own way. We see that adaptation is something totally different from a process of conquest.

See the "Notes de missiologie" by l'Abbé Jules Monchanin, and the beginning of his article on "L'Église et la pensée indienne" in the *Bulletin des Missions* (December 1936), 254: "The Christianization of Indian thought presupposes that one has first tried—setting aside the accidental, the dross, failed impulses—to grasp it in the essence of its movement; that one next tries to rethink Christianity in the inexhaustible newness of the inspired writings; that one confronts it, finally, with the spiritual history of India in order to take it up, purify it, transfigure it. . . . Would it not be a fruitful method to base ourselves on Hinduism and Christianity taken as closely as possible from their sources, on Hinduism not yet crystallized into impenetrable orthodoxies but multiple and welling up, on Christianity at the conclusion of Revelation, not yet engaged in the Mediterranean civilization but already possessing the fullness of its truth and its life? The original Christianity and the Christianity of all time, susceptible to appearing traditional and new in the intellectual modes of India—original and of all time. . . ."

if it is not up to us to fix in detail the form, the time and the place, we no longer have the right to withdraw before them. The choice of the missionary Church is only between boldness and abdication. If she were to listen too much to the voices of current wisdom, not only would she be condemned to stagnation but she would admit to being human. Unfaithful to her mission, she would, moreover, commit the sin against the Spirit.

Let us recognize, then, that they are right who, supposing Christianity to be human, believe it incapable of conquering the world spiritually and who outline for it its own area of dispersal, as for Buddhism and Islam, by a kind of equitable division. They are being logical with themselves. Let us, too, be logical, let us understand that transcendence and universality go hand in hand, and let us not fear to draw the conclusions of so fundamental a truth. Let us recall, with Saint Augustine, that the Church, by right, speaks all languages, that she is that Ark in which all human diversities are to find a place, that Banquet Hall where the varied dishes come from all creation. Let us repeat with Benedict XV that she is essentially neither Latin nor Greek nor Slavic but catholic.[27] Spouse of Christ, her visible catholicity is the normal expression of her inner wealth, and—it is again Benedict XV who teaches this to us—her beauty must be resplendent in variety: "*circumdata varietate*".[28]

II

I must now approach, in this second part, a subject that it is impossible for me to pass over in silence without betraying the cause of the missions, I would even add: without betraying the Church. For I would betray her if, in discussing as I was asked to do the validity of the Catholic missions in the face of the objections that are made to them, I were to appear to ignore the fact that a brutal objection is rising up today, which intends indeed not to remain enclosed within

[27] *Motu proprio* of May 1, 1917, instituting the Sacred Congregation for the Eastern Church, A.A.S. (1917), 530. Cf. the *Encyclique sur saint Ephrem*, October 5, 1920, A.A.S. (1920), 466.

[28] Speech to the Consistory on March 10, 1919 (A.A.S. [1919], 98). These summary indications will be completed by the important study by Msgr. Paul M. A. Mulla, "Perspectives d'après-guerre en pays de mission et conditions d'une évangélisation libre et efficace" published in 1943 in the *Studia Missionalia* in Rome (1:137–65). See also in the *Studia Missionalia* in Rome (1:137–65). See also below, Appendix, pp. 423–27, the opportune supplementary reminders of Father Jean de Menasce.

the spheres of pure thought. We must take care not to be among those Christians of whom His Holiness Pius XII complained very recently, in his Christmas Message (of which only a false summary was available to most Catholics in France). "When earthly authorities make their power felt," the Pope says to us, "these Christians steal away in a timid flight", and, by their silence, they themselves become "the intermediaries for theories and prejudices issuing from circles foreign and hostile to Christianity."[29] We are referring, as you have guessed, to the racist objection. In our exposition of it as in our criticism of it, we will hold strictly to what concerns our subject.

To place it in its full light, let us quote first of all this passage from a book that has known the greatest publishing success of our day:

> From time to time, the illustrated newspapers place before the eyes of our good common people the portrait of a Negro who, in such and such a place, has become a lawyer, a professor or a pastor (let us say: or priest, or bishop), or something of the kind. . . . These common people, in the process of decline, do not have the slightest suspicion of the sin that is thereby committed against reason, for it is a criminal madness to dress up a being, who by his origin is half-ape, to the point that he is taken to be a lawyer. . . . For it is not a question only of dressing him up, as one would a poodle, nor of a scientific education. If one would devote the same care to the races endowed with intelligence, any of their representatives whatever would be a thousand times more capable of obtaining similar results.[30]

Certainly this is not because a man becomes powerful as his thought assumes an intrinsic value of which it was until then deprived. The sentences we have just read are nonetheless quite the opposite of a flash of wit. They are part, if we may say so, of a "system", the whole of which must be brought to mind before judging them.

This system is entirely taken up in the first proposition of the Syllabus that the Sacred Congregation of Seminaries and Universities sent on April 13, 1938, to our Catholic Faculties as well as to those of the entire world, enjoining them to apply their efforts to fight against the doctrine thus denounced. "The human races," says this first proposition, "by their natural and immutable characteristics, are so different

[29] French translation in *La Croix* of January 16, 1941, and *Semaine religieuse de Lyon*. (This text itself is not absolutely complete.)

[30] *Mein Kampf*, French trans. (Sorlot), 428–29.

that the most humble among them is farther from the most elevated than from the highest animal species." There is, then, no human race. Racial differences are essential. The races form a hierarchy that is not a simple contingent product of history but is given once and for all, in a way that nothing can change. In this hierarchy, the Nordic, or Aryan, race occupies the summit; the black race is at the bottom. Physical differences include with the same rigor psychic, intellectual and moral differences, for there is but one life, which has its mysterious expression in the blood. There are all kinds of consequences deriving from this in the various domains of activity. As for religion, notably—this is the fifth proposition of the Syllabus—it "is subject to the law of race and must be adapted to it". This is, in fact, what the principal theoretician of race, Alfred Rosenberg, says: "Religion, like aesthetics and folklore, is essentially relative, national, because it is a product of the blood." Whence, particularly, some consequences for the superior race, whose duty is summed up in an exclusive cult of itself, the scorn of inferior races and the search for the domination to which its superiority predestines it. Nothing is more exalting than to think of "the vocation of a supreme race, of a people of lords, who will dispose of the resources and possibilities of the whole earthly globe".[31]

Rosenberg compares the discovery of racism to the discovery once made by Copernicus. Biological truth, he adds, will not be stopped today by the Church any more than astronomical truth was. For the Church has nothing to oppose it with except a "senile doctrine".[32] She distributes as spiritual food a universalism inherited from Israel that would lead Europe to its ruin if it were to triumph. Doing so, the Church "takes up a position against Europe itself". But Europe will be defended, and universalism will be vanquished.[33]

---

[31] Ibid.

[32] Cf. Edmond Vermeil, *Les Doctrinaires de la Révolution allemande*, 235 and 250.

[33] Rosenberg, Nuremberg Discourse, September 6, 1938, against the Catholic authorities who "have allied themselves with Marxist atheism, which they feign to combat mercilessly but whose universalist attitude they in fact share. . . . A senile doctrine does not want to give in to the vision of a new awakening. The science of the races was not discovered in church pulpits; so the latter are not competent to judge it. . . . The universalist doctrine has long been distributed as spiritual nourishment. Many people have died of it, according to an old French proverb. . . . Despite that, Europe has never ceased to resist attacks aiming at the roots of its power. At present, it is beneath the sign of the racist idea that the great process of cleansing the European awakening is unfolding. . . ."

Cf. the *Nationalsozialistische Monatshefte* (November 1938), "L'Église romaine se détourne

It is this universalism that inspires the Church in her absurd missionary undertaking. Instead of wasting her time founding missions for Negroes or other people of color who have no need of them, she would be better advised to work for the physical and moral health of the peoples of Europe, who are "the receptacle of the spirit". Even if her activity were only a wasted effort! But, as we said just now, it is a criminal folly. A crime against Europe first of all, because the Christian spirit tends to make the superior nations forget their true mission and to establish between themselves and inferior peoples sacrilegious bonds: Does the Church, in fact, not maintain that a community exists of all those who have received baptism? A crime, too, against the Negroes, for, by bringing them closer to our civilization, "she makes of these healthy, although primitive and backward, men a species of lazy half-breeds." Besides, baptism cannot transform a Negro, nor can education civilize him, nor can instruction even penetrate his brain. The racial laws are "of iron". This base being has no intelligence. The Aryan must make him his slave by avoiding any contact with him.[34]

Appeal as constantly as racists may to what they call "the undeniable results of the science of the races", if we deduct from their theories the part of literary Christianity and that of ideological or political propaganda (not to speak of blasphemies), nothing remains to which the name of science applies. The writings of their three prophets: Count Arthur de Gobineau, Houston Stewart Chamberlain and Alfred Rosenberg (a Frenchman, an Englishman and one from the Baltic states!) are a mass of fantastic assertions and often of outrageous errors. None of these three authors has a solid scientific education.[35] If, moreover, they

---

de l'Europe": "Among the great ideological powers that are irreconcilably opposed to a community of white people defined by Nordic blood, there is the Roman Church. The vehement attacks by the Pope against the adoption of the racist idea by Fascism. . . . The direction of the world Church has demonstrated in a very clear way that she has decided to oppose by all means a reconstruction of Europe inspired by the spirit of the North. In doing that, the Roman Church is taking a position against Europe itself." (This journal, edited by Alfred Rosenberg, was "the only official ideological journal of the National-Socialist party".)

[34] *Mein Kampf*, 401. Gunther Hecht, "Le Problème des races dans les colonies" (quoted by J. M. Sédès, "Le Racisme en Afrique", 38–41). In 1915, the *Alldeutsche Blatter* was already becoming indignant about the egalitarian errors engendered by the gospel, which make of a baptized Hottentot the brother of a German Christian (Raoul Patry, *La Religion dans l'Allemagne d'aujourd'hui* [1926], 172–73).

[35] See the articles by Pierre Charles and Doctor Ernest Van Campenhout in the issue devoted to racism by the *Nouvelle revue théologique* (1939). Gobineau himself, who lacks neither

are agreed in proclaiming the absolute superiority of a predestined race, their agreement ceases as soon as it comes to giving a precise designation of it: proof that it was not the observation of facts that led them to their theory. For Gobineau, for example, the "Arians" (this is what he always says) are very far from being confused with the modern German, while the Jews form one of their branches.[36] For Rosenberg, on the contrary, the latter constitute the most unclean race, a kind of "body of Satan" that, in the manner of ancient Manicheism, he opposes to the mystical body of the Aryan community. . . .[37] It is true that we are here in the region of symbols and myths, and more than anything in that of actual judgments: and, too, is not everything mythical in that brain that gave birth to *The Myth of the Twentieth Century*? Not daring to reject into outer darkness a man whom, despite everything, humanity proclaims as great, or perhaps hoping thereby to favor a movement of "Nordic Christianity", the same author makes Jesus an Aryan. But this is in order to add that his authentic doctrine has been lost: from the time of Saint Paul, Christianity has been perverted by the twofold Jewish and Socratic element; a twofold ferment of universalist spirit that Catholicism developed to the maximum and which it is in the end necessary to reject.[38]

To criticize in detail their scientific claims would be to speak too seriously of such lucubrations. If we question true scholars, all would reply first of all that no "pure races" exist today; racists, moreover, find themselves obliged to agree;[39] so, following Chamberlain, they

talent nor a certain erudition, does not draw his doctrine from a truly scientific study. He himself has said of his work, in the foreword: "It is the expression of instincts I brought along with me at birth."

[36] Count Arthur de Gobineau, *Essai sur l'inégalité des races humaines*, 2 vols. (Paris, 1853).

[37] The same antithesis in *Hitler*, etc. Cf. Vermeil, *Doctrinaires*, 226–28.

[38] Vermeil, *Doctrinaires*, 232–33. These affirmations are borrowed by Rosenberg from Chamberlain. Among the Christians of Germany, several, reviving Gnostic doctrines or Marcionism, rejected the Old Testament and made Jesus' teaching "an Aryan protest against the Jewish spirit" (Party, 163–65). The New Testament criticism and the ideas concerning primitive Christian history held by contemporary racists were inspired particularly by the fantasies of Chamberlain and Nietzsche. For more details, see *Israël et la foi chrétienne* (1942), first chapter: "Un Nouveau 'front' religieux".

[39] Thus H. F. Günther, official theoretician of racism: "Nearly all Germany, whether it represents the pure 'Nordic' type or not, is cross-bred and contaminated by suspect elements, by corrupting or degrading influences. Corporally and spiritually, all men of today are hybrid products, and they are continually exposed to dangers of aberration" (Spenlé trans., in *Le Pensée allemande de Luther à Nietzsche*, 190). Gobineau thought that the cross-breeding was

refer "in advance" to their ideal of racial purity. The different attempts made to classify races will convince us then that this is a complicated work, for which science does not have the means today of obtaining a successful conclusion. Above all, no criterion, whether paleontological, biological or psychic, exists that permits us to suppose that there are human races that are essentially different from each other.[40] As for the idea of an essential superiority of one race with respect to others, superiority going to the point of constituting a true difference of nature, it is with even greater reason insupportable.

Before coming to experience, which must be the judge here in the final event, let us make a twofold remark. In the first place, whether it be monogenism or polygenism—a question that science has not at all resolved and undoubtedly is not close to resolving—the question of the unity of human nature does not necessarily depend on it. In order for humanity to form but a single family—let us say, in the spiritual sense, a single race—in the unity of its origin and of its divine destiny, it is not absolutely necessary for all the individuals who ever composed it and who compose it still to descend from one, unique couple, or even from one branch or line, and more than one wise man of pagan antiquity had already risen to the idea of a relationship of all men, outside of any question of origin and blood.[41] In the second place, the somatic differences that one observes between human groups, even if they were much more considerable, would not necessarily include the irreducible differences that one speaks of in psychic structures. In other words, no absolute correlation exists between "psychism" and "blood". Do we not know that man of any race is much closer, somatically, to anthropoid apes than the latter are to other mammals? That is a tangible fact, which racism fails to recognize. "Zoologically speaking,

---

so far advanced that one could not go back and that humanity was in consequence doomed to an irremediable degradation.

[40] For example, Ernest Van Campenhout, *Le Problème des races au point de vue anthropologique*, 201 and 202: "It is impossible to imagine pure races. . . . As for the superiority of 'pure' races over crossed races, this is, at the very least, an audacious affirmation. . . . The racist tendencies expressed by German anthropologists and politicians do not rest on any scientifically demonstrated fact." See also J. Deniker, *Les Races et les peuples de la terre*, 2d ed. (1926).

[41] Cf. Marcus Aurelius, *Thoughts*, 12, 26: "You have forgotten what sound relationship reunites every man with the human race: a relationship, not of blood and birth, but participation in the same intelligence. You have forgotten that the reasonable soul of each is a god, a derivation of the supreme Being."

humanity represents an exceptional and strange group: necessarily differentiated within itself without ceasing to be mutually fruitful, hardly separated anatomically from other primates."[42] Isn't the whole paradox of the "phenomenon of man" contained in a way in this observation, so strongly exploited by the works of Father Teilhard de Chardin?[43]

It is at least obvious from these various remarks that the racist affirmations are unfounded. Experience—that resulting from history and that offered by actual observation—permits us to add that they are false. Even in the case of populations of the black race that are generally more backward, the verdict of experience is perfectly clear. What would it be if we did not give such an advantage to the adversary by restricting ourselves only to these extreme cases? For let us not forget that what is actually at stake is not only the fate of a few small tribes in the center of Africa or Oceania: it is the fate of the Chinese, it is the fate of our Algerians, it is the fate of the Czechoslovakians and the Polish, the fate too, perhaps tomorrow, of the "denordicized" French. . . .[44] A man who had at his disposal the most extensive and varied means of information was able to write:

> It is an error to consider the indigenous as men of an inferior race and beings of a limited mind. Long experience teaches us, on the contrary, that the peoples of the Far East or of the Australian hemisphere are not always inferior to the inhabitants of our lands; that they can even rival them in intellectual acuity; that, if we encounter in men living in full

---

[42] Pierre Teilhard de Chardin, "Les unités humaines naturelles", *Études*, 240 (1939), 11.

[43] Apart even from biological considerations, the differences of mental structure between the various human groups have at times been greatly exaggerated. Some have used the theories of Lucien Lévy-Bruhl on the "primitive mentality" in order to preach a politics of segregation, to enlarge the trench that separates the civilized from the "savage" and to relegate the latter to the fringes of humanity. That was one abuse against which Lévy-Bruhl protested and which helped to make him tone down more and more the formulas of his early works. See in particular his explanations in *Nouvelle revue française*, September 1, 1933. One of his disciples, M. G. van der Leeuw, wrote recently in the same sense: "No serious scholar will maintain that there are two kinds of men, one of which differs essentially from the other. The different state of primitive man signifies at the same time his union with us. Our research must not be restricted to the Papuans and the Andaminites, we must extend it even to ourselves . . ."; *La Mendicité primitive et la religion*, 21. (We can see the criticism of Lévy-Bruhl's theory in Henri Bergson, *Les Deux sources*. . . , 145–60.)

[44] There were numerous allusions, after June 1940, in German newspapers to this "denordization" of France. The nazi jurists judged that the old juridical notion of slave had to be reestablished, in the strictest sense, in modern law, in which it would be applied no longer to individuals but to peoples. The use is generalized from the distinction between *Herrenvolk* and *Disnervolker*.

barbarism an extreme slowness of intelligence, that is, so to speak, unavoidable, since they restrict the use of their intelligence to the demands of their daily life, which are, moreover, minimal.

And to these findings, recorded in the encyclical *Rerum Ecclesiae*, Pius XI could add his personal testimony: "We have almost beneath our eyes numerous indigenous to whom, in our Colleges of the Eternal City, the most varied sciences are being taught; now, not only do they prove equal to the other students by the liveliness of their minds and their scholarly success, but they often excel and surpass them."

The black himself is often very gifted, "very capable", writes a good judge, Father Pierre Charles, "of attaining in all domains the same results as the white, provided that the chances are equal".[45] One great missionary, the Venerable Father Francis Libermann, had noted this in the last century: "The blacks are no less intelligent than other peoples."[46] The populations of Africa were, from earliest times, handicapped by climactic and geographical conditions, notably by the isolation in which vast desert regions had kept them from the "Mediterranean Lake":[47] we know, however, that before the tenth century—

[45] "Une Élite sociale, l'exemple du clergé indigène", *Semaine social* of Marseille (1930), collected in *Missiologie*, 1:113. Likewise: "L'Unité intellectuelle de l'espèce humaine", in *Les Race humaines* (Louvain: Aucam, 1930), and "Préjugés de race", *Dossiers. . .*, 77–80.

See also, in the supplement to the *Union missionnaire du clergé* (April and July 1932), "L'Enquête sur l'évolution intellectuelle de l'Afrique", notably the report of P. Charles: "Possibilités et facteurs de cette évolution." "Every year institutes of higher learning . . . form a good number of Blacks who are perfectly equal to all intellectual situations. . . . Dr. Jubuyu, Dr. Molema, Dr. Aggrey, to cite only three, . . . are pure-blooded Africans. It is impossible, reading their works, to doubt that they are not one of us. At Kigantu, where for five years the University of Louvain has set up an immense medical establishment and a school for indigenous nurses, the first three black candidates, who, after three years of special studies, passed the legal examination, were all three remarkable, and the first perfectly exceptional. I can affirm, with evidence in hand, that the examination was not easy and that the program of studies alone would have made many others, even though sceptics, shrug their shoulders . . ." (147). "There is nothing ridiculous", concludes P. Charles, "in wishing for the Blacks of Africa the facilities of university education lavished in Europe on so many very mediocre Whites" (153).

[46] *Notes et Documents*, 8:227. Father Francis Libermann added: "On the islands of Bourbon and Mauritius, they learn Christian doctrine with ease. . . . Their sensitive nature seems to be made for the Catholic truths. Often they make responses full of clarity, wisdom and intelligence. It is necessary to teach them, it is true, in a very simple manner and to speak their coarse language . . . ; but for the substance of the truths, they understand perfectly and render an account of it with intelligence and fidelity."

[47] Maurice Delafosse, *Les Nègres*, 10: "If so many of the black tribes of our times singularly resemble what we are right to imagine they were several centuries before Jesus Christ, and if

before any Arab or European intervention—the peoples of Central Africa had achieved a degree of culture sufficient to constitute stable states, comparable to the Eastern or European states of the same period. The Vai of Guinea, the Bamoum of the Cameroons, outside of any external influence, invented systems of writing that were entirely original. Others among these people have not only a popular but a scholarly literature, written and oral. With some of them a highly elevated feeling of patriotism has developed.[48] In Rhodesia, imposing traces of a purely African civilization have been found. . . .[49]

If it is necessary to carry the debate from the field of intelligence and culture to that of heroism—a heroism that includes physical courage but which goes immensely far beyond that—it would undoubtedly be enough for minds not numbed by passion to hear recalled the Christian life and martyrdom of a certain number of "half-apes" from Uganda!

There is no question, of course, of contesting the interest that is paid to the science of heredity and of races, no more than to its possible applications, for example, in the matter of so-called "racial" politics; but that has no connection with the racist doctrine. Can we not, without being socialist, accord a great theoretical and practical interest to social problems, and would the recognized importance of the social sciences necessarily entail the truth of such a socialism? Or, indeed, is the fact of admitting that a Jewish question exists equivalent to a profession of anti-Semitism? These examples must place us on our guard against a confusion of words from which racism profits in order to adorn itself with a scientific clothing to which it has not the least right.

Neither is there any question of denying the difference or even the inequalities that, for congenital or historical reasons, can exist between

---

others, although they have achieved undeniable and very appreciable progress, are certainly less advanced than most of the peoples of Europe in the field of agriculture and industry, it is not difficult to perceive the reason for it without having need to resort to the argument of congenital inferiority. The Negroes of Africa, isolated by the Sahara from the Mediterranean Lake, which has been, for millennia, the sole vehicle for world civilization, could not, in the absence of any emulation created by constant external contacts, achieve the progress that, for example, our ancestors of Gaul, under the influence of the Roman civilization, were able to achieve. . . ."

[48] Delafosse, *Les Nègres*, passim.

[49] Ruins of Zimbabwe. Cf. *Anthropologie*, 41:667. When the Portuguese navigators, in the sixteenth century, went down the western side of Africa, they found in several places organized kingdoms that have since disappeared: Msgr. Le Roy, *Le Religion des Primitifs*, 431; Léo Frobenius, "L'Art africain", *Cahiers d'art* (1930), 398–400.

different human groups. Recognition of them is perfectly compatible with the recognition of the essential dignity of any human person. "Are the children of the same family all equally strong and intelligent?" Do they all have the same native or acquired dispositions? And is it not precisely this diversity of physical and spiritual gifts that gives each his value? But if it is true that within mankind the varieties are numerous and strongly pronounced, this truth is not to be considered without the complementary truth already established by simple biological observation, which is the following: divergent human branches never separate, as they would do elsewhere in the animal kingdom: the branching, which is, in fact, very elaborate, is carried out in a phenomenon of "palmation". "From the point of view of systematics, humanity represents the remarkable case of a extraordinarily spread-out animal group in which the crossings continue to be made between branches that, normally, should have been long since dissociated."[50] Thus biology itself seems to teach us already that man is not solely dependent on biology, it implies to us that the law of his conduct and the conditions of his progress must be sought in another order. If we believe that not all finality is absent from nature, will we not admit that this "elasticity", unique of its kind, which maintains the physical cohesion of the whole human range, constitutes the sign of the solidarity that must reign between all the human "races", that is to say, to speak more precisely, between the different "ethnic groups"? Is it not an invitation to exchanges that might establish them increasingly in a common spiritual atmosphere? In fact, is it not thanks to such exchanges that the most vigorous branches have been constituted, those that are shown historically to be the most progressive? Their original qualities and excellent living conditions are not enough to explain their fortune: the latter is the product, not of a segregation, but of a synthesis.[51]

---

[50] Teilhard de Chardin, "Unités", 18. Rosenberg proclaims no less, in his pseudo-scholarly assurance: "The natural laws, such as they are manifested in the life of plants and animals, are also verified in the human race." Nuremberg congress, September 1933.

[51] We are leaving completely aside, as outside our subject, the question of the physical relations, properly speaking, of the crossed or mixed races.

An interesting example can be brought forward here. "Without a doubt", writes René Grousset, *Bilan de l'histoire*, 15–16, "the primitive Indo-European society, such as the famous Meillet reconstituted it by linguistics, could be, from the intellectual and moral point of view, full of promise. But this promise . . . could be kept by the Indo-Europeans only there where their genius was made fruitful by contact with the old southern empires. Such was the case of the Latins, Greeks and the old Iranians, civilized respectively by the Etrus-

From solely the scientific point of view, man, then, presents himself already in a totally different way from an animal, and great teachings already unfold from this simple finding:

> As a paleontologist [writes Father Teilhard de Chardin], I have no illusion about the inexorable fact and forms of biological concurrence. But, in this same capacity, I absolutely refuse to transport bluntly the mechanical laws of selection to the human domain. For, if nature teaches us clearly that there is a universal fight for life, it teaches us no less categorically that, in passing from one stage of existence to another, living properties subsist only in being transformed or transposed. Exploitation and mutual suffocation can be the rule between infra-human zoological groups, because the latter are continually going to supplant each other and diverge from each other. In the case of the human network, by contrast, if the latter progresses only by converging, fraternal emulation must be substituted internally for hostile concurrence. . . .
>
> Pursued on the bases of the most biological roots, the problem of the races, of their appearance, of their awakening, leads us thus to the point of recognizing that the only climate in which man can continue to grow is that of self-sacrifice and renunciation in a sentiment of brotherhood. In truth, at the speed at which his awareness and his ambitions grow, the world will explode if he does not learn to love.[52]

"It is absurd", wrote Rosenberg, "to want to constitute a people of brothers with humanity." That is of course because such an ideal, even to suppose all peoples docile to the Church, will never be fully incarnated. It is no less certain that each human group, in order to be able to play its note in the concert and furnish its part in the exchanges, must fortify itself and defend itself. In addition, the task of the man of state, that of the colonizer, is not that of the leader of the Church or of the missionary. The question, however, remains: Does the ideal of fraternity not open to the human race the only way of salvation?

I understand very well that the racist is assured that his superiority will give him the advantage in the battle. That may be so (although one could not guess what will become of him when the antagonistic racism he has caused to rise elsewhere is unleashed). . . . But at what

---

cans, the Minoans and the Assyro-Babylonians. On the other hand, the Indo-European peoples who remained in their native climate, the Germans, Baltics and Slavs, stayed barbarians until the day when they accepted, directly or through an intermediary, the Mediterranean influence."

[52] Teilhard de Chardin, "Unités", 28 and 30.

price? What will result from his success if not a terribly impoverished and mutilated, terribly animalized humanity? Just as the missions appeared to us recently as a duty of the Church to herself, so we must recognize that humanity fulfills a duty to itself in the respect and the service of its humblest members. It is by this that it is ennobled. When our ancestors dreamed of converting to Christ the "monstrous peoples" who, in their imagination, filled the hidden regions of Africa and Asia, cyclops, cynocephalae, sciadopodes, . . .[53] in their naïveté they worked far better to construct the white civilization than if they had decided to exterminate them or reduce them to slavery. One could condemn the poor quality of the science on which racism presumes, but one is right to demand it to account for the ideal that it claims to promote. What is the worth of its will for power, which is achieved in a carnivorous morality?[54] In the name of what will it make us believe that pride and hardness do more than charity and justice to humanize the strange animal that we are?

It replies to us, in the final analysis: it is a faith. "Race, rather than a philosophy or a knowledge, is a profession of faith. . . . Today a new faith is rising: the myth of blood; a faith that, with blood, safeguards the divine essence of man; a faith based on this evidence that the Nordic blood represents the mystery that dispossesses and replaces the old sacraments."[55] That is in fact clear. In truth, the debate is neither scientific nor even philosophical. A refutation cannot suffice because it is only negative. To faith, one must oppose faith. To the racist faith, our Christian and Catholic faith. When we speak of "neopaganism", that is not a polemical expression. In a renewed form, it is indeed the ancient pagan ideal that is waking to reject Christ. The ancient Fate is recalled today, the liberating Word is repudiated. "The time of the Cross", we are told, "is past." It is for our hearts as Christians to prove that it does not pass.

From which comes the epic grandeur of the fight in which we have participated in the course of these recent years, when, armed solely

[53] Saint Augustine, *De Civitate Dei*, 1–16, c. 7, n. 1. Pseudo-Augustine, *Sermon* 37, Ratramnus, *Epistula de cynocephalis* (*Monumenta Germanica historica, Epist.*, 6:155). Isidore of Seville, *Étymologiae*. . . . Cf. Charles, *Dossiers*, 48. The Eastern Acts of Saint Andrew and Saint Bartholomew speak of the conversion of cynocephales. See also the famous "Portail de la Pentecôte" at Vézelay.

[54] Racism appears here as a simplistic and popularized Nietzscheism, grossly transposed.

[55] *The Myth of the Twentieth Century* (Munich, 1933), 117–18.

with the word, Pius XI set our old Catholic *Credo* in opposition to the new *credo* of racism. Already, in the encyclical *Mit brennender Sorge*, he rose up solemnly against "the vain attempt to imprison God, the Creator of the universe, the King and the Lawgiver of all peoples, before whose greatness the nations are 'like a drop of water in the bucket' (Is 40:15), in the narrowness of the blood community of a single race". Nearly at the eve of his death, the old Pope returned to it with an insistence and energy increased by the growth of the danger. Profiting by each occasion, he exclaimed his faith in discourses that should have caused an immense stir throughout all Christianity. . . . But, unfortunately!, one part of Christianity was already submitting to the oppression, and with us, with us, must it be said? too much, more or less conscious, complicity stifled the echo of this great voice. . . .[56] We must recall in particular the three discourses declared on July 15, 21 and 28, 1938, before three different audiences, all three on the theme of Catholic universalism. "Never," confided Pius XI to the Ladies of the Cenacle, "never before have we thought about it with so much clarity, in so absolute a fashion, one would be tempted to say, with such intransigence; and since God has had the grace to grant us this light, we wish that all our children should have their part in it, for all have a particular need of it in these times." These three discourses are an ardent commentary on the words of Jesus: "Euntes docete omnes gentes" and the article of the *Credo*: "Credo Ecclesiam catholicam." To this precept, to this faith, is opposed today a haughty spirit of separatism that constitutes "a form of true apostasy" and which, "because it is neither Christian nor religious, ends by being not even human".[57] Catholic means universal, no other translation is possible, and Christ wants his Church, going to all men, to gather them all together in one

[56] Thus in October 1938 a weekly journal, the one most frequently read by the clergy, inserted an article in which it was explained that the condemnation of racism was an unimportant episode: "I know that the National-Socialist leaders are not very happy about it, but I think in my own heart that the Syllabus of Pius IX condemned as well many other things rather forgotten by our bishops." Despite the very pale suggestion of a reservation in a note, the journal made this article very nearly its own, introducing its reproduction as a "rectification" on its part in order to excuse itself for having previously spoken of nazism with too little favor. . . . (*L'Ami du Clergé* [1938], 643–47, reproducing an article published in the *Revue hebdomadaire*.)

[57] Already on February 24, 1934: "We are living through tragically historical hours. . . . We are living in times when racial pride is exaggerated to a pride of thoughts, doctrines and practices, which is neither Christian nor human."

and the same love. Addressing on July 28 the students of the Roman College of the Propaganda, Pius XI once again poured out his soul, and the doctrinal fullness of his expression was at the time wholly vibrant with moving accents, which transform this official text into a great human document:

> No separatism! We want nothing to separate the human family. We consider racism to be a barrier erected between one man and another, between one nation and another. . . . They forget that mankind, all mankind, is one, single, great and universal race—although that expression, "human race" is not very attractive. . . . Men are above all a great and unique family of living beings. . . . Naturally there is a place for special races, as for so many other varieties. Just as in musical compositions there are variations in which the same theme always returns but with different intonations, so there is in mankind only one, single, great, universal, catholic family. . . .
>
> What is the Church doing, what is the Holy See doing, what is the Pope doing at the Propaganda, where there are students from thirty-seven nations? It is easy to see: all are sons of the same mother, all are equally dear to her, all are nourished at the common table of the same truth and wrapped with the same benefits. The Propaganda puts into practice the only racism conformed to human dignity and the human reality, for the human reality consists in the fact that the children of all these races are men, not beasts or any other kind of beings, and human dignity consists in this, that all make up a single family, mankind.
>
> It is thus that the Church teaches us to think, to feel, to treat things. It is her reply to the discussions that are shaking the world at present. Such is the true and healthy racism. From her point of view, all men are the object of the same maternal affection; all are called to the same light, all are invited to being, each in his land and his race, the spreaders of this very great and magnificently maternal idea, which is already human before becoming Christian. . . .

This is how one witness of the faith speaks. This is how the Church, which some have at times wanted to oppose to Christ, defends the deposit she has received from him. On the lips of Pius XI, we have gathered the perfect echo of the Apocalypse, describing the host of the elect, that "immense throng, that no one could count, from every nation, every tribe, every people and every language";[58] the perfect echo of the symbolic account from the Acts of the Apostles, enumer-

[58] Rev 7:9.

ating the Parthians, Medes, Elamites, Arabs, Libyans, Armenians, who crowd around Peter on the evening of Pentecost to receive baptism;[59] the perfect echo of the declaration of Paul to the Colossians: "There is neither Jew nor Greek, neither barbarian nor Scythian, neither free man nor slave; you are all one in Christ Jesus."[60] The perfect echo, we can add, of the Prophecy that once resounded in Israel and which the Church has the mission to fulfill. So let us understand that other cry of the same Pope, weighted with a very necessary and very profound meaning: "Spiritually, we are Semites!"[61]

At the beginning of the preceding lecture, we said that this special teaching of missionary theology was a paradox, nearly a scandal. It seems to me that after what we have seen this evening, this judgment can be reversed. Much rather we can say: a sign of the times. Such a study comes in time to draw and concentrate our attention on the points of our faith that are today the most threatened. To speak in general, the great fact of the missions tends to develop the awareness and the love of the *Ecclesia catholica* in the faithful people, and it is natural that this Pope, who was to condemn racism, should also be the one to be hailed with the name of "Pope of the missions".

Two things, in ages past, have too often made us more or less lose the missionary Church from view. It was first of all the indispensable specialization of the members in so vast a body. But it was also, let us recognize, our making ourselves comfortable in the womb of the Church, which seemed to us "established", our withdrawal into a "familiar" Christianity. The open religion par excellence, Christianity also tends always to be closed up in our narrow souls, and, while the best of us go out so that Christ's order might never remain without fulfillment, we give in to this tendency. Even today, are we awake enough? Are our eyes and our hearts open enough? A booklet with the title "Catholics, Are We Christians?" was written a few years ago. Another booklet could also be requested, for a no less timely examination of conscience: "Christians, Are We Catholic?"

Christians of France, in the misfortune that has struck our land, we have undoubtedly not been insensitive to the evils that struck the Church at the same stroke: the disruption of religious life; the dangers

[59] Acts 2:9–11; and 2:5: "Devout men coming from all the nations under heaven."

[60] Col 3:11.

[61] Discourse to the Belgian Catholic Radio pilgrimage, September 6, 1938.

for—and already, in various regions, the persecution of—Catholic Action; the troubled souls, scandalized by the lie; the destruction of old Catholic countries like Poland; and the supreme Pastor cut off from a vast part of his flock. . . . Have we thought about the terrible repercussions of the catastrophe, if it were to be definitive, throughout the mission lands? Are we gripped with anguish at the idea that the Catholic work par excellence might be compromised by the world and that the hope recently called by Msgr. de Solages, in interpreting the thought of the Pope, the "great hope of the twentieth century" might be disappointed? In particular, have we imagined the tragic situation of those missionaries of our own, forced to consider the possible abandonment of lands where their apostolate would no longer be tolerated? the abandonment of churches, some of which are among the most flourishing in the world? and to leave them in whose hands? We do not know what God holds in reserve, and we may be permitted to hope that he will not allow the shadow of a new paganism, coming from the old Christian Europe, to extend over the entire world (and even then, we well know that all would not be lost). But this is on condition that, instead of giving way to despair, we stand by our Church and that her conscience might resound through all our consciences.

O Holy Church, missionary Church, you are for us the permanent revelation of the true God! You show us the Father by teaching us that all the children of men are his children. You show us the Son, in whom we have adoption, and who through you seeks tirelessly to gather together his dispersed members. You show us the Spirit, devouring Fire whose ardor burns so pure and so strong in the heart of our most heroic brothers through whom you are present everywhere. . . . As Saint Augustine already said to you, "By a bond not only of common life but of true brotherhood, you unite citizens to citizens, races to races, in a word, all men to each other, by reminding them of their common origin."[62] Motherly Church, you who once awakened barbarous Europe to the awareness of its mission, you who patiently modeled our souls and our customs, see today your children grown old and blasé. Consider their wounds, give them a youth that is new and more beautiful. Have pity on those among them who turn from your gospel to listen to the tempting voices coming from their more distant past. Do not leave adrift those who, in their presumption,

[62] *De moribus Ecclesiae catholicae.*

have thought that your role was finished and that they could henceforth pass you by. You alone are capable of drawing us out of the paths of perdition where we have lost our way. O Mother, "great majestic Mother, at whose knees we have all been taught" human dignity, the value of every soul and universal brotherhood; may your missions be a teaching that is ever near to us; through them, may we know ever better what is required of each of us by our name, *Catholic*.

Appendix

The *Nouvelle Revue de science missionnaire*, which appeared in Switzerland from the beginning of 1945, published in the course of its first year two extremely important articles by Father Jean de Menasce, O.P., professor at the University of Fribourg: "*La Théologie de la Mission selon M. Kraemer*" [The theology of the mission according to M. Kraemer] and "*Polarité de l'activité missionnaire*" [The polarity of missionary activity]. The first is devoted to discussing the work of H. Kraemer, *The Christian Message in a Non-Christian World* (London, 1938), which applies to missiology the theses of "dialectical theology". The second draws attention strongly to certain superficial ways of missionary adaptation; it points out the possible deviations of this and appeals to the exercise of the theological virtues against the ever-recurring dangers of activism and pragmatism. We can quote here only a few short passages from these articles.

1. The central idea of [H. Kraemer's] work is that the Christian message, because divine, encounters in humanity nothing that prepares for it, nothing that contradicts it, just as its acceptance cannot fail to shatter all that is human by condemning the world that is sin and all sin.

This is because in fact the world, and particularly "the religions", are, entirely, a rejection of God, revolt and negation, even and especially when they seem to call for his mercy and his salvation: an attitude that is not only ineffective but blasphemous. The sin in which the world is set permeates its acts of religion with self-seeking; it exalts man, who dares to believe himself capable of giving worship to God. His homage is equivalent, by the fact of this presumption, to a reverse idolatry. It is precisely where "the religions" seem to be closest and most similar to Christianity that they are farthest from it, that they are satanical parodies of it. The missionary, then, encounters no preparation in the world; he himself constitutes the point of contact. . . .

What is called "adaptation" has its *raison d'être* on the human plane: the missionary, in transmitting his message, must strip it of what has been added to it or of what acclimates it in his place of origin: he must, in order to translate it, decant it first of all. But Christianity, "crisis" and condemnation of the world, is not, to the degree in which the mission is accomplished well, foreign to the new Christianity in which it is sown in the way peoples or historical traditions are foreign to each other. One recovers through this bias all that seemed forever excluded from the missionary enterprise in virtue of the principle enunciated at the beginning. There is no preparation for revelation in the pagan world, but that is because there is none in the Christian world either. On one side just as on the other, it is the reign of the dialectical condition. . . .

Constantly when one lays bare the articulations of different religious thoughts, one strives to show that their apparently sound parts are precisely those that best reveal the mark of man's revolt against God, of his presumption to substitute himself for God. In addition, one specifies indeed that this is a question of complete indissolubles, of unbreakable blocks of which nothing could subsist after the "judgment" of the Christian message. The religions represent an option that is formally anti-Christian.

Henceforth it is no longer a question of a "search for God" to which the missionary would come to offer his collaboration, of a "pooling" of religious experiences destined to enrich one another mutually. The missionary is not there to seek God but to obey the precept to preach; there is nothing in common between what he brings and what his partner "seeks"; he does not propose any fulfillment to him because there is no expectation of it. Finally, since there are no sound elements to retain from this world of sin, where infidelity necessarily becomes "totalitarian", corrupting the thought and the heart from top to bottom, neither can there be a question of a sorting out between the true and the false, the sound and the corrupt. . . .

There is something sound and refreshing in the way Mr. Kraemer wants to affirm the scandal of Christianity, in the trust that he places in the integral and generous preaching of the Christian message whose duty obliges the missionary to a humility and a corresponding understanding, in the condemnation he brings to bear against any apologetic accommodation of the Christian truth that would tend to water it down, to render it inoffensive and sterile. The Word, like the Spirit who animates it, is indeed a sword for him. He knows that the Cross of Christ accompanies the true missionary and governs his field of apostolate.

But because the transcendence of revelation is grasped above all by contrast with the psychologizing and cultural naturalism of Protestant liberalism, because its affirmations are postulated on an indictment, not on a contemplation, it must be admitted that the opposition that Mr. Kraemer plans between revelation and the world appears at the very least coarse and, so to speak, anthropomorphic. The gratuitous intervention of God in this human universe, which is the work of his creation and which, despite its sin, he continues to maintain in being, the infinite distance that separates the supernatural from the natural, is not exhausted by the effect of contrast and destruction in which Mr. Kraemer's analysis takes delight. . . . The transcendence of revelation not only stands up against sin and condemns it but radically governs all created nature, even that undamaged by sin. It governs it, however, in another way, since the supernatural raises nature by respecting it with a delicacy that is itself a mystery of faith. This divine operation, which makes the creature participate in its very nature, is under the sign of Wisdom. An incomprehensible reality, of course, but of positive content and fullness, and in consequence less susceptible of pathos than the notions that directly express negation, destruction, opposition. As for all theologies (and all philosophies of the Nietzschean type) which start from sin instead of from God and which, by that fact, remain radically anthropocentric, despite all efforts that inspire them to return to God in himself, one can say that here the good is conceived on the model of evil, that its absolute character is characteristic of negation, not of fullness. The rejection of man and his judgment appear, as it were, more topical than the creative and loving initiative of God: the tone is given neither by the first verse of Genesis nor by the first verse of the Gospel according to Saint John. The biblical anthropology is amputated by its premises.

I am not resisting the impression that Mr. Kraemer's attitude, despite its tone of defiance and its joy in scandal, belongs to the apologetic order; we are living in a time when No seems more nourishing than Yes. . . .

I believe that Mr. Kraemer has done very well to reduce the problem of adaptation to the "translation" of the Christian message by the missionary into indigenous terms and, on the other hand, to the creation, by the new Christians, of a temporal life inspired by Christianity, in which the latter appears in the multiple social and cultural inventions of the peoples. He has seen very well, in particular, the difficulties of this "translation", which is required both to transmit notions that are intelligible, that is to say, to use terms (and gestures and customs, for "language" must be taken in the large sense) already on hand, and not to blur the Christian newness that a presentation with too much "local color" risks diluting excessively. Converts are very sensitive to this latter danger: the revelation for which they have suffered seems to them compromised by the fact of being expressed in terms that are too common, departing too much from the ambiguous. They shrink from too rapid a cauterization of the rending caused by the Cross. We know that solely on the linguistic plane, the missionary often hesitates between the adoption of indigenous terms that must be distorted to make them render the Christian notion, and the importation of totally foreign terms, borrowed from European languages and thus deprived of indigenous resonances, semantically "hard". There are no other rules but those that a concrete situation inspires; each language, each civilization offers particular possibilities. The evolution of customs and linguistic usages in the pagan environment can make an indigenous term available or, on the contrary, stamp it as incapable. The same is true for usages. . . .

Catholic doctrine and practice are here equally opposed to Protestant liberalism, which is prompt to acclaim the grace in often questionable manifestations, and to the narrow and, despite everything, anthropomorphic pessimism that comes to limit the doctrinal perspectives of Mr. Kraemer.

2. In certain periods, the missionary was little concerned with examining the human cultures of the peoples he was evangelizing and with doing them justice; he tended to carry on regardless, considering above all the transcendence of his message, not daring to stop at the strangeness in which he smelled superstition, and, by that very fact, all the less open to the cultural values he rightly sensed beneath the domain of pagan religions. Perhaps, too, the missionary had trouble setting Christianity free from the cultural aura of the Europe of his time, from the civilization from which he had departed, which was Christian, certainly, but not exhausting all Christian culture. Which of us is perfectly safe from this lack of the sense of the relativity of the cultural? But very quickly the Christian psychologist must recover his balance, become aware, in this new context, of the dynamics of the faith, of the varied stages of its preparation and its stabilization, of its individual and social acclimatization. Today one can even say that the pendulum has arrived at the other extremity of its course: it is a question only of methods of approach, of adaptation. The pedagogical preoccupation carries it along, it is enough to note the place that this preoccupation occupies in the missionary literature of our time. Today the age of the school is succeeding the age of the mission conceived as pure preaching; and this is very good, on condition that the primacy of what constitutes the heart of preaching is maintained, which is to say, the primacy of appealing not only to the gifts and pedagogical knowledge of the missionary, which remains, despite everything, of the human order and, even supernaturalized, of the moral order (full of technique as well), but still more to his theological life, properly speaking.

Let us note, moreover, that this only slightly restrained humanism to which we are alluding is at times opposed to true humanism in an unforeseen way. The missionary of apostolic soul, who has been taught that it is necessary to use human cultures for the ends of the apostolate, often risks seeing the goods of culture as pure "utilities", mere "bait" with which his preaching is clothed, without respecting it, without suspecting the proper finality of it. . . .

Only the wholly supernatural purity of an intelligence penetrated by faith permits one to avoid the twofold reef of failing to recognize the "preparations" of the cultural order and the strictly "utilitarian" use of this same order. The second attitude is no less simplistic than the first and exposes the mission to terrible mistaken judgments. . . .

. . . In this regard, I am persuaded that the contemplatives, when they become apostles, have more discernment than allegedly practical men, that they are freer and more judicious in their choice of instruments; more anchored in the end, they have more freedom with regard to the means, because they grasp them in their relativity as means, while respecting their own value. The hierarchy of values is established only from the top, only the highest value can supply a valid hierarchy. . . . The progress of ecclesiastical sciences on the positive (historical and philological) plane in Catholic university programs cannot be praised enough: but might there not be a need of being counterbalanced by a more profound, more contemplative view of the realities of the faith and of theology? . . .

2. Letter to My Superiors (Lyons, April 25, 1941)

My Reverend Father,

Pax Christi

Undoubtedly it would be better for the reflections that follow to be signed by some other name than mine. I know only too well that, for more than one reason, I should be the last to claim a hearing. But I dare to beg you to forget for the moment who I am in order to consider only the things themselves. If the form in which they are presented in this paper seems to lack serenity, may your kindness attribute it to the twofold effort, moral and physical, that I have had to exercise in order to express them. One sole desire has sustained me in this effort: that of serving, through my poor means, the Church of Christ in her present distress. And I know that when such a cause is in question, a Jesuit can always, whatever his faults or awkwardness, freely address his Superiors with confidence.

Please receive, my Reverend Father, the testimony of my filial submission *in Christo et in Ecclesia Christi.*

H.L.

This letter was welcomed by Father Joseph du Bouchet, who was then my Provincial. This was also true of my Rector, Father Auguste Décisier and Father Fontoynont, Prefect of Studies . . ." (*Résistance chrétienne à l'antisémitisme* [Librairie Arthème Fayard, 1988], 33; [English trans.: *Christian Resistance to Anti-Semitism* (San Francisco: Ignatius Press, 1990), 27, note 7]). "I can affirm, speaking only from my direct and personal experience, that their attitude, taking into account the differences of their temperaments, was the same that Father du Bouchet had shown toward me. Whether it was a question of Father Décisier, who was at first my Rector, then my Provincial, or of Father Charles Chamussy, who succeeded him as Rector at Fourvière. Both, moreover, willingly followed the advice of Father Fontoynont, who had great moral authority with them and who was completely behind the most uncompromising spiritual resistance" (ibid., 134 [126]). Cf. *Mémoire sur l'occasion de mes écrits* (Namur: Culture et Verité, 1989), 235 [English trans.: *At the Service of the Church* (San Francisco: Ignatius Press, 1993), 231–32].

I

The war of conquest being waged today by Hitler's Germany is for it only one stage conducted in the forward progress of a revolution which, before being an anti-French, for example, or an anti-English fight, is an anti-Christian revolution. It is a phenomenon of enormous proportions, whose expansion, moreover, does not depend solely on the success of the German armies. It is related to communism, although the latter is rather the fruit of too much intellectuality while nazism marks, on the contrary, a brutal return to instinct. But to find some analogy for it in history, it would be appropriate, besides, to call to mind both the first century of Islam and the Lutheran Reformation.

To the philosopher, to the theologian, to any man who reflects on his action, a phenomenon of such dimensions poses a long series of problems. An effort of understanding and of "criticism", that is to say, discernment, is imperative in order to free the elements in it that are valid and to prepare, insofar as is possible, the necessary adaptations and assimilations. But such an effort is quite contrary to a surrender. It could not serve as a pretext to inhibit the movement of Christian reaction without which all is lost. To have any chance of reaching a successful conclusion, it must be exercised under sound conditions, which demands above all clearsightedness and firmness. Let us be able, then, first of all to look the danger in the face.

For eight years, religious persecution has been rampant in Germany, and its effects are going to get worse. In 1937, Pius XI could say in his speech to the Christmas Consistory: "Seldom has there been a persecution as grave, as terrible, as sad in its deepest effects. It is a persecution in which neither the use of force nor the pressure of threats nor the traps of guile and lies is lacking." Since then, the grip has tightened. The war itself has not brought any loosening of it. Just yesterday, the Archbishop of Freiburg-im-Breisgau, Msgr. Grôber, long reputed to be one of the most "conciliatory" of the bishops, wrote of his grief "at seeing nearly everywhere around [him] only ruins and plundering". "I myself", he admitted, "had hoped with unpardonable optimism that at least the present conflict would have favored an appeasement: but I was mistaken." Other German bishops and the Austrian bishops are coming forward, too, to make their complaints heard in pastoral letters.

The ruins in fact are immense. Everywhere religious schools have been closed or transformed, Catholic associations are dissolved, the Theology Faculties suppressed one after the other, religious orders hindered in a thousand ways in their apostolate, the Catholic press reduced to nothing. Measures are taken against all the Christian personalities who are not yet cut down or exiled. In most of the cases, simple police operations are enough for everything, the nazi state not troubling itself with legalities. Periodically, great campaigns are unleashed: trials by "slogan", by customs, by "political Catholicism". . . . The end is less to destroy Christianity completely than to debase it. It is denounced as a contemptible thing at the same time as there is an attempt to ruin all its centers of influence, of culture, of strong spirituality. Everywhere a pagan teaching is imposed. Childhood and youth are systematically dechristianized, and the apostasies multiply. . . .

Now, in order to understand the significance of this persecution, and in order to draw the consequences from it that would be useful to our conduct, it is essential to make two remarks here.

In the first place, it is not a question only of a persecution exercised by a state in some way from the outside upon the Church, like so many others have been in other centuries or in other lands. There is nothing comparable here to "Gallicanism" or to "Josephism". Even the anticlerical laicism of Combism or the *Kulturkampf* of Bismarck are wide of the mark. For it is a question *of a formidable pagan thrust that uses the most powerful means of both seduction and constraint that have ever been brought together.* We are in the presence of a body of anti-Catholic and anti-Christian doctrines that the Church has already condemned twice (not to speak of many other less formal documents): in the encyclical *Mit brennender Sorge* (March 14, 1937) and in the Letter of the Sacred Congregation of Seminaries and Universities (April 13, 1938). Now these doctrines are systemically applied, through a singleness of purpose, with a cunning ability and a total lack of scruples. They inspire customs and laws (for example: sterilizations and medical murders) without the least freedom being left to consciences to discuss or protest.

In the second place, this undertaking concerns not only Germany, even with Austria added to it, but extends to all the peoples over which

Germany exercises, in varying degrees, its power and influence. Witness what has been happening in Italy for several years. Witness the atrocities occurring in Poland for a year and a half, what is happening in Alsace, in Lorraine, in Luxembourg for nearly a year. There would already be many sad additions to be made to the two very instructive articles published by Father Lebreton in *Études* last year. In addition, the nazi leaders have made no secret of it: it is from all of Europe that they have very consciously undertaken to uproot what remains of Christian faith.

It would be, then, a serious error to believe that our country, at least in its still Catholic elements, is protected from the danger of Hitler. The danger not only exists, but, in some zones, the ravages have begun. If the danger of persecution, properly speaking, is still in the future, the (more serious) enterprise of corruption is already at work today. Because it is forbidden to denounce it in public, many do not suspect it and so cannot be on their guard against it. The victor's seizure of all the organs of information and thought is particularly heavy with consequences here. Experience shows it: very quickly, even when one has begun to see clearly that all that is printed or declared at the present time is falsified by such a seizure, one comes to submit to the effect of it: one lets oneself fall asleep through the silences imposed, then to be formed, more or less, by the propaganda. . . .

Let us not forget, however, that the latter is going to be intensified even more. Under the present conditions, the economic or political "collaboration" in which we are engaged with Germany (and on which I have nothing to say here) includes by the force of things a "cultural collaboration" on which the nazis insist no less, which is to say, frankly speaking, an opening without defense of our unfortunate country to the Hitlerian virus.

II

This virus is already at work. Hitlerism is beginning (1) to impose its methods and ideas (let us say, its passions) on us, and at the same time (2) to subjugate the Church.

1. I will bring forward only a few examples. We have on our soil the frightful regime of concentration camps for foreigners and also,

for some time, for the French. Certainly it can take root only with the help of a rigorous order of silence: the conscience of too many Frenchmen would revolt against a regime so contrary to any idea of justice (only the police reign there) and humanity (the conditions of life are in many cases physically and morally appalling). But it is taking root.

Another example. We are being led little by little toward a cult of the state that is contrary to Catholic doctrine and that, for over a century, has often been condemned. This cult is insinuating itself thanks to certain confusions: certain sentiments of a wholly different nature are being exploited toward this end, such as love of the wounded homeland, the very legitimate need for a strong authority, attachment to the man who took the helm at very critical times. . . . There is also talk of an inevitable evolution of our societies from an individualist form to a "communitarian" form—which is incontestable. But what they want in reality to lead us to is a whole concept of society, let us even say of being, that crushes the human person (and, with him, the family), because, first of all, it denies the transcendent God. "The history of men", René Château, for example, recently wrote, "is one and indivisible; arbitrary limits cannot be fixed to it, and to refuse to see that, after Christianity, a wholly new civilization is being born would be to close one's eyes to reality; for example, the notion of the state is a conquest of the species that goes beyond the abstract anarchy of Christian and Judaic philosophies." So, the slope down which we are being carried is that of collective apostasy.

Still another example: the propagation of anti-Semitism. This is rampant in its most contemptible form, through a campaign destined to rally public opinion to its side: the press, pictures, cinema (a repugnant film imported from Germany has just appeared in Lyons), and it is beginning to be rampant as well in an unjust form in arbitrary laws. Let us recall the decree of the Holy Office of March 21, 1928: "The Apostolic See condemns in the clearest possible way hatred directed against the people who were once the chosen people of God, that hatred which is today referred to under the name of anti-Semitism." But should a Catholic need an express condemnation in order to disapprove of a campaign that arouses the basest passions or to be concerned about legislation that strikes one whole category of Frenchmen indiscriminately, with retroactive effect, without any regard to their merit or lack of merit, solely because of what is called their "race"? The measures are already much more severe in the "occupied zone", and there is no attempt to hide the fact that the other zone will follow suit and that the result will be one single legislation for the whole of Europe. . . .

2. At the same time as the wave of neopaganism is thus rising in France itself (and everything makes one fear that this is only the weak beginning), the Church is being increasingly hampered. The process has already begun with us by which she was dispossessed of her most elementary freedoms in Germany. On the most serious and current religious questions, pastors cannot instruct or publicly warn their faithful nor can theologians give doctrinal studies that would be opportune. Here are two very recent examples. In Paris, a study by Father de Montcheuil on "Nietzsche and the Critique of the Christian Ideal", a wholly objective work containing not the least political allusion, has been integrally suppressed (by the syndicate of editors responsible before the occupying authorities). After I myself was asked for a study on the principal objections made to the Catholic missions, I was then warned that it was necessary to delete anything that dealt with racism, which is to say, the most virulent of these objections; I then left no more in my text than the official teaching of the Church in its generality; despite that, it was necessary to forego any publication because, Msgr. Chappoulie wrote to me, "the adversaries of the Church too easily found in it the ideas that they are combating, and we would risk provoking complications or reprisals." The broadcasts of the Vatican Radio, which give some precise news on the religious situation, are jammed, and if someone succeeds in listening to them, he can communicate them only in secret. The newspapers do not have the right to reproduce the words of the Pope himself, unless the censor lets them pass, and then it is at times nothing but a false summary, worse than silence.

A more serious thing, at a time when the Pope is already in a situation little compatible with his entire independence, we are no longer free to communicate with him. No secret is assured, not only in ordinary correspondence with the Roman congregations for the day-to-day administration of ecclesiastical matters, but even in those of the bishops with the head of the Church for the major interests of the faith. *Catholic unity is thus being gravely attacked*, especially as these obstacles coincide with an invasion of ideas and passions that tend to destroy the sense of this unity in consciences. Now, it is important to observe, and the knowledge of what has been done in Germany for some years must open our eyes here as well: such a lack of freedom *is not at all a simple fact resulting from the state of war*. It results from the *application of a system that would be rendered only more strict by a Hitlerian peace.*

III

In the face of so tragic a situation, how can we fail to be surprised to perceive only so few signs of uneasiness in Catholic and even ecclesiastical circles? Without stopping their intrigues in other respects, the nazis seek to put our vigilance to sleep, and nearly everything is taking place as if they were succeeding. It seems that we have become, in large measure, dupes of the necessity in which we find ourselves of participating in the official lie. It seems that we, too, are letting ourselves be misled by forced optimism and that we are suffering from that enervating euphoria which, in the very midst of misfortune, has invaded a part of our people. Many priests are extremely ignorant of the situation or prove to be sceptical about facts that are nevertheless, unfortunately, well established; the very horror of these facts makes them sink at times into their scepticism. For a long time a very skillful propaganda has been exercised over them, and as most do not suspect how far the art of Hitler's lie goes, it has often had only too much success. Who, for example, even thought to remark on the pernicious role played in this regard, from 1938 on, by the powerful *Ami de Clergé*, once reputed to be so wise? Today, moreover, the old, ever-recurring illusion of the support of authority makes us forget all the rest. Are there not priests who imagine that a Hitlerian order would favor religion? And have they not gone to the point of spreading word in the presbyterates that, in case of a German victory, a concordat could be signed that would assure salaries to the clergy?

Do our spiritual leaders share, even a little, such a state of mind? This is the question which we cannot keep from asking ourselves today, in the depths of our souls, and which I humbly beg permission to ask, in all simplicity as well as in all respect. We hear some of them publicly express satisfaction with the present situation from the religious point of view; hyperboles abound on their lips and in their writings; they speak freely of "providential defeat", of "miracles", and so forth. But not the most timid reminder of doctrine, the most modest warning, at least in public, has yet reached us. It does not seem that most are concerned with enlightening their clergy on the present situation of Catholicism and on the danger to the faith. Priests and faithful are thus left without any warning, without direction, while outside all the allurements are attracting them. Many are suffering from it, some are becoming discouraged, the body as a whole is left to its unconcern. Do we not risk sliding in a way, without perceiving it, right up to the day when, abruptly, without preparation, we could find ourselves called upon to confess our faith?

Will it then not be too late for many? Will the apostasies that we have noted in Germany and Austria (and already, although these cases are undoubtedly very rare, in Lorraine) not be renewed then with us? For, while waiting, our souls are being undermined by propaganda in a thousand forms, which alone has the right to be expressed and which will be made ever more seductive and intimidating in order to pass next, if necessary, to extortion and threat.

The history of what has happened elsewhere must make us fear that these perspectives are not fanciful. The bishops of Holland have already had to forbid the affiliation of Catholics to the nazi party under pain of being refused the sacraments. Even with us, alarming signs are growing. In occupied France, if our information is accurate, several bishops have already been subjected to definite extortion. In Paris, while the archbishop presides in his cathedral over an inoffensive concert given by the "sparrows" of Ratisbonne, conferences by the infamous Rosenberg, intellectual director of the nazi state and eager enemy of Christianity, are announced. Isn't the attitude of Cardinal Baudrillart, with which we are all familiar, and that of several other ecclesiastics, secular and religious (such as Father Gorce especially, at the M.T., or Father B . . .), by its very nature making his task easier? In *La Gerbe*, a newspaper founded in order to rally the guardians of the old Catholic tradition in Germany, articles are already appearing that openly preach apostasy: Is this not a sign that souls are not in a state of resistance? In Lyons and in all unoccupied France, a series of pernicious leaflets are spreading with impunity, some of them even using the authority of the Church in order to spread more easily among Catholics. It is significant that the "national" censor, who proves so severe in religious matters, lets such a flood of ignominies pour out. But how does it happen that our religious leaders do not seem to be concerned about it? Are they aware, for example, of what *Gringoire* or *l'Émancipation nationale* or *l'Union française*, and so on, are publishing?

As rare as weakening within the Church of France has been up until now, thank God, great publicity has been given it, which makes it more harmful, while total silence reigns with regard to the condemnations and warning cries of the supreme authority, which do not date only from yesterday, moreover, and which would be of such pressing timeliness for us. During this time, emissaries seek to reassure the bishops and religious superiors, to blunt at least their spirit of resistance. There is a desire to involve them in negotiations which, if they consented to them, could go to the point of treason toward their brothers in the episcopacy of Germany. Influence is brought to bear on them by a government that can do nothing but bend to the orders it receives. There is even speculation at times about their "supernatural spirit" in order to distance them from what is called a "political Catholicism" and thus to turn them aside from their primary duty. Skill is used in diverting their uneasiness to other objects. Around some, it already seems almost that recalling the teachings of the gospel and the papacy is done from a "bad spirit". Or rather, those who resist excessive force for strictly religious motives are slanderously denounced as lacking civic loyalty. Those who do not hide their Christian anguish are treated as though they were troubled by political passions. Naïve intermediaries (even among good religious) are always found to bring to the ears of Superiors schemes invented by the fertile tricks of the adversary. Will the experience that has already borne such bitter fruit elsewhere be renewed in the Church of France? "We have been miserably deluded", Cardinal Innitzer was forced to state scarcely several months after the installation of the nazi regime in Austria. "The hatred of National Socialism, equal to that of communism, has been unleashed without restraint against the Church. . . . *The bishops have been loyal and confident; they have been systematically abused. It is necessary that this be known.*" Why must a number of French priests and religious refuse to know this today? What terrible tomorrows do not risk being prepared by this morbid anesthesia?

In consequence, must there not be, first of all, a primary effort made to inform ourselves? to know, for example, the religious history of Germany during these past ten years, that of Austria during the past three years, and so forth? to know the writings of the principal nazi theorists, the primary applications of racist doctrines, the current proceedings and themes of the propaganda used in France, the undertakings to seduce youth, the identity and the merit of particular groups of journalists who have influence on Catholic opinion, and so forth?

Would there not be reason to watch more jealously than ever over our spiritual liberty, insofar as it depends on our vigilance? The service of our country itself demands it: with all the more reason the service of the Church. "God loves nothing so much here below as the freedom of his Church." The concern not to cause any difficulty to the government, as legitimate as it may be, or not to "displease" it, must never be the supreme concern, any more than the concern to know what attitude might be the most "useful" should be. Could these truths, which no one in the Church questions, not be treated, however, with a livelier feeling? And, to take one example, would it not be good to renounce more resolutely gestures such as that of the *Cité nouvelle*, allowing itself to be burdened, from the very outset, with constraints that could become severe?

Should we not also be reminded more that acts can be contrary to Christianity even when they do not attack institutions or men of the Church? Just as the official honors that the latter may receive do not necessarily coincide with a Christian revival, so it is not only when our persons begin to suffer that Christian morality and the faith itself are in peril. Whenever charity and justice are affected, not only in fact and in passing but in virtue of a principle, the Church is affected by that very fact. What is done today, for example, against the Jews could be done tomorrow against us, the same kind of horrors have spread in Germany to both them and the clergy: now, what right will we have to complain tomorrow if we accommodate everything today? Besides, we do not delude ourselves: the anti-Semitism of today was unknown to our fathers; besides its degrading effect on those who abandon themselves to it, it is anti-Christian. It is against the Bible, against the Gospel as well as the Old Testament, against the universalism of the Church, against what is called the "Roman International"; it is against all that Pius XI, following Saint Paul, claimed as ours the day he cried out: "Spiritually we are Semites!" It is all the more important to be on guard, for this anti-Semitism is already gaining ground among the Catholic elite, even in our religious houses. There we have a danger that is only all too real.

Youth in particular is in danger of letting itself be caught up by this, just as by this whole neopagan ideal, which on certain sides knows how to be very seductive. Certainly a restricted elite, formed before the war, particularly in the specialized movements of Catholic Action, is solid. But how small this dam is against the tide that is beginning to mount! This is not the place to examine how a more deeply and integrally lived Christianity, offering less of a hold to the caricatures of the adversary, presupposing perhaps more of reform in our habits and methods, must constitute the sole complete safeguard. But at least, in what concerns the clergy and the young religious, should we not think of inculcating more strongly in them the Christian principles that are in danger of being clouded, in the confused atmosphere that we are all breathing despite ourselves? Would there not be in any case more timely virtues to preach to them than the "virtue of flexibility" at a time when many are being brought without really realizing it to "float with every wind of doctrine"?

If I were asked now why I am writing these things, I would answer that each one always bears his little part in great collective responsibilities, and that in times of exceptional crisis like the one in which we are living—"tragically historic times", as Pius XI has already said—it is a more urgent duty for each to become aware and act in consequence. By thus drawing attention to the present religious situation and to the attitude that, in my opinion, it should arouse in us, I have, moreover, no intention of lodging complaints against anyone with any kind of commotion, condemnation or noisy intervention. I do not expect or desire any activity of the political order, any impossible "crusade" from our spiritual leaders. What I would simply like is for them to be more fully informed so that they might better give knowledge of the danger to those who are uninformed, that they might be better even in encouraging our faith and in helping us save our souls; so that the impression that Catholicism is abdicating in the face of the terrible upheaval of the world may not gradually enter consciences. Powerless to reach those whom I would, nevertheless, have liked to help inform, it is naturally to the Superiors whom God has given me that I turn. I feel encouraged by the thought that my concerns respond to their own concerns and that this report is going in some way to anticipate their desire and be useful to them. After all, would they not have reason to complain, absorbed as they necessarily are by the everyday concerns of their charge, if they were to note later that they had not been able to bring a remedy to the evil when there was still time because those of their inferiors who had the means had not taken the initiative to inform and alert them?[1]

[1] Father Provincial had also written me on November 1, 1941, with respect to something else: "I take advantage of this occasion to tell you how evocative and fine I found your article in *Cité nouvelle* ('Le Combat spirituel')."

With respect to another article, "Pour Christ et la Bible" (*Vie spirituelle,* [June and July 1942]), at first rejected by the Vichy censor, here is what the Father Provincial also wrote me:

From the Rev. Father Joseph du Bouchet, Provincial.

Lyons, December 18, 1941

My Reverend and dear Father, P.C.

As soon as I learned about the incident provoked by your article, I immediately made known to Father Desbuquois my desire to be familiar with it. This is to tell you how much your package corresponded to my affectionate curiosity. I am very sincerely grateful to you for having thought yourself to satisfy me. What I have read surpasses my expectations. I liked it as soon as I saw your fine title. And after having read it, I am more than ever convinced that, for the honor of God and Holy Church, such ideas must succeed in being published.

We have just had a first failure; but I remain persuaded that the final word has not yet been spoken, and, one way or another, such truths must be heard.

Thanking the good worker for Holy Church and the Society, I repeat, dear Father, my very devoted affection in our Lord.

3. Christian Explanation of Our Times

This attempt at an explanation is not offered as a complete explanation. In proposing to seek out some of the causes of the contemporary crisis, in view of better defining it and of helping to bring some remedy to it, it deliberately leaves aside the economic factors, with their thousands of social and political effects and repercussions, in order to pay particular attention solely to the religious factor. It is enough to say that it calls for many an important extension. It is subject, as we well know, to the laws of perspective, laws as pressing in the order of the spirit as in the order of matter. But we nevertheless believe that such a "partiality" is not totally arbitrary, because the religious factor is in fact the essential factor, that which basically governs all. As soon as we step back enough and consider a human problem, whatever it might be, in its relation to the total problem of human destiny, is it not always this that compels our attention, since the religious problem and the problem of destiny are but one?

Causes of the Contemporary Crisis

Our disaster has forced the most benumbed among us finally to become aware of this crisis. But it is of far greater extent than this. It does not date from 1940 or from the few preceding years. It is not only a French crisis. It is a crisis of civilization, begun long ago and felt by all the peoples of Europe. The shock is especially severe for

---

Lecture to the École des cadres d'Uriage (1941). Published twice in 1942: under the title "Vocation de la France" and under the title: "Explication chrétienne de notre temps" (Paris: Éditions de l'Orante, 1942. Cf. *Résistance chrétienne à l'antisémitisme* [Librairie Arthème Fayard, 1988], 111 [English trans.: *Christian Resistance to Anti-Semitism* (San Francisco: Ignatius Press, 1990), 103]).

On the various editions of this lecture given at the École d'Uriage at the request of Hubert Beuve-Méry, see *Résistance chrétienne*, 111 and note 1, p. 121 [English trans.: 103 and note 1 on that page]. Father de Lubac points out on this occasion the complete agreement of Father Victor Dillard with the view expressed in these pages: "It is necessary at this moment to fight, for we bear a crushing responsibility, and we must use all the freedom that remains to us in order to write and to cry out" (quote from Father Dillard, *Résistance chrétienne*, 111 [English trans.: 103]).

us French, since it has come later and since our illusion was more prolonged. A certain easiness of life, coming from the favorable geographical conditions of our country, from our relatively temperate psychology, coming too from the transitory advantages won for us by the 1918 victory, delayed for us a little while the hour of great upheavals. Now, the day of reckoning has arrived for us too. Now it is not only what has been called the bourgeois civilization that is over. We do not have merely a matter of a crisis of liberalism or of democracy or of a failure of a certain intellectualism that, by its excesses, has falsified life. Nor would it be enough to say, with Charles Morgan: "Our folly does not surpass that of our ancestors, but the instruments are more destructive; our civilization is equipped for suicide, which was not the case in other times."[1] No. It is from within that the whole edifice of European civilization seems to be collapsing. The fundamental values by which, across various regimes and with various success, numerous generations have lived seem today to be vanishing, leaving us in a kind of chaos.

Now, if one seeks the causes for this, one perceives four principal ones, which are also but one, for they are in close connection with each other. They are linked together in the course of four stages which, as is normal in things of the spirit, succeed each other less than they overlap each other, although there is a very real order between them.

At the root of everything, it must be said, there is a failure among Christians. Certainly, the Church has promised them eternal life; in each generation she gives birth to new saints; and the present generation counts perhaps more of them than many others. But there has been no promise that each generation would as a whole be faithful or that there would not be collective defections, almost total, long eclipses of the faith and of Christian life. Once, Europe was Christian: more or less, of course (one is never perfectly Christian), but in the end it formed one faith, one morality, of the governing principles. It formed one consciousness, one unity. Troubles and wars, always endemic, were not enough to take this consciousness away from it or to destroy this unity; as serious as they were, they were not fatal maladies. Now, in the course of these recent centuries, the living and active faith, the total faith that alone is fully worthy of the name, gave way in two essential points. On the one hand, with many it came to be no more

[1] *Le Fleuve étincelant*, French trans., 26.

than an habitual faith, that is, simply one of tradition and conservation, and in consequence it came to be deprived of any real efficacy, because it was no longer a principle of life and invention. It is necessary to go even farther: with a great number, it was then no longer anything but hypocrisy, a whole faction of the so-called "ruling" classes uniting a personal scepticism to the famous maxim: "A religion is necessary for the people." On the other hand—this is the second weakening—those very ones who sincerely remained believers were often no longer concerned with Christian virtue and Christian spirit except within the limits of their private life, as if Christianity were deprived of principles for governing the life of either state or business. This was (to use two convenient words by enlarging their meaning a bit) the era of Machiavellianism in politics, then of liberalism in economics. Through a true "treason of the clergy", the best of religious life tended too often to seek refuge in a kind of disincarnated mysticism, leaving the "century" to its path to perdition. Justice and charity were understood only as purely individual obligations. The profound meaning of the Church, which is fraternal community, was lost. . . .

An especially serious weakening since it coincided with a period when the world was in a state of change. The prodigious development of science and technology was then overturning society, and a whole series of new ideas, born in part at least from Christianity, began to impose themselves on the consciousness of the middle-class or popular masses. Ideas of freedom, equality, brotherhood, at the time of American independence and the French Revolution; the idea of nationality; the idea of progress; ideas of social justice and then of an international society. . . . Christian in their origin, these ideas were detached from that origin and professed by men who, in the majority, were not believers. These were laicized ideas, and for all that very often sterilized and falsified, having become ineffective and indeed dangerous. Ideas fallen to the rank of ideologies and utopias, "Christian ideas gone mad", according to the often-quoted expression by Chesterton. The hesitant or contrasting attitude of Catholics with regard to them, then, is understandable. With some, sympathy or even enthusiasm; with others, condemnation or at least mistrust. The former, more attentive to the Christian inspiration of such ideas and not wishing to despair of returning rectitude and efficacy to them; the latter, struck more by their hidden perversion and more fearful of the falsehood of all ideology. Neither the former nor the latter having the power to recapture their heritage or to recognize that they are united in this common possession. So, in the face of a divided century, the Catholics were no less so. These hesitations and this contrast explain in large part the history of Catholicism for a century and a half, particularly the history of French Catholicism, and we also find many a trace of them in the alternate directives emanating from the hierarchy of the Church.

Yet—we are coming to the third cause—another work of disintegration is in process. A faith that is not active, a faith totally turned in on the "private", a faith hesitating about its consequences is a faith that defends itself poorly. Hence its withdrawal in the face of a vast movement of thought that was a particularly negative movement. Modern philosophy acts particularly like a critic. In a manner that is more positivistic and scientific in some, more rationalistic and idealistic in others, its overall action remains corrosive. One of Joseph de Maistre's statements has become even more true than when he made it: "Since philosophy has eroded the cement that united men, there are no more moral aggregations."[2] This whole work of thought, whose greatness we must not fail to recognize, is paid for in practice by the loss of the living God. The world then becomes a world of abstractions, when it is not absurdly reduced to a world of phenomena. In losing its mysterious innermost depth, it has lost its soul. Man is isolated, uprooted, "disconcerted". He is asphyxiated: it is as if emptiness had been formed in him by an air pump. . . . The consequence is not only a social imbalance. The world itself appears "broken". There is, at the innermost part of consciousness, a metaphysical despair. It was of this hunger and this thirst that the prophet Amos once spoke: *absolute* hunger and thirst, because they are a futile hunger and thirst *for the Absolute.* Hunger and thirst that, in many cases, do not even know themselves to be such but that leave on the deepest palate a taste of death.

It is then that substitute faiths inevitably present themselves to fill this tragic void. Such is the fourth and final period of the process. Man is not satisfied by ideologies cut off from any source of real efficacy: the hour must come when he is disenchanted with them. He lives still less from criticism and negations. He does not live by laicism and neutrality. Inevitably something like a great call for air is produced in his inner void, which opens him to the invasion of new positive forces, whatever they might be. The latter conquer him all the more quickly,

[2] *Considérations sur la France*, chap. 5. *Oeuvres*, 1:65.

the more coarse and virulent they are. Cut off from a higher life, he gives in to the brutal pressures that, at least, give him the feeling of a life. Having abused criticism to make truth itself vanish, he now dislikes using it to protect his mirages. A troubled credulity succeeds his faith. *Rationalism has expelled mystery: myth takes its place.* We know great examples of this.

This chain of causes dates far back. Although everything is dependent in history, one can, with sufficient reason, take as the point of departure the dissolution of Christianity around the beginning of the sixteenth century. At that time two great fractures were produced almost simultaneously: on the one hand, the Renaissance and, on the other, the Reformation. These two words have a positive sound, and, in fact, to rediscover the treasures of ancient culture and to renew the Church by eradicating abuses and by separating the usury of centuries from her was in itself excellent. It has been well said, and with truth, that neither "Antiquity" nor "man" was then to be rediscovered absolutely, and that the "abuses" were at that time less serious than they have been in other periods: there was nonetheless room for an equally salutary twofold undertaking. But, in fact, the movement of the Renaissance, even without considering its most serious excesses, ended in denying the ideal of Christianity, the whole life of men in society being thenceforth uprooted from the maxims of the Gospel as well as from the direction of the Church. As for the movement of the Reformation, in consequence of the attitude adopted in the final analysis by its two greatest protagonists, Luther and Calvin, it ended in schism and in the triumph of religious particularisms. Thus divided in itself at the same time as it was expelled from one whole half of man, Christianity necessarily found itself doubly weakened. Despite the delays, the partial revivals, palliatives, even brilliant intermediaries, the consequences of this twofold fracture have not ceased to unfold. Machiavellianism has reigned in the part of man that was abandoned to it, and as it is impossible to live indefinitely in two parts, it ended in expelling Christianity from the other part. What was at first a simple empirical recipe, a collection of maxims for the use of a prince without scruples, has gradually become a system, a totalitarian doctrine.

Must such a diagnosis breed pessimism? Are we at the bottom of an abyss without hope? No. This process of decomposition is full of seeds of progress. The preceding analysis, even if it is accurate, does not say everything, and it would be to falsify it to take it for a picture of history in miniature. We must also keep from any "retrospective illusion". No more than others do for the future must we project the ideal of a golden age into the past. Medieval Christianity was not a perfect success, far from it. It had its weakness and its tares. All was not absolutely Christian! In other respects, in the course of these recent centuries, science and philosophy, national thrusts and social movements have not failed to bring many invaluable elements for the spiritual enrichment of man. We have become more aware of ourselves and of the earth that bears us. Nor has the moral conscience been without affirmation and deepening in several domains. All these gains have not been without intoxication, without disorder, without disastrous oversights, or finally without catastrophes. But in themselves, they remain gains, and they can, if rectified, contribute to real progress. Ever unhealthy and ineffective, the defeatism to which some are in danger today of abandoning themselves would also be an error. Father Teilhard de Chardin has risen against it in a study he has devoted for the past four years to *the present crisis*, a study which retains much of its timeliness. There is a belief, he wrote, "in the approach of a human failure. The collapses of the past are recalled; the physical and moral signs of decadence are enumerated. Intellectual myopia in all that. Let us put these events back into the total phenomenon. Their irregularities become insignificant in the majesty and sureness of the overall movement. Life has gone around or reversed all the obstacles that it has encountered for millions of years. . . . What is happening today that is so critical in the West must be a crisis of progress. Despite all contrary evidence, we can and we must believe it: we are advancing."[3]

These optimistic reflections are not made from the point of view of Sirius. But they are from a naturalist used to calculating on a vast scale and for whom millennia count little. One single precision must be brought to it. If, in fact, the ascending movement of life, whatever the accidents and apparent setbacks there might be, is irreversible, with the apparition of man, a new element comes into play. To benefit from this ascending movement, man must commit himself freely, if his very progress is not to risk turning against him. Let us say, then, that if the present crisis does not denote an inevitable progress, at least it is for us a certain condition for progress. And that must be enough to give us courage.

[3] "La Crise présente, réflexions d'un naturaliste", *Études* (October 20, 1937), 152.

The Christian Vocation of France

For a spiritual and metaphysical crisis, only a remedy of the same nature is appropriate. For a crisis of growth and progress, a remedy that would consist in a mere movement of return to the past could not be appropriate. On the one hand, then, we do not have only, or even essentially, to find some formula of political organization or social technique (even if this be a pressing task); rather the essential problem is a problem of education, and the latter is itself governed by a problem of thought. And, on the other hand, if it is true that we have to go back, beyond the errors and dislocation of these recent centuries, to a distant past whose lessons remain vivid, this could not be with the claim to make it live again as such. No more, for example, than France dates only from 1789 did it become extinct or renounce itself at that time. No more than Europe was founded in the sixteenth century has it ceased to live since then. The dreams of reaction or of restoration are utopias that are as vain and as pernicious as the dreams in the opposite direction. In making an effort to rediscover the spiritual sources of our civilization, we will not forget, then, that it could not be a matter for us of borrowing ready-made solutions from the past but of rediscovering an ever-open truth so as to set ourselves to work.

Let us state to begin with that our European civilization is basically Christian. It would be foolish to seek another basis for it. It is no less foolishly irresponsible than thinking we could maintain it at all costs, coping with the crisis in which it is foundering by continuing to dismiss or neglect Christianity itself. One does not live indefinitely from the perfume of an empty vase. . . .

Of the three principal contributions that are commonly said to have formed Western man—Greece, Rome and the Gospel—the third is the essential contribution. It is of a different order than the other two. To Greece we owe especially our logical reason; to Rome, our maxims of law and government; but to the Gospel we owe our very idea of man. If we deny the Gospel, we are lost. Certainly it is not enough to give us all the principles necessary to organize our earthly existence: "My kingdom", says Christ, "is not of this world." But it must penetrate that existence entirely with its spirit.

Now (to say it in passing) the Gospel is the flower and supreme blossoming of the Bible. The God of Jesus is the God of the prophets, who concludes by revealing himself. Jesus has not come to reject but to carry out the heart of the message of which the people of Israel were the bearer. He came to assure its success by detaching it from its cultural and national connections.

The thought very recently expressed by André Siegfried in an article published by the *Revue des deux mondes* is quite accurate. Mister Siegfried would like a complete Western education to include a series of pilgrimages to the principal places that symbolically call to mind the origins of our civilization. That series would have to end, he says, in the pilgrimage to Jerusalem. And he adds: "Would I be paradoxical in suggesting that it is not Jesus Christ alone whom it is appropriate to seek there? Not that his place is not essential, but must we associate with one place the One who did not want any other limits for the religion of the spirit than those of humanity itself? In all the trips I have made to Jerusalem, I have felt the importance of the Old Testament. Finally, it was at the mosque of Omar, before the Rock of Abraham, that I seemed to feel the most profound emotion."[4] Abraham, who, because he believed in the call of the one God, was worthy to be called "the father of believers", was worthy also, in fact, for the same reason, to be called one of the fathers of our civilization, and it is still his heritage that we must defend today, or rather rediscover and use.

What is true in general of Europe is even much more true of France. There exists, between the destinies of Christianity in the world and the destinies of our country, a connection that is undoubtedly not absolutely necessary but in fact very close. This connection is founded on history at the same time as on a series of natural affinities, which are the sign of a true *vocation.* "When a people has lost the sense of its proper vocation," it has been written, "the homeland crumbles and disappears."[5] All measures of protection or even of "rectification" are in the long run powerless; all the "Maginot lines", whether they be military, political, diplomatic, moral or "racial", are then ineffective. Now, the vocation of France is a Christian vocation, and is so in a twofold sense. Called from its cradle to Christianity and long formed by it, France has also received a certain genius that carries its children either to spread this Christianity around them or to propagate in the world the great human values that we owe to Christianity. This is

---

[4] "La Civilisation occidentale", *Revue des deux mondes* (September 15, 1941), 137.

[5] Jean Mouroux.

shown by certain constants of our history and by our national temperament. We will keep to only two examples here, for symbolic reasons.

In the twelfth century, between 1110 and 1120, in the area around Paris, a monk, Guibert de Nogent, wrote the history of the first crusade. He entitled his work: *Gesta Dei per Francos*. "The interest of the book", Georges Goyau has written, "responds to the splendor of the title. At the same time we see the national spirit born in it and the idea of the vocation of France blossom." Guibert is a sincere historian. He does not hide the fact that during the course of the crusade more than one of his compatriots proved insolent or a plunderer. But the essential thing, he thinks, is that at the voice of the leader of Christianity, which had resounded in France, the French "showed to other peoples the paths of the East". Thanks to the French, these peoples have walked "under the impulse of God, far from their native countries, not through a desire for vain renown or out of an avidity to acquire new riches, or in order to push back the frontiers of their nation, or even to defend freedom and the public welfare, but for God." In these explanations, as already in the four words of his title, Guibert de Nogent "enclosed not only the soul of a period but the soul of a people".[6]

If we turn a century and a half later, we meet the reign of Saint Louis, that high point of the Middle Ages, that time to which, according to the expression of Émile Mâle, France "was the conscience of Christianity". France at that time influenced all of Europe through the threefold prestige of its art, its charitable institutions and its thought. The pontifical legate Eudes de Châteauroux writes that France "is the oven in which the spiritual bread for the entire world is baked". The University of Paris was the great center for the diffusion of Christian thought, and it welcomed into its midst masters as well as students from all nations. Many great men of that time were not French by origin; but it was in France, it was in Paris that they were formed and matured; it was from there that they radiated out in turn; in brief, it was there that they reached the universal. In a parallel way, with Saint Louis dying at Damiette, the idea of crusade was purified and began to be transformed into the idea of mission.

This fortunate success of the French thirteenth century under Saint Louis was more than a fortunate success. It was more, too, than a French success. It thereby placed in relief one of the permanent traits of our

[6] Georges Goyau, *Histoire religieuse de la Nation française*, 181–82; cf. 266.

history. Authentic French nationalism is never turned in on itself. It is not satisfied in itself. Through a kind of expansive generosity, it is always, by the same stroke, in some way a universalism: either because there is a preestablished harmony between our national temperament and the universalism of the religion of Christ or because this religion has so formed us from the cradle that it has become for us, in that at least, even when we seem to have forgotten it, like a second nature. More than any other modern language, the French language is marked by this character of universality; our literature and our philosophy are as well; many of our institutions equally so. This can be noted without chauvinism. Sylvain Lévi, our great Indianist, who had disciples and friends throughout the entire world, recently remarked precisely with respect to the studies of Indianism that have so flourished in Europe for a little more than a century: "France", he wrote, "seeks the human spirit across space and time. It is interested in India just as it is interested in China. In India, while Germany is passionately attached to the Veda, considered as an Indo-Germanic document, French Indianism is above all attracted by Buddhism, the only product of Indian genius that is on a universal order through its inspiration and its history; and, within Buddhism itself, its constant predilection runs to the so-called 'septentrional' Buddhism, which has covered an area of much more extensive propagation."[7] Sylvain Lévi paid honor to the "classical tradition" on which France is nourished. One part goes back just as certainly to the Christian tradition.

For a "Catholic" Renaissance

It is important, in any case, to understand this French universalism—which could so easily deviate—according to the Christian universalism from which it sprang. Now the latter bears a name: Catholicism.

Today, in current acceptation, "Catholicism" is used in opposition to the other Christian confessions: Protestantism, Orthodoxy. . . . This is not the proper and original meaning. From her very beginnings, the Church was called *katholikè*. The first author in whom we find this term is Ignatius of Antioch, who is of the generation that immediately follows that of the disciples of Christ. The word existed in the com-

[7] "Parts respectives des Nations occidentales dans l'indianisme", *Scientia* (1924). *Mémorial Sylvain Lévi*, 116–17.

mon language, derived from the adverbial expression *kath'olou*, which evoked the idea of a whole, of a totality. "Catholic", then, means "universal", as Pius XI reminded the whole Church with so vigorous and so moving an emphasis. But this very universality is not any universality whatever. Catholicism achieves the character neither of a cosmopolitan individualism nor of a kind of unitary socialism. The Catholic Church, according to the very etymology of these two words, is *that which calls all men to unite in a single spiritual whole* in which they will find life and salvation. She is equally concerned about each person and about the unity of the whole. And it is not enough to say that she is concerned about both. Person and Whole: not only does she refuse to sacrifice one of these two values to the other, but she ensures them and exalts them, one by means of the other.

The human person is conceived in the Church as having an absolute value, because he is created in the image of God, whose characteristics he reproduces by his spiritual properties of reason and freedom. Whence his eminent dignity; whence his call, his "vocation" to a transcendent destiny, surpassing all the limitations of earthly ends. Inserted into time, the person breathes in eternity. "God", says the Genesis account, "made man in his image and likeness." The Christian tradition comments: God made man in his image, that is, spirit like him, in view of leading him to his likeness, that is, to make him participate in his Life. There is, then, in all men a sacred part, which by right eludes any enterprise of slavery or monopolization: "To Caesar what is Caesar's, but to God what is God's." The depth of the human soul belongs only to God. Such is the final reason for that essential freedom that no one has the right ever to alienate and that assures us a being, a consistency, an inviolable interiority.

On the other hand, the value of the community is no less absolute. Beings do not exist independently from each other. They neither live nor develop alone. Spiritual beings, persons, even less. Ontological solitude would be their annihilation. If we exist through God, then we exist as well through one another. This essential community of persons is translated on the outside, in the conditions of present life, by a whole series of social bonds. Necessary bonds, "natural" bonds, which it is a matter less of forming than of recognizing and perfecting by organizing them. We cite only the most necessary, the most "natural" of all: family bonds and bonds of one's homeland. Each time they are relaxed, it is the persons themselves who are affected by it. But, for the person to find his complete blossoming, for him to achieve full interiority, full possession of himself, he must be taken up into a more immense and profound community, into a community of a different nature: not simply earthly, like those of family and homeland, but a community of an eternal essence, like the person himself. Such is the Church, that Church which the Apostle Paul called the "Body of Christ" and which we also commonly designate as being the "Mystical Body of Christ". She has her visible and temporal aspect, indispensable insofar as the persons for whom she forms the bond are themselves engaged in earthly affairs, but this reference is not the only one, nor, at bottom, the principal one. It is only partial and transitory. In her final reality, the Church is, according to our faith, nothing but the community of persons, the society of men gathered together in Christ for all eternity. She is the environment within which each human person must become himself, be enlarged, so to speak, to the dimensions of the world and deepened to the dimensions of God; and the good of this community, or universal common good, coincides in the final analysis, in a perfect way with the personal good of each.

In fact, if we question history, we note that these two essential values: person and community, were revealed by Christianity, which made them arise, in a way, at least in all their fullness, just as it is Christianity alone that shows and assures the bond between them. Outside of Christianity, the individualistic spirit and the communitarian spirit always more or less exclude each other or are obstructed by limiting each other. This is because the individual that one takes to be the end is not authentically a spiritual person but a center of egotistical appetites, or rather the community that one prefers to him is neither the universal community of persons nor a community sharing his spirit and concerned to serve him. While, in the Christian conception, Person and Community are perfectly the function of each other and imply each other rather than exclude each other. Christian revelation

> has expanded to the utmost the horizons of the human community into which every "I" is born, and at the same time it has consolidated to the maximum the existence of this I, a tiny element of this community. Revelation of universal brotherhood in Christ, such are the two poles (which it is impossible to dissociate). The term "person" is perfectly suited to signify the twofold property that we thus hold of our supernatural destiny: on the one hand, it serves to mark for us that each of us acquires, by reason of this destiny, a value incommensurate with all the rest of

> nature, to such a degree that it becomes for all the object of sovereign respect; and, on the other hand, in this absolute value communicated by Christ, our freedom finds the sole end worthy of it: to achieve among us a perfect community.[8]

Thus, in the Church, the two movements of interiorization and universalization by which the being is personalized always go hand in hand. Such is the twofold action of the Spirit whom Christ, before dying, had promised to send to her. This is what stands out, for example, in the Pentecost account in the Acts of the Apostles, or again in the account that Saint Paul himself gives of his conversion and of his vocation as apostle. The Holy Spirit, "Spirit of Christ", is that which interiorizes, by making the teachings of the gospel penetrate ever more deeply into the spirit, and it is at the same time that which universalizes, by giving ever more awareness of our divine relationship to all.

Person and Community: these two poles whose balance and tension constitute man are, then, interdependent. On one condition, nevertheless: that their unique foundation, which is God, be recognized. Without God, without this personal and transcendent God in the world, this Spirit and Father God, who reveals himself first to Abraham, to Moses and to the prophets and who is made definitively manifest in Jesus, this God of the conscience and of reason who has scattered everywhere signs of his presence but who uncovers his whole face and compels attention with a necessary firmness only within the Christian faith, without this God the human problem, even in the structures of the earthly city, finds no solution. It is, then, not only the series of ever-recurring difficulties and more or less fortunate and stable compromises that are inherent in the temporal condition, but the absolute alternative, that very one in the midst of which we are bitterly struggling today: either the person is crushed by a system that makes of men a society of termites, or, on the contrary, the human community and the national communities of which it is composed are dislocated by an anarchical liberalism—which is no less fatal to persons themselves. One oscillates from individualism to so-called civilizations "of the masses", from social oppression to libertarian explosions or to slow disintegration.

On the other hand, without this twofold concern for personal inte-

[8] Gaston Fessard, *Pax Nostra*, 39–40.

riority and spiritual community, there is no longer any true belief in God. For, just as it is not enough to cry "Lord, Lord!" in order to enter into the Kingdom of heaven, it is not enough to pronounce the name of "God" in order truly to believe in him. Beneath that word can also be hidden some pagan divinity: any idol whatever, any mythical ideal, in which man objectifies one of his dreams or one of his passions that close him off from himself.

Thus, in the work of reconstruction that is imperative today for any man of good will, that is imperative in a particularly distressing way for us French, but also for which the very vocation of our country assures us a particularly efficacious role, any account of the necessary tasks (accounts that vary infinitely according to the personal situation and profession of each) must be inspired by this Christian spirit, by this "Catholic" spirit that is the spirit of our European civilization and our French tradition. Its essential characteristics fit into the three following points: respect for the person, openness to a spiritual community, belief in God. Such is, so to speak, the essence of the program of this "human revolution", the necessary condition for the good orientation and lasting success of "national revolutions". By clinging to this, France will find herself again, she will find herself faithful to the best of her past as well as to her permanent vocation. Since Christ, it is no longer possible to go back, all human society must participate in the new spirit he has introduced into the world, and the crises that it encounters must be for it the occasion of becoming more deeply aware of this.

If it is necessary to sum up in one word this new spirit brought by Christ, this spirit that our contemporary world suffers from having renounced and that France, more than any other nation without a doubt, is called to give back to it, we would pronounce the word *charity*. The strange sweetening of this word, the finest and the strongest of all, is one of the most striking signs of the Christian decay of these last centuries. For many, unbelievers and believers alike, it has for a long time scarcely evoked anything but a more or less pharisaical gesture of almsgiving; people freely set it in opposition to justice, or rather see in it only sentiment, especially a kind of pity, an amiable but feminine virtue, quite incapable of constructing anything. Now charity is the whole of Christianity, because first of all it is the very Being of God. The Apostle Saint John proclaims it: "God is Charity (Agapē)." Charity is the good of the being, it is the principle of unity. The primary mystery of our faith, which is the mystery of the Trinity, tells us that God is one in three Persons: this unity is possible only because the bond of these three Persons is a bond of love, charity. Now, man is made in the image of God. Between men, then, the same bond must reign as between the Divine Persons: "Be one as my Father and I are one", says Jesus to his disciples. The social bond, which arises first from all sorts of natural necessities and then is fastened humanly by all sorts of contracts and exchanges, must then be made perfect in charity. Of course, since we are made of matter and subject as well to the tyranny of immoderate tendencies, we could not, without a utopia, claim to establish on earth the reign of pure charity. There is no human society without a thousand "social constraints"; there is also an order to observe within charity itself, which, to be universal in principle, must not be indistinct in fact; finally, this charity would be false if it did not presuppose the foundation of justice, to which one opposes it only when one does not understand it. But, beyond the indispensable constraints, beyond the legitimate particularities, beyond justice itself, which is not a principle of union, or rather already within them, informing them and orienting them, giving them a direction, charity must be the end aimed for. Just as it is also already at work each time a human task is accomplished in a spirit of service, each time a man devotes himself to a common cause in a brotherly spirit.

The Catholic Church has no other end but to teach and remind the world of this charity; but to offer it this supreme value, which is the law of its salvation.

Two important remarks could take the place of a conclusion.

In the first place, if it is true that temporal problems can find their final solution only through the solution of the total problem of destiny, it is no less true that the latter must be resolved for itself. The "increase" is given only to those who seek purely "the kingdom of God and his justice". The efficacy of the Christian faith on the temporal plane can be only a result, and if this efficacy proves so problematical, this must without doubt be attributed to the lack of disinterestedness on the part of believers. If we fail so miserably to bring a little balance to our world, it is perhaps because we do not know well enough how to detach our gaze in order to see higher and farther. Let us distrust any search that is overly anxious and too exclusive about efficacy. Let us not forget, either, that the criterion of this efficacy is but an easy thing to determine, and that much apparent success can be misleading, while true long-lasting successes are prepared in adversity.

Let us next note that to speak of a Christian vocation of France and of the "Catholic" ideal that must be its own is in no way to claim that, on the political plane, France must be in allegiance in some way to the Church considered as a visible society. On the contrary, little would be more detestable or, at the same time, more dangerous than what is called clericalism. Besides, we believe we can say that this is the unanimous sentiment of those who would have the right to speak in the very name of the Church. Msgr. Jules Saliège, Archbishop of Toulouse, wrote again recently: "The Church disapproves of clericalism, and we do not want it at any price." Certainly, it must not be denied that there was formerly and that there still is among some members of the clergy a tendency toward clericalism; it will always exist in some measure, because that is a human tendency, and the members of the clergy are men; but those who would give in to it would not have the spirit of their Church, and, in addition, they would lack clarity of vision. For the clericalization of the state inevitably means putting the Church under the control of the state. Now, if the Church really intends to contribute, more than any other body, to the national recovery, she knows that she can do so only in freedom. She must be able to devote herself freely to her task as educator in order to help the country remake itself by helping it go beyond itself. She could never consent to be, in a France systematically turning back on itself, the more or less recognized conservator of a kind of "Christian folklore": that would be to betray both her divine mission and France itself.

One thought has often come to my mind in the course of these recent months. It is only a dream, but it is not absolutely forbidden to have dreams, provided they do not mask the conditions of reality. I was musing, then, on the prodigious power there would be, for the revival of our country and for the future peace of the world, in a generation of young Frenchmen *who took Christianity seriously*. I saw these young Frenchmen, reflecting on the profound causes of our present misery, determined to bring true remedies to it, desirous, for that purpose, of being formed themselves, first of all, at the same time as they acquired a thorough competence, each in his own field. They were not organized into a party, most were even little occupied with politics, but all were of an irreproachable and complete loyalty to their own task and their social duty, ever concerned about human relations with men, very alert to the spiritual dangers that threaten us today. I did not see them all practicing believers in the current meaning of the expression, but, recalling the words of Saint Augustine about those who seem to be in the Church and who, in reality, are outside and about those who seem to be outside and who, in reality, are within, it seemed to me that all these young men were really Christians, and that this was what made them more French, and that the Church, which has the right to anticipate, recognized all of them to be her own. And, carrying my gaze ten years, twenty years, thirty years forward, I perceived each of their activities, although without a concerted plan, rejoin the activities of others in a more and more closely woven fabric: I saw each of their initiatives, just as each of their examples, reunite with those of others in order to give rise to even more. So a vast and irresistible movement would arise from which the country would come out reconciled, enlarged, returned to its destinies, not for undertakings of brutal conquest or disorder, but in order to add new, more beautiful and more fruitful episodes than all the preceding to the *Gesta Dei per Francos*.

4. A New Religious "Front"

Historical Note

The circumstances in which this text was written somewhat explain its genre and tone. They also explain why I could not then take the time to retrace the genesis of the current of ideas that we were having to combat in all its immediate violence. So I will be permitted to provide today some indispensable supplementary information in this historical appendix. Without seeking to be complete or to specify all the lines of influence connecting the authors I am going to point out, I will distinguish, in a schematic way, a French line and a German line. The latter, because of its more determining importance, will hold our attention at somewhat greater length.

We know that for Auguste Comte monotheism constitutes "the Western illness", source of all kinds of extravagant aspirations and "anarchical utopias". Europe owes this evil to Christianity, which had received it from the Jews. So Comte never speaks of Jesus except with a disdain full of bitter hatred, and if he shows, on the other hand, admiration for the "Catholic system", it is insofar as he believes he perceives that this system, distantly prepared by the Apostle Paul (that Paul whom Nietzsche will accuse in the opposite sense of having corrupted the message of Jesus), succeeds in thwarting the God of the Bible and the gospel. When he praises the Catholic priesthood, it is because he sees in it the true heir of "social polytheism", and this praise is an exact

---

Text published in *Israël et la foi chrétienne*, by Henri de Lubac, Joseph Chaine, Louis Richard, Joseph Bonsirven (Fribourg: Éditions de la Librairie de l'Université [Luf], 1942), 9–39, and notes pp. 155–65. According to André Latreille, this text, published in Switzerland, circulated in occupied France. (Cf. *Résistance chrétienne à l'antisémitisme* [Librairie Arthème Fayard, 1988], 65, note 21 [English trans.: *Christian Resistance to Anti-Semitism* (San Francisco: Ignatius Press, 1990), 59–60, note 21].)

This text from 1941 continues, in fact, with a few supplementary notes, the articles published in *La Vie spirituelle* (June 1942: 542–50, and September 1942: 201–12; cf. *Christian Resistance*, 103–8). We have added to it as an appendix the additional note which Father de Lubac himself had supplied for the article at the time of its republication in *Affrontements mystiques* in 1950 (127–30).

copy of what he gave the priests and pagan antiquity. In the doctrine of the Incarnation, in the Catholic cult of the Virgin and the saints, he sees so many breaches made in the monotheistic absolute, so many toothing stones for the edifice of the true religion, which will establish the "real homogeneity between the adorers and the adored beings".[1] For the divinity must be "composed of its own adorers".

The essence of these views is taken up again by Louis Ménard, the "pagan mystic". According to Ménard, if Christianity has borrowed from the Jews "its traditions and its legend, through its dogmas it is tied to Hellenism, whose legitimate successor it is"; for "the dominant trait of Judaism is the height at which it places the divine idea; between its God and man, the distance is infinite; Christianity, on the contrary, has for its fundamental dogma the adoration of the Man-God".[2] Jules Soury, whom we quote below, is no less dependent on Comte. He, too, saw in Jesus a dangerous Jew, and if he sounds the assembly of the Aryans against the Semites, it is in order to lead the assault, more or less directly, against the idea of God, "abstraction of abstractions, quintessence of subtle essences, nothingness of nothingnesses". It is, on the other hand, the influence of Wagner that explains the lucubrations of Joséphin Péladan. After having proclaimed "Latin decadence" in a series of novels, the latter undertakes to "deliver the Gospel from that rapaciousness, Mosaism." Such is the object of a bizarre work entitled *Terre du Christ* (1901), in which he strives to dissociate the two Testaments and to show "that the Office of Holy Week borrows its expression as well as its doctrine from ancient India, that the Christian origins are all pagan, that there is not a straw of Jewishness at the sources of the Religion".[3] One can imagine what a fantastic Christianity results from such a demonstration. . . .

With the school of l'Action française, we return to the line of Auguste Comte and Jules Soury. It is too well known for there to be any reason to speak of it at length. It is in the collection of the first years of *l'Action française*, when it was, not a journal, but a review, as well as in the first works of its members that it is advisable to study its

[1] See *The Drama of Atheist Humanism* (San Francisco: Ignatius Press, 1995), 139–79.

[2] Sources of Christian dogma, in *La Critique religieuse*, first year (1879), 385.

[3] Joseph Buche, *L'École mystique de Lyon*, 283–84. There are some similar traits in the Belgian Edmond Picard. The latter, in an introduction to François Bournand's work, *Les Juifs et nos contemporains* (1898), explained the whole history of Europe since Salamis on the basis of the fight between Aryans and Semites.

doctrine. The anti-Semitism manifest there is just as well, and just as explicitly, anti-Christianity. "Jerusalem", "the Hebrew Christ", "the scourge of charity", "the monotheistic coalition" are designated there as objects of horror. As with Comte, "Rome" is, moreover, exalted there against "Geneva", but this Rome is not a Christian Rome, and when we read for example from the pen of one of the leaders of the school: "I have always considered that Catholicism saved the future of the human race", the perspicacious reader is invited to go on: it saved it from Christianity. The beginnings of the school were influenced by the thought of Nietzsche: this is especially apparent in Hugues Rebell and Pierre Lasserre;[4] but its principal theoretician wants to owe nothing to German thought, and he affects not even to know how to spell the name of that "strange writer of the Slavic race", "of that ingenious, eloquent and rather subtle Sarmatian".

Rémy de Gourmont and Jules de Gaultier are rather close to l'Action française. In *Les Juifs* by Louis Rougier, the theses of the school are set forth without any cautionary introduction. They are found again substantially in *Le Problème juif* by Georges Batault (1921), where "Greco-Roman values" are opposed to "Jewish values", where the triumph of the "exclusive and jealous God of the Jews" and the invasion of the spirit of the ancient prophets at the beginning of our era are deplored.

For modern Germany, the first name that must hold our attention is that of Hegel. Not that we must make this philosopher the initiator of an anti-Semitic propaganda, but his explanation of the spiritual genius of Israel is in fact one of the origins of the movement of ideas that occupies us. Here is how he speaks of the ancient Jews in his *Philosophy of history*:

> If the spiritual was still limited by the fact of nature with the Phoenician people, it proves, on the contrary, to be completely purified with the Jews: the pure product of thought is itself thought, arrives at consciousness, and the spiritual develops, resolved to the highest degree upon the encounter with nature and with its unity with it. . . .
>
> The spiritual immediately repudiates the sensate, and nature is lowered to an exterior thing and deprived of the divine.[5]

[4] Several traits in G. Bianquis, *Nietzsche en France, l'influence de Nietzsche sur la pensée française* (1929), chap. 14.

[5] *Vorlesung über die Philosophie der Geschichte*; French trans. by Gibelin: *Philosophie de l'histoire. La Judée*, 1:200 and 201.

For the first time, then, in the midst of the Jewish people, a divorce is produced between the spirit and nature, or, if one wishes, between reflection and life. That is progress, but it is at the same time a danger. It constitutes in a way a separated Infinity, which leaves the universe deprived of the divine and made by it an object without beauty. "This total reflection", comments Jean Hyppolite, "is the spirit of the Jewish people. Life has been broken, nothing but the relations of master and slave are conceivable between beings. . . . Life is no longer immanent to living things, but the infinite is beyond." But in addition, after having fixed the modalities of nature and vital relations by making things of them, the Jewish people "were not ashamed to desire these things as being gifts from the master": and we have there the principle both of a disturbing imperialism and of an industrial domination of nature. The world is no longer loved, it is used and possessed. Such is the deep meaning of Hegel's words on the great ancestor of the race: "Abraham did not want to love."[6]

Hegel had already outlined this thesis in the works of his youth. The rupture with nature seemed to him to explain the character of Jewish prophetism, in which he wished to see only a cold fanaticism. Sensitive to "the great tragedy of the Jewish people", he nevertheless refused to admit that it, like Greek tragedy, could arouse fear or pity; for these two feelings, he said, are awakened only by the fatal error of a beautiful being; but the spiritualistic abstraction that characterizes the genius of the Jews dismisses beauty: so "their tragedy can awaken only horror." And, wishing to embrace in an overall view the strange destiny of these people, the young Hegel wrote: "All its consecutive states, including the miserable and sordid state in which it is still found today, are only the consequences and developments of its original destiny: an infinite power to which they are opposed in vain." This destiny, he concluded, "abuses them and will abuse them until they are reconciled with it in the spirit of beauty and, through that reconciliation, suppress it."[7]

Several of these traits foreshadow Schopenhauer. In the latter, anti-Semitism is flaunted, violent, and it is mixed with hatred of all faith in God. The fundamental Judaic idea is, he recognizes, theism, "naked theism": now theism is "absurd and revolting", so that Judaism is "the

---

[6] Cf. Jean Hyppolite, *Introduction à la philosophie de l'histoire de Hegel* (1948), 44–46.

[7] Hegel, *L'Esprit du christianisme et son destin*, French trans., 19–24.

coarsest of religions".[8] It is an idolatry, for there is idolatry "from the moment one is faced with a personal being to whom one sacrifices, whom one invokes, whom one thanks".[9] And the idol of the Jews is the worst of all, for, through its exclusive claims, it engenders in its adorers an unbridled imperialism, and, as it claims to be creative, it establishes them in a detestable optimism with regard to this world.[10] Schopenhauer pursues it with a kind of rage. Believing quite wrongly, after a rather hasty reading, to smell a deist in Taine, he exclaims: "And again God and God! Everywhere this old Jew lets himself be seen, he spoils everything: let the door be shut in his face!"[11] Another day, to the same correspondent who he suspects interprets Kant in a too dogmatic a sense, he addresses this diatribe:

> The "thing in itself", for you, is the absolute, the veiled ontological proof on which the God of the Jews rides. And you, you walk before him, like King David before the holy ark, dancing and singing, with a wholly glorious air. And yet, despite the definition that was to make him unshakable: "primitive, eternal being, which has not begun, which cannot perish", he has been well and truly rejected by Kant. He has been conveyed to me in the state of a dead body, and when the odor of it returns to me, as in your letter, I am seized with impatience. . . .[12]

The whole misfortune of Christianity is not having known how to break with the Jewish Bible. The only true Christians were the Gnostics: in their mystical pessimism, they understood the heart of the new religion better than those "twelve Philistines from Jerusalem", with whom the Church has wished to claim kinship.[13] They saw that "the

---

[8] *Parerga und Paralipomena*, French trans., *Dialogue sur la religion*, Dietrich, 39 and 164; *Fragments pour l'histoire de la philosophie*, n. 13, Bossert, 295.

[9] *Parerga, Sur le théisme*, Dietrich, 98.

[10] *Cf. Parerga, Dialogue sur la religion*: "The impression that the study of the Septuagint has left me with is a warm affection and a profound respect for the *megas basileus Nabouchôdonosor.* I reproach it nevertheless for having treated a little too gently a people in possession of a god who granted them or promised them the lands of their neighbors. . . . May every people in possession of a god who makes neighboring lands so many 'promised lands' find in time their Nebuchadnezzar and, in addition, their Antiochus Epiphanius!" (Dietrich, 66). . . .

[11] To Frauenstaedt, August 17, 1855, Jean Bourdeau, *Schopenhauer, Pensées et fragments*, 48–49.

[12] Similarly, August 21, 1852, Bossert, 288.

[13] *Die Welt also Wille und Vorstellung*; French trans. by Bourdeau: *Le Monde comme volonté . . .*, 3:434; cf. 427–28 and 432–22. Adolphe Bossert, *Schopenhauer*, 93; Pierre Godet, *La Pensée de Schopenhauer*, 339ff.

Old and New Testament are diametrically opposed to each other and that their reunion forms a strange centaur".[14] How the core has subsequently been separated from the skin! At that time they would not have failed to recognize, beneath the superficial diversity of myths, the profound relationship of the religion of Christ with the religions of India, Brahmanism and, even more, Buddhism. Who knows even if Jesus, "raised by Egyptian priests whose religion was of Hindu origin, might not have taken from them the ethic of India and the notion of the avatar, which he might then have tried to accommodate with the Jewish dogmas and to graft onto the ancient trunk"?[15] In any case, "like a perfume of flowers carried from distant tropics across mountains and torrents, one senses in the New Testament the spirit of Hindu wisdom". . . .[16]

Thus do we see formed in Schopenhauer a Christianity of accommodation which, in his successors, will take many diverse and at times opposed forms, but in which the constant will be his horror of the God of Abraham, Moses and the prophets—which is as much as saying, of the God of Jesus. The anti-Semitism whose channel we are following here is one of the most notable aspects of the decision made to obtain in the European consciousness "the death of God".

"During the thirty years that followed the apparition of the *Parerga* and up to the first flashes of the sudden vogue of Nietzsche, Schopenhauer was the most widely read of the German thinkers."[17] Heinrich Heine, in whom the voice of the great modern apostasy was stronger than that of his race, was already explaining in terms, which must have struck Nietzsche, that if ancient Rome perished, it was because it was devoured by Judaic spiritualism:

> The dismembered lion of Judah, by gratifying the Romans with its spiritualism, perhaps wanted to avenge itself on the enemy conqueror as the dying centaur once did when it cunningly bequeathed to the son of Jupiter the robe tainted with its own blood, which was so fatal to him! And truly Rome, the Hercules of the peoples, was so powerfully consumed by the Jewish poison that its helmet and its armor fell from its sagging limbs and that its great imperial voice, which had dominated in battles, was

[14] *Parerga, Rationalisme*, Dietrich, 114–15; *Sur la religion*, 99 and 108.
[15] *Sur la religion*, Dietrich, 106.
[16] Ibid., 104. *Le Monde comme volonté*, 3:416, etc. Bossert, 294.
[17] Theodore Ruyssen, *Schopenhauer*, 367.

weakened and changed into humble murmurs of paternosters and into cadences of eunuchs.[18]

The "savage anti-Judaism" of Wagner[19] has the same origins and the same consonances. If Wagner "oscillates from Siegfried to Wotan, from the joy of living to disenchantment, from optimism to pessimism, from Feuerbach to Schopenhauer", he does not cease to bear a grudge against the Christian religion "for proposing for the adoration of the believer an abstract and unintelligible God beyond the sensible and real universe" and for creating in that way an antagonism between man and nature.[20] The wrong goes back to the first apostles, who thought they were making Jesus larger by making him the descendent of David, the successor of the prophets, the son of the Jewish Yahweh. So the Jewish spirit invaded nascent Christianity. It has subsequently penetrated it more and more deeply, particularly within the Catholic Church. The Galilean mildness has been repulsed like Greek beauty, and this was the triumph of the farsighted beast of prey, for the degeneration of humanity. Yet Wagner does not wish to despair: if he abandons an overly heterogeneous, overly semitized Latin civilization to its fall, he wants to place his confidence in the idealism of the Germanic race. Mixed with the "blood of Christ", Aryan blood will be regenerated: such is the message of *Parsifal*.[21]

Lagarde and Dühring give evidence of a more brutal logic. "My conservatism", says the former, "is reactionary on this point, since it goes back to the days of the Salian and Saxon emperors and since it would like to cancel all that has happened from their time to ours."[22] And Eugen Dühring, in a thought of more universal appearance: "The people will have finished with the Jewish spirit only when they have chased from their brain that secondary aspect of Hebraism that is present, which is to say, the Christian spirit."[23] But the one who, on top of Nietzsche, was to be the link uniting Schopenhauer and Wagner, on the one hand, and the theoreticians of National Socialism, on the other, was Houston Stewart Chamberlain.

---

[18] *De l'Allemagne*, 1884 ed., 1:190–91.

[19] Edmond Vermeil, *L'Allemagne*, 198.

[20] Henri Lichtenberger, *Richard Wagner poète et penseur*, 189, 300–301.

[21] Ibid., 108, 361–64, 400–401, 427–28, etc.

[22] Paul de Lagarde, *Deutsche Schriften*; quoted by Bernouilli, *Revue de métaphysique et de morale* (1918), 547.

[23] *Cf. Les Juifs*, Présences series, 21.

The merit of this English author, who was raised in France and finally settled in Vienna, is not equal to his success. His *Assises du XIXe siècle*[24] is nothing but a brilliant work of popularization. The racism of Gobineau is mixed with, transformed into that of Wagner. Schopenhauer is more than once followed and quoted. We find in it, brewed into a more or less coherent and always arbitrary synthesis,[25] all the anti-Semitical themes that we have just gone over. We will not waste our time in analyzing it. Let us merely say, briefly, that for Chamberlain Christianity derives from a threefold origin; through its Aryan origin, the true one, it is an excellent religion; through its Jewish origin, it is perverse; through its Mediterranean origin, it is contemptible. It is in its Catholic form that the Jewish and Mediterranean factors have especially corrupted it. In itself, it is wholly mystical, a close relative of Brahmanism and old Germanism. It is this pure essence that must be rediscovered within a select race. Jewish monotheism, which was imposed on Europe, not as an ennoblement, but as an impoverishment of religious life, will be eliminated; the "unique God" of the Jewish prophets will be replaced by the "one God" of Aryan mysticism. The true Jesus will be rediscovered—just the reverse of the Jesus of Nietzsche—an august figure, remarkable for his combativeness, and about whom there is not the least reason to admit that he was of the Jewish race.[26] Then his words "the kingdom of God is within us" will be understood, that is, that the divinity of nature is what man furnishes it from his own substance. The two terms of faith and religion will be stripped of their Semitic sense. Giving life again to myths that the Judaic poverty had taken all color out of, returning to men "the lively emotion of the great cosmic mystery",[27] the religion of the future will mark a vigorous rebirth of idealism. It will be revealed as "capable of

[24] *Die Grundlagen des neunzehuten Jahrhunderts* (1899). French trans. by Robert Godet, *La Genèse du XIXe siècle*, 2 vols., 3d ed. (1913).

[25] "The author", the foreword tells us, "did not imagine for a minute that his book possessed any scientific value. . . . We beg the reader, then, not to be mistaken about the role of the notes that lend certain pages a false look of erudition." And a little farther on: "It is not as a scholar that I have attacked these subjects; it is as a child of the present. . . . It is not as a pontiff of superhuman objectivity that I have formed my judgments; it is from the point of view of an aware German."

[26] *Genèse du XIXe siècle*, Godet trans., passim, particularly 285–99.

[27] Ibid., 529 and 563, etc. What Chamberlain, like so many others, rejects is that kind of sterilization of the mythological instinct worked by monotheism. He does not accept the injunction of the prophet (Hab 2:20): "Let all the earth be silent before Yahweh!"

evoking eternity in a kiss and of bringing redemption in the space of a flash of lightning". In this regenerated Christianity, which no humanitarian verbiage will spoil, the heroes of the Aryan race will be associated with Christ in one and the same cult, suited to assuring the triumph of the Germans in their battle for the world empire.[28]

From Schopenhauer to Chamberlain, the perspective has moved. This is because the first was impressed by Buddhism, as Eugène Burnouf, in particular, has just revealed,[29] while the second was inspired by the more recent works of Paul Deussen on the religion of the Véda. Thus the acosmism of the former became a naturism in the latter, and the Jews, accused by the one of believing too much in the value of this world, now see themselves reproached above all for their transcendent abstractions. Schopenhauer was scandalized by their appetite to conquer: Chamberlain discerns a "latent Aryanism" in the most ancient parts of the Old Testament, those in which this appetite is most manifest. But what importance do these differences have? The opposition to authentic Christianity is no less strong in either one of them; and in both, this is but one with the hatred of Israel.

At least Chamberlain, like Schopenhauer and like Wagner, remained in fact on the level of dreams and aestheticism. He did not go any farther, as have innumerable authors who go on to quote them as their authorities, the most important of whom, by reason of the official role he has played, is Alfred Rosenberg,[30] the great adversary of Jewish universalism and of Christian love. We are well enough aware of parallel efforts, whether founded to revive a frank paganism or to sift out a so-called Nordic Christianity, freed from the "Syrian Jahweh" whose reign is sustained by "an Etruscan pope". . . . These are yesterday's

[28] On Chamberlain, cf. Seillières, "La Religion impérialiste", *Revue des deux mondes*, 1903 and 1904. Henry Rollin, "H. S. Chamberlain 'prophète' du racisme", in the *Temps* (February 28, 1934). The twofold hatred that Chamberlain bears Israel and Catholic Rome culminates in his hatred for the Society of Jesus, that society founded by two men of whom the first was the non-Aryan Basque Ignatius Loyola, "type of the anti-German", and the second, his secretary Polanco, "pure Jewish blood only lately converted". "Those", he says, "who pass by phenomena of this kind without paying attention have no feeling for the majesty of facts" (709–21).

[29] From 1844 on, Schopenhauer refers explicitly to the master work of Eugène Burnouf, *L'Introduction à l'histoire du bouddhisme indien.*

[30] By the very title he chose for his work, *The Myth of the Twentieth Century*, Rosenberg marks his plan to follow Chamberlain. He had devoted an initial work to him, in which he celebrated him as a prophet.

facts. They are associated with persecutions for which they are presented as the doctrinal justification.

It is repugnant to us to move about again in this bloody filth by rereading these blasphemous pamphlets.[31] We will note in conclusion that, while this kind of doctrinal anti-Semitism has always remained, in France, an abstract theory or literary speculation, it found in Germany a vast acceptance and aroused powerful movements. We do not believe the reason for this is to be found on the side of the respective situation of the Jews in the two countries. But while France is a country that was latinized and Christianized everywhere, to its deepest layers, the Germanic sensibility remained largely accessible to the evocation of its ancient heroes and its ancient cults. Cultism is for us only archeology: on the other side of the Rhine, the voices of Siegfried and Wotan are still capable of awakening an echo.[32] We, too, have our own demons. Only the law of Christ can exorcise them all.

A New Religious "Front"

I

Changing of a label on a bottle does not change the contents of that bottle. Calling the God of the Christians or the law that rules them "Jewish god" or "Jewish morality" does not change the character of that God or of that law. Because it is launched under a name that is sadly in the style of anti-Semitism will not make anti-Christian propaganda less anti-Christian. It will only be more perfidious, more dangerous

---

[31] See, among others, Albert Béguin, "Le Néo-paganisme allemand", *Revue des deux mondes* (May 15, 1935); Helvétius, "La Mystique de la vie dans la révolution nationale allemande", *Esprit* (1934).

[32] This is what Heinrich Heine had already noted, in the very pages where he orchestrated the anti-Semitic theme associated with that of the "death of God": *De l'Allemagne*, 1884 ed., 2:42: "No! the memories of the ancient Germanic beliefs are still not entirely extinguished. There exists in Westphalia old men who still know where the old idols are buried. On their deathbed, they tell it to their last grandson, and the latter carries this holy secret in his heart like a treasure. In Westphalia, the Saxony of the ancients, all that is buried is not dead. When one travels through the old oak groves, one still hears the voices of the ancient centuries, the profound magic words in which runs more life than in the whole literature of the Brandenburg March. An indefinable feeling made me tremble when I roamed beneath the shadows of its old forest. When I passed before the Siegburg, my guide said to me: 'This is where King Wittekind lived!' and he sighed deeply. He was a simple woodcutter, and he carried a large axe. . . ." We will make allowances, of course, for literary romanticism.

because less directly apparent and less frank. Many Christians, too little aware of their faith and too attracted already by a host of ideas and sentiments that are little compatible with it, or simply too ignorant of the "malice of the century" and too little on guard against its artifices, will be in danger of taking this coarse bait. Instead of immediately provoking a salutary reaction, the attack thus risks weakening from the beginning some of those at whom it is aiming in order then better to corrupt them. This is what has happened more than once in the past. This is what has been happening again for some time.

They speak, for example, of a "Jewish idealism", which would supposedly act "like a poison on peoples who accepted Jews into their midst". They denounce the harmful force in this idealism that supposedly suggested to the Jews "to place outside the world a creative Power without which the world could not exist and to install it in a position of absolute preeminence with regard to all beings and all things". They complain that this "gratuitously invented" Being then dominates the whole individual and social life of those who have imagined it. They denounce as so many "failures of energy" the fact that Hebrews alleviated slavery, the fact that they introduced asceticism, that they gave precedence to the "moral man" over the "physical or psychic man", that they forbade homicide and lust, that they spread a "mystique of humility". . . . They are surprised that men have thus been capable "of sacrificing their human and vital interests for abstract considerations about the Beyond". They grow impatient particularly with this word "justice", which "reappears in every line of the prophets and the Psalms". They proclaim that people are lost in advance who let themselves be seduced by the Jewish chimeras to the point of accepting the idea of social justice and believing in the right of the weak, and so on.[1]

In simpler terms, what can we say, except that Christianity is the enemy? Whether it did or did not receive this heritage from Israel can have little importance for the moment: our goal is not to sift through the sieve of historical criticism a literature that manifestly belongs to another genre and demonstrates other concerns. But what would remain of our Christian faith if one were to uproot from it monotheism, the Decalogue, universalism, belief in eternity? Is God any less our

[1] The quotations in this paragraph are drawn from the work by M. Fayolle-Lefort, *Le Juif cet inconnu*, published (of course) in the *Le Temps nouveaux* series.

God because a blasphemer affects to call him Jehovah?[2] Apart from any consideration of the events that can explain such a campaign and which magnify its repercussions, it will then be understood why the Christian conscience makes its protest heard and why the alarm is being sounded.[3]

Undoubtedly, a few veils have been drawn here and there, in order to create an illusion. Thus what is called Christian charity has been freely exalted at the expense of Jewish justice. We are told how Christianity "instinctively rebelled" against the latter, and we are invited to admire how, "with a slight push", it transformed it into the former. If there is still a question, in the Sermon on the Mount, of "those who hunger and thirst for justice"—they forget to mention at the same time "those who suffer persecution" for it—the meaning of the word, they tell us, is "ambiguous", and when Saint Paul speaks in turn of the "justice of God", his sole thought is to combat thereby this "Judaic justice". In brief, thanks to the Gospel, "something greater was substituted for justice. Charity made its appearance in the world."[4] But, we ask, what charity? Solely that, they respond to us, which maintains the social order by "refusing all rights" to the lowly, while toning down what might have been too cruel in the invitation that it makes to them to resign themselves. We have often heard such a description of "charity", but not from the mouths of the Doctors of the Church! and the fresher appeal to a few exegetical fantasies will not make it any more authentic. Christians who let themselves be taken in by such a poor caricature would have to be very poorly instructed in their religion, very poorly formed by it.

[2] Cf. the sermon by Msgr. Franz Rudolph Bornewasser, Bishop of Trèves (Cathedral of Trèves, November 30, 1941), protesting against the speeches delivered at Trèves and at Coblence on November 22 and 23, in the course of which the speaker had exclaimed: "Jehovah, this is the end of your day! Jehovah, you have lost your game! Jehovah, all is over for you!" (In the Swiss Catholic weekly *Schildwache*, issue of February 21, 1942.) Did the blasphemer suspect that he was repeating, more awkwardly, the remarks of a Jew? Cf. Heinrich Heine, "De l'Allemagne depuis Luther", *Revue des deux mondes* (1934), 4:408: "It is the old Jehovah himself who is preparing to die. . . ."

[3] "In its essence", wrote Abbé Charles Journet, "whether it knows it or not, and it is known by all its inventors, anti-Semitism is more than anti-Semitism. It is anti-Christianity. How can one hate the promise without hating the fulfillment? hate the Old Testament without hating the New?" "Antisémitisme", in *Nova et vetera*, Catholic journal for French Switzerland (July–September 1941), 229.

[4] Fayolle-Lefort, *Le Juif.*

Besides, we have but lately known several similar schemes. Must we recall what Jules Soury wrote in 1878?

> When Titus went up to the Capitol, he dragged behind his triumphal chariot and showed to the City and to the world, among other spoils from the Temple of Jerusalem, the golden table, the seven-branched candelabra, the purple veils from the Holy of Holies and the book of the Law. The Jewish Bible, the Torah of Yahweh, conquered, torn, captive, in chains, what a triumph for the ancient world and for our Aryan race! The triumph scarcely lasted: today again, after eighteen centuries, the old Hebrew book is the most implacable enemy of our race and our civilization. When will humanity be allowed to see a new Titus enchain the Bible?[5]

We understand well what the "old Hebrew book" symbolizes here, and that it is not only Judaism. . . . But, whether in Soury himself or particularly in those who were inspired by him, the veils of the illusion offered ordinarily had a slightly different color. The line of combat did not follow exactly the same outline. Charity was then treated no better than justice. "Jewish visions" and "Christian sentiment" were equally proscribed in their corrosive purity; "Christian anarchy" was as detested as Jewish prophetism. But glory was given to the Church for stamping them both out together. None of the "relics of the narrow cenacle of Jerusalem" managed to find favor; the most ill-treated of all was faith in the one God, in the Absolute. But Catholicism, they added, was so adept at "organizing the idea of God" that it succeeded in "taking away his poison"; it enveloped the Absolute so well in "legions of intermediaries" that it found means of neutralizing it, and it was thus that Rome saved us from Jerusalem. . . . In a similar way, according to others, "Romanism" was the dike that prevented humanity from "crumbling ever more and more" in trying "to realize the fantasies of an Asiatic dream". Thanks to it, "Europe", although "nominally Christianized", could continue to live "off the few drops of pagan elixir that it saved from the jealousy of our converters". Thanks to it, the effects of Christianity, that "religion of slaves", and of its "perverse sentimentality" were at least toned down.[6] So spoke Rémy de Gourmont around the beginning of the century. It was not so long

[5] *Essais de critique religieuse*, 26–27. Cf. *Campagne nationaliste* 1902.

[6] Rémy de Gourmont, *Le Chemin de velours*, 13th ed. (1924), 309–17: "Sur le christianisme".

ago that another theoretician, Jules de Gaultier, proposed to us a still bolder series of "dissociations". While admitting, too, that Christianity was essentially Judaic, he wanted an appeal to be made to the Jewish elite as well as to the "conservatives" and to the Churches of all confessions, "which have never been anything but the means of preventing Christianity from making its way", in order to assure the triumph of the "anti-Christian reaction". . . .[7]

Already dated remarks, for the most part, and ones we would have liked to let fall into oblivion. We might have hoped to be spared them henceforth. But here they are, finding a new posterity. The remarks that succeed them today and that are sometimes inspired by them can no longer be taken as remarks by aesthetes. Neither the form in which they are clothed nor the circumstances that support them permit that. They play their role in a large-scale offensive that has forces of all kinds at its disposal. Their very coarseness encourages their spread. It is no longer, then, a time for indulgent illusions. These new blasphemies must not find us less alert than before. Let us say rather: they must find us more alert.

We find here, moreover, a new protagonist arising who does not mince words. Henri de Montherlant does not hesitate to confide to the readers of *La Gerbe*[8] that the evils from which we suffer come from the "Christian values" we have accepted. He also brings his brilliant collaboration to the anti-Christian campaign methodically led for a year by the *Nouvelle revue française*. From a writer of this class, we might have expected, perhaps, a little more subtlety in thought and "breadth" in attitude. Superb insolence was enough for him. He quickly had Jesus Christ, the "celebrated Jew", executed. To believe him, our national defeat would be a defeat of Christianity, that is to say, first caused by him. Christ would thereby find himself judged—judged and condemned. When the Wheel[9] turns, is not the one who comes to rule always right and the one who is crushed always wrong? In that case,

[7] Jules de Gaultier, *Nietzsche* in the series *Les Maîtres de la pensée antichrétienne* (1926). Cf. the speech to Parliament by Deputy Allard, in January 1903: "I myself am not anti-Semitic, I have only one reproach for the Jews, that of having poisoned Aryan thought, which is so noble and broad, with Hebrew monotheism." Quoted by Georges Sorel, *Réflexions sur la violence*, 6th ed., 335, note 1. See also Regnard, in *Revue socialiste*, 5:499.

[8] Issue of October 2, 1941.

[9] With a capital. Presented in this way, and augmented by a little solar mythology, its appearance is thought to be more noble.

doubly wrong, for the present event, this triumph of the "pagan", is "just": is not the pagan, healthy and virile, right as opposed to the Jew, feminine and sick? France was Christian, which comes back to saying that it was Jewish. One had to foresee what happened: *in hoc signo fuges* (*sic*).[10] Will we remain indifferent under the pretext that it is still here a question of Jews?

II

This debate is purely about religion. It has often been said, in fact, that if one rejects belief in God, it is largely for reasons of the social or political order: yet, for all that, belief in God is nonetheless rejected in the most formal and explicit way. And if one truly does so only because of abuses, why always consider these abuses as if they were the authentic fruits of religious teachings confined to the Bible and the Gospel? One need only read, moreover, to ascertain that the quarrel made with Christianity goes far beyond questions relating to public life: it is a question of the whole man and of his spiritual life. Are the problem of immortality and the problem of sexual morality, for example, political problems, with which a Christian would not, as such, have to be familiar? But, to keep to what is in fact the most obvious, does one believe that in the past, when Celsus, Porphyry or Julian attacked Christianity, it was not also, among other major reasons, because of the transformations that this new faith was introducing into society? Their "aristocraticism" was shocked by a religion that was addressed to the common people; the "Christian chimera" seemed to them a public danger, and they saw in it both a "sickness" and "sedition".[11] A little later, in the time of Saint Augustine, was it not particularly because of its action, judged to be deleterious, on the destinies of the Empire that the pagan intellectuals attacked it? The sole, fundamental

[10] *Nouvelle revue française* (November 1, 1941): "Le Solstice de juin" (published later in a volume of the same title). Cf. the reflections made on this subject by Cardinal Gerlier, in his *Allocution aux hommes*, at the time of a pilgrimage to Fourvière on Sunday, December 7: "Should there not be enough respect owed to what is most sacred in the depth of our souls and to what can safeguard the brotherhood of hearts in our suffering France to preserve us from such statements! Let us take care: such an aberration could well become more serious than defeat, for defeat is a catastrophe from which we rise every day, while this anti-Christian work would become an intoxication from which we could die." *Semaine religieuse du diocèse de Lyon* (December 12, 1941), 30.

[11] Origen, *Contra Celsum*, l. VIII, c. 2 and 14, etc. Cf. Pierre de Labriolle, *La Réaction païenne*, 152 and 168.

reason for the sack of Rome by Alaric, in their eyes, was the abandonment of the ancient national divinities. . . . Was this a reason why someone like Origen or Cyril should be silent? And should the *City of God* henceforth be condemned in principle as a work of political controversy?[12] In the whole history of religious persecutions, there was not one that did not have political motives or pretexts—nor do we see, moreover, how it could have been otherwise. The Christians of the first centuries were pursued by Roman magistrates for the crime of high treason, *titulum laesae augustioris majestatis.*[13] Will we say, then, that there were never any true martyrs? As if it were not precisely of the essence of the Christian faith to entail consequences for the conduct of one's whole life, for one's social life as well as for one's individual life!

Of course, clearly we do not have to canonize all the consequences that could be drawn from this. We have the right to judge that there were some that were indiscreet and rash, that there were also some that were false. We know that, outside the traditional interpretation and control of the teaching Church, the Scriptures can be poorly understood. Nor do we forget that the demands of Christianity, without ever abdicating, must always, in practice, come to terms with the laws and the resistances of human nature and that, in order to undertake effectively to Christianize institutions and customs, as much prudence, patience and "realism" is required as ardor and generosity. Experience is enough to warn us, in addition, that nothing is more dangerous than to want to impose norms of Christian origin on a society that no longer really lives by Christianity. Finally, within Catholic orthodoxy itself, and notwithstanding the at times very clear directives of authority, such as those of the great pontifical encyclicals, there is still room for a great diversity of tendencies and schools. This is to say that on more than one point we might actually come to agree—although not at all in the same spirit—with the very ones who are here attacking our faith.[14] But from them to us there would nonetheless remain the whole distance of that faith. There would remain the whole opposition

[12] The historical record of the great work by Saint Augustine can be seen in the recent *Saint Augustin* by Canon Gustave Bardy.

[13] Tertullian, *Apologeticum*, c. 28; cf. c. 10: *Sacrilegii et majestatis rei convenimur.*

[14] Likewise, if it were necessary to see only a chronicle or an analysis, we would be the first to recognize the justice of a few caustic traits in the writing quoted by Henri de Montherlant. Let us not confuse the protestation of outraged faith with the scandal of conformism.

between those who want to belong to Christ and those who reject him as poisonous.

They would serve us a Christianity of ceremonies or even of "devotion". They would encourage it as needed. But it would have to be without intransigence and above all without efficacy. Is this not how the matter was once understood by those emperors and scholars who would have asked no more than acceptance of a cult of Christ alongside cults of Isis, Cybele and Mithra? After an initial period of hesitation, they would have tolerated it, protected it even, provided that it remain "inoffensive". They would have enrolled it in its turn after so many others, they would have absorbed it into their state system. But it is not a trivial or unimportant thing to believe that "Christ is Lord"![15] Christianity is not at all inoffensive. Christianity is demanding. Christianity is not satisfied with ceremonies and devotions. It would never have been itself if, at the same time as it undertook to transform the inner man and in consequence of that transformation, it had not in fact placed its mark on the relations between men. Without going beyond some simple statements of fact, what could terms such as Christendom or Christian civilization really signify otherwise? Now, it is precisely this Christian civilization, the little that is ever achieved of it or what still remains of it, in any case it is its very inspiration, its soul that is resented today. What they hold against Christianity is not at all abuses or distortions, it is the most authentic principles and the most upright spirit. For us, therefore, it is not a question, "as in other times, of maintaining the fight against deficient or altered forms of religious civilization, most still keeping a soul of truth and justice inherited from Christianity or unconsciously drawn from its contact; today, it is the very substance of Christianity, the very substance of religion that is at stake." This grave warning, given on a solemn occasion from the pulpit of Notre Dame de Paris by the one who was soon to become Pope Pius XII,[16] is of still greater urgency today. Yes, the debate with

---

[15] Cf. 1 Cor 12:3; 1 Jn 2:22; Acts 17:7. "*Kurios Christos.* Christians have endured the death of martyrdom because of this brief formula. The pagans could not understand that the Christians should prove to be so narrow and were not willing at any price to say: *Kurios Kaisar.* The imperial functionary thus said to the old Polycarp of Smyrna appearing before him: 'What is so terrible about saying *Kurios Kaisar* and making a sacrifice?' (*Martyrium Polycarpi*)." O. Cullmann, "Les Origines des premières confessions de foi", in *Revue d'histoire et de philosophie religieuse* (1941), 93–94.

[16] Cardinal Pacelli, Speech delivered at Notre Dame de Paris on July 13, 1937 (*Documenta-*

which we are concerned is purely about religion. But it is also about total religion.

When it is pointed out to us, then, that we must now choose between "Europe" and "Judea", let us understand this: the choice that is proposed to us is between Christianity and paganism. Thus, under Julian the Apostate, it was necessary to choose between the camp of the "Galileans" and that of the "Greeks".[17] When the modern European is invited to reject the "Jewish poison", let us not be fooled by the phrase: nothing less than the definitive apostasy of Europe is being demanded.[18]

"At the beginning of our era", they explain to us, for example, "the European spirit" was subjected to a first assault by "Mosaism". Will we be naïve enough not to understand this language? What other meaning can it have if not that paganism was then subjected to the assault by a nascent Christianity? They consent to repeat it to us, moreover, in terms that are a little clearer by specifying that "Jewish values undertook the corruption of the European conscience" at the very moment when "Christianity spread over the totality of the Greco-Latin world."

Here again, let us note, certain reservations are introduced, or rather certain semblances of reservations, which would hope to appease certain scruples. Soon they let us understand that true Christianity, at bottom, has nothing to fear from this revenge that Europe wants to take today because even at the time of the Renaissance "[Christianity] was stripped nearly entirely of what remained to it of Hebraism",[19] which is to say, that, turning its back on the Gospel, it was transformed, in its Catholic form, into a kind of neopaganism. This is the thesis that is naturally proposed to peoples of the Latin tradition, students in Roman law. Soon, on the other hand, for the use of peoples who inherited the Protestant spirit, "star of Judah and Rome" are mixed into a single entity.[20] Catholicism is then attacked with violence, as having

---

tion catholique, 38:261). Words recalled by Msgr. Durieux, Archbishop of Chambéry, in the speech delivered to the solemn opening of the Catholic Faculties of Lyons on November 17, 1941.

[17] Julian, *Letter 84* (Bidez ed., 144). Philostorgius, *Histoire eccésiastique*, l. II, c. 14, etc. Cf. J. Bidez, *Vie de l'empereur Julien*, 49. *Labriolle*, 422.

[18] Or at least, if it is a question of de Montherlant, for several seasons. But, he adds, when Christianity returns, "will we be there to 'betray' once again?" (loc. cit., 526).

[19] Fayolle-Lefort, *Le Juif.*

[20] *Hitlerjugend* (the official organ of nazi youth), quoted by the *Documentation catholique* (1936), col. 1058. On the contrary, Heinrich Heine once wanted to see in Catholicism a

developed to the utmost the seed of universalism contained in the Old Testament and as being, in consequence, no more than a "judaized Christianity".[21] Some, then, give the Christian religion credit for having been paganized late in life, in its Catholic and Roman tradition. Others reproach it for having, from the beginning, with Saint Paul, given the authentic Christ the slip, who was, to believe them, not at all Semite but Aryan,[22] and they exalt a stillborn Christianity which they reconstitute according to their fantasies, a wholly "positive" Christianity that would supposedly have been the vehicle of the values of "Nordic Hellenism". . . . It is in this spirit that some undertake, as they say, to "disencumber religious teaching from its Judeo-Eastern residues".[23]

Many variations on these fundamental themes are worked out. Did not one of these "historians", seduced for several years now by the "Aryan" charm,[24] urge us just the other day to renew from top to bot-

"gnostic Indian spiritualism" and in evangelical Christianity a "Judaic and deist spiritualism", 1:496.

[21] Alfred Rosenberg, *The Myth of the Twentieth Century*. Likewise, the speech of September 6, 1938, etc. As early as 1899, at the anti-Semitic congress of Hamburg, the idea that Christianity had to be purged of any Jewish element had been launched. Several months later, it was taken up by Houston Stewart Chamberlain, in *La Genèse du XIXe siècle*. The latter saw in Catholicism in general, and more particularly in the Jesuit Order, the ally of Jewish power and the adversary par excellence of Aryanism: Do the Jesuits not issue from the collaboration of two men, one a Basque and the other a Jew: Ignatius Loyola and his secretary Polanco, that is to say, of a non-Aryan and an anti-Aryan? (*Genèse*, French ed. by Robert Godet, vol. 1, 3d ed. (1913), 709–21.

[22] Chamberlain, *Genèse*, 285–99: "We do not perceive the least reason for admitting that the relations of Jesus Christ were of the Jewish race. . . . It is so probable that Jesus did not have in his veins a single drop of Jewish blood that this probability is nearly equal to a certitude. . . . This purely negative result has nonetheless a considerable price. It contributes to rectifying to an important degree our knowledge of Christ, making it easier for us, therefore, to understand the power exerted up to the present day by this figure."

[23] Freyberg, first minister of Anhalt, quoted by Ernest Kiesewetter, "Réflexions sur le néopaganisme allemand", *Dossiers de l'Action populaire* (June 10, 1937), 1283. Cf. Rosenberg, *Myth*, 604, on Jesus: "The powerful preacher, enflamed by anger . . . , that is the formative ideal that emerges from the Gospels for us; but not the sacrificial lamb of Jewish prophecy, nor the crucified. And if this ideal cannot emerge from the Gospels, then the Gospels, too, are dead." And Chamberlain, *Myth*, 276: "Another trait of Jesus must be stressed . . . : his combativeness."

[24] Already in 1935, Charles Autran had testified to his enthusiastic adherence to pan-Iranism with his *Mithra, Zoroastre et la préhistoire aryenne du christianisme*, a work in which he explained that the "Semitism" of biblical doctrines had been greatly exaggerated, that Christianity had above all spread the "marvelous Aryan doctrines" in the West, that in everything that had contributed to its formation, all was Iranian or Iranized.

tom our conception of Christian origins in order to account for them by a whole series of factors in which the Semitic factor was lumped together with the rest? And did he not propose that we draw from that a new humanism, "Eurasian humanism", as vast as it is diverse, destined undoubtedly to replace the Christian humanism of our ancestors?[25] Grandiose, rather hazy views at which we may smile. But also, with some, pernicious myths that serve precise designs. Neither the alleged modern Catholicism nor the alleged primitive Christianity is the Christianity of the Church, the Catholicism of Christ. What we have there are only words, signs of a mind that has been misled or that is destined to lead the reader astray. Once again, will they be capable of doing so with Christians who do not want in advance to be deceived?

III

It is all too easy to perceive the circumstances, of a wholly different order than intellectual, to the rescue of which such theses are being mobilized. If the clerics did not always betray them, as Julien Benda wished recently to persuade us, every time they go down into the arena, we could no longer affirm that this descent was always the unalloyed work of a cleric. The race of "theologians of the prince" has never been lacking when there was need of it. It is anxious not to prove unworthy today. But neither has this race ever invented anything that leaves its mark on the history of thought. Across these theories that profess to be in turn religious philosophy, sociology, history or exegesis, it is particularly the great voice of Nietzsche that still makes itself heard. Mixed, certainly, with other voices, and terribly "vulgarized" as well as corrupt in more than one aspect; one can imagine the anger that would have swept that great loner travestied in this way as a master against such a generation of "disciples". But it is nonetheless recognizable. This face of Zarathustra that a child shows to the prophet in a mirror, at once alike and disfigured.[26]

[25] Charles Autran, "Des Origines du christianisme", an article published (naturally) in the *Nouvelle revue française* (June 1, 1941). Father Vincent has just given a vigorous and spiritual refutation in *Vivre et Penser, recherches d'exégèse et d'histoire*, first series (1941), 265–74.

[26] *Also sprach Zarathustra*; French trans. by Albert: *Ainsi parlait Zarathoustra*, second part, 109–10.

Christianity may have formed itself in reaction against Judaism. The latter may have combated it relentlessly at the time of its first expansion. Nietzsche nonetheless discerns more than one continuity between them, more than one profound relation. In his eyes, it is "Jewish astuteness" that has "staged the Christian ideal".[27] The religion of Christ is, according to him, only an "immense act of vengeance perpetrated by the Jews against the splendor of the ancient world. The Israelites carried out their designs with a supreme Machiavellianism: they crucified the founder of Christianity and denied his religion so that other peoples would swallow without any mental reservations the bait that was offered them."[28] This undertaking was most secret, most profoundly conceived, most tenaciously carried out. Seething Jewish thought advanced under a strange and masked phantom that it called Jesus. A marvelous means of seduction invented by Israel to serve its spite![29] Let us admire here, comments Charles Andler very accurately, the black magic of this great secret politic of hate. . . . Now the deadly poison distilled by the Jewish soul was spread into the entire body of humanity. Europe, America and, almost to begin with, Africa have been Jewish ever since. . . .[30] For Christianity is not at all, as some could believe, "a movement of reaction against the Semitic instinct; it is the very consequence of it, one more conclusion in its terrifying logic".[31] "A form of emancipated Judaism",[32] but Judaism all the same.[33] It constitutes the vengeance of Israel.[34]

Let the God of the Christians be, for example, this god of the poor, of sinners, of the sick. A "good" god, god of a degenerate race, the pale ideal of an ebbing life. Shall we oppose his character of "goodness" to

[27] *Der Wille zur Macht*, no. 372; French trans. by Bianquis: *Volonté de puissance*, 1:172.

[28] Cf. Lou Andreas-Salomé, *Friedrich Nietzsche in seinen Werken*; French trans., 222.

[29] *Zur Genealogie der Moral*; French trans. by Albert: *Généalogie de la morale*, 47–48.

[30] Charles Andler, *Nietzsche*, vol. 6, *La Dernière philosophie de Nietzsche*, 158–60.

[31] *Der Antichrist*; French trans. by Albert: *L'Antéchrist*, no. 24, *Le Crépuscule des idoles*, 271. Cf. *Généalogie de la morale*, 1:8: "Let us not believe in particular that this love was the contrary of that thirst for vengeance, the opposite of that Jewish hatred. No. This love is a product of that hatred, like its triumphant leaves. . . ."

[32] *Der Wille zur Macht*, no. 383; Bianquis trans., 1:176.

[33] Erich Ludendorff would write one day: "The Bible contains the purposes of the Jews, and the Christian dogma serves to propagate them." *La Source sacrée de la force allemande*. Cf. *Le Figaro* (April 6, 1937), p. 3, col. 2.

[34] According to Jules de Gaultier (*Nietzsche*, 158), this idea is a "blazing flare projected into the night of History and suited to illumine it."

the character of justice that the god of Israel had? Not at all. We are, on both sides, dealing with the same "moral" god. God at once just and good, who by these two traits joined together is opposed to the aggressive god, to the strong, brave, superb and proud god, to the god who is cruel when he wishes, to the god of the noble peoples in whom life is rising. Wherever he may go through the world and whatever may be the number of those who rally around him, this god remains Jewish and his kingdom remains a kingdom of the ghetto.[35] There should be no objection to the fact that Plato and then Aristotle were already conceiving of a god who might be considered the ancestor of the God of the Christians: insofar as this Greek god appears transcendent, which is to say, a stranger to the life and the healthy passions of this world, he is himself the fruit of a first contamination of Hellenism by the Jewish spirit. Plato, "that anti-Greek, that Semite by instinct", is "the great bridge that leads to corruption".[36] Do we not know, besides, that the decadence of the most noble of peoples begins with Socrates?[37]

Along with the Jewish god, it was the whole Jewish conception of salvation that Christianity adopted in order to impose it on other peoples. It was the Jewish idea of sin.[38] It was the Jewish idea of sacrifice. It was also the whole Jewish morality, if not in its external details and prescriptions, at least in its basic inspiration: a morality of feelings, a morality of the weak and of slaves, which is substituted for the heroic morality of the Greeks.[39] Christian charity is a "Judaic charity",[40] "smoldering under the ashes of humility and misery" in the little circles of the Diaspora.[41] The sign of the Cross is the symbol of

[35] *Der Antichrist*, nos. 16 to 19; Albert trans., 260–64.

[36] *Der Wille zur Macht*, nos. 380 and 393; ibid.: Plato had been "contaminated by Jewish bigotry [in Egypt]" (1:176 and 180). He, in turn, contaminated stoicism (*Werke*, 15:330).

These views were taken up again by Alfred Rosenberg, H. Heyse and several others. "Plato", he said, for example, "is of all the Greek sages the one who brought back the most ideas, and the most singular ideas, from Asia." Insofar as one experiences more or less sympathy toward these Platonian conceptions, one will speak of an Iranian Asia or of a Semitic Asia.

[37] We know that, from the time of *Die Geburte der Tragödie*, Nietzsche took a position against Socrates.

[38] *Die fröhliche Wissenschaft*, no. 135; French trans. by Vialatte: *Le Gai savoir*, 108–9.

[39] See particularly *Jenseit von Gut und Böse*, *Zur Genealogie der Moral* and *Der Wille zur Macht*, passim. Cf. Yves de Montcheuil, "Nietzsche et la critique de l'idéal chrétien", in *Cité nouvelle* (June 25, 1941).

[40] *Morgenrothe*, no. 334; French trans. by Albert: *Aurore*, 297.

[41] *Der Wille zur Macht*, no. 373. "Nothing Greek or Hindu or, particularly, German here.

the transmutation of all the ancient values fraudulently carried out by the Jewish mind.[42] Nietzsche trembled at seeing "the somber propylaea of Jewish salvation" rise on the horizon of history.[43] He quite particularly blamed the Apostle Paul, "that most ambitious and most importunate of souls, that mind as full of superstition as cunning", that "outspoken, pernicious head", that "counterfeiter", that "ingenious model in hatred", for the determining role that he played in the formation of the new cult.[44] He denounced him, as well as Socrates, as a "decadent".[45] Before Paul, there was still only a handful of sectarians, whose influence was not at all assured or was perhaps exercised in another sense. But Jesus was for Paul "a mere 'motif' on the basis of which he composed his music".[46] Paul thus became "the inventor of Christianity", through which the Jewish people, more precisely, "the Jewish priesthood", could proceed to the spiritual conquest of the world.[47] It is time to work a new transmutation of values. It is time to reject not only the dogmas and the precepts of Christianity but, more radically, the quality of soul that engendered them. On the ruins of an abolished Christianity, a thought at last "purified of the *moraline*" must be set up, which comes back to saying purified of the "*Judaine*".[48]

It matters little that in all this Nietzsche is not what one might call "original". It matters little that, just before him, Eugen Dühring had written, in speaking of the Christian religion: "The people will have finished with the Jewish spirit only when they have chased from their brain that secondary aspect of Hebraism that is present."[49] We could

The hymn to charity composed by Saint Paul has nothing Greek in it; it is a Jewish blaze of the eternal Semitic flame" (Bianquis trans., 1:173).

[42] *Jenseit von Gut und Böse*, no. 46; Albert trans., 89.

[43] *Morgenrothe*, no. 321; Albert trans., 291. Cf. *Menschliches, Allzumenschliches*, I, no. 113: "What a shivering wind reaches us from all that!" (French trans. by Desrousseaux: *Humain, trop humain*, 149).

[44] *Der Wille zur Macht*, nos. 358 and 366; Bianquis trans., 1:168 and 170.

[45] Ibid., no. 415, 1:190.

[46] *L'Antéchrist*, 300–302.

[47] *Morgenrothe*, no. 68; Albert trans., 75–79. Cf. *Le Voyageur et son ombre*, no. 85, Albert trans., 278.

[48] Cf. *Ecce homo*, Albert trans., 42. Already too, with Nietzsche, the admiration of that "miraculous paradox" constituted by the Renaissance papacy: *Der Antichrist*, no. 61.

[49] *La Question des Juifs au point de vue de la race, des moeurs et de la civilisation* (1881). Nietzsche affects a profound distrust with regard to Dühring: *Jenseit von Gut und Böse*, no. 204; Albert trans., 182.

note many other "sources" of his thought in the literature of his times. He borrows a part of his radicalism from his friend the Protestant theologian Franz Overbeck, his views concerning Paul and the Jews from the essayist Paul de Lagarde,[50] and the elusive Jesus whom he imagines late in life looks like a brother to that Prince Myshkin whom Dostoyevsky had just depicted.[51] He did not study the Christian origins like he had done for the Greek civilization. Despite the form of some of his assertions, he does not intend to develop a historical thesis: *he constructs a myth*, and he animates this myth with all the power, all the violence of his own thought. So it is even less appropriate to take up one's position on the ground of history in judging *The Antichrist* and the numerous other texts that prepare this long invective than it is for *The Birth of Tragedy*. It is not even on the ground of ideas or of an "objective" truth in which Nietzsche did not believe. The only ground possible is that of Nietzsche's personality.

To what a distance from his miserable followers do we find ourselves then suddenly transported! Let us note first of all: Nietzsche always refused to let himself be carried like them into anti-Semitism. "The battle against the Jews", he wrote, "has always been a mark of base, despicable and evil natures, and the one who participates in it at present gives proof of a vulgar mentality."[52] He saw in it a lack of imagination and a "twistedness"[53] and missed no opportunity to crush the anti-Semites with his scornful sarcasm.[54] His hatred of the Jewish spirit could be expressed with a mad violence; it did not assume vile

[50] Paul de Lagarde, *Über das Verhältniss des deutschen Staates zur Theologie, Kirche und Religion* (1873). Cf. Andler, *Nietzsche*, vol. 2, *La Jeunesse de Nietzsche*, 2d ed., 369–63. The expression "Judaine" is due to Lagarde, an expression that Nietzsche copies in forging that of "moraline". Nietzsche perhaps also owes something of his hatred for the "ugly little Jew" to Renan.

[51] Cf. Charles Andler, "Nietzsche et Dostoïevsky", in *Mélanges Baldensperger* (1930).

[52] *Oeuvres posthumes*, Bolle trans., fragment 678.

[53] *Ecce homo*, 107. He detested it particularly in his brother-in-law Foerster, and one of the essential points of his "racism" consisted in protesting against the mixture of Jewish and Prussian blood. Cf. Charles Andler, "Nietzsche et l'histoire de la civilisation", *Revue de métaphysique et de morale* (1928), 189–91. Nietzsche, in fact, made a great case for the Jewish people and their qualities; cf. *Morgenrothe*, no. 205: "In the Jews of today, the resources of soul and spirit are extraordinary . . ." (Albert trans., 227–30).

[54] *Volonté de puissance*, 2:210: "Anti-Semites do not pardon the Jews for having spirit—and money. Anti-Semites, another name for 'poor in spirit'. He denounces in pan-Germanism and anti-Semitism 'the two great German blunders' " (Jean Edouard Spenlé, *La Pensé allemande*, 176).

forms. And one must say as much, too, of his attitude with regard to the Christian faith. The feeling that the frenzy of his blasphemies inspire in us is not disgust but rather a kind of holy horror. And despite everything, we cannot keep from feeling a persevering sympathy in his regard. This is not so much because, during the period in which he wrote his last pamphlets, he had lost all power to control and correct himself;[55] for, well before that spring of tragic euphoria in 1888, when his lucidity was morbidly sharpened before sinking, he many times expressed a heinous rejection of Christian values. It is not only because he "brought forth his thoughts in suffering" and truly "wrote with his blood".[56] Nor is it only because he never wanted to prove vulgar in his appreciation of Christianity[57] or because he was able more than once, as in a flash of lightning, to render it justice.[58] But, as several of his biographers have remarked, following Nietzsche himself, "his thought is an arena in which opposing forces combat each other", and, just as an imperious power rises in him "against those he loves at the very moment he loves them",[59] this power draws him as mysteriously toward the beings and the values against which it is unleashed, at the very moment of its greatest unleashing.

He could have said of Christ, of that Hebrew Christ, heir of the prophets, of the true Christ, the Christ of the Gospel and of the Church, whom in his dawning madness he attacked both as the answer and as

[55] Daniel Halévy insists with reason on the fact, in a work written before the posthumous influence of Nietzsche had attained a radiance that attributed a perhaps exaggerated importance to his whole "final philosophy", his "knock at the door" philosophy. *La Vie de Frédéric Nietzsche* (1909), 363.

[56] *Die fröhliche Wissenschaft*, foreword, no. 3; Vialatte trans., p. 12. *Morgenrothe*, no. 591 (posthumous edition): "I am not aware of what purely spiritual problems can be. . . . All truths are for me bleeding truths." *Zarathustra*, 1: "I like only what is written with his blood. Write with blood, and you will learn that blood is spirit." Letter to Overbeck, April 19, 1883: "In this book, there is much blood."

[57] Letter to Pierre Gast, 1881: "I have perceived, dear friend, that in my book (*Aurore*), this perpetual inner discussion with Christianity must seem to you bizarre and even painful. But the latter constitutes the best particle of ideal life that I have known; even as a small child, I explored it in many a nook, and I believe that never, in my heart, have I proved vulgar in its respect."

[58] Thus in an unpublished work of later years: "The two forms most worthy of man that I have encountered in my life were the *perfect Christian* . . . and the *perfect artist* of the romantic ideal, which I have often found, moreover, to be well below the Christian level" (*Oeuvres posthumes*, texts translated by H. J. Bolle [1934], 52).

[59] Charles Andler, vol. 2, *La Jeunesse de Nietzsche*, 83. Cf. also Ernst Bertram, *Nietzsche, essai de mythologie*, Pitrou trans., 91 and 166 (with a strong touch of the extreme).

the antagonist, what he had once written of Socrates: "I will admit it! I feel Socrates so close to me that I nearly always have to fight against him."[60]

IV

He also wrote: "In the Jewish Old Testament, the book of divine justice, there are men, matters and discourses of so great a style that the Greek and Hindu literatures have nothing to rival them. One stops with fear and veneration before these prodigious traces of what man was in other times. . . . The taste for the Old Testament is a touchstone for knowing what is great and small."[61]

Up until now, we have defended only Christ, attacked beneath the features of a "Jewish god". But we must now recognize that his adversaries are often right when they see in many points of his doctrine a contribution owed to Israel and first inscribed in the Jewish Bible.[62] So the defense of Christ would be incomplete if it did not extend to those who prepared for his coming, and to the whole order of things which he himself proclaimed that he had come, not to abolish, but to fulfill. Would the New Testament be understood without the Old? And has not the Church from the beginning retained and canonized this Old Testament, claiming it as *her* Scripture?

From the beginning, however, there have been Christians who wanted to break with the "Jewish books". Those whom we call the "Gnostics" could not persuade themselves to attribute the same "author" to them as to the books that contained Christian revelation. What a contrast between the warrior god who is shown in it on nearly every page and the God of Jesus! A cruel and evil god, declared the intransigents, influenced by a dualist metaphysics; at least, an exclusively just and rigorous god, said others; in any case, a mere demiurge, to whom it is impossible to grant the highest divinity. It is this point of view, altogether and in its most radical form, that Jacques de Lesdain adopts today when, in a recent article in the new-style *Illustration*, he

[60] Fragment from 1875: *Science et sagesse en conflit*. Cf. Andler, vol. 3, *Le Pessimisme esthétique*, 130.

[61] *Jenseit von Gut und Böse*, no. 52; Albert trans., 97.

[62] There is an obvious partial truth in this assertion by Renan. *Marc-Aurèle*, preface, p. v: "Christianity begins in the eight century before J. C., at the moment when the great prophets, taking possession of the people of Israel, make of them the people of God, charged with inaugurating pure cult in the world."

is moved to find, in leafing through the Bible, so many "legends of massacres", so many "bestial massacres", so many orders to overrun the homes of neighboring peoples, and when he concludes from this that no other people except the Jewish people "plunges its roots into an origin that is so troubled, so pestilential".[63] This was, in the last century, the point of view of the Fourierist Alphonse Toussenel, in his violent work on *Les Juifs, rois de l'époque*:

> The people who did the great things recorded in the Jewish books must be called the people of Satan. . . . Satan, the god of armies, the god of carnage, the malicious god, the jealous god, the iniquitous god. . . . No, the God of the Gospel is not the same as the one who instituted slavery and ordered his faithful to exterminate without pity all those who do not pronounce *shibboleth* purely.[64]

This is also the point of view of Edmond Picard, who exclaims on the same subject, in the long chapter of his *Synthèse de l'antisémitisme* directed against the Bible: "It is brutal, it is cruel, it is barbarous, it is savage!"[65] It is as if we are hearing the "impieties" once offered by "Marcion, Valentin and Basilide", exclaiming that the god of the Jews "taught cruelty through his Scriptures, since he commanded his adorers to walk on the heads of their enemies and to hand over to torture the leaders of the lands they invaded by violence".[66] A point of view much less in accordance, by contrast, with that of contemporary authors who preach the rejection of the Old Testament because they see in it an obstacle to the glorification of the instincts of force and to the propagation of a heroic and warlike morality that is not at all concerned with "justice". . . . But is not one of the arts of a well-orchestrated campaign to use the most diverse means, and if necessary the most contradictory, in order to converge at the same end?[67] We had to expect there to be, thus, an antibiblicism of the right, for aristocratic

[63] "Nos anciens maîtres", in *L'Illustration*, of September 13, 1941.

[64] *Les Juifs, rois de l'époque*, 184. See also Tridon, *Du molochisme juif* (1884).

[65] Brussels, 1941. As early as 1898, Edmond Picard sought to explain the whole history of Europe after ancient Greece as a continual war between Aryans and Semites.

[66] Origen, *Homily 12 on the Book of Joshua*, no. 3. Cf. *Homily 10*, no. 2; *Homily 5 on Leviticus*, no. 1.

[67] A similar example is offered us by the *Nouvelle revue française* of November 1, 1941, in which Mr. Drieu la Rochelle reproaches Mr. de Montherlant for his "too belatedly renewed sally with Nietzsche" on the "celebrated Jew". (A very amicable quarrel, moreover, as can happen between men of the same views.) Drieu la Rochelle proposes to see in Saint Paul the one who, on the contrary, "Hellenized" Christianity, which was at first wholly

intellectuals, and an antibiblicism of the left, for the use of the masses and for sensitive hearts.[68] Did we not contemplate just a short while ago two kinds of pictures of "Jewish Christianity" for the use of two different peoples? *Discordia concors.*

We know how the Fathers of the Church defended the Jewish Bible against Gnosticism, either by making appeal to the idea of divine pedagogy and graduated revelation, or by having recourse to the symbolism that discerns in the account of external actions a prefigurement of the spiritual realities to come,[69] or still more often by mixing both interpretations together.[70] They continued to run into objections of a historical order only in passing, although one of Marcion's disciples, Appelles, had already raised more than one, transforming the wholly religious criticism of his mentor into a criticism of frankly rationalist appearance.[71] A kind of Voltairian seer, Appelles seems to have formed a school.[72] It is thus that, after him, the Neoplatonian Porphyry tried to show, in his turn, the improbabilities and contradictions of the biblical accounts. Yet this was only a slight suggestion of the difficulties that the progress of science, joined with the development of an "independent" exegesis, were one day to amass on this subject. For around three centuries, these difficulties, so to speak, never ceased to grow, to the point of provoking within the Church a veritable "crisis" of the Old Testament.[73] The result of this crisis, which was to reach its culminating point in the days of Modernism but which it would be premature to say we have yet fully overcome, was not only that the

Judaic. Christianity and paganism are a part, he thinks, of the same vast whole, they are two brothers; so "Christian France" does not have to fear opening itself to a "pagan Germany". Finally, "It is not only a Semitic Asia but also and without doubt much more an Aryan Asia" that we have given Christianity. *Christianisme et paganisme*, 610–15. Once again, one thinks of a beak-like nose. . . . Nietzsche had also said that Christianity was "a fragment of Eastern antiquity" (*Werke*, 1:515).

[68] There were, moreover, instances of interference between them, and Alphonse Toussenel was already writing, for example "Whoever says Jewish says Protestant."

[69] Thus also Origen, *Homily 12 on the Book of Joshua*, no. 1: "See, ungrateful heretic, how the new things agree in all points with the ancients: to the ancients was promised the kingdom of the holy land; to you, through the Gospels, is promised the kingdom of heaven."

[70] For example Saint Irenaeus, *Adversus Haereses*, l. 4, c. 15, no. I: *Lex, et disciplina et prophetia.*

[71] Cf. Origen, *Contra Celsum*, l. 5, c. 54; *Second Homily on Genesis*, no. 2; etc.

[72] Origen, *Second Homily on Genesis*, no. 1.

[73] An initiation to the present state of criticism will be found in the work by J. Coppens, *L'Histoire critique de l'Ancien Testament* (Tournai-Paris, 1938).

Old Testament became for many sincere believers an embarrassment rather than a support in their faith. Little by little, people got out of the habit of keeping for it the place that it traditionally occupied in religious instruction, both in preaching and reading as well as in prayer. It was a cumbersome treasure which people no longer knew how to use. By that very fact, a certain disaffection followed, so that the adversaries of our faith were able to attack it, in an offensive otherwise more serious and more fundamental than all those of the historians and critics, without ever arousing the anxiety one would be right to expect.

For the most violent assaults that are today directed against the Bible are very different from the old ones. They no longer concern, as in the times of the Fathers, the facts of Israel's history testifying to a rather coarse state of customs or religious conceptions superseded by Christianity. Nor do they bear, as was still the case recently, on questions of text, date or historicity. The principal attack is led neither in the name of historical criticism nor in the name of a more purified religious ideal, which would still be due to the gospel. Bolder, more radical, it aims right at the heart. It wishes to demolish what, in the Old Testament, is already, to speak like Saint Augustine, *of* the New Testament. Starting from the moment when Yahweh is affirmed in all his greatness, in full historical light, it begins to speak of a "falsified", "unnatural" notion of God. It does not reproach Israel, like others have done and still do, for having kept mythical elements in its belief and practices redolent of idolatry in its cult: it reproaches it, quite on the contrary, for "its extreme sterility" in matters of imagination and for the "impoverishment of religious life" that would result from its "narrow and curious notion of a creator".[74] It blames it for not having consented to remain in the presence of the world as "in the presence of an insoluble enigma" and for having exhausted "the lively emotion of cosmic mystery" by raising its unique God above the universe, and for thus having, in the final analysis, understood by religion "something completely different from the rest of men".[75] What it blames it for, then, is what is most incontestable as well as most spiritual in the Bible. For its very transcendence. For its permanent values, those that Christianity had only to confirm while fulfilling

[74] H. S. Chamberlain, *Genèse* 300, 305, 316.

[75] Ibid., 532, 529, 562.

them. In brief, what it reproaches Moses and the prophets for is having prepared the way for Christ. For, so to speak, having come before him.[76]

Thus the positions have been entirely reversed.[77] We are still so little accustomed to it that this new kind of offensive risks finding us dazzled at times. But it is important to recover our balance. No Christian must let himself go so far as to think that a movement of withdrawal with respect to the Old Testament would leave his faith intact. Under present conditions, less than ever. The Bible of the Jews, we are also told, in order to detach us from it, was received into the new cult only as a result of a "pure accident": the fact that Jesus of Nazareth was born in Palestine; but its use should have been banned by the Christian churches, for it is truly a "monstrosity" to sing the praises of "an Aryan god" with Jewish songs! We know just how far such invitations would lead us—and is not everything already lost in one stroke, if what we are authorized to preserve in Christianity is nothing any more but the cult of an "Aryan god"? We reject as stupidity as well as blasphemy this contradiction they are trying to set up between a "Semite Old Testament" and an "Aryan New Testament".[78] We maintain the indissoluble bond between our two Testaments, always, in the final analysis, interpreting the Old by the New, but also always basing the New on the Old. In the light of Jesus we will be able to contemplate their "harmony". We will thus remain faithful to the teaching of Saint Irenaeus, which was that of all our Doctors: "The writings of Moses are Words of Christ."[79] There is only one single Scripture for us—*christianas litteras utriusque Testamenti*—which, as an entire whole, is sacred to us. We will not allow Scripture to be touched any more than the Church. We will not allow Scripture to be touched any more

[76] If, with Ptolemy, the ancient author of the *Letter to Florus*, and with Saint Irenaeus, we distinguish three parts in the Law of Moses (the first two parts, moreover, capable of coinciding in part): the "precepts of servitude" destined only for a time, symbolic observances, devoted to spiritual transfiguration, and the laws "of nature and freedom", which the Gospel will sanction, we will say that it is this third part that is presently attacked. On this whole problem, see the little work by Cardinal Faulhaber, Archbishop of Munich (French trans. [Paris: Sorlot, 1935]): *Juifs et chrétiens devant le racisme*.

[77] Cf. Nietzsche, *Ecce homo*, 147: "Before my eyes, everything was turned upside down." Cf., with respect to Nietzsche, Jean de Pierrefeu: "a complete turn-around of ideas and moral sentiments", *Les Nouvelles littéraires* (1927).

[78] Edmond Picard, *Synthèse*.

[79] Saint Irenaeus, *Adversus Haereses*, l. 3, c. 12.

than the Eucharist. In each of these three mysteries, in each of these three states, it is the Word of God we are defending.

Now this fight will not be without fruit. It will oblige us to have a more lively and more joyous awareness of the essential message of our Holy Books, at times obscured by so many problems, so many discussions and critical studies.[80] With what flashes of fire the Bible accentuates the divine action throughout the world! And how this history is ours, since the day of creation! The faith of Abraham is already our faith. In its fundamental precepts, the law of Moses is still our law. The great men of Israel are truly Fathers. The prophets shake us still today with the great lessons God charges them to give his people. They console us in our distress and reawaken hope in us. The gentleness of the breeze in which the Spirit comes to visit Elijah announces to us the gentleness of our Christ. The "roaring" of Amos arouses us to justice, yet Hosea prepares our souls for love. The majesty of the God of Isaiah makes us bow down with him before the thrice-holy Face. Jeremiah hollows out a new dimension in our hearts. Job exhorts us to a manly patience. The Psalms nourish our prayer every day. Daniel and the Maccabees teach us fidelity. And everywhere, from one end to the other, the fidelity of God is revealed:

> The counsel of Yahweh stands forever,
> and the designs of his heart from age to age![81]

In truth, all of this is our heritage. All of this has become our flesh. We will no longer allow them to tear it away from us. And if it is referred to as a pretext for anti-Semitism, we will repeat the perfectly just cry of the great Pius XI: "Spiritually, we are Semites!"

---

[80] "The best way to serve a cause", wrote Nietzsche, "is to attack it, to hunt it down with a whole pack": *Volonté et puissance*, 325.

[81] Ps 32:11. Cf. Paul Claudel, in the collected work *Les Juifs, Présence* series 1937), p. vi: "The continual study I make of the Bible has penetrated me with the predominant importance of Israel from the point of view of God and humanity. It is Israel, with a heroic courage and an intellectual boldness that would be inexplicable without a vocation from above, which has always maintained, against the seductions of Greece, the idea of a personal and transcendent God, superior to all the superstitions of paganism. And it is precisely this paganism, reborn in the lowest and most hideous form, that is coming once again to collide with this unshakeable rock."

5. Spiritual Warfare

Every age has its heresies. Every age also sees the principle of assaults against the faith renewed. For a long time—since its very foundation—Christianity has never ceased to be attacked, but it is not always from the same side or by the same kind of adversaries or with the same weapons. At times it is the historical foundations of our beliefs that seem shaken: biblical criticism and exegesis, the history of Christian origins, that of dogmas and of the institutions of the Church, furnish the field for the battle. At times the latter shifts to the metaphysical plane. The very existence of a reality higher than the things of this world is then denied or declared unknowable, and thought falls back on immanent positions; or rather, it claims, on the contrary, to invade the entire field of being and to leave nothing outside the grasp of a reason that must understand everything: and consequently, without prejudice to more particular objections against some specific dogma, it is the very idea of a mystery to be believed that disappears. Historians and metaphysicians are often, in turn, relieved or replaced by politicians: the latter attack the Church instead, attack what they call her thirst for earthly domination; many of them, not content with opposing any interference of the Church in the state—"clericalism"—want also to destroy any Christian influence in the progress of human affairs, and the most ambitious go so far as to reject, for the benefit of the state, that distinction between temporal and spiritual that the world owes to the gospel. Finally come the objections of the social order, objections so strong, so insistent, that they have more than once seemed preponderant. Just recently, again, was not the primary concern of a number of disciples to prove, through the exposition of Catholic social doctrine and through an effort at social accomplishments, that religion is not the "opium of the people", that the Church is not disinterested in the fate of man on this earth and that, mother of all, she is not at all in league with the rich and the powerful?

None of these kinds of objections has been superseded today. There is not one of these different sectors on which we should relax our

Cité nouvelle (1943), 769–83.

vigilance. Yet the principal attack comes from elsewhere. What is in the forefront, if not always in appearance at least in reality, is no longer a problem of the historical, metaphysical, political or social order. It is a *spiritual* problem. It is the total human problem. Today, the fight against Christianity is waged not only with regard to one of its foundations or to one of its consequences: it is aimed directly at the heart. The Christian concept of life, Christian spirituality, the inner attitude which, above any particular act or any external gesture, defines the Christian: this is what is at issue. How timid, then, appear those men who, for example, fought against the Church while wanting to preserve the gospel!—or those who claimed to be free of any authority, of any faith, but who still called for principles derived from a Christian source! "Free thinkers" who were much less bold, even much less "liberated"! Those who now succeed them do not fail to mock their lack of logic as well as their impotence and to include them in the same reprobation as believers. As for them, they do not intend to be content with "the shadow of a shadow". They have no desire to be nourished by perfume from an empty vase. They put another liqueur in the vase. It is *all* Christianity that they abrogate, and that they replace. Jesus had worked a "reversal of values": it is a reversal of values that they work in their own turn. To the ideal Christian, they oppose a pagan ideal. Against the God adored by the Christians, they proudly set up their new divinities. In doing this, they are aware that they are attacking the essence and sweeping everything away with one stroke, for they profess with Schopenhauer that "it is the spirit and moral tendency that constitute the essence of a religion, and not the myths with which they are clothed."[1]

I

The Bond of Warfare

Such was the conviction of Nietzsche, and such was his plan. The God whose death Nietzsche announces and wants is not only the God of metaphysics; he is, precisely, the Christian God. Hostile to Christianity since the time he lost his faith, when he was around twenty years old, Nietzsche set up in opposition to it a *non*-absolute. His negation,

[1] Schopenhauer, *Die Welt als Wille und Vorstellung*, supplement to vol. 4, chap. 48; French trans. by Burdeau: *Le Monde comme volonté et comme représentation*, 3:434.

immediately radical, would become increasingly violent and frenetic. His last writings are full of cries of hatred and invectives. But never did he take the trouble to outline any refutation whatever.[2] For him, as well as for a Comte or a Feuerbach, it was already done. Christian history could only be a legend, and its dogmatics, a mythology. It was useless, then, to waste time with it. "This mythology which Kant himself did not completely abandon, for which Plato prepared Europe, to its misfortune . . . , this mythology has long since served its time."[3] So, indeed, it is not to this that his interest turns. "This whole absurd residue of the Christian fable", he also says, "these cobwebs of concepts, this theology are scarcely important to us; it would be a thousand times more absurd for us to lift our little finger to combat it."[4] The essential question is not there. It is not a question of truth—is there only one truth?—but a question of value.

> Up to now, the assault against Christianity has not only been timid, it has been based on the wrong premises. Insofar as one does not feel the *morality* of Christianity to be a *capital crime against life*, its defenders will have a good chance. The single problem of the "truth" of Christianity —the existence of its God or the historicity of its legend, to say nothing of its astronomy and its science of nature—is a very secondary problem insofar as one does not call into question the value of Christian morality.[5]

"Does Christian morality have any value at all, or is it a profanation and a shame, despite all the sanctity of the means it uses to seduce?" There, then, for Nietzsche, is the true problem, the only problem. We know how he resolves it. "War against the Christian idea," he exclaims, "against the doctrine that makes beatitude and salvation the end of life, against the supremacy of the simple in spirit, the pure of heart, the suffering, the failures. . . . When and where have we seen a man worthy of the name resemble this Christian ideal?"[6] He is not fighting against belief in God: "What does God, belief in God, matter to us, in our time? God is today nothing but a word grown pale, not

---

[2] "I am speaking", he said, "only of *lived* things, and I am not presenting any cerebral process" (*Also sprach Zarathustra*, appendix, n. 5; French trans. by Betz: *Ainsi parle Zarathoustra*, p. 3).

[3] Nietzsche, written in 1885, *Der Wille zur Macht*; French trans. by Bianquis: *Volonté de puissance*, 1:70.

[4] Written in 1887–1888, ibid., 1:185.

[5] Written in 1888, ibid., 1:140.

[6] Written in 1887, ibid., 1:184.

even a concept."[7] But what he is fighting, and what, he says, "one should never cease to fight in Christianity", is "its ideal of man"; "that ideal whose morbid beauty and feminine seduction, slanderous and insinuating eloquence charm all the laziness and vanities of weary souls—and even the strongest have times of weariness". What he is fighting is "confidence, candor, simplicity, patience, love of neighbor, resignation, submission to God, a kind of disarmament, of repudiation of self", all these virtues which Christianity proposes to man in order to tempt him. The institution of such an ideal, by serving the little and the weak, has threatened the vigorous exceptions with death; it has compromised the great human successes, "as if this unpretentious, puny of soul, this virtuous, average animal, this docile sheep of a man not only had preeminence over the race of crueler, greedier, more daring, more extraordinary, and by this fact a hundred times more vulnerable, men, but even as if he were the ideal, the end, the norm for man in general, the supreme good".[8]

Nietzsche was aware of being an initiator along this path. "No one yet", he said, "has considered Christian morality as something beneath him. . . . Up till now, Christian morality was the Circe of all thinkers. They placed themselves in its service. Who then, before me, has gone down into the caverns where the breath poisoned by this kind of ideal springs from, the ideal of the slanderers of the world? Who then has merely dared suspect that these caverns were there?" He considers that for this it was necessary for him to have "absolutely unheard-of loftiness, good distance vision, psychological depth".[9] Certainly Nietzsche flatters himself. To tell the truth, Christian morality had never completely lacked such adversaries. Recall, for example, not to go back to the early centuries, the pagan impulse of the Renaissance, with a Machiavelli setting "our religion", which "places supreme happiness in humility, abjection, the scorn of human things", in opposition to the ancient religion that "made the sovereign good consist in greatness of soul, strength of body and all the qualities that make man formidable. . . ." In the eighteenth century, in the group of political

[7] Ibid. He also said as early as 1873, in the same spirit: "Christianity will soon be ripe for historical criticism, that is to say, for the dissection table" (2:59).

[8] Written in 1887–1888, ibid., 1:185–86.

[9] *Ecce homo*; French trans. by Albert, 170–71. Cf. *Der Antichrist*; French trans. by Albert: *L'Antéchrist: Le Crépuscule des Idoles*, 293: "Christian values and noble values: we others, free spirits, we have been the first to reestablish this contrast, the greatest there is!"

writers who moved around Diderot and the Baron of Holbach, several professed an anti-Christianism that was just as decided: such as Grimm, treating the Christian dogma of "base and ignoble mythology", reproaching it for exercising "the most sinister influences" and for teaching "debasement, ignominy, servitude", denigrating "the spirit of Christian charity" and declaring "that the spirit of the gospel could never be allied with the principles of good government".[10] But, these "philosophers" were of too base a quality to have any chance of carrying the elite away for long. As for Machiavelli, he had betrayed the depth of his thought only in rare passages; he did not usually pose as a master of moral philosophy but only of politics. We must, then, agree: never before Nietzsche had so powerful an adversary arisen, conceiving his plan in so clear, so full and so explicit a way, and pursuing it in all spheres with so much systematic and reflective ardor. Nietzsche is deeply conscious of his mission as a prophet. He is legislating for times to come. "Another ideal", he said, "runs before our steps, amazing, seductive and rich with dangers . . . the ideal of a spirit that plays naïvely, that is to say, without intent, through excess of force and fecundity, with all that has until then been called sacred, good, intangible, divine." He considers himself called to inaugurate a new era, "to set the first question mark in place, to change the destiny of the soul, to make the needle advance, to raise the curtain on the tragedy".[11] With him, eternal paganism proudly rears its head, but he clothes it, too, in a new outfit. He prepares to remodel individual life and inner feelings as well as public life and acts of power. He takes on, for new conquests, the destiny of humanity.

We will not explain Nietzschean anti-Christianity once again,[12] that appeal to a creative, powerful, heroic life, that morality of force and of hardness, that accusation of "feeling" borne against the founders of Christian morality and first of all against the great prophets of Israel, that opposition of the "nobility" of the Greek heroes to the "baseness" of the Christian slave, that exaltation of Dionysius, the god of orgiastic and ever-reviving life, in contrast with the scorn of the Crucified who,

---

[10] Friedrich Melchior Grimm, *Correspondance littéraire*, vol. 5 (April 1763), 261, 264, 265.

[11] *Ecce homo*.

[12] Refer particularly to the study by Father Yves de Montcheuil: "Nietzsche et la critique de l'idéal chrétien", *Cité nouvelle* (June 25, 1941). In 1901, Alfred Fouillée was defining Nietzscheism as a "neopagan religion": "La Religion de Nietzsche", *Revue des deux mondes* (February 1, 1901), 587.

on the tree of the Cross, "the most poisonous tree of all trees", is "a curse for Life". . . .[13] It is enough to note the extreme gravity of the attack. It is not addressed, like others, to a few specialists of history or metaphysics, its action does not remain confined first to intellectual circles, but, without needing the interpretation of men of science, it comes to shake souls. It is the spiritual elite at whom it is aimed, and when it attains its aim it succeeds in perverting them by sparing them the sense of being demeaned. Like everything that is of the spirit, even though it insinuates itself everywhere, it is difficult to grasp, so it has time to work immense ravages before the first alarm is sounded. Under the cover of impeccable formulas of faith, at times even to the benefit of an apparent redoubling of orthodoxy, souls can be already corrupt. Intellectual laziness is, moreover, a powerful preservative against many objections, the concern for social security can become a very strong argument in favor of religion, but neither intellectual laziness nor the concern for social security protects against the invasion of the pagan spirit. To the complicity that the latter has always found in our nature, Nietzsche's strength has been in adding others, by making appeal to our instincts of greatness.[14]

That he has succeeded only too well in this is obvious from the facts. His influence is universal today. Neopaganism is the great spiritual phenomenon of our time. Despite the horror and vulgarity of the forms with which it is clothed while being spread, it continues to attract noble souls to itself, at times even Christian souls, whose blindness makes one shudder. For forty or fifty years, many young men have begun to think that a "profound distrust of man" had to be the prerogative of "great souls"; many have begun to dream of "heroic ecstasies" and to regret "the pride of ancient heroes";[15] many have made reflections similar to those that Rainer Maria Rilke noted, after an enthusiastic reading of the new prophet:

> The one who is adored as the Messiah makes the whole world a hospital. He calls the weak, the unfortunate, the infirm his children and his beloved. And the strong? . . . How could we ourselves, then, rise if we lend our

[13] Nietzsche, written in 1888: *Volonté de puissance* 2:345. Cf. *Ecce homo*, 176: "Have I been understood: Dionysius in front of the Crucified."

[14] Cf. *Zarathustra*, appendix, no. 11: Betz trans., p. 302: "All my books until now have been nets I have cast: I was hoping to catch some men with profound, rich and exuberant souls."

[15] Cf. Gustave Thibon, *Destin de l'homme*, 78.

> strength to the unfortunate, the oppressed, to lazy wretches, deprived of sense and energy? Let them fall, let them die, alone and miserable. Be hard, be terrible, be without pity! You must go forward, forward! Few men, but great men, . . . will build a world with their vigorous, muscular, dominant arms upon the bodies of the weak, the sick and the infirm![16]

Others, after having repeated the cry: "The gods are dead, long live the Overman!", celebrate the new Nietzschean ideal in terms with which one must be familiar, if one wishes to understand some of the dominant facts of our contemporary history:

> Nietzsche announces the impending return to the ideal, but to an entirely different and new ideal. To understand this ideal, there will be a category of free spirits, fortified by war, solitude and danger. Spirits who will know the wind, glaciers and snow of the summits and will be able to measure without trouble the deepest abysses. Spirits endowed with a kind of sublime perversity and who will deliver us from the love of neighbor and from the desire for nothingness in order to return to the earth its goal and to men their hopes.

Even in France, from the beginning of this century, the Gospel of Zarathustra found a smaller but not muted echo in several cenacles. The Nietzschean current came to mix its waters with one of the arms of the great positivist river. It is thus that a Hugues Rebell began to pursue "that Christian spirit, with which everyone today is infected", he said, "including the men who call themselves its enemies".[17] A Pierre Lasserre, author of an admiring work on *La Morale de Nietzsche*, reproached Christianity for having made a mystery of suffering and for having in a way "made the eyes of the suffering ugly":

> Cruelly pursued by the arrows of Apollo, Christian eyes have become full of anger, hatred and despair. . . . Suspicion and spite inhabit them. . . . If at times they seem finally to have found repose, if they surrender, calm, serene, ethereal, take care! It is then that they express the most knowing and the most proud malice! They want to persuade you that they have forever thwarted the enemy, that already they are paying attention to the first glimmers from the beyond. . . . The hatred that I read in these kinds of Christian eyes is precise, it is the quintessence of the Christian hatred

---

[16] Rilke: *Les Apôtres*, new ed., 1896. Quoted by Christine Osann, *Rainer Maria Rilke, destinée d'un poète*, French trans. (1942), 47.

[17] Hugues Rebell, *Union des trois aristocraties*, 21.

> against the earth. It is when they are the most gentle that Christian eyes are the most devious. . . . Basically, is it not a supreme, cunning trick of incurables to begin to love the sickness and to exalt it?[18]

A laborious exercise of rhetoric, an unwieldy imitation by a disciple without genius? Undoubtedly. The effect of such writings was not, however, negligible. But today, it is a question of a very different matter! Christianity is beleaguered everywhere, and the heart of numerous baptized has already begun to surrender. Accounts of apostasy circulate. The intoxication manages to make even the wisest stagger. . . .

II

Nietzsche's feelings with regard to Jesus always remained mixed. So, too, his judgments on Christianity. He saw in it less a *false* ideal than a *worn-out* ideal. "It is our most severe and refined pity", he says for example, "that prevents us today from still being Christians."[19] It is, then, with the Christians of our times, it is with us that he is angry. His cutting scorn is aimed at our mediocrities and hypocrisies; he aims at our weaknesses embellished with fine names. Can we blame him completely? Must everything that "bears the name of Christian today" be defended against him? When he exclaims, for example, speaking of us: "They would have to sing me better songs to teach me to believe in their Savior. His disciples would have to look more saved!",[20] how dare we be indignant? To how many of us does Christianity appear in fact "like something great, expansive, to which we can surrender ourselves entirely with joy and enthusiasm"?[21] Do the infidels who come into contact with us every day observe on our faces the radiance of that cheerfulness that twenty centuries ago seduced the elite of pagan souls? Are our hearts the hearts of men resurrected with Christ? Are we, in the midst of the century, witnesses to the Beatitudes? In brief, we discern well the blasphemy in Nietzsche's terrible sentence and in its whole context: But does it not oblige us to discern as well, in ourselves, what has been able to push Nietzsche to blasphemy?

---

[18] Pierre Lasserre, in *L'Action française*, 5:277.

[19] Nietzsche, *Zarathustra*, appendix, no. 165; Betz trans., p. 326.

[20] Ibid., 99.

[21] Msgr. Bruno de Solages, *Pour rebâtir une chrétienté*, 245.

Such is the tragedy of the present situation. Whatever the past may be, we are told, the Christianity of today, *your* Christianity is the enemy of Life, because it is itself no longer living. "I see", Jacques Rivière was saying as early as 1907 in a letter to Paul Claudel, "that Christianity is dying. . . . We do not know what these spires, which are no longer the prayer of any of us, are still doing over our cities; we do not know what these great edifices mean that today enclose stations and hospitals and from which the people themselves have chased the monks; we do not know what these turgid stucco crosses of a revolting art demonstrate on tombs."[22] And without doubt Claudel's reply to this cry of anguish was good: "Nothing of the truth is seen in the number of people it persuades." But if those who have remained faithful to the truth seem themselves without "virtue", which is to say, without inner strength, will the abandonment of others not seem justified? Now, the grounds of the verdict are such that it often makes us agree with it. Almost daily experience shows that some of the hardest reproaches made of us come both from our worst adversaries and from men of good will. The tone, intention, profound inspiration are different, but the judgments are, in the final analysis, the same. A surprising but significant convergence. Among the best of those whom we thus disappoint, some of the most clearsighted and most spiritual find themselves caught between two contrary feelings: we see them seduced by the gospel, whose teaching appears to them still full of power and newness; attracted by the Church, in which they sense a more than human reality and the only institution capable of bringing, along with the remedy to our ills, the solution to the problem of our destiny. But, on the threshold, there are those who stop: the spectacle we offer them, we the Christians of today, "the Church that we are", this spectacle repels them. They then come to think and "to say that what still remains of the evangelical ideal in the world survives outside our camps".[23] It is not necessarily that they condemn us: it is rather that they cannot take us seriously. Does history condemn Romulus Augustule for not having revived the work of Caesar or Augustus? It

[22] Jacques Rivière, letter to Paul Claudel, March 17, 1907. *Correspondance de Jacques Rivière et de Paul Claudel*, 15. Cf. Alain-Fournier (Easter 1907): "That Mass this morning, frighteningly garbled, without grandeur, without desire, disgusted me. Everything was ugly, and I felt so strongly that no one understood a thing about it any more." J. Rivière and Alain-Fournier, *Correspondance*, 3:93.

[23] Msgr. de Solages, 238.

notes merely that in this final heir of the Empire, the vigor had been exhausted. . . . So, too, of us and the Church we represent, in the eyes of some of our contemporaries: their feeling is composed of a mixed admiration and contempt.

Whence comes the temptation that lies in wait today for some of us. While the great mass continues to grow duller, blaspheming every day a little more the Lord with whom it claims kinship outwardly while understanding him less and less, while devout circles, the "edifying" circles, so often give proof of such a mediocre quality of education and spiritual life, there are in the Church men who see, who understand, who reflect. There are Christians who refuse to protect their faith with a shield of illusions. "Yes," they say to themselves, "it is only too true. . . . Taken as a whole, our Christianity is insipid. Despite so many fine efforts to give it life and freshness, it is enervated, habitual, rigid. It is effeminate. It falls into formalism and routine. As we practice it, as we think about it at first, it is a weak, ineffective religion; a religion of ceremonies and devotions, of decoration and vulgar consolation, without serious depth, without a real grasp of human activity, at times even without sincerity. A religion outside of life, or that places us ourselves outside of life. There, then, is what the gospel has become in our hands, what this immense hope has become that had been raised above the world! And what is to be said of this alternative, indeed of this mixture of politics and devotion, in which religion is at pains to find a place? Do not many of us profess Catholicism today for the same reasons of inner comfort and social conformism that would have made them reject, twenty centuries ago, the unquieting newness of the Good News? Can we recognize the breath of that Spirit who was to recreate all things and renew the face of the earth? The evil is as serious, although of another nature, with the most "practicing" as with the worldly. The most virtuous themselves are not always the least unaffected. Impatience with all criticism, the futility of all reform, fear of intelligence, are they not manifest signs? Clerical Christianity, formalist Christianity, narrow and rigid Christianity. . . . The great current of Life, which is never interrupted, seems for some time to have deposited it on the bank. . . ."

It is at this point in their reflection, when courageous lucidity begins to change into satirical distortion, that the temptation insinuates itself. The temptation to "cast longing eyes", as the prophets once said, on the side of the new paganism, in order to steal something of that strength and that life with which it appears to be suffused. Imperceptibly, the reproaches made against *our* Christianity are transformed into criticisms of Christianity itself. After having denounced the negative way in which we often practice the Christian virtues, they come to accuse the "negative virtues" that make up the Christian. The satire of the false Christian, who, being "neither of nature nor of grace", is a diminished being, ends in joining the Nietzschean satire of the authentic Christian afflicted with "hemiplegia". There are some strange consonances between the remarks one picks up when people painfully pour out their souls in confidence or from sudden slips on the lips of some young Christians and the caricatured depictions spread, for example, through a work like the *Livre des vivants et des morts.*[24] In the end, this can be apostasy once again. Cases are not unheard of. They make manifest, in a strong condition, a disposition that, in a weak condition, is already widespread.

It would be of no use to blind ourselves to the causes of so profound a malaise. No more than we should refuse to see the good that exists in the adversary would it be good to steel ourselves to our own deficiencies. Such an attitude has only the appearance of the fearlessness of faith. The faithful soul is always an open soul. But, on the other hand, it would be no less fatal to lose the least amount of confidence in the resources of our Christian heritage in order to put ourselves in search of an external remedy. If we want to rediscover a strong Christianity, that "high-powered Christianity" of which there has been so much talk, our first concern must be not to let it be shifted, as is threatened today, into the direction of a Christianity of power. Otherwise, the anticipated cure would only be an aggravation of the evil. If the search for a Christianity by force were not a betrayal, it would at the very least be a reaction of weakness.[25] Is it not clear, in fact, that in this

---

[24] Raymond de Becker, *Livre des vivants et des morts*; see, for example, 52–54 and 154. If we come down another degree, here is what we can read in a very recent work: "An idea is true when it is affirmed forcefully. . . . Uttered from the mouth of Christ, Christianity is true, no doubt about it. But who would dare to maintain that it is true, uttered twenty centuries later by the mouth of one of its alleged disciples? The man closest to Christ in the future will be the one who will throw Christianity to the ground. . . . How will the Church survive, since the Spirit is leaving her? This retraction, this disgust of those who are noble, is the arrow of death in her side."

[25] We could read recently, in an excellent religious bulletin, this account of a men's retreat that had just taken place: "Retreat devoted to the search for a mystique of power, drawn from our Christian and French heritage." The statement was undoubtedly too naïve to be

case, wanting despite everything to remain Christian, one could never propose anything but a pale imitation of the ideal of Power that is being advanced as a conquering hero? One would then be twice conquered in advance. Instead of giving new value to Christianity, as one proposed, one would have weakened it by distorting it. What is at issue is something quite different. It is a matter of returning to Christianity its power in us; which means, above all, of rediscovering it such as it is in itself, in its purity and in its authenticity. In the final analysis, what we need is not even a more virile, or more effective, or more heroic, or stronger Christianity: it is to live our Christianity more virilely, more effectively, more strongly, more heroically if need be. But to live it as it is. There is nothing to be changed, nothing to be added; it does not need to be adapted to the fashion of the day. We must return it to itself in our souls. We must return our souls to it.

The question, once again, is a spiritual question, and the solution is always the same: to the degree we have let ourselves lose it, we have to rediscover the *spirit* of Christianity. To do so, we have to steep ourselves in its sources, and above all in the gospel. This gospel, such as the Church never ceases to offer it to us, is enough for us. But, ever new, it must always be rediscovered. The best among those who criticize us sometimes know how to appreciate it better than we. They do not reproach it for its would-be weaknesses: they reproach us, we ourselves, for not taking advantage of its power. Will we be able to understand the lesson? Lord, if the world is seduced by so much prestige, if it knows today such an offensive return of paganism, it is because we have let the salt of your doctrine lose its savor. Lord, today, like yesterday and all times, there is salvation only in you—and who are we to dare debate or revise your teachings? Lord, keep us from such an illusion and return to us, if need be, not only a faith submitted to but an ardent and concrete esteem for your gospel!

Christianity, if we go directly to its essence, is the religion of Love. "God is Love," says the Apostle John, "and whoever dwells in Love dwells in God, and God dwells in him."[26] Any greater awareness of our faith must make us understand this better. We must not, of course, misunderstand anything about the conditions of this love and of its

---

offensive. But it conveys a tendency, a warping that is observed on all sides, and which are not always equally inoffensive.

[26] 1 Jn 4:16.

natural foundations; in particular of justice, without which it is only a false love; we must beware of its counterfeits, whether gross or subtle, which are today so numerous, or of successes that are too easily obtained. But, in the final analysis, everything is for it. It is the absolute to which all is ordered, in relation to which all must be judged. Now, people are seeking today to steal this primacy away from it, at times by violent assaults, at times by a thousand more subtle ways. The prestige of Power insinuates itself into the very hearts of Christians, and it banishes or at the very least diminishes the esteem of Love. Against these assaults, may the Holy Spirit communicate to us the gift of power! But against the most insidious attacks, may he communicate to us also the gift of Wisdom, to make us understand in what Christian Power consists! The latter is not to be set up beside or in the face of Love, like an antagonist: it is to be cultivated at its service.

In the present state of the world, a virile and strong Christianity must go to the point of being a heroic Christianity. But this epithet is a qualification, it must not be a definition—in which case it would be a falsification. In particular, this heroism will not consist of speaking constantly of heroism and of being delirious about the virtue of power—which would perhaps prove that one was submitting to the influence of someone stronger and that one was beginning to resign. It will consist *first of all* in resisting with courage, in the face of the world and perhaps against oneself, the force and the seductions of a false ideal in order to maintain proudly, in their paradoxical intransigence, the threatened and ridiculed Christian values. With a humble pride. For if Christianity can and must assume the virtues of ancient paganism, the Christian who wants to remain faithful can only reject with a categorical *No* a neopaganism that is constituted against Christ. Gentleness and goodness, delicacy toward little ones, pity—yes, pity—toward those who suffer, the rejection of perverse means, the defense of the oppressed, humble devotion, resistance to lies, the courage to call evil by its name, the spirit of peace and concord, openness of heart, the thought of heaven . . . : that is what Christian heroism will save. This whole "morality of slaves" will make it obvious that it is a morality of free men, that it alone makes man free.

It was not promised to Christians that they would always be in the majority (rather, the contrary was proclaimed to them). Nor that they would always seem the strongest and that men would never be won over by any other ideal but theirs. But, in any case, Christianity will never have any real efficacy, it will never have any real existence and will never make itself any real conquests except by the power of its own spirit, *by the power of charity.*[27]

[27] These pages had already been written when we had the opportunity to read the responses given by Stanislas Fumet, P. Dunoyer de Segonzac and Jean Lacroix, as well as by Joseph Colomb, 11ff., to the question posed by *Jeunesse de l'Église*: "Has Christianity emasculated man?" Although our point of view differs a little from theirs, the convergence of thoughts seems perfect, and, for a more thorough discussion of some of the points touched on here, we refer the reader to these responses.

6. *Homo juridicus*

It is easy to make fun of the *homo juridicus*, "the man who has rights, who thinks only of his rights", the man "whose arrogant vapidity, seated as queen over the universe, has forgotten that heroic ecstasy of the being who receives or who conquers something gratuitous, mysterious, virgin". The joking is, of course, not without purpose, and it is not bad to recall that right, even incontestable right, is not everything. But in portraits of this kind, a little talent is enough to make the irony carry farther, perhaps, than one had foreseen. Make fun, then, as much as you wish, of that insupportable and ridiculous being who always claims what he calls his due. Who would want to take up his defense? But fear, too, to introduce, by this bias, a criticism of right itself. It can become an idol, but it is nonetheless a sacred thing. When I read, from the same ironic pen, that "the instinct of right kills love", when I see that through false antitheses one risks inspiring, in the name of a "heroic politics", the scorn of a politics based on justice, I cannot help being uneasy. I think the expressions at least are unfortunate, and I wait for expressions to balance them. When, in addition, I hear the ideal exalted of those "warriors of long ago" who proceed "in pursuit of some unforeseen favor, edged with danger, of a destiny higher than man, which can give everything to everyone but which owes nothing to anyone", it seems to me that there is something nonsensical in that, which is perhaps not an indication of a happy encounter with the true.[1]

We know the violent reproaches that were addressed in the course of the last century to the Christian doctrine of love. People like Proudhon and Renouvier accused it of being contrary to justice. This was to make a surprising mistake about its authentic tenor and to misunderstand the very demands of charity.[2] Are we going to revive this

Cahiers de notre jeunesse, no. 17 (March 1943), 12–14.

[1] Cf. Gustave Thibon, quoted by the *Cahiers de sainte Jehanne*, February 1, 1943. It is undoubtedly not misunderstanding; it is rather, it seems to me, a very acute and very exacting sense "of the just and of the unjust" that at times pushes Mr. Thibon to his excesses. He is a remarkable detector of illusions, a little in the manner of Guilloré. But this sort also contains its illusions.

[2] Gabriel Madinier has proved this perfectly against Charles Renouvier, in his fine book *Conscience et amour*. In what concerns Proudhon, cf. *Du vrai réalisme, Cahiers du Rhône* (1943).

quarrel and give these reproaches an appearance of reason by taking up on our own account the opposition of two virtues? That would certainly not be any more to the profit of love than to right! Can one, moreover, think that the hour is very propitious for this arraignment of the "instinct of right", when the world is at this point in total disorder because of its failure to appreciate it? If one feels a desire to imitate —or counterfeit—the curse launched by Péguy against the modern world, other points of application would be, it seems, more happily chosen.

Since the Nietzschean intent runs through this "heroic" prose that bewails "the coming of right", let us oppose to it that authentic thought of Nietzsche, whom Minerva did not fail to visit occasionally: "In truth, no one has a higher degree of right to our veneration than the one who possesses the instinct of justice and the power to accomplish it. For, in justice, the highest and rarest virtues are united, as in an unfathomable sea that receives rivers from all sides and absorbs them into itself."[3] Since the epoch of "ancient heroes" is evoked with regret, let us refer to those ancient times, let us reread the *Gorgias* and the *Republic*, as Father Festugière recently invited us to do, let us listen to the divine Plato affirm to us "that there exists a justice that is ever true, ever valuable, independently of human circumstances that assure its triumph and defeat in turn, and that the just in the gallows, tortured by the hangman, is happier than the unjust victor, because he possesses the sole absolute Good, which does not perish."[4] Which of us would wish to scorn such a teaching as conveying an already "modern" sound? Let us say, rather, with several Fathers of the Church, that it is already Christian before the term existed. And since we are finally among Christians, since those who address us are Christians like us, let us read ourselves, and let us invite them to read with us, the Message that Pius XII addressed to us this last Christmas.[5] None of us,

[3] Nietzsche, *Unzeitgemässe Betrachtungen*, no. 2.

[4] André-Jean Festugière, *Le Sainteté* (1942), 116.

[5] Radio message on Christmas Eve 1942. "At the present time", the Pope also said, "the juridical sense suffers frequent and grave attacks. . . . To remedy this situation, it is necessary to reconfirm the value of the fact that the juridical foundation is the sovereign domain of God; that the juridical order eludes the arbitrariness of men; that its power of protection and repression extends to the indefeasible rights of man and defends them against the attacks of any human power whatsoever. From a juridical organization willed by God flows for man the inalienable right to juridical security and, in consequence, to a 'domain of well-defined right, protected against any arbitrary attack'."

undoubtedly, will be tempted then to speak derisively any more. . . . "For social life", said the Pope, "to attain its end, it is essential that a juridical statute serve it as an external support, as refuge and as protection." The primary thing to promote today, he also said, is "respect for the practical exercise of the fundamental rights of the person". Finally, he reminds us, with an insistence that is all the more lively as this truth seems today the more threatened, even in the consciences of believers, that Christian doctrine

> does not allow alternatives: love or right, but the fruitful synthesis: love and right. In both, the twofold irradiation of the same spirit of God, reside the program and the mark of the dignity of the human spirit; both are mutually integrated, cooperate, animate each other, support each other, give each other a hand in the life of concord and peacemaking: right clears the way for love, love tempers right and elevates it. Together they make life ascend into that social atmosphere where, notwithstanding the deficiencies, the obstacles, the harshness of this earth, a fraternal community of life becomes possible.

We well know—unfortunately we need only open our eyes!—that the world is not ruled according to these principles (the Pope knows it undoubtedly as well as we all do!). We know, too, that contestations of rights often generate wars. That justice without love is a lure, and that the pure defense of acquired rights will never be right in opposition to life. Nor are we unaware of cynicism or hypocrisy, we are blind neither to the distortions nor to the caricatures. But is the acknowledgment of evil a reason to blaspheme the good? And can the very extent of its ravages be a motive to discourage us from bringing the remedy for it?

> From a juridical organization willed by God flows for man the inalienable right to juridical security and, in consequence, to a domain of well-defined right, protected against any arbitrary attack.
>
> The relations of man with man; of the individual with society, authority, civic obligations; the relations of society and authority with individuals must rest on a clearly specified juridical basis and be entrusted, at need, to the safeguard of judicial authority.

This "Christmas message" can now be read in the translation with commentary just given in *Renouveaux* (March 1, 1943).

V

THE THOUGHT OF FATHER TEILHARD DE CHARDIN

1. Tradition and Innovation in the Position of the Problem of God in Father Teilhard de Chardin

Introduction

In one of its principal aspects, the entire work of Father Teilhard de Chardin can be considered as a vast proof, renewed in a scientific perspective, of the immortality of the human soul and of the existence of God; a proof completed by an effort to advance to the threshold of the Christian faith. Such was, in any case, one of the constant intentions of its author. This can be clearly deduced from his numerous personal affirmations as well as from an examination of his writings. We see it manifest itself rather early. The lines of it are already drawn, for example, in the major study on *L'Hominisation*, a rough sketch of the successive studies on the *Phénomène humain* [*The Phenomenon of Man*], dated May 6, 1923.[1] But it is from around 1930 that it is accomplished with full amplitude: thus first of all in *L'Esprit de la terre* (1931) and in the series of similar papers that followed it at brief intervals,[2] particu-

---

This article is a report presented to the sixth International Thomist Congress on September 11, 1965, in Rome, in the great hall of the Palace of the Cancelleria, at the request of Father Charles Boyer, S.J., secretary of the Academy of Saint Thomas Aquinas and organizer of the Thomist Congress, at the insistence of Paul VI.

[1] *Oeuvres*, 3:75–111.

[2] Ibid., vol. 6. Cf. Étienne Borne, "Matière et esprit dans la philosophie de Teilhard de Chardin", *Recherches et débats*, 40 (1962), 50: "Teilhard's progress . . . unfolds in a vast proof of the existence of God."

larly in *Comment je crois* (1934). It is enough to glance at the subtitles of this last little work[3] to ascertain this immediately.

From this fundamental plan, let us take the expression, one among many others, in a text dated Peking, October 9, 1936, which was written for the Roman congregation *De Propaganda Fide*, at the request of the apostolic delegate in China: *Quelques réflexions sur la conversion du monde*. A program is sketched there that Father Teilhard de Chardin thought should be accomplished in three stages, or by three successive steps—philosophical, dogmatic and moral:

> A first step would consist in developing (along the lines of the *philosophia perennis*: primacy of Being, Act and Power) a correct Physics and Metaphysics of Evolution. I am persuaded that the loyal interpretation of the new acquisitions of Science and Thought lead legitimately, not to a materialistic Evolutionism, but to a spiritualistic Evolutionism. The World that we know does not develop by chance, but it is structurally dominated by a personal Center of universal convergence.[4]

We will not here go into the details of the argumentation itself. That would take a long study, which should be combined with a study of the whole Teilhardian thought. Moreover the proofs set forth by Father Teilhard de Chardin are varied, and the exposition of each is once again varied, at least in the nuances of its expression, according to the points of view adopted and the interlocutors at whom the author was aiming during the course of his life.[5] Nor will we institute a critical examination of these proofs, any more than we will take them, as such, into our consideration. We would merely wish to outline the curve of them and to bring out their principal points by considering them, so to speak, from outside—a little in the manner in which Teilhard had a habit of considering man himself, as an objective phenomenon, so as to note their most general characteristics.

---

[3] We have analyzed this opuscule in *La Prière du Père Teilhard de Chardin*, "Le Signe" series (1964), second part: "Note sur l'Apologétique teilhardienne" [English trans.: *Teilhard de Chardin: the Man and His Meaning* (New York: Hawthorn Books, 1965), part two, chapter one: "Note on Teilhard's Apologetics", 129–32].

[4] *Oeuvres*, 9:161.

[5] The explanation of three proofs will be found in: Msgr. Bruno de Solages, "Les Preuves teilhardiennes de Dieu", in the collected work *L'Homme devant Dieu*, "Théologie" series (1964), 125–32.

The "Initial Postulate"

At the point of departure, Father Teilhard usually asks that he be granted one thing—one single thing: what he calls either a "postulate" or a "fundamental option" in favor of being, or of the goodness of being, of the value of being; sometimes he also says: "faith in the world", in the goodness of the world. This initial request is dictated to him by the experience of his contacts with certain unbelieving minds. Some prove ready to grant this postulate immediately, which thus provides a common ground for subsequent research. But others are more recalcitrant. He wrote on May 11, 1923, on the boat that took him to China, "between Saigon and Hong Kong":

> Last night, a long conversation with Doctor X . . . and another passenger about subjects of moral philosophy. We came to ascertain that we differed on points as fundamental as: "Is it better to be or not to be?" I really believe, in fact, that a fundamental option in all thought, a postulate that is not demonstrable but from which all derives, is found there. If one admits that being is better than its contrary, it is difficult to stop without going all the way to God. If one does not admit that, discussion is no longer possible.[6]

This lesson was not lost. In several of his writings, Father Teilhard insists on warning his reader formally: "No reflective construct would be possible without the initial choice that makes us incline, heart and reason, toward being rather than toward nonbeing";[7] or again: "Is being good or bad? That is to say, is it better to be than not to be? Despite its learned and metaphysical form, this dilemma is essentially practical, and it represents the fundamental alternative on which, implicitly or explicitly, every man, by the very fact that he was born, is forced to declare himself."[8]

"Faith in being", or "faith in the world": this is still, at least apparently, only a point of departure. But, step by step, this initial faith

---

[6] *Lettres de voyage* (1951). Cf. our work, *La Pensée religieuse du Père Pierre Teilhard de Chardin* (1962), 261–62 [English trans.: *The Religion of Teilhard de Chardin* (New York: Desclée, 1967)].

[7] *L'Énergie humaine* (1937); *Oeuvres*, 6:173.

[8] *La Grande option* (1939); *Oeuvres*, 5:61. Cf. 9:68 and 110. Cf. *Le Christianisme dans le Monde* (1933): any hypothesis that "would make the Universe absurd" must be eliminated: *Oeuvres*, 9:136.

(whose nature it will be necessary to specify) will necessarily produce faith "in some final consummation of *everything* that surrounds us".[9] Its content will be revealed only little by little: nevertheless, in reality, it is already, in one sense, pregnant with everything. To the degree, in fact, that the proof is developed, the "initial faith" from which one has departed is going to experience a series of enlargements, precisions, explanations, indeed, changes ("sheddings"), so that at the end of the chain of reasonings the one who has followed Teilhard will be able to say with him that he now believes "in the goodness and in the (not primary but) final value of things":[10] for they will henceforth appear to him to be founded in God. This is what Pastor Georges Crespy observes, in his thesis on the *Pensée théologique de Teilhard de Chardin*, in analyzing the little work entitled *Comment je crois*, which begins with a profession of "faith in the world": "Teilhard", he concludes, "has the courage to have confidence to the very end in his initial intuitions, he has secretly foreseen that the end would justify all."[11]

The "Third Abyss"

The being from which we are setting off, that in which we are plunged before even having begun to think or act, is presented at first to us as an evolution. That, in Father Teilhard de Chardin's judgment, is more than a scientific conception; with reference to the progress of science, it is an acquisition of consciousness, whose perception, still confused, increasingly compels attention.[12] His whole concern, from then on, is to establish that this evolution does not happen "by chance". It becomes intelligible to anyone who takes the trouble to read the signs; it offers a meaning, because it has in itself a meaning. Its significance is in its direction. It culminates in man, and in consequence, man is the key to the universe.

The tradition of the spiritualist philosophy, very especially in its Christian form, made man "the king of creation". Now, in the judgment of a number of modern thinkers, this tradition was entirely bound

[9] *L'Énergie humaine*, loc. cit.

[10] *Lettres à Léontine Zanta*, "Christus" series, (1965), 89: letter of August 22, 1928.

[11] Paris: Éditions universitaires, 1961, 105. See *La Prière du Père Teilhard de Chardin*, 151–54 and 220.

[12] Cf. *Du cosmos à la Cosmogénèse* (1951); *Oeuvres*, 7:265. See also 5:335.

up with static representations of ancient cosmology: when the latter fell, the former fell by that very fact. At the time when Father Teilhard began to write, one work which popularized this theme with eloquence was having a great success: *Les Affirmations de la conscience moderne*, by Gabriel Séailles.[13] It is still today the opinion of many scholars, who find allies in many a philosopher little concerned with cosmology. Teilhard does not seek to defend an ancient position against them by a defensive apologetic that would resemble rear-guard fighting. He undertakes to demonstrate scientifically not only that the ancient tradition about man was not destroyed by the advent of a new age but that it was to find itself more firmly established, although in a completely new form. Evolution such as he explains it is a "great orthogenesis, of all that lives, toward more immanent spontaneity".[14] Across the growing complexification of organisms and finally of the nervous system, it is a "rise in consciousness": the axis of "cosmogenesis" can be thus defined.[15] To the two infinities of Pascal, to the two abysses of greatness and littleness, must not only be added but opposed a third, which reverses the whole situation: the infinity of complexity.[16] This "third abyss", which is an "abyss of synthesis",[17] ends in being hollowed out in man, in whom the evolution finally becomes conscious of itself:[18] "In the human spirit, as in a unique and irreplaceable fruit, is found gathered together the whole sublimated life, that is to say, the whole

---

[13] See especially 26–31, 4th ed. (Paris: Armand Colin, 1909).

[14] *Le Phénomène humain, Oeuvres*, 1:164. Cf. *Le Groupe zoologique humain* (1965 ed.), 121–23.

[15] *Le Phénomène humain*, 152, note 1: "The galaxy of living forms constitutes . . . a vast orthogenetic movement of involution of an ever greater complexity and consciousness."

[16] *Le Place de l'homme dans l'Univers, réflexions sur la complexité* (November 15, 1942); *Oeuvres*, 3:312–19. *La Centrologie* (December 12, 1944); *Oeuvres*, 7:103–4. *Comment je vois* (August 26, 1948), nos. 1–5. *Le Groupe zoologique humain*, 21, etc.

[17] *L'Atomisme de l'Esprit* (1941); *Oeuvres*, 7:35.

[18] Cf. A. D. Sertillanges, O.P., who is inspired by Teilhard, in *Dieu ou rien* (Paris: Flammarion, 1933), 1:117: "Intelligence . . . is, in the phenomenon, the supreme success of life on earth." To Auguste Valensin, December 31, 1926: "For over two years, I have had the impression of being gradually drawn toward the study of Humanity, not prehistoric, but *present*." Norbert M. Luyten, O.P., "Réflexions sur la méthode de Teilhard de Chardin", in the *Festschrift* offered to Father Bochenski (Fribourg, Switzerland, 1965), 294: "Throughout his paleontological work, Teilhard perceives man as the point of convergence of this immense evolutional process. . . . This man is not only the one whose fossilized remains he encounters, in such and such an excavation, he is also, and even more, the man who lives today. For, the latter is for Teilhard an unshakable conviction, if we can read the fragments the past has bequeathed to us, he is a function of the present that we have under our eyes."

cosmic value, of the Earth."[19] "In truth," Teilhard concludes, "I doubt that there is any moment more decisive for the thinking being than when, the scales falling from his eyes, he discovers that he is not an element lost in the cosmic solitudes but that a universal will to live converges and is homonized in him":[20]

> Since Galileo (according to Freud's remark), man had not ceased to lose, one by one, in the eyes of Science, the privileges that had until then made him be regarded as unique in the world. *Astronomically*, at first, to the degree (as and with the Earth) he was drowned in the enormous anonymity of the stellar masses; *biologically*, next, to the degree (as a totally different animal) he was lost in the host of species, his sisters; *psychologically*, finally, to the degree an abyss of the Unconscious was opened in the heart of his *I*: by three successive degrees, in four centuries, man, I say indeed, had seemed to be definitively dissolved again into the common of things.
>
> Now here, in being placed back in the crucible, this same man is in the process of reemerging, more than ever, *as the head of nature*: since, precisely in order to be recast with the general current of a converging cosmogenesis, he is acquiring in our eyes the possibility and the quality of forming, in the heart of time and space, *a singular point of universalization* for the very material of the world. . . .[21]

Pascal and Voltaire, for once in agreement, as we have said, saw man crushed by the universe. Pascal saved the dignity of man by considering the thought in him, which a number of our contemporaries no longer know how to do. But, by this consideration, he was not able to save man: all he granted him in the final analysis was the knowledge that

[19] *L'Esprit de la terre*; *Oeuvres*, 6:35.

[20] *Le Phénomène humain*, 30. "Not simple progress of life, but *blossoming* of all life", comments Jean Piveteau, in speaking of the appearance of man (Colloque de Vézelay, 1965).

[21] "Les Singularités de l'espèce humaine", *Annales de Paléontologie*, 12 (1955), 51. *Évolution de l'idée d'évolution* (1950): "Initially, that is to say, one century ago, Man was considered first of all as a simple observer, then, after Darwin, as a simple branch of Evolution. Now here, in very consequence of this incorporation in the Biogenesis, he begins to perceive that through him passes the principal trunk of the tree of earthly Life. Life is not diversified by chance, in all directions. But it allows us to see an absolute direction of progress toward the values of growing consciousness; and, on this principal axis, Man is the most advanced end we know. . . . There he is in the process of taking the head: not in stability but in movement; no longer in his capacity as center, but in the form of an arrow of the World in growth. Neoanthropocentrism, no longer of position, but of direction in Evolution" (*Oeuvres*, 3:349).

he is crushed by the universe, while "the universe knows nothing of the advantage that it has over him".[22] "What is a man in the infinite?" The real superiority of this man, his victory over the blind forces of the universe, was truly reestablished only by faith. This is what Pascal had just seen with the shattering of the ancient cosmology: "The eternal silence of these infinite spaces frightens me. . . ." Since Pascal and since Voltaire, science has progressed; after space, it discovered duration; the shattering of the ancient cosmology reached its climax, and man seemed lost even more, if possible, in the midst of the universe.[23] Once again, "a properly revolutionary scientific progress overturns the idea that man forms of himself and of his situation in the world"; once again, "through this revolution the confidence that spirit has in spirit is placed in question."[24] It is then that Teilhard, in posing the infinity of complexity as the culmination of the cosmic evolution, reestablishes man, by the same stroke, not only in his dignity but in his effective domination. He well sees: "The Universe is an immense thing in which we would be lost if it did not converge on the Person";[25] but all his effort ends precisely in establishing this convergence.

Did he fully establish it? Pascal saw "only infinities on all sides", which enclosed him "as an atom and as a shadow that lasts only an instant without returning"; the universe that he described was a world that had "lost all structure".[26] Was Teilhard, by examining the laws of evolution, to return a structure to this world? Was his theory of hominization absolutely proved, at least in its essential line of argument? It would be worth the trouble to examine it seriously. At least, in judging it, one cannot claim that he did not try to demonstrate it. Let us simply note here that Pascal and Voltaire have nothing to say to us against it: for neither Pascal nor Voltaire knew "the new crisis of the spirit" that Teilhard wished to face, and neither Pascal nor Voltaire could foresee "the change of perspective" thanks to which Teilhard believed he could conclude that "there is henceforth,

---

[22] And again: "Through space, the universe includes me and engulfs me as a point; through thought, I understand it."

[23] *La Peur de l'existence* (1949); *Oeuvres*, 7:191–95.

[24] Étienne Borne, *De Pascal à Teilhard de Chardin* (Clermont-Ferrand, 1962), 36 and 42.

[25] Letter of 1935.

[26] M. de Gandillac, "Pascal et le silence du monde", in *Blaise Pascale, l'homme et l'oeuvre*, Cahiers de Royaumont, Philosophie, 1 (1956), 342–85. Cf. Georges Poulet, "Pascal et la sphère admirable", *Esprit*, 233 (December 1955), 1833–49.

in our eyes, a Past and a Future, which is to say, a growth of the World."[27]

"The Rise of the Spirit"

In the Teilhardian universe, Cosmogenesis culminates in Anthropogenesis.[28] So the cosmological proof of the existence of God that Teilhard is going to construct on this foundation will be just as well named an anthropological proof. As well and better still. It in fact passes through man, through the human spirit, which is "spirit of the Earth".

We should not take this last expression, or similar expressions, as signifying that the spirit is a product of matter. That would be a gross mistake. The evolutionist perspective renewed, for Teilhard, the manner of understanding the classical distinction between matter and spirit: it in no way abolished this distinction. If this has at times been poorly understood, it is because a metaphysical implication was immediately given to explanations that were brought forward on the phenomenal plane. Father Teilhard, however, never ceased to explain himself in this regard. As early as November 1917, he wrote: "Of course, consciousness must not be considered a mere resultant. . . . [It is] the appearance in the world of something quite new. . . . [It is] a new substance."[29] The unifying force of the multiple, the spirit cannot be "composed of the multiple". It appears "laden with remains of matter", but not made of matter. It emerges experientially "on more and more synthetized matter", but this does not signify that matter, without anything more,

---

[27] "L'Incroyance moderne, cause profonde et remède", *La Vie intellectuelle* (October 25, 1923). Cf. Étienne Borne, *De Pascal*, 49: "The problem of time could not be symmetrical with that of space. While Pascal found in extension only a mute indefinite, vainly rebegun, in which no situation is qualitatively privileged, in which nothing can be said to be a beginning, middle or end, Teilhard de Chardin describes a duration that develops to a rhythm of increasing acceleration toward a last and final end which will then be well named 'the Omega point'. . . ." "The last word of the philosopher Pascal was a question. . . . The last word of Teilhard the philosopher is an affirmation . . ." (50).

[28] *Comment concevoir et espérer* (1950), *Oeuvres*, 5:372.

[29] *L'Union créatrice; Écrits du temps de la guerre* (1965), 177–78. He even adds—but we are still not at this point of our itinerary—that this presupposes a "properly creative activity". Note of February 18, 1916: "The world is a series of things that were created for the benefit of each other, life for the benefit of a certain dynamic equilibrium—spiritual thought for the benefit of a certain cerebral development—grace for the benefit of a certain moral perfection. . . ." Cf. Étienne Borne, *Recherches et débats*, 40:57: "The duality of matter and spirit is in no way suppressed by Teilhard", etc.

is being changed into spirit. Between the two, there exists a whole complex network of "liaisons" and "oppositions". The spirit is no more matter than the "inside" of things is their "outside". Of course matter and spirit are not like "two compartments", or "two things": but precisely such a dualism, far from assuring the existence of the spirit, would materialize it. And of course, too, there is in being itself a certain concrete unity of the without and the within, of the matter and the spirit: it could even be noted, not, however, without regard to Teilhard, but with regard to Claude Bernard and Father Sertillanges, that this was "basically what Saint Thomas was already teaching".[30] It is nonetheless certain, for Teilhard, that "all consistency comes from the Spirit",[31] or, what amounts to the same thing, that "if things hold and hold together, it is only by reason of complexity, *from above*",[32] materialism being only an illusion, due to a "coarse view of things"; or again, that "the sole consistency of beings is given them by their synthetic [synthetizing] element, that is to say, through what is, to a more or less perfect degree, their soul, their spirit."[33]

But what is no less certain is that we are always seeking consistency with respect to and on the basis of the material universe. For we reason on the basis of the senses. We do not have the intuition of pure spirit. "No spirit (even God in the limits of our experience) exists, or could exist, by construction, without a multiple that is associated with it."[34] In other words, to borrow the language of our classical philosophy, it is only as a function of the world that, through a rational induction, we can pose the existence of God. And the same is likewise true, in the first place, *mutatis mutandis*, for all spirit.

Now, the rise of the spirit (that is to say, of the reflective consciousness and of freedom) on the basis of light, and synthetizing matter, is an *irreversible* rise. This irreversibility is exactly what we call,

[30] J. G. Donders, P.A., *L'Intelligibilité de l'évolution selon A. D. Sertillanges, O.P.*, thesis at the Gregorian University (1961), 3 and 21.

[31] Letter of May 4, 1931: "He does not see that the Cosmos holds together, not by matter, but by spirit" (*Lettres de voyage*, 149), etc.

[32] *Le Phénomène humain*, 37. *Du Cosmos à la Cosmogénèse* (1951), on the *Materia matrix*; "the point of final equilibrium of the cosmic Movement" is on the side "of the superstructure, or of the 'super-compound', which is to say, of the spirit." *Oeuvres*, 7:266–67.

[33] *Science et Christ* (1920); *Oeuvres*, 9:55. Cf. Pierre Smulders, *La Vision de Teilhard de Chardin* (Paris: Desclée de Brouwer, 1964), 71–78.

[34] *Esquisse d'un Univers personnel* (1936); *Oeuvres*, 6:747; *L'Union créatrice* (1917); *Écrits du temps de la guerre*, 178–79.

and what Father Teilhard himself also calls at times, immortality.[35] In other words, in the cosmos, at the end of cosmogenesis, the victory of "convergence" is assured over dispersing entropy, over "usury and universal disintegration".[36] In short, the victory of the spirit over matter.

Teilhard, then, couples the classical idea of the immortality of each spiritual soul with that of a collective immortality. He couples it, but let us observe, he does not replace it. For "the spirit of the Earth" has nothing of an undifferentiated collective reality: it is composed of personal spirits. The process of spiritualization is in fact, identically, a process of personalization; it ends in "the incommunicable singularity of each reflective element",[37] and that is one of the senses in which the Teilhardian expression "personal universe" must be understood. The irreversibility of the cosmos is, then, in the final analysis the personal immortality of all the souls that compose it. In the end, in fact, the cosmos, in its very unity, is essentially "a world of souls".[38]

The fight is "engaged, in the universe, between the unified multiple and the unorganized multitude".[39] A grandiose duel, which extends across the whole duration of the cosmic evolution and which must be terminated by the definitive victory of the unified multiple, that is to say, of the personal Spirit. Father Teilhard described it in a series of expositions endlessly resumed, with an ever-increased effort at precision. Thus, in 1951, in an essay on the *Convergence de l'univers*:

> A certain fundamental law (becomes visible to us), affecting the entire world. No longer merely, in the Universe, as they continue to repeat, the despairing entropy, inexorably bringing all things back to the most elementary and most stable forms. But, emerging across and above this rain of ashes, a kind of cosmic vortex, in the midst of which the material of the world, by a preferential utilization of chance, twists and winds more

[35] So the third paragraph of *Comment je crois* (1934) is entitled: "Faith in immortality". Cf. *L'Énergie humaine* (1937): "The cosmic phenomenon of spiritualization must be irreversible"; *Oeuvres*, 6:196. See also 3:322–23; 9:125, 279–80, etc.

[36] *Les Singularités de l'espèce humaine* (1954); *Oeuvres*, 2:304.

[37] *Le Groupe zoologique humain*, 154.

[38] *La Vie cosmique* (1916); *Écrits du temps de la guerre*, 37, etc. *Note sur le Christ universel* (1920): "the value of souls *in se*, which is to say, the value of the World . . ."; *Oeuvres*, 9:42. Cf. *La Prière*, 166–68.

[39] *Le Phénomène humain*, 58.

and more closely around itself in ever more complicated and centered combinations.[40]

"So that incorruptibility in which ancient philosophy discerned with good reason the most characteristic attribute of the spiritual reappeared in Thought", after an eclipse that many thought definitive.[41]

A Proof of God

Once this irreversible convergence of the universe, or again, "the cosmic drift of complexity-consciousness", is established, we arrive at the last link of the chain that ends in the necessary affirmation of God.

A point, in fact, must be attained where the human consciousness is achieved. "There is before us . . . a critical and final point of ultra-hominization, corresponding to a complete reflection of the noosphere about itself";[42] let us also say, to sum up long explanations that do not enter directly into our present perspective, a point of perfect personalization, in a unity that is the opposite of a homogeneous identity. A *processus in infinitum* is impossible.

This achievement, or this "complete reflection", is the primary meaning that Father Teilhard attaches to what he calls the "Omega point". "Higher pole of human coreflection", "summit of hominization", such a point is still immanent. But just as it was impossible to tend toward it indefinitely without ever attaining it, so it is equally impossible to hold to it. Let us see the demonstration of this in a page from the *Esquisse d'une dialectique de l'esprit* (1946). Among the varied forms that clothe in Teilhard the proof of the existence of God, we undoubtedly have there, if not the most technical, at least the most systematic, the one of his particular views that depends the most on the human future,

---

[40] *Oeuvres*, 7:302–3. *Le Groupe zoologique humain*, 37: "Our World is truly something that is arranged." *Les Singularités*; *Oeuvres*, 2:304.

[41] *Esquisse d'un Univers personnel* (1946); *Oeuvres*, 6:87. One final time the dilemma will be posed, and the duel described, in *Le Christique* (1955): "Entropy or convergence? In other words, is it in the direction of the unarranged-unconscious (materialist solution) or, on the contrary, of the Arranged-conscious (spiritualist solution) that the Universe, balanced on itself, ultimately falls?"

[42] *La Convergence de l'Univers*; *Oeuvres*, 7:302. Cf. François Meyer, "L'Évolution se dirige-t-elle vers un terme défini dans le temps?", *Cahiers Pierre Teilhard de Chardin*, 4 (1963), 90–98.

such as he elaborated it especially in the second part of his career. It is thus, too, in our opinion at least, the form that is the most subject to contestation:

> The natural evolution of the biosphere is prolonged in what I have called the noosphere, but it takes a clearly *convergent* shape, delineating upward a *point of maturation* (or of collective reflection). . . . [At this point] reflective humanity collectively remains alone before itself. It is impossible, under these conditions, to imagine a subsequent complexification determining a higher consciousness. Our law of recurrence automatically ceases to function. . . . So that . . . man is seen to flow toward a terminal position where:
>
> 1. organically, he can go no farther (even collectively) in complexity, then in consciousness;
> 2. psychically, he cannot agree to retreat;
> 3. and cosmically, he cannot even remain in place, since, in our universe "entropy", to cease to advance, is to fall backward.
>
> What does this say if not that, having arrived at this ultra-critical point of maturation, the curve of the phenomenon of man pierces the cosmic phenomenal system and postulates the existence, before and beyond, of some extracosmic pole where the whole reflective incommunicable successively formed in the Universe . . . in the course of evolution is found integrally collected and definitively consolidated?[43]
>
> Seen in ascending, from our side of things, the apex of the evolutionary cone (the Omega point) stands out at first on the horizon as a focus of simply immanent convergence: humanity totally reflective on self. But, if we look more closely, it is clear that if this focus is to hold together, it presupposes, behind it, and deeper than it, a transcendent, divine nucleus.[44]

This is, as we have said, only one of Teilhard's forms of argumentation. It presupposes a vision of the future "extrapolated on the curve constructed with givens offered to actual observation".[45] For more than one reason, such an extrapolation, practiced with so much boldness, might seem debatable,[46] and as, in the judgment of Father Teilhard

[43] Cf. *Vie et Planètes* (1945); *Oeuvres*, 5:155–56. *Le Phénomène humain*, 251–58, etc.

[44] *Oeuvres*, 7:151–52. *Super-Humanité* (1943); 9:208. *Le Groupe zoologique humain*, 155.

[45] Aldo Locatelli, *Dio e miracolo conoscibile al di la della scienza* (Éd. La Scuola cattolica, 1963), 121.

[46] We have explained this in *La Pensée religieuse* . . . , especially chap. 19: "Une extrapolation risquée?"

himself, it is hardly more than "possible",[47] it without doubt does not constitute an entirely sufficient foundation. He did not fail to acknowledge this on several occasions, notably in *Le Groupe zoologique humain*, where, after having taken up in more detail and with all possible rigor the argumentation that we have just read, he concludes in prudent and measured terms: "Up to the new order, modern Astronomy does not hesitate to consider the existence of a kind of primitive Atom in which would be gathered together the entire mass of the sidereal world brought back several billion years. Symmetrically, in a way, with this primordial physical unity, is it not curious that Biology, extrapolated to the extreme (and this time toward the future), leads us to a similar hypothesis: that of a universal Center (which I have called Omega), no longer of physical exteriorization and expansion, but of psychic interiorization . . . ?"[48]

But, as we have also said, we find in Father Teilhard other, simpler, forms of argumentation, whose power to convince seems more universal. Msgr. Bruno de Solages has summed up three principal ones, with his customary vigor and clarity, by indicating the passages to which one can refer in order to complete the explanation. He has designated them by the following names: (1) Proof by human action, or "the Absolute, postulate of Evolution";[49] (2) Proof by the efficient and governing causality, or "God, first Mover of the ascending Evolution"; (3) Proof by the aspirations of the human soul, or "to love God, condition of the ultimate unification of a convergent noosphere".[50] Other commentators, like Father Maurice Corvez, O.P.,[51] or Father C. Valverde Mucientes, S.J.,[52] distinguish these proofs in a slightly different way. In

[47] *Réflexion sur la probabilité scientifique et les conséquences religieuses d'un Ultra-humain* (1951); *Oeuvres*, 7:279–91.

[48] 157–58.

[49] We have sketched a critical examination of this in chapter 16 of *La Pensée religieuse*: "Foi et intelligibilité".

[50] Msgr. Bruno de Solages, "Preuves", 59. The author takes up the subject again in greater depth in a work that is to appear shortly.

[51] *De la science à la foi, Teilhard de Chardin* (1965), 150–53: a. Demands of an accomplished convergence; b. in the more precise perspective of thought; c. in the more precise perspective of love.

[52] Father Valverde, of the University of Comillas (Spain), presented to the International Thomist Congress in Rome (September 1965) a report on *Evolucionismo Teilhardiano y quinta Via* (*Acta* 1:295–301). In another report from this same congress, the Abbé Marcel Duquesne, of the Catholic Faculties of Lille, made a similar comparison ("La Preuve de Dieu par le gouvernement des choses").

the actual thought of their author, they are not, moreover, adequately distinct from each other.

What, through all of them, Father Teilhard wanted first of all to show his contemporaries, and what we retain above all, is that, as he said in 1945 in *Action et activation*, "the problem of a first Mover and of an ultimate future Collector does not diminish; it grows, on the contrary, in importance and urgency with the formidable increases imposed by Science on our representations of the Universe."[53] And it is before this problem that he insisted on placing and on leaving his listeners or his readers, even when the subject treated seemed to be primarily of pure science. Whence, for example, the last page of the *Groupe zoologique humain*, a summary of lectures given at the Sorbonne in the course of the winter of 1950–1951 "for advanced students",[54] in which he gave in particularly technical terms the résumé of his vision of the universe.

> At the risk of being powerless to form the keystone for the Noosphere, "Omega" can be conceived only as the *point of encounter* between the Universe that has reached its limit of centration, and *another Center* that is still deeper, a self-subsistent Center and absolutely ultimate Principle of irreversibility and personalization: the only true Omega. And it is in this point, if I am not mistaken, that above the science of Evolution . . . the problem of God, Mover, Collector, and Consolidator, in advance, of Evolution fits.[55]

The Attributes of Omega

The preceding texts already enumerate several attributes of this divine Omega, "the only true Omega". Without doubt, such a "Center", such a "Pole", such a "Focus", "in itself, and by definition, is not directly perceptible by us"; for it is a matter of an "extracosmic Energy in its origin (although immanent and in its end)".[56] The analysis of evolutionary movement and of its demand for intelligibility does not suffice, then, to make us penetrate "the inner nature of Omega"; but

[53] *Oeuvres*, 9:226.

[54] Claude Cuénot, *Pierre Teilhard de Chardin* (1958), 336–37.

[55] In 1951, ed. of 1956, 162. Cf. *Comment je vois* (1948), no. 13.

[56] *Comment je vois*, no. 20. "L'Union créatrice", in *Écrits du temps de la guerre*, 181–84.

it allows us, nevertheless, to "formulate several conditions that it must satisfy in order to fulfill its role."[57]

The first of these conditions, or the primary attribute of Omega, to point out is its very reality, or its actuality: "Ideal Center, virtual Center: none of that can suffice. To the present and real noosphere must correspond a real and present center. To be supremely attractive, Omega must already be supremely existent."[58] There is in it a "power controlling time and chance", alone capable of providing a guarantee of success to our spirit. This is, as we have seen, "a first mover and an ultimate collector", in other words, at once Alpha and Omega, "sole origin, sole issue, sole end".[59] This "primary Being" is of all necessity a "personal [or 'ultra-personal'] Being", since it is a "personalizing Focus".[60] It is a "real pole of convergence", "Center different from all centers, since it 'over-centers' by assimilating them, Person distinct from all persons, since it ends by uniting them".[61]

This is a major affirmation for Teilhard, one to which he never ceases to return: "A world imagined as drifting toward the impersonal . . . would become unthinkable and unlivable at the same time",[62] and "the personal elements of the universe would return to disorder (which is to say, nothingness) if they did not encounter, in order to rule them, the already-actualized supra-personal. In the world around us must, then, be found, in order to balance our action, not only the anticipation but also the recognizable face of a universal personality."[63] In other words, we must pose a God who is "supremely personal, from whom we are distinguished all the more as we lose ourselves the more in him".[64] "Ultimate Center", consequently, Omega must be conceived

---

[57] Smulders, *La Vision*, 278–79; "Here the movement of Teilhardian thought does not differ essentially from the forms of a classical apologetic."

[58] *Le Phénomène humain*, 299–300. *La Messe sur le Monde* (1923): "The work of the World consists, not in engendering some supreme Reality in itself, but in being consummated through union in a preexisting Being."

[59] *Action et activation*, August 9, 1945; *Oeuvres*, 9:226. *La Vie cosmique*; *Écrits*, 5 and 183. *L'Union créatrice*, etc.

[60] *Comment je crois* (1934). *Sommaire de ma perspective phénoménologique du monde* (1954), 2, etc. *La Transposition conique de l'action* (1942): "ultra-conscious, ultra-personal, ultra-actual"; *Oeuvres*, 5:121.

[61] *L'Énergie humaine* (1937); *Oeuvres*, 6:180.

[62] *Le Rebondissement humain de l'Évolution* (1947); *Oeuvres*, 5:265.

[63] *Esquisse d'un Univers personnel* (1936); *Oeuvres*, 6:89.

[64] *Le Phénomène spirituel* (1936); *Oeuvres*, 6:136.

as "supreme personality". It is "an apex of transcendence", a "primordial transcendence", a "transcendent reality".[65] In brief, "autonomy, actuality, irreversibility and finally transcendence: the four attributes of Omega".[66]

This fourth attribute, which discourages us in advance from enclosing "the inner nature of Omega" in a rational definition, does not, however, leave us in a pure state of ignorance in its regard. This Being who is "not only at the head of all series, but . . . in some way, exceptional [*hors série*]", this Being who alone "finds in himself his proper consistency",[67] is a mysterious Being: he "does not present himself to our finite beings as a ready-made thing that must be embraced", but he "is for us eternal discovery and eternal growth. The more we believe we are understanding him, the more he reveals himself to be other. The more we think to hold him, the more he withdraws, by drawing us into the depths of himself. . . ."[68]

We will note that, here and there, Father Teilhard de Chardin affirms, about the Omega point, that it is "partially transcendent, that is to say, partially independent of the evolution that culminates in It". This is because he joins together, or rather he still keeps united, following the logic of the discovery, the two meanings that he has successively recognized for this word Omega. In other words, he speaks then, not of God alone nor of the world alone, but of "their point of encounter", and he cannot forget, as a good method, that it was *first* the unified world, the world come to its end, that he naturally designated by this symbolic appellation. The rest of the text from which we borrowed these preceding words shows this to us rather clearly. In fact, he says to us, "if Omega did not escape, in some way, the conditions of time and space, it could be neither already present to us nor capable . . . of founding the hopes of irreversibility without which, beginning with man, centrogenesis would cease to function. It is thus that, through a face of itself [= its divine face, God], different from that under which we see it formed [= its cosmic and human, Omega, 'immanent' face], it

[65] *Esquisse d'un Univers personnel* (1936); *Oeuvres*, 6:103. *Du Cosmos à la cosmogénèse* (March 15, 1951), 7:271, etc.

[66] *Le Phénomène humain*, 305; "necessarily autonomous central focus" (292, note). *La Place d l'Homme dans l'univers* (1942): "Irreversible focus"; *Oeuvres*, 3:323. On the simplicity and "complexity" of the Being of God: *Esquisse d'un Univers personnel*; 6:75 and 86.

[67] See also *La Centrologie*, no. 24; *Oeuvres*, 7:119.

[68] *Le Milieu divin*, 175.

emerges forever above the world from which, however, from another angle, it is in the process of emerging. . . ."[69]

In other words, again, this complex Omega, at the end of the argumentation that takes its point of departure from the observation of the cosmos on the way to unification, appears like "a system centered on centers, but" centered itself on "a Center of centers". "Center of higher order", the latter "awaits us—already it appears—not only beside but *beyond* and *above* ourselves."[70]

. . . And, if we had set forth the other aspects of the Teilhardian proof, we would see better how the actuality of Omega is the actuality of love; how its personality is the personality of love, how its power of attraction, activation and union is the power of love; how, finally, Omega is love itself, at once "lovable and loving".[71]

Reason and Revelation

We have already seen several times, and we will see again through some of the passages that have just been quoted, that the necessity of posing the existence of God on the basis of the observation of the World in convergent evolution depends, above all, in Father Teilhard's eyes—above all, though not uniquely—on the necessity of posing a unifying Being. It is principally in his unifying function that God is attained.[72]

Now, Christian Revelation teaches us, on the other hand, that God created the World in a thought of love, so as to unite it with himself; that the accomplishment of this divine plan was worked out through the Incarnation; and that it is through our union accomplished in Christ (Mystical Body) that each of us finds himself united to God.

Father Teilhard de Chardin always professed a strict idea of revelation, recognized in its twofold character, intellectual (which does not

[69] *La Centrologie*, no. 24; *Oeuvres*, 7:119.

[70] *Comment je vois*, no. 20. *Réflexions sur le bonheur*; *Cahiers*, 2:63.

[71] *Le Phénomène humain*, 299–300. *Les Singularités de l'espèce humaine*, Appendix, March 25, 1954; *Oeuvres*, 2:373–74. Father Teilhard, as we see, did not try to imitate the gesture that aims ambitiously at "overcoming the ultimate value of love and transcending the transcendence of the personal God", a gesture that in reality "lets itself docilely be carried away by a pre-Christian and prepersonal spiritual current": Jacques-Albert Cuttat, introduction to R. C. Zaehner, *Inde, Israël, Islam*, trans. Eva Meyerovitch (1965), 17.

[72] We should remember that, in the language of Father Teilhard, unification and identification are opposed to each other. The first is as well differentiation, personalization. Supremely unifying, God is "supremely personalizing": *Comment je vois*, no. 20, etc.

exclude affective) and supernatural. He knows that it is "affirmation from above" and that it culminates in "the fact of the Incarnation".[73] So, when he says, in *Le Christique* (1965): "In the final analysis, the cosmogenesis, after having been discovered, following its principal axis, biogenesis, then noogenesis, culminates in the christogenesis that any Christian reveres", he does not mean to suggest that it is through a natural dialectic that the passage is effectuated in our spirit from noogenesis to christogenesis. Certain abridged explanations, for which he situated himself immediately in the point of view of faith, misled some commentators. Yet, as Mme. M. Barthélemy-Madaule remarked, "it is often we ourselves", in the summaries that we make of his thought, "who mix the levels, who work out too soon, not a synthesis, but a mixture, to be surprised, then, at the confusion."[74] Father Teilhard himself criticized those who, he said, "naïvely" confuse "the levels of the Real" and who make, for example, of Christ, "a physical agent *of the same order* as organic life or ether": one who seemed to him "blameworthy and laughable".[75] He usually distinguished clearly the two domains of what he called the "heavenly truth" and the "earthly truth", or "the taught" and "the found", or again "the divine sphere" and "the cosmic sphere". To verify this, one need only observe the composition of some of his writings; how, for example, he introduces "The Christian Phenomenon" following the long analysis of the "Phenomenon of Man", either in *Le Phénomene humain* itself or in *Les Singularités de l'espèce humaine*; or rather, how he appeals to "the Christian mystique" at the end of his "Reflections on happiness"; or again, how, in the second part of *Comment je crois*, he leaves the paths of individual experience and rational demonstration in order to question history.

To describe this divine revelation, he spoke of "Omega being reflected, *being revealed*, affectively and intelligibly, on the reflective surface of the noosphere".[76] With clear precision, he wrote: "The whole value of Christianity, its whole power to raise souls, depends on the fact that it is presented as an Imposition from above, as from the Other . . . ,

[73] *Essai d'une dialectique de l'esprit* (1946); *Oeuvres*, 7:154–56. *Comment je crois* (1934): "And since in that way there is now outlined for me a higher sphere of the Personal and personal relations, I begin to suspect that attractions and directions of an intellectual nature could well envelop me and speak to me."

[74] *Teilhard de Chardin et la pensée catholique, Colloque de Venise* (Paris, 1965), 88–89.

[75] Letter of May 25, 1923.

[76] *Comment je vois*, no. 22.

already *actuated*, constituted, *extra nos*: such is the essence of the idea of Revelation."[77] But he also said: "The Christian has only to meditate on his *Credo* to find, in the Revelation he admits, the unhoped-for accomplishment of the dream to the threshold of which philosophy logically leads him."[78] He knows, in fact, that the reality of Christ can in no manner be *deduced* from the World, but he also knows that Revelation consolidates, extends, achieves the work sketched by the reason. He discovers with joy a "remarkable similarity" between the dogmatic perspectives and the conclusions or the ultimate hypotheses to which the study of the phenomenon of man leads him, a similarity that he attributes with good reason to the "influence" and the "radiation" of Christian revelation. Between reason and faith, as between nature and grace, if there is discontinuity, distinction and hierarchy, there is also just as much harmony. Teilhard insists, and without doubt excessively at times, on the second of these two aspects, but without failing to recognize truly the first.

The Christic Omega

"In any hypothesis, the world demands to be centered in order to be thinkable." Yet, it could be so by many more or less imperfect ways which are difficult for us today to imagine. "The 'gracious' characteristic of the world consists precisely in the fact that the place of universal center was not given to any intermediary whatever between God and the universe"—which, consequently, had not obtained a perfect "centrality"—"but that it was taken by the Divinity itself, which thus introduced us . . . into the heart of his immanence."[79] In other words, "in place of a vague focus of convergence required as an end to [the] Evolution, the personal and definite reality of the incarnate Word, in whom all assumes consistency, appears and becomes estab-

[77] See the terms cited in Maurice Blondel and Pierre Teilhard de Chardin, *Correspondance commentée* by Henri de Lubac, chapter entitled: "Descente et Montée dans l'oeuvre du Père Teilhard" (129–53). As Georges Crespy well says, 107, Teilhard: "does not conceal the 'passage to another genre' that constitutes the act of faith. . . ."

[78] *Mon univers* of 1924: *Oeuvres*, 9:81. We can apply here what Father Henri Bouillard said with respect to Blondel, in *Blondel et le christianisme* (1961), 162: "To state that the mystery of the Mediator resolves the philosophical enigma is not to require the Incarnation, it is to profit by the light that its notion brings and that one has found from another source."

[79] Loc. cit., 84.

lished."[80] "Naturally", then, there would be "only the expectation of a unification: without Christ, the cosmos would not have any natural Omega; it would remain open"; but in our present situation, "the Incarnation has so well *recast* the Universe in the supernatural that, *concretely* speaking, we can no longer seek, or imagine, the elements of this world, having gravitated toward some center, without the elevation to grace."[81]

Hence the Teilhardian formula: "The revealed Christ is nothing but Omega";[82] or similar formulas. The "gap" from the natural order to the supernatural order has been bridged. "Under the illuminating influence of grace, our spirit recognizes in the unitive properties of the Christian phenomenon a manifestation (reflection) of Omega on the human consciousness, and it identifies the Omega of the reason with the universal Christ of revelation."[83] After having quoted the Pauline texts that were so dear to him: "In eo omnia constant [In him everything continues in being]" (Col 1:17); "Ipse est qui replet omnia [All are complete in him]" (Col 2:10; cf. Eph 4:9); "Omnia in omnibus Christus [Christ is all in all]" (Col 3:11), Father Teilhard could exclaim: "It is the very definition of Omega." Jesus, incarnate Word, dead and resurrected, has become "the universal Christ". It is he who gives everything its consistency, who unites all beings and influences them all, "physically" (with the precisions that we will see later on). The universe is "christified".

"Through the Incarnation, God descends into nature in order to superanimate and bring it back to him. . . . In itself, this dogma can

[80] *Hérédité social et progrès* (1938); *Oeuvres* 5:51. Such is the "Christian humanist's" vision of things .

[81] Note of October 17, 1918. *L'Union créatrice* (November 1917): "Christ, of course, is not the Center that all things, here below, could *naturally* aspire to espouse. The destination of Christ is an unexpected and gratuitous favor from the Creator. It remains true that . . ." (*Écrits du temps et de la guerre*, 195). Reasoning from within our world, Father Teilhard will no longer usually consider, then, the hypothesis of "any intermediary whatever" or of a "vague focus of convergence". He had done so once, at least, in *L'Ame du Monde* (1918). See there the note that precedes this writing in *Écrits du temps de la guerre*, 217–19. Teilhard's thought is here, to some extent, an echo of Pierre Rousselot's, as explained by the unpublished study on "Idéalisme et Thomisme", written in 1908 and corrected in 1911.

[82] *Mons Univers* of 1924; *Oeuvres*, 9:82 (January 29, 1918): "Christ, through his gospel of renunciation, constituted a new Omega in the Kosmos, but it is for us (*Vos estis sine intelligentia?*) to make the union between this Omega and the natural future of the Kosmos." Cf. *Le Phénomène humain*, 332, note.

[83] *Ma position intellectuelle* (New York, April 1948).

be accommodated to many different representations of the experiential world." The Christian has never had trouble thinking within the framework of a static universe, and Father Teilhard de Chardin was not naïve enough to imagine that a Saint Paul or a Saint John must have conceived of universal evolution in advance; he was not audacious enough to believe that in conceiving of it himself he obtained a more profound view of the mystery than theirs. On the other hand, he had proof that, in a universe such as materialistic evolutionism conceives it, "Christianity would be suffocated". Now, humanly speaking, the risk, not long ago, was serious; it was imminent. "In the human view, a universe *in genesis* irresistibly takes the place of the static universe of the theologians. And, in turn, from this new intuition, a special mystique also inevitably emanated: more or less adoring faith in the earthly and cosmic future of evolution. . . . The universe once set in motion, a kind of Divinity, entirely immanent to the world, tends progressively to be substituted, in the human consciousness, for the Christian transcendent God. . . ." Hence Father Teilhard's undertaking, an undertaking in consequence of which he can, it seems, legitimately ask: Does the dogma of the Incarnation, although not dependent in itself on any of our representations or on our scientific hypotheses, "not find its climate better adapted within the . . . perspectives . . . of a universe carried along by the Spirit"?[84] We understand better now the meaning and the interest of the text already quoted:

> Under the illuminating influence of grace, our spirit recognizes in the unitive properties of the Christian phenomenon a manifestation (reflection) of Omega on the human consciousness, and it identifies the Omega of the reason with the universal Christ of revelation.[85]

Father Teilhard considered, then, that transformism, more seriously studied and understood, was revealed appropriate "to furnish an excellent basis for thought and Christian practice":[86]

> Not only, on experience, does traditional Christology prove capable of tolerating an evolutionary structure of the World; but also, contrary to all expectations, it is in the midst of this new organic and unitary milieu, it is to the benefit of this particular curvature of Space linked to Time,

[84] *La Mystique de la Science* (1939); *Oeuvres*, 6:220–21.

[85] *Ma position intellectuelle* (April 1948); text published in *Les Études philosophiques* in 1955, under the title of *Le Pensée du Père Teilhard de Chardin par lui-même*, 580.

[86] *Que faut-il penser du Transformisme?* (1930); *Oeuvres*, 3:122.

that it develops most freely and most fully. It is there that it assumes its true face. . . . Christianity and Evolution: not two irreconcilable visions, but two perspectives made to fit and, mutually, to complete each other.[87]

Here, now, in the satisfaction of having utterly turned around a critical situation, the apologist lets himself be carried away to some excess, contrary to the more measured affirmations he had first uttered. One thing at least, nevertheless, seems very certain. Not only does the formula, that, in the end, the Christ of Revelation is none other than the Omega of Evolution, understood as Father Teilhard explains it, offer nothing disquieting or even, to tell the truth, paradoxical, but, short of admitting some untenable system of "double truth", it is imperative. The Omega of the Apocalypse and that of Evolution cannot be two distinct and rival summits. It is indeed the Omega, discovered in its transcendence at the end of rational inquiry, and no other, of whom the Christian, enlightened by his faith, can say that it has, or that it is, a "trinitarian focus". There is only one, single God. The God of faith cannot really be other than the God of reason. The God of Abraham, Isaac and Jacob is perhaps not "the God of philosophers and scholars": he is in any case the same as the God of science and philosophy.

From Science to Philosophy

Among the characteristics of Teilhardian proofs of the existence of God, we will call attention in particular to two.

Let us note, in the first place, that these proofs profess to be scientific. In order to establish the nature of evolution, the superiority of man, the progress of the world to spirit, the terminal convergence, and so on, Father Teilhard de Chardin constantly refers and wants to refer uniquely to one "law of experiential recurrence, verifiable in the phenomenal field, and appropriately capable of being extrapolated to the totality of space and time". This law of recurrence is enough for him, he says, for it "presides over the formation of beings"; it is according to this law that "the cosmos was constructed".[88] He rules out

[87] Response to an inquiry from the journal *Esprit, Catholicisme et science* (1946); *Oeuvres*, 9:238–40. Cf. *Réflexions sur deux formes d'esprit* (1950); 7:236.

[88] *La Vie cosmique* (1916); *Écrits*, 9.

any a priori, geometrical "synthesis" on the basis of any definition of "being", in order to keep "strictly" to the examination and arrangement of appearances, which is to say, of "phenomena". Despite some excess, here and there, in the presentation of his method—as when he declares that he is confining himself expressly "to the level of facts, that is to say, to the domain of the tangible and photographable"—he nevertheless sees well that his science, or, as he says, his phenomenology, which unites synthesis to analysis and which poses a "within" of things, goes beyond the widespread concept today of "positive science". It is related, he himself explains, to the "physics" of the ancient Greeks and of the medievals. If he does not enter into the paths of an "abstract metaphysics", he very much intends to seek a kind of "universal explanation", by building up, through a "physics of the Spirit", an "ultra-physics of the universe".[89] And he sees perfectly well that in this way it ends in the "World of actual Science exactly reversed".[90]

About which, a certain number of questions can be posed, which are interconnected:

1. In what measure is it legitimate to introduce synthesis into a science that claims to be rigorous?

2. Can there be a scientific proof of God? If one claims that there can be, is that not a return to the "confused thinking" that characterized, according to some, the rational efforts of the great theologians of the Middle Ages, beginning with Saint Thomas?

3. Yet, did Father Teilhard not precisely, through his conception of an evolutionary and convergent universe, discover a new way, a legitimate way, for the passage from science to philosophy? In other words, did he not succeed, not only through a mystical view but by a properly rational path, in lifting "the irritating veil of phenomena", in tearing "the impermeable membrane that the Phenomenon extends between us and all that is above the human spirit"?[91]

We will leave these questions hanging. It would be impossible to reply to them in depth without first raising all sorts of problems of methodology, which we cannot go into here. As for the third, it

[89] *La Centrologie*, December 13, 1944, introduction; *Oeuvres*, 7:105–6. *La Place de l'homme dans l'univers, Réflexions sur la Complexité*, November 15, 1942; *Oeuvres*, 3:306. *L'Union créatrice, Écrits . . .*, 180, and other similar texts.

[90] Letter of February 25, 1929.

[91] Letter of November 20, 1918, *Genèse d'une pensée*, 334. *La Peur de l'existence*, January 26, 1949; *Oeuvres*, 7:196.

would require besides a thorough examination of the whole Teilhardian thought. We will quote only three opinions, corresponding closely to the three questions asked.[92]

Teilhard, says Father Norbert M. Luyten, O.P., "exploded the methodological frameworks in which the sciences as well as philosophy seemed to be enclosed";[93] very soon, expecting "little from an ever more elaborate, *detailed research*", he understood that "to make science go forward and to prevent it from *withering* . . . , it would be necessary to *enlarge the object* and *change the methods*, to arrive at a *more profound and more synthetic* study"; if he used at times "defective methodological processes", he nonetheless had the merit of "providing us with indications of the highest interest for the future of science, if only by posing, in a blunt way, the problem of a synthesis of our knowledge".[94] And another Dominican, Father Maurice Corvez, whom the idea of a "scientific proof" of God in no way frightened: "With a superior mastery, Father Teilhard cleared a way of access to Christianity especially adapted to a category of scholars, geologists, paleontologists, biologists, but very practicable also for those whom the History of nature and life interests, to say as much for all minds endowed with an authentic general education."[95] Finally, Mme. Barthélemy-Madaule: "We must agree that our old categories are too rigid to express that slow maturation, that moment when, in a field that still remains phenomenal, a sense that is already philosophical is in the process of emerging."[96]

It could in fact very well be that, through his phenomenological method, rigorously applied to the description of our universe, Teilhard succeeded in breaking "the magic circle of phenomenalism, the one that, we are assured, would invincibly limit our gaze to a horizon of finite radius":

[92] We broached the subject several times in *La Pensée religieuse* . . . , especially in chap. 15 ("Un Renversement de méthode"), in Blondel and Teilhard de Chardin, *Correspondance commentée*, 109–26: "Envergure et limites de l'oeuvre teilhardienne".

[93] *Teilhard de Chardin et la pensée catholique, Colloque de Venise*, 19.

[94] "Réflexions sur la méthode de Teilhard de Chardin", in the volume of *Festschrift* offered to Father Bochenski, 295 and 317.

[95] *De la science à la foi*, 9.

[96] *Colloque de Venise*, 33. A judgment similar to that brought by Father Sertillanges on Claude Bernard would be applied freely to Teilhard: "He throws a bridge between physiology and metaphysics": *La Philosophie de Claude Bernard* (1964), 7.

> What could not be said, still recently, about our powerlessness to go beyond . . . an elementary vision that was already that of very first human consciousness, that is to say, about the impossibility in which we would find ourselves of advancing one step toward the direct or indirect perception of what is hidden behind the veil of sensible experience? Well! It is precisely this so-called fissureless envelope of the pure "phenomenon" that is pierced, at least in one point, since it is by nature irreversible, by the surging trajectory of human evolution. What there is beyond and behind, of course, in this henceforth identified transphenomenal, we do not see, any more than, once the form of the Earth is recognized, we can foresee the landscape still hidden beneath the horizon. But at least we know that something exists beyond the circle that limits our view: something where we will emerge. And this is enough for us not to feel confined any more.[97]

We will nevertheless admit that Father Teilhard himself has scarcely explained, in its principles if not in its applications, the method that would show the validity of this result.

Teilhardian Optimism

The second characteristic will detain us a little longer.

In presupposing, as we have seen, from the point of departure, a faith in the value of being, Father Teilhard presupposes the three notions of being, truth and value, indissolubly united. This is almost the equivalent of the three transcendentals of the Scholastic theory: *ens, verum, bonum* (the idea of worth being able to unite in itself the good and the beautiful, the latter being too often neglected). Now this is a primary aspect of that fundamental optimism that everyone agrees to recognize in Teilhardian thought, whether to praise or to blame him, and of which we consider here only the two faces under which it is presented in our subject.[98]

Under the aspect we have just mentioned, Teilhardian optimism, let us remark, is simply confused with the rejection of the absurd. He himself warns us of it. If he uses here the word "faith", it is, as he explains

---

[97] *Le Rebondissement humain de l'Évolution et ses conséquences* (September 23, 1947); *Oeuvres,* 5:268–69.

[98] On several other aspects of this optimism: Jean Bastaire, "Teilhard l'impatient", *Cahiers universitaires catholiques* (December 1965–January 1966), 146–59.

again, in a wholly analogical sense[99] and because in fact, as experience has shown him, it is always possible for man, even though he contradicts himself implicitly by that very fact, to deny his trust in reason and to judge that reality is fundamentally "absurd" and "nauseating"; reason itself, in its spontaneous use, feels less repugnance in accepting total absurdity than such a partial absurdity narrowly circumscribed. But Father Teilhard nonetheless maintains that "under its most enveloped form", this "initial faith does not differ perceptibly from acquiescence to a scientific truth",[100] although the temptation might be strong, at certain moments, to abandon it by giving in to intoxication.[101] He also observes, what seems to constitute a better expression of the same idea, that without such a faith "the world, in becoming a thinking world, would logically return to dust."[102]

When Father Teilhard de Chardin returned from China to Paris, in 1945, at the end of the Second World War, he reacted very strongly against the existentialist, atheistic and pessimistic wave, which was at that time breaking over Europe. In several debates, he "steeled himself", as Pascal said. It was in large part because of this that, before his work was truly known, a simplistic legend was born in his regard. Since then, the idea has spread of a certain "Teilhardism", characterized by a facile optimism. Now, this is not even a caricature: it is a falsification. For Father Teilhard de Chardin, facile optimism was not only naïveté, inexperience or stupidity: it was sin.[103] He fought against the myths that projected a "golden age" in the future. Against the "pessimists" or the "jaded", against the "*bon vivants*" or the "sensualists", he called for, not "optimists", but "the ardent".[104]

In fact, he was expecting for humanity, rather, "some inner conflicts still more violent than those we now know". He thought that a universe, such as he conceived it to be, "on its way to conscious concen-

[99] Cf. *La Prière du Père Teilhard de Chardin*, second part, chap. 3: "Foi et analogie".

[100] *Comment je crois*.

[101] He wrote to Father Auguste Valensin, May 27, 1923: "At any price, I believe, it is necessary to cling to faith, *in one direction*, and *in one end*, away from human (even natural) disturbance, since without this faith, nothing more comes to legitimate to our reason the law of our action. But, at first glance, appearances are contrary, and crumbling, divergence, might seem to dominate the history of Life."

[102] *L'Énergie humaine* (1937); *Oeuvres*, 6:173–74.

[103] Cf. *La Lutte contre la multitude*; *Écrits*, 120–22.

[104] *Réflexions sur le bonheur* (Peking, December 28, 1943); *Cahiers Pierre Teilhard de Chardin*, 2:55–58.

tration . . . , is precisely that which must most naturally and most necessarily suffer''.[105] He professed that suffering "increases in quantity and acuteness at the same pace as consciousness rises, in the course of the ages''. He also proclaimed that "moral effort is necessarily accompanied by sacrifice'', that "the highest life is attained by a death'', that "perfection is tied to suffering'', that there is "no progress in being without some mysterious tribute of tears, blood and sin'', and he welcomed from his faith, in order to live it with intensity, the teaching that all the "prodigious spiritual energetics'' of Christianity was "born on the Cross''.[106] Without the adherence of the soul to the "already recognizable face of a universal personality'', he judged it impossible to "preserve the powers accumulated in the heart of the individual, societies and world itself from the worst digressions''.[107] Around the "adorers of progress'', he seemed "to suffocate under too low a sky'', and he said he experienced "a feeling of asphyxiation''.[108] The horror of a "closed world'', the terrible solitude of a humanity unified without God, "the essential fear of the reflective element in face of an All that in appearance is blind'', the despair of feeling enclosed in "the cosmic balloon''—he never ceased to summon them, from the time of *La Grande monade* (1918) up to the time of *La Fin de l'espèce* (1952) and *La Barrière de la mort* (1955). He himself profoundly felt the human anguish, the anguish of all times and that in particular of our times: it is present everywhere at the foundation of his work, and it often comes to the surface of it.[109] Yet, instead of being swallowed up by it, instead of taking pleasure in it, or instead of being content to bewail it, he sought to overcome it, in a rational and Christian manner. Noting that modern man, despite all his science and all his powers, is "sad'',

[105] *Esquisse d'un univers personnel* (1936); *Oeuvres*, 6:105; "Nothing more beatifying than the union attained: nothing more laborious than the pursuit of the union."

[106] *Les Singularités*, 43. *Genèse d'une pensée*, 278. *Parole attendue* (1940); *Cahiers*, 4:28. *La Vie cosmique*; *Écrits*, 54–57. Preface to Marguerite Teilhard de Chardin, *L'Énergie spirituelle de la souffrance* (1951), 9–11. *Mon univers* of 1924; *Oeuvres*, 9:88–92 and 97–102, etc. He well knew, too, that Christian charity is not natural to man—and he has even been reproached, very inconsiderately, for having stated that with realism. *Fiunt, non nascuntur christiani.*

[107] *Esquisse d'un univers personnel*; *Oeuvres*, 6:89.

[108] *Comment je crois* (1934).

[109] See, for example, *Le Coeur de la Matière* (1950), 32. Already *La Grande monade* (1918); *Écrits*, 237–48. *Le Milieu divin*, 172: "So that I do not succumb to the temptation to curse the Universe and the one who made it. . . ." Cf. *La Prière du Père Teilhard de Chardin*, 121–23. M. Barthélemy-Madaule, *Bergson et Teilhard de Chardin* (1962), 411–21. Claude Cuénot, "L'Angoisse contemporaine, un essai de réponse", in *Cahiers de vie franciscaine*, 33 (1962).

he wanted to rescue him from his sadness. He undertook to "save the thinking Earth from the *taedium vitae*",[110] and to work in us a "reversal of fear".[111]

As for his basic optimism, fruit of his "fundamental option" for being, this optimism that says Yes to creation, thus ratifying "the primordial choice implied in the World of which we are the reflected elements",[112] it could be rather justly compared to that of a Saint Thomas Aquinas. In both, it is related to a certain "taste for being" which, before influencing their doctrine, characterizes their deepest personality.[113] By this trait, as by many others, the thought of Father Teilhard de Chardin is worthy of fitting, more than one still usually thinks, into the scope of Thomistic thought.[114] And this taste for being, which is also natural, is transformed and blossoms, in his prayer, into a "taste for Being", a "profound taste", a "feeling that Being is infinitely more rich and renewing than our logic", which, at the very time of trial, maintains it in joy.[115]

Yet, would it not be, on the other hand, a very great, and very debatable, optimism to believe, as Father Teilhard did, that the triumph

---

[110] *La Fin de l'Espèce* (December 9); *Oeuvres*, 5:395. Cf. *Le Goût de vivre* (November 1959); 7:239–51. *Le Retentissement spirituel de la bombe atomique* (1946); 5:184–85.

[111] *La Peur de l'existence* (1949); *Oeuvres*, 7:197.

[112] *Réflexions sur le bonheur* (1943); *Cahiers*, 2:60.

[113] Cf. Pierre Rousselot, S.J., *Études* of September 5, 1911: "Who would make our contemporaries feel this taste for being, this profound and inexpressible love of being, this ardent optimism, this grave, profound, nearly infinite tenderness for humanity, which is exhaled from all the pages of the Angelic Doctor?"

[114] Cf. Étienne Borne, *De Pascal à Teilhard de Chardin* (Clermont-Ferrand, 1962), 67–68: "In spite of the questionable polemics that obscure our view, it is within the Thomist tradition, many traits of which, however, are allergic to Teilhard de Chardin, that Teilhardian thought is situated: rehabilitation of a nature in itself trustworthy and good, rational description of man and the world according to concepts borrowed from an experimental and positive science, proof of the existence of the absolute by the very movement of things that designate a first mover or an Omega point, all these traits are common to Saint Thomas Aquinas and Teilhard de Chardin." See also M. Labourdette, O.P., *Le Péché originel et les origines de l'homme* (1953), 127 and 145–46. Olivier A. Rabout, O.P., *Dialogue avec Teilhard de Chardin* (1958), 167. Claude Cuénot, *Situation de Teilhard de Chardin*, Bulletin de la Société industrielle de Mulhouse, no. 712 (1963), p. 25, and, quoting É. Borne, 26. Blondel and Teilhard, *Correspondance commentée* (1965), 96 and 99–100, etc.

[115] Letter to Léontine Zanta, January 26, 1936, 127–28, etc. Cf. March 16, 1919: "What nourishes my whole interior life is the *taste* for *Being*, satisfied in God, Our Lord"; "May Our Lord guard the taste for Being in me, and the vision that the Being is he!" See *Prière*, 95.

of the spirit over entropy is assured? Such is the second aspect to be considered.

The response to this doubt would come back to deciding whether the Teilhardian vision of the universe, whether his "spiritualist evolutionism", is proved or, at least, probable. We believe that, in essence, it does more than balance the materialistic theories and that its soundness does not depend on final extensions of the system. Let us simply remark here that this second kind of optimism links up precisely, no more than that, with the "optimism" of the whole tradition of spiritualist philosophy that, by different paths, affirms the immortality of the human soul. Just as Saint Augustine, Saint Thomas or Descartes professes that the soul is immortal, so Teilhard professes that the progress of the cosmos, giving birth to beings endowed with a spiritual and personal soul, is an irreversible progress. His context is no longer individual and static; it is collective and dynamic, but on both sides the final affirmation is the same.[116] By means of his "phenomenology", he wants to bring the same response "to the old problem (so parascientific in appearance) of immortality",[117] and the "energetic" way adopted most often by him in his argumentation is a close relation of the Thomist argumentation by the *desiderium naturale*, of which one commentator recently wrote that it constitutes "an apodictic demonstration".[118] Yet, in a more concrete perspective that recalls more directly that of Christian revelation, he seeks to show how, in a "unique and supreme event, . . . the historical must join together with the transcendent". "An opening exists", an "issue"; Thought will not suffocate, "stillborn, in a self-abortive and absurd universe"; there is for us, in the future, "not only survival but *super-life*"; such is, for Teilhard, the conviction that founds an "absolute optimism".[119] And it is through this that he wanted "to give hope to

[116] He wrote, on February 25, 1929: "It seems to me that I have nearly brought into focus a certain "Physics of the Spirit". . . . It is a kind of reduction of the Universe to the spiritual on the physical (not metaphysical) plane, which has, for me, the fortunate corollary of legitimating the conservation of persons (which is to say, the 'immortality' of souls) in the Universe."

[117] *L'Activation de l'Énergie humaine* (1953); *Oeuvres*, 7:413.

[118] Joseph Perini, C.M., "Utrum argumentando ex desiderio naturali immortalitatis, S. Thomas apodictice evincat animan humanam esse immortalem", in *Divus Thomas* (Piacenza, 1965), 383: "Certissime agitur de demonstratione apodictica, quae sc. ex se valet gignere in intellectu perfectam certitudinem." Cf. *La Pensée religieuse*, 253–60.

[119] *Le Phénomène humain*, 258–59.

human research".[120] "To know that we are not imprisoned. To know that there is an issue, and air, and light, and love, somewhere beyond all death. To know it, without illusion or fiction!"[121] In a world "open at its apex *in Christo Jesu*, we do not risk dying of suffocation! And, on the other hand, coming down from these heights, there is not only air, there is the radiation of a love that comes down."[122]

Option and "Segregation"

Yet, since the spirit, being reflective consciousness, is essentially freedom[123]—the "rise of interiority" being identically a rise "of freedom" —all that in no way prejudices the final fate of each individual person, which is to say, the positive or negative sign that must mark his definitive consummation. For, on the basis of man, and through man, "evolution now has to make its own choice";[124] each can use well or poorly this formidable power that is free will: a moral and religious option, constantly called to mind in Teilhard, either with respect to individuals of every period or with respect to the final human generation. We even find it in contexts where it would not seem to be indispensable. So it was, at the end of the Sorbonne lectures, which were of great scientific technicity, devoted to the *Groupe zoologique human*. After having shown that there must be, for the human race, an "issue", through which, at the end of its course, it can escape "total death", Father Teilhard adds, returning to our present day: "Nothing could apparently prevent the human race from still growing (just like the individual man, for good . . . or for evil). . . ."[125]

---

[120] Letter of April 10, 1934; *Lettres de voyage*, 1923–1955 (1961), 176, etc. Cf. *Lettres à Léontine Zanta* (1965), 134–35.

[121] *Le Goût de vivre* (1950); *Oeuvres*, 7:246.

[122] *Le Christique* (1955).

[123] *L'Hominisation*; *Oeuvres*, 3:103 and 107. *Le Groupe zoologique humain*, 132, 154–55, etc.

[124] *Place de la technique dans une biologie générale de l'humanité* (1947); *Oeuvres*, 7:168.

[125] 161. Cf. *La Vie cosmique* (*Écrits*, 56): "All energy is equally powerful for good and for evil." *Mon Univers* of 1924; *Oeuvres*, 9:112–13. See *La Prière*, first part, chap. 13. It is in this sense that Teilhard would have agreed to say with Albert Vandel ("L'Évolutionnisme du Père Teilhard de Chardin", in *Les Études philosophiques* [1965], 463): "Man can succeed in everything but also fail in everything." Likewise, in saying that "one would rather prevent the Earth from turning than humanity from being totalized", or again, that the human group cannot "escape certain irreversible laws of transformation", he really intends to say nothing that would be "a humiliating attack on our freedom": *Les Directions et les conditions de l'avenir*

This dramatic alternative is also presented, at various times, as that of the attitude of the Titans or of Prometheus, or of the attitude of Jacob; that of "revolt" or of "adoration"; of "arrogant Force" or of "evangelical holiness"; of "arrogant autonomy" or of "loving excentration"; of rejection or acceptance of Omega.[126] Beyond the "ambiguous term" of "Spirit of the Earth", the dilemma is posed between the "spirit of force", which is a "spirit of autonomy and solitude", and the "spirit of love", which is a "spirit of service and gift".[127] Father Teilhard expresses at times the hope that, through the effect of spiritual progress, the whole of humanity will incline more to the saving option; but, even then, he always maintains the necessity of the option. "The world does not open itself, for him, like a flower, when it touches the inevitable end of its history; it divides again in a kind of ultimate branching before blossoming in the warmth of Christ."[128] If there is, then, a philosophy for which "evil fades away like a shadow in proportion as thought proves capable of extending its empire forward", this philosophy is not his.

In Teilhardian language, there is a key word, with analogical hierarchical meanings, that serves to show the agreement of this real alternative, that is, of the risk of damnation, with the infallibility of God's work. It is the word "segregation", correlative of the word "aggregation".

Provided one eliminate from it any quantitative connotation, Teilhardian "segregation" could be compared with the biblical idea of the "Remnant" of Israel. We should also note that it is found in all modes as in all levels of being: there is a geological segregation,[129] a cosmic segregation, a spiritual segregation, a christic segregation. In all orders

---

(1948); *Oeuvres*, 5:295–98. The fixed anti-Teilhardian prejudice has nonetheless made an intelligent man write: "The conception of the assured, irreversible Noogenesis could well be only a metamorphosis of quietism, where Pelagianism fatally leads" (André Thérive, in *Écrits de Paris* [February 1964], 102).

[126] See *La Pensée religieuse*, chap. 10, "Évolution et liberté"; Blondel and Teilhard, *Correspondance commentée* (1965), 91–94 and 151. Cf. *Note sur le Progrès* (1920); *Oeuvres*, 5:31, etc. "Born with intelligence, the temptation for revolt must constantly vary and grow with it" (C. Cuénot, *Situation*, 11).

[127] *Le Retentissement de la bombe atomique* (1946); *Oeuvres*, 5:187.

[128] Georges Crespy, *De la science à la théologie, essai sur Teilhard de Chardin*, Cahiers théologiques, 54 (Neuchâtel, Switzerland: Delachaux et Niestlé, 1965), 105.

[129] *Le Phénomène humain*, 123 and 161. *Bulletin de la Société géologique de France* (1946), 501, etc. Blondel and Teilhard, *Correspondance commentée*, 93–94.

as in all degrees, "the creative synthesis involves a tearing away, all aggregation being accompanied by a segregation."

Cosmic segregation: our universe is composed, in a way, of two parts, at first mixed (Teilhard even says once: of two universes), which go on disentangling themselves, separating themselves. The split proceeds to the very roots: on one side, the "cosmos that is segregating itself by life", then by thought; on the other, "the cosmos that is not connected, not informed, that dies and is dispersed". We recognize here what he calls elsewhere the arranged and the unarranged, or, in dynamic terms, the two great inverse phenomena of Convergence and Entropy.[130]

The same law is verified analogically in the spiritual life. Father Teilhard notes, for example, that his instinctive tendency as a believer is to "integrate all in Christ". But that, he immediately specifies, in no ways signifies that he would want to "keep all". He knows that integration, as universal as it may be, essentially includes a segregation, which is to say here, in a correlative fashion, a "renunciation". What he desires, what he is striving after, is, through a process that could also be compared with a distillation, to "obtain the whole *nisus*, the whole impulse and power of life of the universe". He would like "no particle of energy to be lost".

The same is true in the end, objectively, for the Body of Christ. In a final state, it is humanity (= the cosmos) consummated in God. But this "total Body" (to speak like Origen) is formed in the course of the ages and finally achieved only by a rigorous segregation. Here again, Father Teilhard insists on being more specific. During the year 1916, at the time when his most personal thought was being formed, he noted (on October 7): "In writing 'Le Monde dans le Christ', I must reveal, simultaneously, *the innervation of all* in Christ or through Christ, *and* the *segregative* character of this organization." This is indeed, in fact, what he did. "The new Earth is in formation everywhere. Around the finished Center, which is the Humanity of Christ (and of his Mother), the nebula is in the process of segregation and concentration, its elements being everywhere, although still mixed and diffused, everywhere separable particularly in their future (much more than in their present: the tares are not yet distinguished adequately from the good grain). . . ."

This doctrine of christic segregation is opposed by Father Teilhard to doctrines of what he calls "false segregation", preached by "false Christs"; for example, to the myth of "future humanity" (not, obviously, that he does not believe in a "human future", but he conceives it otherwise and does not make an absolute of it). He also opposes it to "pagan pantheism", which excludes the very idea of segregation and considers "only fusion with the initial Whole: and then, neither true degree in being, nor progress, nor lateral clusters, *nor decrease*". And this doctrine also makes it possible for him to distinguish clearly between the two connected but very different truths, which more than one theologian of our time has difficulty not confusing: on the one hand, the assumption of all human nature by the Word of God made flesh, from which results an essential and inalienable relation of all men to Christ, and, on the other hand, the constitution of the Mystical Body of Christ, in which no man is member by the sole fact that he is a man.[131] In other words, if Christ appears to Teilhard "haloed with the glory of the world", this means for him "haloed with all there is of the elect in the Real".[132]

Analyzing this same idea of segregation a little more closely and from another point of view, Father Teilhard found himself led to recognize that it implied the following three principal elements:

> 1. Initial union with the Whole (and thus at least radical coexistence with it forever);
>
> 2. Tendency toward separation, isolation, the sacrifice of many things constituting the Whole, and the progressive accomplishment of this isolation;
>
> 3. Finally, progress, not toward individual scattering, but toward the strictest communion with a new, more reduced but more purified, more homogeneous, more organized Whole. And these diverse elements, in the fundamental segregation in which the life of the cosmos is engaged

[131] This is the doctrine of the Fathers of the Church. Thus Saint Hilary of Poitiers: "Ipse autem, universitatis nostrae in se continens ex carnis assumptione naturam; —Naturam in se universae carnis adsumpsit; —omnium nostrum corpus adsumpsit" (Migne, PL 10, 409; 9, 1025; CSEL 22, 108), etc. Origen, *In psalmum* 36, hom. 2, n. 1: "Christus enim, cujus omne hominum genus, immo fortasse totius creaturae universitas corpus est" (Migne, PG 12, 1330). Cf. Saint Cyril of Alexander, *Contre Nestorius* c. 1, c. 1 (Migne, PG 76, 17). Saint Thomas, *Summa, tertia pars*, q. 8, art. 3: "Accipiendo generaliter secundum totum tempus mundi, Christus est caput omnium hominum, sed secundum diversos gradus. . . ."

[132] Letter of October 9, 1916. *Genèse d'une pensée*, 166. *Le Prêtre* (1918): "You have revealed to me the essential vocation of the World to reach completion through a chosen part of its whole being in the fullness of your incarnate Word"; *Écrits*, 286.

(like the success of the tree in its seed), are called respectively: love of the world, sacrifice, formation of the Body of Christ.[133]

"The movement that incorporates the universe in Christ is in reality a segregation", and "that is a formidable mystery."[134]

With the benefit of these analyses, which do not cease to guide his thought, although the word segregation itself may become less frequent from his pen,[135] Father Teilhard de Chardin can repeat after Saint Paul: "And God will be all in all."[136]

Conclusion

We said in beginning that the whole work of Father Teilhard de Chardin could be understood, considered, from a certain slant, as a renewed effort to establish the existence of God through the transmission of a proof of the irreversibility of the cosmos, which is to say, of the immortality of personal souls, so as to lead men then to Christ. In concluding, we can say again, in perhaps more current language, that this work is an unceasing dialogue with one of the most widespread varieties of atheism of the twentieth century. It is a *real* dialogue, undertaken and pursued during several decades with numerous representatives of this atheism, encountered either in the world of scholars or among men formed in the school of an atheistic science. Anyone who knew the life of Father Teilhard well, as well as his writings, could place here a long series of proper names; he could well recall concrete circumstances,

[133] Notes of February 8 and July 19, 1916, April 9 and November 16, 1918.

[134] *Les Noms de la matière* (1919); *Écrits*, 429. Letter of January 9, 1917: "The true earth for me is the elect portion of the Universe, still spread a little everywhere, and on its way to a slow segregation, but which little by little takes on body and shape in Christ" (*Genèse d'une pensée*, 213).

[135] It is found again in *Le Milieu divin*: "The complete process from which the New Earth is gradually born is an *aggregation* coupled with a *segregation*" (187); "Segregation and aggregation. Separation of the evil elements of the World, and 'coadunation' of the elementary Worlds that each faithful spirit constructs around itself in work and in difficulty . . ." (195).

[136] When Paul also says, Romans 11:26: "All Israel will be saved", he does not also claim to decide the fate of each individual. Cf. Saint Augustine, *In Joannem*, tract. 6, no. 26, with respect to schisms, by allusion to Song of Songs 6:9: "Why have you torn my dove? No, you have not torn her: you have torn your own entrails; for, while you have been torn, the dove has remained intact." See our *Catholicisme*, "Foi vivante" series (Éd. du Cerf, 1965), chap. 8, 174–76. [English trans.: *Catholicism* (San Francisco: Ignatius Press, 1988)].

conversations and real debates, which were not all without a happy result. The often personal tone given to the argumentation is, we would say in passing, thereby explained. Father Teilhard de Chardin is not an armchair philosopher: he is a man who speaks to men.

This dialogue is never a dialogue of accommodation or ease. Much less, of concession or resignation. Pierre Teilhard approaches his interlocutor with the greatest human sympathy; he places himself on the same line of departure with him, he steers his course with him. But he respects him and loves him too much to support him in his illusions. As for him, he does not give in to any relativism. Modest, although ardent, in the proposition of his personal views, he nonetheless considers himself right in having his own language, which he strives to explain better. He does not suffer, in his convictions, from any inferiority complex. He does not reduce his faith in Christ to the possession of some "value", of which a spirit of poverty would induce him to deprive himself in order better to entertain the values of others. . . . "No one", he could say, "has ever taken me to be of little faith." His dialogue—which must end at least by being a wholly serious dialogue on the intellectual plane—is always a dialogue of defiance. That is a healthy example for us today.

One can call attention in Father Teilhard, alongside some eminent merits, a certain number of tendencies that, freed by their isolation, could lead to abusive consequences. Many deficiencies can also be pointed out. Concerning the subject treated here, several of these deficiencies are due to the fact that the links of the scientific chain developed by the argumentation do not all appear perhaps of equal soundness, or of an equally proven soundness. Others are due to the fact that Father Teilhard, a man of science and intuition, was rather little concerned with the formal aspects of philosophical knowledge. His thought is not usually "critical and reflexive".[137] With respect to some of such expositions, Father Maurice Corvez speaks, with good reason, of philosophically "naïve" proof, and his philosophy is in fact "naïve", a little like the painting of the customs officer Rousseau (which does not mean at all that he was himself naïve, nor even that he was not aware of certain problems, but only that he did not treat them *ex professo*). But when a "naïve" philosophy is that of a man in whom "inner revelation and scientific experience are associated in a unique man-

[137] Étienne Borne, in *Recherches et débats*, 40 (1962), 64.

ner",[138] it has the chance of containing a more powerful truth and of acting more effectively on the progress of thought than many more ambitious philosophies.[139] And the seriousness put by Father Teilhard de Chardin into his opposition to atheistic materialism confers on his work a weight that many apparently more subtle works will never have. This is why many, today, consider it necessary to take it seriously.

[138] Helmut de Terra, *Mes voyages avec Teilhard de Chardin*, trans. André Tintant (Paris, Éd. du Seuil, 1965), 136.

[139] Father Norbert M. Luyten has judiciously noted in this respect that "through fear of an overly naïve—or overly difficult—cosmology, our thought has become in large part acosmic and remains imprisoned by a rather insipid self-reflection." Teilhard, he concludes, has at least the merit of indicating "the immense and urgent task that awaits us". *Teilhard de Chardin, Nouvelles perspectives du savoir?* (Fribourg, Switzerland, 1965), 66–67.

2. The Contribution of Teilhard to the Knowledge of God

It is necessary to begin by saying: in what concerns our knowledge of God, Teilhard's work does not contribute, and does not claim to contribute, in essence anything that might be described as properly new.[1]

Is it a question of the ways by which man arrives at knowing God? Teilhard admits, on the one hand, that human reason is capable of rising to the certitude that God exists; on the other hand, he judges that this existence is not, however, obvious by itself and that our reason arrives at knowing it only at the end of a dialectical process.[2] This process assumes various forms in his work, it includes various itineraries, but the point of departure is usually taken in the experience of the sensible world. There we find again the themes familiar to the greater part of the School. It is in particular the position of Saint Thomas Aquinas.

Is it a question of the idea of God in which this work of human reason ends? The principal attributes that Teilhard recognizes in God are those that the most traditional philosophy recognizes in him: autonomy, actuality, irreversibility, transcendence.[3] They will be strengthened, completed, unified, sublimated, by Christian revelation, which teaches that God is Love.

Is it, finally, a question of the inner knowledge that man can acquire

---

An abbreviated version of this text was published in *Teilhard de Chardin*, "Génies et réalités" series (Paris: Hachette, 1969), 193–214. We give here the *whole* text of the article.

[1] Restricting ourselves to rather general considerations in what lies before us and able to quote only rather few texts and to give few details, we allow ourselves to refer the reader, once and for all, to our works on Teilhard: *La Pensée religieuse du père Pierre Teilhard de Chardin* (Paris: Aubier, 1962) [English trans.: *The Religion of Teilhard de Chardin* (New York: Desclée, 1967)]; *La Prière du père Teilhard de Chardin* (Paris: Fayard, 1964), 2d ed. 1968 [English trans.: *Teilhard de Chardin: The Man and His Meaning* (New York: Hawthorn Books, 1965)]; *Teilhard missionnaire et apologiste* (Toulouse: "Prière et vie" ed., 1966); *Maurice Blondel et Pierre Teilhard de Chardin*, correspondence with commentary (Paris: Beauchesne, 1965); "Teilhard et Monchanin", in *Images de l'abbé Monchanin* (Paris: Aubier, 1967); *L'Éternel féminin, Étude sur un texte du père Teilhard de Chardin* (Paris: Aubier, 1968).

[2] *Comment je vois* (1948), no. 20.

[3] *Le Phénomène humain*, 305; *Esquisse d'un univers personnel* (1936); *Oeuvres*, 6:103; *La Centrologie*, nos. 20–24, 7:117–19; *Du cosmos à la cosmogénèse* (1951), 7:271.

or rather receive in the depths of himself of the divine presence and action? Teilhard, like many others, is here in keeping with the great Christian mystics. Their experience is in some measure his own. He was nourished on their works, and he recognized them as masters and older brothers. More than once, he evokes the "God of the Mystics". He invokes their testimony. Above all, it is to Saint Paul and Saint John that he refers; but he is also aware of his affinity with "the Greek Fathers", most especially with Gregory of Nyssa. He appreciates profoundly, among others, Ruysbroek, Angela de Foligno, Teresa of Avila, Father Surin[4]—and, of course, he is a disciple of Ignatius Loyola, the mystic of the *Contemplatio ad amorem*. Like them all, he recollects himself—in opposition to all "immanentism", which he sometimes had to reject as a temptation—in the sense of the "divine Omnipresence".[5]

It is nonetheless true that Father Teilhard's work is extremely personal. So it would not be surprising if, on the subject that concerns us here, this work did not offer us a certain number of original traits. These are the traits of which we will now make an inventory.

We have said that Teilhard took his point of departure in sensible experience, in this world that surrounds us and that compels our attention, as a given. But, instead of considering the simple fact of *movement* in it, in the manner of the ancient philosophers, he considers that great *evolutional* movement in it which authorizes him, he thinks, to say that the universe *is* this Evolution. From this comes the title of one of his writings: *Du cosmos à la cosmogénèse* [From the cosmos to cosmogenesis]. And it is, at first, less as a first principle of movement that he conceives God (unmoving mover, propulsive force, first cause), than as the Being who assures the definitive success of evolution, or of the "cosmogenesis"[6] (Omega point, attractive force, final cause). Such a point of view is that which several theologian-philosophers

---

[4] He invokes their authority. *Le Milieu mystique* (1917): "No one will understand, I think, the great mystics, neither Saint Francis, nor Blessed Angela, nor the others, if he has not profoundly understood that Jesus must be loved like a world." *Écrits du temps de la guerre*, 167; cf. 293, *Le Prêtre*: "Christ is loved like a Person and imposes himself like a World."

[5] *L'Atomisme de l'esprit* (1941), 7:61; *Genèse d'une pensée*, 393; *Le Messe sur le monde* (1923); final prayer.

[6] At times the end is taken, as here, in its most vast extension; at others, he designates the first stage, to which noogenesis and christogenesis succeed (= constitution of the "Mystical Body").

freely adopt today, in speaking of God, as of the "absolute future" of man.[7]

On the other hand, the very conception of Evolution worked out by Teilhard—a conception that we do not at all have to explain here—makes his cosmology develop into an anthropology. If man is, in one sense, the product of the universe, in another, more profound sense, the universe is explained by man. The latter is, in nature, neither an epiphenomenon nor a paraphenomenon; he is *the* phenomenon, central, axial.[8] If it is necessary, then, to see, first of all, how the spirit is born from matter, it is in order to recognize next that "all consistency comes from the Spirit", that "the cosmos, not through Matter, but through Spirit".[9] The proof of God, which is at base evolutional, will, then, be transformed and, from a cosmological proof, will become an anthropological proof. Man is "the Spirit of the Earth",[10] he carries the destiny of the world that has given birth to him—and the final destiny of man is in God.

That is the source of an important difference with the classical point of view. We know in fact that the cosmological proof of the ancients led to the affirmation of a Being whose attributes did not, at least directly, include personality. We know the difficulties encountered more than once by the representatives of Christian thought—encountered by some still today, when they are not sustained in their effort of thought by a living tradition—in making the personal God of the Bible and the absolute of their philosophy coincide in one and the same Being. In Teilhard's case, it is not enough to say that this difficulty is overcome: it must be said that this difficulty does not exist. And by that we do not wish merely to signify that, because of his Christian education, as he himself declared, he experienced no embarrassment of a psychological order in addressing God as a "supreme Someone".[11] The whole movement of his thought obliges him to conceive his God only as a personal God, "supremely personal and supremely personal-

[7] Thus E. Schillebeeckx, in *L'Église dans le monde de ce temps* (Mame, 1967), 158: "This absolute future that God himself is for man. . . ." Obviously this is no more a complete "definition" of God for Schillebeeckx or Rahner than it is for Teilhard!

[8] *L'Hominisation* (1923), 3:75–112, etc.

[9] *Mon univers* (1924), 9:77–79; *Le Phénomène spirituel* (1937), 6:123; *Lettres de voyage* (1931), 140.

[10] *L'Esprit de la terre* (1931), 6:23–58.

[11] *Le Coeur de la matière* (1950), 3d part.

izing".[12] To assure the success of universal evolution is, in fact, for him, to assure the irreversible character of the personalization of the universe. Bergson said that the universe is "a machine to make gods". Teilhard would not take up the expression as his own: in his eyes, the universe is merely a machine to make persons. It "converges on the Person".[13] But it is necessary that God exist in order for this personalizing action of the universe to be effective, irreversible and definitive.

Certainly, Teilhard will criticize certain forms of representation that tend, if overemphasized, to make God a kind of great Individual—such as the gods of mythology are. In a phrase where one senses the polemical point, he will declare the time to have passed when one could conceive the divine Being as "a great proprietor of the neolithic age".[14] Perhaps it was wrong to believe, or to give the impression, that this was above all, for humanity, a question of age; it linked more than it should the constant necessity of purifying the idea of God to the increased knowledge we have today of the universe. In reality, however, he agrees in his criticism—which is in no way negative—not only with all minds that have reflected somewhat on the mystery of God but with all sincerely religious souls; he knows perfectly well that this criticism affects neither the God of philosophy nor the God of the Gospel and of the Christian tradition, which are obviously for him, as for any Catholic, the one and only true God. His criticism of "neolithic paternalism" tends to restore the authentic notion of the "divine paternity", in which he sees the very essence of the message of Christ.[15] Like many others, he distinguishes carefully the two notions of individual and person; he notes that, in our present condition, they imply each other, but he judges at the same time that individuality, as such, is a provisional thing, tied to the limits of spatio-temporal existence, limits from which man hopes to free himself and which it would be absurd and blasphemous to attribute to the divinity.[16]

---

[12] *Comment je vois* (1948), no. 20; *Comment je crois* (1934); *Esquisse d'un univers personnel* (1936), 6:89; *L'Énergie humaine* (1937): "Person distinct from all the persons it completes by uniting with them", 6:180; *Le Sens de l'espèce chez l'homme* (1949), 7:210, etc.

[13] November 15, 1935.

[14] To Léontine Zanta, January 26, 1936, p. 127, etc.

[15] *L'Énergie humaine* (1937), 6:193.

[16] *Le Phénomène humain*, 286–93; "The true Ego grows by inverse reason of 'Egotism'. In the image of Omega, which attracts it, the element becomes personal only by being universalized." (*La Centrologie* [1944], no. 28, 7:124–24. *Esquisse d'un univers personnel*, 6:81–82.)

We should also note another characteristic of the Teilhardian proof, a characteristic that is affirmed more and more with the years. It is an "energetic" proof. Teilhard's point of view was at first, not more "intellectual", but more "intellectualist". Supposing the being of the world to be intelligible and good, which is to say, permeable to the mind and better than nonbeing (heir of the old Scholastic thesis *ens et verum et bonum convertuntur* as much as a reflex of fundamental optimism), one could only reject the hypothesis according to which this being would end, *simpliciter*, in defeat. "Unless one is determined to admit that the cosmos is an intrinsically absurd thing, the growth of the Spirit must be held to be irreversible";[17] there is, then, nothing to do but seek the conditions of this irreversibility; now, step by step, we arrive at the conclusion that it is unthinkable without God. But, to the very degree the cosmological proof was transformed or extended into an anthropological proof, it is within the human consciousness that the problem came to be posed in its liveliest sharpness. From an objective point of view, one passed to a reflexive point of view. In other words, the problem of evolution in general, or the problem of the future of the world, became the problem of human action —or, more precisely,[18] the problem of the "activation of human energy".[19]

In man, evolution became conscious. A "formidable faculty" arose, that "of measuring or criticizing life", and in consequence "of lending oneself to or recoiling from the effort".[20] In principle, this new condition of the cosmos, this new phase of its history, began with the earliest days of "hominization". Yet, up to our own era, man could continue to act more or less by instinct, because he was still thinking, in his action, only of the maintenance or the embellishment of his life. But here, now, we have arrived at a degree of reflection that, coinciding with the discovery of universal evolution, makes him consider necessarily, in all clarity, a new form of action: that which Teilhard names

---

[17] Cf. *Oeuvres*, 3:322–23; 9:125 and 279–80, etc.

[18] Equally in morality, as in politics and economy, it appeared to Father Teilhard in a clearer and clearer light that for a practical science of man it was necessary to pass from a "problem of balance" to a "problem of energy". Letter of November 22, 1936.

[19] *Action et activation* (1945), 9:221–29; *Le Goût de vivre* (1950), 7:237–52; *L'Énergie d'évolution* (1953), 7:381–93; *L'Activation de l'énergie humaine* (1953), 7:407–16; *Contingence de l'univers et goût de survivre* (1953); etc.

[20] *L'Hominisation* (1923), 3:105–6. Cf. *Oeuvres*, 6:155; 9:178, 180, 391.

"true action", or "the search for more-being", fruit of "the passion to grow".[21] By that very fact he is placed before the gravest of alternatives. For such an action, the only one worthy of humanity, will become impossible for him if he cannot believe in "some absolute value" of the evolutional movement that he has a duty to pursue. He could, he would commit himself in the process of this "true action" only with the ulterior motive of accomplishing, according to Thucydides' expression, "a work for always", of contributing to "the preparation of something unique and indispensable for the fullness of the real".[22] Otherwise, it would be—both metaphors are Teilhard's—a strike or paralysis. In brief, "reflective action and total, foreseen disappearance are cosmically incompatible." It is necessary, then, for the world to come to a successful end, for its movement to be irreversible, which is to say, for it to be the bearer of "some absolute value", thanks to a definitive end; which obliges us, at the risk of a desperate halt of the vast human adventure, to set the Omega point such as Teilhard defines it in a second stage of his demonstration.[23]

In a first stage, in fact, Omega is still immanent. It is posed, in the future, as the unified world, come to its end. It is the "superior pole of human coreflection", or again, the point of "complete reflection of the noosphere on itself".[24] Such a terminal unity, or "total synthesis",[25] is, moreover, quite the contrary of a reduction to homogeneity: it is, Teilhard says, "a centered system of centers"; it is a universe of persons, or, as he likes to say, "a world of souls".[26] But as certain as it is that evolution is on its way to this end, it seems just as impossible to think that, by itself, this end can be maintained and eternalized, insofar as one considers it from within a universe whose law is entropy: "To stop going forward is to go backward." One cannot then avoid admitting "some extracosmic pole where one finds integrally collected and

---

[21] *Comment je crois*; *La Place de l'homme dans l'univers* (1942), 3:322–24; *L'Énergie humaine*, 6, 172–75; etc.

[22] *Action et activation*, 9:224; *La Place de l'homme dans l'univers*: "Man (whatever Jeans and Langevin think) will never agree to work like a Sisyphus", 3:323; etc.

[23] *Le Groupe zoologique humain*, ad. of 1956, 157–62; *Le Phénomène humain*, 254–59; *Les Singularités de l'espèce humaine* (1954), 2:357–62; etc.

[24] *La Centrologie*, nos. 18–19, 7:117. Cf. *Le Phénomène humain*, 289.

[25] *L'Énergie humaine*, 6:180.

[26] Cf. *La Vie cosmique*, chap. 3; *Écrits*, 36–39; *Allocution de mariage*, June 14, 1928; Letters of February 25, 1929 and August 24, 1934; *Sauvons l'humanité* (1936), 9:189; *La Mystique de la science* (1939), 6:222.

definitively consolidated the whole reflective incommunicable successively formed in the universe . . . in the course of evolution".[27]

"At the risk of being powerless to form the keystone for the noosphere, 'Omega' can be conceived only as *the point of encounter* between the universe that has reached its limit of concentration and *another Center* that is still deeper, a self-subsistent Center and absolutely ultimate Principle of irreversibility and personalization: the only true Omega. . . ."[28]

"Seen in ascending, from our side of things, the apex of the evolutionary cone (the Omega point) stands out at first on the horizon as a focus of simply immanent convergence; humanity totally reflected on self. But, if we look more closely, it is clear that if this focus is to hold together, it presupposes, behind it, and deeper than it, a transcendent, divine nucleus."[29]

"If Omega did not escape, in some fashion, conditions of time and space, it could neither be already present to us—nor would it be capable (since subject itself entirely to the inexorable entropy) of founding the hopes of irreversibility without which, on the basis of man, centrogenesis would cease to function. It is thus that, through one side of itself, different from that under which we see it being formed, it emerges forever above a world from which, however, from another angle, it is in the process of emerging."[30]

In other words, Omega, "the only true Omega", is necessarily Alpha.[31]

We are only giving a summary of the major features of Teilhard's argumentation, or rather, one of the schemas of his argumentation. Here again, as new as the elements used might be, and as personal as the reflection that assembles them may be,[32] it is not difficult to per-

---

[27] *Esquisse d'une dialectique de l'esprit* (1946), 7:151–52. Cf. *La Vie et planètes* (1945), 5:155–56; etc.

[28] *Le Groupe zoologique humain*, 162. Cf. *Comment je crois*, no. 13.

[29] *Esquisse d'une dialectique de l'esprit*, 7:152.

[30] *La Centrologie*, no. 24, 7:119. Cf. "It is *the dilemma of action*. To believe in the World, one must believe in God . . ." (November 10, 1917).

[31] See also *L'Énergie humaine* 6: 183; *L'Esprit de la terre*, 6:56; *Esquisse d'une dialectique de l'esprit*, 7:158; etc. See above, note 3.

[32] Let us point especially to the "existential" appearance with which Teilhard often imprints his dialectic; rather than the unfolding of a "chain of reasons", the latter is presented as a "psychological axis of spiritual progression toward God". This is not because he wants to make a show of himself; but, persuaded that "man is essentially the same in everyone",

ceive in the Teilhardian thought a twofold precedent, let us say even a twofold source—that he himself willingly admitted elsewhere. He was not, in fact, unaware of the great Thomist thesis of the *desiderium naturae*, which undoubtedly held a certain place in the teaching that he had received and that, in any case, his friend Pierre Rousselot had helped to revive; nor in admitting that "the universe could not, by construction, deceive the consciousness that it engenders", he was not thinking that Saint Thomas was lapsing into a "bad pragmatism",[33] and the "absolute strike" that he was calling for as a threat was not to proceed from a frustrated sensibility but from a scandal of the intelligence; it would not be a withdrawal before the perceptible horror but a halt before the absurdity of absolute death. To be "thinkable", the world had to be "livable".[34] On the other hand, Teilhard had meditated on the "problem of action", following Maurice Blondel, whose influence on him was profound. Although he transposed the Blondelian themes into a wholly different framework of thought, they remained determinative for him: two months before his death, evoking the great project of "spiritual energetics" for which he had as yet written only rough drafts, he would say that this energetics is "singularly related to the Blondelian Metaphysics of action".[35]

Let us point out, finally, one trait that, too, stands out increasingly in the idea of God proposed by Teilhard; a trait that he himself simplified, schematized, hardened, to the point of giving it the appearance of a slogan. His God, he says, is both "God from above" and "God from ahead". This could be translated, although it means being more specific: the God of metaphysics is also the God of "metachronics".[36] In fact, if man is to be raised above himself, it is equally necessary for him to proceed forward, in front of himself: the temporal progress of the world is a preliminary condition of its culmination in God. In other words, "the human forward" and the "Christian above" must

---

he hopes to arouse in the other an experience similar to his own and to unleash in him a similar series of thoughts, by making manifest in him "the trace, in [his] heart, of the uneasiness and the expectation that mark the religious state of the world today". This trait, which we can only point to, would deserve an attentive study.

[33] To Léontine Zanta, October 3, 1923, and August 23, 1929, pp. 61 and 105.

[34] *La Peur de l'existence* (1949), 7:197–98.

[35] To Msgr. Bruno de Solages, February 8, 1955. Cf. already *Comment je crois* (mimeo., 19); *Le Goût de vivre* (1950), 7:239.

[36] Cf. Dom Christopher Butler, *The Idea of the Church* (Baltimore: Helicon Press, 1962).

be "combined": which is to say that the second must be incorporated in the first, "without being immersed in it"! but by "supernaturalizing it".[37] This is an imperative conclusion if, on the one hand, one has taken seriously the fact of universal evolution, directed toward the greater-being and taken in charge by the human race, and if, on the other hand, in a Christian perspective, one considers the destiny of humanity as a collective destiny. To make the Earth mature in order to prepare for its ecstasy in God: other words from Teilhard expressing the same idea. But let us not risk a misunderstanding here. Teilhard also says that it is necessary to combine faith in God and faith in the world. That does not mean that his "God from ahead" is the world! No more than the "God from above" is a being who, starting from the world, had risen above the world is the "God from ahead" a God who would progress across time in order to attain an end beyond time. It is not appropriate to attribute to God this twofold movement, which is man's. Teilhard's God is the God toward whom man is on his way through the twofold, combined movement that carries him both toward the above and ahead.[38] Teilhard was always searching for "the Issue" (this was already, in 1918, the theme of *La Grande monade*):[39] now, this "Issue" is "both above and ahead". The total unity of which humanity dreams, and which it can realize only in God, shines both "at the zenith and at the horizon". In other words, God is both "*beyond* and *above* ourselves",[40] beyond and above the world. And this is why he can be at the "heart" of the world. "Omega, that in whom all converges, is reciprocally that from which all radiates. It is impossible to place it as a focus at the apex of the universe without diffusing at the same time its presence within the least step of evolution."[41]

---

[37] *Le Coeur du problème*, 5:348.

[38] Always under the action of God, whose initiative is primary. For details, see *Maurice Blondel et Pierre Teilhard de Chardin*, 129–53: "Descente et montée dans l'oeuvre du père Teilhard".

[39] In 1918, *Écrits*, 233–48. This word "issue" is frequent in Teilhard; it is the sign of his central preoccupation. Cf. *Le Goût de vivre* (1950), 7:246: "To know that we are not imprisoned! To know that there is an issue and air and light and love, somewhere, beyond all Death. To know it, without illusion or fiction!"

[40] *Réflexions sur le bonheur* (1943); Cahiers Pierre Teilhard de Chardin, 2 (1960), 63. For the "God of the ahead", see also the *Coeur de la matière*.

[41] *L'Énergie humaine*, 6:183.

This "Issue", Teilhard specifies, has a name: it is Christ, at once "Savior of individual souls" and "ultimate mover of the anthropogenesis".[42] Here we are, then, in full Christianity. Teilhard always had a concern to discern, in his thought, the contribution of rational reflection (based on experimental knowledge) and that of Christian revelation (received in faith). He often criticized the illusion of those who, confusing "naïvely the levels of the real", did not see the difference between "the taught" and the "found", between "truth that is worked out on Earth" and "truth descended from heaven".[43] "In no domain", he says, "do Science and Revelation encroach on each other—duplicate each other": that should be "an obvious fact" for all.[44] Besides his declarations on the subject, it is enough to glance, for example, at the way in which he introduces the consideration of the "Christian phenomenon" as an epilogue to the *Phénomène humain*, or in which he appeals to "the Christian mystique" at the end of his *Réflexions sur le bonheur*, in order to understand that he does not intend to mix levels and methods, as is the eternal temptation of concordism.[45] But coherence is not concordism. With everything that, from whatever source it derives, penetrates to the interior of the spirit, the spirit cannot do otherwise, in order to assimilate it, than to organize it in a coherent way with its previous acquisitions. "[All] the different meridians must necessarily meet somewhere on a pole of common vision."[46] And the truth received by

---

[42] On the Christ Omega: *Mon univers*, 9:82–88.

[43] *La Maîtrise du monde et le règne de Dieu* (1916), introduction; *Écrits*, 67.

[44] *Ma position intellectuelle* (1948); *Les Études philosophiques* (1955), 580–81; *Le Phénomène humain*, 315–17; *Barrière de la mort et co-réflexion* (1955), appendix: "Science et révélation, 7:426–29.

[45] It has been written that in Teilhard "the science of the scholars has been . . . carried away and absorbed in a great torrent of enquiring meditation in which science, faith, mysticism, theology and philosophy in a diffuse state are inextricably mixed and confused"; that would be a "sin against the intellect", a sin that Teilhard supposedly committed "in an entirely innocent manner", "the idea of a specific distinction between the different degrees of knowledge having always remained perfectly foreign to him"; yet, "in itself", such a sin would be "irreparable". The sin of interpretation that such a judgment comprises can be said (this time in all truth) to be entirely innocent, in the sense that Teilhard's declarations and explanations have remained until now perfectly unknown to its author; but, on the other hand, it would be completely reparable. Cf. Jacques Maritain, *Le Paysan de la Garonne*, 176–77.

[46] *Ma position intellectuelle*. Loc. cit. Cf. *Le Phénomène humain*, preface, 22: "Like the meridians as they approach the poles, science, philosophy and religion are bound to converge as they draw nearer to the whole. I say 'converge' advisedly, but without merging, and without ceasing, to the very end, to assail the real from different angles and on different planes."

revelation is fruitful. It must become the principle of understanding all that is real.

Faithful to this structural law of thought, as to the Catholic doctrine on the harmony of the two orders, "natural" and "supernatural",[47] Teilhard thus worked out a synthesis for himself, a synthesis in which the givens of his faith play a major role.

What his faith teaches him is first of all that God is Love. This revelation comes to confirm the conclusions to which his dialectic had led him. What, despite everything, remained abstract and could, in consequence, seem "vague" and "conjectural" now appeared to him in a warm light.[48] God is loving, God is lovable.[49] The collective experience of Christian love, coming from God, permits the believer to penetrate a little into this twofold mystery. And this twofold mystery enlightens everything.

If it is true that "union differentiates", and even that, on the higher level of being, "union personalizes",[50] does this law that results from the whole Teilhardian dialectic not find its perfect realization in God? It is the mystery of the divine unity in the Trinity of Persons. "The differentiating and communicating action of love" reveals itself in its pure state, in its absolute strength.[51]

If our world exists, fruit of a creation which everything prompts us to think free and yet everything dissuades us to believe arbitrary, is this not because it is the fruit of love? Are we not led to understand that, at this depth, "supreme necessity and supreme freedom" meet, or rather to "recognize the presence of the free as the infallible sign of an associated love"?[52]

For this world has no other end but to be finally united with the divine life. We had succeeded in posing, in virtue of a rational demand, a supreme, personal and transcendent Center, capable of gathering into itself each of those personal centers that we are in the process of be-

---

[47] See several texts in *Pensée religieuse*, chap. 11: "Nature et grâce".

[48] Cf. *Hérédité sociale et progrès* (1938), 5:51; etc.

[49] January 19, 1929; *Lettres de voyage*, 118.

[50] *La Grande option* (1939), 5:73–78; *La Centrologie*, nos. 27–28; 7:122–25; *Les Singularités de l'espèce humaine*, 2:368–69; etc.

[51] *Introduction à la chrétienne* (1944). Cf. *L'Énergie humaine*: "Union differentiates. Love is only the concrete expression of the metaphysical principle. . . . Not only does love have the virtue of uniting without depersonalizing, but it ultra-personalizes by uniting", 6:189–90.

[52] *Comment je vois*, no. 28.

coming: now this supreme Center takes on life and shape before our eyes. And we understand that the final unity to which we are invited "is in no way a pantheism" or an "identification" that would dissolve us into an ocean of amorphous being:[53] quite the contrary, it is to fulfill us in our ontological difference, so perfectly that the Pauline vision of the "God all in all"[54] can become ours, without any false prudence coming to deaden the boldness of it. While waiting, this vision that is profiled against the horizon of the future, "far from letting the soul be engulfed in a vague and indolent union, pursues it ever higher on the precise roads of action".[55]

All along this road, it is still the Christian faith, the faith in a "Lovable and Loving"[56] God, that sustains us. Here Father Teilhard becomes particularly energetic and insistent. For a whole mass of "new believers in humanity", he says, "the Gospel is only a dangerous opium. But how do they not see that, without Christianity, the world becomes unbreathable twice over? Unbreathable, first because it is desperately closed ahead, faced with a total death. And unbreathable, too, because there is no living warmth in it any more to animate its frightful mechanism."[57] In brief, a world wholly "secularized", from which Christian faith had disappeared, would be both an "entirely disintegratable world and a frozen world"; it would be a "universe without heart and without issue".[58]

We have entered into an active and accelerated phase of scientific research and social organization. Both are factors of progress. In themselves, they are not, then, to be feared. Teilhard engages the Christian, on the contrary, to contribute to them with all his fervor. He even charges him with the responsibility of making them come to a successful conclusion. For the evolution of the world, in this twofold form with which it is presently clothed, would be doubly fearful if personal love were to be banished from it. The cult of science and the cult of

---

[53] Teilhard opposes the mysticism of (personalizing) unification to the mysticism of (depersonalizing) identification. It is a theme to which he returns endlessly, from *La Vie cosmique* (1916) to the end of his life.

[54] 1 Cor 15:26–28. Cf. Teilhard, *Journal*, April 7, 1955, 5:404–5.

[55] *Mon univers*, 9:87. Ibid.: "The danger of false pantheisms has disappeared; and yet we protect the irreplaceable power of religious life that the pantheists monopolize unjustly."

[56] See also *Le Phénomène humain*, 297.

[57] *Trois choses que je vois* (1948).

[58] *Le Coeur du problème*, 5:344. This is why, "taken completely alone, faith in the World is not enough to move the Earth ahead."

society, such as their practice takes shape today in an important part of humanity, would lead us in the end to a hopeless situation. Here, for the first of these two cults:

> Whether it be by depersonalizing collectivization of individuals or even by the non-neutralized threat of a total death, there is not a single one of the "religions" born up to now from Science in which the universe does not become desperately frozen and desperately closed (which is to say, in the end, uninhabitable) ahead, in its "polar" zones. That is the truth![59]

And here, now, for the second:

> What makes pure collectivity monstrous is that, multiple by nature, it has neither thought nor heart, nor face, to which, *by the depths of our being*, we can cling. Society can well suffocate us in its innumerable arms: it can neither reach us nor bring us together by the marrow of ourselves. Stopped on the collective, humanity, so exalted for two centuries, is a frightful Moloch. We can neither love it nor be loved in it. That is why it mechanizes us instead of bringing us to completion.[60]

And Teilhard, then, to conclude that "only love, definitively, thanks to its specific and unique power to 'personalize the complexes', can perform this miracle of superhumanizing man across and by means of the forces of collectivization", just as "it alone, in the course of a still more decisive phase, can open for him access to Omega."[61] That is why the role of the Christian in our world is irreplaceable.

> Only the Christian in the world, *hic et nunc*, because he is given the power to place, not only a vague and cold *Something*, but a warm and precise *Someone* at the apex of space-time, finds himself in a position to believe *thoroughly* and (a still more important psychological event) to dedicate himself *with love* to (not merely more personalizing but personalized) evolution.[62]

---

[59] *Le Christique* (1955). Cf. *La Mystique de la science*: "Basically, no mysticism can live without love. The religion of science had thought to find a faith, a hope. It died for having been closed to charity. More humanity is conceivable without science. But more science is possible without any religion that animates it. Of this religion in science, Christianity is an exemplary form", 5:222–23.

[60] *L'Atomisme de l'esprit* (1941), 7:54.

[61] *La Centrologie*, no. 29, 7:126. *Esquisse d'un univers personnel* (1936), 6:104.

[62] *Introduction à la vie chrétienne. L'Énergie humaine*: ". . . Not the force above us, but Love—and then, to begin, the recognized existence of an Omega that makes a universal Love possible. The vice of modern social doctrines is to present an impersonal Humanity to the ambitions of human effort", 6:188.

The urgency of the Christian faith, then, has never been so great. "Far from contradicting modern aspirations for the future", this faith is presented "as the only attitude in which a spirit ardent for the conquest of the world can find the total and complete justification for his conviction".[63] If it is true, in a general way, that "religion responds to an essential and continually growing function of universal evolution"—for faith in God, assuring an absolute end to this evolution, is "the only possible mover of reflective life"—it is Christianity that, among the religions presently existing, appears, for the reasons just expressed, to be "the only presently viable form".[64] Once again, in this new phase of universal history in which humanity comes to be engaged, at a time when evolution is becoming more clearly and more profoundly aware of itself, thus coming face to face for the first time with dramatic problems of an immense extent, Christianity manifests, to whoever is capable of seeing, "its singular and unique aptitude for finding at the heart of itself and for presenting to us, precisely at the point named, what, in order to be able to act and adore thoroughly, our nature absolutely requires".[65] In revealing itself "capable of justifying and maintaining in the world the fundamental taste for life", as well as in rendering each of the members of humanity capable of really loving all others in the "loving Focus of all convergence", it "responds exactly to the doubts and aspirations of an age abruptly awakened to the consciousness of its future".[66] In brief, "Christianity is, by its very structure, the religion exactly cut out for an Earth awakened to the sense of its organic unity and its developments."

Under these conditions, one understands why Father Teilhard on several occasions hailed it as, in concentrated formulas, "the specific religion of evolution", or "the very religion of evolution".[67] By doing so, he obviously did not mean a kind of religion that would make Evolution its divinity—any more than in speaking, for example, of Catholicism as the religion of Spain, one would claim to designate a kind of religion that would adore Spain in the guise of God! He merely means the religion evolution needs, the religion perfectly adapted to

[63] *Introduction à la vie chrétienne. L'Heure de choisir* (1939), 7:26.

[64] *L'Esprit de la terre*, 6:52–53. To Léontine Zanta, April 3, 1930, 114. Cf. *Le Christianisme dans le monde* (1933), 9:132–33.

[65] *L'Etoffe de l'univers* (1953), 7:406.

[66] *Christologie et Évolution* (1933).

[67] Ibid.

men who have become aware of this evolution. Those who know the Teilhardian work as a whole know that in it we find this formula or similar formulas taken in various senses, sometimes even opposed to each other. It is thus that, in his first writing, *La Vie cosmique* (1916), Teilhard observes in some of his contemporaries a "religion of divine evolution"—but this is to reject it immediately, because in such a religion "the person counts for nothing".[68] Yet, continuing to observe the world around him and to examine its profound orientations, he believes he can perceive a great fact that imposes itself on the reflection of the Christian: "The world is in the process of being converted spontaneously to a kind of natural religion of the universe that turns it unduly away from the God of the Gospel. . . . We have seen a new faith positively born and constituted around us during this past century: the religion of evolution."[69] A phenomenon of this extent cannot be superficial, and it could not be explained solely on the basis of a perverse will. It is the sign of a profound need of the period. As apologists have always done in such cases, Teilhard is, then, going to take this into account; he is going to seize the very expression in which this need is expressed in order to rectify its meaning. It is not an accident if it is encountered, in both of its two meanings, on precisely the same dates and in writings of a completely apologetic character: in 1933–1934 first, then in 1955. What is true here also applies to the word "pantheism", which Teilhard rejects in its current meaning but which he would nevertheless like to retain, for a literal fidelity to Saint Paul, in a Christian sense.[70] Two conceptions face each other, but not like two contradictory ideas formulated on the same level. Christian truth is inclusive: in rejecting error, it claims to give satisfaction more profoundly to precisely what was just in the tendency that was coming to light through it. But as always, too, in such a case, it can succeed in this only through an effort of thought that obliges it to develop. Teilhard remembers Newman here, whose doctrine he had pondered at length. He judges that real development cannot consist solely in a more subtle analysis of the dogmatic given, but that it includes a posi-

---

[68] *Écrits*, 34: "Fugitive whirlwind immediately vanished in the total current . . . , the individual has importance and a future only in relation to the general progress."

[69] Response to the enquiry about the present reasons for unbelief (1933), 9:153. *Comment je crois* (1934).

[70] Cf. *Pensée religieuse*, chap. 14, 215–27; *Prière*, 32–39. Following Blondel, he will speak of "Panchristism": *Quelques réflexions sur la conversion du monde* (1936), 9:163; etc.

tive contribution, thanks to all the elements coming from human experience, which the divine truth assimilates in new syntheses. Nothing is changed in this divine truth itself, and no more today than in any other period has it lost anything, "quite the contrary, of its absolute seductive value".[71] Still it is necessary to show this, by stressing how it responds to the problems and aspirations of the period. When Teilhard strives in his way to do so, by presenting Christianity as "the very religion of evolution", he is thereby trying, as he tells us, only to prove its "extraordinary power of adaptability and control", a power that proceeds from its "transcendence".[72]

But Christianity is not only a doctrine, as high as one may esteem it; it is not only a bunch of beliefs, it is a reality, a personal reality. Christianity is Christ. Christians are not charged with transmitting to the world some fine and generous ideas about love: they have to spread the love they have received. They have to live with the life of Christ and give witness thereby to the fecundity of that life. Father Teilhard, who is a realist, stresses this reality of Christ forcefully.

Which is to say, first of all, that for him the whole "Christian phenomenon" rests on the fact of Jesus, this fact that he admits equally both in its historical reality and in the dogmatic interpretation of Christian tradition. Admitting "the palpable and verifiable truth of the evangelical event",[73] he professes that, in this event, God "truly inserted himself in the cosmos",[74] that "the transcendent became partially immanent", that he "descended into nature in order to superanimate it and to lead it to him".[75] It is in acting with full knowledge of the case that he rejects Modernism, in its twofold form, critical and mystical. For Modernism, Jesus is "a fruit of human, immanent evolution"; for Teilhard, as for any Catholic, he is "the encounter of the ascending

---

[71] *Le Coeur du problème*, 5:339.

[72] Ibid. and *L'Étoffe de l'univers*, 7:406. Cf. *Le Christianisme dans le monde*, on Christ: "*He is never at fault.* [He possesses an] undefined capacity for conformity with any physical and psychological order of our universe", 9:143. To complete these overly hasty explanations, it would be necessary to appeal as well to texts where the Incarnation is in question: God is becoming incarnate in the world, it is God inserting himself into evolution and sanctifying it. See below.

[73] *Le Milieu divine*, 141. Cf. October 26, 1943: "Christus mole sua stat."

[74] Note of July 14, 1920.

[75] *Esquisse d'une dialectique de l'esprit*, 7:155–56; *Que faut-il penser du transformisme?* (1930), 3:223.

participated being and the *unparticipated* Being to whom he is returning". While the Modernist "volatilizes" Christ and dissolves him in the world, Teilhard, who feels "fundamentally other, helping God", would like "to concentrate the world in Christ". But that would be only a dream, let us say a myth, a gnosis, an ideology, or, as Teilhard says, an "imagination", without the historical reality of Jesus of Nazareth, true man and true God. "If our Lord Jesus Christ has no personal and objective reality, the whole Christian religious current evaporates."[76]

As in the question of the divine personality, there is a convergence here, a complicity between the faith of Teilhard and the main inclinations of his thought: realism, biologism, historicism, personalism.[77] "In virtue of the very characteristics that would seem at first to particularize him too much, *a historically incarnate God* is on the contrary the only one who can satisfy, not only the inflexible rules of a universe where nothing is produced or appears except by way of birth, but also the irrepressible aspirations of our spirit."[78] Teilhard knows very well, on the other hand, what the unbelieving intelligence of his century sets in opposition to Christianity. But he has his response; he has sound criteria for confirming it in his faith. He explained himself again one last time, shortly before his death, in *Le Christique*. He had once translated, in his own way and for his personal use, the beautiful text of the Letter to the Romans: "I know that nothing in the world is violent or glittering or excessively vast enough to uproot us from our Lord or to eclipse him for us or *to make us depart from him*: neither angels nor life nor death nor height nor depth, nor the abysses of the past nor the revelation of the future (τὰ μέλλοντα) is capable of separating us from the Charity of our Lord."[79]

---

[76] Notes of June 9, 1919, and December 12, 1920. *Introduction à la vie chrétienne*: "To suppress the historicity of Christ (which is to say, the divinity of the historical Christ) would be to make all the mystical energy accumulated for two thousand years in the Christian phylum vanish instantly into the unreal. Christ born of the Virgin and Christ resurrected: the two form but one inseparable piece."

[77] October 21, 1945: "The necessary Revelation of Omega is unimaginable biologically, evolutionally, without a 'humanization' of the 'Jesus' type. Why would this not be precisely Jesus? Jesus, the initiator and the ever-growing *Object* of Super-Charity. . . . Without the historical and trans-historical Jesus, evolution loses *all its warmth of real life*. . . ."

[78] *Le Coeur de la matière* (1950).

[79] Note of October 31, 1920; Rom 8:38. Cf. *Christologie et Évolution* (1933): "No, neither height nor breadth nor depth risk ever separating us from the adoration of Jesus . . . provided we trust in them *to the end*." It would be appropriate to set forth here the principal traits of the Teilhardian Christology. We must forego this, for lack of space.

Such is the base on which the doctrine of the "universal Christ" and of the "divine milieu" is built: "The immense enchantment of the divine milieu definitively owes all its value to the humano-divine contact that is revealed in the Epiphany of Jesus. . . . The mystical Christ, the universal Christ of Saint Paul can have sense and value in our eyes only as an expansion of the Christ who was born of Mary and died on the Cross."[80] "But it is necessary to explore the cosmic depths of Christ."[81]

As we see, Teilhard gives Saint Paul as his reference. He would have been happy to find a confirmation of one of the essential points of his doctrine in the reflection of a recent exegete, Charles Harold Dodd, author of a little work on *The Meaning of Paul for To-day*: the Person of Jesus Christ is, in Paul's eyes, "intensely individual as well as magnificently universal".[82] The Teilhardian doctrine of the "Mystical Body" contains, moreover, nothing very original in relation to the traditional doctrine that is elaborated on the basis of the Pauline texts on the "Body of Christ". But it is coupled with a doctrine developed at greater length, the doctrine of the "cosmic Body", which, while having an equally Pauline origin, offers distinctive traits.

It is rooted in a spiritual experience that controls all its aspects and all its developments: "The one to whom it is given . . . to see Christ as *more real* than any other reality in the world, Christ everywhere present and everywhere increasing, Christ as ultimate determination and plasmatic principle of the universe, that one truly lives in a zone where no trouble of multiplicity reaches and yet where the work of universal completion is pursued the most actively."[83]

It also results from a reflection prompted by discoveries of modern science on the cosmic immensity, leading to the submission of the hypothesis of a plurality of worlds. "Through his Incarnation, Christ inserted himself not only into humanity but into the universe that bears humanity."[84] All things, Saint Paul tells us, find their consistency in him. He is the Center of creation. Henceforth, will it be enough to

[80] *Le Milieu divin*, 141.

[81] Note from 1919.

[82] French translation (1964), 119. *Mon univers* (1924). "It is impossible for me to read Saint Paul without seeing appear beneath his words, in a dazzling way, the universal and cosmic domination of the incarnate Word": 9:84.

[83] "Note sur l'Élément universel du Monde", December 22, 1918; *Écrits*, 362.

[84] Ibid.

say that he has taken all men upon himself and to speak of an "earthly body" and an "earthly nature" for him? Teilhard in no way wanted to act contrary to the declarations of the Council of Chalcedon, distinguishing in Christ two natures, divine and human. He merely wanted, through a few paradoxical expressions, accompanied besides by linguistic precautions that limit the range of it,[85] to "sub-distinguish" within the "human nature" of the incarnate Word "an 'earthly' nature and a 'cosmic' nature",[86] or again, to draw the attention of theologians to the cosmic "face" or "function" of the humanity of Christ. Hence the expression "cosmic Body", which is frequent in the early writings[87] but subsequently abandoned. His goal in that was clear, and he never ceased to express it: if Christ sustained only the Earth, he would be smaller than the world; now his greatness, his unicity, his central position, his universal principality and his universal lordship must always be maintained.[88]

It is a similar concern to maintain integrally the doctrine of Saint Paul (and of Saint John) that prompts Father Teilhard to explain the idea of the "universal Christ" as that of the "Evolver Christ".[89] The passage from one to the other is simple. In a universe conceived as evolutional, how can Christ's control over it be preserved if not by conceiving it in some way as directing the evolution of this universe. Is this not the only way of complying fully with the affirmation of the "essential perfecting function assumed by the resurrected Christ at the center and summit of Creation"?[90] In brief, after having posed the problem: "What must Christology become (*in order to remain itself*)?",[91] Teilhard strove to specify that, for him, it was not a matter of anything but "*preserving* in Christ the very qualities that are the basis for his power and our adoration".[92] That is certainly not minimism; but if, in one sense, as he believes, his Christ appears to have increased,

[85] *Comment je voix* (1948), no. 31. *Le Christique* (1955).

[86] To Father André Ravier, January 14, 1955. "A Mgr Bruno de Solages", January 2, 1955. Cf. *La Prière*, 51–54.

[87] *Forma Christi* (1918); *Écrits*; 338–39. *L'Énergie humaine* (1937); 6:146. *Écrits*, 47, 128, 165, 196–97, 408.

[88] Note from February 24, 1918, etc.

[89] "Le Christ Évoluteur", *Cahiers Teilhard de Chardin*, 5:17–28. Cf. *Teilhard missionnaire et apologiste*, 24–30.

[90] Ibid.

[91] Letter of December 9, 1933.

[92] *Comment je crois* (1934). Cf. *Teilhard missionnaire et apologiste*, 37–42.

it is, he notes with reason, "by remaining what he was, or, to put it better, *so as to remain* what he was".[93]

In his enthusiastic terminology, Teilhard comes then to speak of the "Super-Christ", as he speaks of "Super-humanity". Such terminology, we admit, has scarcely any appeal for us, but he in no way intends thereby to introduce—if there be any need to spell this out—either any other humanity but ours or any other Christ, for whom the one adored by the Christians would be only a precursor! "By 'Super-Christ'," he protests, "I absolutely do not mean to say *another* Christ, a second Christ different from the first and greater than he; but I mean *the same* Christ, the Christ of all time, revealing himself to us beneath a form and dimensions, with an increased and renewed urgency and area of contact." And again, as if foreseeing the erroneous interpretations to which his thought would give rise: "Not another Christ, I repeat. But the same Christ, ever and always; and all the more the same as it is precisely in order to guard his essential property of being *coextensive with the world* that we have been led to make him submit to this prodigious enlargement."[94]

"Coextensive with the world", but as dominating it, animating it, directing it. Henceforth, if Christ is "universal", the universe can be loved; if he is "evolver", as Teilhard had presented him as early as his first essay (1916), "evolution is healthy."[95] The Christian places himself, through faith, in this "central place where the heart of the world converges in the descending radiation of the Heart of God".[96] In his eyes, "the universe takes the form of Jesus—but, O mystery!, the one who is discovered is Jesus crucified."[97] There is no danger, then, for him, of letting himself become intoxicated or "captured by a pagan naturalism" or "carried away toward a materialistic conquest of the Earth. Does the universal Christ, in all his glory, not always emerge from the Cross?"[98]

---

[93] "Quelques réflexions sur la conversion du Monde" (1936). Letter of November 17, 1947. Cf. "La Prière au Christ toujours plus grand", in *Le Coeur de la Matière* (1950), *in fine*.

[94] *Super-Humanité, Super-Christ, Super-Charité, de nouvelles dimensions pour l'avenir* (1943), 9:208, 212, 193: "In these three expressions, the preface "super" is used to mark, not a difference of *nature*, but a *degree* of fulfillment and of more advanced perception."

[95] *Écrits*, 49. On "the love of Evolution": *Du Cosmos à la Cosmogénèse* (1951), 7:275.

[96] *La Messe sur le monde* (1923), "final prayer". Cf. "Le Prêtre" (1918): "Christ is loved as a Person and imposes himself like a World"; *Écrits*, 293.

[97] "Le Prêtre", *Écrits*, 288.

[98] "La Parole attendue" (1940); *Cahiers Pierre Teilhard de Chardin*, 4:28. *Le Milieu divin*,

For the universal Christ, Christ the evolver, is always Christ the redeemer of the Catholic tradition, seen in the new perspective of the cosmogenesis, which gives his Cross "a new gravity and beauty". Victorious over evil, which is to say, "over Pain, Sin and Death", "the crucified God"[99] appears to us, as "the most powerful spiritual Mover (because the most valorizing and the sole 'amorizing') of ultra-hominization". "That is my faith," Teilhard concludes, "the one I would so like to confess publicly before dying."[100]

The Teilhardian doctrine, as we saw above, always tended to concentrate itself more in an "energetics". The latter, in turn, is summed up, at its peak, in the discovery of the "prodigious spiritual energetic born from the Cross".[101]

The slow formation of the cosmos, the evolution of life, the unfolding of human history, the maturation of the noosphere only set by stages the natural *conditions* for the "excentration" that marks the definitive passage "beyond the future",[102] "that unique and supreme event in which the historical must become fused together with the transcendent".[103] Our effort sets these conditions; but the end is given by God: we can only receive it. Man constructs only the divinizable, the "Christianizable".[104] Between "the force of human propulsion"

118: the Cross is "the sublimation of the law of *all* life". Cf. *L'Heure de choisir* (1939): "As far back as it appears to us, life has never succeeded in rising except through suffering, across evil—by following the road of the Cross"; 7:20.

[99] Teilhard writes: "*qua* crucified", using this detail borrowed from Scholastic language, so as to show well that it is to the mystery of the Cross, in all its Christian specificity, that he adheres.

[100] To Father André Ravier, Holy Friday, April 8, 1955 (he was to die on Easter Sunday, April 10). "To purify" and "to vitalize": the two functions that "are already presented to our heart as equipollent and conjugate" to the Redeemer: "Le Christ Évoluteur", *Cahiers*, 5:25.

[101] *L'Énergie spirituelle de la souffrance* (1950), 7:256.

[102] *Les Conditions psychologiques de l'action humaine* (1949): "A universe that is not impersonal and closed but open, beyond the future, onto a divine Center", 7:185. The *Messe sur le monde* (1923): "The World can be reunited with you in the end, Lord, only through a kind of inversion, of returning, of excentration in which not only the success of individuals but the very appearance of all human advantage founder for a time."

[103] *Trois choses que je vois* (1948). *Le Coeur du problème* (1949), 5:348. *Réflexions sur la probabilité scientifique et sur les conséquences religieuses d'un ultra-human*: ". . . not excluding the Supernatural, but requiring, on the contrary, as necessary preparation, the maturation of an Ultra-Human", 7:289–90. Other texts quoted and commented upon in *La Prière*, 134–40.

[104] He also says: "supernaturalizable", "omegalizable". See *Maurice Blondel et Pierre Teilhard de Chardin*, 32–33 and 74. Jacques Maritain says very justly, in *Le Paysan de la Garonne*, 381,

and "the ascensional Christian force", between "the genesis of humanity in the world" and "the genesis of Christ in his Church", there is a relation of "coherent subordination";[105] between human progress and the reign of God, a "hierarchical conjunction".[106] It is not on our "activities" that our hope is founded but on our "passivities", if they are united to the supreme passivity of Christ on the Cross, which coincides with the supreme activity.[107] And already, by anticipation, before the "total metamorphosis", this obscure world in which we are still plunged can become for us, beyond itself, a "divine milieu", because, on the day of the Incarnation, "the radiation of love" descended to us.[108]

It is in this "divine milieu" that "the Holy Presence"[109] shines. The gaze of faith, which is a gaze of purity, penetrates it. In it, whatever its form, prayer is realized. In it is already sketched, contrary to all titanism or all deceptive prometheism, "the happiness of adoring".[110] "Nothing lives or acts more intensely, in the world, than purity and prayer, suspended like a calm light between the universe and God. Across their serene transparency, the creative wave unfurls, charged with natural virtue and grace."[111]

---

that "the advent of glory will not be the fruit of cosmic evolution but the fruit of its transfiguration through an act of God." This is precisely Teilhard's thought, which he very wrongly believed he had to oppose.

[105] *Trois choses que je vois.* "Hérédité sociale et progrès" (1921), 5, 50–51.

[106] "Le Christ Évoluteur" (1942), *Cahiers Pierre Teilhard de Chardin*, 5:27. Hence the "marvelous conjunction" that seems to him to be effectuated for the Christian between "cosmic sense" and "christic sense" (christic = theocosmic).

[107] *Le Milieu divin*, second part. *La Signification et la valeur constructive de la souffrance* (1933), 6:64–66. Cf. *Maurice Blondel et Pierre Teilhard de Chardin*, 75–76.

[108] *Le Christique* (1955); *Le Milieu divin*, 117, 177 and 202.

[109] "*Jesus solus, solus Jesus.* . . . The Holy Presence should gradually absorb me in itself. . . . May these days, gently, return me in him, to him. . . ." Retreat of 1948, first day, August 30.

[110] *Réflexions sur le bonheur* (1943), Cahiers Pierre Teilhard de Chardin, 2:69–70; *L'Esprit de la terre*, 6:54; *Comment je crois* (1934); *Le Christique* (1955); Cf. *Maurice Blondel et Pierre Teilhard de Chardin*, 152–53.

[111] *Le Milieu mystique* (1917); *Écrits*, 162–63. Various texts in *La Prière*, passim.

3. Note on Teilhard and the Problem of Evil

In a letter of January 2, 1952, Teilhard pointed to "the greater importance that the explicit consideration of evil holds in my thought". The place that it had always held was already great. The nature of a work such as the *Phénomène humain* did not allow him to consider all aspects of it. The *Milieu divin* could be more explicit—although this kind of "treatise of perfection" is addressed to a Christian already firmly engaged in the path of salvation. The evil, not only that of suffering or that of physical death but, if one dare say it, the evil par excellence, the evil enemy of God, Sin, is brought forth there in gripping characteristics. It is to this that the author devotes, with such courageous vigor!, the whole final section, with the significant title: "The Outer Darkness and the Lost Souls", some of the most severe teachings of the gospel. The powers of evil are shown to us at work in the Universe, and "are not only impersonal forces of deceleration and deviation: there are obscure presences around us, mixed in the luminous Presence of God". In certain beings, "evil has become, as it were, incarnate, substantialized". Under their influence, as Scripture teaches us, the end of time will be marked by a profound schism. From the beginning of our race, a mysterious original fault has come "to complicate and worsen" the situation of man, and it is to its burden that we must attribute so many of the "disconcerting excesses in the overflowing of sin" that we must indeed note. The genesis of the world is pursued, but it does not proceed, in fact, without a "definitive loss": "There are shadows, not only lower, but outer." We are, then, invited to reflect with gravity on the "mystery of the damnation" that the defection of fallen spirits cuts "in the midst of the Mystical Body", to see how "the damned is excluded from the luminous face and from the beatitude" of the Pleroma. Such can be the end of each of us: called to "aggregation", we risk "segregation". A structural element of the universe, hell exists.

It could not be said that he failed to understand the drama of Christ

---

Unpublished.

in his struggle with man's rejection and with his sin. His vision of the world is dramatic. "O Jesus, I want at least to make the *ever-menacing gravity of Condemnation* enter into my usual view and practice of the World." "The fires of hell and the fires of heaven are not two different forces but the contrary manifestations of one and the same energy." He will repeat to the end that, if man grows, it is "for good or *for evil*". He will beg for the salvation of all through "a bold prayer" (191–92).

4. Letter to a Council Father from Whom I Had Just Heard, in the Aula of Saint Peter's, an Intervention Unfavorable to Teilhard

Rome, October 22, 1965

. . . The kind words you spoke the day before yesterday about the *periti* encourage me to write to you.

You forcefully recalled, in your intervention, the existence of evil in the world and the influence that demons exert in it. Please allow me, undoubtedly along with many others, to express my gratitude to you for this. But, if you would also allow me, I will add that you would be delighted if you knew that this all-too-certain truth was recalled no less forcefully by Father Teilhard de Chardin.

Of course, in his writings of science and scientific philosophy, Father Teilhard did not usually have occasion to speak of these things. But in the *Milieu divin*, a religious work, which he particularly valued, he invites his reader to meditate on the mystery of evil, on the disorder manifested in the world, a disorder whose cause he sees not only in a clearly recalled original fault but in the action of evil personal powers (demons). And in this same *Milieu divin*, as in several other writings, very far from teaching any kind of "Origenism" (if one understands by that the doctrine of apocatastasis), he insistently places us before the formidable eventuality of damnation. No contemporary religious writer, to my knowledge, has spoken of the dogma of hell with so much courageous firmness as Father Teilhard.

What is called his "optimism" is at first opposed to all the atheistic pessimisms, whether they proceed from scientific milieux (as in Henri Poincaré) or from more recent philosophical currents (as with

---

Unpublished text. Already, in the Council itself, one orator (who was not French) declared in the Aula in 1965, believing to launch an arrow against Teilhard: "Haec terra numquam paradisum erit!" As he was not resolutely prejudiced, nothing was easier, through an exchange of letters, to enlighten him, and a little later I had the pleasure of receiving his visit, in Saint Peter's, at the tribune of the *periti*: he seemed very pleased to know Teilhard a little better. (*Teilhard posthume* [Paris: Fayard, 1977], 147.)

Sartre); he also reacts against certain deviations of thought among believers, in the name of the Christian faith and hope, founded on the definitive victory of the resurrected Christ. But he absolutely does not suppress the drama of the human existence. The inevitable option between Good and Evil (between Revolt and Adoration), producing the alternative between salvation and damnation, is constantly evoked in the Teilhardian writings, even in those that do not appeal directly to the light of Revelation.

Having no book here, I cannot indicate to Your Reverence the numerous texts on which I base myself here. (A certain number are cited in my work on *La Pensée religieuse du Père Teilhard de Chardin* [1962], a work that had been requested of me by my Superiors, in France and Rome, and which has received their entire approval.) But the sole reading of the *Milieu divin* (in its final chapters) can suffice for what is essential. I know that mistakes with respect to Father Teilhard are frequent, as much because of so-called disciples (some of whom, in the German language, seriously betray his thought) as because of certain detractors. That is why I feel obliged to offer you humbly this testimony. It comes from someone who is not particularly "Teilhardian" but who has sufficiently known the person and work of the Father to have had the opportunity not to be seriously mistaken about them.

Please accept, my most Reverend Father, the expression
of my profound respect and devotion
in Christo Jesu.

P.S. You quoted, if I remember correctly, the *Hymne à la matière*. May I draw your attention to the fact that this Hymn is often reproduced in a way that is doubly incomplete? On the one hand, certain verses are omitted, precisely those that evoke the dangers of Matter, the necessity of fighting it and of resisting its attractions. On the other hand, they forget to say that it serves as the conclusion to a symbolic study on *La Puissance spirituelle de la Matière* [The spiritual power of matter], from which it follows that this Hymn is placed on the lips of a Christian who has passed through the stages of ascesis and sacrifice. It is a little in the same manner that Saint John of the Cross exclaims, paraphrasing Saint Paul: "Mine are the heavens, mine is the Earth. . . ."

5. Teilhard and Newman

From the time of his studies, Pierre Teilhard de Chardin, like, and even more than, his friend Pierre Rousselot, had acquired a true English education. The list of English authors with whom he was familiar —in addition to technical works, among which we rank the famous monograph of A. White, *Warfare of Science with Theology*—would be long. Among those he read with particular interest, between around 1910 and 1920, figure the names of Newman, Kipling, Wells, Benson —as well as some Americans: Edgar Allen Poe, Emerson and William James.

Newman held an unrivalled place in his estimation. It was perhaps Auguste Valensin who first got him to read Newman, at the time of their philosophy studies on Jersey. In any case, in the theological milieu of Ore Place, he could not fail to meet him. There can be little doubt that he read the two important articles that Father Léonce de Grandmaison devoted, in *Études* of 1906, to "John Henri Newman considéré comme maître" [John Henry Newman considered as master].[1] There was often talk among his professors and working companions of the way in which Tyrrell and Loisy had used Newman and abused his doctrine. Teilhard greatly admired him. In October 1911, he was delighted to go visit the place that preserved his memory at Oxford. Each time he encountered him, he felt his sympathy grow and his community of ideas with him become closer. He wrote in 1919 that Newman's *Apologia* was one of those essential books that are in some way necessary, the only ones that should be written.[2] In his *Essay on Development*, Teilhard likewise recognized a work born of the very needs of his inner life. He saw in it a man seeking the solution of the religious problem, of the total problem, such as it arose in his life. It was to this that he himself aspired when he undertook in 1916 his first essay on "*La Vie cosmique*" [The cosmic life]. Two other things in Newman attracted him. This man knew how to free himself from

Unpublished text.

[1] *Études*, 109 (1906), 721–50.

[2] *Blondel et Teilhard: Correspondance* (Beauchesne, 1966), 104–5.

disputes that were too particular in order to get down to fundamental, "organic" problems, to those problems in which the primordial interests of the Kingdom of God are involved. In addition, without being shaken in his faith, he felt objections keenly; so he trembled at seeing young, open minds on the point of wrestling with the religious crisis of their times, and true success seemed to him to be in courageous and bold studies, outside any intellectual "enclosure". In the years that followed, Teilhard very often reflected on the question of doctrinal development; in a completely different context of situation and ideas, he understood that for him, too, it was a vital question, and one could say, although he seemed to forget him late in life, that Newman was one of those who nourished his thinking.

During the war of 1914–1918, he wrote to Father Victor Fontoynont (March 15, 1916): "I have gone back, through need and reason, to think and to pray, excited now and then by the reading of one of those books (the only ones that should be written) in which a life is revealed, Newman's *Apologia*. . . ." On February 2, 1916, he was already writing to Marguerite Teilhard: "I have still not left Newman's *Apologia*. . . ."

On July 22, 1916, again: "To relieve the boredom of the trenches, I have read *Newman catholique* by Thureau-Dangin. More than ever I have sympathized with the great Cardinal, who was so bold, so believing, so 'full of life and thought', as he himself said—and so contradicted at the same time. And I felt, once again, in the depths of myself, the breath that calls one to the great work of the reconciliation between the supreme and definitive Love of God and the lower (but legitimate and necessary) Love of Life embraced in its natural forms. A host of ideas from Newman . . . so large, so straightforward, so realistic, . . . have entered into my mind as into a dwelling long since inhabited by them. And it was all the more comforting for me to find this community of inclinations and opinions since the one who felt them so keenly experienced with difficulty, without being scandalized, the harsh temptation of having been born before his time and the season of his thought."

On December 5, 1916: "*He and I*, Newman says somewhere in his *Apologia*, in speaking of the profound feeling he had experienced at a given moment of the two sole Essentials in view—those in which all the rest are summed up and between which all the rest are ordered." (February 28): "The more I read Newman, the more I feel a relationship (how humble, to be sure!) between his mind and my own.

And one consequence of this harmony is the exhilaration his example communicates to me of accomplishing *my* work."

It was in Newman that he had read this thought by which he was always inspired: "Those who wish to make a truth triumph before its time risk ending up heretics" ("Genèse d'une pensée", 145).

6. The Deepest Spirit of Teilhard's Work

"My faith must imply the (official) Church and her directions over me, in the highest degree" (October 20, 1943). This is why he did not want to risk, by detaching himself however slightly from the community of the faithful, "being the *cymbalum tinniens* of which Scripture speaks". Now, he knows himself to be fallible, like any man: "Happy are we for the authority of the Church! Left to ourselves, how far would we risk being cut adrift?" He even went so far as to say that his own temperament made the protection of this authority even more necessary for him than for others (*Teilhard et notre temps* [Paris: Aubier, 1971], 119).

"It seems to me that I have rarely worked as entirely for God alone. I have confidence that he will give me the light and strength to end well what I desire to do *only for him*" (Peking, February 8, 1940, in writing the *Phénomène humain*).

"I hope that the Lord will help me, since it is only so as to try to make his face seen and loved that I have gone to all this trouble . . ." (NLV, 41–42, to M. T.-C., March 7, 1940).

Witness could be given that the "unique" goal of his action in the world was to "make the Face of the Lord seen and loved" there. In an essay that he contemplated in 1937, it was into the "final chapter on the Love of God" that he wanted to put all his care, "the rest being a pedestal of blocks already known"; likewise, at the end of his life, he wanted to conclude his work with a writing wholly consecrated to the "Love of God". He was not granted the time to do so. But he was able to do better: to accomplish fully the hope he had always entertained of overcoming to the end any conflict, outer or inner, "by means of love".

VI

FIGURES

1. Abbé Jules Monchanin

In 1932, on Passion Sunday, Abbé Jules Monchanin, on the point of dying, received the last sacraments from the hands of Abbé Édouard Duperray. "Consecration to India" he would note, "for death and for life, according to God alone." He survived. That same Passion Sunday, in 1939, a letter from Father Kalathil was delivered to him, inviting him to come: "Today, the granting of my prayer: the call from India. God is good! . . . I am in peace and a kind of essential joy. I know more than ever that God is waiting for me."

Nothing could less resemble a search for an "experience" than this departure for India of a priest in whom all those who approached him recognized an exceptional being, radiating intelligence as well as charity. Never more than in his case would the mysterious word *vocation* be confirmed.

It will soon be twenty years since he died, exhausted by the gift of himself to India, just as he had nearly missed dying in Lyons, in 1932, exhausted by the gift of himself to all the poor, to all the seekers of God, who came to him from everywhere, in his humble vicar or chaplain's room. He had published almost nothing. He left only a few writings. But these few (outlines of conversations, personal notes, personal letters) are of a density as well as of a rare quality that the perspective of time only better highlights. Here we have gathered together the texts that concern India. The collection of them has been patiently prepared by Mlle. Suzanne Siauve, Doctor of Letters, member of the French School of the Far East, who knew Father Monchanin closely when she was in the service of the *Institut français d'indologie* at Pondichéry. We have here a perfect edition in all respects. Indianists, who already know the strictness and the penetration of Monchanin's views, find in it many invaluable notations. Missionaries will draw from it, or renew, their purest inspiration. The work will be read with passion, not perhaps by the curious or by innovators, but by those thirsting for mysticism. It will not leave indifferent any of those who are devoted to a thorough exploration of the problem, more present than ever, of the meeting of cultures, any of those who are sensitive to the resonance of any profoundly human thought.

"Not only for the Church of India but for the universal Church, the witness of Abbé Monchanin has been and remains of an incalculable value." A mere review cannot analyze all the aspects that come together to verify this judgment stated by Father Pierre Fallon in the preface. The reader will pardon us if we must restrict ourselves to pointing out one or two features from among the most characteristic and most timely.

Abbé Monchanin wanted "to become as Indian as he could", to feel and to suffer like the Indians, "to think according to the traditional categories of their civilization", to bury himself (that is his word) in the Indian earth and work to implant the Church in it. But as much as he sought a synthesis, so much did he fear confusion. Contrary to certain Europeans giving in to the "dizziness of Vedanta", he experienced (it is again he who tells us this) "a growing horror of confused forms of thought", of "that which is beyond thought", which, most often, turns out to be only "this side of it" where everything is drowned. This was not only on his part a need for intellectual clarity: it was a demand for loyalty, "both vis-à-vis Christianity, whose essence cannot be mutilated, and vis-à-vis Hinduism, whose fundamental error cannot be hidden". He was not afraid of repeating this, on a memorable occasion, in the public homage he gave to Mahatma Gandhi on February 21, 1948, and the nobility of his attitude, joined to a sympathy that his audience sensed to be total, allowed him to make himself understood:

> Christians do not have to hide the face of their Christ, who is not the god of myths but the Absolute who took upon himself the whole man and all men so as to save all and who made himself Become so as to deify the totality of Creation. A unique event. He is the older brother of the human race, the unique Incarnation of all time, of whom the unique Church is the Mystical Body and of whom we are all the very unworthy members.[1]

[1] *Hommage à Gandhi*, February 20, 1948. In this same speech, neither did he fear to say:

As these last words show, Abbé Monchanin was always, in the most complete sense of the word, a man of the Church. It was at the reading of the encyclicals of Benedict XV and Pius XI that his missionary vocation was awakened. It was always marked with the seal of catholicity. Passing through Rome, he insisted on seeing the Pope, if only for "a flash". For more than ten years, as he had done in Europe, he gave himself in India to parish ministry among the poor. Mysticism is not a flight: it is ecclesial and—as we see, indeed, today, it is all one—dogmatic. "Christian mysticism", he declares, "is trinitarian or it is nothing." And again: "Hindu thought, so profoundly centered on the Unicity of the One, . . . could not be sublimated in trinitarian thought without a crucifying night of the soul. It has to submit to a noetic metamorphosis, a passion of the spirit."

In March 1950, he finally obtained permission to withdraw to a hermitage: the "ashram of Saccidânanda", which is to say, the monastery of the Trinity. This was, without any pretensions, a "minuscule attempt at profound Christianity grafted onto profound India". Silence, prayer, waiting. . . . What a "disagreeable surprise", the day he saw the photo of his ashram, taken by a visiting Jesuit, in a Spanish journal! "Publicity is always corrupting". . . . May we be far from the restless and the vagabonds! To whoever wanted to obtain from him some oracle, he replied: "Prophet I am not, nor am I from a school of prophets." Let us gather together the final words he said in public, in Madras, in December 1956, although he was already consumed by sickness:

> Our task is to keep all the doors open, to await with patience and theological hope the hour of the advent of India in the Church, so as to realize the fullness of the Church and the fullness of India. In this centuries-long vigil we remember that very often *amor intrat ubi intellectus stat ad ostium* (Love enters where the intellect remains at the door).[2]

"Another doctrine wanted and continues to want a society without classes and without a state. If the end can be considered pure, at least in its philosophical heights, the means are only too often trickery, lies, force and war."

[2] "La quête de l'Absolu", *Indian Culture and the Fullness of Christ* (Madras: The Catholic Centre, 1956), December 6–13.

A very recent example of the numerous errors that have long been spread about the life of Abbé Monchanin in India:

"The Kurisumala Ashram, founded in 1950 by Don Jules Monchanin and by the Benedictine Henry Le Saux"!

On Father Le Saux

(*by Abbé Jules Monchanin*)

"Undoubtedly you already know through Abbé Duperray or Marguerite Adiceam the tribulations of the Shantivanam. Particularly the departure (temporary but which will nevertheless become definitive) of Father Le Saux, who is following his own line and wants to live as a Christian hermit in the midst of Hindu spirituals. Serious divergences between us have thrown a shadow over us these past years: I believe that he is going too far in his concession to Hinduism, and it seems to me increasingly doubtful that one can rediscover the essence of Christianity beyond the *advaitá* (nonduality of Shankara). The *advaitá*, like yoga and more than it, is an abyss. Whoever plunges into it, with a feeling of dizziness, cannot know what he finds in fact. I fear that it is *himself* rather than the living and trinitary God."

To Mlle. C. Bouiller
July 12, 1957

September 5, 1989

Very dear Father,

I think that it is opportune to publish Father Monchanin's note.

Father Le Saux, who had sent me his correspondence with the Abbé, had suppressed the next to the last letter in which the latter reproached him—severely but fraternally—for that departure (that *flight*) at the moment when Monsignor was sending him the best priest of the diocese. . . . India is fashionable. In *La Croix* of Sunday the third, there is an entire page on "The Ashram, Crossroads of the Spirit", which ends with a passage from Father Monchanin: "Words of a Pioneer". The article is by Father Bruno Chenu.

E. Duperray

2. Msgr. Paul Mulla-Zadé

Even within the Church, and even in clerical circles, the name of Paul Mulla (1881–1959) is very little known today in France. Nevertheless, in more than one regard, it would eminently merit being so, and this is suggested by even a first glance at the study that Msgr. Charles Molette has devoted to him. Director of the Archives of the Church of France, Msgr. Molette does not intend to give us some general biography, suitable to satisfy the lazy curiosity of the public thanks to the pungency of a few adventures—although the latter were not lacking in the existence of Méhémet-Ali Mulla-Zadé, this Turk born on Crete (in Candia) in 1881, who, fervent Moslem in his youth, received baptism in Aix-en-Provence in 1905 and died in Rome in 1959, after long teaching Islamology at the Pontifical Oriental Institute.

What the author offers us, then, at the end of minute research conducted with a wholly scientific rigor, without sacrificing anything in vividness, is essentially a dossier of a few memoirs and abundant correspondence, with a sober commentary on the whole, but always with precision and along with a coherent narrative, which allows us to enter inside a spiritual adventure. Throughout the many slight or serious events of an exceptional existence, we are, in a way, present at the unfolding of a long drama of conscience with unexpected developments. We are thereby, too, invited to reflect, with respect to a very particular but one might say exemplary case, on the most profound conditions that are and will always be, in the most diverse historical situations, at the basis of an Islamo-Christian dialogue. And here, these two objects are but one: for all happens "within a man's conscience". Just as the author has proceeded throughout his enquiry with the critical rigor characteristic of him, so too he has been able to make use of a spiritual discernment that cannot fail to retain or awaken the interest of those who, perhaps at first without knowing it, would be capable of following the reflections of a sound mind or participate in their own way in the inner debates of an upright and delicate soul.

Preface to Charles Molette, *La Vérité où je la trouve. Une conscience d'homme dans la lumière de Maurice Blondel.*

In reading these often very engaging texts, I could not keep from remembering an analogous, somewhat later case—especially since the analogy, to some extent, is also filiation. I knew Msgr. Paul Méhémet-Ali Mulla-Zadé. I also knew, and better, Father Jean Mohammed Abd-el-Jalil, a Franciscan, his junior (1904–1979). Now both also knew each other well. One can say of the former just as it has been said of the latter that, once he became a Catholic, he "worked unceasingly to destroy the misunderstandings that exist between believers of the two monotheisms", while following basically, heroically, the same call, "without syncretism or eclecticism": which is shown from the very first by their common insistence on writing out their signature. Like the young Cretan Turk had done first, after several years of inner searching, the second received baptism. They both encountered similar obstacles, which were at times close to tragic. Just as the one had quickly become a professor of Islamology in Rome, the other was not long in becoming so in Paris.

But a closer and stronger link had previously united them: the spiritual quasi-dependence of the second in his relations with the first. When Mohammed, in the course of his years in Paris from 1925 to 1928, was still questioning himself, he had had recourse through correspondence to Msgr. Mulla. He himself recounted it: it was the latter who "had guided me in a decisive way toward baptism". Jean-Mohammed had even learned later—what he would also specify in writing—that, at the time, "Msgr. Mulla was submitting my objections to Maurice Blondel, who suggested responses or references to him." He would remark that in fact these letters received from Mulla "are Blondelian" and would relate another fact discovered later still, which attached him more personally to Blondel, awakening in his regard an even livelier gratitude.

It seemed to me that it might be good for this spiritual genealogy to be recalled here. It is not without reason that I have spoken of the "quasi-dependence" of the young baptized in relation to his elder. In reality—and despite their very different human temperament—they were rather brothers. They were so both because of what they both received so discreetly from Blondel and through their common, ever-proclaimed fidelity to the best of what they owed to Islam.[1] This is

[1] On the relations, which became increasingly close, between Blondel and Mulla, the doc-

what Msgr. Molette's work, whose importance is capital, permits us to appreciate even better.

umentation gathered together in this book is abundant. For Abd-el-Jalil, see "Recueil Jean-Mohammed Abd-el-Jalil", 3d vol. in the *Nouvelles de l'Institut catholique de Paris* (1980), 224 pp.; more particularly: 207–23: "Témoignage d'un tard venu à l'Église" (published first in *Évangile aujourd'hui*, Cahiers de Vie franciscaine, 54 [1967/II]).

3. *As If He Saw the Invisible*

A little book was published this spring, little but weighty with experience, ripened over a long period in reflection and prayer underlying an already long life in the apostolate. The author of it is Father Jacques Loew, a Dominican, whose studies on the Dockers of Marseille and the *Journal d'une mission ouvrière* are well known. The title was inspired by the words that the Letter to the Hebrews says of Moses, the leader of the chosen people across the desert: "As if he saw the invisible, he held firm." No work seems to me better adapted to the needs of the Christian who wishes even today to be truly a witness of Jesus Christ. "What type of apostle will carry God to the world today? How can we take up a position at the height required to love this world and yet not let ourselves be engulfed by it? How can we resemble it and yet be different from it? be thoroughly engaged in it and yet make manifest that God is the only Absolute?" This is what he explains, following Saint Paul, the great Apostle, the most timely mentor.

I want to restrict myself here to only one very short chapter, almost a parenthesis, of this book—because in this parenthesis he has treated a subject whose urgency seems extreme. We are suffering from an illness that gets worse every day, a veritable epidemic that is in the process of consuming us. *Murmurs and murmurers*: in a dozen pages, Father Loew proceeds to a perspicacious analysis of this evil, "a cultivation of dissatisfaction raised to the ranks of virtue". Such, indeed, is in fact one of the present characteristics of our French Catholicism, capable of drying up the vital sap that gives, on the other hand, so many signs of vitality. Father Loew, in describing this, makes undoubtedly only one mistake: he who knows how to speak frankly and who, on occasion, even uses slang, speaks here through euphemisms.

"Murmurs"? The stage of murmurs has well passed. . . . We are much rather besieged with deafening cries. It is an incessant concert of recriminations. Everything in the Church is the object of criticism: both institutions and men, both acts and words, both intentions and

---

Jacques Loew, O.P., *Comme s'il voyait l'invisible. Un portrait de l'apôtre d'aujourd'hui*, "L'Évangile au XXe siècle" series (Paris: Éd. du Cerf. 1964), 240 pp.

methods, both the past and the present. People scarcely trouble themselves about studying or reflecting. They receive docilely from any mouth, provided that the words that leave that mouth come to enrich their arsenal. It is a conformism of criticism, a vast, collective neurasthenia. There is no longer any concern about being just, or often about being reasonable. They keep themselves in such a disposition of mind that everything, in the Church, appears in a pernicious light. Nothing is easier, in truth, than to give in to such an optical illusion. But nothing is more sterilizing, and all the fine plans for reform that one constructs are from then on only a utopia.

Father Loew judiciously recalls on this subject the words of Father Chevrier: "One who demolishes does more work in one morning than one hundred masons do in a day." In this atmosphere of unhealthy criticism it is not only the rectitude of our Catholic spirit that is attacked: our faith itself is placed in danger. In the desert, the children of Israel murmured against Moses and Aaron; Father Loew reminds us, too, of the reply made by the two men of God: "Who are we? But it is not we, but indeed Yahweh, whom your murmurings assail" (Ex 16:8).

I was thinking of this yesterday in reading the following lines from a recent discourse by Paul VI, who confirms the diagnosis made by Father Loew. The Holy Father evokes there the love of the Church and the Papacy that inspired the action of Catherine of Siena in so troubled a period of the Church's history.

> One can [he says], one must love the Church and the Papacy, even if their face be veiled by human infirmities. This is perhaps the lesson that so many modern men, who nevertheless say they are Catholics, do not well understand, occupied as they are and almost impassioned to seek criticisms that are not always serene or even always objective. Jesus says one day: "Happy are those who will not be scandalized because of me!" The history of the Church gives us occasion to meditate on these words, and the son of the Church, who understands her truly and brings the testimony of his charity to her, will still find in her today a source of beatitude.

Let us hold on to these last words in particular. The one who always criticizes can well be satisfied, too satisfied with himself: he does not know the joy of the true disciple of Jesus Christ. He is deprived of one source of beatitude. He does not enjoy any of those fruits of the spirit that are, according to Saint Paul, writing to his dear Galatians

(Gal 5:22–23), "charity, joy, peace, patience, kindness, goodness, trust in others, gentleness, self-control".

Chance, which sometimes does many things, made me reread on the same day an older text, drawn from a personal letter, recently published. The author of it is Father Teilhard de Chardin. It was during the war of 1914. A priest then for five years, stretcher-bearer in a regiment of riflemen, Father Teilhard wrote to his cousin Marguerite Teilhard-Chambon: "Happy those who suffer at not seeing the Church as beautiful as they wished, and who are only more submissive and suppliant to her. This is a profound sorrow, but one of high supernatural value."[1] In his subsequent life, he was to encounter many other occasions to apply this line of conduct and to experience this sorrow and this beatitude. On this point as on many others, Father Teilhard de Chardin's example, which cannot be contested even by those who contest certain aspects of his thought, should serve as a subject of meditation today.

Undoubtedly it is not to the readers of *Vie chrétienne* that these reflections should be addressed. But perhaps they are better prepared than others to understand their urgency. Perhaps, too, they are more apt to carry them out by beginning the corrections that are imperative among us.[2] For it is high time, if we do not want to agree to let the Christian life become insipid and corrupt in our land, that resolved Christians reunite to lead their brothers into a change of attitude. They will be able to show them that, escaping a morbid criticism, they are in reality less credulous, less timid, more lucid, more truly "adult". Their words, like their action, will be to build up, not to destroy, and through them the Spirit of the Lord will pursue his work.

---

[1] Letter of July 4, 1915, *Genèse d'une pensée*, 72.

[2] They might be encouraged by a few pages published in the *Cahiers universitaires catholiques* (April–May 1964): Jacques Perret, "Tristesse et action de grâces avec saint Augustine", 373–77. The article gives more than its title seems to promise, for it is of the most urgent timeliness.

4. *Love and Responsibility*

It is not normal for a mere priest, whom, moreover, no particular competence recommends, to preface the work of a member of the episcopal corps. The thing would even be completely improper if it were not a matter simply of presenting to the French-speaking public the translation of a book already published in another language (Polish), a book whose merit has no need of being recalled to those familiar with it. We would nevertheless have hesitated to sketch these few lines if not for the insistent request addressed to us by His Excellency Bishop Karol Wojtyla himself. But since it was indeed necessary to obey him, we are happy, we admit, that the occasion is thus offered us to render public homage to one of the artisans of the current conciliar work. For we have had the opportunity for some time to see at close range —and this sight is the source of great comfort to us—the Christian vigor as well as the clearsightedness with which he applies himself to the examination of the most serious subjects yet to be studied.

The subject treated in the present work is precisely one of the most important and the most discussed among them. Much has been written during these recent years about the problems concerning love, chastity, marriage, procreation and the family. We hope not to offend anyone by stating that it has rarely been done with so much care in analysis and rigor in thought; with an equal concern to integrate these problems and their very diverse aspects into an overall vision of human reality. Psychology, metaphysics and morality are successively employed. The biological and medical givens, treated in a separate chapter, are in no way neglected. The most delicate, pungent descriptions alternate with the most robust dialectic. The role and value of sexuality are fully recognized, especially since the latter is never separated from the subject that it affects and which is responsible for it. So the eminent dignity

---

Preface to the work of Karol Wojtyla, *Amour et responsabilité: Étude de morale sexuelle* (Paris, dated June 12, 1965). On the relations of Father de Lubac with the future Pope John Paul II, notably during the Vatican II Council, see *Entretiens autour de Vatican II*, 46–48, 59, 109–10, 126. See also *Mémoire sur l'occasion de mes écrits* (Namur: Culture et Verité, 1989), 175–77 [English trans.: *At the Service of the Church* (San Francisco: Ignatius Press, 1993), 171–73].

of man, such as the Church of Christ promotes and defends it, is admirably brought out.

The author, however, does not address himself solely to believers; at least he does not appeal first to their faith. He does not proceed according to the teachings of Scripture but through the paths of rational argumentation. He says nothing, for example, of Pauline mysticism. Without excessive accommodation to the place of current modes of language, he has nonetheless assimilated the best of modern reflection, particularly of phenomenology, and he knows how to utilize both the philosophy of Aristotle and, even more, that of Saint Thomas Aquinas to make the latent personalism spring forth.

Such a book as this is well suited to show everyone that the most classical tradition offers incomparably more resources to thought, in this domain as in many others, than a certain critical attitude, which is too widespread today, allows one to acknowledge. No one, in any case, after having read it closely, could give way any longer to those facile diatribes, those caricaturing pamphlets against traditional theses, which dishonor even some of our Catholic publications. No one could any longer, in order to get rid of it, reduce to a biological order, modeled to the taste of the individual, what is in reality the very order of existence, subject to personalist norms.

The doctrine set forth by the Archbishop of Cracow might seem austere. It is, however, that of a man who cares about man; that, too, of a pastor of souls who is not unaware either of the weaknesses of human nature or of the means of grace that come to his help. It is the doctrine of a realist as well as of a man of faith. It does not claim, moreover, to settle by the sole play of a few principles the whole variety of innumerable particular circumstances. Clearly we could not foresee the spontaneous application of this by populations who have never been touched by the Good News or who have become insensitive to it. Undoubtedly we can expect that the myriad voices of publicity will sing few praises of it. Perhaps it will even be judged too hard by some clerics. Yet we do not doubt that, on the other hand, it will convince many serious minds, concerned to found the relations of the couple on a complete, coherent and thorough anthropology. Nor do we doubt that it will be welcomed with joy by numerous Christian homes, happy to find here the rational justifications and enlightenment of what their moral health and the instinct of the Spirit had already made them understand in the depths of their heart.

If the conciliar *aggiornamento*, launched by John XXIII and pursued with tenacity by Paul VI, is necessarily to be basically an interior renewal, according to the evangelical spirit, Msgr. Karol Wojtyla's work must contribute greatly to it. It is suited to dissipating some of the illusions that would compromise it. Among many signs, in fact, that maintain our hope today, there are also a few others that arouse some uneasiness. The Holy Father alluded to this last month in saying: "Whoever would see in the Council a relaxing of the internal commitment of the Church toward her faith, her tradition, her ascesis, her charity, her spirit of sacrifice and her adherence to the Word and to the Cross of Christ, or even an indulgent concession to the fragile and versatile relativist mentality of a world without principles and without transcendent end, or a kind of more convenient and less demanding Christianity, that person would be in error." It is against one of these errors of interpretation that Msgr. Wojtyla places us on guard. He does so, moreover, in a wholly positive way, without entering into any controversy, through the simple exposition of a long-matured doctrine. He will give courage to many. Contrary to what would inevitably happen if men of the Church let themselves be carried away, under the pretext of an opening to the world, by the easiness of a lukewarm Christianity and by the indulgences of a morality without dignity, he engages us in the way that must render our faith more "contagious". The work is of a nature to make one reflect seriously and to guide upright souls toward the light of the Gospel.

5. *The Joy of Believing*

Madeleine Delbrel had published in 1957, by Éditions du Cerf, *Ville marxiste, terre de mission*. If this book created such a stir it is because a long experience had been condensed in it, that of a whole life of devotion and reflection. After her death, a collection appeared through Éditions du Seuil, under the title *Nous autres, gens des rues* (1966); and here, in 1968, we have the same publisher offering us a second collection: *La Joie de croire*. It is here that the secret of Madeleine Delbrel is revealed at its foundation. True spiritual books are rare. This is one. It is among the most beautiful. It is made up, as we are told, of bits and pieces: little newspaper articles, meditations, conferences, poetry, personal letters, personal notes, sketches. . . . Nothing more commonplace, more simple—but just as the Gospel, of which it is the fruit, is simple and commonplace. For nearly twenty centuries, the same miracle continues, and while today many educated men seem no longer to understand anything in the four little books that convey to us the message of Christ, the inexhaustible fecundity of these four little books is imperative today, in the most immediate and the most burning timeliness. Yet, Madeleine Delbrel tells us, "the law of Christ can be lived only by humble and gentle hearts", in the image of the Heart of Christ.

Madeleine Delbrel was a realist. Her spirituality is not a dream, cerebral or sentimental. She knows that "any relationship to God will be pierced by a doubled-edged blade: joy and the cross"; she warns us that "without solitude we could perhaps never know if we have tried to love God or if we have created literature, philosophy or historical novels." Her behavior reminds us, too, of one of the essential conditions of any apostolate. She understood that fidelity to the gospel does not go without fidelity to the Church. Witness this letter, as admirable as it is strange, from 1952: "Sharing for eighteen years the life of a population not only without faith but without a Christian memory: bound very profoundly to what the Church, in France, conveys that is *nova* and *vetera*, persuaded that our fidelity demands a missionary

---

Madeleine Delbrel, *La Joie de croire* (Paris: Éd. du Seuil, 1968).

thrust that is ever more ardent as well as an ever stronger rootedness in obedience, I desired to go to Rome, in the name of us all. . . . So that this might be an act of faith and nothing more, I arrived in Rome in the morning; I went immediately to the tomb of Saint Peter. . . . I remained there the whole day, and I left again for Paris in the evening."

What greatness in this simple gesture! What a lesson for us! It will be more powerful for maintaining the cohesion of the Church than the many contrary gestures today to disintegrate her.[1]

[1] Father de Lubac returned several times, with admiration, to the Roman pilgrimage of Madeleine Delbrel. On the life and work of the one whom Father Gaston Fessard called the militant of Ivry and whose figure his work *De l'Actualité historique* (1960) greatly contributed toward revealing to the Church of France, see Christine de Boismarmin, *Madeleine Delbrel, rues des villes, chemins de Dieu*, 1904–1964. Introduction by Jacques Loew. (Paris: Éd. Nouvelle Cité, 1985.) With a bibliography.

"Rome is for me a kind of sacrament of Christ-Church", as M. Delbrel summed it up in a striking way (cf. *La Joie de croire*, 3).

6. *Existence and Eternity*

Msgr. Fernand Guimet died accidentally in Gaète on June 21, 1973. He was born in Varennes-Saint-Sauveur, in the Louhans Bresse region (Saône-et-Loire) on April 27, 1909. After higher studies in rhetoric at the *Institut catholique* in Paris, ordained priest on March 27, 1937, he first exercised parish ministry as vicar at Saint-Pierre-de-Châlon. He was then director of the major seminary of Autun, superior of the Ozanam School at Mâcon, where he had done his secondary studies, then he had for many years (1946–1963) the office of vicar general. In 1963, he was dispatched to Paris as chaplain of the University Parish for higher education. Finally, in 1970, he succeeded Father Delos, O.P., as ecclesiastical counselor to the Ambassador of France to the Holy See. He had degrees in classical letters, philosophy and theology and had a diploma in Eastern languages from the *Institut catholique* in Paris. He had in his youth taken an active part in the beginnings of the JEC. His courageous charity and chaplaincy of the maquis of Saône-et-Loire during the dark years 1940–1944 earned him the Legion of Honor for military considerations.

One of those who knew him closely, Canon Bernard Lambey, depicts him to us as an indefatigable reader, a writer who was exacting to the point of scruples, an untiring seeker, interested in an astonishing way in everything and everyone, concerned about making ideas spring forth and about opening his interlocutor to a Christian vision of life and the world. He was deeply convinced that in order to be a priest today, the service of the gospel of Jesus Christ demands a labor of knowledge, for which no amount of generosity can substitute. So he strove to make each one understand the necessity of pausing a little, in the whirlwind of life—even in the midst of apostolic work—in order to study, reflect and pray. So he questioned that impoverished faith, which becomes mere religious sentiment, or an impulse without form, or even simple communitarian warmth, or, worse yet, slogans for action. The necessities of the various ministries that were confided

---

Fernand Guimet, *Existence et éternité* (Paris: Éd. Aubier Montaigne, 1973). Cf. *Mémoire sur l'occasion de mes écrits* (Namur: Culture et Verité, 1989), 229 [English trans.: *At the Service of the Church* (San Francisco: Ignatius Press, 1993), 225].

to him, to which he dedicated his whole soul and on which there is no need to dwell here, did not allow him to carry through to completion the thesis that he had only just barely started on John Duns Scotus. But the all-too-rare studies that he published, on the trinitarian doctrine of Richard of Saint Victor, on Scotus' theology of love, on "philosophy, theology and contemplation" . . . , sufficed to attest, among experts, to the exceptional quality of his thought.

At the time of his death, the present work was already in proofs. The three studies of which it is comprised, each one of which forms a whole, are closely connected: the deepening of the Christian idea of Tradition (often so poorly understood) leads the reader to perceive the insufficiency of the theologies of Event and Word and to introduce him to a meditation, which culminates in spiritual directives, on the divine Transcendence and the mystery of the Holy Spirit in the Church. There is no book more truly one.

Can one, the author nevertheless asks with humor, "conceive of a theme less timely?" On the contrary, one perceives quickly that from the center where he situates himself, it is at the heart of timeliness that he unceasingly aims. In some one hundred thirty small pages, he has succeeded in enclosing the entire Catholic synthesis, such as our times, in the midst of a chaos of opinions and research, needs to see and feel it in order not to let anything be lost from its eternal value. A very rich thought is unfolded there, or rather is concentrated there, whose contemplative serenity is united to a sharp perception of the present situation. Served by very sure language, this irenic thought makes manifest its rigor in its rejection of ready-made conceptions as well as dichotomies, oppositions and perpetual exclusions that characterize so many publications of misleading ostentation. It dismantles, by overcoming them, the very frequent illusions of a criticism or an analysis that would wish to be taken as sufficient. It also rejects compromises and equivocal understandings by the frankness with which —without a shadow of polemical spirit—it opens and pursues the essential debates. Let us say, finally, that it is expressed in a fine, classical style, without any searching after originality, but in which judicious formulas abound. Long, perfectly constructed sentences at times sustain in their meanderings, without omitting any nuance, the course of this thought that is ever in progress.

Now that Msgr. Guimet, whose modesty was extreme, has gone, we do not hesitate at all to say: he has left us a masterpiece. It is the fruit of an attentive observation and a long-matured reflection, but also of prayer, suffering and love. It is one of those texts, seldom very numerous but the most invaluable of all, that fully honor the sacred name of "theology". Through this text, a living being once more communicates to us in its totality the Christian mystery that he lived. His pages, for example, on the divine depth and human proximity of the mystery of the Cross, reach the sublime.

Each generation has its light and its darkness. It has been justly said of Fernand Guimet, priest of Jesus Christ, that a light both prestigious and discreet emanated from his person. It has been extinguished to the eyes of our flesh. But in this little book, which is, in a way, his testament, it will shine again. It will continue to radiate, clear and warm, for the benefit of the coming generation. It is even today one of the signs, one of the realities that sustain our hope.

7. *Life and Faith*

Our archbishop has won for himself one more reason for our gratitude by giving us this little book which discusses "Christian coherence" in thirty brief chapters. Each of us can receive it as a true *pastoral letter*, personally addressed to him. Each of us can draw from it what we all have the greatest need of today, in the midst of whirlpools and temptations of all kinds, for the fidelity—which is to say, for a deepening —of our Christian life. Whatever might be the diversity of our opinions, our activities, our tendencies—and we know that this diversity is great and that it is at times manifested in dramatic confrontations—each of us, without exception, needs to hear himself called back, with renewed illumination that corresponds to the present situation, to the same gospel; to hear the same call coming from Christ. What peace, what freedom in our hearts, what new strength, what effectiveness in our search for union, a search ever to be taken up again, always to be extended, if we decide—if I, if I myself decide, for it is I, personally, who am addressed here—to make this living message enter into us!

When he speaks to us of the Holy Spirit, of prayer, of fraternal charity, of conversion of heart, of hope . . . , Cardinal Renard speaks as a true pastor. This is what gives his words a persuasive warmth. He confides to us in passing, in a few lines, what the role of the bishop is, particularly as defender, but even more as promoter of unity. He has the courage to say how much this unity is threatened, ridiculed, when, losing the sense of the eucharistic mystery yet thinking to work for the renewal of the Church, one comes to the point of making it a sacrament of division. And is this not also a very salutary warning that he addresses to us, when, in the face of so many projects, criticisms, plans for reform, in the face of this fever of ideologies whose least misdeed is to lose us in abstraction, he quotes these words from an old bishop: "What a lot of architects, and how few masons!"

One senses, in reading him, that this pastor personally loves each of the sheep confided to him by the Lord; that he would like to be able

---

Cardinal Renard, *Le Vie et la foi* (Desclée de Brouwer, 1973).

to know them all personally. The dimensions of a large diocese do not permit him to do so: so then he addresses each one through writing; through this book he speaks to each "head to head" and "heart to heart".[1]

[1] I would have to use a whole dossier here to make known the activity shown by Cardinal Renard to cope with the insane undertakings aimed at destroying the Catholic faith. It is still too early to publish the numerous texts that attest to the clearsightedness, courage and suffering of the Archbishop of Lyons and member of the French Episcopal Conference, which I have witnessed during these years. If I collaborated a little with him, it was he who took the initiative, as some of the letters he addressed to me between our conversations will verify (H.L., 1989).

8. *Church of France, Take Care Not to Lose the Faith*

Father Gaston Fessard died, on June 18, 1978, at the moment he was putting the finishing touches to this already completely written work. It is a fraternal duty for us to devote ourselves to its publication, a duty especially urgent since the author attached, in complete personal disinterestedness, an extreme importance to it. He wanted it to be published quickly. After having already submitted it, according to his usual custom, to several parties for our criticism, he had asked us to reread it after its completion, as needed, and to correct it again. In a fraternal friendship of nearly sixty years, we have often worked together,

---

Preface to a posthumous book by G. Fessard, *Église de France, prends garde de perdre la foi* (Paris: Julliard, 1979).

This work was written not only with the permission but with the encouragement of Father André Costes, Provincial of France for the Society of Jesus. Although no review or the least mention was made of the work in the principal French journals of the Society of Jesus, Pope John Paul II read Father Fessard's book very attentively before undertaking his first trip to France from May 30 to June 2, 1980, as Father Roger Heckel was to confide to us on the evening of Friday, May 30, 1980. Although without any real basis in fact, some good observers compared the title of Father Fessard's book and the sentence with which the Pope ended his speech at Bourget (June 1, 1980): "France, elder daughter of the Church, are you faithful to your baptism?"

The correspondence between Father Fessard and Father de Lubac, from December 3, 1922, to October 8, 1977, comprises several thousand pages and has been almost entirely preserved.

Father Fessard died on Sunday, June 18, 1978, at Trinité de Porto-Vecchio (Corsica) as he was placing the finishing touches on his book: *Église de France, prends garde de perdre la foi.* His funeral was celebrated in the Church of Saint Ignatius in Paris, on Thursday, June 22, 1978. It was on the same day, in the morning, that Jeanne Hersch handed the manuscript to Father de Lubac.

After having met with the refusal of three large Parisian publishers, two of whom were Catholic, the posthumous book of Father Fessard was published in several weeks at Éditions Julliard, by Bernard de Fallois, upon the intervention of Raymond Aron, who also devoted a column to it in *L'Express* of May 12–18, 1979 (cf. our study: "Praxis marxiste et discernement chrétien", in *Plamia*, 15 rue Porto-Riche, 92190, Meudon, no. 53, Christmas 1979, p. 56, note 12). On Father Fessard, see also *Mémoire sur l'occasion de mes écrits* (Namur: Culture et Vérité, 1989), 50, 66, 168–71, 192, 197–98, 277–83, 386–94 [English trans.: *At the Service of the Church* (San Francisco: Ignatius Press, 1993), 51, 65, 164–67, 188, 194–95, 276–81, 389–96.

in total intellectual sympathy as well as in total freedom of judgment, each in relation to the other. His principal field of study was not mine, and I could in no way rival his power of thought; but our fundamental preoccupations were commonly held. He himself was aware, besides, as he even declares here, of broaching only one of the aspects of the present situation in this final writing, the fruit of his deep faith and his intense love of the Church. This aspect, however, is not a minor one, and the alarm—for that is what it is—that Father Fessard sounds, if one really consents to hear it, can have a salutary effect, accompanied as it is from one end to the other by a rigorous reflection.

Father Fessard's vocation was essentially doctrinal. But one should not imagine that this was in the least to the detriment of his social sense or apostolic ardor! As a young collegian, he had been haunted by the problem of social justice, and this obsession never left him. Later, he envied (if one may use this word here) the first worker-priests. Although very sparing with confidences, he nevertheless told me this more than once. A metaphysician, theologian and distinguished spiritual director, he was, as a true Jesuit, attentive to the most profound needs of his times. So he refused to lock himself into an intellectual work whose value was recognized by the best judges, even among the most opposed to our faith. This is because he had discerned very early the most insidious peril: that perversion of spirit that today threatens not only the Christian faith but all humanity, which would end in reducing it to a mass with bowed heads, destined for the worst slavery.

Upright and courageous as well as perspicacious, as he proved on several occasions, this great servant of the Church, who was too often misunderstood, is still rendering her an eminent service beyond the grave.

9. Homage to Hans Urs von Balthasar

Some ten years ago we wrote a few pages on the occasion of the sixtieth birthday of Hans Urs von Balthasar.[1] They were nothing but a testimony. If it had been a question of explaining and appreciating the work of von Balthasar, how insufficient they would have been! How much more would they be so today! During these ten years, the monument offered to our sight has been considerably amplified. With the first panel of the projected triptych concluded (*Herrlichkeit*), the construction of the second has been briskly undertaken (*Theodramatik*), and so on.[2] But in particular, outside of any quantitative consideration, the greatness of the work increasingly compels attention. It does so in spite of the discretion that keeps its author from any publicity sprees, in spite of the secret hostility that superiority, even when it is modest, always arouses in spite of the inattention of a certain number of professionals who do not recognize one of their own in this unclassifiable man. Even in France, despite the regrettable insufficiency of translations, made in scattered order and distilled into a rhythm of hopeless slowness, the thought of von Balthasar is gradually permeating the spirit of a young elite.

And giving it an overall look, I believe I can discern in it, in fact, among others that would take too long to describe, two fundamental

---

Text published in *Communio* (1975), 86–89.

On the work of von Balthasar, see also *Paradoxe et mystère de l'Église* (Paris: Aubier, 1967), 180–212: "A witness of Christ in the Church: Hans Urs von Balthasar. Cardinal Lustiger has said on several occasions the importance that the pages of Father de Lubac had for him, the reading of which had led him to undertake the study of *La Gloire et la Croix*. It was, moreover, thanks to the perseverance and intervention of Father de Lubac with superiors of the Society of Jesus that the complete translation of the large work of von Balthasar could be finished and published in the 'Theology' series, the suppression of which had been decided upon."

On H. U. von Balthasar, see also *Mémoire sur l'occasion de mes écrits* (Namur: Culture et Vérité, 1989), particularly 153–54 [English trans.: *At the Service of the Church* (San Francisco: Ignatius Press, 1993), 150–51]. Father de Lubac gives there as an appendix the complete text of the letter sent by von Balthasar to his confreres on the occasion of his leaving the Society of Jesus in March 1950 (371–75 [English trans.: 370–75]).

[1] Reproduced in *Paradoxe et mystère de l'Église* (Aubier, 1967), 180–212.

[2] Cf. J. M. Faux, *Gloire et liberté*; on several recent publications of H. U. von Balthasar: *Nouvelle revue théologique* (June 1975).

traits that have begun to stand out more in the course of this past decade and that are gaining in strength and timeliness.

On the one hand, instead of leading a series of rear-guard attacks against the representation of Christian origins such as some think results from contemporary criticism in its multiple ramifications, or being content to discuss one after another of its many details, to show at length its arbitrary excesses, von Balthasar, with an astonishing sureness of vision, makes the essence of this criticism his own; he swallows it whole, so to speak, he digests it—he himself pursues it with wisdom; but, through a faultless discernment, he draws from it a vision totally different from that which some might have thought. The Person of Jesus radiates with a brilliance that is particularly incontestable in its relation to the interpretations which the writings of the evangelists give us. There is a reversal of perspective there owing to an analysis that recalls, in an even more fundamental domain, the process Newman applied to the development of dogma. The operation, without any artifice, is conducted with rigor, and the mind that seeks to understand experiences a lively satisfaction in it. Never has anyone brought out so powerfully the unity of convergence between the two Testaments and that of the different parts of which the New is composed. Never has the mysterious focal point that is, not the consequence, but the source of that unity been made more perceptible to the historian: the unfathomable Figure of Christ, object of the faith of the Church. All the recognized diversities, in which a myopic criticism can perceive only oppositions, rendering incomprehensible the Christian Event in its origins as well as in its developments and its extraordinary power, are resolved in a higher harmony, which imposes itself on one's gaze like a revelation. In this exemplary case, one feels forced to admit that—according to the title of one of von Balthasar's own works—*the truth is symphonic.*

On the other hand—this is the second trait—instead of wearing himself out like so many others in the effort to rejuvenate the old Scholasticism for better or worse by a few borrowings made from philosophies of the day, or even of renouncing, again like so many others, any organized theological thought, von Balthasar makes a fresh start at outlining an original synthesis, of radically biblical inspiration, which sacrifices nothing of the elements of traditional dogmatics. His extreme sensitivity to the developments of culture and to the questionings of our age inspires such boldness in him. His intimate knowledge, attested to by his earlier works, of the Fathers of the Church, of Saint Thomas Aquinas and of the great spiritual leaders, allows him to attempt the venture. It is on them that he has long been nourished; he is their successor today, without any servility just as without any betrayal, so much has he assimilated their substance. Such an undertaking, in which one would seek in vain for the least concession to modern "gnoses", is also very far from sporadic, short-lived attempts that rather resemble individual fantasies or that, proceeding from a resentment with regard to Tradition, most often minimize or secularize the given of faith to the point of making it disappear.

These two fundamental traits that I am describing perhaps in an awkward or in any case summary way seem to me all the more remarkable since they correspond exactly to the two fundamental needs of Christian thought today, and since they began to be sketched even before the last council had invited theology, too, to make its *aggiornamento*. It is a mark of great necessary and fruitful undertakings to arise in this way, without anyone paying attention to them at first, without their initiator himself conceiving a plan of it at first, without the goal toward which they are tending being at first clearly perceived. They take shape and develop through a growth that is, in a way, natural, and not, as it were, on command.

Not only are the divine origin of the Christian faith and the Christian authenticity of theology, through the twofold effort that has just been described, in no way compromised: but the first is placed in a new light and the second is freed, in a climate of spiritual objectivity, from naturalist and objectivist consequences which, in modern times, are often cumbersome and even a little distorted. The incompressible life of Tradition carries it above a frightened conservatism. It is a fact that Scholasticism, such as it had ended in being codified and of which nearly all serious attempts at rejuvenation for nearly a century have been stopped by an authoritarian assault, appears today to be discredited. The phenomenon is of such breadth that it would undoubtedly be useless to waste one's time weighing down with minutiae the part of injustice and incomprehension (a certainly considerable part) that it conceals. Interesting in terms of history, such an effort at discernment would be at least incapable, in itself, of arousing new life. Disputes have taken possession of this great body, used like a cadaver to be dissected, and many now have the impression of being before a great void. Few among them seem to suspect that all around them, on the same tested foundations,[3] a new edifice is rising, gathering together the most precious part of the apparently dissipated heritage, at the service of an intact and revitalized faith. But the admirers themselves of von Balthasar's work at times see in it scarcely more than a series of fine, stimulating books on broad, more or less timely subjects; they do not discern the true significance of it.

Through that work, however, as the years pass, Hans Urs von Balthasar appears more and more clearly to us as what he always was: in the broadest and finest sense of the term, a man of the Church—a man of communion—"catholic".[4] And in the trial that the Church is going through today, torn apart by her own children—a trial whose gravity escapes no one, whatever might be the interpretation that one proposes for it and whatever might be the phraseology with which one happens to cover it, everything shows that he was himself acutely aware, before God, of the role that his qualifications as a theologian made it a duty for him to assume. Hence, on the periphery of his more scholarly works, but not at all peripheral to his essential aim, the series of small volumes, simpler and more accessible, but no less important or less personal: such as this *Einfaltungen* [English trans.: *Convergences*], this *In Gottes Einsatz leben* [English trans.: *Engagement with God*], or these *Klarstellungen* [English trans.: *Elucidations*]; or again this *Der antirömische Affekt* [English trans.: *The Office of Peter and the Structure of the Church*], so painfully current. Hence the long and persistent effort deployed for the creation of that international theological journal which, under the title *Communio*, hopes to serve to strengthen the intellectual and spiritual vitality of Catholicism. Hence so many humble tasks, preaching, personal conversation, work in commissions, symposia. In all that, the most virile firmness of thought, but at the same time a constant serenity, a freedom entirely independent of any partisan spirit, the sincere, never discouraged search for conciliatory views, a generously comprehensive understanding in the face of all situations, a heart open to whoever comes to him. "I had the impression of having known him always", one of his visitors said recently, marveling at his friendly reception soon after their first meeting. "It seemed to me", he also

[3] See in particular the fine book dating from 1947: *Wahrheit*, vol. 1: *Wahrheit der Welt*, which is too little known today, despite its French translation, under the slightly misleading title: *Phénoménologie de la vérité* (Beauchesne, 1952).

[4] Cf. his last little book: *Katholisch, Aspekte des Mysteriums*; "Kriterien" series, 36 (Einsiedeln, 1975).

said (and we will end with these picturesque words) "I was taking a walk with a Father of the Church, wandering among the Helvetians, one who would count among his ancestors both the Magi kings and William Tell."

Appendix

From von Balthasar

Zurich, July 1950.

Very dear friend. I could scarcely believe what you wrote to me. It is bewildering, totally incomprehensible. But it is indeed that form of martyrdom that must seal your work. You are already the victor, nothing will stop the progress of your ideas. These signs of weakness will only accentuate the truth you are defending. And you who told me that one was protected within the Society!

I am finishing my Karl Barth, which is basically a discussion between him and you. I would like to dedicate this book to you, he owes you almost everything. Don't lose courage, continue to work as if there were nothing, so many friends surround you and will want to help you. I am doing what I can to make your influence spread in German countries.

If you have the time, write more to me: Who must leave Fourvière? Rondet? Bouillard? I am afraid that Karl Rahner will be very discouraged now, he who is nearly our only hope. He must be supported—you must both be helped.

Your "Conclusion" has been translated and is going to appear in *Christ heute*, with the approval of Aubier.

If you are in Paris this summer, I will return to see you. I am praying for you. Be cheerful.

All good to you.

Balthasar.

EPILOGUE TO PART TWO

The Texture of a Work and Its Unity

It would be fruitless to seek in such a diverse collection of writings the elements of any truly personal philosophical or theological—or, as some have said, "gnoseological"—synthesis, whether to criticize or to adopt it. In this multi-colored fabric gradually formed according to teaching assignments, ministries, situations and appeals of all kinds, it nevertheless seems possible to me to discern a certain texture which, come what may, creates a unity. Without claiming to open up new avenues of thought, I have sought rather, without any antiquarianism, to make known some of the great common areas of Catholic tradition. I wanted to make it loved, to show its ever-present fruitfulness. Such a task called more for a reading across the centuries than for a critical application to specific points; it excluded any overly preferential attachment to one school, system, or definite age; it demanded more attention to the deep and permanent unity of the faith, to the mysterious relationship (which escapes so many specialized scholars) of all those who invoke the name of Christ, than to the multiple diversities of eras, milieux, personalities and cultures. So I have never been tempted by any kind of "return to the sources" that would scorn

---

Excerpt from *Mémoire sur l'occasion de mes écrits* (Namur: Culture et Vérité, 1989), 146–49 [English trans.: *At the Service of the Church* (San Francisco: Ignatius Press, 1993), 143–46]. To understand better what Father de Lubac says here of the period after the Council, one should note that these pages were written at the end of 1974 and the beginning of 1975, while the thirty-second General Congregation of the Society of Jesus was being held in Rome, during which Paul VI himself, faced with the seriousness of certain orientations, took the initiative of intervening directly in a decisive manner. On this period of the Church's history, one will find in the book by Gérard Leclerc, *L'Église catholique (1962–1986). Crise et renouveau* (Paris: Denoël, 1986), a number of pieces of information more or less forgotten or willingly passed over in silence in most of the books published in France during this period. One will not find in this work, however, nearly any information on the internal crises of the great religious orders after the Council.

later developments and represent the history of Christian thought as a stream of decadences; the Latins have not pushed aside the Greeks for me; nor has Saint Augustine diverted me from Saint Anselm or Saint Thomas Aquinas; nor has the latter ever seemed to me either to make the twelve centuries that preceded him useless or to condemn his disciples to a failure to see and understand fully what has followed him.

When I left Jersey (I was then twenty-seven years old), where a Suarezian spirit still reigned, I had been put down severely as a Thomist (of a Thomism, it is true, revitalized by Maréchal and Rousselot). At that time, this was called "not holding the doctrines of the Society". I have never renounced that fundamental orientation. I even believe that I have worked (with varying degrees of success) to lead minds back to the authentic Saint Thomas, as to a master considered ever-current. As for the "Thomism" of our century, I have too often found in it a system that is too rigid and yet at the same time not faithful enough to the Doctor it claims as its authority. I have also seen it raised too often (in complete good faith) like a pavilion to cover the most diverse merchandise to be able to take it seriously. I have known a traditionalist Thomism à la Bonald, a Thomism as patron of *L'Action française*, a Thomism as the inspiration of Christian Democracy, a progressivist and even a neo-Marxist Thomism, and so forth (to say nothing of innocent fantasies such as the Thomism of the scout rule, among others). And no salvation outside of each in its turn. I have read, from the pen of a theoretician rejecting any fidelity to Catholicism, that he would never forget his debt of loyalty to the doctrine of Saint Thomas Aquinas. I have more than once observed a "Thomism" that was scarcely more than a tool in the hands of the government, the rallying point of a party, the password of a troop of ambitious careerists, or even the empty shell of a thoughtless conformity, the padlock closing the door to all understanding of the thought of others. Even today, despite all the supervening changes, this still makes it difficult for me to be very loud in proclaiming that I am a Thomist. Besides, to each his task! I have never claimed to be doing the work of philosophical systematization or of theological synthesis. That is not out of contempt on my part, quite the contrary. But, leaving this twofold kind of task to others with the necessary gifts, it is in a more general way to the great tradition of the Church, understood as the experience of all Christian centuries, coming to enlighten, orient, expand our poor little individual experience, to protect it from aberrations, to open it to the paths of the future, that I once again recently made appeal in the introduction to *La Foi chrétienne* [English trans.: *The Christian Faith*], just as I had done long before in *Catholicisme* [English trans.: *Catholicism*].

What I have more than once regretted in highly regarded theologians, experienced guardians, was less, as others made it out, their lack of openness to the problems and currents of contemporary thought than their lack of a truly traditional mind (the two things are, moreover, connected). I inwardly reproached them for not having an acute enough awareness of what they were representing or should have been representing: like those Romans who seem to be ignorant of their claims to Christian nobility, taking no interest deep in their heart either in the catacombs or in the mosaics of the churches of their city, and who, going up to the Cadius [Monte Celio], crowd along the same pavement that Saint Gregory once trod without being in any way affected by it. They were, for me, in Péguy's sense, the "moderns". Such a state of mind, which was too generally widespread in dominant spheres during the preparation for the Council, was in my opinion at the root of a contempt that was not without grave consequences. It was the state of mind that characterized the party (I believe that word is appropriate here) that had hoped to control, not to say confiscate, the Council and that was, from the very first session, spectacularly overcome. But in the consequence of the confusion that I have just pointed out, it seemed in its defeat to entail the defeat of Tradition as well, although the latter, on the contrary, was in fact liberated. A necessary reaction, a condition of the desired "opening", was taken to be revolutionary, and, in public opinion, which was very poorly informed, it was the tradition of the Church herself, with all her fertile but misunderstood richness, that seemed to be crushed. Many were no longer attentive to the very work of the Council, to the substance of its teachings, to the spirit that emanated from it: for them, through them, it was a new "modernity", in restless excitement but without a compass, that triumphed over a petrified modernity.

What can be said, since then, of the new powers of the day, who, in the reverse situation, suffer from a blindness that is more dense and all the more confident! What I had wanted to offer as savory nourishment and, as it were, a propelling force, I see them push aside as a dry fruit or reject as a cumbersome burden. Despite the efforts of the better interpreters of the Council and above all the efforts of him who through his supreme office never ceases to guide us in its wake, I see with sadness the spread of an indifference, when it is not a flaunted scorn or a resentment full of bitter hatred, with respect to this tradition, which alone has the promise of life and of renewal because it is the bearer of eternity.[1] At the same time, I see a harsh demand for "pluralism", which, in its worship of differences, shatters the harmony of the great Catholic concert and tends, not to enrichment, but to the dislocation of Unity.[2] How I would like to be able to cry out with the same persuasive tone to those of my brothers who are letting themselves be seduced by this music of perdition what in the last century Newman declared to his contemporaries!

> There is [he said] a depth and a power in the Catholic Religion, a fullness of satisfaction in its creed, its theology, its rites, its sacraments, its discipline, a freedom yet a support also, before which the neglect or the misapprehension about oneself on the part of individual living persons, however exalted, is as so much dust when weighed in the balance. This is the true secret of the Church's strength, the principle of its indefectibility, and the bond of its indissoluble unity. It is the earnest and the beginning of the repose of Heaven.

[1] "Tradition", wrote Maurice Blondel in *Histoire et dogme*, "anticipates the future and prepares to illuminate it through the very effort it makes to remain faithful to the past." See also the little book by Msgr. Guimet pointed out above, *Existence et Éternité* (1973), for which I wrote a brief introduction.

[2] There, it is a question of something quite different from a legitimate, inevitable and desirable "pluriformity", all the elements of which constitute, as it were, so many converging lines.

In fact, it is not by following cleverly devised myths that we made known to you the power and coming of our Lord Jesus Christ, but for having been eyewitnesses of his glory. For he received honor and glory from God the Father when the voice coming from the magnificent splendor of God said to him: This is my beloved Son in whom I am well pleased; listen to him. And we ourselves heard this voice coming from heaven when we were with him on the holy mountain. And we hold to be all the more certain the prophetic word, on which you are right to fix your gaze as on a lamp shining in a dark place, until the day dawns and the morning star rises in your hearts. *First of all, know well that no prophecy from Scripture is a matter of any personal interpretation. In fact, no prophecy has ever been produced by man's will, but it was moved by the Holy Spirit that holy men have spoken on behalf of God.*

2 PETER 1:16–21

"As an epilogue to the fourth volume [of *Exégèse médiévale*]" notes Father de Lubac in his *Mémoire sur l'occasion de mes écrits* (84–85 [English trans.: 84]), "I transcribed in capital letters a text I consider to be one of the most beautiful of the New Testament. It is by a late, unknown author, at times considered insignificant. This anonymous person, clothed with the great name of Peter, was nonetheless a mind of astonishing perspicacity and depth. He has left us in a few lines one of the most decisive and I would dare to say one of the most intelligent professions of faith, still perfectly adapted to the situation of today." We reproduce it here according to the Vulgate Latin, simply placing in italics the sentences kept as an epilogue to *Exégèse médiévale.* The text from 2 Peter 1:19–21 is quoted in no. 11 of the dogmatic constitution *Dei Verbum,* on Divine Revelation, of the Second Vatican Council. The text from 2 Peter 1:16–19 constitutes the second reading of the Mass of the Transfiguration of the Lord, August 6, in the Roman Catholic liturgy.

Index